# THE
## INSIDERS'®
## GUIDE
### TO
# Nashville

## THE
# INSIDERS'®
## GUIDE
### TO

# Nashville

*by*
*Jeff Walter*
*and*
*Cindy Stooksbury Guier*

The Insiders' Guide®
An imprint of Falcon® Publishing Inc.
A Landmark Communications company
P.O. Box 1718
Helena, MT 59624
(800) 582-2665
www.insiders.com

Sales and Marketing: Falcon Publishing, Inc.
P.O. Box 1718
Helena, MT 59624
(800) 582-2665
www.falcon.com

•

SECOND EDITION
1st printing

•

©1999 by Falcon Publishing, Inc.

•

Printed in the United States
of America

•

Cover photos, clockwise from top left: *Grand Ole Opry*, courtesy of Gaylord Entertainment/Donnie Beauchamp; Parthenon, courtesy of Nashville Convention & Visitors Bureau; Gary Chapman, Sam's Place concert at Ryman Auditorium, courtesy of Donnie Beauchamp; Gaylord Entertainment Center (Nashville Arena). Spine photo: courtesy of Nashville Convention & Visitors Bureau/Gary Layda

Publications from *The Insiders' Guide*® series are available at special discounts for bulk purchases for sales promotions, premiums or fundraisings. Special editions, including personalized covers, can be created in large quantities for special needs. For more information, please contact Falcon Publishing.

**ISBN 1-57380-118-6**

# Preface

Welcome to the second edition of *The Insiders' Guide® to Nashville*!

If you're reading this, it's likely because you are either visiting or planning to visit Nashville or are a new resident. Or perhaps you are a Nashville native or well-entrenched transplant who wants to learn more about our great city. Whatever the case may be, you have come to the right place.

This book is loaded with information about Nashville — from its interesting history to its neighborhoods, and from its recreation opportunities to its colleges and universities. The pages are packed with helpful Insiders' tips and suggestions too.

Of course, we haven't forgotten the music. If you're just visiting, that's probably what brought you here in the first place. If you're a resident, that also may be why you're here.

Nashville is known worldwide as Music City U.S.A. This is the home of country music and the *Grand Ole Opry*. We are proud of our musical heritage and the role the city and its people have played in creating what has become one of the most loved and most listened-to genres of music. In this book you'll find page after page of information about Nashville's music culture. We'll tell you all about the *Opry* and other music attractions, the best places to hear live music and our favorite music events and festivals; we'll even give you the country music stars' perspectives!

The spotlight is always on Nashville's music business, but as you'll see when you flip through the pages of this book, there is much more to Nashville than music. Nashville is a leader in education, publishing and healthcare, and manufacturing contributes greatly to the economic base. Our population continues to grow because the word is getting out that Nashville is a wonderful place to call home —

it has the just-right combination of big-city and small-town qualities that makes it appealing to longtime residents, former big-city dwellers, relocating companies and other newcomers.

In writing *The Insiders' Guide® to Nashville*, we've tried to cover just about every topic we could think of, from a real Insider's viewpoint. Since we are Nashvillians — albeit transplants from East Tennessee and Kentucky — we feel especially qualified to tell you about the good burger joints, the best golf courses, our often woeful traffic jams, our arts scene, the healthcare industry, the many houses of worship and all the other subjects you'll discover in this book.

When we first took on the task of writing *The Insiders' Guide® to Nashville*, we were honored and humbled by the chance to highlight the best and brightest of our wonderful city. There is just so much to tell about Nashville. Even for someone who knows all the city's big attractions, all the interesting nooks and crannies, all the little out-of-the-way shops and diners, and all the best resources, this task was at times almost daunting. At the same time it was a labor of love.

We went to work — researching, traveling, phoning and writing — to try to present you with thorough, up-to-date, usable information. We haven't attempted to cover every place in Nashville, but if you explore the many chapters in this book, we guarantee you'll make some new discoveries and learn new things. We encourage you to use this book as a guide to learning more about Nashville and its surrounding area. We hope to spark your interest in the city and perhaps lead you to some new experiences.

Tell your friends about *The Insiders' Guide® to Nashville*. Before long, you and everyone you know will be Nashville Insiders!

# About the Authors

## Jeff Walter. . .

Jeff Walter is a writer, editor, songwriter and musician. A West Virginia-born Kentuckian who moved to Nashville to pursue a music career, he is co-author of Insiders' Guides to both Nashville and Lexington, Kentucky. He also has ghostwritten books on business and personal/professional development during a career that has followed him — along with his restless energy and desire for new challenges — among newspapers, freelance writing, marketing and corporate communications.

Walter, a University of Kentucky graduate, began his journalism career at this hometown newspaper, *The Daily Independent*, in Ashland, Kentucky, where he worked as a sportswriter. When he moved to Lexington to complete his degree at UK, he joined the staff of the *Lexington Herald-Leader*, where he worked for seven years at various positions including copy editor. At the end of 1990, burned out on the newspaper business, he left the *Herald-Leader* and started his own copywriting business, Vital Communications, which provided advertising and communications services for a variety of corporate clients.

As a freelancer, Walter began a continuing relationship with WYNCOM Inc., a diverse leadership communications and training company whose services include marketing, promotion and production of public presentations featuring such top business authors and speakers as Stephen Covey, Tom Peters and Ken Blanchard. In addition to the aforementioned, he has worked on projects with legendary UCLA basketball coach John Wooden and noted newswomen Linda Ellerbee and Catherine Crier.

Walter's work has been honored by the International Association of Business Communicators and the Lexington Advertising Club. His song "Baby Ain't a Baby Anymore," which he wrote with Olin Murrell, won first place in the country category of the Austin Songwriters' Group's 1996 competition. He is also co-founder of the Lexington Fiction Writers Group.

In Nashville (where he has on occasion been mistaken for hit songwriter Bob DiPiero), Walter has focused as much of his energies as possible on his music. Meanwhile, he's also worked as a copy editor at *The Tennessean* daily newspaper; written medical news and features, jacket copy for Christian books and music publicity; and driven a 500-mile-a-day courier route delivering pharmaceuticals throughout Western Kentucky.

Now he's playing bass guitar and writing songs for Scarecrow Junction, an original country-folk-rock band, while also getting his music publishing company, Jack and Jenny Music (named for his mom and dad), up and running. In his spare time, he enjoys playing and watching sports (especially Kentucky Wildcat and other Southeastern Conference basketball), reading, concerts, cooking and travel. He lives in the Donelson area of Nashville with his artist wife Roberta, a retired schoolteacher; their son Reece, a budding artist and musician in his own right; and a husky-collie mix named Lyle.

What he'll do next is anybody's guess.

# Cindy Stooksbury Guier . . .

Cindy Stooksbury Guier has called Nashville home since 1987. She grew up with an appetite for books and a propensity toward writing, but it was her love of music, interest in the music business, and influences of her musical family that led her to Music City U.S.A.

After graduating with a degree in communications from the University of Tennessee in her native Knoxville, Guier set her sights on Nashville. She soon landed a position in the editorial department of BPI Communications, publisher of such top entertainment industry magazines as *Billboard*, *Amusement Business* and *Hollywood Reporter*.

Guier covered all facets of the world's entertainment business, from annual events to concerts and attractions to conventions. She carved a niche covering the music industry, with an emphasis on the country and contemporary Christian genres.

Guier has interviewed, written about and/or photographed everyone from country music legends such as Roy Acuff and Minnie Pearl to superstar Garth Brooks, to rockers Alice Cooper and R.E.M., to Christian pop's Amy Grant and Michael W. Smith, as well as top record company executives, concert promoters, talent agents, songwriters and others involved in the business of music.

She is a big fan of Nashville events and has covered such annual happenings as Summer Lights, the Country Music Association's Fan Fair, the Gospel Music Association's annual convention and Dove Awards show, and the Nashville entertainment Association's Extravaganza showcase. She has also worked as a writer and photographer for record companies and recording artists. As a freelance writer and editor, Guier also covers the tourism industry, including articles and travel guides.

Guier and her husband Russ live out in the country "in a little corner of paradise" just beyond west Nashville. They share their home with their Border Collie Ally, and a large aquarium full of assorted saltwater fish, sea anemones and other ocean creatures. In their spare time the Guiers often can be found hiking the trails at Radnor Lake, biking at Warner Parks, listening to some of their favorite live music at the Bluebird Cafe and the Station Inn and exploring all the wonderful things Music City has to offer.

Photo: Cathy Summerlin

The Hermitage, Andrew Jackson's home, remains
one of Nashville's most popular attractions.

# Acknowledgments

## Jeff Walter

I've had a lot of help putting two editions of this book together. The list below is, unfortunately, bound to be somewhat less than complete. To anyone whose name I've omitted, please accept my apologies in advance. Deadlines can do terrible things to one's memory.

Thanks to Bob DiPiero, Larry Wall and Steven Womack for graciously agreeing to be interviewed for Close-ups. And to all the other people who took time out of their busy schedules to add to my grasp of a diverse and complex town (especially when I was on deadline and needed information now): I really appreciate it.

It has been my pleasure to share authorship of two editions of *The Insiders' Guide to Nashville* with Cindy Guier. She's been here longer than me and knows more about this great town, has extensive insight into the entertainment industry, is full of ideas, makes an excellent sounding board, and answers my e-mails and phone calls even when she's on deadline. She's a great writer and friend, and she and hubby Russ are also cool people to see a Steve Earle/Del McCoury show with.

Cathy and Vernon Summerlin — two fine writers in their own right — were instrumental to the first edition. The book's first edition (and, by natural extension, the revision you now hold in your hands) wouldn't have gotten done without Cathy's meticulous research. Vernon, meanwhile, was generous in his sharing of knowledge about Nashville-area lakes and fishing opportunities. Look for their regional travel books at your favorite bookstore. Thanks, Cathy and Vern!

Jenni Frangos, my editor for this second edition, has been a paragon of patience, understanding and even mercy. Thanks, Jenni, for the skillful editing and alert eyes. Thanks as well to my previous editors and other contacts at The Insiders' Guides: Beth Storie, Theresa Chavez, Dan DeGregory, Dave McCarter, Annie Kao and Eileen Myers.

My musical pursuits, while not directly linked to this book, have nonetheless added tremendously to my overall view of Nashville. So I'd like to acknowledge my co-writers, musical collaborators and mentors, including my fellow "residents" of Scarecrow Junction: Frank James, Frank Pilgrim and Johnny Joe Weyers (extra special thanks to better halves Barbara, Debbie and Erica); Steve Goetzman; Forest Borders (and Reba); Olin Murrell (and Molly); Larry Wayne Clark and Maggie Ross; Bob Dellaposta; and all the great musicians, singers and demo producers I've had the opportunity to work with in Music City.

*The Tennessean*, *Nashville Medical News*, *Tennessee Medicine*, *Country Songwriter* magazine, Thomas Nelson Publishers, Journal Communications, Express Courier and Manpower have helped pay the bills. Thanks to all of you.

Thanks, Mom and Dad and Amy and Bruce, for coming to see the Walters in Nashville and letting me show you around. (We're still waiting for Scott, Sheila and Steve.)

The entire Walter clan would like to thank everyone who has helped make Nashville home, including Gini and Larry Thompson (it's so nice, Gini, to have a friend, Realtor and book resource all wrapped up in one person!); and our new neighbors Don and Anne Shepherd; Keith and Heather Seger; and Dan, Pam, Daniel and Jared Schafer.

And I'd like to thank, most of all, Roberta Jo and Reece, for loving and understanding me enough to put up with my hermit-on-deadline behavior, not to mention making the full-time move from our Kentucky home so I could pursue a music career. It ain't easy being my wife or my son, but you two are GREAT at it (and this is truly a "Great Adventure" we're on together). I love you both with all my heart and soul.

# Cindy Stooksbury Guier

So many people shared their time, insights, knowledge and perspectives with me during the preparation of this book. There isn't room on this page to thank everyone, but I am very grateful to all of them.

I wouldn't have been able to take on this project without the love, support and encouragement of my wonderful husband, Russ. Thank you for your endless optimism, encouragement and dependability, afternoon shoulder rubs at the computer, much-needed vacations, computer expertise and for being willing to live among stacks of notes and papers and for several months. I'm so fortunate to have you in my life.

It was a pleasure working with editor Jenni Frangos, who is not only a great editor but also has an amazing knowledge of practically everything. Thanks again to Cathy Summerlin, who provided excellent research on the first edition of the book (which saved me weeks of time on this edition!)

It was great working again with the multitalented co-author Jeff Walter. It's been fun getting to know you and your family, Jeff.

So many people — hundreds, literally — were willing to take time to answer questions and provide information for the book. I am especially grateful to author and historian Ridley Wills II for graciously and generously giving of his time and for sharing his knowledge of Nashville history with me on more than one occasion.

Thanks to the Metropolitan Historical Commission for providing brochures and other information on Nashville history. The staff at the Nashville Room of the Ben West Library was very helpful in directing me to all the right resources. Thanks to the staff at the Nashville Convention & Visitors Bureau, Nashville Area Chamber of Commerce and other area Chambers for providing lots of facts and info.

Thanks also to the Tennessee Department of Tourist Development and the Greater Nashville Regional Council. The Metro Parks staff, especially Barry McAlister and John Flowers, and the whole crew at Warner Parks, was a big help in providing details about Metro Parks, and Thurman Mullins at Tennessee State Parks was especially helpful too.

Real estate agent extraordinaire Julie Casassa of Shirley Zeitlin and Co., was a big help in tracking down information on area real estate sales. Thanks also to Mark Deutschmann at Village Real Estate Services.

Ronnie Pugh and Kent Henderson at the Country Music Foundation Library and Media Center are always ready to help me track down info on country music. Thanks also to the Country Music Association and all the record label staffers who pitched in with info; CitySearch, a fun online resource for all things Nashville; and Jill Green at the Tennessee Association of Broadcasters.

Once again, we couldn't have prepared this book without the help of many Nashville Insiders. Thanks to you all. And to the readers, I hope you have as good a time reading this book as I had writing it!

# Table of Contents

# Directory of Maps

# Nashville Region

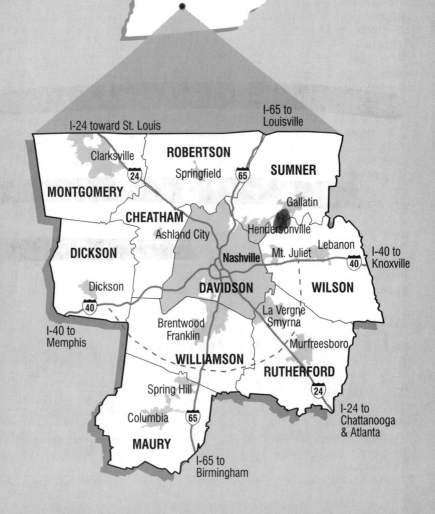

I-24 toward St. Louis

I-65 to Louisville

Clarksville

**ROBERTSON**

Springfield

**24**

**65**

**SUMNER**

**MONTGOMERY**

Gallatin

**CHEATHAM**

Ashland City

Hendersonville

Lebanon

**DICKSON**

**Nashville**

Mt. Juliet

I-40 to Knoxville

**40**

Dickson

**DAVIDSON**

**WILSON**

**40**

I-40 to Memphis

Brentwood
Franklin

La Vergne
Smyrna

Murfreesboro

**WILLIAMSON**

**RUTHERFORD**

Spring Hill

**24**

Columbia

**65**

I-24 to Chattanooga
& Atlanta

**MAURY**

I-65 to Birmingham

# Downtown Nashville

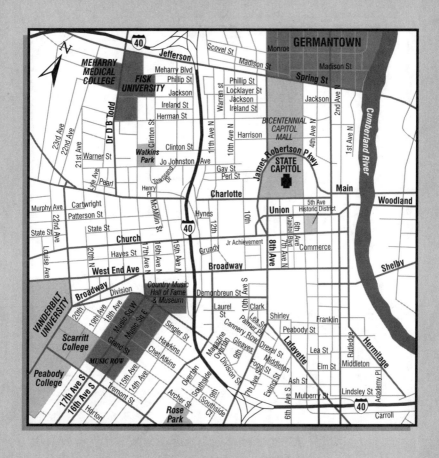

# Nashville
# Citywide

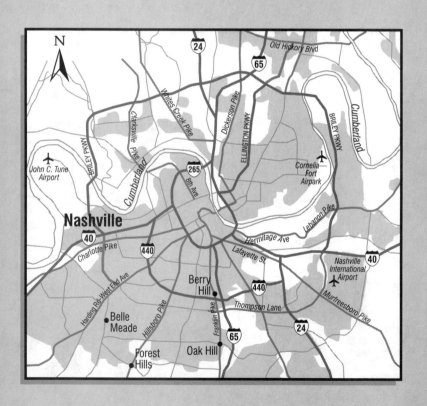

# Historic Nashville

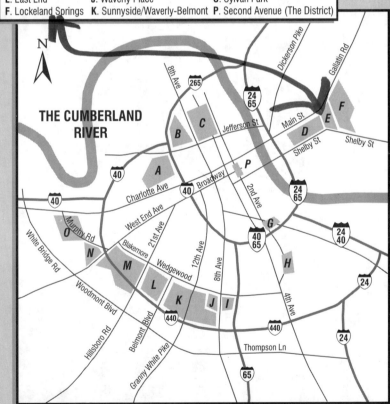

## Historic Nashville Neighborhoods

**A.** Fisk-Meharry
**B.** Buena Vista
**C.** Germantown
**D.** Edgefield
**E.** East End
**F.** Lockeland Springs

**G.** Rutledge Hill
**H.** Cameron-Trimble
**I.** Woodland-In-Waverly
**J.** Waverly Place
**K.** Sunnyside/Waverly-Belmont

**L.** Belmont-Hillsboro
**M.** Hillsboro-West End
**N.** Richland-West End
**O.** Sylvan Park
**P.** Second Avenue (The District)

THE CUMBERLAND RIVER

We're pleased that,
whether you are a
visitor, a newcomer or
even a longtime
resident, you have
chosen the Insiders'
Guide to Nashville to be
your companion here.

# How to Use This Book

*T*he *Insiders' Guide® to Nashville* is meant to be used, and used often. It is not a coffee-table book (even though we believe it will add a certain grace and elegance to your table — and when friends ask about it, you can tell them where to get one of their own). Just be sure to take it with you whenever you go out, so you can avoid potentially unpleasant conversations like this:

"Honey, what was the name of that little barbecue place that sounded so appetizing?"

"It's in our *Insiders' Guide.* Didn't you bring it?"

"I thought *you* had it."

"Aarrgghh!"

Obviously, *how* you use the book is not nearly as important as *that* you use it. That said, we'd like to make a few suggestions that will help you make the most of this book, so you soon will feel like an Insider yourself.

First of all, experience the book on your own terms. There's nothing that says you have to read it straight through. Obviously, if you and the family are hungry right now, you'll want to go immediately to the Restaurants chapter. If you're looking for something exciting to do, turn to Attractions or Kidstuff or Recreation or Nightlife. In the mood to discover why Nashville is known worldwide as "Music City"? We've devoted a hefty chapter to that subject, and you may be surprised at the diversity of sounds you can find here. Need a way to get from point A to point B? Then you may want to go first to the Getting Around chapter. Or you might choose to take the casual approach and simply flip through the book, skimming the pages to see what catches your eye.

We've designed *The Insiders' Guide® to Nashville* to be self-contained. That means each chapter essentially stands on its own, so wherever you start reading, you'll find the information you need to enjoy that aspect of Nashville life. And there are lots of cross-references.

While our primary focus is Nashville and Davidson County, we'll also take you throughout the rest of the eight-county metropolitan statistical area — Cheatham, Dickson, Robertson, Rutherford, Sumner, Williamson and Wilson counties. You'll visit towns and communities such as Hermitage, Old Hickory, Brentwood, Franklin, Hendersonville, Goodlettsville, Murfreesboro, Lebanon, Springfield, Smyrna and Madison, to name a few. And our Daytrips chapter will take you to some great places a little farther away, but still within easy driving distance.

Don't hesitate to personalize this book — make it your own! Scribble notes in the margins, circle places you have visited, underline points of interest. Heck, there's a chance that, somewhere along the way, you might disagree with something we've said. That is to be expected in any forum where someone dares to make subjective judgments. Go ahead, write something like "They're way off base on this one!"

You might also discover some diner or nightclub or getaway that has escaped our notice. Make a note of it and, if you would be so kind, share it with us so we can include it in our next edition.

Please remember that, in a rapidly growing metropolitan area such as Nashville, things are bound to change. By the time you read this book, there will be new places to visit and experiences to savor — and, unfortunately,

Photo: Curtis Hilbun/Dollywood

In and around Nashville, you can find museums and other attractions dedicated to your favorite performers.

some old favorites that might have bid us fare-well. Menus will be revised and schedules al-tered. It's always a good idea to call before visiting an attraction or restaurant. And, again, feel free to share your experiences with us, so we can keep *The Insiders' Guide® to Nashville* as accurate and up-to-date as possible.

Address all correspondence (complaints as well as information and especially fan let-ters) to:

*Insiders' Guides®*
*Falcon Publishing*
*P.O. Box 1718*
*Helena, MT 59624*

A final thought: if you enjoy *The Insiders' Guide® to Nashville*, you might be interested to know that Insiders' Guides are also avail-able for many other American cities. See the back of this book for ordering details. And also be sure to visit The Insiders' Guides Online[SM] at www.insiders.com.

We're pleased that, whether you're a visi-tor, a newcomer or perhaps even a longtime resident wanting to see whether you've been missing anything, you have chosen us to be your companion here in Nashville. We sin-cerely hope we're able to make your stay a pleasant one.

Nashville is a place where, fortunately, quality of life and cost of living don't go hand in hand.

# Area Overview

Welcome to Nashville!

In the more than 200 years since its founding in 1779, the community now known worldwide as Nashville, Tennessee, has earned fame and prestige in many areas, in the process earning a proportionate number of nicknames. "Music City USA" . . . "Athens of the South" . . . "Wall Street of the South" . . . "The Buckle of the Bible Belt" . . . "City of Parks" — those are just a few of the names affixed to Nashville throughout its history.

The problem we have with such nicknames is that each is severely limited, generally paying tribute to only one facet of what is truly a multifaceted metropolitan area. At the same time, we appreciate that each of these names, in its own way, serves as a tribute to some of the accomplishments that have made our city great. In other words, it is significant that Nashville has inspired so many terms of endearment, and so we'll look at these nicknames in greater detail later in this chapter.

But first, we'd like to take time to point out something that, although you probably already know it, can occasionally get obscured by all the hype. And that is: Nashville is a *wonderful* place to live or to visit.

This is the friendliest city in the United States, according to a 1995 edition of NBC's *Dateline*, based on a study by Fresno State University. You might say that Nashville is the embodiment of Southern hospitality. Waitresses call you "honey" while serving you down-home delicacies like fried chicken, made-from-scratch biscuits, grits and country ham. People smile and speak to you on the street, and are generally willing to give you the time of day, or directions if you need them. Adding to the laid-back, hospitable atmosphere are antebellum mansions, some of which could have been used as sets for *Gone With the Wind*; elegant Victorian homes; and lush flowering gardens. Many business people wear cowboy boots with their suits. (If you're thinking now that we're merely catering to stereotypes, rest assured that these scenes are all very real, although they're only a part of the big picture. There are, of course, plenty of Nashvillians who wouldn't be caught dead in cowboy boots, for example, and many who prefer to dine on Continental cuisine and live in modern condominiums. Such is the diversity that characterizes this town.)

This is a place where, fortunately, quality of life and cost of living don't go hand in hand. According to something called the ACCRA Cost of Living Index, for the third quarter of 1997, Nashville's cost of living was at 95.6 percent, compared with the national average of 100 percent. (By comparison, New York was at 226.9 percent, Boston at 138.5 percent, Austin at 98.9 percent, Birmingham at 98.4 percent, to name a few.) In Tennessee, you pay no state income tax — although, if some politicians have their way, this may soon change. And Nashville's per capita income rose 13.1 percent between 1991 and 1993, the largest increase among the nation's 80 largest metropolitan areas.

In 1995, *Fortune* magazine ranked Nashville as the top relocation destination in the country. And a 1998 poll by the New York-based research firm Louis Harris and Associates found "Nashville" to be the ninth-most-popular response to the question: "If you could live in or near any city in the country except the one you live in or nearest to you now, what city would you choose?"

Of course, with attractions like the *Grand Ole Opry*, the Country Music Hall of Fame and Museum, the Ryman Auditorium, historic Belle Meade Plantation, The Hermitage estate of Andrew Jackson and countless museums, art galleries and outdoor recreational activities, Nashville remains a top tourist destination among Americans as well as visitors from other countries.

Whether you're here on vacation or you're planning to make a home here, you'll find a wealth of opportunities in practically any area that interests you, from education to recreation, from child care to retirement.

## Some Basic Facts

Nashville, the capital of Tennessee, is the center of a metropolitan statistical area (MSA) covering 4,135 square miles and eight counties: Davidson, where Nashville is located; Cheatham; Dickson; Robertson; Rutherford; Sumner; Williamson; and Wilson. Other cities in this rapidly growing area include Ashland City, Charlotte, Dickson, Springfield, Smyrna, Murfreesboro, Gallatin, Hendersonville, Portland, Brentwood, Franklin and Lebanon.

In addition, two other counties — Maury, with its county seat of Columbia; and Montgomery, with its county seat of Clarksville —

are considered part of the "Nashville economic market."

Nashville/Davidson County has a combined metropolitan government. The estimated 1998 population of Nashville/Davidson County was 538,796. That population makes Nashville the second-largest city in Tennessee, after Memphis, and Nashville's 533 square miles make it one of the United States' largest cities in area.

The population of the eight-county MSA is 1,151,858; the population of the Nashville economic market is 1,359,748. That's a lot of people, and those numbers continue to grow rapidly. Nashville is one of the fastest-growing large cities in the nation, with vigorous population growth that has continued for more than three decades. Rutherford County, the fastest-growing county in Tennessee, and Williamson County, meanwhile, are among the 50 fastest-growing counties in the nation.

Nashville itself has a diverse ethnic makeup, with blacks comprising about a quarter of the population, and other ethnic groups such as Asians and Latin Americans also present in growing numbers.

## A Progressive and Sophisticated City

When Nashville and Davidson County formed their combined city/county metropolitan government in 1963, it was one of the first of its kind. The act served a dual purpose: increasing a tax base that had been dwindling because of numbers of people moving from the city to the suburbs, and eliminating much duplication of services, thus resulting in a more efficient form of government. It has since become a model for other metropolitan governments around the country.

Nashville has proven to be a progressive and sophisticated city in other ways, such as race relations and urban development. During the turbulence of the civil rights movement, the city made great strides without the violence or threats of violence that other Southern cities often suffered. Desegregation of pub-

Items paying homage to country music's giants can be found throughout Nashville.

lic schools began in 1957, in response to a class-action suit filed by a black man named A.Z. Kelley who wanted his son to attend a neighborhood school rather than be bused across town. In 1960, after several peaceful sit-ins at downtown lunch counters, desegregation also began taking effect in public facilities, a process that was largely complete by the summer of 1963. And in 1967, Vanderbilt University's Perry Wallace became the Southeastern Conference's first black basketball player.

The early 1950s witnessed the Capitol Hill Redevelopment Project, one of the nation's first federal urban renewal projects. Through this and other similar undertakings, the city has largely demonstrated that it understands the challenge of balancing the sometimes conflicting goals of progress and preservation. During the late 1970s, a commission studying Nashville's long-term development adopted the motto "Celebrating the Past While Looking into the Future." Now, nearly two decades later, those words still serve to describe Nashville's philosophy.

Downtown Nashville today is a vibrant, thriving area that is a blend of old and new. While many of the old buildings that line Broadway have changed little since the turn of the century, steel-and-glass skyscrapers loom nearby. Just down the street from the legendary honky-tonks where many of yesterday's country singers and songwriters first plied their trade, you'll also find newer, hipper attractions like Hard Rock Cafe and Planet Hollywood. The Ryman Auditorium, a true landmark that since its completion in 1892 has served as a tabernacle, assembly hall and theater as well as onetime home of the *Grand Ole Opry*, is beautifully restored and still playing host to a variety of entertainers.

Another example of Nashville's ingenuity in forging onward while honoring its illustrious past is the Bicentennial Capitol Mall State Park (see our Parks chapter), which opened in 1996. This Tennessee state park, just north of the State Capitol downtown, was built on land that had long been considered too swampy for development. As the town's skyline grew during the building boom of the 1950s and '60s, the State Capitol disappeared from view on three of its four sides — east, west and south. The north side is now a 19-acre commemoration of Tennessee's first 200 years, highlighted by such features as a 200-foot granite map of the state embedded in a concrete plaza; a Visitors Center; 31 fountains representing Tennessee's major rivers; a Walk of Counties with a time capsule from each of the state's 95 counties; a Wall of Tennessee History; and an outdoor amphitheater. Looming proudly over the park from atop downtown's tallest hill is the beautiful State Capitol.

Nashville's inventiveness will be further tested as we advance into the 21st century. As with any metropolitan area, Nashville must find creative and progressive ways to answer questions related to such vital issues as continued growth and modernization, race relations, education, crime, poverty and homelessness. Obviously, many of these issues are related. Like our counterparts nationwide, we must find better ways for people from various backgrounds to live together in harmony, while equipping themselves with the knowledge and skills they need to build better lives.

Now, about those nicknames . . .

## "Music City USA"

From Roy Acuff, Minnie Pearl, Ernest Tubb and Hank Williams . . . to Garth Brooks, Wynonna Judd, Alan Jackson and Shania Twain, Nashville has long been known as the world's capital of country music. While much of today's country music has drawn its share of detractors who say it has grown fluffy and insignificant, the fact remains that today's "new country" performers succeeded in bringing country music to a new generation of CD- and cassette-buying fans. The challenge now for the country industry is to continue to reach new fans while producing recordings of musical and lyrical substance.

At the same time, many artists in the wake of multimillion-unit-selling superstars such as Brooks and Twain feel the industry is fraught with unrealistic expectations. Recently, it has not been uncommon for artists to sell a million copies of a recording and still get dropped by their record label. In reaction to such developments, a recent trend has been for artists to start their own labels. Labels such as John Prine's Oh Boy! Records; Steve Earle's E-Squared Records; and the Dead Reckoning label, which is owned by a group of artists, have proven that, with drastically more modest budgets for recording and video sessions, it's possible to sell far fewer units while not

## Nashville Notables

Not surprisingly perhaps, the renowned musicians and music-industry giants who hang their hats in Nashville make up a veritable who's who list. But throughout history as well as today, Music City also has been home to numerous notable non-musicians who have marched to the beat of their own drummers. Famous Nashvillians outside the music industry include:

• James Robertson and John Donelson, who led Nashville's first settlers to the area;

• Andrew "Old Hickory" Jackson, hero of the Battle of New Orleans and seventh president of the United States;

• James K. Polk, 11th president of the United States;

• Andrew Johnson, 17th president of the United States;

• Sam Houston, who led the Texas army to victory over Santa Anna after the defeat of the Alamo;

• John Bell, U.S. congressman, speaker of the House and senator who ran unsuccessfully for president in 1860 against Abraham Lincoln;

• Thomas Hart Benton, U.S. senator and onetime friend of Andrew Jackson, who later shot Jackson during a brawl in Nashville;

• Gilbert Gaul, renowned Civil War painter;

— continued on next page

• William Walker, a soldier of fortune who became president of Nicaragua but was executed by a Honduran firing squad four years later when he tried to become Honduran president;

• Felix Grundy, prominent lawyer, congressman, senator and U.S. attorney general;

• Wilma Rudolph, who ran for three gold medals at the 1960 summer Olympics in Rome;

• Vice President Al Gore;

• Fred Thompson, Watergate investigator, U.S. senator, part-time actor and, some have said, future president;

• Grantland Rice, the sportswriter who first wrote of the University of Notre Dame's "Four Horsemen of the Apocalypse";

• Jesse and Frank James, who lived here under assumed names during the 1870s;

• Frank Andrews, successor of Gen. Dwight D. Eisenhower as Army commander of the European theater and namesake of Andrews Air Force Base in Maryland;

Vice President Al Gore cut his political teeth in Nashville.

• Robert Penn Warren, Vanderbilt University alum and Pulitzer Prize-winning author of *All the King's Men*;

• Ron Mercer, former University of Kentucky basketball star and current NBA star,

• Oprah Winfrey, actress and TV talk-show host.

only making a decent living, but also maintaining one's artistic integrity.

Of course, the streets of Music Row have long been a magnet for singers and songwriters who dream of following in the footsteps of their musical heroes. What many people fail to realize is that Nashville offers a wide diversity of music in addition to the country for which it is best known. In the early days of the city's development as a center for recorded music, pioneers such as producer Owen Bradley and guitarist Chet Atkins eschewed "pure" country in favor of a sound that combined so-called hillbilly music with pop, gospel and other influences. This was in the 1950s, and the result was the "Nashville Sound."

Today the sounds coming from Nashville are more diverse than ever. You'll find not only country, but also rock 'n' roll, blues, soul, gospel, jazz, funk, folk and even rap. While some of these styles have yet to make a major impact in the recording industry, they are adding to an eclectic live-music scene, and the annual Nashville Music Awards, or NAMMYs as they're unofficially known, are a testament to this diversity.

The Nashville Area Chamber of Commerce lists more than a dozen major record labels, more than 80 smaller labels, along with about 175 recording studios, 290 music publishing companies, 21 major booking agencies, 10 record manufacturers, 23 theatrical talent agencies and 40 record promotion companies. These numbers, while constantly changing and surely outdated by now, provide a glimpse into the vastness of the area's music and entertainment industries. See our Music City chapter for more information, including a wealth of details about opportunities for both fans and practitioners of music.

While we're still on the subject of entertainment, it seems appropriate to mention another related nickname often used to describe Nashville. "Third Coast" is a reflection of the fact that our city, like its counterparts on the

East and West coasts, is a major player in the entertainment industry. This ain't New York City or Los Angeles — quite frankly, we think that's a very good thing — but there is a lot going on here. Nashville's role in the entertainment industry has expanded well beyond music and into film, video and other forms of art and entertainment.

## "Athens of the South"

It's easy, we confess, to be a little skeptical about titles like this. After all, Lexington, Kentucky, about a 3½-hour drive northeast, has long perpetuated its claim to the title "Athens of the West," which was bestowed back when it was still a thriving frontier town. How many Athenses can you have in one region? But we have to say that Nashville is worthy of its Athenian title. The city is brimming with arts, culture, learning institutions and classical Greek architecture, and by the late 1800s people were calling it "Athens of the South" (we're not sure who said it first, though Jesse C. Burt, in his 1959 book *Nashville: Its Life and Times*, attributes it to Philip Lindsley, a highly influential educator). In 1897, Nashville made the title tangible by celebrating its 100th birthday around a full-size replica of the Parthenon in the middle of Centennial Park (see our History and Parks chapters for details).

In Nashville and the rest of Middle Tennessee, education for all ages is a priority. We particularly realize the importance of higher education, as our nearly 20 accredited colleges and universities, with a total enrollment of more than 85,000 students, will attest. In the Nashville metropolitan statistical area, almost 45 percent of adults 25 and older have at least one year of college education; and more than 45,000 people have graduate or professional degrees.

Vanderbilt University has been ranked among the nation's best; its schools of education, medicine, business and law have also been ranked near the top. Vanderbilt is the largest private employer in Middle Tennessee and the second-largest private employer in the state.

Meharry Medical College is the largest private, historically black institution dedicated solely to educating healthcare professionals and scientists in the United States.

Nearly 15 percent of all African-American physicians and dentists practicing in the United States are Meharry graduates.

Fisk University, like Meharry, is renowned for its contributions to minority higher education. One out of every six of the nation's black doctors, dentists and lawyers is a Fisk graduate. The school has also gained nationwide attention for its Fisk Jubilee Singers and its collection of modern and African-American art.

Nashville has also made substantial contributions to primary education. In 1855 it became the first Southern city to establish a public school system. In 1963, Susan Gray, an educational researcher at the city's Peabody College, introduced a program for disadvantaged preschoolers that became the prototype for Head Start. Peabody College, which became a part of Vanderbilt in 1979, remains a leading center for training teachers.

For more information on education in Nashville, see our Education chapter.

As for the arts and culture, Nashville has a ballet, a symphony orchestra that plays at the Tennessee Performing Arts Center and area outdoor venues, a Broadway Series, an opera company, several theater groups and numerous art galleries. For more information, see our Arts chapter.

Incidentally, the Athens comparison even extends to food. As you'll discover in our Restaurants chapter, you can dine on falafel, tabouli or a Greek salad in Nashville.

## INSIDERS' TIP

**Union soldiers brought baseball to Nashville during the Civil War, playing in the area where the Bicentennial Capitol Mall State Park now stands. In the early 1900s, Nashville had a Southern Association team that played at Sulfur Dell Park, in the same area, and won championships in 1901, 1902 and 1908.**

# "Wall Street of the South"

Music and entertainment are just a part of Nashville's economy — and not even the largest part at that. The same creative flair, innovation and energy that go into great music have also made the area a leader in such industries as healthcare, publishing, tourism and insurance. The diversity of the local marketplace has given us the ability to weather economic downturns.

The nicknames "Wall Street of the South" and "Financial Center of the Southeast," while no longer as accurate as they once were, are reflections of the influence that banking has had in contributing to the area's growth. Even today, finance, insurance and real estate are responsible for more than 35,000 jobs. Government, education, automotive and other manufacturing and communications are responsible for hundreds of thousands more.

But the field that Nashville is really dominating is healthcare management. Vanderbilt University & Medical Center employs more than 12,000 people. Columbia/HCA Healthcare Corporation, the nation's largest for-profit healthcare company, has its headquarters in Nashville and employs more than 8,000 here. There are more than 250 healthcare management companies in the area as well as about 70 other health-related firms. Other major employers in the field, with a combined workforce of several thousand, include St. Thomas Hospital, Baptist Health Care Systems and Centennial Medical Center. See our Healthcare chapter for more details about Nashville's offerings in this area.

For years, Nashville has been the largest publishing and printing center in the South. Much of this is attributable to the city's status as "The Buckle of the Bible Belt" (see subsequent section), but now a number of national secular publications are printed here as well.

Today, it might be appropriate to bestow a new nickname: "The New Motor City." We made that one up, but it's not that much of an exaggeration. The nearby Nissan plant in Smyrna and the Saturn plant in Spring Hill are helping the region make a name for itself in the automotive industry. In addition to employing more than 15,000 people, these plants have also attracted suppliers and related businesses to the region.

Nashville's central location makes it a great distribution center by land, by air and by water. The three major interstates — I-24, I-40 and I-65 — that converge here are ideal for trucking. Nashville is home of the largest CSX rail yard in the Southeast; Nashville International Airport, in addition to transporting passengers, handled about 185,000 tons of cargo in 1995-97; and the Cumberland River remains a viable option for some types of shipping.

*Fortune* magazine has ranked Nashville the nation's second-best city for its pro-business attitude. *Inc.* magazine named Nashville one of the 10 best cities in which to start a business. And Cognetic Inc., a leading national small-business-research group, named Nashville one of the top three U.S. "hot spots of entrepreneurial activity." And, at this writing, Nashville was making plans for the arrival of a Dell Computer plant.

Publicly held firms based in Nashville include Shoney's, O'Charley's and Cracker Barrel — see what we mean by Southern hospitality? — as well as Dollar General, Service Merchandise and Thomas Nelson Publishers.

According to the Nashville Area Chamber of Commerce, 170 new businesses have relocated to Middle Tennessee since 1990, while more than 330 existing businesses have expanded. In that same period, more than 100,000 new jobs have been created. One reason for all this growth is that the largest segment of Nashville's population falls within the

## INSIDERS' TIP

More than 6 million people helped Nashville celebrate the state's 100th anniversary in 1897, one year late. The Centennial Exposition was held in Centennial Park, where a plaster reproduction of the Parthenon had been built for the occasion. That replica was replaced by the current steel-and-concrete building in 1931.

Photo: Cathy Summerlin

The district along Second Avenue has shops, restaurants and clubs in revitalized 19th-century warehouses.

25 to 44 age range, which translates into a ready labor pool.

## "The Buckle of the Bible Belt"

At one time, Nashville was said to have had a higher ratio of churches to people than any other American city. Many of those were located, appropriately enough, on downtown's Church Street.

Today there are more than 800 houses of worship in Nashville, spanning an array of faiths that extends even to Buddhism and Hinduism. The vast majority of area worshipers remain Protestants, however, and some have gone so far as to dub Nashville "the Protestant Vatican."

The Baptist Sunday School Board, the publishing arm of the Southern Baptist Convention, employs more than 1,300 people at its Nashville business and publishing facilities. The National Baptist Publishing Board, established here in 1896, is the nation's oldest and largest religious publishing and printing corporation owned and operated by blacks. Although The United Methodist Publishing House, the largest agency of the United Methodist Church, was not formed in Nashville until 1968, several of its predecessors were based here as early as the 1830s. Thomas Nelson Publishers, also based in Nashville, is the world's largest publisher of Bibles and other religious literature.

Opportunities for a religious education abound in Nashville, too, from the collegiate level down to the primary. Church-affiliated colleges and universities include David Lipscomb University, founded by the Church of Christ; Belmont University, which is affiliated with the Tennessee Baptist Convention; Free Will Baptist Bible College; and Trevecca Nazarene University.

For more information about the religion scene in Nashville, see our Worship chapter.

# "City of Parks"

If you equate "quality of life" with recreational opportunities, Nashville is just the place for you. With several thousand acres of municipal parks and state parks, two large recreational lakes and miles of undeveloped land you can find practically any activity you can imagine. Whether you prefer peaceful nature walks replete with flora and fauna or more physical activities such as swimming, tennis, golf or ice skating, Nashville's parks are sure to have what you're looking for.

Percy Warner Park is the city's largest, at more than 2,000 acres; combined with the adjacent Edwin Warner Park, they comprise one of the nation's largest municipal parks. J. Percy Priest and Old Hickory Lakes add a wealth of water activities to the mix. Eight state parks in the metropolitan statistical area offer even more outdoor opportunities, including birdwatching, hiking, camping and learning about the state's history.

The beauty of Nashville's gardens, such as Cheekwood — Nashville's Home of Art and Gardens (see Attractions), is renowned among lovers of flowering plants. Elsewhere, there are seemingly countless playgrounds and ball fields.

If you like to watch sports as much as play them, you're also in luck. Nashville has become a mecca for professional athletics. Foot-ball fans rejoiced when, after a long period of debate, it was announced that the National Football League's Houston Oilers would relocate to Nashville. After an interim season in Memphis, the Tennessee Oilers moved to Nashville in 1998, changing their name to the Tennessee Titans at the end of the 1998-99 season. They began the 1999-2000 season in their new stadium, Adelphia Coliseum, on the east bank of the Cumberland River.

Nashville is also home to an expansion National Hockey League franchise, the Predators, who began play here in the 1998-99 season. Sports fans can also go to Greer Stadium to root for the Nashville Sounds, the AAA affiliate of major-league baseball's Pittsburgh Pirates, or cheer for the Nashville Kats arena football team, which began home play in 1997 at Gaylord Entertainment Center (the former Nashville Arena).

The college athletics scene is thriving as well. For more information, see our Spectator Sports chapter.

As you can see, Nashville lives up to its many nicknames, and it's sure to inspire even more as time goes by. It's a great place to make music, learn, work, worship, play or be yourself. At the risk of sounding like a broken record (which we suppose is appropriate), we'll again state that Nashville is a wonderful place to live or to visit. Whatever your reason for being here (or planning to be here), for however long, enjoy your stay. This city has a lot to offer. Once again, welcome to Nashville!

With just a little practice and some practical knowledge, you'll soon find your way anywhere you want to go in metropolitan Nashville.

# Getting Around

Question: How do you get to the *Grand Ole Opry*?

Answer: Practice, practice, practice!

OK, it's an old joke, slightly paraphrased. But we use it to make the point that, with just a little practice and some practical knowledge, you'll soon find your way without problem to the Opryland area, the downtown/Music Row area or anywhere else you want to go in metropolitan Nashville.

If you do happen to lose your bearings, don't lose your cool. Stop and ask directions — remember, you're in the land of Southern hospitality! It's reassuring to note that, in Nashville, it seems almost *everyone* is originally from somewhere else. Which means that, like you, they've been lost before and may get lost again. This town is a magnet for talented, creative people seeking fame and fortune, personal fulfillment, an exciting lifestyle . . . or maybe just a great place to live. If they've been able to find their way from Point A to Point B in their quest, they're usually more than happy to share the benefit of their experience with you.

Once you understand a few of the ground rules, such as the names and directions of the interstates and primary crosstown routes, you'll discover that getting around in Nashville is a bit like life itself: you're bound to make a few wrong turns along the way, but you'll be wiser for the experience. (Hey, do you think there might be a song in that?)

Of course, if you prefer, you can leave the driving to somebody else. Nashville has a number of transportation alternatives. We'll tell you about them later in this chapter.

## Knowing the Laws

A night in jail, or even a ticket from a police officer, might be fodder for a great country song, but you'd still probably rather avoid these situations if possible. Therefore, it pays to know the following laws pertaining to getting around in the fine state of Tennessee.

• **Driver licenses.** A valid Tennessee driver license is required for anyone who lives here and wants to drive. If you've moved here from another state and have a license from there, you'll need to apply for one here within 30 days. Please note that different classes of licenses are issued depending on what type of vehicle you drive. Class D, the most common, is for regular passenger vehicles, pickup trucks and vans; Class A, B and C licenses are for various types of commercial vehicles; and Class M licenses are for motorcycles.

• **Driving under the influence.** Driving under the influence of alcohol or drugs in Tennessee is a serious no-no. The minimum penalty for a first conviction is 48 hours in jail, a

$350 fine and the loss of your license for a year. In addition, there can also be considerable court costs, fees for an alcohol safety course, increased insurance premiums and other expenses. So just don't do it.

• **Buckling up.** State law requires the driver and all front-seat passengers to wear a seat belt. Children 4 or younger must be in an approved child car seat; those ages 5 through 12 must be buckled up or in a car seat.

• **Headlights.** When it's raining, snowing or otherwise precipitating enough for you to be using your windshield wipers, the law requires you to have your headlights on as well.

• **Watching your speed.** It's never fun to get caught speeding, but the law provides for even stiffer penalties for those who go too fast in school zones or construction zones. Speeding in a school zone while children are going to or from school or are at recess is considered not just speeding, but reckless speeding, which automatically results in six points being added to your driving record. Speeding in a construction zone when workers are present will get you a minimum fine of $250.

• **Turning right on red.** Tennessee law permits right turns at a red light after coming to a complete stop, unless otherwise posted.

# Interstates, Major Highways, Bypasses and Crosstown Routes

Nashville's location at the confluence of three major interstates means that getting into or out of town by ground is generally convenient. That's not to say that you won't run into congestion during peak hours — you will, although state and federal highway officials are always working on ways to make area traffic flow more smoothly. (We're giving the Tennessee Department of Transportation, commonly known as TDOT, the benefit of doubt here; in the interest of full disclosure, however, you'll often hear TDOT described in less-than-flattering terms when road construction projects — like the simultaneous 1999 work on interstates 65, 40 and 24 — result in major gridlock around town.)

Interstate 65, which runs north–south, connects Nashville with Bowling Green, Kentucky, and, ultimately, the Chicago area to the north. Going south, it leads to Birmingham before winding up in Mobile, Alabama. Nashville-area exits, from north to south, include Old Hickory Boulevard/Madison (Exit 92), Briley Parkway/Dickerson Pike (Exit 89), Trinity Lane (Exit 87), James Robertson Parkway/State Capitol (Exit 85), Shelby Street (Exit 84), Wedgewood Avenue (Exit 81), Armory Avenue (Exit 79), Harding Place (Exit 78) and Old Hickory Boulevard/Brentwood (Exit 74).

www.insiders.com
See this and many other **Insiders' Guide®** destinations online.
Visit us today!

Interstate 40, a major east–west connector, links Nashville with Knoxville and, eventually, Wilmington, North Carolina, to the east; and with Memphis and — if you're in the mood for a *long* drive — Barstow, California, to the west. Nashville-area exits, from east to west, include Old Hickory Boulevard (Exit 221), Stewarts Ferry Pike (Exit 219), Nashville International Airport/Donelson (Exit 216), Briley Parkway (Exit 215), Spence Lane (Exit 213), Fessler's Lane/Hermitage (Exit 212), Second Avenue/Fourth Avenue (Exit 210), Demonbreun Street (Music Row)/Broadway/Charlotte Avenue/Church Street (Exit 209), 28th Avenue (Exit 207), 46th Avenue/West Nashville (Exit 205), Briley Parkway/White Bridge Road/Robertson Avenue (Exit 204), Charlotte Pike (Exit 201), Old Hickory Boulevard (Exit 199) and Bellevue/Newsoms Station (Exit 196).

**INSIDERS' TIP**

Check out the changing rainbow of colors created by the Airport Sun Project, a massive, three-part sculpture at Nashville International Airport.

Photo: Cathy Summerlin

The Nashville Trolley offers a handy means for seeing downtown Nashville as well as the Music Row area.

Interstate 24 is a diagonal route running northwest–southeast. It will take you from Chattanooga in the southeast to Clarksville or, going farther northwest, to near St. Louis. Nashville-area exits include, from northwest to southeast, Briley Parkway (Exit 43), Murfreesboro Road (Exit 52), Briley Parkway/Airport (Exit 54), Harding Place (Exit 56), Antioch/Haywood Lane (Exit 57), Bell Road (Exit 59) and Hickory Hollow Parkway (Exit 60).

The two major bypasses are Interstate 440 and Interstate 265. I-440 connects I-40 in west Nashville to I-65 in south Nashville and I-24 in the southeastern part of the city. Its exits are at West End Avenue (Exit 1), Hillsboro Pike/21st Avenue (Exit 3) and Nolensville Road (Exit 6). I-265 links I-24/I-65 in the north with I-40 in the west, where I-440 also joins the party. I-265 has one exit of its own: Eighth Avenue.

Construction is also under way on another bypass, controversial loop — this one about 30 miles outside Nashville. Now called State Route 840, it is being built to federal standards and will probably be called Interstate 840 one of these days after it is completed — that is, if it is ever completed. As proposed in its entirety, State Route 840 is a 185-mile loop around the metropolitan Nashville area, connecting interstates 24, 40 and 65 to the north as well as to the south of Nashville. At this writing, the section of State Route 840 linking I-40 east and I-24 east has been completed, and the rest of the southern part of the loop is either under construction or under contract. The loop is controversial for a number of reasons, including the impact it would have on rural farmland, its contribution to "urban sprawl" and alleged violations of environmental laws. Opponents of State Route 840 have filed lawsuits that have slowed work on the project.

Other major highways running through Nashville include U.S. highways 31, 41 and 70.

Briley Parkway, also known as Tenn. Highway 155, encircles Nashville and bisects all three of its major interstates. Beginning in the east at its juncture with Charlotte Avenue, it runs northeast to meet I-65; heads southeast, briefly following the Cumberland River through the Opryland area and meeting I-40 near Nashville International Airport; then continues south before turning back east, crossing I-24 and becoming one with Thompson Lane. Thompson Lane becomes Woodmont Boulevard, which becomes White Bridge Road northeast of West End Avenue and runs to Charlotte Pike, completing the Tenn. 155 loop.

Harding Place begins in the southwestern part of the city as Harding Pike (U.S. Highway 70 S.), then branches east from U.S. 70 S. and becomes Harding Place. After crossing Granny White Pike (12th Avenue) in south Nashville, it inexplicably becomes Battery Lane for a brief stretch before resuming as Harding Place when it crosses Franklin Road, which is known as both Eighth Avenue and U.S. Highway 31. Harding continues east, then veers northward and becomes Donelson Pike.

Old Hickory Boulevard is even more perplexing. Beginning in the southwest, at Tenn. Highway 100 on the west side of Percy Warner Park (see our Parks chapter), it runs east until it crosses Nolensville Road (also known as Fourth Avenue or U.S. Highway 31 Alternate), and changes its name to Bell Road. But wait . . . it's far from through. Back near where we started, Old Hickory also heads north from Tenn. 100 at Edwin Warner Park (see Parks) before turning into River Road. It also seemingly just materializes just east of Charlotte Avenue's juncture with I-40, then heads north. Up north, way north, Old Hickory masquerades as Tenn. Highway 45. It passes, from west to east, across Dickerson Pike (known variously as U.S. Highway 31 W., U.S. Highway 41 and Tenn. Highway 11), I-65 and Gallatin Pike (a.k.a. U.S. 31 E. and Tenn. Highway 6), through the Madison and Old Hickory areas of metropolitan Nashville. It then heads southeast, crossing Lebanon Pike (U.S. Highway 70, Tenn. Highway 24) in the Hermitage area and, still acting as Tenn. 45, crosses I-40

near J. Percy Priest Lake on its way out of town. (Finally!) A word to the wise: just because you've been on Old Hickory once before and are now on it again doesn't necessarily mean that you're anywhere near where you were the first time. In other words, you probably shouldn't use this boulevard as an orientation point.

# HOV Lanes

Nashvillians are seeing the appearance, along all three major interstates, of so-called HOV lanes, which are intended to reduce both traffic congestion and auto emissions during peak times by encouraging car pooling. HOV stands for "high-occupancy vehicle". Because of federal air-quality standards, the U.S. government requires the state to build these lanes any time it uses federal money to widen an interstate in an urban area. Basically, you're rewarded for being in a vehicle with two or more people by being allowed to drive in the less-traveled inner lane, marked with a white diamond painted on the pavement.

If you're driving alone during peak traffic hours — from 7 to 9 AM Monday through Friday for traffic inbound to Nashville, and from 4 to 6 PM Monday through Friday for outbound traffic — stay out of any lanes marked with a diamond. In other words, you must have two or more people in your vehicle (children count) to drive in an HOV lane at these times. Exceptions are granted for buses, motorcycles and emergency vehicles. Trucks with three or more axles cannot use the HOV lanes during these hours, regardless of how many passengers they have. Failure to abide by these restrictions can earn you a $50 fine.

# Local Streets

The Cumberland River, which played such an important role in the founding of Nashville, remains an important orientation point for residents and visitors. If you're trying to figure out the way the streets are laid out, start at the river, which runs north to south through the center of town. West of the river, or on the downtown side, numbered avenues run parallel to the river. East of the Cumberland, however, it is streets and not avenues that are numbered, though they still run parallel to the river.

Three bridges cross the Cumberland in the downtown area; from west to east, they are: Jefferson Street, Woodland Street and the Memorial Street. A fourth bridge, at Shelby Street, is being converted into a pedestrian bridge; meanwhile, work is expected to begin in 2000 on a new six-lane bridge, part of a $55 million Gateway Boulevard project.

Primary downtown streets running perpendicular to the numbered avenues include James Robertson Parkway, which circles the State Capitol; Union Street; Church Street; and Commerce Street. Broadway serves as the north–south dividing line.

You'll notice that, in the downtown area, many of the numbered avenues are one-way, so pay attention to make sure you're not turning the wrong way.

The numbered avenues generally change names as they head out of town. For example, 1st Avenue becomes Hermitage Avenue and then Lebanon Road; 2nd Avenue actually merges with 4th Avenue before changing into Nolensville Road; 8th Avenue becomes Franklin Road. This phenomenon is not limited to numbered avenues downtown, either. It's a simple fact of Nashville that many roads change names, some several times. After a while, you'll get used to it.

You'll also notice that many a road is referred to as both a "pike" and a "road" or an "avenue," depending on which sign or map you're looking at. For example, Charlotte Avenue is also Charlotte Pike, Hillsboro Pike is also Hillsboro Road, and Murfreesboro and Nolensville roads are also known as pikes. There are many other examples of this; in some cases the "pike" designation is more common; in other cases "road" or "avenue" is favored. The "pike" references are holdovers from older days when roads were often known as turnpikes. Don't worry too much about which word you use.

# Buses

If your group would like its own bus for travel inside or outside Nashville, you can find more than three dozen companies listed in the Yellow Pages under "Buses — Charter & Rental." Many of these offer guided tours of the Nashville area; for more information on these, see our Music City chapter.

### Greyhound Bus Terminal
**200 Eighth Ave. S. • (615) 255-3556**

From its Nashville terminal, Greyhound offers service to more than 2,000 destinations in the continental United States, including Memphis, site of the closest Amtrak station (see next section).

# Trains

Nashville does not have passenger train service. If you're interested in traveling by Amtrak, however, you can make your own arrangements for getting to Memphis, site of the closest Amtrak station.

# Public Transportation

### Metropolitan Transit Authority
**1011 Demonbreun St. • (615) 862-5950**

Metropolitan Transit Authority, Nashville's public transportation system, serves about 40 bus routes citywide. About a half-dozen of these are "express" routes between two points, and a dozen are "limited service" routes. The system has five shelters and 16 park-and-ride lots.

Regular bus fares for 1999 are $1.45 for adults and 70¢ for seniors; adult express fares are 30¢ higher. Several package deals, such as 20 fares or unlimited fares for a month, are also available.

Nashville Trolley Co., another service run by MTA, offers downtown and Music Valley

---

**INSIDERS' TIP**

**Nashville's famous skyline can help you get oriented if you momentarily lose your way. Or you can always stop and ask someone for directions — remember, you're in the land of Southern hospitality.**

Drive (Opryland area) fares for $1, or an all-day pass for $3. Trolleys run every 10 minutes. Yet another MTA service, Accessride, provides door-to-door van service for disabled people who qualify.

The MTA landport on Demonbreun features a lower level with 175 parking spaces for van or car poolers or people taking a direct shuttle to Nashville International Airport, and an upper level where you can wait in air-conditioned comfort for your transportation to arrive.

Also in the works from MTA is a commuter rail system that is scheduled to be in operation as early as 2002.

For more information, call the MTA offices — or pick up a system map and schedules at the landport or at the general office at 130 Nestor Street.

# Taxis

Taxi fares in Nashville are regulated by law. The meter starts at $1.50 when you get in the cab, and you'll pay $1.50 a mile to your destination. When traveling from the airport, a $1.20 tariff is added. A fare from the Opryland area or the airport to a downtown location will run somewhere between $15 and $20.

It's best to reserve your cab at least 30 minutes in advance. Near popular downtown restaurants, you'll often find taxis waiting at the curb, however, so you might not have to call. By law, taxis are not supposed to "cruise" for customers, but visitors from big cities generally don't know this, and the law is not regularly enforced.

Many companies take credit cards, but others do not; sometimes that decision is left to the discretion of the individual driver, so it's a wise idea to specify that you plan to use a credit card when you call or before climbing into a cab.

Some Nashville cab companies include Allied Cab Company, (615) 244-7433; All American Taxi, (615) 865-4100; Checker Cab, (615) 256-7000; Grand Old Taxi, (615) 868-

8080; Music City Taxi, (615) 262-0451; United Cab Co., (615) 228-6969; and Yellow Cab Metro Inc., (615) 256-0101.

# Limousines

Nashville is a town of stars and special occasions, which means it's a limousine kind of town. The Yellow Pages list nearly three dozen limousine services, most of which are available 24 hours a day, seven days a week. All accept major credit cards. As with any other service, you get what you pay for, and prices cover a wide range. Expect to pay more during peak times such as prom and graduation season, the December holiday season and during big events — just try getting a last-minute limo for the Country Music Association Awards, for example. And, during such times, you often have to make your reservations as much as four months in advance.

Standard features in most models include television, stereo (many with CD player and tape deck), privacy partition, moon roof and cellular telephone. If you're looking to travel in style, you can rent stretch models for up to 10 people with additional luxuries including double bars with crystal champagne glasses. Some companies also offer specials that include dinner. A number of companies rent basic sedans, like Lincoln Towncars or Cadillacs, as well as limos; these, of course, will be nice but without all the luxuries of a limo.

Prices range from about $50 an hour for a six-person model to $100 or more an hour for a 10-person stretch with all the amenities. Also plan to add a driver gratuity of 15 percent to 20 percent; some companies will automatically add this to your bill. Most companies have a three-hour minimum on weekends and a two-hour minimum during the week. Weeknights during non-peak seasons are generally a little cheaper; if you can, plan your special night during the week to increase your chances of getting what you want.

Here are a few of Nashville's limo companies: Capitol Limousines Inc., (615) 883-6777;

---

**INSIDERS' TIP**

Interstates 440 and 265, both bypasses, can help you avoid traffic tie-ups if you're driving across town.

Carey Limousine, (615) 360-8700; Celebrity Limousines Inc., (615) 316-9999; Deep South Limousines, (615) 361-0401; Precious Cargo Limousine Services, (615) 885-9680; and Town & Country Limousine, (615) 826-8844.

# River Taxis

Opryland USA offers two "river taxis" that connect the Opryland area with downtown; both one-way and round-trip fares are available. Tickets are available at Opryland or, if you're downtown, at the Ryman Auditorium. Board the river taxis downtown at Riverfront Park. (See our Attractions chapter for related information.)

Round-trip tickets are about $13 for anyone 12 and older, $10 for children ages 4 through 11 (kids younger than 4 ride free); one-way fares are $9 and $7. For more information, call Opryland USA at (615) 871-6100.

# Airports

## Nashville International Airport
**I-40 and Donelson Pk., 8 miles southeast of downtown • (615) 275-1610 (Metro Nashville Airport Authority)**

"It sure wouldn't hurt to have wings," Mark Chesnutt sang in a recent country hit. Fortunately, Nashville International Airport has plenty of wings: 16 airlines serving 91 markets, with an average of 390 daily arrivals and departures. More than 8 million passengers flew from or into Nashville International in 1998. The airport also handles tons upon tons of cargo.

While these figures might still be a far cry from Chicago's O'Hare or Atlanta's Hartsfield, they show significant growth from humble beginnings. When the airfield opened in 1937, it was known as Berry Field and occupied just 337 acres. In the 60 years since then, Nashville International has undergone numerous expansions, developments and renovations to become a state-of-the-art facility that now sits on 4,480 acres. Additions in recent years include a concourse connector and an International Arrivals Building. The airport contributes $2.3 billion and more than 15,000 jobs a year

to the Nashville area economy. Its efforts were rewarded in early 1998, when a nationwide study named Nashville International the fourth-best airport in the country.

The Metropolitan Nashville Airport Authority — an independent, self-financing organization in operation since 1970 — owns and operates Nashville International and the John C. Tune general aviation airport (see next listing) without the help of local property-tax dollars. The Authority has more than 250 full-time employees at Nashville International, where it maintains its own state-certified aircraft rescue, firefighting and law enforcement division. Numerous U.S. cities and the governments of Bermuda and Canada have studied the Authority as a model airport governance organization.

Nashville International Airport will be putting on a new face for the new millennium. A $35 million dollar expansion project, which began in the summer of 1998, will be completed in summer 2000. The changes will give airport visitors expanded parking facilities, widened roadways in front of the terminal, and covered pedestrian walkways that will connect the second and third levels of the short-term parking garage to the ticketing and baggage claim levels.

The Metropolitan Nashville Airport Authority is also improving airport services with the expansion of air cargo facilities. In July 1999, the Authority announced its purchase of the business interest of the Vernon Williams family, which operated air cargo facilities at Nashville International under a lease agreement dating back to 1968. This acquisition will allow the airport to keep pace with the growing demands of shippers and remain competitive with other cities and airport worldwide.

The airfield itself has four runways with lengths up to 11,000 feet. Parallel runways allow for simultaneous landings and takeoffs. The 820,000-square-foot terminal consists of three levels: ticketing, baggage and ground level. There are 47 air carrier gates, with a capacity for 13 more. Covered short-term parking and full-service ground transportation are available.

As of August 1999, the airport offers non-stop flights to a total of 47 markets. And you'll be happy to know that this airport, which prides itself on efficiency and customer service, is generally known for on-time performance.

Airlines serving Nashville International Airport include Air Canada, (800) 776-3000; American and American Eagle, (800) 433-7300; Comair, (800) 354-9822; Continental, (800) 525-0280; Corporate Express, (800) 555-6565; Delta, (800) 221-1212; Delta Express, (800) 325-5205; Northwest, (800) 225-2525; Skyway, (800) 452-2022; Southwest, (800) 435-9792; Trans States, (800) 221-2000; TWA, (800) 221-2000; United, (800) 241-6522; and USAir and USAir Express, (800) 428-4322.

## Getting To and Leaving the Airport

Nashville International is 8 miles southeast of downtown Nashville at Interstate 40 and Donelson Pike. It's also near the intersection of two other major interstates: I-65 and I-24.

Once you've driven onto the airport grounds, simply follow the signs to short-term, long-term or satellite parking; arrivals; or departures. If you're waiting to pick up someone from an arriving flight, look for the blue and white signs leading you to the free "Waiting Area," then wait in your vehicle until your passenger shows up.

Metropolitan Nashville Airport Authority Police are charged with the responsibility of reducing traffic congestion in front of the terminal. It's a responsibility they take seriously. Unless you're loading a passenger on the arrival ramp or unloading one on the departure ramp, stay out of these areas. Otherwise, the police will politely direct you to one of the parking areas or the waiting area.

The airport facilities include ramps and elevators for travelers with physical handicaps, and complimentary parking is available for vehicles with handicap license plates or decals. Each airline makes its own arrangements for helping disabled travelers get to and from planes. Contact your airline in advance for more information on the services it offers.

## Parking at the Airport

Your first 30 minutes of parking are free at all Nashville International lots, including the covered short-term garage. After that, you'll pay up to a maximum of $18 a day in the short-term area, $1 an hour up to $7 a day in the long-term area, or $1 an hour up to $5 a day in the satellite lot about a mile from the terminal. If you park in the long-term or satellite lots, you can catch a complimentary shuttle to and from the terminal.

## Ground Transportation from the Airport

Various taxi services are available at the ground level; just get out by the curb and wait. Please note, however, that the ground transportation area is one level below the baggage claim area, so you'll have to take the escalator or elevator after picking up your luggage.

Taxi meters start at $1.50 and are $1.50 a mile afterward. A $1.20 tariff is added to fares leaving the airport.

Most hotels in the Briley Parkway/airport area offer free shuttle service to their guests. Gray Line Airport Express, (615) 275-1180, which serves hotels downtown and in the Music Row and Vanderbilt areas, offers $9 one-way and $15 round-trip fares.

If you'd prefer to captain your own ship, on-site rental car agencies include Alamo, (615) 275-1050; Avis, (615) 361-1212; Budget, (615) 366-0800; Dollar, (615) 275-1005; Hertz, (615) 361-3131; National, (615) 361-7467; and Thrifty, (615) 361-6050. All of these rental agencies have convenient locations at the airport.

## Enjoying Your Time at the Airport

While you probably don't want to spend any more time in the airport than you have to, Nashville International has taken pains to ensure that your stay is as pleasant as possible. You'll find plenty of opportunities to tend to your needs in the areas of food, drink, shopping and other diversions — while appealing to your aesthetic sensibilities.

The modern terminal, designed by New York architect Robert Lamb Hart, features a large central atrium with sloping skylights that contribute to a general atmosphere of openness and accessibility.

The Arts in the Airport program brightens the concourses with visual arts ranging from paintings to sculpture to photography as well as frequent live musical performances. The Airport Sun Project is an ambitious light sculpture created by Dale Eldred and dedicated in 1989. The sculpture illuminates three areas of the terminal, using safety-glass panels, white painted steel frames, mirrors and diffraction panels to turn sunlight into a spectrum of colors that is an ever-changing work of art. Art lovers of all ages will also enjoy the three-dimensional mosaic sculptures by Sherri Warner Hunter — like the Airport Sun Project, a permanent acquisition.

Numerous services are available for airport visitors. Business travelers can find computer phone line hookups in specially designated areas throughout the terminal. Internet and e-mail access is available through new kiosks on the baggage level and airport concourses. Other consumer services include on-site rental cars, a host of restaurants and a food court, and specialty shops for tourists and golfers. There is a free children's play area on the ticketing level of the concourse connector. You'll also find two lounges, several news and gift shops, a bank, three ATMs, a welcome center, lockers, public telephones, courtesy and hotel phones, tele-services for the hearing impaired, first aid, shoe shines and a meditation room.

## John C. Tune Airport
**110 Tune Airport Dr. • (615) 350-5000**

John C. Tune Airport is a 399-acre general aviation reliever airport in west Nashville, 9 miles northwest of downtown. It opened in July 1986 and has undergone several expansions since, including the completion of a new, 36,000-square-foot terminal in October 1995. Nearly 100 aircraft, mostly private, are based here. Facilities include rental car delivery by Enterprise, a full-service maintenance facility for piston-powered aircraft, a helicopter service and a flight school.

The story of Nashville is full of fascinating characters, and the plots are filled with action, battles, victories, defeats, mysteries, political intrigue and romance — something for everyone.

# History

You don't have to be a history buff to become engrossed in the history of Nashville. It's as exciting a tale of drama and adventure as any you'll find at the theater or on TV. And it's a true story to boot. The story of Nashville is full of fascinating characters, and the plots are filled with action, battles, victories, defeats, mysteries, political intrigue and romance — something for everyone.

The story of the founding of Nashville is full of suspense and adventure. It is a story of courage and determination, hardship and hope. Land lured the first settlers west in 1779. They were looking for a new place to call home and were willing to give up their homes, chart territory unknown to them and brave whatever circumstances they might encounter — all for their dreams of a better future.

In this chapter, we tell you that story and highlight some of the people and events of the years to follow that made Nashville the interesting, dynamic city it is today — a place that continues to lure new "settlers" with its promise of a good life.

## Prehistory

Those early settlers in 1779 weren't the first to inhabit the area that is now Middle Tennessee. The land was first a home, hunting ground and burial ground for prehistoric Indians. Evidence of large Paleo-Indian villages has been found that suggests these early peoples lived in the area 11,000 to 12,000 years ago. The Mississippian culture of Indians, known as Mound Builders, inhabited the area from about A.D. 1000 to A.D. 1400. By A.D. 1200 their large villages, some occupying hundreds of acres, could be found throughout the area.

All that we know of them is what we have learned from the evidence they left behind. The Mound Builders buried their dead in stone-lined graves, covering them with earth. Many of these large, distinctive burial mounds, known as Temple Mounds, have been found at the village sites and along area rivers. Near the Harpeth River in west Nashville is Mound Bottom, a ceremonial site a couple miles upstream from the Narrows of the Harpeth State Historic Site. A historical marker on Cedar Hill Road off U.S. Highway 70 W. tells about that site. Burial grounds were found at the mouth of Stones River (across the Cumberland River in the Edgefield area) and at other sites in and around Nashville.

Additional evidence — tools, weapons, pieces of pottery and jewelry — left behind by the Mound Builders and other early Indians has been found. This evidence testifies to the intelligence and sophistication of these early "Nashvillians," some of whom are believed to have been influenced by Mexican culture.

Around the middle of the 15th century, the Indian villages mysteriously disappeared, and the area became a hunting ground for various tribes. Cherokee, Chickasaw, Creek and Shawnee shared the land, hunting the plentiful supply of buffalo, deer, bear, wild turkeys and geese. The Shawnee, the last Indians to have any sort of settlement in the area, were eventually driven out by Cherokees from the east and Chickasaws from the west in the early 1700s. The Cherokee and Chickasaw continued to use the land as a hunting ground and a place to trade.

In the late 1600s and early 1700s, French traders from Canada and what would become Louisiana established a trading post next to a high bluff along the Cumberland River near a salt lick (where animals came for a necessary supply of salt) and a sulfur spring. The spot, later known as French Lick, was just north of where the downtown area is today. A Frenchman, whose name is apparently unknown, established a trading post in 1710 to trade with the Shawnee and was soon joined there by a young French-Canadian named Jean de

Charleville. Charleville, only 14 when he arrived at the salt lick, eventually succeeded the Frenchman at the post.

Around 1769, while the area was still being shared by various Indian tribes, another French-Canadian fur trader arrived. Jacques-Timothe De Montbrun, a tall, athletic, dark-skinned man, came to French Lick from Kaskaskia, Illinois. He built a hut at French Lick and spent many winters buying furs from the Indians, which he would then sell in New Orleans. He finally settled in the area in the late 1780s and later operated a store and tavern at the square, where Second Avenue N. is today. Although his grandfather was the first Canadian to achieve nobility and De Montbrun himself was a lieutenant under George Rogers Clark and lieutenant governor of the Illinois District, De Montbrun preferred a more rugged lifestyle. It is said that he once lived or sought refuge from Indians in a cave on the banks of the Cumberland River, about a mile north of Riverfront Park. De Montbrun, later known as Timothy Demonbreun (pronounced Di-MUN-bree-un), is often referred to as the "first citizen" of Nashville. A historical marker has been placed at Third Avenue N. and Broadway to mark the site of his home; another marker at First Avenue at Riverfront Park tells about Demonbreun's Cave.

As Demonbreun and the other traders bartered with the Indians at French Lick, others ventured into the area in search of food and furs. Between 1769 and 1779, "long hunters" — explorers from the colonies of North Carolina and Virginia who lived and hunted in the wilderness for months, or even years, at a time — could be found here. Among these early travelers to our area were John Baker, Abraham Bledsoe, Joseph Drake, Kasper Mansker and John Rains. When these hunters discovered a salt lick, it usually was named after them; such names as Drake's Lick, Bledsoe's Lick and Mansker's Lick were bestowed by a group of hunters in 1771. Some of the long hunters are legendary. Uriah Stone, for whom the Stones River is named, reportedly was ribbed for some time after his furs

and hides were stolen right out from under him as he was preparing to head down river. And legend has it that Thomas Sharpe Spencer, a large man known as "Big Foot," lived for months in a hollow sycamore tree. Spencer, who planted corn at Bledsoe's Lick, where Sumner County is today, is credited with being the first white person to plant in Middle Tennessee.

# The Settlement

During the 1770s, the colonies along the East Coast in Virginia and North Carolina were becoming crowded. Settlers began hearing the call of the West. In those days, the area we now know as East Tennessee was "The West", and some people settled there in the early 1770s. The leader of the Watauga settlement in this area — Capt. James Robertson — would soon play a starring role in the history of Nashville.

In the spring of 1775, just weeks before the American Revolution began, Richard Henderson, a North Carolinian who was president of the Transylvania Land Company, met with Cherokee leaders at the Watauga River and convinced them to trade the land between the Ohio and Cumberland rivers for a few loads of guns, ammunition, rum and other goods. It turned out that the deal wasn't so simple, as Henderson's claim to the land was challenged by everyone from officials of Virginia and North Carolina to the British to the Chickasaws. In 1777, Henderson met with Robertson and Col. John Donelson, two men who eventually helped him secure his claim to the area along the Cumberland River.

In 1779, Henderson sent 35-year-old Robertson to find a suitable spot to build a new settlement. The Wataugans were being crowded by the growing settlements in their area, threatened by the Indians and were frightened of the nearby British early in the war. Robertson, a farmer, explorer, surveyor and negotiator with the Cherokee and Chickasaw, was the right man for the job. In early 1779, he and eight scouts made the trip to Cumberland country; their instructions were to locate a spot for the Wataugans to settle and to stake their claim on the land by planting a crop of corn.

They chose the area at the French Lick, and Robertson called the spot The Bluffs. Leaving three men behind to tend the corn, Robertson traveled up the Ohio River to obtain "cabin rights" from George Rogers Clark, and the rest of his entourage returned to Watauga in August. They told the people of the great river, the streams and creeks, the fertile and uncultivated land, canebrakes of 10 to 20 feet in height, the bountiful supply of fish, and the buffalo and other wild game that came to the salt lick. The salt spring near the bluffs meant a great deal to them as well: salt was a precious commodity, used in preserving meat.

It was decided that the Wataugans would move to The Bluffs in two groups. The trip through the wilderness was deemed too difficult for women and children, so the first party, led by Robertson, was made up of men and boys; the women and children would come later on boats, led by Donelson. In October 1779, the first group, a few hundred strong, set out, taking with them horses, cattle, sheep and pigs. They traveled a difficult, wintry route of 300 to 400 miles, following trails made by buffalo and early hunters through Kentucky and thick wilderness areas. Several families joined them along the way. They traveled for weeks, enduring bitter cold and heavy snows in one of the worst winters they had seen. Despite the difficulty of their journey, they made good time, and everyone arrived safely at The Bluffs.

It is generally thought that the group arrived at the north bank of the Cumberland River on December 25, 1779. When they reached the river, it was frozen, so they walked across with livestock in tow and settled on the opposite bank. That was the beginning of Nashville.

A few days before Robertson's party arrived at The Bluffs, Donelson and the second Watauga party had begun their 1,000-mile river journey. Donelson, in his mid-50s, led a group of more than 200 women, children, elderly men, slaves and their belongings in a 33-boat flotilla that departed December 22. Among the passengers was Donelson's 10th child, 13-year-old Rachel, who would eventually marry Andrew Jackson before he was elected seventh president of the United States. Donelson, a land speculator and surveyor who had served in the Virginia House of Burgesses before coming to Watauga, led the assortment of canoes and flatboats down the Holston River, down the Tennessee, up the Ohio and up the Cumberland. The group faced many more hardships than Robertson's party did.

They were short on river navigation skills — no one in the party had ever traveled the rivers — but they weren't going to let that stop them. The weather, however, was a different story. Only 5 miles into their voyage, severe weather forced them to stop and set up camp for two months. They resumed their journey in late February 1780, but didn't arrive at French Lick until two months later. The severe winter wasn't the only hardship they faced, as Donelson recorded in his journal. Numerous Indian attacks and frostbite claimed lives. One of the more horrifying incidents was the slaughter of a boatload of the travelers by Indians. Twenty-eight members of the entourage had contracted smallpox and were traveling together on a boat that brought up the rear of the flotilla. Indians captured their vessel, and the other travelers listened in horror as they were killed. The rest of the group wondered if they would soon meet a similar fate.

Hungry and exhausted, their provisions nearly gone, the crew pressed on, unsure of what the next bend in the river would bring. At one point, several groups, faced with dangerous rapids, opted to change course. Some headed down the Mississippi to Natchez, while others turned toward Illinois. "I am determined to pursue my course, happen what will," wrote

## INSIDERS' TIP

In 1784 Nashborough became Nashville. The English "borough" was replaced with the French "ville," most likely as a sign of appreciation for France's assistance during the American Revolution against Great Britain.

Donelson on Wednesday, March 15, 1780. He and his party finally arrived at The Bluffs on April 24, 1780.

On May 13, 1780, 256 men from the settlement signed the Cumberland Compact, which spelled out the rights of the settlers. The original document, representing the first civil government in Middle Tennessee, is preserved today in the Tennessee State Library and Archives. The settlers claimed land and built clusters of cabins in the area. High on the bluff on the west bank of the Cumberland they constructed what would become the capital of the settlement, Fort Nashborough, named in honor of Revolutionary War Gen. Francis Nash of North Carolina. The fort was reconstructed by the Daughters of the American Revolution in 1930. The current representation of the fort, built in 1962, features five reproductions of original Nashborough cabins and is open to the public (see our Attractions chapter).

As the settlers were busy building their new town, hard times were headed their way. The American Revolution continued, and Nashborough settlers were attacked by Indians, who had received arms from the British and Spanish. It soon became impossible for settlers to farm or hunt. Indian attacks caused Robertson to move his family to the safety of Fort Nashborough, while the Donelson family moved to Kentucky. In April of 1781, Indians attacked Nashborough in the "Battle of the Bluffs." Robertson's wife, Charlotte, was the hero of the day, saving the fort by turning a pack of angry, growling dogs on the attackers. It is said that after this battle, only 70 of the original 400 to 500 settlers remained in the area; other survivors had moved to safer areas. The Robertsons were among those who stayed. (The settlement faced its last severe attack in September 1792.)

In 1783 the American Revolution came to an end; the colonies had won their freedom. Also that year, the North Carolina Legislature created Davidson County. A year later, the legislature established the town of Nashville; the population was 600.

In the years that followed, Nashville grew rapidly, expanding beyond the boundaries of a frontier crossroads into an influential western town. In 1785, Presbyterian minister Thomas B. Craighead arrived to lead Davidson

Academy, Nashville's first school, and Dr. John Sappington, the town's first physician, arrived. In 1788 future U.S. president Andrew Jackson came to serve as the public prosecutor. He would have a lasting influence on Nashville as well as the entire country. Also in 1788, a man named Robert "Black Bob" Renfroe, a free African American, opened a tavern on the public square; it wasn't uncommon to find Jackson there.

Fifteen to 20 percent of Nashville's first black settlers were free, and they had voting privileges until 1835. In the late 1790s to early 1800s, there may have been as many as 200 free blacks in Davidson County. They could own property and attend school. Some operated businesses, such as barbershops and rooming houses. Sara Estell, for example, owned an ice cream parlor on Fifth Avenue N. and catered the firemen's functions. From 1833 to 1856, free African Americans conducted schools for black children in the Cedar Street neighborhood in view of the capitol, where Charlotte Avenue is now. In 1791, slaves accounted for one of every five residents in Davidson County, and by 1800, one of every three residents.

# The Jackson Era

In 1796 Tennessee became the 16th state in the Union. Nashville's first church — a Methodist church built near the courthouse, jail and stocks — was built that year too. Three years later, the town's first newspaper was printed. Between 1796 and 1800, Davidson County's population grew nearly 170 percent, from 3,600 to 9,600. In 1800, only 400 of the 9,600 Davidson Countians resided in Nashville. The city was on its way to becoming a leader in the Western territory and soon would be the focus of national and international attention.

Andrew Jackson is credited for much of the city's growth and influence during the first half of the 19th century. After arriving as a 21-year-old public prosecutor, he achieved success quickly, and, in part because he often accepted land grants as payment for his services, became very wealthy. Upon his arrival in town, he boarded at the home of John Donelson's widow (Donelson was mysteriously killed in 1786 while en route from Kentucky to

Photo: Tennessee State Library and Archives

This late 19th-century scene depicts the northeast corner of Fourth Avenue and Union Street in downtown Nashville.

Nashville), where he met and fell in love with the Donelsons' daughter Rachel, who had separated from her husband, Lewis Robards. Jackson and Rachel Donelson Robards were married in 1791, and repeated their vows in 1794 after discovering — amidst something of a social scandal — that Rachel's divorce from her first husband had never been made official. The Jacksons' marriage remained a topic of gossip for quite some time.

Other soon-to-be prominent Nashvillians during this time included John Overton and Sam Houston. While boarding at Donelson's, Jackson met young attorney Overton, a fellow boarder who arrived in 1789. Overton eventually became a well-known lawmaker, judge and key advisor to Jackson during his presidential campaigns. Overton and Jackson were partners in many land deals. Overton also is known for his home, Travellers Rest, today a National Historic Place at 636 Farrell Parkway off Franklin Pike. Another of Jackson's friends and supporters was Sam Houston, an interesting (to say the least) character. After moving to Nashville, Houston served as district attorney and served two terms in Congress before being elected Tennessee's governor in 1827. By the early 1830s, he had left Tennessee and the governorship, living for a while

with the Cherokee and then moving to Texas, preparing to lead the area to its independence from Mexico. He served as president of the Republic of Texas, and then as a senator and a governor for the state of Texas. He was ousted from his post as governor for refusing to join the Confederacy.

As Jackson was becoming the star of the day, Nashville continued to grow. Manufacturers and mercantile firms sprang up among the town's four brick buildings, frame houses and numerous cedar log homes and stores. Among them were a cotton-spinning factory, cotton gin factories, coppersmiths, cabinet makers, silversmiths, blacksmiths, a tannery and a nail factory.

In 1806, the community was incorporated as a city, and Joseph Coleman was elected the first mayor. Before 1810, a fire-fighting force was established; the state's first bank, the Bank of Nashville, was founded; and the first book to be produced in Nashville was published. By 1810, Nashville's population was approaching 2,000. Residents of the city lived mainly near where First, Second, Third and Fourth avenues are today.

Its location along the Cumberland River made Nashville a prime city for trading. Boats loaded with flour, tobacco, cotton, iron and other products left for New Orleans each spring, and before long a regular trade was established between the two cities.

Meanwhile, Jackson, who had served in the U.S. Senate and as a justice of the state Supreme Court, was preparing for battle. In 1812, Congress declared war on Great Britain, and the War of 1812 was begun. Jackson, a colorful figure described as both a "roughneck" and a "gentleman," became a national hero for his role in the war, leading American troops to victories over the Creek Indians (British allies) and over the British themselves in New Orleans in 1815. News of a peace treaty signed two weeks before the New Orleans battle didn't reach the battlefield in time, so Jackson's last and greatest military victory was actually won after the war had ended.

Jackson had a reputation among his troops as a tough-as-nails military man, and, after one of his soldiers said he was as tough as hickory wood, Jackson's nickname became "Old Hickory." Numerous reminders of the nickname remain throughout Nashville today.

In 1824, despite winning the popular vote, Jackson lost his bid for the presidency of the United States to John Quincy Adams, but he returned victorious in 1828, becoming the first man from west of the Appalachian Mountains to be elected president. More significantly, however, was his role in the founding of a new Democratic party characterized by a spirit of reform and interest in the welfare of the common man. The roots of today's Democratic Party date back to this time. Jackson was elected to a second term as president, serving through 1837. His wife, Rachel, died of a heart attack in December 1828, before his first inauguration.

Having a hometown hero in the White House did much to boost Nashville's reputation. While president, Jackson made several trips to his plantation, the Hermitage, 12 miles northeast of Nashville, often entertaining renowned guests there. When his term was up, he returned to the Hermitage, where he worked to promote other Democrats such as Tennessean and later Nashville resident James K. Polk, who was elected president in 1844. Jackson died at his home June 8, 1845, marking the end of an era of Nashville history. He is buried next to his wife at the Hermitage garden.

Nashville saw much progress during that era. Before Jackson's terms in the White House, the city became a center of trade. On March 11, 1819, residents gathered along the banks of the Cumberland to welcome for the first time the *General Jackson*, the first steamboat to arrive in the city. The luxurious, $16,000 *General Jackson*, named after Andrew Jackson, was no doubt quite a sight. Soon Nashville was engaged in a prosperous river trade with ports along the Ohio and Mississippi rivers. In the 1840s, Nashvillians were making 15-day round trips to New Orleans by steamboat, some outfitted with music, gambling and various amusements. They could travel to Memphis or St. Louis in 10 days, and to Pittsburgh in five.

Other signs of growth during this time: the completion of Nashville's first publicly owned waterworks in 1833; the founding of the first insurance company, Tennessee Marine and Fire Insurance Company, in 1833; Nashville's growth as a religious community and religious publishing center; and the construction of turnpikes such as the Franklin, Murfreesboro and Gallatin pikes in the 1830s, and Nolensville, Charlotte, Lebanon and White's Creek pikes in the 1840s, all of which are key roads leading to and from the downtown area today. A toll bridge was built across the Cumberland River in 1823, and in 1853, a suspension bridge connected the downtown area with the Edgefield area to the east. Methods of communication and transportation were improving too: Nashville received its first telegraph in 1848 and the first steam engine, the No. 1, arrived in 1850, ordered by the Nashville and Chattanooga Railroad, which was completed to Chattanooga in 1854.

By 1840, the city had a population of 6,929 — a 25 percent increase from the 1830 census. In 1843, Nashville was named the permanent capital of Tennessee, chosen because city officials had offered a 4-acre plot of land for the Tennessee State Capitol. Construction of the impressive capitol began July 4, 1845, following the design of architect William F. Strickland of Philadelphia, an authority on Greek Revival architecture. The building was completed in 1859.

In 1850 the population topped 10,000 for the first time. The Nashville of the mid-1800s boasted schools, churches, newspapers, gas-

# The Maxwell House:
# Much More Than Coffee

When John Overton Jr. began construction on his downtown luxury hotel in 1859, many locals derisively referred to the project as "Overton's Folly." After all, Nashville at that time had a population of fewer than 17,000 and little apparent need for such a showplace. Time would prove these naysayers wrong, however, as the Maxwell House Hotel would develop a national reputation — and a name that today lives on, most notably in a popular-brand beverage.

Close-up

But we're getting ahead of the story. The completion of Overton's hotel, designed by Isaiah Rogers of Cincinnati, was significantly delayed by the outbreak of the Civil War. The first residents of the unfinished building were Confederate troops, who dubbed it Zollicoffer Barracks in honor of Gen. Felix K. Zollicoffer, a former Nashville newspaperman who had joined the rebel army as a volunteer. By 1862, the building, like the rest of Nashville, had fallen into the hands of Union troops, who used it first as a barracks, then a hospital and, finally, a prison. It was in this last configuration that tragedy struck the building, as several Confederate prisoners reportedly were killed when a stair collapsed in September 1863.

After the war, construction resumed, and in September 1869, the Maxwell House Hotel officially opened at the corner of Cherry (now Fourth) and Church streets. It didn't take long for the new hotel to establish itself as a place for the elite to meet. The dining room became famous not only for its menu's quality, but also for its quantity, with sumptuous spreads of rich foods, especially during holidays and other special occasions. "Christmas menus might offer a choice of as many as 22 meats, including

— continued on next page

Photo: The Maxwell House Hotel

The Regal Maxwell House today continues the tradition of the original Maxwell House.

roast quail, Minnesota venison, Cumberland Mountain black bear and broiled pheasants," according to a history of the hotel prepared by today's Regal Maxwell House Hotel (more on that later).

Several U.S. presidents stayed at the Maxwell House, including Tennessee's own Andrew Johnson, Hayes, Cleveland, Benjamin Harrison, McKinley, Theodore Roosevelt, Taft and Wilson. The wide range of other prominent politicians, civic and business leaders, socialites and entertainers who sampled the hotel's hospitality include social reformer Jane Addams, actress Sarah Bernhardt, orator William Jennings Bryan, Wild West star Buffalo Bill, opera star Enrico Caruso, inventor Thomas Edison, auto maker Henry Ford and the famous midget Tom Thumb.

As you've probably guessed by now, the hotel also became noted for its coffee, provided by local entrepreneur Joel Cheek. That Cheek-Neal brand of coffee was served to President Theodore Roosevelt when he visited Nashville on October 22, 1907. This was a major event to Nashvillians, and crowds lined the streets to watch the popular president arrive. After speaking briefly at the Ryman Auditorium, Roosevelt traveled on to the Hermitage, where he had breakfast at Andrew Jackson's former home. Asked for his opinion of the Cheek-Neal coffee he had been served, the president pronounced it "good to the last drop." Advertising copywriters have been known to kill for phrases like that, of course, and those words have served as a slogan for the Maxwell House brand ever since.

On August 1, 1928, the giant General Foods Corporation bought the Cheek-Neal Company for a price — in cash and General Foods stock — that was reported to be around $45 million, at the time the largest financial transaction in Nashville history. The fortune generated by this sale, incidentally, lives on in Cheekwood — Nashville's Home of Art and Gardens. Cheekwood is the former estate of entrepreneur Leslie Cheek, who earlier had the foresight to invest in his cousin Joel's coffee company. (For more information about Cheekwood, see our Attractions chapter.)

As for "Overton's Folly," the original Maxwell House Hotel lived on for many more years, being converted into a residential hotel in its later years. The Maxwell House literally went out in a blaze of glory on Christmas night 1961, when it was destroyed by fire. The corner of Fourth and Church streets is now occupied by a bank and office building commonly referred to as the SunTrust building. But the Maxwell House name lives on, not only in a bestselling coffee brand, but also in another Nashville hotel. In 1979, the Clarion Maxwell House Hotel opened at 2025 MetroCenter Boulevard; in 1991, under new ownership, it became the Regal Maxwell House, which advertises "plantation grandeur" and "continues to uphold the standards of Southern elegance and hospitality." Enjoy a meal in Praline's, the hotel restaurant, and be sure to try the coffee, which remains "good to the last drop."

lit streets and an educated, wealthy contingent of citizens. The first permanent Roman Catholic Church in the state, St. Mary's Catholic Church, was completed in 1847. Numerous Protestant churches and a small Jewish community could be found here. Schools included University of Nashville, formerly known as Davidson Academy and Cumberland College; Nashville Female Academy, which was founded in 1816 and by the 1850s had become the largest school for girls in the South; Tennessee School for the Blind, founded in

1846; the University of Nashville medical school, founded in 1851; and Hume School, the first public school, which opened in 1855 at the northeast corner of Eighth Avenue N. and Broad Street.

Nashvillians were interested in more than studying, though. In the 1850s, they could claim a variety of cultural interests and activities. The beautiful Adelphi Theater, the city's premier entertainment venue, opened in 1850 in the area of Fourth and Charlotte avenues, where the Municipal Auditorium is today, and began offering top-notch entertainment. Residents flocked to hear Jenny Lind, the Swedish soprano, perform there in 1851, and in 1854, an Italian opera company offered Nashvillians their first live opera experience. The theater also booked regular performances by theater companies with known actors.

There was much to enjoy about life in Nashville in the mid-1800s. The city was thriving. In 1860, it was the eighth-largest city in the South and had two publishing houses, five daily newspapers, five banks and numerous mills, factories, breweries and wholesale houses. But the city's growth and prosperity was about to come to a halt — and it would remain there four years.

# The Civil War Years

Historians say the Civil War had several causes; political, governmental and economic forces that continued to separate the North and the South were at work. Most agree, however, that the issue of slavery was at the root. The debate over slavery had been growing for years.

Nashvillians had long discussed the issue, and they watched as the nation became divided. Though slavery was allowed in this Southern city, slave owners made up a minority of its total population of 16,988 in 1860. Included in that number were 3,211 slaves (nearly 19 percent of the population) and 719 free blacks. Nashvillians, and indeed Tennesseans in general, were certainly not at the front of the line of those wanting to join the Confederacy: Tennessee was the last state to secede from the Union and the first to rejoin after the war ended. Early on, the city had been committed to the Union. Nashville had held pro-Union meetings and at one point even rejected the governor's idea to secede. Nashvillians favored the idea of slavery, but surely not enough to go to war over it.

On April 12, 1861, Confederates attacked Fort Sumter in Charleston, S.C., marking the beginning of the Civil War. Three days later President Lincoln called for Union troops, and the Confederate states took this as a sign to prepare for battle. Virginia, Arkansas and North Carolina pledged their allegiance to the South, joining South Carolina, Mississippi, Florida, Alabama, Georgia, Louisiana and Texas. On May 6, Tennessee became the 11th and final state to join the Confederate States of America, led by their president, Jefferson Davis. The vote in Nashville was 3,029 for secession and 250 for the Union.

As its young men signed up to serve the cause, Nashville mobilized quickly and became a key center for the manufacture and storage of weapons and other supplies to support the Southern army. But Nashville didn't remain a Confederate city for long. When Union troops captured nearby Fort Henry and Fort Donelson, gaining control of the Cumberland River to Nashville, they had a clear shot at the city. There was no way the Army of Tennessee could defend the capital city, so the Confederate commander ordered his troops to exit. When the troops abandoned Nashville, the city panicked. While some citizens boarded the first trains out of town, others packed what belongings they could onto wagons and carriages and fled. They cut the ties on the suspension bridge and set fire to the railroad bridge. Rioting and looting broke out. On February 24, after Federal troops had closed in, Nashville Mayor Richard B. Cheatham surrendered the city.

Nashville's position along the Cumberland River plus its good road and railroad links to other major cities made it a prime target and a highly desirable western base for the Union. The troops girded the city with a string of forts, including Fort Negley, the largest of the fortifications. Trenches and rifle pits surrounded the city. Nashville was secure.

In March 1862, President Lincoln appointed Tennessee native and former governor Andrew Johnson to serve as military governor to the state. Johnson's goal was to reclaim Tennessee's loyalty to the Union. Johnson required all government officials and other professionals to sign an oath of loyalty to the United States, arresting and imprisoning those who refused. During the occupation, more than 8,000 blacks sought refuge in Nashville, tripling the black population to more than 12,000. They helped fortify the city against attack and served in the Federal army. Two thousand assisted in the construction of Fort Negley. Thousands more served in combat.

Serving as a Union base took a toll on Nashville. Buildings and homes were destroyed to make room for forts. Churches and other buildings were taken over to serve the military's needs. More than half the city's trees were cut down. Some of the citizens managed to make a living supplying the citizens and military with supplies and services or working for federal operations.

When Union Gen. William T. Sherman marched through Georgia, leaving Atlanta in flames in November 1864, Confederate Gen. John B. Hood turned his troops north toward Nashville with the plan of recapturing the city. He thought he might then be able to join Robert E. Lee in Virginia and pursue Ulysses S. Grant. General George H. Thomas, who had more than 70,000 soldiers, was prepared to defend Nashville. Hood's soldiers numbered 23,000. Hood's plan was, obviously, a misguided one. He thought he could lure the Federal troops south and then attack Nashville. On November 30, Hood's Confederate soldiers met with a Union force at the Battle of Franklin. Hood attacked and, in less than six hours, lost 6,252 of his troops, including 12 generals. The Union lost 2,326 men.

The Union force withdrew to Nashville. Hood advanced. By December 2, the Confederates had settled into a position in the hills just south of town. They waited. Thomas waited too, unwilling to attack until the time was right. On December 8, Nashville was hit by a severe ice storm. Both armies were immobilized but remained ready. On December 15, after the ice thawed, Thomas and his Union soldiers attacked the Confederates. Moving from the river toward the south and the east, the Federal forces pushed Hood's troops back. One day later, Thomas wiped out three Confederate positions, and the rest of the Southern forces retreated to the south. The death toll from the two-day Battle of Nashville was 6,000 for the Confederates, 3,100 for the Union.

The Battle of Nashville was the last major conflict of the war. On April 9, 1865, Gen. Robert E. Lee, leader of the main Confederate army, surrendered to Gen. Ulysses S. Grant at Appomattox Court House, Virginia.

# Athens of the South

On April 15, 1865, six days after Appomattox, President Lincoln died after being shot by John Wilkes Booth. Andrew Johnson, former military governor-turned-vice president, became the 17th president of the United States, the third Tennessean to go to the White House. As Johnson set out to restore the Union, Nashville began its restoration. It had fared much better than some Southern cities had during the war, but there was damage to repair. The next two decades would produce a truly revitalized Nashville, a city that would be a leading commercial center and a growing center of higher education for blacks and whites.

Highlights of the early postwar period include the appearance of mule-drawn street cars in 1865; the state's ratification of the Fourteenth Amendment to the U.S. Constitution, which took effect in 1868, providing citizenship for former slaves and delivering them full civil rights; and the stabilization of Nashville's city government in 1869. In September 1869, Nashville's elegant new Maxwell House Hotel made its official debut. The under-construction hotel had been used by Confederate and then Union troops during the war. The hotel soon became one of the most popular in the country, welcoming presidents and other high-profile guests.

In 1866 a new suspension bridge was completed. Tolls paid for its construction. The prices to cross included 75¢ for a four-horse carriage, 15¢ for a horse and buggy, 5¢ for a person traveling on horseback and 1¢ for a hog; pedestrians could cross free.

Progress continued, and Nashville's population boomed. Between 1860 and 1870, the population in the city alone jumped more than 52 percent to 25,865. Crowded conditions on the waterfront area, lack of a sewer system, poor water quality and lack of regulations on industries made for an unhealthy environment. Several cholera epidemics broke out in the years before and after the war; one epidemic claimed the lives of 1,000 people.

Nashville's economic growth continued, and the city made great strides in education. Once known as a frontier crossroads, then as French Lick and The Bluffs, Nashville would soon become known as the Athens of the South for its abundance of colleges and universities. The postwar period marked the opening of such institutions as Fisk University, Vanderbilt University, Meharry Medical College and Peabody College.

Blacks and northern missionaries started several colleges. The first was Roger Williams University, in 1864, originally called the Nashville Normal and Theological Institute. In 1866 a free school for blacks, Fisk School, now known as Fisk University, opened its doors. The school was named for Clinton B. Fisk, an official with the Freedmen's Bureau for Tennessee and Kentucky, a federal agency that served the needs of newly free blacks. Classes initially were held in a Union military hospital on Church Street. That first year, as many as 1,000 African-American men, women and children signed up for classes. In the 1870s, the school's wonderful chorus, the Jubilee Singers, saved the financially failing university. The group, founded in 1867, toured throughout the United States and later around the world, raising enough money to purchase a 25-acre campus and fund work on a new school building. On January 1, 1876, Jubilee Hall opened — the country's first permanent building constructed for the purpose of educating African Americans. Today, it is a National Historic Landmark.

Another school for blacks was Central Tennessee College, established in south Nashville in 1865. The school later moved to College Street and in 1900 changed its name to Walden University before closing in 1915. The university's medical department evolved into Meharry Medical College, which offered the country's first medical education program for African Americans. Today, it is the country's largest private medical school for blacks. The medical school was organized in 1876 and named for the family that generously helped support it. Meharry moved to northwest Nashville near Fisk University in 1931.

Vanderbilt University, on a 75-acre campus west of downtown, opened its doors in 1875. (Today, the nationally prominent school is the largest among Nashville's many colleges and universities.) It was founded in 1873 with a gift of $1 million from Cornelius Vanderbilt to Methodist Bishop Holland N. McTyeire, Vanderbilt's wife's cousin by marriage. McTyeire represented Southern Methodists who were planning to build the Central University of the Methodist Episcopal Church South. Following Vanderbilt's conditions, the board of trustees appointed McTyeire board president for life; they changed the name of their planned university to Vanderbilt University in appreciation for Vanderbilt's assistance.

Nashville's oldest college, the University of Nashville, evolved into a well-known teacher training institution after getting aid from a fund established by George Peabody of Massachusetts. The literary department of the former Cumberland College and Davidson College separated to become the Tennessee State Normal College in 1875, later becoming the George Peabody College for Teachers. In 1979, Peabody College became part of Vanderbilt University.

Other schools during the postwar period included Saint Bernard Academy, a school for girls founded in 1868, and Ward Seminary, another school for girls. Ward later merged with Belmont Junior College for young women, established in 1890, to form Ward-Belmont. Watkins Institute was a free vocational school for adults; the institute rented unused space in its large building to businesses. In 1891 David Lipscomb College got its start as the Nashville Bible School; it was named for the late Church of Christ minister Lipscomb.

Nashville's public schools grew after the war as well. In 1874 high school classes of the city's first public school, Hume School, moved to the adjacent Fogg School. In the early 1890s, there were approximately 8,000 students enrolled in public schools in Nashville. There were also a number of private academies.

By 1897 Nashville had earned a reputation as the Athens of the South.

As Nashville grew as an educational center, its population exploded. By 1880, when the city celebrated its 100th anniversary with the month-long Nashville Centennial Exposition, the population had increased to 43,350; Davidson County's population was 79,009. In the next 10 years, the city's population grew 75 percent, totaling 76,168, while the county's population grew to 108,174. Nashville's African-American community accounted for nearly 40 percent of the population by 1890. By then, electric trolleys had replaced the mule-drawn streetcars, and the city had telephone service. In 1890 Nashville's first football gamed pitted Vanderbilt against Peabody. Also that year, General Hospital opened with 60 beds. Nashvillians had been enjoying professional baseball for years, played since 1885 at Sulphur Dell Park — today, site of the Bicentennial Capitol Mall.

The year 1892 marked the premiere of one of Nashville's most famous landmarks — the Union Gospel Tabernacle, later renamed Ryman Auditorium. Riverboat captain Thomas G. Ryman built the facility after being inspired by Georgia evangelist Sam Jones, a traveling Southern Methodist minister. Ryman wanted a permanent site for Jones's revivals and other religious gatherings. Jones preached there on a few occasions, but by 1900, the building was gaining a reputation as a premier theater in the South. It hosted theatrical and musical productions and political rallies. After Ryman died in 1904, the venue was renamed for him. It served as home to the *Grand Ole Opry* from 1941 to 1974. Today it is on the National Register of Historic Places and, since reopening in 1993 after a renovation, is one of Nashville's

most popular entertainment venues. (See our Arts and Culture, Music City U.S.A. and Attractions chapters for details.)

Historic happenings of 1896 included the first automobile to be driven in Nashville and the founding of the National Baptist Publishing Board, dedicated to the publication of religious materials that would serve the African-American community. The next year, Nashville would host its biggest party yet.

# Centennial Exposition

Tennessee marked its 100th anniversary as a state in 1896, but had to wait until 1897 for the party. From May 1 to October 31, 1897, Nashville hosted the Tennessee Centennial Exposition in West Side Park, now Centennial Park. Officials had begun planning the event in 1893, but a lack of funds forced them to delay the festivities for a year. Support from the railroad companies helped ensure the exposition would be a success.

The six-month celebration, produced at a cost of more than $1.1 million, featured numerous exhibits, amusement rides, dancers and a dazzling display of lights. The centerpiece of the exposition was a replica of the Parthenon, the temple of Athena, goddess of wisdom, that stands on the Acropolis in Athens, Greece. Nashville's replica, built following plans provided by the king of Greece, was intended to be a temporary structure, like the exposition's exhibit buildings that were constructed of wood and plaster. During the Centennial Exposition, the Parthenon housed works of art.

The Tennessee Centennial Exposition was hailed as a success. It welcomed more than 1.7 million visitors from around the world and was the first such event in America to earn a profit.

After the exposition, the exhibit buildings were torn down, but Nashvillians were fond of their Parthenon, a symbol of the city's reputation as the Athens of the South, and let it stand. The City Parks Board rebuilt the facility out of concrete after it began to deteriorate in the early 1920s. The exterior of the Parthenon features 46 Doric columns and two pairs of bronze doors, each weighing 7.5 tons. Inside are marble floors, a ceiling made of cypress and, the highlight, a magnificent, 42-foot statue of Athena, completed in 1990. A wide selection of art can be found in the Parthenon's art gallery. Today, another restoration project continues at the popular attraction, which makes quite an impression as the focus of Centennial Park. (See our Attractions chapter for more information.)

# A New Century

At the beginning of the 20th century, Nashville's population was 80,865, while Davidson County's total stood at 122,790. The city was on the verge of major growth, soon to become a leader in finance, insurance and publishing.

One of the highlights of 1900 was the premiere of Nashville's new Union Station train shed at the corner of Broad and Walnut streets. The official dedication of the spectacular new Romanesque building took place October 9, 1900. Construction had taken more than two years and involved the razing of more than 200 buildings at the site. Atop the building's tower stood a 19-foot copper figure of Mercury, the Roman god of commerce and travel and messenger to the other gods. (The statue was blown down in a windstorm in 1952; a new Mercury was installed in 1997, only to be damaged by the spring 1998 tornado that swept through downtown Nashville. A repaired Mercury graces the tower today.) Union Station provided an important link to the country's leading railroad cities.

The downtown area continued to grow. In 1903, the 360-foot-long, 75-foot-wide Arcade, a modern two-level, glass-covered mall boasting 40 stores and occupying about an acre of space, opened between Fourth and Fifth avenues N. The $300,000 project was similar to popular shopping areas in the Northeast. The first skyscraper, the 12-story First National Bank (Bradford Building) at Church Street and Fourth Avenue N., was constructed in 1904 by

banker Frank Overton Watts, and the city's Carnegie Library opened at the corner of Eighth Avenue N. and Union Street. That same year, the names of downtown streets were changed to numbers. The Hermitage Hotel opened downtown in 1910.

Banking was big business for the city, and Nashville became one of the South's leading financial centers. Insurance was also big business. By 1903, two major insurance companies — National Life and Accident Insurance Company and Life and Casualty Insurance Company of Tennessee — had been formed. Nashville also was growing as a center of distribution for a number of goods. Leading commercial activities included the production, processing and/or distribution of grain, groceries, dry goods, lumber, and boots and shoes. In the printing and publishing fields, Nashville companies offered everything from popular magazines to religious publications, the latter produced by its numerous religious publishing houses. Business growth was accompanied by growth in education, communication, transportation, religion and culture.

Two disasters made Nashville headlines in the second decade of this century. One was the flood of 1912. In the early morning hours of November 5, the southeast wall of the round limestone reservoir on Eighth Avenue S. cracked, spilling 25 million gallons of water down the hill into the area's homes. The city repaired the damage, and the reservoir is still in use today. On March 22, 1916, a fire erupted in east Nashville. It reportedly started in a mill on First Street, and before long, winds had swept the flames throughout the area. The fire burned for four hours, killing one person, destroying nearly 1,000 buildings and leaving 3,000 people homeless.

A little more than a year later, in April 1917, the first World War began. Nashvillians gave their enthusiastic support to their country, as some 15,000 men and women from Davidson County volunteered for service. The Old Hickory Powder Plant, a U.S. government facility that manufactured smokeless powder for the Allied forces, was built in 1918 at Hadley's Bend on the Cumberland River. DuPont, which had built the plant and the town around it — Old Hickory — purchased both after the war ended in 1919.

# Segregation, Whiskey and Women's Rights

Racial segregation continued to grow during the early 1900s, as a number of laws were established that restricted the rights of black citizens. In 1905, Nashville's African-American community began a boycott of electric streetcars after a law was passed requiring separation of black and white passengers on them. At the time, blacks made up more than 30 percent of the city and county populations. Sadly, segregation continued to become more severe and for some time remained an issue of primary concern only to the population that suffered its unfair consequences. (It wasn't until the late 1950s that city schools were desegregated, and following sit-ins at lunch counters in downtown stores and other nonviolent protests beginning in 1960, public facilities were finally open to all citizens by 1963.)

A positive change came about as a result of another social issue of the early 1900s: women in America won the right to vote. Nashville played a key role in the women's suffrage movement. Suffragists had been gathering steam across America, and in 1914 the National American Woman Suffrage Association held its national meeting at Nashville's Hermitage Hotel. Nashville women who were influential in Tennessee's suffrage campaign included Anne Dallas Dudley and Catherine Talty Kenny, prominent in the Tennessee League of Women Voters. In 1918 that organization merged with another group of suffragettes, and the newly formed group was headed by Kate Burch Warner. That same year, President Woodrow Wilson announced his support for the movement.

By March of 1920, 35 states had approved passage of the 19th constitutional amendment, which would make it illegal to deny women the right to vote. One more state was needed for the amendment to become law. Suffragettes, led by Carrie Chapman Catt, targeted Tennessee, which had more than 60 chapters of the suffragist organization. In July and August of 1920, making the Hermitage Hotel their headquarters, they pushed for the state's legislature to vote in favor of their cause. They won, and on August 18, 1920, Tennessee cast the deciding vote, becoming the 36th state to ratify the 19th amendment.

The issue of temperance — total abstinence from alcoholic beverages — had been debated for years. The city's first temperance organization had been formed in 1829, 50 years after the first settlers arrived. These early efforts had little effect. By the early 1900s, Nashville had more than 150 saloons. By 1909, 11 years before Prohibition (1920 to 1933), the Tennessee Legislature declared it illegal to sell alcoholic beverages within 4 miles of a school or to manufacture alcoholic beverages. Only a handful of states had taken this route of total prohibition. The rules were loosely enforced in Nashville until the national Prohibition amendment outlawed the manufacture, sale and transportation of alcohol. Bootleggers took over after that, however.

# Grand Ole Opry

Nashville's population had passed the 100,000 mark in 1910, and by 1920, 118,342 lived in the city, while 49,473 more lived in Davidson County. Automobiles had all but replaced horses and wagons on city streets, and Nashville had its first symphony orchestra.

During the '20s, a new type of music was beginning to develop: old-time music, later called hillbilly music and eventually known as country music. A Nashville-based radio program would have a lot to do with the development of this emerging music genre.

Nashville's famed *Grand Ole Opry* premiered in 1925. Interested in radio as an advertising medium (the first commercial radio station, Pittsburgh's KDKA, had signed on the air in 1920), the prosperous National Life and Accident Insurance Company launched radio station WSM on October 5, 1925. The station's call letters came from the insurance company's slogan, We Shield Millions. The station played a mixture of live classical, jazz and other pop music, with a few banjo players, fiddlers and other performers of newly popular "old-time tunes" thrown in here and there. Soon after WSM hit the airwaves, popular Chicago radio announcer George D. Hay came to Nashville's fledgling station and started a show similar to the *WLS National Barn Dance* he had hosted in Chicago.

On November 28, the station showcased the talents of 78-year-old fiddler Uncle Jimmy Thompson and his niece/piano accompanist, Eva Thompson Jones. With 1,000 watts, WSM had one of the strongest signals of any station in America, and that night, listeners from around the country called and sent telegrams with their enthusiastic praise of the program. The *Grand Ole Opry* was born.

The *WSM Barn Dance*, as it was called for a time, began airing its old-time music program every Saturday night, mainly featuring local amateur acts. Among the early stars the show produced were Thompson and Uncle Dave Macon. The *Barn Dance* became the *Grand Ole Opry* in December 1927. The name change came about when, one evening, after an NBC classical music program from Chicago had aired, Hay introduced a short program of music from *Barn Dance* regulars by saying, "For the past hour, we have been listening to the music taken largely from Grand Opera, but from now on we will present the Grand Ole Opry!" Soon after that the program expanded to a four-hour broadcast, and WSM became a 5,000-watt station reaching 50 percent of America.

After relocating a few times, including a stint at the War Memorial Auditorium, the *Grand Ole Opry* moved to the 3,000-seat Ryman Auditorium in 1941. The Ryman became known as "The Mother Church of Country Music." In 1974, the *Opry* moved to a specially built, state-of-the-art production facility at what was then the Opryland theme park, where it continues to entertain country music fans old and new

and remains the longest-running radio program in America. (See our Music City U.S.A. chapter for details.)

# Depression, Suburban Growth and World War II

While the *Opry* was putting the spotlight on Nashville and making stars out of the show's early performers, the nation's economy was spiraling toward disaster. The stock market crash of October 29, 1929, sent the country into the Great Depression. Nashville was by that time an established financial center, and the bank failures, layoffs and business failures didn't leave the city untouched. One of the biggest stories to come out of Nashville during this time was the collapse of Caldwell and Company, led by Rogers Caldwell and Luke Lea, in 1930. When their financial empire fell, it sparked a series of bank failures — as many as 120 in seven states.

In 1933, newly elected Democratic president Franklin D. Roosevelt announced his New Deal, a program of economic and social policies designed to get America back on track. Nashville benefited from the creation of the Tennessee Valley Authority, the Works Progress Administration and similar organizations and programs. The WPA, created in 1935, meant jobs for Nashvillians and improvements throughout the city, such as renovation of existing streets, construction of miles of new streets, construction of a new airport (named Berry Field, in honor of WPA official Harry S. Berry) and improvements to the Warner Parks and other public parks.

Making headlines along the way were the 1933 tornado that destroyed hundreds of homes in east Nashville, American Airlines initiating passenger service to Nashville's new airport in 1936 and the 1938 establishment of the Nashville Housing Authority. In 1937, Nashville artist William Edmondson became the first African American to have a one-man show at New York's Museum of Modern Art.

During this time, Nashvillians had been leaving the central city for the suburbs. In 1930, Nashville's population was 153,866, while the total for Davidson County was 222,854. By 1940, Nashville's population had grown 9 percent, to 167,402, while Davidson County's grew 15 percent, to 257,267. Areas such as Belmont Heights, Sylvan Park and west Nashville became popular. In 1938, west Nashville's Belle Meade was the first of the residential areas to incorporate as a city.

When Japan bombed Pearl Harbor on December 7, 1941, igniting World War II, Nashville was on its way toward recovery from the Depression; the war gave the city the push it needed to get back on its feet. While thousands of residents headed off to war, area manufacturers went into wartime production. Among the many manufacturers were the $9 million Aviation Manufacturing Corporation of California's Vultee Aircraft, which built military aircraft and employed 7,000; Nashville Bridge Company, which built navy minesweepers, barges and other vessels; and General Shoe Corporation (Genesco), which made footwear for military personnel. The Middle Tennessee area, with its varied terrain, was chosen as the site of the world's largest military training efforts, which brought in hundreds of thousands of army personnel. Thousands more, stationed at nearby military camps, descended on Nashville on the weekends for entertainment. More than 1 million came through Nashville during the first year of the war.

Nashville prospered during the war, and by September 2, 1945, when Japan signed its surrender to the Allied forces, the Depression was just a memory. In the following years, Nashville's insurance business boomed. By the early 1960s, the city was home to eight insurance companies (including giants National Life and Accident, and Life and Casualty) that had more than $2 billion in assets.

The postwar period also saw Nashville's growth as a religious center. A number of missionary-training colleges were opened, religious publishing houses flourished, and denominational headquarters were established in the city. Nashville also had a huge number of churches. "The Protestant Vatican" and "Buckle of the Bible Belt" were added to Nashville's list of nicknames.

During the 1940s, Nashvillians began using TVA's electricity in their homes; downtown traffic jams were common; buses replaced the city's electric streetcars; the city's first recording studio, Castle Studio, opened; the

Children's Museum, later known as the Cumberland Science Museum, opened; a new Nashville Symphony was founded; Roy Acuff emerged as a country music star (and ran unsuccessfully for governor in 1948); and Hank Williams made his *Opry* debut and had his first hit single, "Lovesick Blues." The audience for the *Grand Ole Opry* had been growing, and in September 1947, *Opry* performers, including Ernest Tubb and Minnie Pearl, performed at Carnegie Hall in New York.

Before the decade was over, the city had approved the Capitol Hill Redevelopment Project, the nation's first urban renewal project. The population grew, and the first parents of the baby-boom generation preferred living in the suburbs. Strip shopping centers and theaters sprang up in suburban Belle Meade and Melrose. Between 1940 and 1950, the city's population increased only 4 percent, to 174,307, while Davidson County's total grew 25 percent, to 321,758. The shift to the suburbs resulted in a housing boom.

The 1950s saw unprecedented growth and change. Nashvillians could tune in to the WSM television station for the first time in 1950. The Capitol Hill Redevelopment Project that took place in the decade revitalized acres of severely neglected property near the capitol; nicely landscaped hills, new buildings and the James Robertson Parkway replaced the slum area that had been known as "Hell's Half Acre." Other urban renewal programs followed, and development in the downtown area increased. The 31-story Life and Casualty Insurance Company building opened in 1957 at the corner of Fourth Avenue and Church Street, giving a new look to the Nashville skyline. It was 409 feet tall, the tallest building in the Southeast until the mid-1960s. In the mid-1950s, the Green Hills Village Shopping Center and the Madison Square Shopping Center opened. The 1950s also brought the interstate highway system, which would greatly influence the lives of Nashvillians as well as Americans everywhere.

In 1950, WSM radio announcer David Cobb referred to Nashville as "Music City U.S.A." for the first time. In other music news, country music fans mourned the death of 29-year-old Hank Williams Sr., who was found dead in the back seat of his car January 1, 1953. Among the growing number of *Opry* performers during this decade were Johnny Cash, The Everly Brothers, Stonewall Jackson, George Jones, Webb Pierce, Jim Reeves, Marty Robbins, Hank Snow and Porter Wagoner.

Social changes accompanied the city's physical changes and the growth in country music. In 1954, the U.S. Supreme Court declared segregation in public schools illegal. In September 1955, Nashvillian A.Z. Kelley filed a class-action lawsuit to end segregation in Nashville schools after his attempt to enroll his son in a "white" school in his neighborhood was denied. That lawsuit eventually resulted in a plan to gradually desegregate Nashville schools, beginning in 1957. Desegregation didn't come that easily, however; for years, threats and violence kept the majority of black parents from enrolling their children in integrated schools. Desegregation of parks and other public facilities continued throughout the remainder of the 1950s and into the early 1960s.

# Highlights of the 1960s

The 1960 census showed a marked change in Nashville's living patterns. The city's population had increased steadily for a century, but in 1960, the number declined 2 percent, to 170,874, while Davidson County's population grew 24 percent, to 399,743. The appeal of life in the suburbs wasn't diminishing. As the demand on city services in the outlying areas increased, the need for change in government became apparent. Nashville Mayor Ben West and Davidson County Judge Beverly Briley were the leaders during the time, and both played important roles in the change.

A city commission in 1915 had recommended annexation and the formation of a consolidated city-county government, but it didn't come about until decades later. In the mid-1950s, Briley advocated a unified metropolitan government for the city and county. The plan, though popular with officials and the media, was nixed by county voters in 1958, but the idea finally won their support after Nashville began annexing large chunks of county land. County residents suddenly found themselves living inside the city — paying higher taxes, but with no increase in services.

After calling for a second referendum, in June 1962 voters approved the merger of Nashville and Davidson County governments. They elected Briley mayor a few months later and elected a 41-member council. April 1, 1963, marked the beginning of the Metropolitan Government of Nashville-Davidson County. The reorganization made Nashville the first city in America to completely consolidate city and county governments; the move was admired by cities throughout the country.

Other significant events during the '60s: track stars Wilma Rudolph and Ralph Boston of Tennessee A&I State College won Olympic gold medals (1960); the municipal airport opened (1961); Congress passed the Civil Rights Act (1964); and liquor by the drink was approved in Davidson County (1967).

In the late 1960s, hospital-management companies were founded here, positioning Nashville as a healthcare-industry capital. Most hospitals at the time operated on a nonprofit basis and were controlled locally by governments, medical schools or churches. As insurance continued to cover a growing proportion of patients' hospital costs, private, for-profit hospital-management companies began to spring up. Three were founded in Nashville in 1968: Hospital Corporation of America, Hospital Affiliates International and General Care Corporation. The first of these, HCA, was founded by two Nashville physicians, Thomas F. Frist Sr. and Thomas Frist Jr., and friend Jack Massey, who had become wealthy from the Kentucky Fried Chicken fast-food business. HCA, the second hospital-management company in the nation, became the leader in its field. The company later acquired GCC, and in the early 1980s, HCA and HAI merged. In February 1994, Louisville, Kentucky-based Columbia Health Care Corporation merged with HCA, forming Columbia/HCA Health Care Corporation. The Nashville-based company is the world's largest for-profit healthcare corporation, managing approximately 300 hospitals.

# Music Capital

By the 1960s, Nashville had already become a music city. The *Grand Ole Opry* had been introducing the nation to new country performers for years, and other industry-related businesses had begun operating. Acuff-Rose Publishing, a leader in country-song publishing, was established by Roy Acuff and Fred Rose in 1943. In the late 1940s and early 1950s, RCA Victor, Decca Records, Capitol Records and Mercury Records had set up shop in Nashville.

In 1952, Owen Bradley, a musician and former musical director at WSM, opened a studio in the basement of an old house on 16th Avenue S., a few blocks from Vanderbilt University. That was the beginning of Music Row, the area where the business of country music is carried out every day. In 1955, Bradley began recording in a Quonset Hut (a half-cylindrical metal building with end walls, originally developed for military uses) next door; the building's excellent acoustics, combined with Bradley's production talents, made it a popular recording site. Bradley sold the studio to Columbia Records in 1962 and moved to Williamson County, where he opened Bradley's Barn, a renowned recording studio that attracted country and rock artists for years.

While Bradley was operating the Quonset Hut in the late 1950s, a guitar player by the name of Chet Atkins joined with RCA Victor to establish another studio. In 1957, Atkins, a versatile musician who could play country, jazz, classical or pop, was producing records and beginning to develop what would become known as the "Nashville Sound," a new style of country music. Atkins and Bradley used new recording techniques and blended pop elements such as background vocalists and horns into their country recordings to produce a more modern sound that became popular with music fans.

As the recording business grew, other music businesses began operating in Nashville. Song publishers, performing-rights organizations and booking agencies came to town, and the Country Music Association was founded in 1958 to promote the growing industry. Country stars also began recording television shows. Popular artists in the 1960s included Chet Atkins, Loretta Lynn, Dolly Parton, Porter Wagoner and Tammy Wynette. Artists such as Jack Greene, Willie Nelson, The Osborne Brothers, Del Reeves, Tex Ritter and Dottie West joined the *Opry*, and Jimmie Rodgers, Fred Rose and Hank Williams were the first inductees to the Country Music Hall of Fame. Pop, rock and folk music artists could be found in Nashville studios too. Bob Dylan, for example, recorded an album here in the mid-1960s.

By 1970, when Nashville's population reached 426,029, and Davidson County's registered 447,877, country music was drawing to the city not only performers and music business professionals, but also plenty of tourists. In 1971, attendance at the *Grand Ole Opry* topped 400,000 for the first time. National Life opened the 380-acre Opryland U.S.A. musical theme park in 1972 and two years later relocated the *Grand Ole Opry* to the new Grand Ole Opry House at the park. Opryland, and the adjacent and enormous Opryland Hotel, an attraction in itself, proved to be huge draws. In the mid-1990s, the park was attracting 2 million or more guests a year, enough to rank it among the country's top 30 amusement parks. Nevertheless, citing poor attendance, officials closed the park for good after the 1997 season.

In the music industry, a number of country artists, including Dolly Parton and Kenny Rogers, were enjoying crossover success on the pop-music charts during the '70s. Barbara Mandrell and Jeanne Pruett joined the *Opry*, and Loretta Lynn and Conway Twitty began recording together, as did George Jones and Tammy Wynette. The first Fan Fair, a convention offering country music fans a chance to meet the stars, took place in 1972 at the Municipal Auditorium downtown; the event would move the larger-capacity Tennessee State Fairgrounds 10 years later.

While some artists enjoyed success with pop-sounding hits, another group of artists moved in another direction. The 1970s also saw the birth of the "outlaw movement," led by such artists as Waylon Jennings, Kris Kristofferson and Willie Nelson. The outlaws didn't conform with the traditional Nashville Sound, preferring instead a rougher, honky-tonk, rock 'n' roll sound. And with their long hair and leather, they didn't conform to the traditional image of the country music star. The new style of country was a big success. By the end of 1975, Jennings and Nelson each enjoyed No. 1 hits. In 1976, *Wanted! The Outlaws*, featuring Jessi Colter, Tompall Glaser,

Waylon Jennings and Willie Nelson, became country music's first platinum-selling album (signifying sales of 1 million units). In 1979 Willie Nelson was named the Country Music Association's entertainer of the year.

The popular film *Nashville*, directed by Robert Altman, was released in the mid-1970s; it received mixed reviews among Nashvillians, some of whom thought the film unfairly and inaccurately portrayed the city.

In the 1980s, acts such as Alabama, Emmylou Harris, The Judds, Barbara Mandrell, Reba McEntire, The Oak Ridge Boys, Ricky Skaggs, Randy Travis and Hank Williams Jr. were among the many country artists winning awards and selling millions of albums; some were pushing country music in a new direction. Artists such as George Strait, Randy Travis and Dwight Yoakam were part of a new traditionalist movement away from the pop-sounding side of country.

In 1987, Willie Nelson's third Farm Aid benefit concert for America's farmers sold nearly 70,000 tickets and grossed nearly $1.4 million, while Alabama, Kenny Rogers and George Strait were the other leaders at the concert box office, earning anywhere from $200,000 to more than $600,000 per concert. At the end of the decade, artists such as Clint Black, the venerable Conway Twitty, Ricky Skaggs, Steve Wariner, Rodney Crowell, Keith Whitley, The Judds, George Strait and Willie Nelson had the top radio hits as recorded by *Billboard* magazine.

Country music phenomenon Garth Brooks emerged as a superstar in the 1990s, alongside the likes of Alan Jackson, Reba McEntire, Vince Gill, Brooks & Dunn and Shania Twain. Brooks has become one of the top-selling artists of all time. By March 1999, four of his albums had sold more than 10 million copies each in the U.S., putting him second only to The Beatles. Today, the top country artists sell millions of albums and can sometimes earn more than $1 million per concert; on an extended tour, an act may earn as much as $10 million, $20 million or even $30 million or more in one year from ticket sales alone. Country music reached a new height in popularity this decade. According to the Recording Industry Association of America, in 1995 country music sales accounted for nearly 17 percent of

all records sold in the United States. In 1996, sales of country music recordings topped $1.8 billion and accounted for nearly 15 percent of all records sold. In 1997, country accounted for 14.4% of record sales, again $1.8 billion-worth.

Television networks such as The Nashville Network and Country Music Television now serve up country music programming day and night, and the CMA's annual Fan Fair brings as many as 24,000 country music fans to Nashville each June. Every Friday and Saturday night, the *Grand Ole Opry*, the show that started it all, still packs 'em in at the Opry House.

While it is undoubtedly the country music capital of the world, Nashville also boasts a strong tradition of gospel and pop music. Today, Nashville is the center of the growing contemporary Christian and gospel music industry, and every year the city hosts the Gospel Music Association's Dove Awards show. You can find every genre of gospel here, from traditional black gospel to Christian rock, pop, country, folk and rap to Southern gospel.

A number of pop and rock artists come here to record, and some call Music City home. Don't be surprised if you find rockers like Bon Jovi or Metallica sitting beside Amy Grant or Wynonna Judd at a music club or coffee shop. For every musician in cowboy boots, you can probably find another wearing leather pants and a nose ring.

Every January, the Nashville entertainment Association (NeA) sponsors the multiple-day Extravaganza showcase of up-and-coming local and regional rock and pop talent. Nashville is also proud of its outstanding songwriting community, which receives national and international acclaim for penning songs in a variety of music genres. The annual Tin Pan South multiple-day music festival spotlights some of Nashville's excellent writers. Nashville is truly Music City. (See our Music City U.S.A. chapter for an even more detailed perspective.)

# A Modern City

Outside the music industry, Nashville has grown tremendously in recent decades. The city had integrated all 12 grades in its public school system by 1970, established the Metropolitan Historical Commission in 1975, wel-

Second Avenue's restored warehouses are now homes to galleries, restaurants and upper-level lofts and condos.

comed the return of professional baseball in 1978 with the minor league Nashville Sounds and in 1979 began its bicentennial celebration, Century III.

At the beginning of the 1980s, Nashville's population was 455,651, compared with Davidson County's 477,811, both showing an increase of 7 percent over the previous 10-year period. Highlights of the decade included the opening of the Tennessee Performing Arts

Center in 1980, the opening of Riverfront Park in 1983, the reopening of Union Station as a hotel in 1986 and the opening of the new airport and the downtown Nashville Convention Center in 1987. An interest in historic preservation that had intensified around the turn of the decade continued, as a number of buildings — the Ryman Auditorium, Union Station and the Parthenon among them — were renovated and reopened. The downtown area also enjoyed a rebirth. From the late 1980s through the 1990s, restaurants, shops, entertainment attractions and other businesses opened along Second Avenue Historic District near the Cumberland River; today "The District" is the hot spot of Nashville, the site of several annual events and celebrations and a popular daytime and nighttime destination for Nashvillians and tourists alike.

In 1996, the year Tennessee celebrated its bicentennial, Nashville opened its new downtown Bicentennial Capitol Mall state park and its $145 million, 20,000-seat Nashville Arena, now called the Gaylord Entertainment Center. In 1997, the city lured the National Football League's Houston Oilers with the promise of a new downtown stadium. Now named the Tennessee Titans, the team was set to begin playing in the new, 67,000-seat Adelphia Coliseum in the fall of 1999.

Nashville is also home to the Nashville Kats Arena Football team, which plays at the new arena. Football isn't the only pro game in town, however. Nashville was chosen as a National Hockey League expansion city in 1997; our NHL team, the Nashville Predators, offers sports fans another big-league choice. Music, education, religion, publishing, healthcare, and now professional sports are the buzzwords of modern-day Nashville.

The next big attraction to come to town will be Opry Mills, the entertainment/shopping/dining destination being built at the site of the former Opryland theme park. In another cultural direction, the Frist Center for Visual Arts will open in 2000 in the historic building that was formerly the downtown post office, making Nashville one of the few U.S. cities with an art gallery with 20,000 square feet of exhibit space.

As we welcome the new millennium, Nashvillians can be proud of their city and optimistic about its future.

## Modern-day Settlers

We say that it's rare to run into a "true" Nashvillian — one who was born and raised here. That's because the city is such a magnet for people from all areas that it seems everyone you meet is a transplant from another city. While Music City welcomes some 9 million tourists each year, newcomers relocate here every day. Quality of life, a low cost of living, a favorable business climate and four glorious seasons are just a few of the reasons that individuals and businesses are making the move to Music City. It's often said that Nashville offers an ideal mix of small-town life and big-city amenities, and it's true. Nashville is one of those rare cities where you can get the best of both worlds. It's a great place to live, work and visit. Those first settlers in 1779 recognized that, just as the more than 1.1 million Nashvillians do today.

If you are interested in learning more about Nashville history, there are many wonderful resources available. The Metropolitan Historical Commission's selection of brochures provided much information for this chapter. So did the many excellent books on Nashville history, such as *History of Davidson County* by Professor W. Woodford Clayton (Charles Elder, 1971, reprint of 1880 edition); *Nashville, A Short History and Selected Buildings* (Historical Commission of Metropolitan Nashville-Davidson County, 1974); *Nashville in the New South, 1880-1930* and *Nashville Since the 1920s* by Don H. Doyle (University of Tennessee Press, 1985); *Nashville: The Faces of Two Centuries, 1780-1980* by John Egerton (PlusMedia Incorporated, 1979); *Nashville: A Pictorial History* by George Rollie Adams and Ralph Jerry Christian (Donning Company, 1988); and *The Grand Ole Opry History of Country Music: 70 Years of the Songs, the Stars, and the Stories* by Paul Kingsbury (Villard Books, 1995). The Nashville Room of the downtown library is a wonderful repository of books, articles, and other publications on the history of the area.

Because Nashville welcomes so many visitors, it is a very good idea to secure your accommodations in advance.

# Accommodations

Nashville-area hotel and motel accommodations are in demand year-round, but with just a bit of planning, you shouldn't have any trouble finding a place to stay in Music City. Most likely, your biggest problem will be choosing from among our numerous and varied lodging options. The Nashville area has about 250 hotels and motels with more than 30,000 rooms combined. Thousands more rooms are under construction. We have everything from the spectacular Opryland Hotel (it's more like a small city than a hotel) to elegant luxury hotels in historic buildings to budget motels and long-term corporate lodging.

When choosing your accommodations, keep in mind that Nashville is pretty spread out. For convenience, you might want a hotel that's closest to your primary interests. Properties are concentrated in three areas: Opryland/Music Valley, near the airport and downtown. As you travel away from downtown in any direction, you'll find a number of motels and a few hotels, most of which are near interstate exits.

Do you want to stay near the *Grand Ole Opry* and Music Valley? Or would you prefer the Music Row/West End area, close to the heart of Nashville's music industry and Music City's top restaurants and nightspots? Maybe you're here on business and would like to room somewhere near the airport or in the downtown business district. Downtown Nashville is also a good choice if you plan to do lots of sightseeing — you'll be within walking distance of historic Second Avenue, the Ryman Auditorium, the State Capitol and other attractions.

Nashville-area hotels and motels serve more than 9 million visitors annually, including tourists and convention delegates. Since it is the country music capital of the world, Nashville welcomes thousands of country music fans each year. June is an especially busy month, when as many as 24,000 country music lovers descend on Nashville for Fan Fair (see our Music City chapter for that story). With convention and meeting facilities, such as the Nashville Convention Center and the Opryland Hotel & Convention Center, the city is also a popular choice for conventions and trade shows.

Because Nashville welcomes so many visitors, especially from Memorial Day through Labor Day, it is a very good idea to secure your accommodations in advance. You definitely don't want to arrive in town without a place to stay, only to find out that Fan Fair is going on and every room in town is booked for a week! If you're coming for Fan Fair, some hotels suggest you make your reservations a year in advance. Country Music Week in October is another busy time. That's when lots of out-of-towners arrive for the CMA Awards and other festivities. December holidays bring many visitors too, especially to the festive Opryland Hotel and surrounding lodgings. During these busy times, you're likely to find that hotel rates are a little more expensive. Nashville's busy season is generally the summer months, however.

In the following listing, we provide a price guide to help you choose a hotel. Our rate information was provided by each property. Most have more than one rate, and in some cases rates span a wide range — from hundreds to even thousands of dollars per night. Our dollar-sign price code indicates these ranges (see following "Price-code Key" gray box). Prices are based on the "rack rate," that is, what one night's stay, double occupancy, midweek in peak season would cost you if you walked in off the street. Most likely, you'll pay less than that, however. Many properties offer lower rates on weekends, and most offer a few discounts. AAA and AARP members, for example, get discounts at many hotels. There are a lot of other discount programs out there, so be sure to inquire about them when you make your reservation. Always ask for the best rate — you can often enjoy significant savings by doing so.

## Price-code Key

The following price code represents the average cost of a double-occupancy room during peak season. Prices do not include accommodations tax. By mid to late 1999, the hotel/motel tax will be 5 percent of the gross room rate, and that's in addition to the sales tax of 8.25 percent.

| $ | Less than $50 |
|---|---|
| $$ | $51 to $75 |
| $$$ | $76 to $125 |
| $$$$ | $126 to $175 |
| $$$$$ | $176 and more |

There are so many hotels and motels in Nashville and surrounding counties that we couldn't possibly list them all and still have this book published before the end of the century, so we have chosen just a portion of the properties in various areas of town. If you have a favorite trustworthy chain and don't see one of its properties listed here, call the chain's central reservation number to find out if there is a location in Nashville.

Unlike most chapters in this book, this chapter is divided into geographic categories — Downtown, West End/Music Row, Opryland/Airport, North, South and Southeast, and West; that's to help you quickly locate a suitable property in your preferred area. Our goal is to provide you with a good selection of accommodations — price-wise and location-wise.

All the hotels in this chapter accept major credit cards, and all offer free local telephone calls unless otherwise noted. Amenities vary widely. Some places offer little more than a bed, while others pamper you with every possible luxury. Virtually all properties in town offer nonsmoking and wheelchair-accessible rooms. At some locations, 75 percent or more of the rooms are nonsmoking, and some have a larger number of wheelchair-accessible rooms and more accessible facilities than oth-

ers. Be sure to state your preferences and needs when making a reservation.

For other accommodations, see our Bed and Breakfast Inns and Campgrounds chapters.

# Downtown

## ClubHouse Inn & Conference Center Hotel
$$$ • 920 Broadway
• (615) 244-0150, (800) CLUB-INN

This hotel's great location at the corner of Tenth Avenue and Broadway puts you within walking distance of Broadway and Second Avenue attractions. The eight-story hotel has 285 rooms, including 12 suites. Amenities include satellite TV, free HBO, an outdoor pool and a small exercise room. The 10,000 square feet of meeting space makes this a good choice for business groups.

If you like to wake up to a hearty breakfast, you can't beat the value of this hotel's free breakfast buffet, served 6:30 to 9 AM weekdays and 7:30 to 10 AM weekends in the Club Grille. Start your day with eggs, bacon or sausage, biscuits, gravy, hash browns and other breakfast favorites. After a long day of work or play, relax with complimentary soft drinks and cocktails at the manager's reception held 5 to 8:30 PM in the Club Grille. Free parking is available in two underground parking lots and one side lot.

## Doubletree Hotel – Nashville
$$$-$$$$ • 315 Fourth Ave. N.
• (615) 244-8200, (800) 222-8733

Recently renovated, this full-service downtown hotel offers 338 nicely furnished guest rooms, including 10 suites. The Doubletree, a contemporary-style, nine-story angular building, sits at the corners of Fifth Avenue and Deaderick and Fourth Avenue and Union. It's is in the heart of downtown Nashville, a short walk from both the State Capitol and Second Avenue entertainment.

The hotel's spacious corner rooms feature large wraparound windows and have a sitting area with sofa. All rooms have coffee makers, hair dryers, two phone lines and TV with free

HBO. You'll be served complimentary freshly baked chocolate chip cookies on your night of arrival.

Extra amenities for guests on the ninth-floor executive level include terry-cloth bathrobes, a free *USA Today* each morning, free breakfast and two free drinks at the Plaza Lounge each night. All guests have access to the indoor pool and exercise room on the second floor. Laundry services are provided.

Breakfast is an additional $9.95 per person. The 75-seat Plaza Cafe serves a full breakfast menu, burgers and sandwiches for lunch and is an award-winning dinner choice. Drinks and sandwiches are available in the Plaza Lounge.

## Days Inn – Downtown Convention Center
**$$$ • 711 Union St.**
**• (615) 242-4311, (800) 627-3297**

This five-story motel at the corner of Union and Seventh Avenue has been around awhile, but its 100 rooms were renovated in mid-1999. Extras include in-room hair dryers, free continental breakfast and free HBO. If you want to stay downtown without spending a bundle, this is probably your best bet. It's right across from Legislative Plaza and the Capitol, and convenient to the Tennessee Performing Arts Center, Ryman Auditorium and other downtown attractions. Interstates 40, 24 and 65 are less than a mile away.

## Renaissance Nashville Hotel
**$$$$ • 611 Commerce St.**
**• (615) 255-8400, (800) HOTELS-1**

Connected to the Nashville Convention Center, this 30-story hotel is a top pick for convention-goers. After a day of meetings and walking the trade show floor you can unwind at one of the many restaurants and nightspots just minutes away. The hotel is a short walk from the Ryman Auditorium, the State Capitol and historic Second Avenue.

With its dramatic four-story atrium, glass walls and glass-front elevators, the hotel has a light, airy and spacious feeling. Lots of convention traffic keeps the pace lively. The hotel's upper floors afford great views of Nashville. Even if you're not staying on one of the loftier

levels, you can ride up to check out the views from the hallway windows.

The hotel boasts 673 deluxe rooms, including 24 suites. All rooms feature remote-control TV with in-room movies, computer data ports, coffee makers and direct-dial phones. Extra amenities include laundry and valet service, complimentary shoe shine, covered parking in the adjacent multilevel garage (there is a parking fee), a gift shop/newsstand, concierge service and free newspapers. Fifty-eight private Renaissance Club-level rooms offer a few extra perks, such as a complimentary continental breakfast and evening hors d'oeuvres in the Club Lounge, comfy bathrobes, express checkout and a Renaissance Club concierge who is prepared to take care of any special requests.

In-hotel dining options include the Commerce St. Bar & Grille, featuring sophisticated Southern cuisine, and the Bridge Bagels and Deli, which, along with the adjacent Bridge Lounge, offers a great view of downtown Nashville from the glass-enclosed atrium. You can also order room service 24 hours a day.

The hotel has award-winning meeting and banquet facilities. With the Nashville Convention Center, the Renaissance offers more than 200,000 square feet of space, including nearly 120,000 square feet of exhibit space. The hotel's elegant 18,000-square-foot Grand Ballroom and 11,000-square-foot Convention Center ballroom are perfect for large gatherings, and the hotel's exhibit hall can accommodate 615 10-by-10-foot booths.

## Sheraton Nashville Downtown
**$$$-$$$$ • 623 Union St.**
**• (615) 259-2000**

This elegant, 28-floor hotel, which changed its name from Crowne Plaza Nashville in August 1999, lures locals as well as business travelers and vacationers. Pinnacle, the hotel's revolving rooftop restaurant, offers a fantastic 360-degree view of the city (see our Restaurants chapter). It's a good choice for special dinners, romantic celebrations or just cocktails. Even if you don't plan to dine here, stop by after dark for a beverage and look out on the twinkling lights of Nashville. The hotel's other full-service restaurant is Speakers Cafe, offering American cuisine for breakfast, lunch and dinner. Sessions lounge, on the first floor, is the spot for cocktails and snacks.

Sheraton Nashville Downtown has 473 rooms and 14 suites, which range in size from 300 to 1,500 square feet. Rooms on the upper floors offer splendid views of the State Capitol and other Nashville sites. Rooms feature remote-control TV, free HBO, video games, voice mail, data ports, coffee makers, hair dryers, irons and ironing boards. De-stress in the exercise room and indoor pool. The hotel offers 2,300 square feet of meeting space and a business center, where you can take care of your faxing and copying. Valet service is available in the adjacent eight-story garage; there is a fee to park.

www.insiders.com
See this and many other Insiders' Guide® destinations online.
Visit us today!

## Union Station Hotel
**$$$$ • 1001 Broadway**
**• (615) 726-1001**

The Union Station train shed opened in October 1900 and pushed Nashville into the 20th century, linking the city by rail to the country's important railroad cities. The Romanesque Revival-style train shed had taken more than two years to complete, and its opening was a grand occasion. When the building reopened as the Union Station Hotel in 1986 after a two-year renovation, it was another grand affair. What had become something of an eyesore was saved by historic preservationists in the 1970s, and today it is a magnificently restored National Historic Landmark. The Union Station Hotel offers what may be the most elegant and luxurious accommodations in town.

Beautiful stained-glass panels adorn the spacious, three-story lobby's 65-foot-high vaulted ceiling, while an abundance of decorative gilded accents lend to the room's classic elegance. Here and there, you'll notice reminders of the hotel's past, such as the ornate clock in the lobby, which years ago was used to time incoming trains.

The seven-story hotel has 124 unique guest rooms, including 13 suites. Some rooms have vaulted ceilings and open toward the lobby. All rooms have exterior views. Rooms are classified as standard, deluxe, premier, concierge and suite, and are priced accordingly. Amenities include room service, valet parking, same-day laundry and cleaning service, overnight shoe shine, voice mail and in-room movies. Copy and fax services are available too. The concierge can arrange for a day of golf at Legends Golf Club or any other course you choose. Guests also have access to Cummins Station Fitness on 10th Avenue.

Union Station's location near downtown puts you just blocks away from some of Nashville's trendiest restaurants and clubs in The District, West End and Music Row areas. You might want to stay at the hotel, however, and enjoy dinner at the on-site Arthur's restaurant, an award winner featuring a prix fixe continental-cuisine menu. The Broadway Bistro is a casual spot for lunch, dinner and cocktails. Breakfast is served in the lobby area each morning for $9.95 per person.

## The Westin Hermitage
**$$$$-$$$$$ • 231 Sixth Ave. N.**
**• (615) 244-3121**

This all-suites hotel, Nashville's last remaining grand hotel, is the only commercial beaux arts structure in the state. The hotel is listed on the National Historic Register. When it first

## INSIDERS' TIP

**If you're visiting Nashville in the summer months, pack clothing suitable for heat and humidity. Nashville's average temperature from June through August is 78 degrees, but the temperature often soars to the upper 90s and sometimes even past 100. When you add to that the often high level of humidity, the temperature can feel much hotter than 100 degrees.**

opened in 1910, the hotel had 250 rooms and featured elegant furnishings imported from around the world. The lobby still boasts Grecian and Tennessee marble, and its three-story arched ceiling is capped by a beautiful skylight designed by Italian artist Hotojy. The walls of the hotel's 2,500-square-foot Grand Ballroom are paneled in Circassian walnut imported from Russia, and the room features an ornately hand-crafted ceiling and other opulent touches.

Over the years, the hotel has welcomed such luminaries as Franklin and Eleanor Roosevelt, John F. Kennedy, Richard Nixon, Al Jolson, Greta Garbo and Bette Davis. Cowboy star Gene Autry once showed up with his horse Champion. Others who have called the hotel home include Jack Dempsey, Minnesota Fats, Al Capone and Mickey Spillane.

The hotel was converted into an all-suite property years ago. A $4 million renovation in 1995 restored the magnificent property to its original splendor. The renovation included improvements to the lobby and a complete overhaul of all 120 suites, including all-new carpet, wallpaper and furniture. Some of the original period pieces remain, such as the lobby's large baroque mirror with gold-leaf frame. Today the hotel has 112 one-bedroom suites and eight two-bedroom suites. All are luxurious and spacious and feature a large living area with work desk, separate bedroom(s) and dressing area. Amenities include two TVs, three telephone extensions, voice mail, coffee makers, hair dryers, irons, ironing boards, small refrigerators and wet bars. The two-bedroom suites feature one bedroom with two double beds and a second bedroom with one king bed plus two separate baths and a shared living area. The plush bedrooms are beautifully decorated in a variety of styles and furnishings.

The hotel's highly acclaimed Capitol Grille was named one of the top 25 best new restaurants by *Esquire* magazine in 1996. The restaurant prides itself on its creative lunch and dinner menus, its extensive wine list and excellent service (see our Restaurants chapter for details). The Veranda is atop the hotel entrance and offers cocktails and light menu items. Just off the Veranda is the Lobby Bar, where you can relax with your choice of bev-

erages while enjoying the sounds of a grand piano. The clubby Oak Bar offers a more intimate atmosphere. The hotel offers room service from 6:30 AM to 10 PM Sunday through Thursday and until 11 PM Friday and Saturday.

Most of the hotel's clientele is corporate, and the hotel offers several meeting and banquet facilities to serve their needs. Guests who want a little recreation have discount privileges at a health club two blocks away and also can visit the YMCA pool on 10th Avenue nearby. The hotel's location on Sixth Avenue puts you within walking distance of such downtown destinations as the Nashville Convention Center, Second Avenue, State Capitol, Tennessee Performing Arts Center, Ryman Auditorium and Printers Alley.

# West End/Music Row

### Courtyard by Marriott – West End
**$$$ • 1901 West End Ave.**
**• (615) 327-9900, (800) 321-2211**
The amenities at this 223-room, seven-story hotel make it popular with business travelers, and it's usually booked solid Monday through Thursday. Each room features a large work desk, separate seating area and coffee maker. If you're not in the mood to go out, you can stay in and watch free Showtime movies. You get a free newspaper delivered to your room on weekdays. Other amenities include a large outdoor pool, an exercise room with whirlpool, a meeting room and free parking. A full buffet breakfast ($6.95 a person) is served in the restaurant weekdays 6:30 to 11 AM and weekends 7 AM to noon. The hotel offers a dinner plan with nearby Valentino's restaurant that allows you to charge meals to your room.

### Days Inn – Vanderbilt
**$$ • 1800 West End Ave.**
**• (615) 327-0922, (800) 325-2525**
This combination hotel/motel has been at the corner of 18th Avenue S. and West End since the 1960s, but it has been recently renovated. Convenient to downtown, Music Row and Vanderbilt University, it's a budget-type property with few frills, but it's bright and clean and has an outdoor pool, free parking, free

Photo: Cathy Summerlin

Some of Nashville's most elegant accommodations are in historic buildings.

HBO and free continental breakfast. The hotel's adjacent restaurant, Basante's, serves authentic Italian food.

## Fairfield Inn – Opryland
**$$$ • 211 Music City Cir.**
• **(615) 872-8939, (800) 228-2800**

The Fairfield Inn, a Marriott property, offers 109 rooms and six suites, a heated indoor pool, fitness center, free deluxe continental breakfast and cable TV with Showtime. There's a free shuttle to nearby Opryland and Nashville International Airport, fax/copy services, and same-day dry cleaning.

## Guesthouse Inn
**$$-$$$ • 1909 Hayes St.**
• **(615) 329-1000, (800) 777-4904**

This comfortable hotel is one block off West End, near Baptist Hospital, Vanderbilt and Centennial Park. It is a good choice for medical guests, but it is just as popular with tourists, business travelers and visiting families of Vanderbilt students. The hotel's shuttle provides free transportation to most major area hospitals and attractions. The hotel has 108 rooms, with seven wheelchair-accessible rooms on the first floor. All rooms are minisuites and feature a kitchen sink, microwave and refrigerator. There are six larger suites that have living rooms with sleeper sofas. Free continental breakfast is served each morning in the dining area just off the lobby. Other amenities include a small gift shop, basic cable TV and free parking. Group rates are available.

## Hampton Inn – Vanderbilt
**$$$ • 1919 West End Ave.**
• **(615) 329-1144, (800) HAMPTON**

A good choice in the West End/Music Row area, this 171-room hotel is at the corner of West End and 20th Avenue S. It's close to popular restaurants and shops as well as Vanderbilt and downtown. You can enjoy a free deluxe continental breakfast in the comfortable lobby, where floor-to-ceiling windows offer a view of busy West End. Other amenities include free parking, free Showtime, in-room coffee makers, hair dryers, irons and ironing boards, an exercise room, outdoor pool and a free *USA Today* weekdays. An extra treat is fresh-baked cookies served 4 to 7 PM Monday through Thursday. On weekdays, the clientele is mostly the business crowd.

## Holiday Inn Select Vanderbilt
**$$$$ • 2613 West End Ave.**
• **(615) 327-4707, (800) HOLIDAY**

This 13-story hotel has a super location on West End, right across the street from Centennial Park and close to Vanderbilt. The hotel is popular with business travelers Monday through Friday. Its proximity to Centennial Sportsplex and Vanderbilt makes it a top choice among sports groups on the weekends. Out-of-towners visiting Nashville for family reunions and weddings often stay here too.

The hotel has 300 rooms, including seven suites. The Cafe Becca serves breakfast, lunch and dinner, while Ivories piano bar, open every afternoon and evening, has live entertainment Tuesday through Saturday nights. Amenities include an outdoor pool, a second-floor fitness center with a good selection of workout equipment, satellite TV with free HBO. Every room has a coffee maker, iron and ironing board, hair dryer and makeup mirror. The executive-level rooms on the top floor have all that plus comfy bathrobes and a complimentary continental breakfast. A computer, fax, TV, tables, books and phone and modem hookups are available in the club room/business center, which all guests can access with their room keys.

## Loews Vanderbilt Plaza Hotel
**$$$$$ • 2100 West End Ave.**
• **(615) 320-1700, (800) 336-3335 (reservations)**

Tasteful, sophisticated and luxurious, Loews Vanderbilt Plaza Hotel welcomes many business guests and VIPs. The hotel was built in 1984 and purchased by Loews in 1989. It is one of the chain's dozen or so U.S. properties. This 340-room, 11-story hotel is part of the Loews Vanderbilt Plaza Hotel & Office Complex, which includes an adjacent 13-story office building and a 750-space parking garage. The complex is conveniently located on West End, within walking distance of Vanderbilt University, Centennial Park and several good restaurants. Downtown Nashville and Music Row are just a minute or two away.

Loews will accommodate virtually any request if you give a little notice. Room amenities include a fax machine, refreshment center, coffee maker, hair dryer, iron and ironing board, dual telephone line with voice mail and computer ports. The Business Class rooms on the Plaza Level feature complimentary in-room coffee and mineral water, evening turn-down service and newspapers delivered to the room. A concierge attends to the needs of guests who stay in the spacious Plaza Level rooms, which also feature a complimentary continental breakfast and evening hors d'oeuvres served in the exclusive Plaza Lounge (it has a great view).

Loews Vanderbilt Plaza has a business center, exercise facility, gift shop, hair salon, 17 meeting and banquet rooms, room service, dry cleaning service and more. The hotel has two restaurants: Ruth's Chris Steak House, a steak-lover's dream, and the nice Plaza Grill. For relaxing after a long day of meetings, try the Garden Bar.

If you want to see more of Nashville, the guest-services department can arrange a car rental or limousine service. Rates for the hotel's enclosed parking garage were $11 per night maximum. Valet parking is $14.

### Quality Inn Hall of Fame
**$$ • 1407 Division St.**
**• (615) 242-1631, (800) 4-CHOICE**
Popular with tourists, this 103-room hotel sits just off Music Row, across the street from the Country Music Hall of Fame. It's not fancy, but it does have an outdoor pool, a meeting room and a laundry room on the fifth floor. There are four large suites suitable for families. Parking is free, and you can enjoy free HBO movies in your room. Just off the lobby is a country music theater featuring live music nightly. The hotel offers free continental breakfast from 6:30 to 9:30 AM.

### Shoney's Inn of Nashville – Music Row
**$$ • 1501 Demonbreun St.**
**• (615) 255-9977, (800) 222-2222**
If Music Row is your destination, you may want to stay at this motel. Just off I-40, Shoney's Inn is a stone's throw from the Country Music Hall of Fame & Museum and convenient to other Music Row sights. When you've

seen and done it all on the Row, head in the other direction for downtown Nashville, less than a five-minute drive away. Or hop on I-40 east to get to the Grand Ole Opry and Music Valley in about 15 minutes. It's not uncommon to see those colorful country music tour buses parked in between this motel and the adjacent Shoney's restaurant, so you never know who you might see here. Touring bands do lodge here frequently.

There are 147 rooms, including six suites and one suite with a whirlpool. All rooms have cable TV, including free HBO. Complimentary coffee and a copy of *USA Today* are available in the lobby. If you want a workout, visit the nearby Cummins Station Fitness for half-price. And, of course, there's a Shoney's restaurant right next door.

# Opryland/Airport

### AmeriSuites
**$$$ • 220 Rudy's Cir.**
**• (615) 872-0422, (800) 833-1516**
Tourists and business travelers alike find this Music Valley property a suitable choice. This five-story, 125-suite hotel sits right off Music Valley Drive across from the Opryland Hotel. It's close to the Grand Ole Opry and the Factory Stores of America outlet mall in Music Valley. The large rooms feature one or two beds; sleeper sofas; a minikitchen with microwave, refrigerator and coffee maker; and a 26-inch remote-control TV with free HBO. There is a complimentary continental breakfast buffet in the lobby each morning, a laundry room, movie rental center and a fitness center. The business center has a computer with Internet access, plus a fax machine, copier and other business necessities. You can pick up a free copy of *USA Today* in the front lobby on weekdays.

### Best Suites
**$$$ • 2521 Elm Hill Pk.**
**• (615) 391-3919, (800) BEST-INN**
This four-story hotel is between Briley Parkway and Donelson Pike, about 5 miles from the Opryland/Music Valley area. Each of its 95 spacious suites has a living room with sleeper sofa, table and chairs, and a kitchenette with

sink, microwave, refrigerator and coffee maker. Some suites also have whirlpool tubs. All rooms feature cable TV with free HBO and a VCR. You can rent movies at the shop on the first floor. If you like a hearty breakfast, you'll enjoy the free full breakfast buffet of eggs, bacon or sausage, biscuits, bagels, fruit and more, served daily from 6 to 10 AM. Complimentary cocktails and snacks are served each afternoon from 5 to 7 PM in the lobby. An indoor pool, fitness center and laundry facility are on the first floor.

## Best Western Calumet Inn at the Airport
**$$-$$$ • 701 Stewarts Ferry Pk.**
**• (615) 889-9199, (800) 528-1234**

A budget-friendly choice, less than a mile off I-40, 8 miles from the Opry/Music Valley area and 12 miles from downtown, this 80-room motel is in a quiet, park-like setting adjacent to Percy Priest Lake. The three-story property, which opened in the early 1990s, has four suites (king suites have a whirlpool and refrigerator), an outdoor pool, free HBO and free continental breakfast in the lobby from 6 to 10 AM daily.

## Best Western Suites – Near Opryland
**$$$ • 201 Music City Cir.**
**• (615) 902-9940, (800) 528-1234**

This five-story, 100-suite hotel is just off Music Valley Drive, right in front of the Factory Stores of America outlet mall. All accommodations feature a microwave, refrigerator, coffee maker, kitchen sink and cable TV with HBO. Four executive suites offer whirlpool tubs and a living room area. Start off your day with the complimentary deluxe continental breakfast available daily from 7 to 10 AM. Amenities include a sauna, gym and outdoor pool. A meeting room accommodates as many as 40 people.

## Baymont Inn & Suites – Nashville Airport
**$$ • 531 Donelson Pk.**
**• (615) 885-3100, (800) 301-0200**

Its proximity to the airport, I-40 and the Opryland complex makes this property a popular choice with business travelers and vaca-

tioning families. Downtown Nashville is only about a 10-minute drive, so out-of-towners will find it easy to zip into town to check out The District or Music Row. This hotel has 146 sizable rooms, including about ten suites. Some suites have refrigerators, microwaves and sleeper sofas. An executive office provides a TV, VCR and conference table that seats 12 people. Business travelers can use the hotel's copy machine at no charge. The hotel's extras include free HBO and Showtime, free parking and an outdoor pool. You don't even have to leave your room to enjoy the free continental breakfast — it will be delivered to you upon your request, 5 to 10:30 AM daily. Free shuttle service to the airport is provided. You can get your 13th night free at one of this chain's locations if you participate in the Club Baymont frequent-stay program.

## Courtyard By Marriott – Elm Hill Pike
**$$$ • 2508 Elm Hill Pk.**
**• (615) 883-9500, (800) 321-2211**

About 2 miles from the airport, this four-story hotel has 145 rooms, including 11 suites. A free shuttle to and from the airport is available. Other amenities include an outdoor pool, indoor whirlpool and exercise room. If you're traveling on business and can't get away for breakfast or dinner, the 40-seat Courtyard Cafe restaurant offers a convenient full breakfast bar each morning and a soup, salad and sandwich bar in the evenings, both for an extra charge. The lounge, next to the restaurant, is open from 5 to 11 PM. Two 30-capacity meeting rooms provide extra space for business travelers. If a visit to the *Grand Ole Opry* is on your itinerary, you'll find it just minutes away on Briley Parkway. If you want to unwind in your room, you can watch free HBO movies. Local calls are 50¢ each.

## Embassy Suites Nashville
**$$$$ • 10 Century Blvd.**
**• (615) 871-0033, (800) EMBASSY**

No, you're not in Miami. Curiously enough, this bright pink nine-story hotel is right here in Music City. You can't miss it. Visible from I-40, the hotel is in the Century City complex off Elm Hill Pike, 1 mile from Briley Parkway. It's about 2.5 miles from the airport and a short drive from the Opryland Hotel and Music Valley attractions. Business travelers and vacationing families will find much to like about this property. Embassy Suites advertises "twice the room, twice the convenience and twice the value" and promises to refund your money if you're not 100 percent satisfied.

Each of the 296 all-suite accommodations features two TVs, two phones, a wet bar, refrigerator and a microwave. A sleeper sofa in the living room is just right for the kids or an extra person in your party. Morning newspapers and free airport shuttles are provided, and complimentary cooked-to-order breakfasts and evening beverages are nice perks. For breakfast, choose from the buffet or order a complete cooked-to-order meal. From 5:30 to 7:30 PM, enjoy complimentary beverages in the hotel's spacious tropical-themed atrium, complete with chirping tropical birds and a babbling brook. Just off the atrium is the Ambassador Grille restaurant, open for lunch and dinner. A lounge area and sports bar are off the atrium. Amenities include a fully equipped fitness center with exercise equipment, sauna, heated pool and whirlpool. The hotel has 14,000 square feet of meeting space and a 500-capacity ballroom. Meeting planners and a catering staff are available for corporate events.

### Fiddler's Inn North
$$ • 2410 Music Valley Dr.
• (615) 885-1440

This 202-room motel has been in business since 1975. It's one of the more affordable choices in the Music Valley area, appealing to families, bus groups and budget-minded business travelers. There are three buildings: two two-story buildings and one three-story building with an elevator. The only extras are an outdoor pool, free Showtime and morning coffee and doughnuts; if you want to spend a little time in more elegant surroundings, the Opryland Hotel is just across the street, offering lots of restaurants, shops and sightseeing. Music Valley attractions are within walking distance.

### Holiday Inn Express – Music Valley
$$-$$$ • 2516 Music Valley Dr.
• (615) 889-0086, (800) HOLIDAY

This no-frills hotel in the Music Valley area

offers affordable accommodations and a location that's convenient to Opryland. Open since the mid-1980s, the three-story hotel has 121 rooms. A complimentary continental breakfast is served on the second floor. A nice outdoor pool with a sunning area is about the only extra here.

### Holiday Inn Express Airport
$$$ • 1111 Airport Center Dr.
• (615) 883-1366, (800) HOLIDAY

About 2 miles from the Nashville International Airport, this hotel welcomes lots of business travelers and airline crews. It's located just off Donelson Pike, about 5 miles from Opryland. When you enter the lobby, you may be surprised to find that this three-story property, open since 1987, has a resort lodge-type theme. It features lots of wood, exposed beams, a brick floor and a stone fireplace in the center of the lobby. The 206 guest rooms are not so elaborately decorated, but they are comfortable and roomy. You can choose a room with two double beds or one king bed. There aren't too many extras here, just a couple to help make your stay more comfortable. All rooms have coffee makers, and a free continental breakfast is served in the atrium. The hotel has an outdoor pool and offers free HBO and pay-per-view movies. Three small banquet rooms are available.

### Holiday Inn Select Nashville – Opryland/Airport
$$$$ • 2200 Elm Hill Pk.
• (615) 883-9770, (800) HOLIDAY

Situated right off Exit 7 of Briley Parkway, this is the closest full-service Holiday Inn to the Opryland area, which is just 2 miles away. The hotel is also convenient to the airport, 2 miles east, and downtown Nashville, 6 miles west. This 14-story property has 384 recently renovated rooms, including four suites. Each room has a coffee maker, hair dryer, iron and ironing board, two data ports for computers and free HBO. Guests on the top-floor executive level are treated to complimentary morning newspaper, coffee and continental breakfast. An indoor pool and sun deck are in the back atrium of the main floor. Nearby are a sauna, fitness center, game room and gift shop. The Ivories piano bar presents live entertainment Tuesday through Saturday nights.

Jackson's Veranda is open for breakfast, lunch and dinner. Dinner highlights include a pasta bar and weekly prime rib special. You can arrange for a car at the car rental desk. Other services include room service, laundry service and a free airport shuttle.

## The Inn at Opryland
**$$$ • 2401 Music Valley Dr.**
**• (615) 889-0800**

Right across Briley Parkway from the Opryland Hotel, this comfortable, three-story hotel is in a great location. Each of the 306 rooms has a coffee maker, hair dryer, voice mail, free Showtime and pay-per-view movies. Faxing and copying services are available at the front desk for a small charge. The hotel is within walking distance of Music Valley shops, restaurants and museums. After a long day of fun at nearby attractions, you can come back here for a relaxing soak in the hotel's whirlpool, or swim a few laps at the indoor pool. A sauna and exercise room offer other opportunities to unwind. The on-site Briley's Restaurant serves a buffet breakfast, buffet lunch and full-service dinner. Pennington's Lounge has live music Friday and Saturday nights.

## Nashville Airport Marriott
**$$$$ • 600 Marriott Dr.**
**• (615) 889-9300, (800) 228-9290**

On 17 acres of rolling wooded hills, the Nashville Airport Marriott offers some of Music City's most comfortable accommodations. It's in the same area as the Music City Sheraton, Embassy Suites and Holiday Inn Select Nashville (see this chapter's respective entries), just off Elm Hill Pike and just a few minutes from the airport or Opryland.

Open since 1987, the 18-story hotel has 399 rooms, including six suites. All rooms have hair dryers, irons and ironing boards, two telephones with voice mail, AM/FM radio, in-room pay-per-view movies and free HBO. Guests

on the 15th- and 16th-floor concierge levels are treated to a few extras, such as terry-cloth robes, turndown service, complimentary continental breakfast, buffet-style hors d'oeuvres in the afternoon and a private bar. Rooms feature views of either the airport area, downtown Nashville or the swimming pool. First-floor rooms have private balconies.

The hotel has excellent recreation facilities, including a sand volleyball court, tennis courts, a basketball court and a health club with workout equipment and separate saunas in each locker room. With 14,000 square feet of meeting and banquet space, this property is also well equipped to handle business functions. The on-site Allies American Grille is open for breakfast, lunch and dinner. Albert's Lounge serves drinks and items from the restaurant menu. A gift shop, room service, guest laundry area, one-day dry-cleaning service, free airport shuttle and free parking are among other extras.

## Opryland Hotel
**$$$$$ • 2800 Opryland Dr.**
**• (615) 883-2211, (615) 889-1000**

The Opryland Hotel is the star of Nashville accommodations. Even if you don't stay at this awe-inspiring property, it's worth stopping by to visit. Thousands of locals, tourists and business travelers drop by every day to walk through and marvel at the three enormous themed atriums. And it's a tradition for Nashvillians to visit during the holidays, when the hotel property turns into a Christmas fantasy land aglow with more than 2 million lights (see our Attractions and Annual Events chapters for more information).

The Opryland Hotel is one of the largest convention and resort properties in the nation and is the world's largest combined hotel/convention center under one roof. The hotel opened in 1977 with a "mere" 600 rooms. Today, it has 2,884 guest rooms (including 200 suites), 600,000 square feet of meeting and

---

## INSIDERS' TIP

**Nashville's only 24-hour post office is the Metro Airport station, (615) 885-9280. From downtown Nashville, take I-40 east to Exit 216B. Go past the airport and take a right at the "air cargo" sign. At the end of that street, turn left. Parking spaces are available.**

exhibit space, 85 meeting rooms, five ballrooms, three indoor gardens spanning 9 acres, 30 shops, 15 restaurants, 10 lounges, three swimming pools and a fitness center. You can get a workout just walking from one end to the other. The three indoor gardens are The Conservatory, The Cascades and the largest, the 4.5-acre Delta, whose 1,500-foot-high roof is composed of more than 650 tons of glass. The Delta even has its own river — big enough to carry passengers on flatboats on a guided tour of the area.

The hotel was designed for meetings and conventions, and more than 80 percent of its guests are here for such events. It has seemingly endless space and virtually every amenity needed for group functions. The largest of the five ballrooms, The Delta Ballroom, has 55,269 square feet of space. The 289,000-square-foot Ryman Exhibit Hall hosts trade shows and other business gatherings. Despite its rather pricey rooms, the award-winning hotel has maintained an above-average occupancy rate of more than 80 percent since it opened.

There are several types of accommodations here. Each of the garden rooms has a private balcony or patio overlooking one of the themed gardens and costs about 20 percent more than the traditional rooms, which have a window view to the exterior grounds. Guest rooms do not mirror the opulence of the lobbies and gardens, but they are very comfortable and nicely furnished.

For the ultimate in luxury, the hotel offers six Presidential Suites, which range from 1,500 to 2,000 square feet in size. These fifth-floor suites have one bedroom with a canopy bed (the bedroom connects with two or three other bedrooms outside the suite), living areas, a full wet bar, baby grand piano, whirlpool bath and at least one fireplace. Some have a full chef's kitchen and a dining room. Presidents George Bush and Ronald Reagan are among the distinguished guests who have stayed in these suites. (President Bill Clinton opted for a more ordinary room, but he did reserve the whole wing in which it was located.) Most Presidential Suite guests, however, are business executives; even celebrities and most VIPs opt for the regular rooms. The rate for these spectacular spaces is $2,000 to $2,500 per night,

with the exception of a bi-level suite, a "bargain" at about $1,300. The regular suites range from about $250 to $750.

Breakfast, lunch and dinner options at the Opryland Hotel are plentiful. Numerous restaurants and lounges offer something for every taste. Among the choices are Beauregard's (see our Restaurants chapter), Old Hickory Restaurant, Rachel's Kitchen, Cascades Lounge, Rusty's Sports Bar and The Pickin' Parlor. The Sunday brunch at Cafe Avanti is a real treat.

The Opryland Hotel offers many package plans that include tickets to Nashville attractions and events. Other discounts are available. Inquire about these when you make reservations. The hotel charges a $5 parking fee.

## Residence Inn by Marriott
### $$-$$$$ • 2300 Elm Hill Pk.
### • (615) 889-8600, (800) 331-3131

It's easy to mistake this all-suites motel for an apartment complex. This property, which opened in the mid-1980s, has 21 two-story buildings with a combined 168 suites, including 42 bi-level penthouse suites. It's about a quarter-mile from Briley Parkway, just 5 miles from Opryland and 2 miles from the airport. The regular suites have a combination living room/full kitchen area with refrigerator, stove, microwave, coffee maker and pots and pans. More than half the suites have fireplaces too, making this an especially cozy choice during the winter. The penthouse suites are more roomy and feature loft bedrooms and two baths. All rooms have irons and ironing boards, free HBO and pay-per-view movies.

Save some money by cooking a few meals in your room. The hotel staff will even do your grocery shopping. Just be sure to give them your grocery list by 9 AM, and they'll deliver the goods by 6 PM the same day; the groceries will be added to your bill. For breakfast, consider the complimentary "extended" continental breakfast, served each morning in the lobby. From 5 to 7 PM Monday through Thursday, you can enjoy beverages and filling hors d'oeuvres in the lobby, compliments of Marriott. If you want to dine out without leaving the neighborhood, there are some moderately priced restaurants within about 1.5 miles.

Amenities at this property include an outdoor heated pool and hot tub. Guests have access to the workout facilities at the full-service Marriott across the street. Free airport shuttle service is provided.

## Sheraton Music City Hotel
**$$$ • 777 McGavock Pk.**
**• (615) 885-2200, (800) 325-3535**

This award-winning hotel is one of Nashville's best. Designed as a Southern-style mansion, the four-story Sheraton Music City sits atop a hill on 23 acres in a business park just off McGavock Pike. It's about a five-minute drive from the airport or Opryland. Downtown Nashville is just minutes away too. Marble floors and dark wood accent the elegant and open lobby, which continues the Southern-mansion theme.

The hotel's 410 rooms offer a variety of accommodations, including about 56 suites. The second-story Club Floor rooms come with extra perks, such as upgraded bath amenities, plush bathrobes, bottled water, turndown service, an iron and ironing board, complimentary newspaper each morning, data ports, voice mail and an in-room printer for fast video checkout. A complimentary breakfast and evening hors d'oeuvres in the Club Lounge are available to Club Floor guests. All rooms are spacious and comfortably appointed with large bathrooms and extra-spacious closets. Rooms also have hair dryers and coffee makers, complete with Starbucks or Maxwell House coffee. Services include room service, free airport shuttle, valet/laundry service and concierge. For recreation, you can choose from the indoor pool, outdoor pool, tennis courts or health club with exercise equipment. The large outdoor pool is in a quiet courtyard just off the lobby.

If you're among the hotel's many business and convention guests, you'll find the services at the Lanier Business Center on the main floor helpful. Printing, faxing, computer work stations, duplicating, binding and office-supply sales are just a few of the convenient ser-

vices available. The hotel has 11,160 square feet of flexible meeting space. Dining choices include the elegant Apples in the Field restaurant, offering gourmet Southern specialties, and the Veranda, a piano bar off the lobby where you can have restaurant items delivered.

## Shoney's Inn
**$$-$$$ • 2420 Music Valley Dr.**
**• (615) 885-4030, (800) 222-2222**

This mid-priced hotel in the Music Valley area has 185 rooms, including 13 suites. It's right in the middle of all the action of busy Music Valley, convenient to the *Grand Ole Opry* and the airport. Business travelers, tour and travel groups, and individual tourists keep this property busy. In fact, if you're planning to stay here in June or any time from September through December, you'll probably need to make your reservations well in advance.

The hotel has 2,500 square feet of meeting space divisible into two sections. A complimentary airport shuttle and Opryland Hotel shuttle provide convenient transportation. Amenities include in-room coffee makers, an indoor heated pool, outdoor whirlpool and gift shop. Other perks include free Showtime and complimentary continental breakfast served in the lobby.

## Wilson Inn & Suites
**$$ • 600 Ermac Dr.**
**• (615) 889-4466, (800) 333-9457**

If you're planning an extended visit, you might want to consider staying at Wilson Inn & Suites. One-third of the accommodations at this five-story, 110-room hotel are suites. Wilson Inn & Suites, established by Holiday Inn founder Kemmons Wilson, is a good value for vacationers or business travelers. Although there are no recreational amenities, this hotel's spacious and comfortable rooms and attention to extras make for a pleasant stay. All rooms come with refrigerators, coffee makers, irons and ironing boards, while the suites

## INSIDERS' TIP

**International visitors: If your passport is lost or stolen, contact your country's consulate in Washington D.C. Find the number by calling (202) 555-1212.**

also have microwaves and hair dryers. The two-room suites have a living room area with a sofa, loveseat, chair and TV. A free breakfast bar with baked goods, fruits, cereals, boiled eggs and beverages is available each morning in the lobby, and each afternoon, guests are treated to free popcorn and punch. Free pizza is served Wednesday night.

## Wyndham Garden Hotel – Nashville/Airport
**$$$ • 1112 Airport Center Dr.**
**• (615) 889-9090, (800) WYNDHAM**

Sitting about one block off Donelson Pike, the seven-story Wyndham Garden is convenient to both the airport and Opryland. The hotel has 180 rooms, including 24 suites. Rooms have coffee makers, irons, ironing boards and hair dryers as well as amenities added with the business traveler in mind, such as data ports, voice mail and extra-large work desks. The hotel has 2,500 square feet of meeting space, an indoor pool, whirlpool and exercise room. Dry-cleaning service, a free airport shuttle and free parking are other pluses. All guests are treated to a complimentary full breakfast in the Garden Cafe, which also serves moderately priced breakfast, lunch and dinner items (no lunch on weekends). The lobby lounge is open afternoons and evenings. Room service is available from 5 to 10 PM.

# North

## Days Inn – Central
**$-$$ • 211 N. First St.**
**• (615) 254-1551, (800) 251-3038, (800) DAYS INN**

This high-rise hotel is within view of downtown Nashville, less than a mile from I-65. The hotel has 180 rooms, some of which feature whirlpools. Rooms facing downtown offer a great cityscape view. Amenities here include an indoor heated pool, game room and lounge. For business guests, there are three meeting rooms — two on the first floor and a larger room on the ninth floor. The hotel provides a complimentary continental breakfast each morning and there's an on-site restaurant that opened in mid-1999. For lunch or dinner, we suggest you venture across the

Jefferson Street Bridge to the historic Germantown district. The Mad Platter and Monell's are two good dining choices there. If you're in Germantown during the daytime, you might want to visit the Bicentennial Capitol Mall and Farmer's Market, both within walking distance.

## Days Inn – West Trinity Lane
**$ • 1400 Brick Church Pk.**
**• (615) 228-5977, (800) DAYS INN**

This 108-room Days Inn is in the Trinity Lane area, just off I-65 and minutes from downtown. You won't find many amenities here, but the super-affordable rates are a great trade-off. It's a popular choice for vacationing families, and it gets a few budget-conscious business travelers too. During warm-weather months, guests can take a dip in the outdoor pool, which stays open until 11 PM. A free continental breakfast awaits guests in the lobby each morning. Surveillance cameras, extra nighttime security and card keys offer a little extra peace of mind. There are several restaurants nearby.

## Days Inn Opryland North
**$$ • 3312 Dickerson Pk.**
**• (615) 228-3421, (800) DAYS INN**

Just a seven-minute drive from Opryland and 10 minutes from downtown Nashville's Second Avenue, this two-story, 46-room motel is the choice of lots of fun-seeking tourists. It's short on amenities but long on cleanliness and convenience. This location received Days Inn's five-star rating, the chain's highest quality rating. Guests who find themselves with a little time to spare here can enjoy the outdoor pool and 48-channel cable TV, including free Showtime. Local calls are 25¢. Help yourself to free coffee, orange juice and doughnuts in the lobby from 6 to 9:30 each morning. Outdoor security cameras and electronic card locks provide extra security. There are plenty of fast-food restaurants, convenience stores, drugstores and ATMs on Dickerson Pike.

## Hampton Inn – North
**$$ • 2407 Brick Church Pk.**
**• (615) 226-3300, (800) HAMPTON**

You'll find the 127-room Hampton Inn – North just off I-65 near Trinity Lane. The five-story hotel is about seven minutes from downtown and about 15 minutes from Opryland, so it gets lots of family vacationers, especially on weekends. Amenities include a fitness room, outdoor pool, pay-per-view movies and Nintendo, and a free deluxe continental breakfast served in the lobby from 6 to 10 each morning.

### Holiday Inn Express – North
**$$ • 2401 Brick Church Pk.**
**• (615) 226-4600, (800) HOLIDAY**

A nice and affordable choice in the Trinity Lane area off I-65, this five-story hotel has 172 rooms and offers easy access to downtown Nashville, about a seven-minute drive. Each room has sliding glass doors that open up to a small balcony, but there's not much in the way of a view. A free continental deluxe breakfast is available 6 to 9:30 AM daily in the lobby. Other amenities include free Showtime, pay-per-view movies and Nintendo, an outdoor pool, fitness room with sauna, and meeting/banquet space. Some rooms have hair dryers.

### LaQuinta Inn MetroCenter
**$$ • 2001 MetroCenter Blvd.**
**• (615) 259-2130, (800) 531-5900**

This 120-room motel has been here since about 1970. In-room coffee makers, free HBO and an outdoor pool are about the only extras, but the rooms are comfortable and the property convenient to downtown. Two two-room suites provide extra space for those who need it.

### Ramada Inn Limited – At The Stadium
**$$-$$$ • 303 Interstate Dr.**
**• (615) 244-6690, (800) 251-1856, (800) 2-RAMADA**

Business travelers and tourists have been relying on this convenient property for about 40 years. Situated on the east bank of the Cumberland River, the four-story hotel was renovated in the mid-1990s. There are 120 rooms, including 14 suites. Some rooms have nice views of the downtown skyline. The hotel is close to I-65 and is only about eight blocks from downtown Nashville. The hotel's indoor guitar-shaped swimming pool is a fitting touch

for a Music City hotel. Guests can also enjoy a free continental breakfast, served daily in the first-floor breakfast room.

### Ramada Inn North
**$$-$$$ • 1412 Brick Church Pk.**
**• (615) 226-3230, (800) 544-6385, (800) 2-RAMADA**

A budget-friendly choice in the Trinity Lane area off I-65, this three-story motel opened in 1975 and has 170 rooms. It may have a new name by the time you read this. Free entertainment is a bonus here. The on-site Broken Spoke — with a sports bar, lounge and Songwriters Cafe — features live bands, karaoke, songwriter showcases and more. If you're not in the mood for nightlife, you can enjoy free HBO movies in your room. Adults who pay the "bed-and-breakfast rate" are entitled to free full breakfast each morning; breakfast costs extra for children. After breakfast, hit the road. Downtown Nashville is less than 10 minutes away, and Opryland and Music Valley are about a 15-minute drive.

### The Regal Maxwell House
**$$$$ • 2025 MetroCenter Blvd.**
**• (615) 259-4343, (800) 457-4460**

One of Nashville's luxury hotels, the Regal Maxwell House carries on a proud tradition. It's the namesake of the famous Maxwell House Hotel (see the related Close-up in our History chapter) that opened in downtown Nashville in 1869. The hotel was the site for many important business and social events, and it enjoyed a national reputation. And yes, the hotel is connected to the famous brand of coffee, although the hotel had the Maxwell House name first. President Theodore Roosevelt, on a visit to Nashville in the early 1900s, commented that the coffee was "good to the last drop." The original Maxwell House was destroyed by fire in 1961. The current hotel opened in 1979; it sits just off I-265, 1.5 miles from downtown.

Atop a knoll overlooking downtown Nashville, this 10-story hotel has 285 spacious and well-appointed rooms, two bi-level suites with two full baths, and two Regal suites with a king bedroom and connecting parlor area. Rooms have card-key locks and in-room voice-mail service. Amenities include an outdoor

Photo: Cathy Summerlin

Luxurious highrise hotels dot the local skyline.

pool, two lighted tennis courts and a health club with sauna, steam room and workout equipment. This hotel has a concierge on call until 11 PM plus room service and valet/laundry service, so you can relax and let someone else take care of the details. Getting around town is easy and stress-free thanks to the hotel's free shuttle, which will take you to any location within a 5-mile radius. On-site Praline's offers breakfast, lunch and dinner. The sports bar-themed Maxwell's Lounge is open daily.

## South and Southeast

### AmeriSuites Nashville/Brentwood
$$$ • 202 Summit View Dr., Brentwood • (615) 661-9477, (800) 833-1516

This all-suite hotel is a nice property that's just off I-65 at Old Hickory Boulevard, close to Brentwood's Maryland Farms and the Cool Springs area. It's 10 miles south of downtown Nashville and 10 miles from Franklin, so while it's popular with business travelers on weekdays, lots of tourists and pleasure travelers stay here on weekends. There are 126 suites on six levels, including 24 business suites that feature a king bed, large desk, chair and ottoman, a small desk and snacks. Standard suites

have a refrigerator, microwave, wet bar, coffee maker and 26-inch TV.

You'll find a fitness center, laundry room, movie rental center and 1,200 square feet of meeting space on the first floor. There is also an outdoor heated pool. The hotel provides free shuttle service to any spot within 6 miles, and you'll find some good restaurants, CoolSprings Galleria mall and other good shopping within that radius. A complimentary deluxe continental breakfast buffet is served daily. On Wednesdays from 5 to 6:30 PM, you can enjoy complimentary beer, wine, soft drinks and hot appetizers during the manager's reception.

### Best Western Music City Inn
$$ • 13010 Old Hickory Blvd. • (615) 641-7721, (800) 237-8124

Convenient to the First American Music Center, Smyrna and LaVergne, Best Western Music City Inn has 137 rooms, including nine suites. It's off I-24 at Exit 62, about 12 miles south of downtown Nashville. Each room has a coffee maker and TV. Rooms with king-size beds have hair dryers. Complimentary continental breakfast is served from 6 to 10 AM daily in the lobby, and there is a welcome reception with cookies and punch daily. There's a fam-

## FRANKLIN
# Marriott.
## COOL SPRINGS

700 Cool Springs Boulevard, Franklin, Tennessee 37067
(615) 261-6100 Fax: (615) 261-6161

*F*ranklin Marriott Cool Springs — Tennessee's newest Marriott. Just 15 minutes south of downtown Nashville, surrounded by gorgeous countryside is Marriott's newest 300 room hotel with over 21,000 sq. ft. of flexible meeting space.

Visitors will enjoy a first-class facility with an indoor pool, exercise room and outdoor sundeck. *Lorraine's Bistro* serves a wide variety of regional cuisines featuring aged Black Angus char-broiled steaks. *The Stirrup Cup* Lounge compliments the restaurant with rich wood paneling and an equestrian theme.

Neighboring attractions include historic downtown Franklin, Civil War battlefields, homes of the nation's leading country and acoustic music artists, 90 holes of premier golf, all located near restaurants, office facilities and the second largest mall in Tennessee.

*Don't sleep just anywhere . . .*

**Franklin Marriott Cool Springs**
700 Cool Springs Boulevard
Franklin, TN 37067
(615) 261-6100 • FAX (615) 261-6161

---

ily-style restaurant on the property and a lounge that features live entertainment nightly. An outdoor pool, laundry room and renovated restaurant are among the amenities.

### Days Inn – Bell Road
**$ • 501 Collins Park Dr., Antioch**
**• (615) 731-7800, (800) 926-8366**
**(800) 325-2525**

Conveniently located at I-24 and Bell Road, this two-story motel offers budget-priced accommodations about 10 miles from downtown Nashville. It's close to Hickory Hollow Mall, First American Music Center and plenty of restaurants. The hotel offers a free continental breakfast in the lobby each morning, but if you're really hungry you might want to go next door to Cracker Barrel.

The hotel opened around the mid-'70s. It has 113 fairly spacious rooms. Cable TV and an outdoor pool are about the only extras.

### Franklin Marriott Cool Springs
**$$$-$$$$ • 700 Cool Springs Blvd., Franklin • (615) 261-6100**

The newest Marriott in the Nashville area, this 300-room hotel features an indoor pool, sundeck, exercise room, and flexible meeting space, and offers easy access to all that Nashville has to offer. There's an on-site restaurant and an equestrian-themed lounge, too.

### Governor's House Hotel
**$$ • 737 Harding Pl.**
**• (615) 834-5000**

Just off I-65 at Harding Place, Governor's House offers easy access to Nashville and Brentwood. There are a few restaurants, such as Darryl's 1827 Restaurant & Bar and Cracker Barrel, nearby on Sidco Drive. Downtown Nashville is just 12 miles north. If you travel south on I-65 for about 10 miles, you'll find the upscale CoolSprings Galleria mall, which is

Many of the finer hotels in downtown Nashville offer accommodations within walking distance of the State Capitol and Second Avenue entertainment.

surrounded by a variety of restaurants — everything from Copeland's of New Orleans and Romano's Macaroni Grill to Taco Bell.

The four-story hotel has 150 spacious rooms, including four suites. Rooms have TVs, but no free movies. Local calls are 50¢. An outdoor pool is available during warm-weather months. The hotel's full-service Dixieland Cafe is open for breakfast, lunch and dinner. The Club Car Lounge is just off the restaurant.

### Hampton Inn – Brentwood
**$$$ • 5630 Franklin Pike Cir., Brentwood • (615) 373-2212, (800) HAMPTON**

Corporate clients doing business in Brentwood's nearby Maryland Farms office park keep the 114-room Hampton Inn – Brentwood busy Monday through Friday, while lots of families and tourists usually arrive for weekend stays. The hotel is right off I-65 in Brentwood. CoolSprings Galleria is about 5 miles south, and downtown Nashville is about a 10-minute drive in the opposite direction.

This four-story property features spacious and nicely decorated rooms plus just enough extras to make sure your stay here is comfortable. You'll find an iron and ironing board in each room, and guests can enjoy free HBO, free local calls and a complimentary continental breakfast in the lobby from 6 to 10 each morning. If you're in the mood for a workout you can visit the nearby Maryland Farms Athletic Club, courtesy of the hotel, seven days a week.

### Hilton Suites – Brentwood
**$$$$ • 9000 Overlook Blvd., Brentwood • (615) 370-0111, (800) HILTONS**

As its name and address suggest, this all-suites property sits atop a hill overlooking Brentwood and I-65. This four-story hotel features 203 two-room suites. The rooms have more than 500 square feet of space and include a bedroom and a living/dining area with a microwave, coffee maker, refrigerator and table with four chairs. Each room also has a VCR. The three King Executive rooms are even more spacious and have boardroom tables. The three Governor's Conference Room Suites have separate meeting rooms.

Since it opened in 1991, this Hilton has welcomed a steady stream of corporate clients on weekdays and vacationing families on weekends. The hotel's amenities appeal to both groups. For recreation, there's an indoor pool, whirlpool and fitness center. After you work up an appetite, you can enjoy breakfast, lunch or dinner in the full-service restaurant in the center atrium area. A cooked-to-order breakfast is included in your room rate. Other amenities include a billiard room, business center, library, gift shop with videos available for checkout and four meeting rooms.

### Residence Inn by Marriott
**$$$-$$$$ • 206 Ward Cir., Brentwood • (615) 371-0100, (800) 228-9290, (800) 331-3131**

Most guests at this all-suites property are here for an extended stay. Some are in town for business functions, and others are relocating to the area. Rates depend on the length of stay; long-term guests might pay as much as 25 percent less than the price code indicates.

This Residence Inn is in Brentwood's lovely Maryland Farms office park. It is a two-story, apartment-type property with 110 suites. The 763-square-foot, two-bedroom, two-bath suites have a kitchen and living room area with sofa bed. The 477-square-foot studio suites have a bedroom and kitchen, and some have sleeper sofas. Most suites have fireplaces, and all have cable TV (no movie channels, though) and free local calls. Extra amenities and social functions, including complimentary continental breakfast and social hour, help you feel at home here. Tuesday night is cookout night, and guests are treated to a free dinner. An outdoor pool, exercise room and recreation area with a basketball court, volleyball court and badminton area are available.

### Brentwood Steeplechase Inn
**$$-$$$ • 5581 Franklin Pike Cir., Brentwood • (615) 373-8585**

One of the Nashville area's rare privately owned and operated hotels, the Steeplechase Inn promises luxury at an affordable rate. It's popular with business travelers, who account for about 70 percent of bookings on weekdays. The hotel welcomes a lot of guests for weddings and family reunions on weekends.

Steeplechase Inn opened in 1986 and features 48 rooms, including 24 suites. The large rooms have 9-foot ceilings, which add to their spacious feel. The decor includes floor-to-ceiling draperies and cherry-wood furniture. The 650-square-foot suites have fully furnished kitchens. Some suites have fireplaces; others have whirlpool tubs. Daily continental breakfast is included in the room rate. Other perks include free access to Brentwood's World Gym (about a mile away), cable TV and free parking.

The inn is off I-65 on the east side of Old Hickory Boulevard. There are plenty of affordable restaurants and good shops across the interstate in Brentwood, and the Cool Springs area, about 6 miles south on I-65, has a great mall and lots of good restaurants. Downtown Nashville is about 7 miles north on I-65.

# West

### Baymont Inn & Suites – Nashville West
$$-$$$ • 5612 Lenox Ave.
• (615) 353-0700, (800) 301-0200

This property is just off White Bridge Road near Charlotte Pike, one block off I-40. If you're not looking for it, you may pass right by, but once inside, you'll find a courteous and helpful staff and nice rooms with lots of extras. This hotel opened in 1988 and has 109 rooms, including about 10 suites. Amenities include a pool, continental breakfast delivered to your room at your request, in-room coffee makers, irons and ironing boards, 25-inch TVs, and pay-per-view movies and Nintendo.

This chain really caters to the business traveler, and about 90 percent of the guests at this location are here for business. The hotel has seven Business First Rooms, each featuring a king bed, spacious work desk, speaker phone, adjustable ergonomic chair and a lamp with a power outlet and modem jack in its base. The hotel allows up to five pages of free inbound faxes.

When it's time for recreation, you'll find downtown Nashville and Music Row about a 5- to 10-minute drive; Opryland is about 15 miles east. Nearby restaurants include Uncle Bud's Catfish and Shoney's. Numerous other good restaurants, including Caesar's, J. Alexander's, The Orchid and Calhoun's, are a short drive down White Bridge Road. Members of the hotel chain's frequent guest program get a free night's stay after 12 visits.

When you stay at a B&B, you get a real Insider's view of an area. It's a great way to experience the local color and flavor.

# Bed and Breakfast Inns

There is something special about spending the night at a bed and breakfast inn. In fact, some travelers refuse to stay anywhere but a bed and breakfast.

Maybe it's the home-away-from-home feeling you get at a bed and breakfast — something you just can't get at a hotel or motel. Or maybe it's the hospitality of the hosts, who welcome you into their homes and treat you like a very special friend. It might be the uniquely decorated guest rooms, the fresh flowers, homemade breakfasts and other attention to detail. Or maybe it's the privacy, the peace and quiet, the relaxing times spent snuggled up in front of a roaring fire or enjoying a soft breeze while you sip a cold drink on a front-porch swing.

More and more people are discovering the delights of bed and breakfast hospitality. Many believe the bed and breakfast inn is a new concept for America and that our inns are copies of European inns, but American bed and breakfasts in one form or another, have been around since the earliest Colonial days. Today they are becoming increasingly popular among business travelers, vacationing families and people looking for a close-to-home weekend getaway.

When you stay at a B&B, you get a real Insider's view of an area. It's a great way to experience an area's color and flavor — a place to become one of the locals for a short time. When you've long forgotten a night in a nondescript hotel, you'll look back with fond memories on your pleasant stay in a special bed and breakfast.

Each inn has its own charm — no two are alike. The innkeepers are just as diverse. Retirees, business executives, secretaries, farmers, teachers, lawyers — friendly people from all walks of life own B&Bs. You'll find some gracious hosts at Nashville-area inns. They are as interesting as their homes, which range from properties on the National Historic Register to modern dwellings with every possible amenity. There are country inns offering spacious, deluxe accommodations as well as cozy, comfortable homes with one or two rooms to rent. Many out-of-towners expect to find large Southern plantation mansions here, but Nashville isn't in the Deep South, and there aren't many properties like that in this area. You will find interesting homes full of character, however.

Business travelers and tourists might enjoy staying at a B&B in or close to the city;

there are several of those to choose from. Those who prefer a country setting will find some excellent choices too — country inns, farmhouses and cabins on the outskirts of Nashville or in nearby towns.

In this chapter you'll find a good selection of B&Bs in and around Nashville. We haven't listed all the available properties, but we have chosen a sample that represents several locations, accommodations and price ranges. Most are less than an hour's drive from downtown.

Here are a few Insiders' tips to keep in mind when choosing a bed and breakfast.

•The "breakfast" part of your bed and breakfast booking might be a made-to-order country breakfast; an owner's special pancake breakfast; a continental-style breakfast of coffee, juice and baked goods; or something in between. If you have any special dietary needs, be sure to let your hosts know in advance; they'll usually make a good effort to accommodate your requests.

•Some bed and breakfasts accept children; some do so only by special arrangement; some do not allow kids at all. If you are traveling with children, be sure to find out if your preferred B&B is kid-friendly. Likewise, if you're looking for a quiet, adult environment, ask the innkeeper if any children will be staying at your chosen inn during your visit. Policies on children are provided for the B&Bs we list.

•If you're traveling with a pet, you can probably find an inn that accepts pets. Be sure to inquire about pet accommodations, especially if your pet is accustomed to staying indoors; some inns only allow them to stay outside. Also, if you have allergies or just prefer not to be around pets, be sure to ask if the owners have any indoor pets. Pet policies are included in our listings.

•Many inns offer some wheelchair-accessible rooms, but some of the older, historic locations may not be fully accessible. Be sure to inquire about this when you call if accessibility is important to you.

•Virtually all area B&Bs are nonsmoking properties, but most allow smoking on the porch, deck or other outside areas.

•Credit card policies vary. Check with the inn when making your reservations to see which, if any, credit cards are accepted. We'll tell you if a listed B&B doesn't accept credit cards.

•Advance deposit and refund policies vary. During certain times of year, policies may be more strict due to the demand for accommodations. Be sure you understand the rules before making a reservation.

•If you would like help booking a room, one of the bed and breakfast reservation services we list can take care of the details for you.

## Price-code Key

The following key is a general guide to what you can expect to pay for one night's stay. The rates are for double occupancy. If you're traveling alone, you can expect to pay approximately $5 to $15 less. Prices are subject to change.

| | |
|---|---|
| $ | $50 to $75 |
| $$ | $76 to $100 |
| $$$ | $101 to $125 |
| $$$$ | $126 or more |

# Associations and Reservation Services

## Tennessee Bed & Breakfast Innkeepers Association
**5341 Mt. View Rd., Ste. 150, Antioch TN 37013 • (800) 820-8144**

This state association is a nonprofit organization established to market Tennessee bed and breakfast inns. Its 100 member inns are fully licensed by the state and have passed the association's biennial inspection program. About 20 are in the Nashville area. Call the toll-free number for a free brochure that describes each inn.

## Tennessee Equestrian Bed & Breakfast Association
**5436 Leipers Creek Rd., Franklin TN 37064 • (615) 791-0333**

There are a variety of bed and breakfast inns in the Nashville area that provide accommodations for horses or that offer their own horses for guests to ride. Contact this association for a listing of horse-friendly B&Bs.

## Natchez Trace Bed & Breakfast Reservation Service
• (931) 285-2777, (800) 377-2770

This service, operated by Bill and Kay Jones, has a directory of some 36 inns in Tennessee, Alabama and Mississippi. All are along the Natchez Trace, a historic route that runs from Nashville to Natchez, Mississippi. About 10 of the inns are near Nashville. Call the toll-free number for reservations, details on homes and a free map of the Trace, or write to P.O. Box 193, Hampshire TN 38461.

# Bed and Breakfasts In and Around Nashville

## A Homeplace Bed & Breakfast
$-$$, no credit cards
• 7286 Nolensville Rd., Nolensville
• (615) 776-5181

The story behind this bed and breakfast is so charming you may want to visit right away. It all started with a quest for apples. Newlyweds Alfred and Evelyn Hyde Bennett got their first taste of bed and breakfast hospitality on their honeymoon in Scotland, where they stayed at a variety of inns. One day not long after their honeymoon, Alfred, a retired minister, and Evelyn, a retired Metro schoolteacher, took a drive in the south Nashville countryside to buy a bushel of apples.

After noticing a crowd and a commotion around the old Putnam family home, they stopped and discovered that the property was being auctioned. There weren't many bidders, even though the property was zoned for commercial use. When they realized the lone bidder planned to demolish the house, the Bennetts began bidding and soon found themselves the proud owners of a 1-acre plot of land containing a couple of structures built in the 1800s. What had started as an apple-gathering excursion ended with the couple buying a new home, soon to be the site of their new business, a bed and breakfast inn.

The Bennetts restored the building and opened A Homeplace Bed & Breakfast in Au-

gust 1990. The building was originally a stage-coach stop; the front of the house was built around 1820 and the back around 1850. It's featured on the local historical society tour, and sometimes individuals just drop by for a look. Guests from as far away as Switzerland and South Africa have found their way here, and the inn has quite a few repeat visitors.

The main house offers three guest rooms, each with a large full bath, canopied double bed, armoire, dresser with wash basin, fireplace and sitting area. Downstairs is the Parlor Suite guest room, which has a library. Upstairs is the Doctor's Room, so named because an out-of-town ophthalmologist-veterinarian stayed there when he had appointments scheduled in Nashville. (He enjoyed his stays so much that he moved his practice to Nashville and now lives near the Bennetts.) The Honeymoon Suite is also upstairs. It features a Victorian couch, an elegant library table and several other interesting antiques. If you stay in this room, ask the Bennetts to tell you the history of the pieces.

Outside, cheerful and colorful flower gardens brighten each side of the main house. In the backyard is the Victorian Cottage, or "gingerbread house," as Evelyn calls it. The cottage, which served as the cook's cottage in the stagecoach days, is suitable for a lengthy stay and features a small kitchen, an antique bed and a bath. Water lily and lotus ponds are nearby. The backyard creek house and gazebo offer a view of the creek, stone fences and meadow. The large gazebo is the setting for barbecues, special receptions and civic group events.

Guests have access to all other rooms in the main house. A piano, TV and VCR are in the living room, and the Bennetts have a dulcimer and accordion available too. Phones are in the living room and dining room. The large front porch has rocking chairs, a porch swing and bench, and is a nice place to take your morning cup of coffee.

Breakfast is a special treat at this inn. Alfred, of Scottish heritage, dresses for the occasion. Attired in his kilt and Prince Charles dinner jacket, he serves a full breakfast. Ham quiche and hot biscuits are specialties. Also on the menu are fresh fruit, country ham, Scottish scones, juice, hot tea and coffee. Waffles and sausage are usually served Sundays. Evelyn gets many requests for her recipes, and she'll be glad to share them with you. Children are accepted here, but pets aren't. Guests who stay in any of the rooms for a week or more receive a generous discount.

This inn is about 7 miles from the Old Hickory Boulevard–Nolensville Pike intersection, about a 20-minute drive from downtown Nashville. Antique lovers will enjoy browsing at the antique malls next door and across the street from the inn. Nearby Franklin and Murfreesboro also have lots of good antiquing.

## Apple Brook Bed, Breakfast & Barn
**$$ • 9127 Tenn. Hwy. 100 W.**
**• (615) 646-5082**

If you're looking for a country getaway that isn't far from the city, Apple Brook is a perfect choice, offering down-home comforts in a relaxing setting just minutes from Nashville's attractions. It's close to Warner Parks, the northern terminus of the Natchez Trace Parkway, Chaffin's Dinner Barn, canoeing on the Harpeth River and more. It's approximately 10.7 miles from the Tenn. Highway 100–U.S. Highway 70 split in west Nashville.

The 1896 farmhouse was covered in brick in the 1960s, and while it has undergone several renovations over the years, it retains that old-time country home ambience. In addition to the farmhouse, Apple Brook's 5-plus acres contain a barn that provides overnight horse accommodations. If you'd rather forget city life for a while, a babbling brook, natural spring and pond reinforce that out-in-the-country feel. Canada geese make their home at the pond, and deer often graze on the lawn — if you peer out your bedroom window at just the right time, you might spy one. When you arrive, you'll probably hear the cackling hens out in the barn.

In the days before running water made its way here, the spring supplied water for a nearby one-room schoolhouse. Longtime teacher Sally Morton sent her students through the apple orchards to the spring to fetch water. When Don and Cynthia Van Ryen purchased the property, they named it Apple Brook after learning about its history.

Open since 1994, Apple Brook has four rooms on the second floor of the farmhouse, and each has a queen-size bed. Each room has a private bath: two rooms have tubs and showers, and two have showers only. The Blue Room features blue walls trimmed in white, with a blue and yellow color scheme. The bath is just next door, and a door in the hallway allows guests to close off this bedroom and bath to create a private suite. The Cardinal Room is decorated in shades of mauve and pink and features a stained-glass cardinal in the window. A canopy bed is the focus of the Tea Rose Room, decorated in mellow cream colors with airy lace curtains. The Peach Room is done in shades of peach and features a wicker headboard. Light, apple-scented lotion in an apple-shaped dispenser is a nice touch in each room. The rooms also have cable TV.

Downstairs is a formal parlor, the kitchen, the dining room (which accommodates up to 12 at one sitting) and a living room with a fireplace. The house is decorated with antiques that the Van Ryens picked up during their travels abroad and other items guests have brought them. Cynthia loves to show off these treasures. In the back of the house there's an Olympic-size swimming pool, or "cement pond" as Don calls it; it's a nice place to cool off on a lazy summer afternoon.

The specialty breakfast at Apple Brook is Don's fabulous apple pancakes, topped with real maple syrup. Another favorite is the bacon that's been smoked over apple wood chips; it's shipped in from northern Wisconsin. The aroma of bacon frying brings guests downstairs in a hurry. It's OK to ask for a second helping — even thirds if you can hold it.

The Van Ryens opened Apple Brook after visiting many B&Bs and hostels in North

**BED AND BREAKFAST INNS • 73**

Some bed and breakfast inns in and around Nashville (such as Hillsboro House, shown here) feature Victorian signature elements such as gingerbread and arched windows.

America and Europe. Don is busy planting and harvesting the garden and renovating the barn to accommodate weddings, receptions and other special functions, but he's not too busy to visit with guests. Hospitality abounds here. The Van Ryens enjoy chatting with visitors, and they make great hosts. Children are welcome by prior arrangement (some dates are reserved for couples only). Pets can't stay in the house, but they can spend the night in the barn.

## Birdsong Lodge
## on Sycamore Creek
$$$$ • 1306 Tenn. Hwy. 49 E.,
Ashland City • (615) 792-1767

This home was built around 1912 by Leslie and Mabel Cheek, of Maxwell House Coffee fame, who used the home as a vacation cabin (see the Cheekwood entry in our Attractions chapter). Today the one-story lodge, which is

on the National Register of Historic Places, serves as a luxurious retreat designed with the sophisticated traveler in mind.

Birdsong is about 25 miles north of downtown Nashville, reached via a private country road off Tenn. Highway 49 that runs along Sycamore Creek. The inn sits behind a gated entrance on 9 acres of woods and open fields. Birdsong has been a B&B for years. In June 1998, George and Elizabeth Trinkler purchased and renovated the inn, adding elegant and luxurious touches such as Persian rugs, antiques and designer bedding. Elizabeth is the great-granddaughter of E.C. Lewis, who ran the Sycamore Mill on the property in the last 1800s, before the Cheeks purchased it. The innkeepers, Robert and Elizabeth Pilling, are friends of the Trinklers and moved up from Florida to operate Birdsong. Robert is a former educational specialist who enjoys birding. Elizabeth has worked as a professional chef, so you can be sure that the meals here are delicious.

The original home, built from red cedar logs cut on the property, consisted of a great room with fireplace and four other rooms. It has been modernized but still retains its historic feel. The home features 10½-foot ceilings with cedar beams. Favorite spots for relaxing are the two large swings on the front screened porch and the "fireside parlor," which has large leaded glass windows and built-in seating beside the massive fireplace.

There are three rooms in the main house and a one-bedroom cottage just a few steps away. Rooms in the main house have four-poster beds, chandeliers, private baths, cable TV and private telephones. Antiques and tasteful artwork adorn the rooms. The private and romantic cottage has a full kitchen, large bath, queen-size bed, sofa bed and fireplace in the living room, plus front and back porches. All guest rooms have nice views of the outdoors. In fact, rooms are arranged so that guests can bird-watch from the comfort of their beds!

www.insiders.com
See this and many other *Insiders' Guide®* destinations online.
Visit us today!

Guests staying in the cottage are treated to breakfast there, while other guests have their choice of breakfast in bed, in the dining room or in the sunroom. Some of Elizabeth's breakfast specialties include crusted French toast in a boysenberry pool, sausage-apple quiche, and omelets, but she will be happy to prepare any special requests.

After breakfast, you can choose to explore the beautiful countryside, relax in a hammock, take a stroll through the gardens or explore the 20,000-acre Cheatham County Wildlife Management Area about 6 miles away. You can swim, picnic, boat and fish at the Cheatham Dam about 5 miles away. Hikers will find country trails to explore nearby. Binoculars are available for birdwatchers. You might also want to play a round of golf at nearby Sycamore Golf Course or head to Music City for a day of fun.

Dinners, available by reservation, are a treat here. The table is set with antique china, crystal and silver. Elizabeth describes the dinners as casually elegant and encourages guests to

dress comfortably and casually if they wish. The nearest restaurants, including the popular Bill's Catfish Restaurant (see our Restaurants chapter), are about 4 miles away in Ashland City.

Although most guests at Birdsong Lodge are business travelers and couples, the inn will accept children ages 14 and up. The only pets allowed in the house are the Pillings' four poodles and two Siamese cats, but guests staying in the cottage might be able to arrange to keep their pets there.

### Blueberry Hill Bed & Breakfast
**$-$$ • 4591 Peytonsville Rd., Franklin • (615) 791-9947, (800) 400-4923 (PIN 7929)**

This inn sits high on a hill overlooking farms and valleys of rural Williamson County. The views are so extraordinary that most guests are content to relax and take in the scenery during their stay. Getting here is a bit of an adventure. The road to Blueberry Hill is steep and rather narrow. The inn is 2.8 miles east of Interstate 65 off Exit 61. When you arrive, innkeepers Joan and Art Reesman will be waiting to greet you. Joan, a retired pediatric nursing instructor, and Art, a retired Vanderbilt University geology professor, have been welcoming guests to Blueberry Hill since May 1995.

The original house was built in 1980 in the Federal style. A recent addition includes a great room with cathedral ceilings and floor-to-ceiling windows, a screened porch and a front deck, all of which take advantage of the magnificent views. The inn offers two guest rooms on the second floor. Each has a private bath, queen-size four-poster canopy bed, antique furniture, gas fireplace, loveseat and TV (no cable). If you want to enjoy the view from your room, reserve the Blue Room, in the front of the house. Special features include three windows, walnut antiques and a stained-glass bath window featuring Jonathan Livingston Seagull. The Berry Room faces the wooded hill in back of the house and is furnished with oak and maple antiques.

In winter, the great room is a popular gathering place. It has a fireplace, grand piano, pub table for games, extensive library, TV, VCR and a good selection of movies. When the weather is nice, guests enjoy the screened porch, which has a wicker swing, and the deck outside the great room. It's also fun to explore the 5-acre property, which has gardens, a goldfish pond, blueberry bushes, bluebird houses and hummingbird feeders. Deer often feed in the meadow.

A candlelight breakfast is served in the dining room, a cozy room featuring hand-hewn beams and a 7-foot, open-hearth fireplace. The Reesmans serve a hearty meal, often including homemade blueberry pancakes, muffins, waffles or coffeecake; an egg dish; sausage, sausage balls or bacon and juice, fruit and coffee.

Children older than 10 are welcome, and on days when the inn isn't busy, younger children can be accommodated. There are no pet accommodations.

## Carole's Yellow Cottage
**$$ • 801 Fatherland St. • (615) 226-2952**

Situated on a corner lot in east Nashville's historic Edgefield, this spacious 1902 Victorian cottage is a popular spot with business travelers and weekend visitors who want to stay close to the city. The house is listed on the National Register of Historic Places and is surrounded by some beautifully restored 19th-century homes. Each spring, the neighborhood has an open house to showcase some of the best. "I feel very elevated, spiritually, to be here," said Carole Vanderwal, who opened Carole's Yellow Cottage in 1995. "Older homes are really a treasure. There are not that many left in the city of Nashville." Vanderwal, who has a degree in Russian language and literature as well as a law degree, works full time for the state of Tennessee. She plans to become a full-time innkeeper when she retires.

This sunny, one-story cottage features specialty millwork in a sunburst design over the front porch entrance; the same design is found indoors in the main hall. The lavender front door is complemented by lush blooms of crepe myrtle during the summer. In the enclosed backyard, a deck looks out on perennial gardens planted with lavender, lilies, antique climbing rose, peonies, yucca, begonia, purple coneflower and herbs. The front yard offers a dramatic view of the downtown Nashville skyline.

Inside, the 2,100-square-foot house features 12-foot ceilings, bedrooms with ceiling fans, central heat and air and original heart-of-pine wood floors. The two guest rooms originally shared one bath, but Vanderwal planned to have a private bath for each room by 1998. She had the weary business traveler in mind when she selected the bedrooms' soothing color schemes. One room has a large double bed, turn-of-the century antiques and a restful buttery yellow and white color scheme; the pale pink and yellow wallpaper features an iris pattern. The other room has one double bed, a futon couch that opens into a second double bed, and a taupe color on the walls, with deep royal blue bed covers, mini-blinds and coordinating wallpaper trim.

The sitting room/library features deep red walls, a loveseat and two chairs. Come here to enjoy a selection of books or watch television before turning in at night. The rooms do not have private phones, but a phone is available. Vanderwal carefully selected original paintings and other artwork for the walls.

Only one pet is allowed here, and that's the resident cat. This bed and breakfast doesn't allow children.

Carole serves a full breakfast each morning. She specializes in whole-grain cooking, so you can expect delicious multigrain waffles or maybe nine-grain toast with eggs and fruit.

## Hancock House
**$$-$$$$ • 2144 Nashville Pk, Gallatin • (615) 452-8431**

Roberta and Carl Hancock have lived in this historic house since the late 1970s. They opened it as B&B 1991 after Roberta, a school teacher for 20 years, decided she was ready for a new career. Roberta and Carl, who was formerly in the tobacco business, spent several months renovating the home and the two-story cabin in the side yard. In 1999 they added the three-bedroom Stone House next door.

Hancock House is a 15-room colonial revival log inn. In late 1800s it was a stage coach stop and toll gate house known as Avondale Station. Over the years two small cabins were attached to the back of the original building.

In between the three structures is a courtyard, just off the dining room. The interior features hardwood floors, exposed beams, fireplaces, log walls, area rugs and period antiques that the Hancocks have collected over the past 30 years.

The main house has four bedrooms, each with a private bath and fireplace. The Chamber room, located on the ground floor, has an antique murphy bed and a whirlpool tub. The Nannie Dunn room, half a flight of stairs off the dining room, has an antique bed. Upstairs are the Bridal Suite, with an antique canopied fourposter bed and a romantic whirlpool for two, and the Felice Ferrell room, named for the home's previous owner, which has an antique elevated bed.

The cabin offers more privacy. It sleeps up to six and has a bedroom, kitchen and den with sofa bed and fireplace. The bath has whirlpool tub and shower. The Stone House has three bedrooms and two baths, each with a whirlpool tub, plus a kitchen, large living room and dining room.

All accommodations include a full country breakfast, served in your room, in the dining room or outdoors in the courtyard. The Hancocks also serve afternoon tea and other beverages and plenty of fresh fruit. Brunch, lunch and dinner are available by reservation. Children are welcome at Hancock House, but there are no accommodations for pets.

## The Hillsboro House
$$$ • 1933 20th Ave. S. • (615) 292-5501

Owner Andrea Beaudet describes The Hillsboro House as a cozy Victorian bed and breakfast for travelers, featuring private baths, feather beds, morning birds and homemade breads. This circa 1904 house is in the heart of Nashville's historic Belmont-Hillsboro District, within walking distance of Hillsboro Village shops, Vanderbilt University, Belmont University and the popular Sunset Grill restaurant. Music Row is just a few blocks away.

Located at the corner of Portland and 20th, just off 21st Avenue, the house was condemned when Beaudet, a former music teacher in Maine, purchased it in 1990. She has since carefully restored it and made it the showpiece of the neighborhood. The cheerful yellow two-story house is trimmed in white and bordered by a cream-colored picket fence. Colorful flowers bloom in the well-tended window boxes, and morning glories climb the trellis on the side of the front porch. In the evening the fragrance of the night-blooming moonflowers fills the air. Herbs and perennials grow in a traditional Victorian garden in the side yard.

Lots of business travelers have made this charming and casual bed and breakfast their home away from home since it opened in 1994. The house is also popular with the neighbors, who send visiting relatives there for the night. "It's more like grandma's house than anything else," Beaudet said. "It's comfortable and cozy. Guests get a good night's sleep, a good breakfast, and they're on their way."

Two parlors are on the first floor. Beaudet keeps a small refrigerator stocked with refreshments in the main parlor. The living room has a fireplace and makes for a cozy spot to relax during winter. Hillsboro House has three guest rooms, each with a private bath. The second-floor Fairfax room features a queen-size feather bed and has country-style furnishings. The bath has a shower only. The spacious Acklen room, also upstairs, has a queen-size feather bed and lots of windows. The connecting private bath has a claw-foot tub as well as the amenities of a modern bath. The downstairs bedroom has a queen feather bed plus a daybed, and the bath has a shower only. All guest rooms have private phones and cable TV. Upstairs is a cozy library nook, a nice spot for working or reading. After a busy day of working or sightseeing, you can return to The Hillsboro House and enjoy a soothing soak in the tub, complete with relaxing homemade bath salts.

## INSIDERS' TIP

**Some bed and breakfast innkeepers have other jobs, so you may have to adjust your schedule (arrival time, breakfast time, departure time) to fit theirs. If this is a concern, be sure to inquire about the host's schedule when making reservations.**

Breakfast is served until about 10 AM. The specialty is carrot-nut pancakes topped with homemade cinnamon cream syrup. Andrea's peaches-and-cream French toast is another favorite. Breakfasts come with freshly ground coffee, juice and sausage or bacon; eggs are usually served every other day. Beaudet's recipes have been featured in several cookbooks, so you can be sure that breakfast is something to look forward to.

Children and pets are welcome at Hillsboro House. Andrea's West Highland Terrier, Bonnie, also lives here.

## The Inn on Main Street Bed & Breakfast
**$$-$$$ • 112 S. Main St., Dickson
• (615) 441-6879, (615) 441-5821, (888) 654-1966 (beeper)**

This inn is about 35 miles west of downtown Nashville in the rural town of Dickson. The landmark 1903 home is surrounded by antique stores, old-timey craft places and the kind of small-town shops you would expect to find along a Main Street in the South. Across the street is the Grand Old Hatchery, a former feed mill that now presents live country music by amateur and "semi-pro" singers and groups. You can stop by and listen to them rehearse on Thursday and Friday nights, or come on Saturday night, when the real show takes place and the room is packed. It's a family-oriented, no-alcohol evening.

When you've taken in the area attractions, you'll enjoy returning to your comfortable accommodations at The Inn on Main Street. The two-story home was renovated before Brett and Misha Lashlee purchased it. They had been visiting bed and breakfast inns for several years, and when this house went on the market, they jumped at the chance to buy it. Brett, who works for an airline, and Misha are both antique lovers, and they have filled the inn with their collection of period antiques.

This inn offers three guest suites. Each has a phone, remote-controlled cable TV, a private bath with modern amenities and a private coffee bar with a coffee pot and a selection of coffees. On the first floor, facing Main Street, are the Civil War Suite and the Walker Suite. The Civil War Suite boasts some of Brett's Civil War artifacts, books and paintings. It has a queen-size canopy bed and the bath has a whirlpool tub. The Walker Suite is named after the family that owned the home; this room was once occupied by Grandma Walker for many years. The Lashlees consider this room the most romantic. It is decorated in *Gone with The Wind* memorabilia and has a cranberry color scheme, hardwood floors, full-size bed, a loveseat and a table for two. The bath has a claw-foot tub. If you choose the inn's "romance package," you'll get accommodations in this room, plus fresh flowers, a box of chocolates, champagne or wine and extra privacy. Both downstairs suites have VCRs; a selection of videos is in the hallway.

Upstairs, also with a Main Street view, is the Noah's Ark room, which is filled with the Lashlees' Noah's Ark collectibles that used to decorate the bedrooms of their two children. In keeping with the theme, everything in this room is presented in twos: two double beds, a table for two, a double sink in the bathroom — too cute! It has a walk-in closet. The Lashlees live in the other suite on this floor. Outside, there are upstairs and downstairs front porches and several picnic tables.

Well-behaved children are welcome at this inn, and pets are welcome but must stay outdoors in the kennel. For business travelers, the inn offers access to fax and Internet lines and provides for other office needs in its mini-office.

This inn offers several packages in addition to the romance package. A Civil War package, for example, includes a guided tour of historic war sites.

Brett and Misha serve a full country breakfast, but can also provided lighter fare on request. Be sure to try Brett's yummy biscuits.

## Namaste Acres Country Ranch Inn
**$$ • 5436 Leipers Creek Rd., Franklin
• (615) 791-0333**

This offbeat bed and breakfast is developing a great reputation, having been featured in *Southern Living*, *Horse Illustrated* and *Western Horseman* magazines. It caters to equestrians but also is popular with casual travelers, hiking enthusiasts, nature lovers and historians.

Bill and Lisa Winters and their teenage daughter Lindsay are the innkeepers. They opened their inn with one guest room, and the business grew from there; today they offer a choice of four unique suites. The property is about 25 miles south of Nashville and 12 miles southwest of Franklin, near the community of Leipers Fork, approximately 1 mile off the Natchez Trace Parkway (see our Daytrips and Weekend Getaways chapter).

The Trace, a 500-mile wilderness route that connected the northwest United States with the new Mississippi Territory in the early 1800s, is a big part of the appeal here. Guests can ride on portions of the original Trace — the same route traveled by Andrew Jackson and Meriwether Lewis. The 450-mile scenic Natchez Trace Parkway was constructed in 1938, and in 1991 a 26-mile trail for equestrians and hikers was created between the Parkway and Namaste Acres. A spur trail authorized by the National Park Service in 1993 allows guests at Namaste Acres to reach the Natchez Trace bridle path directly from the inn property. Guests can sign up for one of two guided trail ride packages for an additional fee. The half-day, 5-mile trail ride covers pine and hardwood forests, open meadows and farmland and crosses creeks and streams. The 2.5-mile ride is enjoyable, but less demanding. Other riding and hiking opportunities are nearby, among them Nashville's Percy Warner Park. Guests who don't bring their own horses can choose to ride one of Namaste Acres's Tennessee walking horses or American quarter horses.

After a day on the trails, you'll enjoy relaxing in your private guest suite. The Dutch Colonial country home offers four suites, each with a private entrance, queen-size feather bed, private bath, fireplace, comfortable seating area with reading material, TV/VCR, CD/cassette player, clock-radio, phone, ceiling fan, mini-refrigerator and coffee maker. Each room is elaborately themed.

The Cowboy Bunkhouse features rough-sawn lumber walls, log/robe bunk beds, a claw-foot tub and a private deck. The spacious Indian Lodge has a Southwestern scheme and is filled with an interesting collection of Native American artifacts and paintings. An upper-level deck provides a nice valley view. The Frontier Cabin features rough-sawn lum-

ber walls, a 12-foot ceiling and hand-hewn beams. This room's private deck overlooks a pool and rock garden. The elegant Franklin Quarters has a peach and cream color scheme and is decorated with Civil War memorabilia and art. The inn also has an exercise nook with workout equipment, a seasonal hot tub, gas grills, horseshoe pit, a fire ring for campfires and weenie roasts, and a tree house and swing by the creek. Equestrians will appreciate the stables, six separate pastures, outdoor riding arena, round pen and horse walker. In the morning, after awakening to the rooster's crow, you can enjoy a delicious and hearty country breakfast — maybe eggs, bacon, ham, sausage, potato casserole and pancakes.

This inn allows children ages 10 and older, but be sure to inquire about that when you make your reservation. If you have pets other than horses, check with the innkeepers before bringing them. "Namaste" — (na-mas-stay), by the way, is a Native American word that is the highest form of greeting — an honorable tribute from one person to another.

## Natureview Inn Bed & Breakfast
**$$ • 3354 Old Lebanon Dirt Rd.,**
**Mt. Juliet • (615) 758-4439,**
**(800) 758-7972**

A quiet country setting and spacious accommodations await you at this bed and breakfast, about 20 to 25 minutes east of downtown Nashville and 2 miles off Interstate 40. The 2,700-square-foot ranch-style home sits on 5 acres among rolling hills and pastures.

The house offers two guest suites, each with a private bath, living room and fireplace; the furnishings feature antiques and original artwork. One unit, with Southwest decor, sleeps six and has a fully equipped eat-in kitchen. It has two bedrooms — one with a four-poster queen-size bed and the other with twin beds and a walk-in closet. The living area has a sleeper sofa, cable TV and VCR.

The other suite sleeps four. The bedroom features a four-poster queen bed. The large living room has picture windows offering a nice view of the surrounding countryside. Instead of a kitchen, this unit has a library, and the living room has a TV. This unit is decorated eclectically with antiques and many pieces from owner Paulette Pettingell's collection of antique glassware. It also has a large deck overlooking the swimming pool. An in-room phone is available at your request.

Pettingell, who holds degrees in biology and botany, opened the bed and breakfast in July 1995. Originally from Illinois, she lived for years in Albuquerque, New Mexico, and taught at the University of Albuquerque. Today she makes her home in a terrace apartment in the back of Natureview Inn. She and her son Rick, who is a professional chef, serve up some delicious morning meals. Their Mexican specialties, such as huevos rancheros, feature the delicious chili peppers that are grown in the high valleys of New Mexico. Other breakfast items include eggs Florentine, pecan pancakes, freshly baked lemon bread and banana bread, and broiled grapefruit grenadine. If you want a real Southern breakfast, you can dig in to a plate full of eggs, pork chops, gravy, hot biscuits and potatoes or grits. Fresh fruit, juice and hot tea or coffee accompany every meal. While breakfast is being prepared, you might enjoy an early-morning walk along the half-mile road that passes by the house.

Natureview has welcomed guests from around the world, including Russia, Germany, England, Scotland, France and just about every state in the country. Most guests are tourists, but some business travelers stay here, and sometimes newlyweds spend their wedding night here. Well-behaved children are welcome, though the inn can accommodate children under age 6 by prior arrangement only. The suite with the kitchen is especially good for families with children. Guests may bring housebroken dogs, but cats must stay at home.

## Peacock Hill Country Inn
**$$$-$$$$ • 6994 Giles Hill Rd., College Grove • (615) 368-7727, (800) 327-6633**

Peacock Hill is one of Middle Tennessee's premier bed and breakfasts. This luxury country inn has been featured in such publications as *Southern Living, Country Accents, National Geographic Traveler* and *Country Inns*. It's on a 700-acre working cattle farm about 45 minutes from downtown Nashville, in between Franklin and Lewisburg.

The historic site was the only farm in the area that wasn't burned during the Civil War. Owners Walter and Anita Ogilvie can tell you all about the interesting history of the property. They can also tell you about the wild peacocks that live here. The Ogilvies opened the inn in the fall of 1994. Walter is a retired CPA and banker, and Anita is a former schoolteacher. When Walter retired in the early 1990s, they decided to renovate the historic buildings at Peacock Hill.

Guests can choose from ten accommodations here, including the renovated 1850s Farmhouse, two-story Log Cabin Suite, two-story Grainery Suite and the 1800s McCall House. The rates for the suites are about 30 percent to 60 percent higher than rates for Farmhouse rooms. All rooms and suites have king-size beds and luxury baths, and TV/VCRs are available.

The Farmhouse has five guest rooms. Each has a private bath with a whirlpool tub and a separate shower. The Anna Virginia Room features a four-poster bed draped in white cotton tab panels, an antique wedding ring quilt and brightly colored pillows, as well as an original stone fireplace and handpainted wood floors. The Kathleen Suzanne Room, a favorite of many guests, is decorated in a spring garden scheme: fresh floral fabrics, green and white checked wallpaper and white shutter headboard behind the bed. The Walter William Room is decorated in Aztec fabrics with a denim comforter on the oak bed. Victorian is the theme of the Hobert Rodgers Room, which features family heirloom antiques, white linens, a crystal chandelier and an Eastlake settee in front of the large bay window. The Anita Katherine Room is a deluxe room featuring a mahogany carved rice bed, a fireplace with hand-painted mantel and other comfortably elegant touches. The room's French doors open to a back deck that overlooks a rock water garden and the hillside. The Farmhouse offers accommodations for adults only.

The Log Cabin Suite is popular with honeymooners and small families. The rustic, early-19th-century log cabin smokehouse, just a few steps through the garden from the main house, has an exposed-log living room with a fireplace. Overlooking the living room is a loft

Peacock Hill is one of the area's best-known country inns. It's about 45 minutes from Nashville, in the small town of College Grove.

bedroom with an iron canopy bed. The large bath has a claw-foot tub and separate shower. The Grainery Suite is the best choice for long stays. It features a "Cottage Toile" bedroom with a fireplace and whitewashed poster bed; a European limestone bath with double whirlpool and separate shower; an upstairs English living area with original poplar floors and painted beams; and a fully furnished kitchenette.

About a mile down the road is the McCall House, a renovated early-1800s house that offers one suite and two guest rooms. All accommodations here are spacious and have fireplaces, large baths, microwaves, refrigerators, TV/VCRs, inside and outside entrances and a private deck or screen porch. The Grand Suite is decorated as a cozy English manor house; the bedroom opens onto a private deck.

The Honey Bee Room has natural pine walls accented with white mantle, trim, drapes and linens. The Blue Willow Room is a tranquil retreat decorated in blue-and-white color scheme. Guests staying in the McCall house have the option of cooking their own breakfast or being served at the Farmhouse.

Breakfast is served on the bright and cheerful sun porch overlooking the garden. The Ogilvies specialize in healthy fare. There's plenty of fresh fruit, yogurt, cereal, fresh breads and freshly squeezed juice, plus a hot entree. A favorite is the Honey Pufffed Pancake, a delicious, rich pancake served in a black iron skillet and topped with creamy, cinnamon-spiked honey butter. Another favorite is the farmer's breakfast, a mixture of farm-fresh eggs, hash browns, onions and peppers, topped with shredded cheese and served hot off the stove in an iron skillet. It's accompanied by hot whole-wheat biscuits. Those wanting a lighter meal will enjoy the light German pancake filled with fresh fruit. Dinners and box lunches are available with advance notice.

After breakfast, we suggest you explore the grounds. When this Insider and her husband celebrated our anniversary here recently, we strolled through the garden then made the 2-mile trek up to Hogg Hill, where the view of the surrounding countryside is spectacular. We were escorted there and back by the Ogilvies' friendly and well-trained Old English Sheepdog. If you're like us, after that 4-mile round-trip, you'll be ready to relax on the front

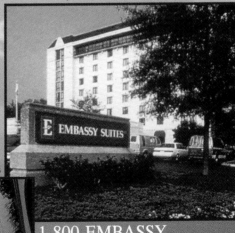

{ *The Sweetest Sounds In Nashville Are*
*The Sweet Dreams Coming From Doubletree.* }

The newly renovated Doubletree Hotel is a highlight on the Nashville skyline located in the heart of downtown near the state capital, Convention Center, Arena, Adelphia Stadium and "The District" with its vibrant nightlife. The Doubletree is only 15 minutes away from the airport and a short drive from Nashville's Music Row, home to attractions like the Country Music Hall of Fame. And as always, in the tradition of the Doubletree, we welcome every guest with freshly baked chocolate chip cookies.

- 338 luxury rooms and 10 suites
- In room movies & coffee makers
- Two phones with data ports & voice mail
- Heated swimming pool & fitness area
- Full service restaurant and lobby lounge

- Iron & ironing board
- Valet parking available
- Writing desk & sitting area
- Same day laundry & dry cleaning
- Am/fm clock radio

# DOUBLETREE HOTEL™

## NASHVILLE

convenient to Interstates 40, 24 and 65
315 4th Avenue North, Nashville, TN 37219
Dial Direct: (615) 244-8200 • Fax: (615) 747-4894

http://www.doubletreehotels.com
http://www.citysearch.com/nas/doubletree

For reservations, call your travel professional or
1-800-222-TREE

*Freshly baked chocolate chip cookies await you at over 150 Doubletree Hotels, Guest Suites and Resorts in the continental U.S., Hawaii, Mexico and the Caribbean.*

# The Sheraton Music City Hotel. A Manor of Style.

*N*estled on 23 acres of rolling hillside, just minutes from Nashville International Airport and seven miles from downtown, you'll find the Sheraton Music City Hotel convenient to shopping, entertainment and sight-seeing. Shuttle service is provided to and from the airport and downtown. There is ample complimentary parking for cars and tour buses.

We offer luxurious accommodations, which include 412 spacious guest rooms and 56 suites, with the finest amenities, including private balconies, three telephones, 24-hour room service, in-room coffee makers and video checkout.

After dining in Apples In The Field, our award-winning restaurant, you'll find one of Nashville's most popular lounges for late-night dancing and fun, and an intimate piano bar for relaxation. We also offer an outdoor pool, lighted tennis courts and outdoor jogging.

For business or pleasure, visit the Sheraton Music city soon and find out why we've earned the reputation of being "Nashville's Cordial Manor."

## Sheraton Music City
### HOTEL
### NASHVILLE

777 McGAVOCK PIKE AT CENTURY CITY
NASHVILLE. TENNESSEE 37214
PHONE: (615) 885-2200   FAX: (615) 231-1120
Internet: http://www.tenn.com/sheraton

# DON'T SLEEP JUST ANYWHERE . . .

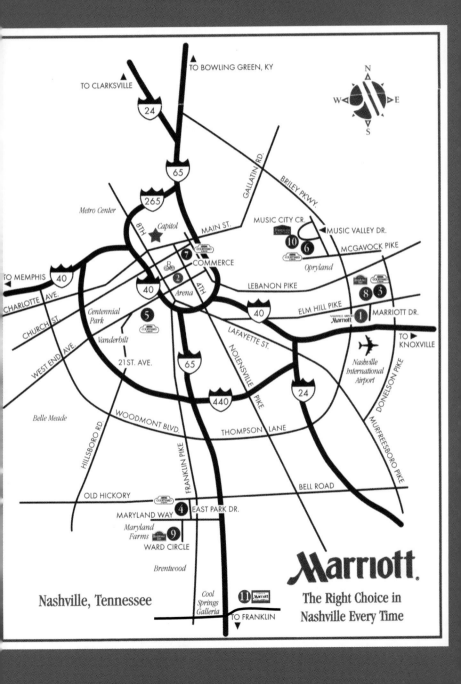

DON'T SLEEP JUST ANYWHERE . . .

TO BOWLING GREEN, KY

TO CLARKSVILLE

24

65

265

Metro Center

Capitol

8TH

MAIN ST.

GALLATIN RD.

BRILEY PKWY.

Music City CR.

MUSIC VALLEY DR.

10 6

McGAVOCK PIKE

COMMERCE

7

Opryland

TO MEMPHIS

40

CHARLOTTE AVE.

CHURCH ST.

WEST END AVE.

Centennial Park

Vanderbilt

21ST. AVE.

2

Arena

40

4TH

LEBANON PIKE

8 3

ELM HILL PIKE

Marriott 1 MARRIOTT DR.

5

65

LAFAYETTE ST.

NOLENSVILLE PIKE

440

Nashville International Airport

40

24

TO KNOXVILLE

DONELSON PIKE

Belle Meade

HILLSBORO RD.

WOODMONT BLVD.

THOMPSON LANE

MURFREESBORO PIKE

FRANKLIN PIKE

OLD HICKORY

BELL ROAD

MARYLAND WAY

4 EAST PARK DR.

Maryland Farms

9

WARD CIRCLE

Brentwood

Nashville, Tennessee

Cool Springs Galleria

11 Marriott

TO FRANKLIN

**Marriott**

The Right Choice in Nashville Every Time

# Residence Inn.
# room to relax,
# room to work,
# room to breathe.

*R*esidence Inn, our all-suite hotel, is the perfect choice for an extended stay, whether traveling on business, pleasure or relocating. Nashville offers its guests two centrally located properties.

Each suite in our residential setting is complete with a fully-equipped kitchen, living area, private entrance, and most have fireplaces. Grocery shopping service, guest laundry and valet service are also available for your convenience.

Add complimentary continental breakfast, weekday hospitality hour and newspaper, swimming pool, heated spa and sport Court®, and you have the perfect choice for your next extended stay.

**Residence Inn – Elm Hill**
2300 Elm Hill Pike, Nashville, TN 37214
(615) 889-8600 • FAX (615) 871-4970

**Residence Inn –
Brentwood/Maryland Farms**
206 Ward Circle, Brentwood, TN 37027
(615) 371-0100 • FAX (615) 661-5714

*F*airfield Inn offers the Marriott services you are accustomed to at an exceptional value.

Comfortable accommodations, free continental breakfast and an indoor pool make this hotel a hit with the whole family. Only minutes away from Opryland, downtown attractions and the Nashville International Airport makes this location not only convenient but economical.

**Fairfield Inn – Opryland**
211 Music City Circle, Nashville, TN 37214
(615) 872-8939 • (800) 228-2800
FAX (615) 872-7230

# Don't sleep just anywhere . . .

The most

*attention*

*you'll get in*

# Nashville

*without a*

*record deal.*

Here, you'll be spoiled — even if we don't recognize your autograph. Personal service. World class food. Elegant surroundings.

The lifestyle that some people in this town have worked years to achieve. We offer valet parking, a fitness center, and we're centrally located in the downtown business district, within easy walking distance of Vanderbilt University and Music Row. To make a reservation call the hotel direct at (615) 320-1700 or 1-800-23-LOEWS.

**LOEWS**
**VANDERBILT PLAZA HOTEL**
NASHVILLE

*2100 West End Avenue, Nashville, Tennessee 37203*
*www.loewsvanderbilt.com*

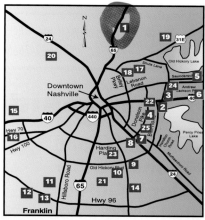

porch swing with a good book and a couple of yummy homemade ice cream sandwiches. What a treat!

Peacock Hill has eight stables for horses. Pets are welcome but must sleep in the barn.

## Ridgetop Bed & Breakfast
**$-$$ • 2141 Columbia Hwy., Hampshire**
**• (931) 285-2777, (800) 377-2770**

This B&B, located in a rustic setting on 170 acres, is about an hour and 20 minutes south of Nashville, between Columbia and Hohenwald. It's only 4 miles from the Natchez Trace and is a popular stopover for people driving and bicycling the Trace. Guests will find acres of woods, trails, clear streams and waterfalls on the property.

Accommodations are available in a cabin, a frame cottage and in the main house, all in a clearing atop the ridge. All have private baths, air conditioning and coffee pots, and are furnished with antiques.

The Swiss cottage can sleep up to four people if the twin beds in the loft are used. The cottage features an antique iron double bed and two rocking chairs. A refrigerator, dishes and sink allow guests to enjoy coffee and snacks in their room. The small loft, reached via a ladder, is just the right size for children. Outdoors, you can relax on the patio or in the nearby swing at the water-lily pond.

The 1830s-era log cabin features a double bed, a rollaway bed, large bath, a fireplace and a front porch with swing. The spacious cabin was reconstructed on site and modeled after an old cabin found nearby.

The guest room in the main house is decorated in the Victorian style, with quality antiques and comfortable chairs. This room has a double bed plus a rollaway bed for extra guests. Old family photos and Civil War literature add interest.

Breakfast is served in the main house and features homegrown blueberries and specialty egg dishes. A favorite is the baked French toast. Owners Kay and Bill Jones welcome children and pets. Bill, retired, is a history buff, while Kay enjoys wildflowers, works part-time and is active with the Tennessee Native Plant Society. They've been welcoming guests to Ridgetop since the early 1990s.

## The Rose Garden
**$$$-$$$$, no credit cards**
**• 6213 Harding Rd. • (615) 356-8003,**
**(615) 401-3857 (pager)**

This 900-square-foot private living suite is just west of the U.S. Highway 70–Tenn. Highway 100 junction near Belle Meade. Owners Jim and Shirley Ruppert, who live on the second floor of the 1960s brick home, say that it is more like a home away from home than a bed and breakfast inn. They frequently rent the suite to long-term visitors or people who are preparing to move into a new home.

It can comfortably accommodate an individual traveler or as many as four adults (no children or pets). It's a popular location for vacationers, business travelers, newlyweds and parents of students, offering a comfortable environment and a considerable amount of privacy. Parents of Vanderbilt students book the suite two years in advance for graduation time.

The suite has a private entrance from an adjoining patio through French doors in the back of the house. Amenities include a brick fireplace with gas logs, a couch, easy chairs, queen-size bed, daybed and twin bed. There's also a full kitchen, including wet bar, microwave and refrigerator; an entertainment area with a TV, VCR and some popular videos; and a bath with shower. The decor includes lots of copper antiques. A five-person hot tub is on the patio. An added attraction is the Rupperts' prize-winning hybrid tea rose gardens, featuring 85 roses. Perennial and shade gardens add to the charm.

In the owners' living quarters, guests have access to a desk, phone, modem, fax, com-

---

## INSIDERS' TIP

If the name of the bed and breakfast contains the word "barn," it usually means the inn has accommodations for guests' horses. Some inns also have horses on site for guests to ride.

puter and copy machine. For recreation, guests can visit nearby Westside Athletic Club or head to the Warner Parks, just a couple minutes away. Breakfast is often continental-style with juice, cereal, muffins, breads, fruit, cappuccino, gourmet coffee and hot chocolate. Sometimes the Rupperts offer their specialty, huevos rancheros. Other popular choices are apple Belgian waffles, spinach quiche and fruit-filled crepes. Inquire about discounts if you plan to stay a week or more.

## Simply Southern Bed & Breakfast

**$$$ - $$$$ • 211 N. Tennessee Blvd., Murfreesboro • (615) 896-4988, (888) 723-1199**

This historic house opened its doors as a bed and breakfast in July 1996 in Murfreesboro's historic district, right across the street from Middle Tennessee State University. It was built in 1914 by the Harrison family, who owned the house for more than 65 years and opened a portion of the third floor as housing for college men. The home's various owners always shared the house with college students. At one point, 16 students lived here, occupying half the second floor and all of the third floor. Today the house welcomes many parents who are in town to visit students. It has also become popular with business travelers and honeymooners. Its location about 30 miles from Nashville makes it popular with Music City tourists who are looking for accommodations outside the Metro area.

Innkeepers Carl and Georgia Buckner visited many bed and breakfasts through the years, and decided they would enjoy running an inn when they retired. They spent about 15 years making plans for their B&B and actively searched for just the right property for about five years. They were delighted to find this historic home and were especially pleased that it had been extremely well maintained. The house was built in a four-square style with Dutch influence and a Craftsman-style interior. The Buckners, who live on the third floor, are proud that "every pane of glass and every piece of woodwork" have survived since the house was built. The wood floors and some of the chandeliers are original as well.

With more than 7,500 square feet of space, this inn offers plenty of room for guests. Georgia describes the home as simple and elegant. There are four comfortable guest rooms and one suite, each of which has a private bath. The rooms, named after Tennessee flowers, are the Tennessee Coneflower Room, Magnolia Room, Redbud Room, Dogwood Room and Azalea Suite. The suite has a queen-size bed and opens into a sun room with a queen-size sleeper sofa, TV and VCR, and a kitchenette with a refrigerator. Two of the other guest rooms have queen-size beds and one has twin beds. The rooms are furnished with an eclectic mix of antiques and more modern pieces. Each room has a private phone with laptop access, a TV and VCR. Some of the baths have claw-foot tubs, some have marble showers and some have combination tub/showers.

A rec room in the basement is equipped with a pool table, player piano, karaoke, vintage Coke machine, a collection of old records and other amusements. It won't be too difficult to get Carl to take a turn on the karaoke. Guests in the mood for quieter enjoyments can visit the main living area and parlor to browse the collection of antique books. Others might prefer to relax in a rocking chair on the large front porch.

At breakfast, the Buckners will prepare a delicious Southern gourmet meal. Georgia loves to cook and enjoys serving a variety of dishes. A favorite of many guests is "eggs in a nest," a special scrambled eggs–cream cheese–herb mixture baked in a sausage cup. Hot homemade biscuits, sourdough bread, sourdough pancakes and banana crepes are other specialties. Other egg dishes, casseroles and bacon are often on the menu too. Ask the Buckners about their recipe books. Their first was titled *A Kaleidoscope of Recipes*, in keeping with a kaleidoscope theme of the house. The second book, which they were working on in 1999, is *Kaleidoscope II: A Collection of Our Guests' Favorite Recipes*.

If special arrangements are made, this inn will sometimes accept children older than age 12, but other accommodations must be made for pets. The Buckners will be happy to arrange guided tours of the area. They can also direct you to Murfreesboro antique stores, festivals, sporting events, concerts and other area attractions.

## Sweet Annie's Bed, Breakfast and Barn

**$$, no credit cards • 7201 Cumberland Dr., Fairview • (615) 799-8833**

This B&B has been featured in *Appaloosa Journal* and *Southern Living* as a haven for horse lovers, but owners Ann and Charles Murphy cater to equestrians and non-equestrians alike. When they first married, they were inspired to open a bed and breakfast with horse accommodations after moving Ann's horses across the country from Virginia to Utah. During that experience, they found that some, but not many, bed and breakfast inns along the way had stables. They operated an inn in Utah during the early 1990s, until Charles, an explosives engineer, was transferred to the Nashville area. They chose the small town of Fairview, just minutes from west Nashville, as the location for their new home and inn.

Sweet Annie's is named for a fragrant flower in the oregano family, which grows in the backyard of this lavishly landscaped property. The Murphys describe their bed and breakfast as a contemporary getaway. It's a peaceful, quiet retreat that's popular with Nashvillians who are looking for a close-to-home escape. The red brick home was built in the 1960s, but the interior was totally renovated in the 1990s. It is decorated in contemporary, pastel furnishings that, along with the many windows, provide a feeling of spaciousness.

There are two guest rooms, one with a king-size round bed and the other with a double bed. The rooms share a bath; for an extra $15 you can have a private bath, if the other bedroom hasn't been rented. The inn offers plush bathrobes, a hot tub, an outdoor swimming pool, a two-level deck and a great room. Most guests make at least one visit to nearby Bowie Nature Park, a great place for horseback riding (you must bring your own horses, though), bicycling, hiking and picnicking. The Natchez Trace Parkway is nearby too. If you prefer, you can relax on the deck or in the shaded backyard.

Spa services such as massages and facials can be arranged with advance notice. Ann, a fitness instructor, personal trainer and yoga expert, cooks healthy morning meals as well as hearty country breakfasts featuring homemade biscuits and muffins. Nighttime snacks and sweets are provided.

The house is on the west end of Fairview, 5 miles from I-40. Well-behaved children are welcome. The Murphys prefer not to have pets in the house, but pets are allowed to sleep in the garage or barn.

## Sweetwater Inn

**$$-$$$$ • 2436 Campbells Station Rd., Culleoka • (931) 987-3077**

You can take a trip back in time and journey down the Mississippi River without ever leaving dry land when you visit this unique bed and breakfast. The three-story mansion was built in 1900 in the elaborate Gothic Steamboat style of the American Revival period. Indeed, it calls to mind a Mississippi riverboat.

Tommy Young and Melissa McEwen purchased this inn in October 1998 from Sandy Shotwall. They had fallen in love with the house when they celebrated their fifth wedding anniversary there the previous year. When they found out the inn was for sale, they knew it was meant for them. Tommy previously managed a lawn and garden shop in Franklin and Melissa was an office administrator for a computer software company in Franklin. Everyone told them they would be naturals at running a B&B: Tommy loves to talk and Melissa loves to cook.

Sweetwater Inn sits on 10 acres of rolling hills surrounded by Columbia farmland, about 45 miles south of Nashville off Interstate 65. Rocking chairs await guests on upstairs and downstairs wraparound porches — an ideal

---

**INSIDERS' TIP**

Your bed and breakfast host can recommend good restaurants, attractions and shopping spots in the area. Be sure to ask about their favorites — there's nothing like a real Insider's view.

spot to relax, enjoy the lovely views and watch sunsets and sunrises. Each of the two large guest rooms and two suites has private access to the second-story porch. The elegantly appointed rooms feature handpainted borders and murals, queen-size beds and private baths. Captain Campbell's Suite is decorated in a Civil War theme, with tasteful and unusual antiques, Civil War prints and books on the Old South. The other rooms offer a more feminine and formal decor. McKibbon's Suite, named for the family that built the house, is the largest room and has a comfortable sitting area.

In the morning, you'll be served early coffee and juice in your room. Then you'll want to come downstairs for a delicious breakfast, which will probably include one of Melissa's delicious casseroles. Breakfast is often served in the dining room, but can be served in the sun room or another more private setting if you prefer. Sweetwater Inn serves dinner by reservation. Tommy and Melissa will also be happy to recommend restaurants.

The inn features two formal parlors and lots of extended living spaces. Outdoors, guests can enjoy a game of horseshoes, croquet or badminton, and there are several nearby attractions to visit. Columbia, the home of President James K. Polk, has many antebellum homes. Antique lovers will find a variety of shops, malls and auctions nearby, and there are golf courses, swimming pools and canoeing all within a 10-minute drive. Because the inn is popular with honeymooners and couples celebrating anniversaries, accommodations for children are available only by prior arrangement. This inn doesn't accept pets.

Although most area campgrounds will be happy, when possible, to accommodate campers who just show up looking for a site, you are strongly encouraged to make reservations.

# Campgrounds

Nashville and its immediate area offer more than a dozen campgrounds, most of which have sites for both recreational vehicles and tent campers. Some camping opportunities are also available at nearby state parks.

You'll notice that the geographic breakdown in this chapter is significantly different from the one we use in other chapters of this book. That's because the private campgrounds are generally concentrated in a few areas, especially around J. Percy Priest Lake and near the Music Valley area.

Although most area campgrounds will be happy, when possible, to accommodate campers who just show up looking for a site, you are strongly encouraged to make reservations. Sites tend to fill up, especially during nice weather. You wouldn't want to load up the family and all your camping gear and head for Nashville only to find nowhere to stay.

We list state park camping opportunities under a separate heading. For more information about recreational and other opportunities in Tennessee State Parks, see our Parks and Recreation chapters.

All campgrounds are open year round unless otherwise indicated. Please note that prices are subject to change; off-season rates may be a little cheaper.

## Private Campgrounds

### J. Percy Priest Lake Area

#### Cook Campground
**3737 Bell Rd. • (615) 889-1096**

Cook Campground has 57 sites that can be used for tent camping or recreational vehicles. There is no electricity or water at individual sites, but several spigots are available. The campground has asphalt driveways, picnic tables, grills, hot showers, two sets of restrooms and a dump station for RV holding tanks. Campers also get free use of Percy Priest's beach, in the day-use area. The rate is $11 a night.

Cook Campground is open May 1 through Labor Day.

#### Nashville Shores Campground
**4001 Bell Rd. • (615) 889-7050**

This campground, known until July 1997 as Hermitage Landing and then briefly as Rainbow Island, is below the dam on Priest Lake. Facilities include a public park with beach, cabins, picnic pavilions and an area for docking sailboats. Sailboats are available for rental.

With the change of name and ownership, major alterations and additions have been made. A massive water park — with water slides, paddle boats, miniature golf, cruises, a food court and more — now anchors the 385-acre site. The existing camping facilities remain, though some have been relocated. Prices are $10 a night for tent camping, $30 for full RV hookups and $95 to $115 for a modern (with heat and AC) two-bedroom cabin that sleeps up to six people.

#### Seven Points Campground
**1810 Stewarts Ferry Pk.**
**• (615) 889-5198**

Seven Points, on J. Percy Priest Lake, has 60 full-hookup sites for RV or tent camping. A dump station is available. Prices are $17 to $21. The campground is open April 1 through October 31.

### Opryland Area

#### Holiday Nashville Travel Park
**2572 Music Valley Dr. • (615) 889-4225**

Holiday Nashville Travel Park offers a variety of options for travelers. In addition to 200 pull-through sites for recreational vehicles and a tent-camping area, the park has chalet-like sleeping huts and park models, which are three-bedroom trailers with living room, dining room, kitchen and bath. Rates range from $20 a night for tent campers to $36.50 for full hookups and $85 for the park models, all based on two people, with no charge for children 11 and younger.

### Opryland KOA Kampground
**2626 Music Valley Dr. • (615) 889-0282**

Opryland KOA features 460 sites for various uses, from tent camping through different types of RV hookups. Twenty-five cabins are also available. There's a grocery store on site, and recreational opportunities include a swimming pool, miniature golf, a game room and two playgrounds.

The campground also contains a 750-seat arena that features live country music seven nights a week. Most shows are free, though there's a charge on those occasions when a legend like Little Jimmy Dickens or Porter Wagoner shows up. Rates are $19.95 for tent camping, $32.95 for full hookups, $36.95 for one-room cabin and $45.95 for a two-room cabin.

### Two Rivers Campgrounds
**2614 Music Valley Dr. • (615) 883-8559**

Two Rivers has 115 RV sites but does not allow tent camping. Full hookups are $27.50, and water and electric only are $25, with discounts for senior citizens or Good Sam members. A pool, game room and playground area are also on site.

## Goodlettsville

### Holiday Rest Campground
**1200 Louisville Hwy., Goodlettsville • (615) 859-0348**

The 105 sites at this campground — 10 minutes from Nashville — include areas for tent camping as well as full RV hookups. Rates range from $16 for tent sites to $34.50 for cab-

ins with full-size bed and bunk bed, based on double occupancy. Holiday Rest also has a pool, and Gray Line Country & Western Tours picks up people for trips to nearby attractions. (For more information about Gray Line and other tour companies, see our Music City chapter.)

### KOA Nashville North Kampgrounds
**708 N. Dickerson Rd., Goodlettsville • (615) 859-0075**

KOA Nashville North has tent sites, full RV hookups and one cabin. There's a playground, and sites contain picnic tables. Prices are $16 for tent sites, $24.50 for full hookups and $34.50 for the cabin.

## Smyrna

### Nashville I-24 Campground Inc.
**1130 Rocky Fork Rd., Smyrna • (615) 459-5818**

This wooded campground, open since 1971, is affiliated with the Good Sam family of campgrounds. It has 155 sites for tent camping and recreational vehicles plus four cabins. Amenities include a swimming pool, grocery store, game room, horseshoe pits and a volleyball court. Prices are $13 for tent camping, $17.50 for full hookups, $20 for single-room cabins and $35 a night for a cabin with kitchenette and bathroom. Discounts are available for Good Sam members.

# Army Corps of Engineers Campgrounds

Corps of Engineers campgrounds must be reserved through the National Recreation Reservation Service, which bills itself as North America's largest camping reservation service. You can make your reservations by calling the NRRS — which offers 49,500 camping facili-

---

**INSIDERS' TIP**

**It's wise to make reservations before traveling to any private or state park campground.**

Cabin rentals are a rustic alternative to tent-camping.

ties at 1,700 locations managed by Corps and the USDA Forest Service — toll-free at (877) 444-6777, or by visiting www.reserveusa.com, a web site with detailed maps, directions, prices, regulations and about anything else you'd need to know. Most of these sites offer ample opportunity for fishing, boating, skiing and swimming, as well as viewing such wildlife as white-tailed deer, rabbits, raccoons, skunks, wild turkeys and squirrels.

Please note that most Corps campgrounds require a two-night minimum on weekends and a three-night minimum on holiday weekends.

## J. Percy Priest Lake Area

### Anderson Road Campground
**3737 Bell Rd. • (615) 361-1980**

Anderson Road offers 37 sites, along with hot showers, dump station, picnic shelter, boat launch and public telephones. The campground is open from late April through early September, and sites and $11 to $13 a night, with a two-night minimum on weekends and a

three-night minimum on holiday weekends. The picnic shelter for up to 60 people can be reserved for $120 a day.

### Poole Knobs Campground
**Jones Mill Rd. • (615) 459-6948**

Poole Knobs, near Smyrna, has 87 camp sites and a group camping area, as well as hot showers, dump station, boat launch, a picnic shelter and public telephones. Fees are $11 to 20 a night. The campground is open from late April through early September.

## Old Hickory Lake Area

### Cages Bend Campground
**Benders Ferry Rd., Hendersonville • (615) 829-4989**

Cages Bend has 43 sites with electric and water hookups for $19 to $23 a night. Hot showers, dump station, boat launch, laundry facilities and public telephone are also available. The campground is open from April through the first of November.

Photo: Donnie Beauchamp/Gaylord Entertainment

Many Music City visitors opt to travel in style with many of the comforts of home.

### Cedar Creek Campground
**Saundersville Rd., Hendersonville**
• **(615) 754-4947**

Cedar Creek has 59 sites with electric and water, as well as hot showers, dump station, laundry facilities, picnic shelter (reservable at $35 a day), playground, boat launch and public telephones. Rates are $19 to $23 a night, and the campground is open from April through the first of November.

### Shutes Branch Campground
**Lebanon Rd. • (615) 754-4847**

Shutes Branch offers 35 sites and a picnic shelter, plus hot showers, dump station, boat launch and laundry facilities. Sites are $11 to $17 a night, and the shelter reserves for $35 a day.

## Nearby State Parks

Tennessee State Park campsites are available on a first-come, first-served basis. While the following state parks are open year-round, many of them have reduced capacity during the winter, with portions of the campgrounds closed. In general, this is from early November through early April, but it really depends on the weather.

For more information about state parks, see our Parks chapter. You can also call the individual park or, if you'd especially like to know about other state parks, call the department at (800) 421-6683.

### Bledsoe Creek State Park
**400 Zieglers Fort Rd., Gallatin**
• **(615) 452-3706**

This 164-acre park on Old Hickory Lake has 114 campsites (102 have water and electrical hookups), picnic tables and grills. Restrooms with showers are nearby. Old Hickory Lake, with two boat ramps, offers opportunities for boating, skiing and fishing. Rates are $14 a day with water and electric hookups, $10 without.

### Cedars of Lebanon State Park
**328 Cedar Forest Rd., Lebanon**
• **(615) 443-2769**

Cedars of Lebanon has 117 campsites, as well as an 80-person group lodge and nine cabins. Campsites with water and electrical hookups are $14 a night for two people, and

50¢ for each additional person. A dump station is available. Cabins are $75 to $90 a night, plus $2 if you want air conditioning. The group lodge is $165 a night for the first 33 people, and $4 for each extra person.

## Long Hunter State Park
**2910 Hobson Pk., Hermitage**
**• (615) 885-2422**

If you like your camping the way it was meant to be — with absolutely no frills — then spend the night at this park named for the long hunters, rugged types who in the early 1700s would go hunting for months or even years at a time. There are no campsites, but there's a little circle at the end of a 6-mile trail where people can pitch tents for no charge. If you're interested, pick up a permit at the visitors center. For organized groups of up to 200 people, there are also some big fields with fire rings and a water tap but no other facilities. Scout groups use the fields for overnight outings where they earn their badges; the cost is $1 a person

Elsewhere in this 2,315-acre park, you'll find 28 miles of trails for day hiking and overnight backpacking, and a 110-acre lake with a fishing pier.

## Montgomery Bell State Resort Park
**U.S. Hwy. 70, Burns**
**• (615) 797-9052**

This 3,850-acre park, north of U.S. 70 and 7 miles east of Dickson, offers 89 RV campsites with electric and water hookups for $14 a night and 27 tent sites (five of them with water) for $9.50. Montgomery Bell State Resort Park also has eight fully equipped two-bedroom cabins (one of which is wheelchair-accessible) that sleep five to nine people apiece. The cabins rent by the week only, from June through August, at $350; the rest of the year, they're $60 to $70 a night with a two-night minimum.

The man the park was named for, by the way, moved to Dickson County from Pennsylvania in the early 1800s and established an extensive iron industry in the area. Laurel Furnace and the old ore pits are still visible. The park, also site of the Cumberland Presbyterian Church's founding in 1810, contains a replica of the Rev. Samuel McAdow's log house and a chapel where summer services are held.

We have virtually every type of restaurant imaginable: ethnic eateries, fine dining spots, barbecue joints, catfish houses, romantic bistros and much, much more.

# Restaurants

Hungry? If you're not right now, you will be by the time you scan through a few pages of this chapter. We're going to stimulate your appetite by telling you about the Southern-style comfort foods, hearty pastas, thick and juicy steaks and burgers, freshly baked breads, tasty vegetarian meals, delectable desserts and spicy international dishes you can find in Nashville.

Nashville has a multitude of great places to eat — so many that we would suggest calling it "Noshville" if that name hadn't already been taken by a Broadway-area deli. We have virtually every type of restaurant imaginable: ethnic eateries, fine dining spots, barbecue joints, catfish houses, romantic bistros and much, much more. We're probably best known, though, for our "meat-and-threes." For those of you who aren't familiar with the term, a meat-and-three is a place where you can get a down-home Southern entree — dishes like fried chicken, meat loaf, turkey and gravy or country-fried steak — accompanied by three vegetables. And when we say vegetables, we mean anything from mashed potatoes, corn and green beans to deviled eggs, macaroni and Jell-O. Corn bread, rolls or biscuits come with the meal too. We have an abundance of these beloved meat-and-threes, places like Swett's, Sylvan Park and Elliston Place Soda Shop. They are longtime favorites, and we highly recommend them for their good home cooking and Southern hospitality.

Some of our restaurants are nationally known (places like the Loveless Café and the Pancake Pantry), and other establishments that started here have gone on to become national or regional chains — places such as Houston's, O'Charley's, J. Alexander's, Uncle Bud's Catfish and Whitt's Barbecue. Nashville is also home to Shoney's, and the great Cracker Barrel is based just east of here in Lebanon. We have several well-known themed restaurants too: Hard Rock Café, Planet Hollywood, Boswell's Harley-Davidson Grill and NASCAR Café, and more on the way.

In this chapter, we're primarily highlighting places that are unique to Nashville. We have lots of fast-food restaurants, fern bars, pizza franchises and family-style eateries, but you already know what to expect from those places. We want to steer you to some of our local favorites. We've arranged this chapter alphabetically by category of cuisine — American, Italian, Meat-and-threes, Mexican, Sandwiches and so on. For information on even more dining options, see our Nightlife chapter. That's where we've listed sports bars, brewpubs, coffeehouses and the like. Many of those places have great food, and they often serve it late into the night; you'll want to add them to your list of favorites.

## Price-code Key

Use the following price code as a general guide for the cost of a meal for two, excluding appetizers, alcoholic beverages, desserts and tip. Keep in mind that drinks, desserts and extras for two can significantly add to the bill and will often put you in a new price category.

| | |
|---|---|
| $ | $15 and less |
| $$ | $16 to $25 |
| $$$ | $26 to $40 |
| $$$$ | $41 to $60 |
| $$$$$ | $61 and more |

Most major restaurants take credit cards and debit cards. Some of the smaller establishments, like a few of the meat-and-threes, take only cash and personal checks. We'll alert you to those places that don't accept credit cards. We'll also suggest whether you should make a reservation. As for smoking, virtually all restaurants offer nonsmoking areas, though sometimes the wait is longer for a seat in a smoke-free spot. Some restaurants have little or no parking, but those in that situation usually offer free valet parking. We'll mention the parking situation if warranted.

Finally, keep in mind that Nashville's restaurant scene seems to be constantly growing and changing. Operating hours change, businesses change hands, chefs play musical chairs, eateries close and re-emerge with new names and menus, and new restaurants open up regularly. If you're planning a special meal out, it's a good idea to call first, at least to make sure of the operating hours.

Enjoy your meal.

## American

### 12th & Porter
$$$ • 114 12th Ave. N. • (615) 254-7236

Funky, hip and brimming with pasta, 12th & Porter is a convenient spot to grab a bite before seeing a concert next door. 12th & Porter classics are the Pasta YaYa, a dish of spinach fettuccine in a Cajun cream sauce with andouille sausage and chicken, and the Rasta Pasta, with chicken, scallops and shrimp. The stuffed filet, with crab meat and brown gravy, is also popular. 12th & Porter has pizzas and a light menu too. Just about anything goes when it comes to attire and accessories, including body piercing and tattoos. 12th & Porter is open for lunch Monday through Friday and for dinner Monday through Sunday. They're open late most nights — until 11 PM Monday through Thursday and until 2 AM on Friday and Saturday.

### Belle Meade Brasserie
$$$-$$$$ • 101 Page Rd.
• (615) 356-5450

This sophisticated, romantic little bistro is one of Nashville's "well-known secrets." Owner Robert Seigel, who also owns the Finezza Trattoria Italian restaurant nearby (see subsequent listing), opened Belle Meade Brasserie in 1989. The restaurant has a loyal following, mostly residents of nearby Belle Meade and Green Hills.

Belle Meade Brasserie serves contemporary American cuisine. There are always plenty of fresh seafood dishes on the menu. The grouper is the best seller. There is also a selection of steaks, lamb, pork, veal and poultry and, of course, pasta. Be sure to sample the restaurant's signature corn fritter appetizers. The wine list has more than 150 selections, and the restaurant has won a *Wine Spectator* Award of Excellence. Belle Meade Brasserie is open for dinner Monday through Saturday. Reservations are a must on weekends.

### Blackstone
$$-$$$ • 1918 West End Ave.
• (615) 327-9969

The fish 'n' chips, artichoke chicken pasta, pork chops, trout and filet mignon are favorites at this comfortable West End restaurant/brewery. Blackstone brews six ales at its onsite brewery, including the award-winning St. Charles Porter.

### Blue Moon Waterfront Café
$$$ • 525 Basswood Ave.
• (615) 352-5892

This delightful, off-the-beaten-path restaurant opened in 1994 and has become a local summertime favorite. Casual gourmet is the best description of the cuisine at Blue Moon, a floating, open-air restaurant at west Nashville's Rock Harbor Marina. Blue Moon is almost always packed, so you can expect a wait of at least 45 minutes (we once came late and had a two-hour wait).

Blue Moon's menu features new American-style dishes — familiar foods presented with a twist. Some of the most-ordered entrees are the Siamese Cat, a sesame seed-encrusted catfish filet served with plum sauce and Chinese spicy mustard; and the pork chop with a port wine reduction sauce. The grit cake appetizers, served with sun-dried tomato mornay sauce, are a specialty, and the upside-down bourbon pecan tart and the white chocolate mousse torte are real treats for dessert.

Blue Moon is open daily from March through October. You won't find it without directions, so here's how to get there: take I-40 west to Exit 204 (White Bridge Road), turn right and get in the center lane to take an immediate left onto Robertson Avenue. Go about 1.5 miles to Basswood Avenue, turn left, then take the first right to Rock Harbor Marina.

## Boswell's Harley Davidson Grill
$-$$ • 401 Fesslers Ln. • (615) 242-6067

You don't have to own a Harley to eat here, although lots of riders do stop by on weekends to refuel. Monday through Friday, you'll usually find the business crowd lunching on one of the two big favorites — "The Sportster" hamburger or "The Fishtails," a fish, fries and hush puppies meal. The grill also serves salads and lots of sandwiches, including barbecue and sausage varieties.

Tables, booths and counter seats provide room for about 60 diners. Harley items, such as old bikes and engines, and memorabilia from the '50s to the '70s adorn the walls of this restaurant, which is in the back of the gift shop. If you're in the market for a Harley, this is the place to get one; you can also stock up on all the necessary accessories — leather jackets, boots, jeans, helmets and T-shirts.

Boswell's is open 10:30 AM to 2:30 PM Monday through Friday, and 8 AM to 2:30 PM Saturday, when a breakfast bar is available. Alcohol is not available.

## Demos' Steak & Spaghetti House
$-$$ • 300 Commerce St.
• (615) 256-4655
$-$$ • 1115 NW Broad St., Murfreesboro
• (615) 895-3701

While its name is frequently mispronounced, Demos' ("DE-mo-SEZ") menu never leaves you guessing. This American-Italian-Greek restaurant, owned by Jim Demos, has lots of pastas with a variety of sauces and four or five steaks that are good for the price. Demos' has a nice, semi-casual/semi-upscale, family-friendly environment. The most expensive entree is $11.95. The blackened chicken pasta and Greek-style chicken salad are good choices. Demos' has a lunch special Monday through Friday from 11 AM to 3 PM, but be prepared to wait for a seat; sometimes the wait is 30 to 45 minutes, and it's always first come, first served. At the downtown Nashville location, the only nearby parking is at meters on the street or in parking lots and garages. Demos' is open daily.

## F. Scott's
$$$ • 2210 Crestmoor Rd.
• (615) 269-5861

Casually elegant, warm and inviting, F. Scott's is considered by many to be one of the best restaurants in Nashville. This is a place where the sophisticated feel comfortable, but it's not necessary to dress to the hilt; you'll fit in, whether you're in jeans or coat and tie. F. Scott's serves American bistro-style food. The menu changes seasonally, but there is always plenty of pasta, chicken, duck, lamb, pork, beef and fresh fish. Grilled tuna on spinach with shallots and pommes frites, roasted butternut squash soup, grilled salmon with purple sticky rice, and center-cut pork chop in orange cumin butter are just a few tempting examples of the contemporary dishes you might find here. F. Scott's has three dining rooms and a jazz lounge with live entertainment each night. In addition to a wonderful dining experience, this is a very pleasant place to stop for a drink. Reservations are recommended.

## Granite Falls
$$ • 2000 Broadway • (615) 327-9250

Granite Falls's patio is always packed at

lunchtime. It's popular with the Music Row and Vandy crowds who like to dine al fresco, and its proximity to the Row means you're likely to spot a well-known face or two here. In wintertime, they turn up the heat and enclose the patio in plastic, so you can still have the feeling — almost — of dining outdoors. If you sit inside, you can color on the paper tablecloths with crayons while you wait for your food to arrive.

Granite Falls is a warm, casually elegant restaurant. It's not necessary to dress up, but many do. It's a suitable place to come after a black-tie event, so you'll frequently see well-dressed customers here. The menu is varied, with a selection of pastas, filets, lamb, fresh fish, sandwiches and salads. The Rattlesnake Chicken Pasta, a spicy pasta dish with chicken and roasted peppers in a cream sauce, is delicious, and the vegetarian Pasta Mediterranean, a combination of artichoke hearts, olives, mushrooms, peppers and other veggies, is good and healthy. Other favorites include the Maryland crab cakes and the tahini chicken salad.

Reservations are recommended on weekends. Granite Falls is open for lunch and dinner daily and also serves a Sunday brunch menu. There is a parking lot behind the restaurant, and valet parking is available at lunchtime Monday through Friday.

### Green Hills Grille
**$$ • 2122 Hillsboro Dr. • (615) 383-6444**

The always reliable Green Hills Grille is a comfortable, family-friendly spot where you can expect good food and good service. The restaurant opened in 1990, and a second one opened a few years later in Huntsville, Alabama. Lots of windows let in the light during the day, but at night the Southwest-themed restaurant is dimly lit and more intimate. They don't take reservations, but if you're coming for dinner, you can call ahead and put your name on the seating list.

Once you're seated, order some of the yummy spinach and artichoke dip for an appetizer. Other popular menu items include the tortilla soup, Chinese grilled chicken, lemon artichoke chicken and tortilla club sandwich with grilled chicken and guacamole. If you have room for dessert, try the Heath Crunch Pie, which is a layer of chocolate ice cream and a layer of vanilla ice cream with crumbled Heath bars, all topped with caramel and hot fudge. Green Hills Grille has some good cappuccino drinks and makes a mean martini. The biggest drawback is the lack of parking spaces, but free valet parking is available. The Grille is open daily.

### Hard Rock Café
**$-$$ • 100 Broadway • (615) 742-9900**

You can't miss the Hard Rock Café — right underneath the huge guitar mural facing Broadway. Rock 'n' roll memorabilia is the big draw here. The Nashville Hard Rock features a large collection (larger than any other Hard Rock) of guitars once belonging to rock greats. Also adorning the walls are gold and platinum records and memorabilia of all sorts, including a suede jacket worn by Jimi Hendrix, a leather coat worn by Elvis, one of James Brown's silk suits and a guitar played by John Fogerty when he was with Creedence Clearwater Revival. In keeping with the rock 'n' roll mood, the music here is loud, and the atmosphere is very lively. About twice a month the restaurant features live country, blues and rock bands.

As for the food, it's all-American: burgers, sandwiches, salads, daily blue-plate specials, homemade soups, malts and shakes, and yummy desserts. The Pig Sandwich — a pulled pork barbecue sandwich — is the Hard Rock's signature item. If you're in a hurry or extra hungry, you might want to call ahead to see if there's a long wait. During summer the line to get in can be long, and the restaurant doesn't take reservations. After your meal, be sure to check out the Hard Rock's merchandise in the historic Silver Dollar building a few feet away.

### Houston's
**$$$-$$$$ • 3000 West End Ave. • (615) 269-3481**

This national chain originated in Nashville. The first Houston's opened here in 1977; today there are nearly 40 of them, with company headquarters in Nashville, Atlanta and Phoenix. Houston's is an upscale fern bar restaurant. The consistently good food and service and the fun atmosphere have made this a longtime favorite. The restaurant is known for its huge specialty salads, like the grilled chicken salad, and it also serves great ribs, steak and chicken. The most popular item on the menu, however, is the spinach-artichoke dip, a Houston's original.

Houston's is a favorite among the business crowd and is known for its great salads. On Friday nights you can find lots of singles and yuppie couples here. There is almost always a wait for dinner; the restaurant doesn't accept reservations, but you can call ahead and put your name on the waiting list.

## J. Alexander's
**$$ • 73 White Bridge Rd.**
**• (615) 352-0981**
**$$ • 1721 Galleria Blvd., Franklin**
**• (615) 771-7779**

J. Alexander's is another local restaurant success story. Since the first J. Alexander's opened on White Bridge Road in 1991, more have sprung up all over the country, from Denver to Fort Lauderdale, Florida. Several have won local "best of" awards. By mid-1999, the publicly traded company had 20 locations and plans for more.

J. Alexander's is known for its casual but nice atmosphere, good service and contemporary American menu. The restaurant has award-winning prime rib, a variety of great salads and homemade dressings, wonderful pasta dishes, homemade soups and made-from-scratch desserts. One of the first restaurants in the area to open its kitchen to the view of diners, it cooks all the grilled products over a hardwood, open grill. Reservations are not accepted, and there is usually a wait for dinner; come early if you want to avoid the crowd. J. Alexander's is open daily for lunch and dinner.

## The Melting Pot
**$$$$ • 166 Second Ave. N.**
**• (615) 742-4970**

This fondue restaurant is a fun spot when you're in the mood for something a little different for dinner, and it's a great place to go with a group. The atmosphere here is casually elegant, relaxed and intimate. Seating is in high-backed booths that offer a sense of privacy. Allow two hours for the complete Melting

Pot experience. The menu is based on courses. The salad course is followed by a cheese fondue course, prepared by the server; during this course you dip bread, apples and vegetables in your choice of four cheeses. For the entree course, you cook your choice of entree in the melting pot in the center of the table. You can cook your selection in a light vegetable broth or the traditional canola oil. Lobster tails, center-cut filet, Cajun-rubbed meats and sausages are just a few of the choices. The final course is the dessert fondue — a variety of chocolate fondues in which you dip pound cake, cheesecake, bananas, strawberries, pineapple and nutty marshmallows. Mmmm. If you want only the dessert fondue, come in the late afternoon or after 9 PM. It's a good idea to have reservations, especially on the very busy Friday and Saturday nights. The Melting Pot is open daily for dinner.

## The Merchants
**$$$$ • 401 Broadway • (615) 254-1892**
**$$$$ • 1717 Mallory Ln., Brentwood**
**• (615) 376-0800**

Downtown Nashville's Merchants is a casual fine dining restaurant that serves American food with a Southern flair. The romantic atmosphere and excellent food make this a good choice for a special dinner. Most people like to dress up at least a bit when they come here. The restaurant occupies three floors of a historic building that once housed a pharmacy and hotel. The second floor is the main dining room — it has a more upscale atmosphere and menu than the first floor; the third floor is a banquet space.

If you're dining on the second floor, try the pan-seared salmon fillet with caper dill beurre blanc atop a bed of linguine with shrimp and scallops, all enclosed in a pastry net, or the Tennessee medallions, sliced beef tenderloin served with fresh apples and a maple Jack Daniels sauce. The Lexington Lamb Chops are a favorite too. On the first-floor Casual Bar & Grill, popular entrees are the New York strip and the Pasta Mediterranean: penne pasta with chicken, feta cheese and pesto cream sauce. First-floor diners will pay about 50 percent less than diners upstairs. For lunch, order the always-in-demand five-pepper chicken. Merchants does a brisk weekday lunch business and opens both floors for the lunchtime crowd. The restaurant has a very good wine selection.

Reservations are recommended, especially on busy Friday and Saturday nights. It's often crowded here on Thursdays too. Merchants is open for dinner daily and has a Sunday brunch from 11 AM to 2 PM.

The Brentwood location, in the Cool Springs area, serves most of the same menu items as the Nashville restaurant and is somewhat more casual.

## Midtown Café
**$$$ • 102 19th Ave. S. • (615) 320-7176**

This small restaurant just off West End has a devoted following of Insiders who like the eclectic American cuisine and casually elegant atmosphere. At lunch, it's a prime spot for high-ranking business lunches, while the dinner crowd ranges from business types to romantic couples, mostly 40-somethings and up. Midtown's crab cakes are great as an appetizer, entree or sandwich. The fresh catch of the day is always in demand, and the Caesar salad is a lunch favorite. Veal, pasta, steaks and lamb dishes round out the menu. Midtown has a nice wine list too. For dessert, the Key lime pie is good. The eatery is open for lunch Monday through Friday and for dinner nightly. Reservations are recommended for dinner.

## NASCAR Café
**$$ • 305 Broadway • (615) 313-7223**

Racing fans will want to check out the NASCAR Café. Open since November 1997, this family-oriented, themed eatery features all sorts of racing memorabilia and attractions. Outside the restaurant, you'll find the Winston Cup champion's car. Inside, cars hang from the ceiling, and multiple attractions keep guests busy before and after their meals. You can have your photograph taken inside Dale Ernhardt's or Jeff Gordon's car, or play one of the racing-themed games. There's also a virtual reality simulator that will allow you and 11 other passengers to experience the thrill of a race from the driver's perspective.

When you're ready to eat, head upstairs to the main dining room. The half-pound NASCAR Burger is a big seller. There are also salads, sandwiches, steaks and the like. Racing clips on the large video screens and loud country music complete the atmosphere.

The restaurant is open daily for lunch and dinner. NASCAR Café plans to offer valet parking in the summer; otherwise, parking is available in downtown garages, lots and at metered spaces.

## The Pineapple Room
**$$ • 1200 Forrest Park Dr.**
**• (615) 352-4859**

The Pineapple Room at Cheekwood features American cuisine with an occasional Southern twist. The glass-enclosed dining room is a nice place to enjoy a lunch during a visit to Cheekwood (see our Attractions chapter for more information on this grand old mansion). The menu features a variety of soups, salads and appetizers, a good selection of sandwiches (from herb-encrusted salmon to a veggie club) and entrees ranging from creamed chicken on egg bread to bourbon maple boneless pork chops..

The Pineapple Room is open daily for lunch and Monday through Thursday for dinner. Reservations are suggested.

## Pinnacle
**$$$$ • 623 Union St. • (615) 742-6015**

The Pinnacle is the revolving rooftop restaurant at downtown Nashville's Crown Plaza hotel. The restaurant serves Southern nouveau

---

### INSIDERS' TIP

Looking for a late-night meal? 12th & Porter, Goten 2 and Sunset Grill have late-night menus, and Cafe Coco is open 24 hours a day. If something a little more downscale is in order, the Waffle House is a perennial favorite. And if you like spicy food late at night, there's Prince's Hot Chicken Shack in north Nashville, open to 4 AM on the weekends.

cuisine, but it's the view that draws many guests. This is a romantic and fun place for dinner. The restaurant, on the 28th floor (300 feet in the air), makes one revolution every 65 minutes, offering a 180-degree view of Nashville.

Prime steaks and fresh fish are top picks here. House specialties include herb dijon-crusted rack of lamb and free-range lemon chicken. The desserts are worth the calories. Reservations are strongly recommended, and business casual attire or better is suggested.

## Planet Hollywood
**$$ • 322 Broadway • (615) 313-7827**

You can't miss Planet Hollywood; it's the restaurant with the huge revolving planet hanging over the sidewalk. Inside, you'll find tons of movie memorabilia — costumes, set pieces and other movie mementos. In 1997 the restaurant added a *Titanic* display after the 60-plus restaurant chain purchased almost the entire set from the movie. Memorabilia is geared to the theme of each dining room — Hollywood Hills, Zebra, Sci-Fi and Adventure. The atmosphere, including the loud music, takes center stage at this restaurant, but Planet Hollywood has good food too — everything from pastas to fajitas to pizzas. The burgers and the Hollywood Club sandwich are favorites. The Chicken Crunch appetizers are a hit too. Expect a wait here, especially in the summer, when lots of tourists are in town. On weekends, the wait averages 30 minutes to an hour. Reservations are accepted for groups of 20 or more. The restaurant is open daily for lunch and dinner.

## Prince's Hot Chicken Shack
**$ • 123 Ewing Dr. • (615) 226-9442**

Why? How? You'll probably ask yourself those questions after biting into a piece of Prince's *fiery* chicken. Why do Nashvillians like this dangerously hot food, and how does the Prince's gang make it so hot? The reasons why might include: it's a challenge; it's a Nashville tradition; it helps sober you up after you've had a few too many. As for the how, the family's not telling what makes the chicken burn so good. Simone Jeffries, whose mother, Andre Prince, has operated Prince's for nearly two decades, says the recipe for the hot stuff isn't

even known by most family members; it's passed down to whomever takes over the operation.

This restaurant, in a little strip shopping center off Dickerson Pike, has been operated by the Prince family for decades. It's been at this location since around 1989. You can order your chicken mild, medium or hot. You can order it plain, but it's still going to be hot because it's cooked in the same vat of oil that the hot stuff is cooked in. If it's your first time here, take our advice and order the mild. Chicken sandwiches — really a quarter-chicken served atop two slices of white bread — come with a couple of pickles. Go ahead and order some extra slices of bread right away. You'll need them. The only beverages available are from the drink machine in the corner. A medium-hot chicken sandwich requires a minimum of two cans of lemonade to douse the fire. Better yet, bring a jug of cold water. Side items like potato salad, cole slaw and baked beans are good to counter the hot chicken. Did we mention that this chicken is hot?

Prince's is open Tuesday through Thursday noon to midnight, and noon to 4 AM (that's right, 4 AM) on Friday and Saturdays.

## Princeton's Grille
**$$$ • 3821 Green Hills Village Dr.**
**• (615) 385-3636**

Princeton's Grille is a great place to go before or after a shopping trip to Green Hills mall. It's located between the mall and the 18-theater Green Hills Regal Cinema, so it's also a good choice for dinner-and-a-movie dates. It's a comfortable, sort of upscale casual restaurant with plenty of recognizable entrees on the menu — chicken tenders platter, prime rib, rotisserie chicken, baby back ribs and vegetarian lasagna, for example. Other choices include barbecued or marinated trout, citrus grilled chicken, grilled salmon and several tasty and filling salads.

Princeton's has a good specialty drink menu, with an extensive martini list. In the summer, you can dine out on the patio or sample a martini or two out there before dinner. A live jazz band performs in the bar nightly. This is one of four Princeton's Grille restaurants, but the only one in Nashville (the others are in

Photo: McNulty Communications

Some area restaurants, like Seanachie, go above and beyond traditional means to stand out in the crowd of Nashville eateries.

Alabama). Princeton's is open daily for lunch and dinner.

## Second Story Café
**$ • 4007 Hillsboro Rd. • (615) 385-0043**

Second Story Café is on the upper level of Davis-Kidd Booksellers in Green Hills. This is a great place to enjoy a meal before or after browsing the fabulous collection of books at Davis-Kidd. It's also a good destination in itself. There are a few tables that overlook the first floor of the bookstore; other tables are just outside the door in the atrium.

Second Story Café is known for its incredibly good chicken pot pie. This is mainly a soup, sandwich and salad place. There is always a quiche and soup of the day and two daily specials. We can't believe they took the cranberry walnut cheesecake off the dessert menu, but the caramel cake, Key lime pie, red velvet cake and German chocolate cake still sit temptingly in the glass case. The restaurant has a selection of beers and wines. Coffees, espresso and flavored cappuccinos and lattes go very well with your newest book purchase (free refills on regular coffee is a nice extra).

On Friday nights, Second Story Café presents a songwriters' showcase. The restaurant also does occasional book signings in conjunction with Davis-Kidd and hosts children's parties, showers, receptions and other special gatherings in the atrium.

## South Street Smokehouse & Crab Shack & Authentic Dive Bar
**$$ • 907 20th Ave. S. • (615) 320-5555**

Don't worry about remembering the whole name. Everybody just calls it South Street. This is a super fun place — a great spot to hang out in the spring, summer and fall because they open up the big garage door windows and let the fresh air in. There is always a lively crowd dining outdoors; this is definitely not the place to have a quiet, romantic meal. South Street is within walking distance of Music Row, and music-business movers and shakers can be found here daily. Tourists have also found out about this place, and lots of country performers show up here too — Garth, Reba, Wynonna and Lyle have been spotted here. Word about this hip place has even spread to the rock 'n' roll world: South Street was selected as caterer for The Rolling Stones when they played Vanderbilt Stadium in 1997, and they catered for the Eagles when they were in town.

South Street serves "urban Southern" cuisine. The smoked ribs are a big hit, and the Deep South platters — like chicken and roasted pepper enchiladas, and crawfish and shrimp enchiladas — are always a hit. The marinated Jack Daniels Strip, a 16-ounce New York strip steak, should please the real meat eaters. The Crab & Slab, a full slab of ribs with king crab, snow crab and Dungeness crab, served with corn and potatoes, is a fun way to feed two to four people. The South Street Rita, a frozen Margarita, is the proper beverage choice. For dessert, get the New Orleans-style bread pudding with Jack Daniels sauce.

South Street serves lunch Monday through Saturday and dinner seven days a week. Seating is first come, first served.

### Sunset Grill
**$$$ • 2001-A Belcourt Ave.**
**• (615) 386-3663**

Sunset Grill is one of Nashville's favorite restaurants. Since it opened in fall 1990, this Hillsboro Village hot spot has developed a reputation as a good place to see and be seen. It's a music-business hangout and draws lots of other business people and sports personalities too. On weekdays when the weather is nice, diners don their dark sunglasses and power-lunch on the patio. In winter, the patio is enclosed for those who prefer a more casual setting than the main dining room. Sunset Grill serves new American cuisine in a casually elegant atmosphere. Any night of the week you're apt to see customers in jeans dining next to a group in tuxedos.

The Voodoo Pasta is a menu staple. It has grilled chicken, baby shrimp, andouille sausage and roasted red pepper marinara sauce dusted with Black Magic seasonings and tossed with Cajun fettuccine. The Vegetarian Voodoo Pasta has zucchini, eggplant, mushrooms and onions. Other menu favorites include Szechwan duck and lamb dijonnaise. There is a good selection of vegetarian dishes, such as Veggies Lee Ann — steamed seasonal veggies over garlic-herb orzo pasta with black beans.

The desserts are beautiful. Try the chocolate bombe, a brownie crust with double-thick chocolate mousse filling, drenched in chocolate glaze. You can also order a large dessert trio for $13, or half-portions for $8. If you want to go all out, order the dessert mirror, 10 full portions of various desserts served on a mirrored tray, for $40.

Sunset Grill has an excellent wine selection — one of the best in town — with more than 200 wines, 60 available by the glass. On Tuesday afternoons in the spring and fall, Sunset Grill offers winetasting classes ($10 per person); seating is limited, so make a reservation if you don't want to miss out. Sunset Grill is one of the few places in town that has a late-night menu. You can order 'til 1:30 AM Monday through Saturday and until 11 PM Sunday.

### Tin Angel
**$$-$$$ • 3201 West End Ave.**
**• (615) 298-3444**

Tin Angel is a casual, cozy restaurant that serves contemporary American cuisine with an occasional international twist. Popular dishes include meat loaf with mushroom gravy and mashed potatoes, Mediterranean pasta and the Mediterranean salad. Tin Angel is one of our reliable standbys — good food, good atmosphere and rarely a wait. Reservations are not accepted. There is a small parking lot in back of the restaurant, and valet parking is available as well. Tin Angel is open Monday through Friday for lunch and dinner, Saturday for dinner and Sunday for brunch.

### The Trace
**$$$-$$$$ • 2000 Belcourt Ave.**
**• (615) 385-2200**

This Hillsboro Village restaurant has become one of the "in" places to dine, and its bar is a favorite among Nashville singles. A windowed wall, white tablecloths and candle-

### INSIDERS' TIP

**Nashville's popular Gerst Haus restaurant, displaced by the new football stadium, is scheduled to reopen in early 2000 at 301 Woodland Street (across from the restaurant's former site).**

light make for a casually elegant atmosphere enjoyed by both the early dining crowd and the late-night bar crowd.

The Trace serves "new American" cuisine, including plenty of pasta dishes. A favorite is the penne pasta with pesto cream sauce, grilled chicken, Gorgonzola cheese and roasted peppers. The beef filet and swordfish are also popular. The Trace has an extensive wine list, with about 40 varieties available by the glass. The Trace is open for dinner daily.

# Barbecue

### Bar-B-Cutie
$ • 5221 Nolensville Rd.
• (615) 834-6556
$ • 501 Donelson Pk.
• (615) 872-0207
### Bar-B-Cutie Express
$ • 1041 Murfreesboro Rd.
• (615) 361-7575

Hickory pit barbecue is the specialty at Bar-B-Cutie, a Nashville favorite since 1948. Barbecue and ribs are most in demand here, but the restaurant also serves a good grilled mesquite chicken sandwich as well as turkey and roast beef. Barbecue plates come with two side items and bread. This is a no-alcohol, family-style restaurant. The dining room is busy, and the restaurant does brisk take-out and drive-through business too. The Donelson Pike restaurant is a little more lively and upbeat. At Bar-B-Cutie Express, the menu is basically the same, but there are no fried items and no drive-through there. Bar-B-Cutie is open daily for lunch and dinner.

### Corky's Bar-B-Q
$ • 100 Franklin Rd., Brentwood
• (615) 373-1020

This Memphis-based barbecue restaurant serves slow-smoked barbecue in a fun, 1950s-style environment. Try the wet and dry ribs, fresh pulled barbecue shoulder, barbecue chicken, beef brisket, tamales and onion loaves. If you have room, you can top off your meal with a serving of fudge pie, a dessert that's as rich and delicious as it sounds. If you're in need of a quick barbecue fix, Corky's has a drive-through. Beer is available. The res-

taurant, right off I-65 southbound at Exit 74B, is open daily.

### Hog Heaven
$ • 115 27th Ave. N. • (615) 329-1234
$ • 998-B Davidson Dr. • (615) 353-3885

This is a good time to apply the don't-judge-a-book-by-its-cover rule. Hog Heaven doesn't look like much — it's a tiny white cinder-block building tucked in a corner of Centennial Park behind McDonald's — but once you taste their barbecue, you'll know why they attached the word "heaven" to the name. This is some good eatin'. Hog Heaven's hand-pulled pork, chicken, beef and turkey barbecue is actually pretty famous among Nashville's barbecue connoisseurs.

The menu is posted on a board beside the walk-up window. After you get your order, you might want to hop on over to Centennial Park and dig in, since the only seating at the restaurant is two picnic tables on a slab of concrete right in front of the window. You can order barbecue sandwiches, barbecue plates that come with two side orders, and barbecue by the pound. The white barbecue sauce is just right on top of the chicken, and the regular sauce comes in mild, hot or extra hot. Quarter-chicken and half-chicken orders are available, and Hog Heaven has spareribs too. Barbecue beans, potato salad, cole slaw, turnip greens, white beans, green beans, black-eyed peas and corn on the cob are among the side dishes. The homemade cobbler is a heavenly way to end a memorable Hog Heaven meal. Hog Heaven delivers to areas nearby and is open Monday through Saturday for lunch and dinner.

A second Hogg Heaven, located on Davidson Drive, just off Charlotte Avenue, opened in 1999. Both restaurants are open Monday through Saturday, 10 AM to 7 PM.

### Jack's Bar-B-Que
$ • 416 Broadway • (615) 254-5715, (615) 228-4600 (catering)
$ • 334 W. Trinity Ln. • (615) 228-9888

Jack Cawthon opened his first barbecue restaurant in 1976 after studying in the barbecue hot spots of Memphis, Atlanta, Texas, Kentucky and the Carolinas. Today he satisfies Nashville's appetite for barbecue at two locations. The Broadway location backs up to the historic Ryman Auditorium, and diners there can sit on Jack's Backdoor Patio, in view of the Ryman's backstage door. Jack's serves Tennessee pork shoulder, ribs cut St. Louis–style, Texas beef brisket, smoked turkey and chicken, and Texas sausage. Side items include baked beans, potato salad and cole slaw. For dessert, try the chess pie, chocolate fudge pie and brownies. Beer is available. Jack's is open daily and also caters.

### Mary's Old Fashioned Pit Barbecue
1108 Jefferson St. • (615) 256-7696

For some real "Insiders barbecue," head over to Mary's on Jefferson Street. This little drive-up restaurant has been a Nashville favorite for some 30 years. Open around the clock, seven days a week, Mary's has some of the best barbecue in town. It was owned for years by Mary Carrethers who sold the business to employee Clark Fizer in 1999 just months before she passed away. Mary is no doubt fondly remembered by generations of Nashvillians.

Clark has spiffed up the place a bit and added a couple of new menu items. There are two drive-up windows, one for the traditional ribs, barbecue, sandwiches, baked beans, slaw and potato salad and one for the newly added fish sandwiches and chicken wings.

### Whitt's Barbecue
$ • 1800 Antioch Pk., Antioch
• (615) 331-5936
$ • 4601 Andrew Jackson Pkwy.,
Hermitage • (615) 885-4146
$ • 2535 Lebanon Pk., Donelson
• (615) 883-6907
$ • 5211 Alabama Ave. • (615) 385-1553
$ • 5310 Harding Rd. • (615) 356-3435
$ • 3621 Nolensville Rd.
• (615) 831-0309
$ • 114 Old Hickory Blvd. E., Madison
• (615) 868-1369
$ • 173 Old Shackle Island Rd.,
Hendersonville • (615) 822-7900
$ • 105 Sulphur Springs Rd.,
Murfreesboro • (615) 890-0235
$ • 206 Warrior Dr., Murfreesboro
• (615) 890-7931

Whitt's has been serving barbecue to Nashvillians for about two decades. It has been voted the No. 1 barbecue restaurant in *The Tennessean* readers' poll for years. You can count on speedy service and quality barbecue, cooked over hickory coals and topped off with a vinegar-based sauce. Whitt's serves pork, turkey and beef barbecue in sandwiches or on plates. The barbecue plate portions are huge and come with two side items and rolls or corn bread. Whitt's miniature chess, fudge and pecan pies are the perfect after-meal treat.

Whitt's is open Monday through Saturday for lunch and dinner. Some locations have dine-in-areas; all have drive-through windows. In addition to the locations listed above, there are locations in Ashland City, Clarksville and Alabama. Whitt's does a lot of catering and can accommodate any size group. The restaurants are open Monday through Saturday.

# Breakfast

### Bruegger's Bagel Bakery
$, no credit cards • 5305 Harding Rd.
• (615) 352-1128
$, no credit cards • 330 Franklin Pk.,
Brentwood • (615) 661-5668

Bruegger's, a bagel chain with more than 850 stores nationwide, arrived in Nashville in October 1995, and it didn't take long for the store to develop a following. The bagels are baked every 20 minutes, guaranteeing you a fresh bagel experience. Bruegger's does a huge breakfast and lunch business, so you might have to stand in line for a minute or two, but not too long — service is usually very speedy. While you wait, you can check out the menu. Choose from 15 or 16 types of bagels, including honey grain, raisin and blueberry, and top it off with one of about 13 varieties of cream cheese. We recommend the honey-walnut cream cheese, but other choices include strawberry, light strawberry, herb garlic, sun-dried tomato, smoked salmon and jalapeño.

Bruegger's also fixes breakfast bagels with egg, cheese and bacon or ham. Bruegger's coffee is a blend of Costa Rican and Colombian beans, reputedly grown at the company's own plantation in South America; we didn't verify that — the coffee's good, and that's good enough for us. Espressos, lattes and other specialty coffees are available.

For lunch, you can create your own deli sandwich or choose from the sandwich specialties. Favorites are the chicken fajita, Greek chicken, Santa Fe turkey and herby turkey — all on a bagel, of course. Bruegger's is open daily.

## Donut Den
**$, no credit cards • 3900 Hillsboro Rd.**
**• (615) 385-1021**

Bagel burnout? How about a doughnut for a change? They're not low-fat, but how many of us don't enjoy sitting down every now and then with a melt-in-your-mouth doughnut or two, and a hot cup of coffee or a cold glass of milk? Donut Den in Green Hills has been a favorite for years. They make 35 or 40 different kinds of doughnuts and also sell muffins, cookies and frozen yogurt. Try the old-fashioned cake doughnut. You can park right out front and dash in for a quick fix day or night, until midnight. If you come around 2 or 2:30 PM, the place will be packed with students from Hillsboro High School right next door. Get there first, while the selection is still good. The Donut Den is open daily.

## Loveless Cafe
**$$ • 8400 Tenn. Hwy. 100**
**• (615) 646-9700**

The legendary Loveless Cafe is the real thing: country cookin' just like grandma's. Take it from a Southerner who spent half her childhood at her grandparents' farm, where there was always a plate full of fluffy white biscuits sitting atop a dish of greasy bacon and sausage in the kitchen. The meals were Southern and country — plenty of fried food and a big bowl of hot gravy, and it was good. The Loveless always brings back memories of Granny's house. If you didn't grow up on a farm in the South, you can get a taste of what you missed when you eat at this little out-of-the way motel restaurant in west Nashville. The Loveless first opened in 1947, and it seems that nothing much could have changed here since then.

If you prefer, you can order a plate full of fried chicken with vegetables like green beans, white beans, corn and mashed potatoes, or country ham and eggs with french fries or a

tossed salad. But, especially if it's your first visit, we recommend the breakfast, which is served all day. Choose from eggs, omelets, sausage, bacon, grits, waffles and pancakes. Plates full of biscuits and bowls of gravy and homemade blackberry and peach preserves come with the meal. If you don't know what kind of gravy you want, try both. For those of you unfamiliar with the gravy thing (and we've learned there are many of you in this boat), sausage gravy is the creamy white gravy made with milk, flour and sausage drippings; red-eye gravy is the oily-looking gravy made from ham drippings.

If you're planning to come here on a Saturday or Sunday, you'll want to call a day or two ahead and make reservations. While you're waiting to be seated, check out some of the photos of celebrities who have dined here. The Loveless doesn't have a nonsmoking section — it's really too tiny for that. This place is very casual; in fact, some guests are surprised at how "down-home" it really is. It's open daily.

## Noshville
**$ (breakfast) • 1918 Broadway**
**• (615) 329-NOSH**

This New York-style deli is famous for its enormous sandwiches, but it also serves a good breakfast. Assorted bagels and cream cheeses, plus eggs, omelets, griddle cakes, assorted toasts and cereal satisfy just about any morning appetite. Read more about Noshville in the "Sandwiches" section of this chapter. The deli is open daily.

## Pancake Pantry
**$ • 1796 21st Ave. S. • (615) 383-9333**

The Pancake Pantry has been a Nashville breakfast tradition for nearly four decades. Locals are willing to stand in line as long as it takes to get a table and a stack of pancakes at this Hillsboro Village restaurant. The line usually snakes out the door and down the sidewalk. We've even stood in line in the middle of winter with snowflakes falling. Urns of complimentary hot coffee are a welcome warmer during wintertime waits.

Once inside, the longtime waitresses will make you feel right at home. In addition to a variety of pancakes, you'll find all the familiar breakfast foods on the menu. Known to draw celebrities on a regular basis, the Pancake Pantry has served everyone from Garth Brooks to Lamar Alexander. Try not to stare. It's a regular meeting place for the music-business pros too. The Pancake Pantry is open daily for breakfast and lunch.

## Provence Breads & Cafe
### $ • 1705 21st Ave. S.
### • (615) 386-0363

Provence is primarily a food store (see our Shopping chapter for more about its great breads), but there are some wonderful breakfast and lunch items here and a few tables. For breakfast, try a marvelous French pastry — perhaps an almond croissant — and a cappuccino. For more on this delightful place, see the "Sandwiches" section of this chapter. Provence is open daily.

## Star Bagel Co.
### $, no credit cards • 992 Davidson Dr.
### • (615) 352-2435
### $, no credit cards • 4502 Murphy Rd.
### • (615) 292-7993
### $, no credit cards • 20 Harding Road
### • (615) 781-2662

In at least one of the local reader polls, Star Bagel earned the distinction of having the best bagels in town. There are all sorts of yummy ones to choose from here. Plain bagels and multi-grain are two of the most-ordered varieties, but try the cinnamon-raisin swirl, sun-dried tomato, wild blueberry and egg ones too. In October, pumpkin-raisin joins the menu for a Halloween season treat. Star Bagel's cream cheeses include light plain, wild blueberry, light spicy cucumber, herb and garlic, olive pimiento and the ever-popular honey walnut raisin.

If a heartier breakfast is in order, you can top your bagels with any combination of eggs, bacon, salami and cheese. For lunch, order from the menu of deli sandwiches such as hot pastrami and Swiss, roast beef and cheddar and tuna melt, or create your own sandwich. Star Bagel is open Monday through Saturday for breakfast, lunch and early dinners (the Murphy Road store is open on Sundays as well). If you want to dine in, go to the larger, more comfortable Murphy Road store.

# Burgers

## Brown's Diner
### $ • 2102 Blair Blvd. • (615) 269-5509

This weathered building, an expanded dining car, is a genuine tavern — what you might call a dive. But it serves what many people consider the best cheeseburger in town. Plenty of seating is available in the dining room, where there's a big-screen TV. But the real atmosphere is in the dark bar (beer only), a popular hangout for songwriters, business people and regular working folk, with a TV that's generally tuned to a sports event. Chili dogs, fried fish and a few sandwiches are among the other menu items, but the burger with fries is really your best bet. This is real Nashville at its most unpretentious.

## Fat Mo's Burgers
### $ • 2620 Franklin Pk.
### • (615) 298-1111
### $ • 1216 Murfreesboro Pk.
### • (615) 366-3171
### $ • 946 Richards Rd., Antioch
### • (615) 781-1830

Insiders may disagree about who has the best burger in Nashville, but there's no argument about who has the *biggest*. When your ads and signs proclaim "the biggest burgers in town!" you have to deliver, and this popular establishment offers the Fat Mo's Super Deluxe Burger, more than 27 ounces of fresh beef cooked up in three patties and topped with grilled mushrooms and onions, barbecue sauce, bacon and jalapeños — enough to feed the whole family. Those with less-hearty appetites (or smaller families) can choose from burgers of *only* 16 or 8 ounces; even the Little Mo's Burger weighs in at 5 ounces, which is bigger than a Quarter Pounder, and it's cooked fresh.

Other sandwiches include fried and grilled chicken, catfish, roast beef, hot dogs and corn dogs. Fat Mo's also has fries in "plain" and "spicy" varieties, onion rings, cheese sticks, fried mushrooms and stuffed jalapeños. And be sure to save room for an old-fashioned milk shake, ice cream cone or sundae. The Antioch and Franklin Pike locations are drive-through only, but you can eat in at the Murfreesboro

Get in line and wait your turn: breakfasts at Pancake Pantry
in Hillsboro Village are worth the wait.

Road restaurant. And while you'll have to wait several minutes for your order, you'll find the difference between Fat Mo's and fast-food burgers to be well worth the wait. (If you're really in a hurry, call ahead; your order will be ready when you arrive.)

## Rotier's Restaurant
**$ • 2413 Elliston Pl. • (615) 327-9892**

The burgers at Rotier's are legendary. Read about them and other Rotier's offerings in the "Meat-and-threes" section of this chapter.

## Sports Page Restaurant and Bar
$ • 419 Union St. • (615) 251-9503

Sports Page Restaurant and Bar is a busy downtown lunch spot. Good sandwiches and burgers and affordable prices bring in all types of people. The ground chuck cheeseburgers come with one of five types of cheese and one of six kinds of bread. Nothing on the menu costs more than $5.50 or $6. Sports Page has a full bar and is open weekdays for lunch and dinner. TVs around the room allow sports fans to keep up with the action.

# Cajun/Creole

### Bro's Cajun Cuisine
$ • 5411 Centennial Blvd.
• (615) 350-8866

The location has changed a couple of times in the past few years, but the delicious food is still the same. Gumbo, red beans and rice, crawfish étouffée, fried catfish on Fridays — all the favorites are still on the menu. (And the rolls of paper towels are still on the tables.)

Don't be put off by the look of the place — it's definitely nothing fancy. Nevertheless, Bro's is one of those Insiders' favorites that has a devoted following. The affable owner, Darrell Breaux, of Lafayette, Louisiana, cooks up authentic Cajun foods with just the right amount of spice. Meals here are very affordable. Call in a to-go order the next time you need lunch in a hurry — it's much better and healthier than fast food. During the holidays, the restaurant sells deep-fried turkeys, injected with onions and seasonings ($40). Bro's is open for lunch Monday through Saturday until about 3:30 PM and on Friday is open until about 7:30 PM.

### Copeland's of New Orleans
$$-$$$ • 1649 Westgate Cir., Brentwood
• (615) 661-8040
$$-$$$ • 909 Two- Mile Parkway,
Goodlettsville • (615) 851-1961

Though Copeland's isn't unique to Nashville, the food at this locally owned franchise of the Louisiana-based chain is too good to leave out of this chapter. Copeland's, right across I-65 from Franklin's CoolSprings Gal-

leria and on Two-Mile Parkway in the Rivergate area, serves delicious New Orleans-style Cajun and Creole food as well as good pastas and all-American favorites. This is an upscale casual restaurant with a lively, upbeat atmosphere. Customers in their best dresses and suits dine alongside others in shorts and hiking boots.

We've always enjoyed our meals here. Some of the top picks on the menu are the shrimp étouffée, crawfish étouffée, shrimp or redfish creole and blackened redfish with lump crabmeat. Steak lovers will appreciate the fact that most steaks here are prime cuts. Entrees come with Copeland's yummy New Orleans biscuits. On Saturday and Sunday, Copeland's has a great brunch; the live jazz band on Sunday is a great touch. The Cajun omelet and the egg sardou are good brunch choices. New Orleans beignets come with each brunch selection. Copeland's is open daily for lunch and dinner.

# Catfish

### Bill's Catfish Restaurant
$$ • 1205 Old Hydes Ferry Pk., Ashland City • (615) 792-9193

Folks from around these parts have been satisfying their catfish cravings at Bill's since 1971. The family-owned restaurant is right off Tenn. Highway 12 in Ashland City, about 20 miles from Nashville. The catfish alone is worth the drive, but the homey, small-town ambience and Southern hospitality make everything complete. Bill's is a favorite of blue-collar and white-collar workers and celebrities. The original restaurant was decorated with photos of the many country performers who dined here, but that restaurant burned in 1989. You can still spot a star here from time to time. Randy Travis, Mel Tillis, Tanya Tucker and Don Williams are just a few of the celebrities who've stopped by.

You can order whole catfish or catfish fillet dinners. They come with your choice of potato, plus slaw, white beans and hush puppies. Bill's also makes its own hickory-smoked pork barbecue. The lunch buffet, available Tuesday through Friday and Sunday for about

$5.95, brings in lots of people with big appetites. The selections vary daily, but there's usually a full salad bar, fish, fried chicken, pit barbecue, corn on the cob, white beans, cole slaw, corn bread, rolls and a dessert — maybe peach cobbler. Blue plate specials and sandwiches, soups and salads are also on the menu. On Saturday nights Bill's has a $14.95 seafood buffet with catfish, two or three kinds of shrimp, scallops, crab legs, stuffed crab, stuffed lobster tails, a variety of vegetables, and they even throw in prime rib for good measure. Bill's is open Tuesday through Sunday.

### Mallard's Restaurant
**$, no credit cards • 101 Sanders Ferry Rd., Hendersonville • (615) 822-4668**

This family-style restaurant serves all-you-can-eat catfish on Fridays after 5 PM. Read more about what's for dinner at Mallard's in the "Meat-and-threes" section of this chapter.

### Mallard's Restaurant
**$ • 3803 Dickerson Pk. • (615) 860-4211**

Though not affiliated, this Mallard's, like the one in Hendersonville, serves plenty of catfish. Again, read more about it in the "Meat-and-threes" listings in this chapter.

### Uncle Bud's Catfish, Chicken and Such
**$$ • 219 Largo Dr.**
**• (615) 781-6811**
**$$ • 358 White Bridge Rd.**
**• (615) 353-0016**
**$$ • 714 Stewart's Ferry Pk.**
**• (615) 872-7700**
**$$ • 277 Gleaves St., Madison**
**• (615) 860-6848**
**$$ • 1214 Lakeview Dr., Franklin**
**• (615) 790-1234**

What started as a little catfish house in Franklin has grown into a bona-fide chain. Uncle Bud's serves good catfish in a fun atmosphere. Popular with just about everybody — young couples, families and senior citizens — Uncle Bud's serves catfish with all-you-can-eat fixins, including white beans, hush puppies, onions, pickles and cole slaw. This place is so popular, there is often a considerable wait, but there are plenty of benches and rocking chairs where you can relax 'til it's your turn

to dig in. Don't forget to bring a cap that you can trade for an Uncle Bud's cap. The staff will hang yours from the ceiling, along with the hundreds of others they've collected through the years. All locations are open daily.

# Chinese

### August Moon
**$$ • 4000 Hillsboro Rd. • (615) 298-9999**

August Moon offers very good Chinese food in a nice environment. It's a favorite of many locals. We enjoy coming here for lunch especially — it's quiet, rarely crowded, and the service is fast and friendly. Five-flavored shrimp and chicken are always a hit. August Moon's dining areas are divided into at least two separate rooms, offering a sense of privacy. It's open daily.

### Chinatown
**$$ • 3900 Hillsboro Rd. • (615) 269-3275**

Considered by many to be the best Chinese restaurant in Nashville, Chinatown, in business here since 1984, is always a great place to satisfy a craving for Chinese. Located in the Hillsboro Plaza shopping center in Green Hills, this restaurant combines an understated elegance, intimate and quite environment, and really good food. There are a lot of lunchtime regulars, but the room never seems to be too crowded, and the atmosphere is always subdued. They serve a lot of Governor's chicken, sesame chicken, rice noodles, sauteed green beans and dumplings. Roast duck is available on weekends. Chinatown is open daily.

### Golden House Chinese Restaurant
**$ • 321-A Harding Pl. • (615) 331-1689**

This casual dining spot has been here since the early '90s. The lunch buffet is a big draw, offering several bars full of food plus a dessert bar for around $5.50 per person. There is a dinner buffet too, with 25 to 30 items, for $7.25, but if you have a favorite dish, order from the menu. Favorites include pepper steak and sweet-and-sour pork. The food is not only flavorful, it is artfully presented. There is a full bar and limited wine list. Golden House is open daily.

Photo: Cindy Stooksbury Guier

There are several restaurants within walking distance from Nashville's famous Music Row.

### New Asia Chinese Restaurant
**$$ • 3744 Nolensville Pk.**
**• (615) 315-0066**

Longing for Chinese food but don't want the MSG and the fat? Head to New Asia, where you can dine on incredibly good, fresh Chinese food. Friendly owner Michael Wong puts the emphasis on healthy here and wants his customers to know that his food is MSG-free (no need to ask). The specialty here is Mongolian barbecue, and this is the only place in town where you can get it. If you order this dish, you'll select from four meats (beef, chicken breast, pork or shrimp) and four sauces (kung pao, five-flavor, house special and teriyaki). Choose any or all, then watch as the chef cooks it up right in front of you on the grill — without oil. It's healthy, low-fat and delicious.

New Asia also offers lunch and dinner buffets with more than 30 items, from soups and appetizers to General chicken, Mandarin fish and the popular chicken cho-cho — grilled chicken on a stick. Buffet prices are $4.95 for lunch, $7.95 for dinner. You can't go wrong if your opt to order from the menu, but you may have a hard time choosing from the 100 differ-

ent selections. The seafood combinations are good, and the sacha beef, Mongolian beef and Mongolian chicken are ordered often. New Asia has two dining rooms; one is available for parties. The restaurant is about a quarter-mile north of Grassmere Park and is open daily.

## Continental

### Arthur's
**$$$$$ • 1001 Broadway**
**• (615) 255-1494**

Arthur's, in the historic Union Station Hotel, is always a perfect choice for a special occasion or important business dinner. White tablecloths, stained glass, candlelight, 24-foot ceilings — this is one of Nashville's most elegant restaurants, yet the feeling is very relaxed. While it isn't necessary for men to wear ties, jackets are preferred. You'll feel most comfortable here if you are well-dressed for the evening.

Arthur's offers a seven-course prix fixe dinner at $60 a person. The menu, which changes nightly, is presented verbally. There are six choices — fresh seafood, beef, lamb, pork, veal, fowl or occasionally wild game. Arthur's is best known for its fish and rack of lamb. The restaurant has an excellent wine list. After your appetizer, soup, salad, sorbet and entree, you can indulge in a flaming dessert (or a different choice) and flaming after-dinner coffee — a perfect ending to a memorable dining experience.

Arthur's is open nightly for dinner. Reservations are strongly suggested.

## The Bound'ry
**$$$ • 911 20th Ave. S. • (615) 321-3043**

The Bound'ry, about a block from the Vandy law school, has become a big local favorite. We've found it's a reliable choice for good food and a great atmosphere. The Bound'ry has several cozy dining rooms, dimly lighted and strung with tiny white lights. We like to dine upstairs on the open-air deck. The Bound'ry serves "global cuisine." From the top-selling planked trout to the Tennessee ostrich, there's something for everyone. The filet mignon, wood-oven pizzas and "wood fish of the day" are among the other favorites. The restaurant is known for its excellent assortment of tapas (a collection of appetizers), and you can create a meal from a couple of these choices, or order a variety to enjoy family-style. The Bound'ry's bar is a hot spot, especially among the singles set. For more on that, see our Nightlife chapter.

## Cafe Lylla
**$$$-$$$$ 2114 Green Hills Village Dr. • (615) 297-5669**

Cafe Lylla is a quaint and romantic cafe specializing in American-influenced European dining. It's located across from the Mall at Green Hills in a small strip shopping center. White tablecloths, exposed brick and mirrored windows help to create a casual yet sophisticated atmosphere. At night, the lights are dim and candles glow on every table, making this a nice spot for a romantic dinner for two.

Favorites from the lunch menu include chicken Nicoise salad, southwestern pita, herb-roasted salmon salad and shellfish stew, also available at dinner. A recent summer dinner menu included rack of lamb with roasted hazelnuts or crusted almonds, baked scallops with roasted garlic sauce and a special: stuffed flounder with lobster sauce, crab and shrimp. For dessert, the crème caramel, raspberry almond tart, tiramisu and raspberry and lemon sorbets are very good.

Cafe Lylla is open Monday through Saturday for lunch and dinner and Sunday for brunch until 4 PM.

## Café One Two Three
**$$$$ • 123 12th Ave. N. • (615) 255-2233**

Café One Two Three is a most-recommended choice for a wonderful dining experience. Another of Jody Faison's restaurants, this is one of Nashville's favorites; it's popular with the music crowd, casual diners and anyone who enjoys good food. Wood floors, a fireplace and a historic hardwood bar contribute to the "speakeasy" atmosphere. Café One Two Three serves Continental cuisine with a regional twist. Portions are generous. Deep South Duck, the rib-eye chop and seafood pasta are among the favored dishes. The white chocolate crème brûlée is a nice treat. Reservations are recommended. The eatery is open Monday through Saturday for dinner.

## Capitol Grille
**$$$-$$$$ • 231 Sixth Ave. N. • (615) 244-3121**

This is one of Nashville's best. Capitol Grille is in the historic Hermitage Hotel and is open daily for breakfast, lunch and dinner. Unlike many hotel restaurants, the Capitol Grille is actually a favorite of locals. Voted one of the top-25 restaurants in America by *Esquire*, this restaurant offers creative dishes, excellent service and a sophisticated atmosphere. Fresh seafood and black Angus steaks are in plenti-

## INSIDERS' TIP

**Sunday brunch plans? Just in case you plan to order a bloody Mary or mimosa, remember that, on Sundays, alcohol cannot be served until noon.**

ful supply. Reservations are suggested for lunch and dinner.

## Jody's Dining Hall and Barcar
**$$ • 209 10th Ave. S., Ste. 201 • (615) 259-4875**

It has taken us locals a while to get used to referring to this restaurant as Jody's. It was originally known as Jules, but when well-known restaurateur Jody Faison took over, he changed a few letters in the name. He also brought some of the menu favorites from the beloved but now-closed Faison's, including the Broken Hearted Fettuccine — a combination of scallops, crabmeat and artichoke hearts in a light cream sauce — and the dessert that everyone loves, The Next Best Thing To Robert Redford, a chocolate mousse treat with a pecan crust, cream cheese, whipped cream and chocolate toffee.

Vegetarians who miss the veggie dishes at Faison's will find several very good selections at Jody's, especially at lunch. The dinner menu has such tempting choices as the signature jerk chicken, chicken Florentine and Faison filet, a filet of beef served with hash-style potatoes, crabmeat and bearnaise sauce.

The atmosphere here is as interesting as the menu. Jody's is in the funky, hip Cummins Station office and retail complex; the building was once a railroad warehouse, and it overlooks the railroad. Jody's has two bars and provides pool tables in the back. The restaurant draws lots of Music Row-ers and Vandyites and is popular with the business crowd at lunch.

Free parking is available in the lot across the street, Jody's is open for dinner Tuesday through Saturday, and for lunch weekdays.

## The Mad Platter
**$$$$ • 1239 Sixth Ave. N. • (615) 242-2563**

Although it has been around since 1989, The Mad Platter found mainstream attention only in recent years. It's now widely considered one of the best restaurants in Nashville and has been voted "best romantic rendezvous" in a local readers' poll. In a historic building in Germantown, two blocks from the Bicentennial Mall, The Mad Platter establishes its ambience with white linen tablecloths, fresh flowers and candlelight. The tiny dining room only accommodates 20 or so tables.

"Gourmet world fusion cuisine" is a perhaps the best description of the food here. The lunch and dinner menus change daily depending on availability of ingredients, but you can expect expertly prepared and beautifully presented dishes. The restaurant grows its own herbs in a garden in back of the building. The Mad Platter's lunch items range from about $5 to $15. A favorite at lunchtime is the Pasta Mad Platter — linguine with sauteed artichokes, mushrooms, sun-dried tomatoes, spinach, onions, garlic, oregano, chorizo sausage and Montrachet cheese. Reservations are required for dinner. The Mad Platter serves lunch Tuesday through Friday and dinner Tuesday through Sunday.

## Mere Bulles
**$$$-$$$$ • 152 Second Ave. N. • (615) 256-1946**

With dining rooms overlooking the Cumberland River, a cozy yet elegant atmosphere and delicious food, Mere Bulles has become a Nashville favorite. Try the pecan-encrusted rainbow trout, filet mignon, sauteed veal medallions or potato-encrusted Norwegian salmon. Mere Bulles (the name means "mother bubbles") has a great all-you-can-eat Sunday brunch. For $23.95 you can get your fill of crab legs, peel-and-eat shrimp, omelets, pastas, fruit, pastries and a number of other tempting, tasty dishes. The wine list has about 250 selections; 20 wines are available by the glass.

Mere Bulles is open for dinner daily. Reservations are a good idea. Whether you come for dinner or drinks, you'll want to wear your "smart-casual" or better attire here.

## Quails
**$$$$ • 4936 Thoroughbred Ln., Brentwood • (615) 376-2799**

Quails is a fine dining restaurant that serves American cuisine with a Continental twist. Creative salads, exotic game, seafood and poultry dishes, all beautifully presented, are the specialties here. Interesting and unusual appetizers include the venison and three-cheese quesadilla. Entrees include free-range pheasant and coconut and pistachio encrusted duck.

Desserts, such as Bavarian chocolate-raspberry ganache, are a hit. The Cappuccino Brentwood (cappuccino with Bailey's and crème de cocoa) or the Quails Cappuccino (with Tia Maria and brandy) offer a delicious end to your meal. Quails is open for lunch Monday through Friday and dinner Monday through Saturday. Reservations are accepted.

## Restaurante Zola
**$$$$ • 3001 West End Ave.**
**• (615) 320-7778**

Voted "the best restaurant that doesn't feel like Nashville" in the *Nashville Scene* reader's poll, Zola offers Mediterranean-inspired cuisine in a beautiful atmosphere. Nationally known chef Debra Paquette opened Zola in the former location of Nashville's beloved Cakewalk restaurant. She had been the executive chef at Cakewalk before leaving to start the successful Bound'ry restaurant.

Zola has become one of Nashville's favorite places to dine. The food is excellent and the service is superb. Zola's menu combines flavors from Spain, France, Italy, Greece, Turkey, Egypt and Morocco, with a dash of the South. Much of the produce is locally grown and organic, and the meats and seafood are shipped in daily. Veal, lamb, rabbit, duck cassoulet and vegetarian dishes are among the favorites. Each menu item has its own suggested wine accompaniments. A sampling from a recent summer menu included Grandma Zola's Paella, a combination of Spanish jambon risotto, mussels, fresh fish, scallops, oysters, shrimp, homemade chorizo and aioli verde; Zolanella, grilled fish drizzled with truffle oil on a bed of greens, black olive croutons, grilled vegetables and portobellos, olives, capers, red onion, tomatoes, prosciutto and tomato reggiano vinaigrette; and the Riviera Filet, a 4- or 8-ounce beef tenderloin with Provencal portobello sauce, fried oysters,

tomato slices, potato corn salad and French green olives.

Zola is open Monday through Saturday for dinner. Reservations are suggested.

## Sperry's
**$$$$ • 5109 Harding Rd.**
**• (615) 353-0809**

This is a neighborhood restaurant, Belle Meade-style. Doctors, lawyers, judges and well-dressed couples have been dining at Sperry's since 1974. Casual dress is OK, but suits and ties and nice dresses are the norm. This is a comfortably upscale restaurant with good food and good service. Deep red carpets and wood tables contribute to the warm and cozy atmosphere. Sperry's is known for its steaks and seafood. Fresh swordfish and tuna, a bleu cheese-stuffed filet and rack of lamb dijon are always in demand. There are daily specials. Desserts like cherries jubilee, bananas Foster, Boston cream pie and Death by Chocolate cake satisfy 37205 (ZIP code) tastes. Sperry's is open every night for dinner.

## The Wild Boar
**$$$$-$$$$$ • 2014 Broadway**
**• (615) 329-1313**

The Wild Boar is the choice when nothing but the ultimate in elegance and extravagance will do. Many consider the food here to be the best in town. The Wild Boar serves contemporary French cuisine in an old European hunting lodge atmosphere. White damask tablecloths, lots of silver and opulent appointments provide the backdrop for a wonderful meal. The chef has created a menu that pleases every palate. Beluga caviar or Napolean foie gras are tasteful appetizer choices. Among the selection of entrees are filet mignon of venison, breast of chicken in puff pastry, sea bass with spinach and mushrooms topped with a fillet of salmon wrapped in puff pastry, and

---

### INSIDERS' TIP

**Look for restaurant reviews by food critic Kay West in the weekly *Nashville Scene* alternative newspaper. Her columns tell it like it is and are always fun to read, although judging by some of the letters to the editor she has a few non-fans out there. She's been known to cause an uproar or two in the local restaurant world.**

rack of lamb. The wait staff's synchronized service is a rare experience in Nashville, and the wine list is exceptional. The Wild Boar is open for dinner Monday through Saturday.

# German

## Old Heidelberg
**$$$ • 423 Union St. • (615) 256-9147**

You'll find all kinds of schnitzels, sausages, sauerbraten and other German foods on the menu at Old Heidelberg. Other favorites are the hasenpfeffer and beef rouladen. For dessert, try the German apple strudel or Black Forest cake. Beer and wine are available, including a good assortment of German spirits.

It gets pretty lively here on Saturday nights, when the restaurant features live music by Austrian accordion players. Owner Helma Ritter, originally from Stuttgart, Germany, sometimes plays the harmonica. Folks like to sing along, and even though there's no dance floor, they sometimes get up and dance. Old Heidelberg is open Monday through Friday for lunch and Thursday through Saturday for dinner. Reservations are recommended for dinner.

# Indian

## The East India Club
**$$ • 4926 Thoroughbred Ln., Brentwood • (615) 661-9919**

The East India Club offers authentic Indian food and good service in a contemporary and casual atmosphere. White tablecloths, subdued lighting and music ranging from classical Indian to Big Band keeps the feeling upscale. Foods have just the right amount of spice. There are several choices, including good seafood and vegetarian dishes. Most popular are the chicken tandoori and the lamb vindaloo.

The eatery is open for dinner Monday through Saturday; reservations are recommended on weekends. An all-you-can-eat, seven-course lunch buffet is available Monday through Friday for $5.95. A 10-course vegetarian lunch buffet is featured from noon to 2 PM Saturday for $6.95.

## Sitar
**$ • 116 21st Ave. N. • (615) 321-8889**

This small and casual restaurant is where many folks go when they have a craving for spicy Indian foods. Business execs, the music-business crowd, performers (Ricky Skaggs is said to dine here often) and students frequent Sitar. The decor features numerous photographs and art from India.

The affordable lunch buffet includes a good selection of items, or you can order most dishes from the lunch menu for $5 or less. For dinner, chicken and lamb dishes are favorites, and there are vegetarian meals here too. Sitar is open for lunch and dinner daily, but hours vary.

# Italian

## Amerigo
**$$$ • 1920 West End Ave. • (615) 320-1740**

Amerigo's Italian food with an American flair pleases just about every palate. The shrimp scampi is always a winner, but other good choices are the chicken Tuscany and veal saltimbocca. The pasta dishes are great and come in small and large portions; unless you're really hungry, order the small. Amerigo has pizzas too, all prepared with a honey-yeast dough, whole-milk Mozzarella and imported Parmesan cheese.

With lots of windows, dark wood and a professional staff, Amerigo has a comfortable dining environment that pleases everyone from business lunchers to families. Free valet parking is available, and there is a small parking lot behind the restaurant. The eatery is open daily for lunch and dinner.

## Antonio's of Nashville
**$$$ • 7097 Old Harding Rd. • (615) 646-9166**

Bellevue residents often lament the lack of good places to eat on their side of town, but they are blessed with this fine Italian restaurant. Antonio's of Nashville serves gourmet Italian cuisine in a casually elegant atmosphere. It's a perfect place for a romantic date whether you're wearing blue jeans, a tux or an evening dress. White linen tablecloths and dim lights set the mood, and the service is attentive but not intrusive.

All foods here are fresh and prepared to order. Beautifully presented pasta, veal, chicken and seafood dishes emerge from the European-style open kitchen. A favorite is the scaloppini Sorrentino — veal layered with prosciutto, eggplant and Mozzarella and sauteed in a white wine and red sauce. The best-selling pasta dish is the cappellini alla giudea, angel hair pasta tossed with artichoke hearts, Italian bacon and green onion in a red and cream sauce. Tiramisu is the ideal end to a meal here, but the fresh berries zabaglione (a sauce of sugar, eggs, cream and Marsala) is a nice alternative. Twice a year — on Valentine's Day and New Year's Eve — Antonio's has a four- or five-course special menu; it's a bit more pricey, but makes for a memorable special occasion dinner. Antonio's is open nightly for dinner. Reservations are recommended, especially on weekends.

## A Taste of Italy
**$ • 73 White Bridge Rd., Ste. 104**
**• (615) 354-0124**

In 1997, the tiny A Taste of Italy opened to good reviews as a market and deli that served dinners by reservation only. The dinners were so successful (and so wonderful) that in 1999 the owners expanded A Taste of Italy to a full-service restaurant serving lunch and dinner six days a week. It's in the Paddock Place shopping center across from Target.

## Basante's Restaurant
**$$ • 1800 West End Ave.**
**• (615) 320-0534**

Basante's is a casual, bistro-style restaurant that serves delicious authentic Italian cuisine. Try the potato gnocchi, angel hair pasta with bay shrimp or fettuccine with Alfredo sauce pancetta. For dessert, you can't go wrong with the tiramisu. Basante's serves 30 wines by the glass. The restaurant is open for lunch weekdays and for dinner Monday through Saturday.

## Caesar's Ristorante Italiano
**$$ • 88 White Bridge Rd.**
**• (615) 352-3661**

Caesar's is loved by about everyone we know. Depending on when you come and where you dine, the restaurant is either intimate and romantic or spirited and lively. It somehow manages to be both a great spot for a romantic dinner and a fun place to take the family. Separate dining rooms help to maintain the mood. On most of our recent dinner visits we have found dim lights, lace curtains, candles glowing on every table and opera and old standards playing in the background.

Warm bread and olive oil arrives right after you're seated. Caesar's has a diverse but pasta-based menu. Especially good are the pastas with Northern Italian white sauces. Try the specialty — ziti alla carbonara, a combination of ziti with fresh cream, asparagus, Italian ham and Parmesan. The ziti Florentine, with sauteed spinach, bacon, ham and onion in a cream sauce, is also quite good. Caesar's also has the expected spaghetti and fettuccine with a variety of sauces, as well as lasagna, eggplant, manicotti and cannelloni. There are several seafood dishes, veal and poultry, pizzas with your choice of about 15 toppings and sub sandwiches. For lunch, Caesar's has an all-you-can-eat buffet, which is tasty but not quite the same as a nighttime meal.

## Finezza Trattoria
**$$-$$$• 5404 Harding Rd.**
**• (615) 356-9398**

Finezza Trattoria is a comfortable neighborhood restaurant. Located right at the Tenn. Highway 100–U.S. Highway 70 split in west Nashville, the restaurant draws lots of regular customers from Belle Meade, West Meade and Bellevue. When you are seated, your server will bring some bread and a plate of olive oil, garlic and freshly ground pepper for dipping.

## INSIDERS' TIP

Loveless Cafe is noted for its biscuits and country ham. (See the Close-up in this chapter for their Blackberry Jam recipe.)

Wine is served in a comfortable-to-hold tumbler.

Finezza's menu is inspired by the dishes of the rustic restaurants in the Italian countryside. Hearty pastas and filling polenta are featured, along with a variety of pizzas, chicken, seafood and veal. The menu is quite extensive. As for atmosphere, Finezza is dark and relaxed, welcoming to families with small children as well as couples on a date. Finezza is open nightly for dinner.

### Gibson's Caffé Milano
$$ • 174 Third Ave. N. • (615) 255-0073, (615) 255-0322 (concert hotline)

Bravo for Caffé Milano! We love this place. It features some of the best concerts in town in an acoustically excellent room, and before the show you get to dine on tasty Italian-American food. Gibson's Caffé Milano is housed in a former brick factory, and the original brick walls are still in place. The open, airy venue, decorated in vibrant colors, features two giant bas-relief works by Italian sculptor Max Squillace, the brother of Caffé Milano founder and former owner Pino Squillace. The restaurant and concert venue is now owned by Gibson Guitar Corp.

One side of the room is occupied by the serpentine bar and open kitchen, where the chef prepares great pizzas in the wood-burning oven, as well as favorites like tri-color cheese tortellini, seared ahi tuna on a bed of pasta, salmon penne with horseradish sauce and grilled medallion of veal tenderloin. Gibson's Caffé Milano has a full bar.

Reservations are recommended. You might want to call as far as a month in advance if there is a show you really want to see. Shows often fill up quickly. Past performers include Chet Atkins, Ricky Skaggs, Larry Carlton, Béla Fleck and the Flecktones, Amy Grant and dc Talk. Meals are not included in the price of concert tickets, which usually range from about $5 to $40. (For more on Gibson's Caffé Milano's concert scene, see our Music City U.S.A. chapter.) Gibson's Caffé Milano is open daily and features concerts Monday through Saturday. On Sundays, a jazz band plays during brunch.

### Mario's
$$$$ • 2005 Broadway • (615) 327-3232

Mario Ferrari opened Mario's in 1965, introducing many Nashvillians to fine dining and Northern Italian dishes. Over the years Mario's has won every major restaurant award and it has an award-winning wine list of more than 700 selections. Mario's has a lot of regular customers who come for the osso buco, pastas and saltimbocca, and the restaurant welcomes many business travelers and special occasion diners. Celebrities eat here too — everyone from Hank Williams Jr. to Al Gore. Mario's has two elegant dining areas: the more intimate lower level and the upper level, where it's easy to see everyone coming and going. Reservations are recommended. Mario's is open Monday through Saturday for dinner.

### Sole Mio
$$$ • 94 Peabody St. • (615) 256-4013

Delicious Italian food, a casually elegant atmosphere and the best view of downtown Nashville await diners here. This restaurant, situated in Rutledge Hill overlooking downtown Nashville, is about one-third windows.

Sole Mio has white linen tablecloths, fresh flowers on every table and, at night, is aglow with candlelight. But there's more to this restaurant that the atmosphere and view. The food is excellent. Sole Mio, owned by Giancarlo and Debra Agnoletti, who moved their restaurant from Northern Italy to Music City in 1995, specializes in handmade and hand-rolled pastas and homemade sauces, fresh fish, veal and chicken dishes and brick-oven pizzas. Lasagna is the signature dish, and the mussels are a favorite as an appetizer. Top dessert picks are the crème caramel and cannoli. There are daily lunch specials and on Saturday and Sunday, Sole Mio has a brunch with a choice of three to four pastas, fresh fish, champagne, bread and salad for $9.95.

It's a good idea to make reservations; the restaurant is often filled even on weeknights. On Friday and Saturday nights, a pianist plays unobtrusive jazz, blues and show tunes. Sole Mio is just up the hill from Riverfront Park at First Avenue South. It is open Tuesday through Sunday for lunch and dinner.

## Valentino's Ristorante

$$$ • 1907 West End Ave.
• (615) 327-0148

Business executives, couples on romantic dates and tourists all come to Valentino's for Northern Italian cuisine in a comfortably elegant atmosphere. Although the waiters wear tuxedos, it's not really necessary to dress up to come here, but many do.

Located in a century-old home that was once a boarding house, Valentino's has three separate dining rooms: a Tuscan-style room, a Romanesque room and the always-popular wine cellar downstairs. Pasta, salmon, stuffed shrimp and rack of lamb are especially popular here. Valentino's does a strong lunch business. Known for its excellent wine list, the restaurant is open weekdays for lunch and dinner and Saturdays for dinner only. Reservations are suggested for dinner. Valentino's offers complimentary valet parking.

# Japanese

## Asahi Japanese Sushi Bar

$$ • 4215 Harding Rd. • (615) 352-8877

Voted the No. 1 Japanese restaurant in one 1997 local readers' poll, Asahi serves some of the freshest and most delicious sushi and Japanese dishes in town. If you're not a sushi eater, try one of the teriyaki bento boxes. The tempura is great too. Beer, wine and several types of sake are available. This relaxed and friendly restaurant is in Belle Meade, at the corner of Harding Road and Harding Place. Asahi is open daily for lunch and dinner.

## Goten Japanese Restaurant

$$$ • 110 21st Ave. S. • (615) 321-4537

Goten ("go-TEN") is the only Japanese restaurant in town that has both hibachi grill cookery and a sushi bar. Goten opened in the late 1980s and has been voted best sushi bar and best Japanese restaurant in local media polls. Dark and elegant, it is more upscale than some Japanese restaurants in town, so you'll fit right in if you dress up just a bit. Of course, in casual Nashville, you rarely have to dress up, so a laid-back look is also OK.

Goten has 11 separate dining areas, all centered around a grill where the chef pre-

pares the food right in front of you. The steak and seafood cooked on the grill are delicious, and the tempura and sushi are favorites too. Goten is open weekdays for lunch and dinner and Saturday and Sunday for dinner only. Reservations are not necessary but are suggested, especially on busy Friday and Saturday nights.

## Goten 2 Japanese Restaurant

$$ • 209 10th Ave. S. • (615) 251-4855

Following the success of Goten Japanese Restaurant, Goten 2 opened in the mid-1990s in Cummins Station. Goten 2 is more informal than the Goten on 21st Avenue S., and the prices are a bit lower. Goten 2 has a sushi bar but doesn't do hibachi cookery — meals are prepared in the kitchen. Goten 2 is a good spot for late-night dining. It's open until midnight most nights and until 1 AM Friday and Saturday nights.

## Ichiban

$$$ • 109 Second Ave. N.
• (615) 254-7185

Ichiban's front display window — filled with Japanese cooking ingredients, cookware and related implements — draws the attention of passersby on Second Avenue, luring in not only Music City tourists, but also lots of local business people and families. The restaurant has many regular Japanese customers; sometimes as many as 50 percent of the diners are Japanese — an excellent testimony to the quality of food here.

Ichiban is a comfortable restaurant with three dining areas. The first floor offers traditional Japanese seating. In back, there's a sushi bar. The upstairs dining room is often used for private parties. Ichiban's shrimp tempura is always a favorite, and the beef teriyaki and chicken teriyaki are excellent as well. The combo dinners, featuring two entrees, sushi, soup and salad, are ordered often. Japanese customers often get the "house specialties." Ichiban is open for dinner daily and for lunch Monday through Friday. Groups of five or more should make reservations.

## Kobe Steaks Japanese Restaurant

$$$ • 210 25th Ave. N. • (615) 327-9081

Kobe Steaks is a local favorite for Japanese hibachi cooking. Kobe has been in Nashville for nearly 15 years and also has restaurants in Atlanta and Dallas. A meal here is as entertaining as it is delicious. The dark, comfortable and spacious bar area is a nice spot to enjoy a cocktail before dinner.

There are eight separate dining rooms, two of which are "Japanese rooms" where you take off your shoes before entering. Rooms accommodate anywhere from 15 to 40 people. Watching the chef prepare your meal is always fascinating and fun. Children especially get a kick out of watching the chef toss shrimp tails behind his back and into his hat. Chicken and steak meals are delicious and the most popular, but the seafood dishes are excellent as well. Meals range from about $13 to $27.

Kobe is open daily for dinner only. You can make reservations for Sunday through Thursday. It gets pretty crowded here on Friday and Saturday nights, so come early if you don't want to wait. Valet parking is available, or you can search for a spot along 25th.

### Koto Sushi Bar
**$$-$$$ • 137 Seventh Ave. N.**
**• (615) 255-8122**

Koto is a favorite among many local sushi connoisseurs. In business here since the mid-1980s, this casual restaurant offers table seating and traditional, shoes-off floor seating. Sit at the sushi bar if you like and watch the chef prepare Koto's specialty. Some of the sushi rolls are named for local celebrities and other regular customers. If you're not into sushi, try the teriyaki dishes. Koto is popular with the downtown lunch crowd and is busiest weekdays from about noon to 1 PM. The restaurant is open Monday through Friday for lunch and dinner and Saturday for dinner only.

### Taste of Tokyo
**$ • 1806 21st Ave. S. • (615) 292-8338**

Casual and popular with the Vandy crowd, this small Hillsboro Village restaurant is almost always busy. Regular customers often call ahead to place their orders or put their names on a waiting list for seats. Taste of Tokyo has about 20 boxes (entrees, soup and salad) to choose from. Sushi, chicken teriyaki and the noodle soup are always in demand. You can order a beer, wine or hot or cold sake with

your meal here. Lunch is served Monday through Friday; dinner is served nightly.

# Korean

### Arirang
**$$$ • 1719 West End Ave.**
**• (615) 327-3010**

Native Korean dishes and traditional open-flame cookery are featured at Arirang, on the corner of 18th and West End. Strips of marinated chicken, pork, beef or squid are grilled over an open flame at your table. Steamed rice, fried tofu and a variety of veggies, such as cucumbers, carrots, bean sprouts, spinach, potatoes and cabbage, are individually prepared in their own sauces. Arirang has a $6 special Tuesday through Friday. Dinner is served nightly.

# Meat-and-threes

### Belle Meade Cafeteria
**$$ • 4534 Harding Rd. • (615) 298-5571**

The Belle Meade Cafeteria has been a Nashville favorite for four decades. Located in the Belle Meade Plaza at the intersection of White Bridge Road and Woodmont Boulevard, the cafeteria serves home-cooked Southern-style favorites in a comfortable atmosphere. Create your own meal here by choosing among entrees such as turkey and dressing, fried chicken, roast beef, liver and onions and baked shrimp, and side dishes like green beans, creamed corn, turnip greens and fried okra. There are daily specials too, like teriyaki chicken with rice and Creole spaghetti. Everything comes with your choice of fresh-baked yeast rolls, corn bread, biscuits or muffins. There are enough desserts to tempt even the most finicky sweet tooth — homemade fruit cobblers, pies, custards and cakes. A lot of regulars who find the full-size meals too filling order the mini-meal — an entree, two vegetables and bread. Belle Meade Cafeteria is open daily for lunch and dinner.

### Elliston Place Soda Shop
**$ • 2111 Elliston Pl. • (615) 327-1090**

Plate lunches and milk shakes are the

# Insider Recipe: Love That Loveless Jam

The Loveless Cafe is probably Nashville's most famous restaurant. It's a little country motel and restaurant out on U.S. Highway 100 at the northern terminus of the Natchez Trace Parkway. Popular with locals and tourists, it serves up *real* country cooking in a down-home dining room.

The Loveless Cafe serves up country cooking.

The Loveless is famous for its biscuits. They arrive hot from the oven, accompanied by dishes of incredibly good blackberry and peach preserves. Before leaving, we usually purchase a jar or two of preserves to take home.

Donna McCabe, who along with her son, George McCabe, owns the Loveless, shared the restaurant's recipe for blackberry preserves with *The Insiders' Guide to Nashville*. You can find more Loveless recipes in a recipe book entitled *Meet Me At the Loveless* (Cool Springs Press, 1998).

### Blackberry Preserves

Yield: variable

10 pounds fresh blackberries
5 pounds sugar

Rinse the blackberries; remove and discard any stems.
Pour the blackberries into a large saucepan. Add the sugar; mix well.
Bring the mixture to a boil, stirring until the sugar dissolves.
Reduce heat and cook until the mixture is thickened and of jam consistency, stirring frequently to prevent the mixture from sticking to the saucepan.

Ladle the mixture into hot sterilized jars, leaving a 1/2-inch headspace.

Seal with two-piece lids.

Process in a boiling water bath for 10 minutes.

This little country motel/restaurant on Highway 100 is popular with locals and tourists.

claims to fame of this 1950s-style diner. One of Nashville's oldest restaurants, Elliston Place Soda Shop first opened in 1939. Little has changed here over the years. The restaurant has had only three owners, and it still has some of its original chairs and booths. The old miniature jukeboxes sit on each table, though they don't work anymore. The big jukebox still spins hits from the '50s and '60s.

Monday through Saturday, diners can choose from four entrees, including daily specials like turkey and dressing, fried chicken and catfish. For the "three" part of your meat-and-three, choose from among 10 vegetables and side dishes including fresh turnip greens, fried corn, baked squash and macaroni and cheese. Your meal comes with corn bread or a biscuit. If you want to indulge further, have one of the soda shop's celebrated shakes. If you drive here at lunchtime, you might want to allow extra time to find a parking space. There are metered spaces on both sides of the street, but they're often filled. Plan to circle the block a time or two.

## Mallard's Restaurant
**$, no credit cards • 101 Sanders Ferry Rd., Hendersonville • (615) 822-4668**

For Southern-style plate lunches and a lake view, eat at Mallard's in Hendersonville. This family-style restaurant has been around more than 20 years; owner Kevin Berry purchased it in 1989. It's at the corner of Sanders Ferry and Gallatin Pike, and nearly every seat has a nice view. Choose from about seven meat entrees, including meat loaf and fried chicken, and about 15 vegetables, including the always-popular squash casserole, spinach casserole and green beans. If you know what's good, you'll be sure to get some pinto beans, because (as any Southerner knows) they are perfect with the fried corn bread, or any kind of corn bread for that matter. On Fridays after 5 PM, Mallard's has all-you-can-eat catfish with fries, cole slaw and hush puppies for $8.50. Mallard's is open for breakfast and lunch daily, and serves dinner Tuesday through Friday.

## Mallard's Restaurant
**$ • 3803 Dickerson Pk. • (615) 860-4211**

Although it has the same name as the Mallard's in Hendersonville, this Mallard's is independently owned by David Vaughn. The two restaurants are not affiliated, but you wouldn't know that by comparing menus. This Mallard's serves traditional meat-and-three meals just like the other one. Choose one of about six entrees, such as roast beef, steak and gravy and catfish, and three of the 12 vegetables and side dishes — perhaps turnip greens, deviled eggs, white beans or applesauce. Rolls and corn bread complete the meal, and if you have room, you might try some of the homemade pie or cobbler. The breakfast menu has the basics, including eggs, bacon, sausage and country ham. Open for breakfast, lunch and dinner daily.

## The Mason Jar
**$ • 750 W. Main St., Hendersonville • (615) 822-0288**

To quote The Mason Jar's Norris Davidson (who is quoting Channel 4's Bill Hall), his place is "a little hole in the wall." Davidson, who owns this tiny meat-and-three with his wife Ruby, has found that a restaurant doesn't have to be big to be a big hit. Including the kitchen area, The Mason Jar takes up only about 1,000 square feet of space; it seats about 75. On the walls are photos of some of the country music celebrities who have taken a shine to The Mason Jar's country cooking — artists like Lorrie Morgan, Bobby Bare, Ronnie McDowell and John Anderson.

Open Tuesday through Friday for lunch only, The Mason Jar offers five or six meat choices daily. Favorites are roast beef, baked chicken and chicken casserole. They come with two or three vegetables and homemade flapjack corn bread cooked on a grill. Mason Jar meals are best washed down with some of the restaurant's "world-famous" iced tea. Regulars know that for dessert, the lemon icebox pie, coconut cream pie and banana pudding can't be beat.

## McCabe Pub
**$ • 4410 Murphy Rd. • (615) 269-9406**

The casual and friendly McCabe Pub is a combination neighborhood pub and sports bar. It's known for great hamburgers, lots of good vegetables (mashed potatoes, green beans, squash casserole, broccoli casserole, sweet potato casserole and steamed veggies to name a few) and great desserts (Hershey Syrup cake, blackberry crunch, sour cream coconut cake and more). The home-cooked plate lunches and dinners, with entrees like fried catfish, pork chops and meat loaf and your choice of vegetables, satisfy nearby Sylvan Park families, couples and singles and lure out-of-the-neighborhood regulars as well, including the Music Row set. See our Nightlife chapter for more on the sports bar scene.

## Monell's
**$$ • 1235 Sixth Ave. N. • (615) 248-4747**
**$$ • corner of 6th Ave. and Church St., downtown • (615) 248-4744**

At Monell's, you sit at a big table with other guests and enjoy an all-you-can-eat family-style meal. Guests pass bowls and platters of food around the table and serve themselves. The food is Southern, with entrees like meat loaf, fried chicken and country-fried steak, plenty of fresh vegetables, home-cooked side dishes, biscuits and corn muffins. Monell's is in Germantown, in a renovated Victorian house next door to The Mad Platter. It's open for lunch and dinner Tuesday through Saturday, lunch Sunday and breakfast Saturday. Lunch is $8 and dinner is $11, including beverage, tax and dessert. By the time you leave, you may have found a new friend or two. Monell's doesn't serve alcohol, but you can bring your own wine. Seating is first come, first served. The 6th and Church location was scheduled to open in August 1999.

## The Pie Wagon
**$ • 118 12th Ave. S. • (615) 256-5893**

This cozy little diner near Music Row has been a favorite among locals for more than 30 years. It's open for breakfast and lunch only — hours are 6 AM to 2 PM — and it packs them in. Don't be surprised if a stranger asks to sit down at your table, if there happens to be a seat available.

The inexpensive, cafeteria-style cuisine is simple home cookin', or comfort food, as some people call it. Lunch entrees might include fried chicken, meat loaf or salmon croquettes, with vegetables/side dishes like real mashed potatoes, green beans, stewed tomatoes, greens and macaroni and cheese. There's also cornbread and homemade desserts. And the

friendly counter workers will treat you like family.

## Rotier's Restaurant
**$ • 2413 Elliston Pl. • (615) 327-9892**

Best known for its hamburgers and chocolate milk shakes, Rotier's ("row-TEARS") is really an old-fashioned meat-and-three. It's been around since 1945 and is one of Nashville's most beloved restaurants. Walking into Rotier's, you'll find yourself in a building that was once a carriage house for a ritzy West End home. Vintage upholstered booths line the walls of the dimly lit space, the TV is always on, and the cash register seems to never stop ringing. A few solo diners or beer drinkers usually sit at the counter bar, while booths full of Vandy students and white-collar and blue-collar workers keep the noise level high and the restaurant staff busy.

If you come for a burger, you won't be disappointed. If it's your first time here, however, you might be surprised to see that the burgers are on bread (some are on French bread), not buns, so they look more like sandwiches. Rotier's cheeseburger, by the way, has been voted best in town by *Nashville Scene* readers year after year. Not only is it scrumptious, it's a bargain at $3.20 to $3.50. To get the full Rotier's experience, you must have a chocolate shake with your burger.

If you're in the mood for some more serious home cooking, Rotier's will not disappoint. This family-owned restaurant has the meat-and-three (or, in this case, the meat-and-two) down to a science. "Meats of the Day" include hamburger steak on Monday, country-fried steak on Tuesday, fried chicken breast on Wednesday, meat loaf on Thursday and salmon croquettes on Friday; all are accompanied by two side items plus rolls or corn bread. Rotier's also has several specials, such as chicken breast, spaghetti and a small sirloin steak. For breakfast, you can order all the traditional country favorites. The eatery is open Monday through Saturday.

## Swett's Restaurant
**$ • 2725 Clifton Ave. • (615) 329-4418**
**$ • Farmer's Market, 900 Eighth Ave. N. • (615) 742-0699**

Swett's is legendary for its meat-and-three

RESTAURANTS • 121

meals. This family-owned restaurant has been serving up Southern food since 1954. Diners choose their meat-and-three in a cafeteria line. Entrees like fried chicken, ham and roast beef, and a variety of vegetables, including potatoes, corn and beans, fill the plates. A meat-and-three meal wouldn't be complete without corn bread, and Swett's has some of the best. Swett's is open daily. The Farmer's Market location serves lunch only.

### Sylvan Park Restaurant
**$, no credit cards • 4502 Murphy Rd.**
**• (615) 292-9275**
**$, no credit cards • 2201 Bandywood Dr.**
**• (615) 292-6449**

Sylvan Park is one of the best meat-and-threes in town, which explains why it's always busy. It has been serving Nashvillians for decades; the current owner, James Lynn Chandler, purchased it in 1965.

Sylvan Park's plate lunches and dinners are served from 10:30 AM to 7:30 PM Monday through Saturday. Entrees vary daily, but there are usually choices like fried chicken, meat loaf, turkey and dressing, roast beef and country-fried steak. They're all accompanied by three vegetables or side items like potatoes, macaroni and cheese, white beans and pinto beans, plus corn bread or biscuits. The star of the dessert menu is the fabulous chocolate pie, but other favorites are the coconut cream, butterscotch, sweet potato and lemon varieties.

### Varallo's Too
**$, no credit cards • 239 Fourth Ave. N.**
**• (615) 256-1907**

Varallo's Too is run by Todd Varallo, grandson of the legendary Frank Varallo Jr., who for years operated Varallo's on Church Street. Known as Nashville's oldest restaurant, the original location opened in 1907 and was operated by the Varallo family until Frank retired in December 1998, ending a longtime Nashville lunch tradition.

Though Frank and his wife Eva are missed by the daily lunch crowd of politicians, judges, lawyers, business executives and blue-collar workers, Varallo's Too is still serving up the tasty food that helped make the family famous.

The signature item here is "three-way chili,"

which is a combination of chili, spaghetti and a tamale originated by Frank Varallo Sr. back in the '20s. The plate lunches feature your choice of meats and vegetables. Favorites like country-fried steak, meatballs, meat loaf and turkey and dressing are accompanied by fresh "creamed" potatoes, turnip greens, broccoli casserole and squash casserole. Daily entree specials include salmon croquettes on Friday. Homemade peach or blackberry cobbler or banana pudding are among the great ways to end a meal here. If you come for breakfast, you can order what Eva Varallo describes as the best hotcakes in town, along with the usual bacon, eggs and biscuits.

You may have seen the Varallo's brand of chili in grocery stores. Although it bears the family name, the Varallos are no longer associated with it, and the chili isn't the same as what you'll get in the restaurant. Varallo's Too is open weekdays only from 7 AM to 2:30 PM.

# Mexican

### Casa Fiesta Mexican Restaurant
**$ • 1111 Bell Rd. • (615) 731-3918**
### Casa Fiesta Mexican Restaurant 2
**$ • 2615 Elm Hill Pk. • (615) 871-9490**

We have a friend from a border town who swears Casa Fiesta's food is the closest thing he's found to home cooking as he knows it. He eats at the Bell Road restaurant at least once a week. Judging from the often-crowded dining room and waiting area, we guess he's not the only one. Casa Fiesta serves the familiar Mexican combination plates — burritos, fajitas, chimichangas, tacos, tamales — accompanied by plenty of rice and beans. They don't forget the cheese either. If the tasty food and icy cold Margaritas don't bring you back, the affordable prices probably will. Both Casa Fiestas are open daily.

### Chez Jose
**$ • 2323 Elliston Pl. • (615) 320-0107**

Fresh, healthy and delicious California-style Mexican fare is the specialty at Chez Jose ("SHAY-ho-ZAY"), a casual, upbeat Mexican restaurant on Elliston Place near Rotier's and Centennial Park. Open since late '95, Chez Jose has won lots of followers for its fresh approach to Mexican food. It's not Tex-Mex, but Cali-Mex — instead of cooking with lard, Chez Jose cooks spice up the food with fruit juices and other flavorful ingredients.

Choose from chicken, steak, shrimp, fresh catch of the day or grilled veggies to design your own taco, burrito or other favorite entree. For hearty appetites, there's the Mexico City Burrito, filled with grilled chicken and steak, plus salsa crudo, guacamole, beans, rice, sour cream, cheese, tomato, lettuce and onions, for $5.95. For kids, there are Itty Bitty Burritos and Itty Bitty Quesadillas. Be sure to check out the salsa bar, where you can choose from all sorts of salsas.

Chez Jose is open daily and does a brisk lunch business to the beat of Mexican music. At night, classic rock plays while college students and families dine in a more relaxing atmosphere. Margaritas, sangrias and bottled beers are available. If we're lucky, there may be more Chez Joses in Nashville soon.

## Es Fernandos Mexican Restaurant
$ • 4704 Gallatin Pk. • (615) 227-3060

This family-owned restaurant that has been satisfying Nashvillians' cravings for Mexican food since 1970. This ultra-casual Mexican restaurant is known for its spicy chili verde and great quesadillas — tortillas filled with any combination of beans, cheese, chicken, beef and fajita steak folded into neat little squares and warmed just enough to keep it all together. They fit nicely in your hand if you're having lunch on the go in the car. Try them red (mild) or green (hot) for a tasty and inexpensive lunch; they're even better on Mondays, when they're only $1.49 each.

Es Fernandos has plenty of other items on its Sonora-style menu: all sorts of tacos, tostadas, nachos, enchiladas, chimichangas, taquitos and more than 10 kinds of burritos. There are also several combination plates served with beans and rice. Daily specials include Taco Tuesday, Green Burrito Wednesday and Salsa Saturday.

Domestic and Mexican beers are available to wash everything down. While this food is served up fast, it's always cooked fresh. A sign at the drive-through reminds customers that the food isn't prepared until they order. Es Fernandos is open daily.

## La Fiesta of Mexican Food
$ • 436 Murfreesboro Rd.
• (615) 255-0539

Generations of Nashvillians know La Fiesta as the place to go for great Tex-Mex food. Decorated in red and green and accented with piñatas, this casual eatery opened in this spot in 1966.The food hasn't changed much over the years. While other restaurants experiment with trendy food combinations, La Fiesta serves up the no-frills lunch and dinner favorites that customers have come to expect.

There are several affordable dinner combo platters. Chimichangas, fajitas, enchiladas, tacos and quesadillas arrive on a sizzling hot plate with plenty of beans and rice. The chile rellenos, stuffed with ground beef and cheese, and the chalupas, with meat, beans and melted cheese with lettuce and avocado dip on top of a corn tortilla, are popular. If you're looking for something on the light side, try the grilled chicken salad topped with honey-mustard dressing.

Open Monday through Saturday, La Fiesta has a full bar, complete with a selection of Mexican beers. Reservations are accepted for large groups.

## La Hacienda Taqueria No. 1
$ • 2615 Nolensville Pk.
• (615) 256-6142
## La Hacienda Taqueria No. 2
$ • 5560 Nolensville Pk.
• (615) 833-3716
## La Hacienda Taqueria No. 3
$ • 1019 Gallatin Pk., Madison
• (615) 868-8327

La Hacienda, a Mexican grocery store, tortilla factory and restaurant, serves up what may be the most authentic Mexican food in Music City. Once you try the delicious, freshly prepared tacos and burritos, you'll never want to return to Taco Bell.

La Hacienda is owned by the Yepez family, who sought to create an authentic Mexican restaurant where customers can feel at home. They opened the original 60-seat location in 1992 next to the grocery store and tortilla factory and later expanded it to seat 250. The casual, bustling dining room is packed at lunchtime with workers enjoying a quick Mexican food fix. If you're dining alone, it's entertaining to sit at the lunch counter and watch the busy cooks expertly prepare the meals.

Lunch or dinner here is a treat. The burritos are pretty famous. They're filled with beans, your choice of meat (chicken, beef, pork, Mexican sausage, tripe, tongue), onions, cilantro, avocado and salsa. Tacos are just as good. We're partial to the chicken tacos — perfect little soft tortillas topped with flavorful shredded chicken, diced onions, fresh cilantro and accompanied by an avocado slice, lime wedge and green and red sauce. "*Muy delicioso*," and they're only 99¢ each. There are several combination platters, including the spicy rotisserie chicken served with rice, beans, corn or flour tortillas and a salad. After your meal, visit the grocery store, where you can pick up a package of tortillas made at La Hacienda Tortilleria. You might even been inspired to take home a Mexican sombrero or piñata. All locations are open daily.

### La Paz Restaurante Y Cantina
**$$ • 3808 Cleghorn Ave.**
**• (615) 383-5200**

La Paz combines creative Mexican fare with a more upscale atmosphere than you find at most Mexican restaurants. Inside it's warm and cozy, even though the rooms are open and spacious and, especially at lunch, somewhat noisy. At night, when the lights are dimmed, you can enjoy a romantic dinner here.

There are a handful of these restaurants in the Southeast. We've eaten at the one in Destin, Florida, and have found the food and service consistently good. You'll find lots of tasty Southwestern and Mexican items on the menu. All foods, including the green tomatillo salsa and spicy red salsa that arrive with your chips when you're seated, are made fresh. La Paz serves traditional favorites — burritos, fajitas, tamales and the like — but often puts a creative spin on them. The California quesadilla, for example, is a pesto tortilla with fresh spinach, pico de gallo, Monterey Jack cheese, guacamole and sour cream. Most menu items are priced between $5.95 and $16.95. La Paz has a full bar, and all imported beers are Mexican. The Margaritas are good. Try the Texas variety — all the good stuff in the regular drink, plus orange juice and orange liqueur.

La Paz is open daily. Reservations are accepted only for parties of eight or more.

### Las Palmas
**$ • 5511 Charlotte Pk.**
**• (615) 352-0313**
**$ • 1400 Antioch Pk., Antioch**
**• (615) 831-0863**
**$ • 15560 Old Hickory Blvd.**
**• (615) 831-0432**
**$ • 803 Two Mile Pkwy., Goodlettsville**
**• (615) 851-7315**
**$ • 1905 Hayes St.**
**• (615) 322-9588**
**$ • 2000 Mallory Ln., Franklin**
**• (615) 771-7014**
**$ • 110 Imperial Blvd., Hendersonville**
**• (615) 264-1919**

Since the Charlotte Pike location opened in 1990, Las Palmas has continued to expand. Now Music City is practically covered with these casual Mexican eateries, which are owned by three Hispanic families who really know how to tempt your taste buds.

Although the line for dinner sometimes extends out the door, customers never have to wait too long for a table. Once you've ordered, don't be surprised if your meal arrives just when you're getting into that Margarita and basket of chips with salsa. What to choose? The Chili Colorado is good — beef tips fried in a red sauce served with beans, rice and tortillas. And you can't go wrong with the quesadillas, chile rellenos and fajitas. The lunchtime favorite is the No. 1: beans, chile rellenos, a taco and guacamole salad. There are 25 dinner combination plates to choose from. All Las Palmas are open daily.

### Rio Bravo Cantina
**$$ • 3015 West End**
**• (615) 329-1745**
**$$ • 1705 Gallatin Pk., Madison**
**• (615) 868-2688**
**$$ • 1634 Service Merchandise Blvd., Franklin • (615) 309-0889**
**$$ • 801 N.W. Broad St., Murfreesboro**
**• (615) 867-3110**

The always-reliable Rio Bravo has been a Nashville favorite for years. The original location was on West End. A lively fiesta atmosphere, border-town cantina decor and freshly prepared meals make it popular with those just looking for a place to hang out with friends as well as those with an appetite for some good food. Rio Bravo, by the way, makes some of the best chips and salsa in town, but be sure to leave room for delicious fajitas, tasty black bean soup, pollo con queso or your favorite combo platter.

The patio, almost always packed, is the happening place here, especially around happy hour. Umbrella-topped patio tables strung with colorful lights fill up fast and make an excellent spot to enjoy a frozen Margarita and rejoice that you're not sitting in West End traffic.

If the weather doesn't permit patio dining, there are several comfortable dining rooms inside. On weekends, you might find squeezing your way through the often wall-to-wall (mostly single) bodies a challenge. The Sunday brunch features more than 50 items.

## U.S. Border Cantina
**$ • 7105 U.S. Hwy. 70 S.**
**• (615) 646-4100**

If the interior of this Bellevue restaurant seems vaguely familiar, it may be because the building used to house a Pizza Inn. That has long been forgotten by most area residents, and this place doesn't have anything to do with pizza now. A welcome addition to the skimpy list of restaurants in this part of town, U.S. Border Cantina has some of the freshest and tastiest authentic Mexican dishes in town. They purchase all produce locally and make a fresh batch of salsa each morning. No canned refried beans either. Owner Jose Naranjo, who has been in the restaurant business for two decades, also has an exclusive line of spices that he uses here.

U.S. Border Cantina has the familiar combo plates with beans and rice but has added some interesting and unique specials to the menu. Shrimp enchiladas, grilled salmon and the pork, chicken or shrimp Paisano Tamales are among the more unusual items. It seems that at least one person in our party is always enticed by the Palomino — enchiladas topped with white sauce. A favorite off the traditional list is enchiladas verdes, three chicken enchi-

ladas covered with white cheese and green sauce, accompanied by rice and beans. There are also some vegetarian-friendly selections. Those who want their Mexican food spicy may find this fare a little on the mild side. There are always affordable lunch and dinner specials on the weekends. Margaritas and Mexican beers are in plentiful supply.

# Pizza

## DaVinci's Gourmet Pizza
**$-$$ • 1812 Hayes St. • (615) 329-8098**

DaVinci's is a great pizza place located in an old renovated house on Hayes Street. Once you taste the fresh, delicious gourmet pizzas, you'll think twice before ordering from one of the national franchises. There are many pizzas to choose from here. The "DaVinci" has tomato sauce, Mozzarella and provolone cheeses, Italian sausage, roasted red peppers and onions. There is also a bleu cheese and spinach pizza, and shrimp and scallop, barbecue, Southwestern and Hawaiian varieties, and you're not likely to find a potato pizza or oysters Rockefeller pizza anywhere else in town. There are plenty of others too.

DaVinci's also makes fresh pesto sauce, which can be substituted for the red pizza sauce. Select your own favorite toppings to create a custom pizza if you like. Vegetables range from black olives to red cabbage, and there are at least eight kinds of cheeses, all the usual meats and a variety of special toppings such as capers, roasted chicken, smoked oysters and artichoke hearts.

Domestic and imported beers are available, and for dessert there's Snickers pie. DaVinci's is open Wednesday through Friday for lunch and nightly for dinner.

## Pizza Perfect
**$ • 4002 Granny White Pk.**
**• (615) 297-0345**
**$ • 1602 21st Ave. S. • (615) 329-2757**
**$ • 3571 Clofton Dr. • (615) 646-7877**

The appropriately named Pizza Perfect has been a favorite for years. Iranian Raouf Mattin opened the Granny White location in 1984, and found a devoted following; it's especially

Photo: Cindy Stooksbury Guier

Sunset Grill's patio is a hot spot for lunch in the summertime.

popular with students from Vanderbilt, Belmont and David Lipscomb. Mattin's former partners, Amir and Ali Arab, own the 21st Avenue store (right in the heart of Vanderbilt) and in 1997 opened the Bellevue location in the small strip shopping center off Old Harding Pike on Clofton.

Pizza Perfect makes delicious pizzas with all sorts of yummy toppings. The round pizzas come in 12-, 14- and 16-inch versions, while the rectangular Sicilian comes in 10-by-14-inch and 16-by-16-inch sizes. We like the Fantasy Pizza, which has pesto sauce, sun-dried tomatoes, roasted garlic and feta cheese, and the Perfect Pizza, the perfect combination of pepperoni, sausage, mushrooms, onion, green pepper and black olives — a 14-inch medium is about $11.75; it's $11.99 for Sicilian style. Pizza Perfect also has calzones, sub sandwiches, spaghetti, manicotti, lasagna and salads.

# Pub Food

### Big River Grille & Brewing Works
$$ • 111 Broadway • (615) 251-4677
This microbrewery and restaurant offers a half-dozen ales, along with such pub fare as homemade sausages, California-style pizzas, pulled pork barbecue, grilled chicken, pasta and sandwiches. There's also a bar and pool room.

### Ireland's
$$ • 204 21st Ave. S.
• (615) 327-2967
From 1947 to 1983 the Bush family operated Ireland's at this very same location. In late 1997 Nashvillians rejoiced when Steve Bush reopened the popular eatery. Once known for its "stake and biskets," Ireland's now serves "steak and biscuits," as well as other Irish and American favorites. Be sure to end your meal with the signature fudge pie.

Convenient to Vandy, Music Row, Hillsboro Village and Green Hills, the cozy and friendly restaurant is a favorite with he college crowd, business workers and families. It's open daily for lunch and dinner.

### Market Street Brewery & Public House
$$ • 134 Second Ave. N.
• (615) 259-9611
You may have sampled bottled Market Street beer, which is available around town as well as regionally. There are many more varieties of it — from lager to nut brown ale to dark — on tap here, at Nashville's first brewpub. (There's even one brew that tastes a lot like vanilla cream soda, if you've got a sweet tooth.) The menu is heavy on the appetizers and sandwiches. The crab cakes are a spicy treat, and the Baron o' Beef sandwich makes a hearty accompaniment to the beer of your choice.

## Seanachie Irish Pub & Restaurant
$$ • 327 Broadway • (615) 726-20006

Once you're inside the Seanachie, you might very easily picture yourself in jolly ol' Dublin. (You'd never guess that this was once the site of a nightclub where males impersonated female country stars.) This old-fashioned pub is largely owned and operated by real, honest-to-goodness Irishmen, and you'll discover many of the same among the regulars.

They clean the lines on the beer taps once a week, which is a very good thing, as a Guinness-loving friends of ours has demonstrated (he's actually Scottish, but that's another story). In addition to Guinness, you can get Harp and Bass on tap as well as Seanachie's own lighter brew.

As for the food, it's hearty, with an emphasis on meat and taters. The beef and Guinness stew is rich and savory, the potato-and-leek soup is a creamy delight, and the vegetable boxty (vegetables folded into a crepe-like potato pancake) and scallop-and-mushroom pie are lighter alternatives that will still fill you up.

# Sandwiches

## Bread & Company
$ • 106 Page Rd. • (615) 352-7323
$ • 4105 Hillsboro Rd. • (615) 292-7323
$ • 18 Cadillac Dr., Brentwood
• (615) 309-8330

Bread & Company introduced many Nashvillians to European-style breads — hearth-baked, crusty and delicious! Not only does this bakery have superb breads and gourmet packaged food items (read about them in our Shopping chapter), but it also has delicious sandwiches and take-home fare.

For lunch, the herb-roasted turkey sandwich is a favorite. Also good are the portobello mushroom sandwich with fresh spinach, provolone, gold peppers and lemon-oregano vinaigrette on farm bread. But wait, there's also the tarragon chicken salad, the low-fat tuna, roast beef with horseradish-chive mayo. You'll probably return often.

Salad selections include the Strawberry Fields, a flavorful concoction of fresh strawberries, avocados, pecans and poppy-seed vinaigrette. The low-fat couscous with sun-dried tomato vinaigrette is a healthy and filling salad choice. Take-away dinners averaging $10 or $11 await you in the glass-enclosed case. Wouldn't poached salmon, penne pasta with eggplant or a chicken pot pie with rosemary sauce, shiitake mushrooms and sun-dried tomatoes be a welcome sight at your dinner table?

## Cafe Coco
$$$ • 210 Louise Ave. • (615) 321-2626

A former coffeehouse, Cafe Coco is now a 24-hour restaurant specializing in Italian and vegetarian fare. During the week, it's usually a busy lunch spot for office workers and employees at the nearby hospitals. Its location off Elliston Place behind TGI Friday's makes it the perfect place for an after-show bite for the Exit/In crowd. Favorite menu items include the Waldorf Elliston Salad, and the Avocado Garden sandwich, a yummy combination of sundried tomatoes, onions, mushrooms, peppers, garlic, guacamole and creamy Swiss cheese grilled between slices of wheat bread. There's also a good selection of coffee drinks. Cafe Coco delivers to the downtown–MetroCentre–I-440–Wedgewood area.

## Noshville
$$ • 1918 Broadway • (615) 329-NOSH

Nashvillians enthusiastically welcomed the arrival of Noshville, an authentic Jewish deli that became an instant favorite. Noshville serves tasty, high-quality food in a lively atmosphere. It's a fun place, and the sandwiches are huge. You really don't need to order the "We Dare Ya" size, unless you're feeding two or haven't eaten in a week or so. Trust us on that one.

With most regular-size sandwiches priced around $7.95, you'll pay a little more here than at other sandwich places, but you definitely get your money's worth. Meats are piled high. A bowl of kosher pickles on the table makes everything complete. Noshville also serves a selection of soups (including matzah ball soup with noodles), salads and entrees like homemade meat loaf, corned beef and cabbage, and pot roast served with a vegetable and choice of potato. There are several smoked fish platters available, and plenty of juices, specialty coffees and desserts (New York cheesecake and rugalach cookies, to name two) on the menu. Noshville is open daily for breakfast, lunch and dinner. (For more on the early-morning munchies at Noshville, see this chapter's Breakfast section.)

## Porta Via International Café
**$ • 7091 Old Harding Pk.**
**• (615) 662-0063**

Porta Via may be Bellevue's best-kept restaurant secret. Located in a small shopping center just off U.S. Highway 70 in Bellevue, this little deli sells delicious "international" sandwiches and salads. Greek, Italian, Southwestern, Mexican, German and American flavors can all be found on the menu. The restaurant is known for its bolillos (stuffed Spanish baguette sandwiches), muffuletta sandwiches and pita sandwiches filled with a fresh and flavorful mixture of ingredients. Gyros, Reubens, Italian hero sandwiches, Philly cheesesteaks and vegetarian sandwiches are among the many choices. Caesar salads, Mexican chicken salads and antipasto make a nice alternative to sandwiches, and Porta Via also has a variety of "Pastabilities," soups and baked potatoes. There are weekday lunch specials, and there is a limited children's menu. Sweets like tiramisu, baklava, cheesecake and cookies, along with a variety of coffee drinks, make a fine finish to a casual and delicious meal.

Porta Via is open daily. The restaurant delivers to a limited area.

## Provence Breads & Cafe
**$ • 1705 21st Ave. S. • (615) 386-0363**

In addition to baking some heavenly breads, Provence Breads & Cafe sells some delectable sandwiches and soups. Lots of transplanted Europeans mingle at lunch with Hillsboro Village area residents, Music Row workers and Vanderbilt students and workers in the lively cafe. A half-sandwich and a bowl of soup satisfy most lunchtime appetites. The soups are incredibly good. There are two soups du jour, and the choices change daily depending on the produce available at the Farmer's Market.

There are about seven sandwiches, all served on freshly baked bread. Try the oven-roasted chicken sandwich with lavender, fresh rosemary, toasted almonds and a drizzle of balsamic vinaigrette topped with tomato, lettuce, Dijon mustard and mayonnaise. Vegetarians will enjoy the Montecito, a sandwich of California avocado, tomatoes, sprouts, red onion, cucumber, sesame seeds, herb vinaigrette and Vermont cheddar. If you're not in a sandwich mood, try one of the cold salads — maybe the lentil salad or shiitake mushroom and fresh fennel linguine salad. Don't forget to take home a crusty loaf of bread for your evening meal. (For more about Provence Breads & Cafe breads, see our Shopping chapter.)

## Rosko's & The Muncheonette
**$ • 2204 Elliston Pl. • (615) 327-2658**

Not only is Rosko's (which changed its name in 1999 when a new owner took over) a great place to buy magazines, newspapers, greeting cards and cigars, but this little shop also has marvelous sandwiches and other tasty things to eat. They also deliver everything they sell, as long as you're within the downtown–MetroCenter–Music Row–I-440 radius. The Muncheonette does a big lunchtime delivery business. If you want to call in an order but don't have a menu, try the famous Looney Tuna, the Turkey Munch or Chunky Chicken Salad sandwich. Everything's made from scratch, and most sandwiches are available in half and whole sizes. Rosko's also has three kinds of wraps (tortillas filled with various ingredients), homemade soups and great desserts. They do breakfast trays of croissants, biscotti, muffins and bagels and put together good party trays, hors d'oeuvres and box lunches.

It's always packed here at lunchtime, with customers vying for the 15 or so indoor counter seats and 12 outdoor seats. Delivery can take up to an hour, so get your order in before you're ravenous. Rosko's is open daily 7 AM to midnight.

## Sammy B's
**$$ • 26 Music Sq. E. • (615) 256-6600**

Sammy B's is a hangout at lunch and after work for music-business types. There's a large bar, an outdoor courtyard that stays busy in the spring and summer, and a contemporary menu featuring a variety of salads, sandwiches

Some of our finest eateries are in unsuspecting locations.

*Photo: Cathy Summerlin*

and favorites like the smoked chicken quesadillas (known on the menu as "The Usual") and pork barbecue roll-ups.

# Steak

## Jimmy Kelly's
### $$$ • 217 Louise Ave. • (615) 329-4349

Steak lovers have plenty of very good restaurant choices in Nashville, but we would have to give Jimmy Kelly's our nod as the best. Generations of Nashvillians will back us up on that. Jimmy Kelly's has been a favorite since 1934; lots of longtime customers dine here regularly. In a Victorian home not far from Elliston Place, the restaurant oozes Old South charm. The specialty is aged, hand-cut steaks, and the corn cakes are legendary. If you're not in the mood for beef, try the veal chops, lamb chops or fresh fish. Jimmy Kelly's is comfortable, the service is top-notch, and the food is great. What more could you ask for? The restaurant is open for dinner Monday through Saturday. Reservations are recommended.

## Morton's of Chicago
### $$$$$ • 618 Church St. • (615) 259-4558

Nashville's Morton's is one of the best in this restaurant chain, which is known for its fine dining, quality service and elegant atmosphere. Real steak connoisseurs know

Morton's as an excellent choice. When you walk into this restaurant, you'll feel as if you've entered an elegant private club. Dark woods, comfortable leather booths, white tablecloths, dim lights and warm brick set the tone.

Morton's is known for its table-side presentation. The wait staff wheels carts of uncooked vegetables and entrees for viewing. The food is prepared in an open kitchen, in full view of the patrons. The restaurant is known for its huge cuts of prime, aged, grain-fed beef. There is also a good selection of fresh seafood and chicken. Morton's has a comfortable bar and a group dining room. It's open nightly for dinner; reservations are recommended.

### Ruth's Chris Steakhouse
**$$$$$ • 2100 West End Ave.**
**• (615) 320-0163**

When it comes to steaks, Ruth's Chris Steakhouse, a Louisiana-based chain with about 70 restaurants, is a favorite for special occasions and business dinners. The restaurant is known for excellent beef and live Maine lobsters that are flown in daily. There are chicken and fish choices too. The ambience is elegant all around — dimly lit, lots of dark wood, dark burgundy chairs, a brass rail bar. The clientele is equally upscale — lots of business owners and business travelers. Ruth's Chris was voted by the *Robb Report*, a publication geared toward the $750,000-and-up income group, as the No. 1 U.S. restaurant, and its signature dessert, Death by Chocolate, was voted the most decadent dessert. Ruth's Chris is open nightly for dinner. Reservations are recommended.

### Stock-Yard Restaurant
**$$$-$$$$ • 901 Second Ave. N.**
**• (615) 255-6464**

They advertise that you never know who you'll see at the Stock-Yard, and it's true. But this restaurant is often so lively and bustling you may not even notice if Reba or the latest country music chart-topper walks by. Music Row's Buddy Killen opened the Stock-Yard in 1979 and has turned it into one of Nashville's best-known restaurants. He sold it 20 years later to Wayne Fricks and Jerry Terrette.

Located in the building that once served as Nashville's stockyards, it's only natural that this restaurant serves steaks. The Stock-Yard is renowned for excellent certified Angus beef, hand-cut and aged for 38 days before cooking. Lobster and other seafood, chicken, pasta and ribs are among the other menu choices.

The Stock-Yard Restaurant is on the second floor of the building, and there is live country music in the second-floor Studio Lounge. On the first floor is the Bull Pen Lounge, which features live music nightly. On the third floor are the banquet facilities and a fabulous wine room (the wine list here is about five pages). The Stock-Yard is open for dinner every night and for brunch on Sunday. Reservations are accepted but not required.

# Thai

### The Orchid
**$$-$$$ • 73 White Bridge Rd.**
**• (615) 353-9411**

Casually elegant and comfortable, The Orchid is a favorite for Thai food. Tasteful watercolors adorn the white walls, and white tablecloths add an upscale feel. The food here is fresh-tasting and not too spicy, though you can order it extra spicy if you like. The Orchid is in the Paddock Place shopping center across from Target. It's open for lunch Monday through Friday and for dinner nightly.

### Royal Thai
**$$-$$$ • 204 Commerce St.**
**• (615) 256-0312**
**$$-$$$ • 210 Franklin Rd., Brentwood**
**• (615) 376-9695**

This restaurant serves spicy, authentic Thai food in a dark, relaxing environment. Imported spices add authenticity to the recipes, which the chefs brought here from Bangkok. The seafood dishes are especially good. Royal Thai, next to Sbarro's on Commerce, has a good reputation but never seems crowded. The restaurant is open for lunch Monday through Saturday and for dinner seven nights a week.

Knowing that the nightlife scene is ever-changing, with new venues coming and going regularly, we recommend that you check out the weekly *Nashville Scene* for an up-to-the-minute rundown of clubs, bars and restaurants.

# Nightlife

While live music is the star of Nashville's nightlife, the city has plenty of other options for nighttime fun. In fact, there are probably lots more places than you ever imagined.

Nashville has all kinds of after-dark destinations. You can dance the night away at a '70s disco or country dance club, catch a game with the gang at the neighborhood sports bar, contemplate a poem during a coffeehouse poetry reading or relax with friends in a cozy pub or bistro.

We've compiled a list of some of places you can go for a night on the town. Knowing that the nightlife scene is ever-changing, with new venues coming and going regularly, we recommend that you check out the weekly *Nashville Scene* for an up-to-the-minute rundown of clubs, bars and restaurants.

Three things to remember:
• If you're going to drink, do it in moderation.
• The drinking age is 21.
• A designated driver is a good thing — if you don't have one, don't drink.

In this chapter, you'll find descriptions of some of the best-known nightspots as well as some of the newer locations; many of both kinds are covered in Restaurants. If you don't find what you're looking for here, check out our Music City and Restaurants chapters. Unless otherwise noted, the following nightspots do not require a cover charge.

## Bars and Pubs

### The Beer Sellar
**107 Church St. • (619) 254-9464**
This casual beer and cigar bar opened in fall 1996 in the space underneath Hooters on Second Avenue; the entrance faces Church Street. The Beer Sellar has what is likely Nashville's largest selection of — you guessed it — beer: 50 draft beers and about 150 bottled

brands, including many imports from Scotland, England, Ireland and other places. They pour a lot of flavored brews too, including cider, vanilla and cherry. The 175-capacity room is frequented by an eclectic bunch, including college students and the over-60 crowd. The 3 to 7 PM happy hour, featuring pints, brings the after-work crowd. Some come just for the tasty sandwiches or to watch a game on one of the four TVs. Darts, a pool table and foosball also provide amusement. Live entertainment — usually a solo singer with guitar — is often featured on Wednesdays, and a $2 cover might be levied those nights. On Thursdays (two-for-one night), there's a $5 cover after 9 PM. As for cigars, the Beer Sellar has a variety, and you can buy and smoke them here.

### The Bound'ry
**911 20th Ave. S. • (615) 321-3043**
Just a few blocks from Music Row, The Bound'ry's bar is a popular gathering place, usually crowded with the young and single. A cozy yet lively atmosphere, well-made cocktails and an extensive selection of beer and wine make this a good place to gather before dinner or a night on the town. The Bound'ry's also a good place for dinner. Weekends are especially busy. When the weather's nice, you can sit outside.

### Café One Two Three
**123 12th Ave. N. • (615) 255-2233**
Off Broadway, Café One Two Three is a tasteful choice for before- or after-dinner drinks. Lots of wood, mirrors and tables make for a cozy and warm atmosphere. You might want to stay for dinner. Café One Two Three is a favorite among locals.

### The Gold Rush
**2205 Elliston Pl. • (615) 327-2809**
The Gold Rush is a Nashville institution — legendary in some circles. An anchor of Elliston

Place, The Gold Rush is frequented by every-one from celebrities to preppy Vandy students to leather-and-chain–clad rockers. It can get downright rowdy late at night. The Mexican food here is tasty, especially the near-legend-ary bean rolls.

## Jack Legs' Speakeasy and Showcase
### 152 Second Ave. N. • (615) 255-1933

Themed to the "roaring '20s," Jack Legs' has a friendly neighborhood bar feel. The club is located in a spacious long room underneath Mere Bulles and is open only on Friday and Satur-day nights. Jack Legs' features live local and oc-casionally national rock, alternative, jazz and funk bands. There's also a game room where you can go if the music's a bit too loud for you. A great sound system, fantastic bar staff and fun atmosphere make this a nice place to spend at least part of your night on the town. There's usually a $3 cover charge.

## The Merchants
### 401 Broadway • (615) 254-1892

The Merchants offers not only a superb dining experience, but also a cozy bar that's a great spot to hook up with friends before a night on the town. The first floor includes a horseshoe-shaped bar, tile and hardwood floors and lots of exposed brick. It comfort-ably accommodates about 180 people. Booths with windows are an excellent vantage point from which to watch all the action at Fourth and Broadway. The Merchants, which is housed in a renovated turn-of-the-century ho-tel, is known for its wine selection and attracts an upscale crowd of people in their late 20s to early 50s. In spring and fall, The Merchants features the Twilight in the Courtyard music series, presenting live jazz and blues artists on the patio for no cover charge.

## Mulligan's Pub
### 117 Second Ave. N. • (615) 242-8010

This cozy Dublin-style pub in the heart of The District features live traditional and con-temporary Irish folk music as well as Ameri-can music from the '60s to the '90s. We've seen it so packed here that you can barely squeeze in.

## Pub of Love
### 123 12th Ave. N. • (615) 256-5683

This tiny neighborhood pub is just off Broadway, across from 12th and Porter. Dark, hip and laid back, the Pub of Love offers a selection of imported brews. The club occasionally offers late-night live music in the small upstairs space.

## Sammy B's
### 26 Music Sq. E. • (615) 256-6600

Its location on Music Row makes Sammy B's a top pick with the music-business crowd for lunch, after-work drinks, socializing and dinner. The outdoor seating area up front is always crowded during the summer, and there's a good bar and cozy, relaxed seating inside. A lively atmosphere and drink specials keep them coming back.

## Seanachie Irish Pub and Restaurant
### 327 Broadway • (615) 726-2006

If you're searching for an authentic and enormous, not to mention fun, Irish pub, look no further. Seanachie (pronounced "shawn-a-key") Irish Pub and Restaurant, which opened in August 1997 at the corner of Fourth Avenue and Broadway, is a true delight. The Irish own-ers spent more than $1 million on renovations to turn the building into a full-service bar and restaurant. "Seanachie" means "storyteller," and this pub tells the story of Ireland. From its cobblestone floors to the Irish antiques and gas lanterns, Seanachie is Irish through and

**INSIDERS' TIP**

**For nightlife of a different kind, book a spot on a nighttime canoe float at Radnor Lake. Call (615) 373-3467 for information.**

Photo: Cathy Summerlin

The Hard Rock Cafe is a popular tourist destination on Broadway, near the river.

through. The owners brought artists from Ireland to help re-create the authentic Irish pub atmosphere. The attention to detail — in both the furnishings and the menu — is impressive. The 200-seat pub features lots of cozy nook seating and a quiet writer's room decorated with commissioned portraits of Irish authors.

At the bar, you'll find a plentiful supply of Irish beers and whiskeys. In addition to a well-stocked bar, Seanachie has some great food. The menu features contemporary Irish foods, including traditional Irish favorites, seafood, lots of potato combos and delectable desserts like potato pudding and truffles.

Seanachie features regularly scheduled live entertainment. You may want to mark your calendar to come here on St. Patrick's Day (March 17). It's sure to be a blowout. The pub prepares for it for months. On September 17,

they even celebrate "Halfway to St. Patrick's Day."

## The Sherlock Holmes Pub
### 206 Elliston Pl. • (615) 327-1047

The Sherlock Holmes Pub is a traditional British pub owned by Terry and Margaret Widlake, England natives who now make their homes in Nashville. Sherlock's has plenty of imported beers on tap, including Guinness, Bass and New Castle Brown Ale, plus such traditional British fare as fish and chips, Cornish pasty, and steak and kidney pie. The pub also serves traditional English teas and scones.

On the Elliston Place Rock Block, in between Rosko's and Exit/In, Sherlock's is a favorite of music-business people and is known to draw its share of celebrities — from Pink Floyd to Kathy Mattea to U.S. Senator Fred Thompson. The crowd is pretty diverse, though, and includes everyone from young families to college students. On Friday and Saturday nights, the pub presents live music, mostly Celtic but sometimes blues or jazz. There's no cover charge, but they do pass the hat for the band. Sherlock's is open 11 AM to 1 AM Monday through Saturday and serves lunch Tuesday through Saturday.

### Tin Angel
**3201 West End Ave. • (615) 298-3444**
This neighborhood restaurant and bar at the corner of 32nd Avenue and West End is a good place to sip a glass of wine and nibble on appetizers — maybe some delicious Brie and bread. Bar stools line the bar, and there are a few small booths nearby that are just right for more intimate conversations. Both the bar and restaurant areas are quiet and usually not crowded. In winter the fireplace up front lends a warm glow and extra-cozy feeling. Casual and romantic, it's a great spot for a date.

### Your Way Café
**515 Second Ave. S. • (615) 256-9682**
This friendly nightspot draws a mixed gay crowd but caters mostly to women. Friday and Saturday nights feature either live music, dance or karaoke. There's a full dinner menu too. There's a $5 cover on live music and karaoke nights.

# Dance Clubs

### The Klub
**207 Broadway • (615) 244-8173**
The Klub, at the corner of Second Avenue and Broadway is a rock 'n' roll bar featuring live music upstairs and downstairs. There's no cover downstairs, but the charge for the bands upstairs is $3 to $5. This bar is popular with locals and tourists, and the age range here spans the gamut: you might find vacationing grandparent–types mingling with mohawk-sporting twentysomethings. Sandwiches and pizzas are the main menu items.

### The Church
**629 Third Ave. S. • (615) 252-4872**
One of the first things late-nighters will notice about Nashville nightlife is that there isn't a whole lot to do late, late at night. One option for serious night owls is The Church, open Friday and Saturday. No, it's not a church service. This after-hours club in a historic church near downtown Nashville has been called the hippest late-night gathering spot in town. The club doesn't even open until 2 AM, and it stays open until 7 in the morning. Hundreds of mostly 18- to 40-year-olds pack in to dance the night and the early morning away to music from the '70s to the '90s. Downstairs is a game room with pool tables and TVs. Outside, on the 600-square-foot deck overlooking the Nashville skyline, you can get some fresh air and, if you're hungry, re-energize with a Bishop Burger.

This is a BYOB club; the bartender sells sodas, juices and other mixers. If you bring beer, they'll provide a bucket of ice for you to keep it chilled. Security is pretty tight here. Owner Tommy Smith, who owned the Elliston Square nightclub in the '80s, keeps a tight rein on the crowd — anyone who even looks like he or she might cause trouble doesn't get in the door. Admission is $5.

Smith also rents The Church for parties, showcases, video shoots, wedding receptions and other events.

### The Chute Complex
**2535 Franklin Rd. • (615) 297-4571**
This Melrose-area club has been here since 1983, drawing a mixed gay crowd. There are five bars in the complex, including a dance club and the Silver Stirrup piano lounge. Entertainment includes recorded tunes played by a DJ, occasional female-impersonator shows and karaoke. There's usually no cover charge, but a $3 to $5 cover may apply for special shows. Hours are 5 PM to 3 AM nightly.

### The Connection of Nashville
**901 Cowan St. • (615) 742-1166**
This place packs 'em in on weekends, when you can find more than a thousand here dancing and partying in three different bars: the country bar, dance bar and show bar. The Connection is known as a gay club, but it's not strictly a gay club. It has a devoted following of locals as well as regulars who come from as far away as Alabama and Kentucky to dance the night away. The country bar is open

nightly and the dance bar, featuring retro music, and show bar, featuring drag shows, are open weekends. There is a $5 cover charge on weekends.

## Graham Central Station
### 128 Second Ave. N. • (615) 251-9593

A sort of one-stop entertainment destination, Graham Central Station offers seven clubs under one roof. There's something for everyone here — from dance clubs to an arcade. Owned by Texas-based Graham Bros. Entertainment, this multilevel entertainment complex next to the Wildhorse Saloon opened in August 1997.

Each club has a different theme and atmosphere. **Bell Bottoms** has a lighted dance floor, boogie cages and a DJ playing disco hits from the '70s, '80s and '90s. **Party on the Roof** is an open-air rooftop bar overlooking the Cumberland; there's live music here on weekends. **Starz** is a karaoke bar featuring six singers and dancers. **Ivory Cats** is a sing-along dueling-piano bar — you probably have to see it to understand. With a boat-shaped dance floor and an ocean mural, **Piranha's**, a Top-40 dance club, will put you in a beach party state of mind. **Metropolis** offers live music and pool tables. Though not owned by Graham Central station, the first level of the club also features the **Second & Goal** sports cafe.

**The Zone**, down in the basement, is a family entertainment-center kind of place, with approximately 8,000 square feet of space filled with interactive videos, virtual reality games and other fun for all ages. There's no cover charge here, but there is usually a cover charge for the rest of Graham Central Station — from $4 to $7, depending on the day of the week.

A lot of local business people stop by for the Friday happy hour. The regular Friday and Saturday crowd is mainly well-dressed 25- to 45-year-olds.

## Have A Nice Day Café
### 217 Second Ave. S. • (615) 726-2233

The yellow, have-a-nice-day smiley face from the '70s is the mascot of this restaurant/dance club, which opened in June 1997. It's all '70s-themed, from the colorful lava lamps to the music to the caricatures of movie stars

and rock stars adorning the walls. There's a disco dance floor too. At 9 each night, the club moves the tables and chairs out of the way to make room for dancing. The signature beverage here is the Happy Bowl, a combination of Kool-Aid and pure grain alcohol served in a fish bowl, and yes, they serve a lot of them. The first one is $13, and refills are $9. During Friday's happy hour, from 5 to 7 PM, you can get a Happy Bowl for $10. Music is all '70s, except for Wednesday nights, when the club ventures into the '80s. There is a cover charge Wednesday through Saturday, ranging from $5 to $7, depending on the night. Those under age 21 can visit on Wednesdays, but their cover is $10

# Country Music Clubs

## Denim & Diamonds
### Madison Sq. Shopping Center, 950 Gallatin Rd. • (615) 868-1557

Denim & Diamonds is part of a chain of clubs in the United States by the same name owned by Graham Bros. Entertainment. This 32,000-square-foot club is actually four clubs in one, offering everything from boot scootin' country line dancing to '70s disco. Denim & Diamonds is the country dance club; if you've never tried line dancing, you can sign up for lessons a couple of nights a week. In **Bell Bottoms Disco Club**, a DJ plays dance hits from the '70s and '80s. **Cocomos** is a Top-40 dance club where you can also participate in all sorts of wacky contests, such as a build-your-own-bikini contest, and vie for big prizes. **Cheers** is a karaoke bar where you can pick from a wide selection of songs, then stand up and make a fool out of yourself as you sing them. One cover charge gets you into all four clubs.

The cover charge is usually $6. Sunday night is for teens only, and the cover is $7.

What to wear? Almost anything goes here, but men will need to don socks if they're wearing sandals, tuck in their shirts and leave the cutoff shirts at home.

## Rodeos Dance Club
### 2265 Murfreesboro Rd. • (615) 361-9777

This 9,500-square-foot dance club ropes

them in with progressive country music dance tunes, free admission for women and drink specials. Country dance lessons are given on Sundays and Thursdays, and on Fridays, the Music City Swing Dance club gives swing dance lessons. The cover charge for men is $5. Parking is free. Rodeos draws a mostly local crowd, but does attract quite a few tour groups in the summer. On a crowded night, there could be as many as 700 or 800 urban cowboys and cowgirls here.

## Silverado Dance Hall & Saloon
**1204 Murfreesboro Rd.**
**• (615) 361-9922**

Wranglers and boots aren't required, but you'll fit right in here if that's what you're wearing. Hundreds of country dance lovers come to scoot their boots at Silverado, a dance club with a big local following. The large club, on Murfreesboro Road near Briley Parkway, holds

about 500 people. It draws all ages, but the later it gets, the younger the crowd. The music is loud. The cover charge is usually $5, but there are lots of specials, including ladies night, college night and drink specials, that allow you to get in and party without spending too much. The club is open Wednesday through Sunday. On Monday evenings, the Nashville Swing Dance Club meets here and gives swing dance lessons.

## Wildhorse Saloon
**120 Second Ave. N. • (615) 256-WILD,**
**(615) 251-1000**

Wildhorse Saloon is a little bit of everything — dance club, restaurant, tourist attraction, concert venue and TV studio. Its location in the heart of The District makes it a popular place for tourists and locals. The multilevel nightspot has a 3,300-square-foot dance floor and state-of-the art sound, lighting and video

Photo: Nashville CVB/Mark Tucker

Second Avenue, a.k.a. The District, is bustling at night.

systems. Fifteen-minute dance lessons are available on weekdays from 4 to 9 PM and on Saturday and Sunday from 1 to 9 PM. The Wildhorse features live music nightly. A rotating schedule of "house bands" brings in some good regional touring groups, some of which have gone on to the big time. Concerts by name country acts are scheduled each Friday night; tickets usually cost $8 to $12. Thursday and Sunday, a $3 cover charge applies at 5 PM. Saturday night, the cover is $6, but you can skip it if you're in before 5 PM.

The Wildhorse also has a lunch and dinner menu, including the specialty "Unbridled Barbeque," plus salads, desserts and a kids' menu. Food is served from 11 AM to 10 PM, but the entertainment and dancing continues until 2 in the morning.

# Dinner Theater/ Comedy Club

## Chaffin's Barn Dinner Theater
**8204 Tenn. Hwy. 100 • (615) 646-9977, (800) 282-BARN**

Established in 1967, Chaffin's Barn is Nashville's oldest professional theater. Feast on the all-you-can-eat buffet, topped off by the house specialty, Southern-style bread pudding, then enjoy a Broadway play. Chaffin's presents a variety of productions, including comedies, musicals and mysteries (see our chapter on The Arts). The MainStage Theatre seats 300; its stage descends from the ceiling. The BackStage Theatre seats 60. Shows are presented in-the-round, so every seat has a good view. Tuesdays through Saturdays, doors open at 6 PM, and the buffet is open until 7:30. The actors and actresses serve as the wait staff. The show starts at 8. There is one Sunday matinee per production. Reservations are required and weekends usually sell out, so call early if you want to attend on a Friday or Saturday. "Dressy casual" is the dress code.

Chaffin's has a full-service bar. The theater is smoke-free, but smoking is permitted in the bar and lobby. Chaffin's is open year-round except major holidays and the first two weeks of January.

## Zanies Comedy Showplace
**2025 Eighth Ave. S.**
**• (615) 269-0221**

Laughing is good for you. If you don't believe it, spend a few hours at Zanies, and see if you don't feel great after the show. No matter who's headlining, you're bound to get plenty of laughs. We've never *not* had a good laugh here.

Near Wedgewood Avenue, across the street from Douglas Corner in the Eighth Avenue antique district, Zanies, Nashville's oldest comedy club, presents nationally known comedians as well as up-and-coming talent. Past performers include Jay Leno, Jerry Seinfeld and Jeff Foxworthy. Photographs of funny people who have appeared at the club line the walls at the entrance. The place is packed when the bigger names appear, so you'll want to get your tickets early and show up early to get a good seat. Tickets usually range from $7 to $10, although special shows cost more.

# Coffeehouses

## Bean Central
**2817 West End Ave., Ste. 109**
**• (615) 321-8530**
**3370 Hillsboro Pk. • (615) 386-0244**

Bean Central, Nashville's first "Internet cafe," roasts its own coffee beans, sells packaged coffee and prepares an assortment of tasty coffee drinks. Tucked among a collection of mostly upscale retail establishments and restaurants at West End's Park Place shopping center, Bean Central is a relaxing spot to enjoy a cappuccino, latte or just a regular cup of joe. A side room with cool piped-in music, large tables, comfy chairs and computers with Internet access invites you to linger and have a second cup. During the day, college students can be found here poring over textbooks and notes or surfing the 'Net, while 9-to-5ers catch up on the latest news as they get a quick caffeine boost. If you're in a hurry, drop by for a to-go cup. Bean Central also has a tempting selection of baked goods and sandwiches. At night, it draws a diverse crowd, everyone from tie-died retro hippies to

# Nashville and The Bottle:
# A Continuing Saga

Nashville, a town often associated with cry-in-your-beer songs, has long had a love-hate relationship with "the bottle." Decades before Merle Haggard bemoaned the fact that tonight the bottle let him down, locals had waged battle — literally shedding blood in one infamous, landmark case — over alcohol sales.

Travelers during the last quarter of the 19th century knew Nashville as a wild, swinging, "anything goes" kind of place. Downtown was home to a number of upscale saloons and gambling establishments, including the popular Southern Turf and, at one time, as many as three tracks for horse racing, which is now illegal in Tennessee.

During these years, naturally, many religious leaders and others objected to the drinking, gambling and carrying on that transpired in the riverfront district. In 1885, steamboat captain Thomas Ryman was persuaded to close the bars and gambling dens on his boats after hearing the exhortations of traveling evangelist Sam Jones. Ryman was so moved by the spirit — and away from the spirits — in fact, that he donated money for a tabernacle. (This building, which now bears the captain's name, later became the home of the *Grand Ole Opry* and is now a popular auditorium for a variety of musical performances. During most shows, ironically, alcoholic drinks are sold in the lobby.)

Anti-alcohol sentiment picked up during the early 1900s, and one of the most vocal prohibitionists was Edward Ward "Ned" Carmack, editor of *The Tennessean* newspaper. On November 9, 1908, Carmack was shot to death downtown by Duncan B. Cooper and his son, Robin, who objected to the editor's often strident stance. The two were convicted and sentenced to 20 years in prison, but Gov. Malcolm Patterson, a friend of the Coopers, pardoned them. The resulting furor helped prompt the passage of a statewide prohibition law that took effect in July 1909. Despite the law, enforcement was often lax, due in part to corruption by local and state officials who disagreed with the ban.

Prohibition remained a controversial political issue throughout the next decade, and one mayor, Hilary E. Howse, was forced to resign from office in 1916 because of his failure to enforce it. He later was re-elected.

One side effect of Prohibition was the birth of the downtown area known as Printers Alley. The alley gradually became a hot spot for speakeasies where illegal alcohol was sold. Prohibition in Tennessee, as nationwide, ended with the 1933 passage of the 21st Amendment.

Of course, the sale and use of alcoholic beverages is destined to forever remain a seed of contention — and, as illustrated by George Jones's drinking-related, near-fatal Lexus wreck in 1999, the connections between booze and country music will never disappear. As for those once-popular cry-in-your-beer songs, they're no longer the country-radio staple they used to be. In today's Nashville, many publishers, producers and record companies who are looking for tunes specifically state that they don't want any songs about drinkin'.

fortysomethings with their kids. The cafe features live music — mainly jazz, Latin jazz and Middle Eastern music — on Tuesday, Thursday, Friday and Saturday evenings. There's also a monthly poetry night.

The West End Bean Central is open 7 AM to 11 PM Monday through Saturday, 9 AM to 5 PM Sunday. The Hillsboro Pike Bean Central in The Glendale shopping center is open 7 AM to 6 PM.

## Bongo Java
### 2007 Belmont Blvd. • (615) 385-5282

This is the home of the Nun Bun, the miracle bun with the face of the late Mother Teresa baked right in. In case you don't know the story, in October 1996, hungry Bongo Java worker Ryan Finney picked out a cinnamon bun to munch on. Before he took a bite, he paused. "It looked kind of weird," said Finney. "I turned it around and thought, 'Oh my God.'" Staring back at him was a doughy rendition of Mother Teresa's face. The bun actually is amazing in its likeness to her.

A wave of worldwide attention followed. The Nun Bun was featured on TV and in newspapers everywhere. Finney, who went to Colorado before the publicity bonanza began, received a call from his mother, who had read his name in the *Boston Globe*. People came to Bongo Java in droves to see the preserved bun, and the coffeehouse sold assorted Nun Bun T-shirts and other merchandise for a while before receiving a letter from Mother Teresa asking Bongo Java to stop the merchandise and promotion. In mid-1997, the bun appeared in a cross-country video produced by a couple of Bongo Java friends. It is now back at Bongo Java.

Other than the Nun Bun, coffee and atmosphere are Bongo Java's claims to fame. The coffeehouse opened in a big old house in the early '90s, right in the heart of the Belmont College area. Open until 11 PM Sunday through Thursday, and until midnight Friday and Saturday, it's a regular hangout for college students and party types, and also draws some college professors and regulars from the neighborhood. When the weather's nice, the front patio is a good spot to hang out; if you want more privacy, the rooms inside the house are cozy and relaxed, with plenty of space between tables. Upstairs, The Bongo Java After Hours Theatre offers a variety of regularly scheduled entertainment, including poetry readings, films, dance and live music. It's open to all ages. The admission price depends on the show; it's usually $4 to $15. Occasionally, bands play outside on the front deck.

A second Bongo Java, known as Fido, is in Hillsboro Village. (See our separate entry.)

## Café Fido and Bongo Java Roasting Company
### 1812 21st Ave. S. • (615) 385-7959

A great place to linger over a latte, Fido, as this coffeehouse is known, opened in October 1996 in the building previously occupied by Jones Pet Store. This is the second of the Bongo Java coffeehouses and is perhaps more upscale than the super-casual Belmont Boulevard location. Located in Hillsboro Village, right next to Vanderbilt University, Fido draws a big college crowd as well as a lot of Green Hills residents, creative artist types and 40-and-older coffee lovers. Fido's spacious, quiet and dimly lit room makes for a relaxing environment where everyone seems to feel comfortable.

There's plenty of freshly roasted coffee plus tea, chilled drinks, fresh pastries and a breakfast, lunch and dinner menu. Fido is open 7 AM to 11 PM Monday through Thursday, 7 AM to midnight Friday, 8 AM to midnight Saturday and 8 AM to 11 PM Sunday.

## The Gibson Cafe and Guitar Gallery
### 318 Broadway • (615) 742-6343

Owned by Gibson Guitars CEO Henry Juszkiewicz, this is both a coffeehouse and a music venue. Tourists and locals of all ages can be found here, and the coffeehouse gets

## INSIDERS' TIP

**Nightclubs occasionally have all-ages concerts. Keep your eyes and ears open.**

Photo: Cindy Stooksbury Guier

There's a songwriter's showcase going on somewhere in Nashville any night of the week.

a lot of before- and after-dinner business from the crowds at Planet Hollywood next door. In the daytime, this is a nice spot to enjoy a specialty coffee drink or have a light lunch. At night, the coffeehouse adds live music to its offerings — everything from reggae to instrumental piano. It's an intimate, smoke-free listening room with a great sound system. Local aspiring performers take the stage every night, usually around 7. Songwriter and open-mic night is Tuesday. There isn't a cover charge. Gibson Cafe has a deli-type menu and a beer and liquor selection.

## Radio Café
### 1313 Woodland St. • (615) 262-1766

Radio Café is a charming, neighborhood coffeehouse at the corner of Woodland and 14th streets in East Nashville, between the historic Edgefield and Lockeland Springs neighborhoods (see our Neighborhoods and Real Estate chapter). The owner, Mac Hill, is a collector of radios, and about 100 of them, dating from the 1930s to the present, are on display. Customers continue to add to the collection, bringing in radios they've found in their attics and at yard sales. The cafe is in a historic

building that for years housed a pharmacy. The same soda fountain fixtures the pharmacy used to make milk shakes 50 years ago now whip up yummy milk shakes and frozen lattes.

Radio Café has a loyal and eclectic clientele. Lots of residents in the diverse East Nashville neighborhoods can be found here daily. Symphony players, other musicians and artists are regulars, and increasing numbers from outside the neighborhood are seeking out this java joint. Doctors and lawyers sip their coffee alongside construction workers and songwriters. Inside, the main room accommodates about 80. If the weather is nice, head to the small outdoor patio.

If you want a little quiet time, come between 3 and 5 PM. That's a good time to relax and read one of the cafe's magazines or newspapers or play one of the board games. Radio Café has live music, including folk, country and gospel, six nights a week; a swing band performs during the Sunday brunch. In addition to the coffee beverages, the cafe has a breakfast menu that includes made-from-scratch omelets, "groovy potatoes" and French toast. Lunch and dinner specialties include fish and chicken dishes, sandwiches and tasty homemade soups. Beer and wine are available. There's live music Monday through Saturday evenings and there's rarely a cover charge. The cafe opens at 7:30 AM weekdays, 9 AM Saturday and Sunday. Monday through Saturday it stays open til whenever the bands stop playing; Sunday it closes at 3 or 4 PM.

## 23rd Psalm Coffeehouse
**2203 Buena Vista Pk. • (615) 259-2323**

A coffee house with a message, this north Nashville venue was founded by former rock, jazz and blues vocalist Ben Houston in 1998. The 23rd Psalm presents live Christian music nightly; musical styles range from alternative rock to Southern gospel to rap. The informal, family-oriented coffeehouse also hosts a monthly community forum on such issues as racial harmony, domestic violence, gang activity and women's health. Proceeds from those events go to various ministries.

23rd Psalm's breakfast menu includes grits, eggs, bacon, ham, pancakes and biscuits. The dinner menu includes traditional family pleasers like spaghetti and meatballs, fried chicken wings, sandwiches and potato salad.

# Sports Bars

## Box Seat
**2221 Bandywood Dr. • (615) 383-8018**

Box Seat, in Green Hills (across the street from Kroger), offers a more sophisticated ambience than most sports bars. This popular bar opened in 1987, but later moved to a larger location nearby. It now seats about 250. Box Seat has been voted the No. 1 sports bar in Nashville by readers of the *Nashville Scene* and *The Tennessean*. Lots of brick and wood set the tone for this warm, friendly hangout, which is popular with the 25- to 55-year-old crowd and is packed when there's a big college or pro sports game. Fifteen TVs, positioned strategically around the room, ensure that you don't miss any of the action. Pool tables and dart boards provide halftime distractions. The Box Seat's in-house smoker produces some yummy barbecue, ribs and brisket. Pizzas from the wood-burning oven plus salads and sandwiches are good too. There's a Friday prime rib special and a Sunday king crab special. The Box Seat is open 11 AM to 3

The Wildhorse Saloon offers food and a 3,300-square-foot dance floor that attract both locals and out-of-towners.

Photo: Gaylord Entertainment Center

Nashville really lights up after dark.

AM Monday through Saturday and noon to 11 PM Sunday.

### Jonathan's Village Café
**1803 21st Ave. S. • (615) 385-9301**

Jonathan's is a combination sports bar/restaurant/all-purpose hangout that's popular with twenty- and thirtysomethings. Its location in Hillsboro Village makes it popular with the Vandy crowd. The bar stays busy, serving up a variety of imported and domestic draft and bottle beers. Two large screens and 17 TVs provide plenty of views of the games.

### Marathon Sports Bar and Grill
**15568 Old Hickory Blvd.**
**• (615) 833-0898**

This fun and friendly neighborhood sports bar has a *Cheers* atmosphere; there are a lot of regulars. Twelve TVs, including one large-screen, plus darts, pool tables, drink specials and more keep the crowds entertained and happy. In business since the early '90s, Marathon's, located in Nipper's Corner, offers about 60 different imported and domestic

beers. The food is the usual sports bar fare: burgers, sandwiches, nachos and other finger foods.

### The McCabe Pub
**4410 Murphy Rd. • (615) 269-9406**

A combination sports bar and neighborhood family restaurant, The McCabe Pub is in the heart of the Sylvan Park neighborhood. Here since the early '80s, McCabe Pub is a true neighborhood bar, with lots of regular patrons who walk over from their homes and socialize, enjoy a beer and maybe catch a game on the tube. The bar seats about 15, while the restaurant accommodates 120. McCabe Pub has a full-service bar with a well-stocked liquor selection and a medium-size wine list.

### Melrose Billiards
**2600 Franklin Pk. • (615) 383-9201**

Melrose Billiards has been in business here since 1942. This combination pool hall/sports bar draws a varied crowd. The approximately 4,000-square-foot facility has 11 pool tables, one snooker table, Ping Pong, darts and three TVs. They have a full bar and a wide selection of beers. If you're hungry, try the specialty here — the chili dog; hamburgers and barbecue are also on the menu.

Hours are 10 AM to midnight Sunday through Thursday and until 1 or 2 AM Friday and Saturday.

### Rivalry's Sports Bar
**1038 Murfreesboro Pk. • (615) 361-5266**

In case the orange caboose connected to this sports bar doesn't give you a clue, Rivalry's is a popular hangout with University of Tennessee football fans. On "Tennessee weekends," the place is packed. There's more than football though — Rivalry's has a 12-foot screen, an 8-foot screen and eight or nine 30-inch TVs, so you can pretty much watch the sport of your choice.

Rivalry's serves up a variety of tasty foods, including Cajun-influenced items. In the spring they have crawfish boils regularly. In addition to sports and food, there are pool tables, pinball and other amusements. On Tuesday nights, the bar presents live music. Wednesday night is family night, when you can get a $5 14-ounce rib-eye steak and play trivia. On Friday and Saturday nights, they turn on the karaoke. Rivalry's has a full bar, of course, and some people just drop by for a beer or two. During the warm months, the outdoor deck is a happy gathering place.

### Sportsman's Grille
**5405 Harding Rd. • (615) 356-6206**

Although you can categorize Sportsman's Grille as a sports bar, most people come for the food. This dark, cozy and casual neighborhood restaurant/bar is family-oriented place with a sports theme. It's on the edge of Belle Meade, right next to the U.S. 70–Tenn. 100 split. If you're so inclined, order up a big frosty glass of Gerst beer before feasting on your choice of catfish, burgers, steak, sandwiches, salads and pasta. If you are a sports fan, you can keep up with the action, since sports are always in the background — on about six TVs positioned around the room.

You'll find a second Sportsman's near Vandy (see the next write-up).

### Sportsman's Grille In The Village
**1601 21st Ave. S. • (615) 320-1633**

Like the original Sportsman's Grille in Belle Meade (see previous write-up), the emphasis is more on family dining than sports at this restaurant/sports bar, which opened in 1991. The dinner crowd makes up most of the business. Since this Sportsman's is in the heart of the Vandy community, you can always find plenty of students, professionals and families here. Ten TVs show sports full time — from Australian-rules football to Davis Cup soccer. On the menu are pasta dishes, steaks, burgers and catfish. Some local publications' readers polls have voted Sportsman's best sports bar, and it also has garnered a nod for best hamburger on at least one occasion.

### Sports Page Restaurant and Bar
**419 Union St. • (615) 251-9503**

Sports Page Restaurant and Bar caters mostly to the lunch crowd, but it does have a full bar and stays open until around 8:30 weeknights. Known for its low prices, Sports Page is usually very busy at lunchtime, when you can find everyone from the mayor to bricklayers dining here on the famous cheeseburgers and getting a sports fix via one of the five TVs. It seats about 125 on two levels.

# Brewpubs

### Big River Grille & Brewing Works
**111 Broadway • (615) 251-HOPS**

This huge, full-service brewpub is across

---

the street from the Hard Rock Café. The beer is good, and so is the food. Eight to 10 ales are available at all times. Billiard tables provide a little recreation, while patrons in the dining area feast on a variety of pizzas, pastas and other tasty entrees.

### Blackstone Restaurant & Brewery
**1918 West End Ave. • (615) 327-9969**

A comfortable, relaxed place to dine and drink, Blackstone offers six ales, brewed at the on-site brewery. The St. Charles Porter was awarded a gold medal at the 1996 World Beer Cup. Blackstone is a little more upscale than some brewpubs. With a variety of reasonably priced lunch and dinner items, it has a busy lunchtime business. It is a convenient spot for Music Row, West End and downtown workers to stop after work. Take a tour of the brewery if you like.

### Bosco's Nashville Brewing Co.
**1805 21st Ave. S. • (615) 385-0050**

Delicious food, great beer and a fun environment make Bosco's a good pick among Nashville's growing brewpub selection. The original Bosco's opened in Germantown in 1992 and was the first brewpub licensed in the state, and one of the first in the Southeast. Bosco's has been at its 21st Avenue S. address in Hillsboro Village since early 1996. You can't go wrong with the pub's wood-fired oven pizzas, pastas and grilled specialties. The best-selling beer is Bosco's trademark Famous Flaming Stone Beer.

### Market Street Brewery & Public House
**134 Second Ave. N. • (615) 259-9611**

This is Nashville's original microbrewery. Market Street Brewery opened in 1989 in one of Second Avenue's 19th-century warehouse buildings. The brewery added a restaurant in 1994. All beers are hand-crafted on the premises, and guests can see the brewing process at work. The most popular brews are the Market Street Pilsner and the Bohannon Vanilla Crème Ale. The pub's menu feature's lots of Cajun specialties plus burgers and a good chicken sandwich. A turn-of-the-century tasting room overlooks the Cumberland River and Riverfront Park.

# Movie Theaters

Nashville isn't lacking in movie theaters. Large multiplexes can be found in every part of town. There are a few theaters, however, that are worth pointing out, because of their quality programming, good value or both. Check local newspaper listings for current schedules or call the listed numbers.

### Watkins Belcourt Theatre
**2102 Belcourt Ave. • (615) 383-9140**

The fate of Hillsboro Village's historic Belcourt has been uncertain for the last couple of years. At this writing, there was a movement to raise funds to save the art house theater, which is in need of renovation. Belcourt found a niche showing the films that don't usually make their way to the big multiplexes in town — foreign language, art and independent films are the focus. The theater has two screens, and the schedule changes frequently.

### Franklin Cinema
**419 Main St., Franklin • (615) 790-7122**

This is the only theater around where you can have dinner and a movie at the same time. Kick back in a comfy chair or sofa and enjoy beer, pizza and other fun food while you watch a movie. Just two blocks off Franklin's historic town square, Franklin Cinema has developed a reputation for showing the more arty films and foreign films. With two screens, it usually offers a more mainstream movie choice as well. Mondays and Tuesdays, the theater serves 99¢ draft beer. On Wednesday, you get free popcorn if you bring your own popcorn bowl. *The Rocky Horror Picture Show* is the feature every Friday night at midnight; tickets for this feature cost $4.50. Regular tickets cost $4.50 before 4 PM; $3.50 between 4 and 6 PM; and $6.50 for ages 12 through 54 and $4.50 for ages 3 through 11 after 6 PM.

## Sarratt Cinema
**24th Avenue S. and Vanderbilt Pl.**
**• (615) 322-2425, (615) 343-6666 (film hotline)**

Vanderbilt University's Sarratt Cinema may offer the best movie value in town. It shows mostly a selection of classics, recent hits and documentaries for $4, or $3 for Vanderbilt students. The theater is in the Sarratt Student Center, a couple of blocks off West End Avenue. Traditionally movies are shown twice nightly Monday through Saturday, usually around 7:30 and 9:25 PM, but the schedule may change with the school calendar. There is a 3 PM matinee on Sunday. About every other Friday and Saturday, Sarratt schedules a midnight movie.

# Music Industry Humor

If you're here for any length of time, you're eventually going to run into somebody in the music business. It's inevitable. This person might be someone rich and famous, or it might be someone who looks like a waiter, cab driver or receptionist but is actually just biding his or her time. (Heck, it might be you!) When you do meet someone in the business, endear yourself to your newfound friend with a little music industry humor. For example:

Question: How do you get a songwriter off your front porch?
Answer: Pay for your pizza.

Q: What do you call a musician who just broke up with his girlfriend?
A: Homeless.

Q: Did you hear about the A&R (artists and repertoire) guy who got hit by a train?
A: He didn't hear it.

Q: How can you tell when a drummer is on your porch?
A: He's got the wrong key, and he doesn't know when to come in.

Q: What's the difference between a fiddle and a trampoline?
A: You take off your shoes before you jump on a trampoline.

Q: How many singers does it take to screw in a light bulb?
A: Just one. She holds the light bulb, and the world revolves around her.

**Running into a music star is just about an everyday occurrence here in Music City.**

# Music City U.S.A.

They don't call it Music City for nothing. Nashville is truly the place to be if you are a lover of music, whatever the style. Whether you're an aspiring singer or songwriter, an aficionado of live music in intimate settings, a student of country music history or a star-struck fan eager to discover more about the lifestyle of your favorite artist, you can find plenty in Nashville to meet your desires. By the way, for insight into Nashville's development as a music capital, check out our History chapter.

If you're a tourist in Nashville, you've probably been keeping your eyes peeled for a glimpse of a country music star as you stroll down Music Row. You might spot someone ducking into a studio or driving by, but you're just as likely (probably more likely) to bump into your favorite star in an ordinary place like the post office, the mall or the grocery store. Running into a music star is just about an everyday occurrence here in Music City. We've rubbed elbows with Lorrie Morgan at a Green Hills department store cosmetics counter, bumped into Steve Earle at the Acklen Station post office, spotted Steven Curtis Chapman at the Nippers Corner movie theater, mingled with visiting rockers R.E.M. on Elliston Place, shopped for Hallmark cards next to members of Petra at CoolSprings mall, sat next to Emmylou Harris at the Bluebird Cafe . . . you get the picture.

In this chapter, you'll find a plethora of attractions, venues and services related to popular music. If your tastes tend toward more highbrow entertainment like opera and classical music, check out our Arts chapter. Or, if you're into dancing to discs spun by disc jockeys, you'll find establishments offering that kind of entertainment in the Nightlife chapter. The main sections of this chapter are as follows:

•**Attractions.** Country music-related museums include general-interest sites, like the Country Music Hall of Fame and Museum and the Grand Ole Opry Museum; a variety of shrines tailored to particular artists; and even a wax museum where you can see (almost) lifelike reproductions of the stars. Tour companies offer packages that will take you to various Nashville attractions and, in some cases, past the current or former homes of an assortment of stars, both living and dead.

•**Record stores.** Yes, we still prefer to call them record stores, even though most of them now deal instead in CDs and cassettes. But there are actually places in Nashville where you can still find vinyl, especially vintage vinyl.

•**Live music.** Here you'll find a world of choices covering practically every musical style you can think of. You'll find venues large and small, including ones specializing in performances by songwriters — and opportunities for you to perform, if that's one of your dreams.

•**Support organizations.** Nashville has numerous support organizations and associations for members of the music industry, and you'll find information about them here.

•**Annual events.** It seems that some kind of yearly festival, concert series, jubilee or other musical event is always going on here, celebrating Nashville's musical heritage, its thriving present and its promising future.

In addition, this chapter contains a number of Close-ups offering everything from history to trivia to helpful hints.

Of course, as we've said elsewhere in this book — and as we'll continue to emphasize

— one of the aspects that many newcomers find surprising about Music City is the sheer diversity of its output. While country music remains by far the most visible (or should we say audible?) style, you can find an eclectic selection that includes about any kind of music you might possibly want to hear. This really isn't a new development, as a quick study of the recording industry will attest. Nashville actually had a thriving rhythm-and-blues scene well before the city became known as the country music capital of the world. From the early days of the city's recording industry on up to today, a stunning array of non-country artists including Burl Ives, Ray Charles, Bob Dylan, James Brown, Leontyne Price, Neil Young, REO Speedwagon, Johnny Winter, Carol Channing, Paul McCartney, Elvis Costello, the Allman Brothers, B.B. King, Dave Brubeck, Joe Cocker, Dean Martin and Yo La Tengo have recorded albums here. While many of these artists have drawn upon country influences on their Nashville records, others have not, simply recognizing the wealth of talent and facilities available here.

Today Nashville is home to a growing number of "old rock 'n' rollers," like Peter Frampton, Michael McDonald, Steve Winwood, Randy Bachman and Steppenwolf's John Kay. Elvis Costello and Mark Knopfler are frequent visitors. More and more people, perhaps, are realizing that, regardless of category, good music is good music, and that music is an international language Nashville speaks fluently.

# Attractions

## Country Music Hall of Fame and Museum
**4 Music Sq. E. • (615) 256-1639, (800) 852-6437 (reservations and gift shop orders)**

The Hall of Fame and Museum, operated by the Country Music Foundation, has welcomed more than 10 million visitors since it opened in April 1967. Today it averages an annual attendance of about 250,000. It is a must-see attraction — the place to go for an entertaining look at country music's past and present.

In late 1999 the attraction is scheduled to move from its current spot on Music Row into a new, $37 million-home at Demonbreun Street and Fifth Avenue S., adjacent to the Gaylord Entertainment Center (the former Nashville Arena). The new, four-story complex will provide triple the exhibit space, allowing the Hall of Fame to showcase much more of its collection, which includes more than one million items. The 105,000-square-foot building will include 45,000 square feet of exhibit space, a 7,000-square-foot conservatory and a 200-seat indoor amphitheater. A visit to this attraction includes tours of the museum, Music Row and the legendary Studio B on Music Row. The sticker you receive at the ticket desk will allow you unlimited access to all these attractions on the day of your visit.

Start your tour at the museum. More than 3,000 items related to country stars are on display. Popular current exhibits include *Marty Stuart Presents: The Treasures of Hank Williams*. This exhibit features a collection of personal and professional memorabilia from Hank Williams, some from Stuart's personal collection. A highlight is the 1948 Packard that Williams rode in to his first *Opry* performance. Song manuscripts, rare film footage and interactive displays are also featured. *Stars & Guitars: The Gibson Centennial Exhibit* is a tribute to Nashville-based Gibson Guitars, which was founded in 1898 in Michigan. A 100-year-old handmade guitar as well as modern guitars donated by B.B. King and other guitar greats are on display.

One of the most popular exhibits is Elvis's "solid gold" Cadillac, which features a 24-karat gold interior, plus a refrigerator, TV, shoe-shine buff and more. The paint is encrusted with gold dust and pearls. The King and his manager, Col. Tom Parker, donated the vehicle to the Country Music Foundation shortly before Elvis's death. The museum also features costumes, original song manuscripts and other items from country's top stars. Guides are on

Photo: Cindy Stooksbury Guier

Many Music Row businesses are housed in renovated buildings.

hand to answer questions and tell interesting stories about the artists and exhibits. Be sure to visit the museum store to check out the souvenirs. You'll find everything from CDs and books about the country music business to guitar-shaped fly swatters.

For the Music Row tour, you'll board a trolley or bus and get a behind-the-scenes look at the entertainment biz. Tours depart every 15 minutes from the stop beside the museum's main entrance. The tour guide will point out the interesting spots along the Row, such as Reba McEntire's new complex, Garth Brooks's office, record labels, publishing companies and recording studios. Bring your camera. During the 20-minute tour, you'll stop at RCA's Historic Studio B, at the corner of Music Square W. and Roy Acuff Place. This is where stars such as Elvis, Dolly Parton, the Everly Brothers, Waylon Jennings and Roy Orbison recorded many of their hits from 1957 to 1977. You can look through the soundproof glass and watch a real recording session take place; sometimes you'll even catch a top star here. A $200,000 renovation in 1995 restored the interior to the studio's original 1960s look and sound. The control room, however, features state-of-the-art equipment. The studio tour lasts 20 to 30 minutes. You can take the Hall of Fame bus or trolley back to your starting point.

Allow at least two hours to tour these three attractions. Tickets are $10.75 for adults, $5.75 for children ages 6 to 12. There is a parking fee in the lots adjacent to the Hall of Fame and Museum. Hours are 9 AM to 5 PM daily. This attraction is closed Thanksgiving, Christmas and New Year's Day.

### Gruhn Guitars Inc.
**400 Broadway • (615) 256-2033**

A must-stop for guitarists or serious music fans, this world-famous store is Nashville's largest guitar dealer. The store specializes in high quality new, used and vintage guitars, banjos and mandolins, with prices ranging from a few hundred dollars to as much as $100,000. Gruhn's has a strong celebrity clientele, but owner George Gruhn is quick to note that his store has "plenty of things that mere mortals can afford." Instruments range from new Martin and Gibson guitars to pre-World War II Martin and Gibson acoustics and 1950s and 1960s electric guitars.

Gruhn opened his first store in 1970 at 111 Fourth Avenue N. From 1976 to about 1993, the store was at 410 Broadway. Today, Gruhn's occupies 12,000 square feet on four floors at 400 Broadway. (Gruhn's has never been more than 100 feet from its original location.) Annual sales run between $5 million and $6 million. In addition to Gruhn, the store has more than a dozen experienced players on staff plus six full-time professionals who work in vintage restoration of the store's products. Hours are 9:30 AM to 5:30 PM Monday through Friday, and 9:30 AM to 5 PM Saturday.

## Hatch Show Print
### 316 Broadway • (615) 256-2805

In business since 1879, Hatch Show Print is the oldest letterpress poster print shop in America (see our Attractions chapter for more information). The shop is best known for its posters of early *Grand Ole Opry* stars. Today the shop is owned and operated by the Country Music Foundation, which operates the Country Music Hall of Fame and Museum (see previous listing). Hatch still produces its trademark posters and other designs. Its 14- by 22-inch posters advertising local rock bands and would-be country stars can be seen in window displays and on telephone poles around town. Hatch sells samples of its posters in the shop. You can drop by Monday through Friday from 9:30 AM to 5:30 PM, and Saturday from 10:30 AM to 5:30 PM. Admission is free.

## Grand Ole Opry Museum
### 2802 Opryland Dr. • (615) 889-3060

Located at the Opry Plaza area surrounding the Grand Ole Opry House, this 12,000-square-foot museum tells the story of the *Grand Ole Opry*, the world's longest-running radio show (see our History chapter). High-tech displays and interactive videos allow you to get involved in the exhibits, which present the story of some of the Opry's legendary early members. There are also exhibits of current Opry stars, including Garth Brooks and Reba McEntire.

The downtown Ryman Auditorium was home to the *Opry* from 1943 to 1974, and the Ryman's back alley entrance is reproduced here as a backdrop for exhibits on the careers of Patsy Cline, Little Jimmy Dickens, George Jones, Jim Reeves, Marty Robbins and Hank

Snow. The Roy Acuff and Minnie Pearl museum collections are now housed at the Grand Ole Opry Museum as well.

Replicas of past and present recording studios are featured too. You'll find a number of video kiosks in the exhibit areas that allow you to look back on country music history via special audiovisual effects. The 10- by 10-foot video wall plays a six-part video on the history of the *Opry* and its international appeal, narrated by Porter Wagoner.

Admission is free. The museum opens at 10:30 AM daily; closing hours vary.

## Jim Reeves Museum
### 2011 Johnson Industrial Blvd., Nolensville
### • (615) 776-5656

The museum is dedicated to *Grand Ole Opry* star Jim Reeves ("Four Walls," "He'll Have To Go"), and is owned and operated by a Nashville businessman. Exhibits include stage clothing, guitars, furniture from Reeves's home, gold records, awards, rare photos, a tour bus and 1960 Cadillac El Dorado. Reeves died in a plane crash in 1964, and a replica of the plane is featured at the museum.

You'll find a good selection of Reeves's records, tapes and CDs in the gift shop. Admission is free. Hours are 10 AM to 5 PM daily, and the museum was closed on major holidays.

## Kitty Wells/Johnny Wright Family Country Junction
### 240 Old Hickory Blvd. E., Madison
### • (615) 865-9118

This free-admission attraction is in Madison, about 10 minutes north of downtown. The museum is near the homes of Wells and Wright. It features awards, trophies, costumes and other memorabilia. There's also a model train layout of the Tennessee Central Railroad, a tribute to Wells's father, Carey Deason, who worked for the railroad for 33 years. A gift shop sells logo merchandise and Nashville souvenirs. Hours are 10 AM to 4 PM Monday through Friday. This attraction is closed December through March.

## Music Valley Wax Museum
**2515 McGavock Pk. • (615) 883-3612**

Alan Jackson, Randy Travis, George Strait, Elvis, Roy Acuff and Minnie Pearl are among the 53 artists represented in wax at this museum. Some of them are dressed in the performers' original costumes. If you want, bring a video camera and record yourself visiting with the stars. MTV did a skit here in 1996 with the wax Dolly and Willie. Be sure to take a stroll on the Sidewalk of the Stars, where hundreds of performers have dropped by to place

their footprints, handprints and signatures in concrete. A gift shop offers Nashville souvenirs and collectibles. Admission is $3.50 for adults, $3 for seniors 65 and older and $1.50 for children 6 to 12. From Memorial Day through October, hours are 8 AM to 8:30 PM daily. The rest of the year, hours are 9 AM to 5 PM daily.

## Ryman Auditorium and Museum
**116 Fifth Ave. N. • (615) 254-1445**

Home of the *Grand Ole Opry* from 1943 to 1974, the Ryman is Nashville's most famous historic attraction. Exhibits and information on the history of the building and country music are displayed on the main floor. Exhibits in-

Once the heart of Nashville's entertainment district, Printers Alley continues to welcome singers, songwriters, locals and tourists to popular venues.

clude memorabilia and photographs of such Opry stars as Kitty Wells, Hank Snow and Ernest Tubb. Among the other attractions are interactive videos narrated by Johnny Cash, Vince Gill and Little Jimmy Dickens, life-size bronze statues of Minnie Pearl and Roy Acuff and a gift shop with a selection of recordings and souvenir merchandise.

You can stop by for a self-guided tour any day of the week from 8:30 AM to 4 PM, but we recommend checking out the exhibits while attending a concert here. Admission is $6 for adults, $2.50 for children 4 to 11. Prices for concert tickets vary. (See our History and Attractions chapters, along with the live music listings in this chapter, for more on the Ryman.)

### Studio B
**26 Music Sq. W. • (615) 256-1639**

See the previous Country Music Hall of Fame and Museum listing in this section for information about historic Studio B.

### Trinity Music City U.S.A.
**1 Music Village Blvd., Hendersonville**
**• (615) 822-8333**

In mid-1994, California-based Trinity Broadcasting Network purchased the late Conway Twitty's estate known as Twitty City and turned it into Trinity Music City U.S.A. Free tours of the Trinity Music Church Auditorium, WPGD Studio and the Twitty Mansion are available at designated times throughout the week. The gardens, gift shop and Solid Rock Bistro are open during regular operating hours: 10 AM to 6 PM Monday through Thursday, 10 AM to 8 PM Friday and Saturday, and 1 to 6 PM Sunday. The state-of-the-art virtual-reality theater features films shot in the Holy Land. Tickets for the film are required and are available at no charge at the theater. Worship services are held in the auditorium Sundays at 2 PM, Tuesdays at 7 PM, and Thursdays at 10 AM. The *Praise The Lord* program is usually taped here Thursdays and Fridays at 7 PM; doors open at 6 PM and admission to the taping is free.

### Willie Nelson Gift Emporium
**2613-A McGavock Pk. • (615) 885-1515**

This museum and gift shop is right behind the Nashville Palace in Music Valley, across from the Opryland Hotel. There are lots of ex-

hibits on Willie Nelson, including awards, guitars, clothing and other personal items. Other displays pay tribute to Patsy Cline, Elvis and other stars. The gift shop has all sorts of souvenir items, including lots of T-shirts and sports merchandise. Admission is $3 for adults and teens, $1.50 for children 6 to 12. Group discounts are available. Memorial Day through Labor Day, hours are 8 AM to 10 PM. Fall and winter hours are 9 AM to 5 PM, but winter closing hours sometimes vary. This attraction is closed on Thanksgiving and Christmas.

# Tours

### Grand Ole Opry Tours
**2810 Opryland Dr. • (615) 871-6100,**
**(615) 871-5642**

Grand Ole Opry Tours offers about eight different tours. The most popular is the Grand Ole Nashville tour, which includes admission to the Ryman museum, a trip down historic Second Avenue, a visit to Music Row, a drive to the Governor's mansion and a look at the homes of several music stars, including Pam Tillis, Ronnie Milsap, the late Minnie Pearl and others.

The Inside Music tour takes you around the city of Nashville, including Historic Second Avenue, and stops on Music Row so you can tour the Country Music Hall of Fame and RCA's Studio B. While on Second Avenue, you'll visit the Wildhorse Saloon, and, just a few blocks away, the Ryman Auditorium.

The Music Country and Country Legends tours take you by many country artists' homes. On the Country Legends tour you'll see the homes of Reba McEntire, Porter Wagoner, Lorrie Morgan and the late Roy Orbison, among others. The Music Country tour takes you past the homes of such stars as Alan Jackson, Dolly Parton, Faith Hill and Tim McGraw, Amy Grant and Alison Krauss.

Other tours available include a tour of Nashville's historic mansions. All tours are $24 per person and last about three hours.

### Johnny Walker Tours
**2416 Music Valley Dr., Ste. 118**
**• (615) 834-8585, (800) 722-1524**

This tour operator offers five tours and one

shuttle. The most popular tour is the Country Music Express tour, which includes a trip to downtown Nashville. A 30-minute stop on Music Row allows time for a quick visit to the Country Music Hall of Fame and Museum or a walk past the many record companies, song publishers and other music businesses. This tour also takes you past some of the city's antebellum mansions and Civil War sites. While in the Brentwood area, you'll see the homes or former homes of such stars as Alan Jackson, Martina McBride, Charlie Chase, Lorianne Crook, Ronnie Dunn and Kix Brooks of Brooks & Dunn, Marty Robbins, T.G. Shepard, George Jones and Randy Travis.

The Ryman/Wildhorse/Downtown Tour is also a popular choice. It includes guided tours of those downtown attractions and allows for you to go exploring for a while on your own.

Other tours include the Music City Dinner Tour, a tour of Opryland's gardens and tours of the stars' homes.

Tour prices range from $19 to $29 for adults; tickets for children ages 6 to 11 are half-price. All tours last approximately three hours. You'll travel in 25-passenger minivans that depart at designated intervals. The vans will pick you up at nearly any Nashville-area hotel, or you can drive to the tour. Reservations are recommended.

The Grand Ole Opry Shuttle provides round-trip transportation from various hotels to the *Grand Ole Opry* on Friday and Saturday nights but doesn't include tickets to the *Opry*. Shuttle tickets are $8.50 for adults, $4.25 for children. If you're departing from and returning to the Opryland/Music Valley area, tickets are $3.50 for all ages.

### Gray Line Country and Western Tours
**2416 Music Valley Dr. • (615) 883-5555**

This tour company offers 13 tours and a few other outings. One of the most popular is the Grand Legends Tour, which includes stops

at the Ryman Auditorium and Country Music Hall of Fame, as well as a trip to the Brentwood area to see some of the stars' homes. The Homes of the Stars Tours takes you past the homes of some of Music City's more contemporary stars such as Amy Grant and Gary Chapman, Vince Gill, Suzy Bogguss, Faith Hill and Tim McGraw, and Kix Brooks and Ronnie Dunn. You'll also see homes of country legends such as Tammy Wynette, Ronnie Milsap, Dolly Parton and the late Webb Pierce. Have your camera ready! There is also a tour of the Opryland Hotel, Grand Ole Opry House and wax museum across the street.

On the six-hour Historical Tour you'll see or visit the Tennessee State Capitol, Ryman Auditorium, Fort Nashborough, The Upper Room Chapel (featuring a replica of da Vinci's *The Last Supper*), the Hermitage and the Parthenon. There's a Jack Daniel's Country Tour, which takes you to Lynchburg to visit the Jack Daniel Distillery. This tour takes about seven hours. Lunch is included during the Historical and Jack Daniel tours.

Most tours depart at 9 AM and 1:30 PM; the tour bus can pick you up at a hotel if you call at least an hour ahead, or you can board at the Gray Line office. Tickets for adults range from $21 to $63 (the latter is for the General Jackson showboat tour, which includes dinner); for children ages 6 to 11, tickets range from $10.50 to $63.

# Record Stores

### Ernest Tubb Record Shops
**417 Broadway • (615) 255-7503**
**2416 Music Valley Dr. • (615) 889-2474**
**1516 Demonbreun St. • (615) 244-2845**

Ernest Tubb founded his downtown store on Commerce Street in 1947. Today the downtown store is at 417 Broadway. It specializes in early and hard-to-find country recordings, but also stocks the latest country hits, so you'll

Ernest Tubb Record Shops specialize in current and classic country recordings.

find CDs and cassettes by everyone from Hank Snow, Webb Pierce and Johnny Bush to LeAnn Rimes and George Strait. The store also has recordings by small label artists such as Mike Snyder and Johnny Russell. Hours of operation vary. Stores open at 9 AM and close at 10 PM. The Broadway and Music Valley stores stay open until midnight on Friday and Saturday. The Midnight Jamboree at Ernest Tubb's Record Shop takes place at the Music Valley Drive location. See our "Live Music" section for more on that.

### The Great Escape
**1925 Broadway • (615) 327-0646**
**111 N. Gallatin Pk. N., Madison**
**• (615) 865-8052**

A bargain-hunter's paradise for some 20 years, Great Escape offers tens of thousands of used CDs, cassettes, albums and comic books. Collectors will find some vintage recordings here, and there is also a selection of new local music that the store sells on consignment. Most CDs cost $6 to $9, while most tapes and records range from 99¢ to $3.99. The store pays cash for used products. Bring a photo ID if you have products to sell. The Broadway store is open 10 AM to 9 PM Monday through Thursday, 10 AM to 10 PM Friday and Saturday and 1 to 6 PM Sunday. The Madison store is open 10 AM to 9 PM Monday through Saturday and 1 to 6 PM Sunday.

### Phonoluxe Records
**2609 Nolensville Rd. • (615) 259-3500**

Phonoluxe sells used CDs, cassettes, albums, videos, DVDs and laser discs. For music lovers on a budget, it's a must-stop. CDs are priced from $2 to about $10, and albums start at $1 and go all the way up to $200 for some of the rare, autographed recordings. Phonoluxe sells current and out-of-print recordings. The store pays cash for your used products (about $5 per CD); just bring a photo ID.

In business since 1987, the store is located between I-440 and Thompson Lane. It's open Monday through Saturday from 10 AM to 8 PM and Sunday from noon to 6 PM.

### Tower Records
**2400 West End Ave. • (615) 327-3722**

With more than 100,000 CDs and cassettes in stock, Tower has the best selection of music in town. Rock, pop, country, world music, folk and bluegrass, classical, opera, Christian and gospel are among the many categories here. Tower also stocks an extensive local music section. Videos are available for sale and rent. The store also has a large CD-ROM collection and carries DVD software. The MUZE machine allows you to search for recordings by artist name, album title, song title or key word. Separate listening rooms plus 22 listening stations allow you to preview selected items before you buy. Tower is open 9 AM to midnight every day of the year.

### Wherehouse Music
**2312 West End Ave. • (615) 320-9788**

The largest of Nashville's seven Wherehouse Music stores, the West End location has 15,000 square feet devoted to practically every music genre you can think of. There are separate categories for blues, R&B, Latin, reggae, classical, New Age, soundtracks, dance and many more. There's a used music section as well. This location is open until midnight every night except Sunday, when it closes at 10 PM.

# Live Music

## Catch 'em If You Can: A Highly Subjective List

Trying to assemble a list of "must see" performers in Nashville is like making a trip to one of those 40-item buffet bars: your plate's simply too small to include everything you like, so you have to make some difficult choices. Please keep in mind that the following list is highly subjective, and that oodles of worthwhile artists and songwriters have been omit-

ted. That said, we don't think you can go wrong with any of these acts, which include bands and solo performers as well as people who have primarily made their mark as songwriters. What we want to do here is turn you on to some people you might never have heard of — people who generally play the small, intimate venues as opposed to the big arenas and stadiums.

For many music lovers, locals as well as visitors, there's nothing quite like the experience of hearing hit songs performed not by the artists who put them on the charts, but rather by the people who wrote them. Generally, when performed live by the writers, the songs are considerably less slick than the radio versions. But what they lack in polish, they more than make up in immediacy, emotional honesty and nuance — traits that often get lost in the layers of production that characterize many commercial recordings. Even if you don't recognize the name, don't let that scare you off from catching a show at one of Nashville's songwriter showcases. Who knows? You just might catch one of today's unsung heroes, or one of tomorrow's songwriting legends.

Here, then, are just "a few" (20, actually) of our favorites:

**BadaBing BadaBoom** plays swing tunes that you'd swear were covers from the '30s and '40s. The twist is they're all originals. Most of the songs were penned by guitarist and group leader Eddie Mugavero, whose lyrics are clever, witty, audacious and wordplay-rich in the tradition of Cole Porter and Tin Pan Alley. (Bring your sense of humor, and don't take personal offense, as one drunk Southerner did, at the gut-bustingly funny "That's What I Like About the North.") The music — made by guitar, upright bass, drums, fiddle, trumpet and two female vocalists — just dares you to sit still. BadaBing, which has released two fine CDs, is one of the most entertaining groups around.

**Marc-Alan Barnett** refers to his music as "in-your-face country soul," and we think that's a pretty good description. Barnett, a soul shouter whose performing style incorporates country, R&B, pop and straight-ahead rock 'n' roll, has great taste in covers; as a staff writer for a small Nashville publishing company, he has also written some fine songs of his own. "Can't Blame Nobody But Me" will send shivers down your spine. Incidentally, two of Barnett's former backup singers are Jennifer and Heather Kinley, the singer-songwriter twins who recently hit the country charts with "Please" and "Somebody's Watchin'."

**Matraca Berg** has been on a hot streak as a songwriter, producing such smashes as Deana Carter's "Strawberry Wine" and "We Danced Anyway," Patty Loveless's "You Can Feel Bad" and Martina McBride's "Wild Angels." But she's a fine singer in her own right, and a writer whose lyrics run much deeper than the typical Top-40 modern country song. Her 1997 album, *Sunday Morning to Saturday Night*, earned critical acclaim if not airplay for its finely drawn character studies of real people living their lives as best they can.

**Dewayne Blackwell** is the jovial, songwriting uncle you probably never had. As the pen behind such classics as "Friends in Low Places," "I'm Gonna Hire a Wino to Decorate Our Home" and "Mr. Blue," he has been recorded by the likes of Garth Brooks, David Frizzell, Bobby Vinton and, more recently, rising country singer-songwriter Michael Peterson. Whether he's making you laugh or touching you with a tender tune of regret like "For a Song," which he wrote and Peterson recorded, Blackwell is a deft turner of phrases and painter of images you won't forget.

**Bob DiPiero** might not be a household name, but he's a modern songwriting legend. At this writing he'd penned 13 No. 1 hits, and by the time you read this, that number will surely be higher. It's enlightening to hear his versions of smashes like "The Church on Cumberland Road." And those who've heard his account of lunch with Vince Gill know he has a killer sense of humor.

**Steve Earle** is one of the most influential songwriters of modern times, in any genre, and one of the fieriest performers. His first album, the 1986 classic *Guitar Town*, established him as an artist who bridged country and rock with gritty stories of drifters, losers and people struggling to make it day by day. Earle, like many of his characters, lived hard, and it almost killed him. But after serving time in prison on drug charges, he's back, clean and sober, writing better and rocking harder than ever before, as powerfully illustrated by his recent albums *Train a Comin'*, *I Feel Alright*, *El Corazon* and the modern bluegrass classic *The Mountain* (recorded with the Del McCoury Band). He still frequently plays small venues in Nashville, but they fill up fast — so when you hear of a Steve Earle show, don't walk . . . run.

**Mark Germino** is a modern-day protest singer with a penchant for Dylanesque wordplay and story songs that describe the plight of the "little man." He can make you think, laugh and cry with songs like "Fire in the Land of Grace," in which the narrator dreams of burning down Graceland, and "Rex Bob Lowenstein," a morality fable about the state of today's radio. Backed by his band, he's also perfectly capable of rockin' the joint.

**Dean Hall and the Loose Eels** are led by the son of the famed "Storyteller," Tom T. Hall. Dean speaks loudest with his guitar, turning out raucous blues with his three-piece band. He sings too, though, and sometimes his lyrics are memorable, as on the hilarious "If You Play One More Country Song (I'm Gonna Have to Kick Your Ass)." The Loose Eels play every Tuesday night at Rivalry's sports bar on Murfreesboro Road.

**Alex Harvey**, as a songwriter, is best known for the classic country songs "Delta Dawn" and "Reuben James." As a performer, he's garnered considerable acclaim among locals for his intense, soulful singing and guitar playing. Like John Hammond, he sometimes appears to be possessed during one of his riveting shows. Harvey's a versatile guy: You can see his acting skills on display (along with those of Levon Helm, Randy Travis, Mark

Collie, Marty Stuart and Travis Tritt) in the Steven Seagal thriller *Fire Down Below*.

**Eric Heatherly**, who recently signed a recording contract with Mercury, seems poised to hit the charts with his hybrid of good, old-fashioned pop and rock 'n' roll. Musical reference points in his original songs include early Elvis, Roy Orbison (whose widow, Barbara, signed Heatherly to a publishing contract), rockabilly, surf (Heatherly plays a mean guitar), country and blues. The result is, in some ways, mindful of Chris Isaak: modern yet timeless, catchy yet ethereal.

**Mike Henderson and the Bluebloods.** Henderson, a co-founder of the artist-owned Dead Reckoning record label, is gaining attention as a songwriter and solo artist as well as with his rockin' blues band, the Bluebloods, which you can catch Monday nights at the Bluebird. John Jarvis, Glenn Worf and John Gardner round out the group.

**Marion James** is a blues veteran and Nashville native who's now several years into the second incarnation of her career. She came up during Nashville's happening blues and R&B scene in the 1950s and, during the 1960s, Jimi Hendrix was actually a member of her band. These days, backed by her band, the Blues Bachelors, she continues to thrill with her forceful, Chicago-style blues, which are reminiscent of KoKo Taylor with more of a gospel influence. Incidentally, James is host of a blues musicians reunion around Labor Day each summer; it's usually held at the Elks Lodge on Jefferson Street.

**Jason and the Scorchers** don't perform all that often in Nashville, but when they do, it's an event — as in a late 1997 show at Exit/In that was recorded for a live album. If you're at all interested in the roots of today's so-called alternative country or cowpunk, you need to check out the Scorchers, local boys who burst onto the Nashville scene in the mid-'80s with a potent mixture of hard rock, punk energy and country twang.

**Angela Kaset**, best known for her Lorrie Morgan smash "Something in Red," writes and performs songs of grace, beauty and sensitivity that hit-makers want to record. That may be why the performing rights organization SESAC named Kaset its 1997 Country Songwriter of the Year. You can hear a pin drop when she's performing one of her often bittersweet adult-contemporary tunes live, spellbinding her audience with only her voice and electric piano.

**R.B. Morris**, a Knoxville native, released his first album, *Take That Ride*, in 1997 on John Prine's Oh Boy! Records. He's a poet and playwright, and his lyrics are literate, vivid and often fanciful. The music is country, folk, rock, blues, Celtic, with a little beat poetry and performance art thrown in. His band, featuring guitarist Kenny Vaughan, can flat-out peel the paint off the wall. Words don't do him justice. Take that ride, indeed.

**Jonell Mosser**, one of the most soulful singers around, is widely known for her testifying backup vocals for Delbert McClinton and others. After one solo project was never released due to changes at the record label, she recorded *Around Townes*, a tribute to Townes Van Zandt that was released before the influential songwriter's death on January 1, 1997. She also sang the leading role in *Tapestry*, a stage tribute to Carole King. Catch her live with her band, Enough Rope, or with her fellow Kentucky natives Etta Britt, Vickie Carrico and Sheila Lawrence, performing as Kentucky Thunder.

**Gretchen Peters** has established herself as one of Nashville's leading feminist voices with songs like Martina McBride's "Independence Day," which tackle difficult subjects such as abuse. But she can also have fun with ditties like McBride's "My Baby Loves Me Just the Way I Am"; and, as her recording of Steve Earle's "I Ain't Ever Satisfied" shows, she also has excellent taste when she covers other writers' material.

**Charlie Daniels says, "If you want to see how much Nashville has grown, take a look at Bob Dylan's *Nashville Skyline* album. It was made in the '70s."**

**Kevin Welch**, another Dead Reckoning co-founder, is a singer-songwriter whose highly acclaimed 1995 album *Life Down Here on Earth* was the label's first release. He plays frequently at the Bluebird, so try to catch him.

**Gillian Welch** (no relation to Kevin) is a graduate of the University of California–Santa Cruz whose parents were Hollywood TV writers. Yet her debut album, *Revival*, which was nominated for a Grammy as best contemporary folk album of 1996, is a convincing blend of Appalachian-style folk, country and spirituals, and her follow-up, *Hell Among the Yearlings*, continued the tradition. She almost always performs live with her songwriting partner, David Rawlings, at local venues including the Station Inn. You'll be mesmerized.

**Joy Lynn White**, dropped from Columbia Records after two underrated albums, rebounded in 1997 with *The Lucky Few*, produced by Dwight Yoakam guitarist/producer Pete Anderson and released on his independent Little Dog Records. White is a redheaded dynamo, full of fire and soul, and her album was one of the best of 1997. She's even better live.

# Places to Hear Live Music

Day or night, it's hard to escape live music in Nashville, even if you'd like to (but why would you?). During the day, someone is always singing country hits to backing tracks, karaoke style, in front of the cluster of souvenir shops on Demonbreun Street. When we recently stopped for lunch at a Chinese restaurant on Murfreesboro Road, a Chinese singer and guitarist was performing classic country and folk hits on a small stage in the dining room. Don't laugh — he was pretty darn good. The point is, live music is such an integral part of this town that you'll find it almost everywhere, from bars, restaurants and coffeehouses to boot and book shops, street corners and churches.

The revitalization of the downtown area —

especially in "The District," which is the name given to Second Avenue, Printers Alley and lower Broadway — has provided a wealth of entertainment opportunities for tourists and locals, and given more performers a place to play. In many cases, there is no cover charge, which means you can hop around from one establishment to another without spending a fortune. Often these performers are playing for free, so if you like what you hear, please drop a bill into the tip jar or in the hat if one is passed around.

When planning this chapter, we had some difficulty deciding how to list the many music clubs that dot Nashville's landscape. We considered breaking it down by genre but ultimately chose not to do that for two primary reasons. First of all, while many of the establishments lean toward a certain genre, like country or blues or rock, many others present a hard-to-categorize variety of musical styles. Secondly, since we've been harping so much on the fact that Nashville is so much more than just country and has so much cross-pollination of styles, we thought it would be a little hypocritical to arbitrarily segregate these places. Please bear with us. While you may have to skim through a few listings to find that honky-tonk you're looking for, you might also unexpectedly discover a blues bar or worldbeat club that really flips your switch. Such is the process of musical discovery, which is one of the things that makes Nashville such a wonderful place.

We list the larger venues, then dive right into the more intimate places. We also provide a separate list of places that hold "open microphone" songwriters nights, where any writer with an instrument and a song or two (and a little nerve) can play.

As far as costs go, in most cases arena shows are going to be priced like . . . well, arena shows, which generally means tickets will run you $20 and more. Cover charges at the clubs and other smaller venues can vary

**INSIDERS' TIP**

Don't miss Dancin' in The District, a series of free concerts at Riverfront Park. It happens every Thursday during the summer, with each show featuring multiple acts.

from "none" to about $10 or even higher for special engagements. Unless otherwise noted, there's no cover at smaller venues.

## Larger Venues

### First American Music Center
**3839 Murfreesboro Rd., Antioch**
**• (615) 641-5800**

First American Music Center, formerly Starwood Amphitheatre, is the area's only major outdoor venue. It has a capacity of more than 17,000, including 5,200 covered seats in the pavilion and a gently sloping lawn where you can spread a blanket and enjoy the music under the stars.

Major concerts in recent years have included the all-female Lilith Fair; Tom Petty and the Heartbreakers; Willie Nelson, Lyle Lovett and Shawn Colvin; Ozzy Osbourne's Ozzfest; Alanis Morisette and Tori Amos; N Sync; Cher; Tina Turner; Counting Crows with the Wallflowers; James Taylor; Lynyrd Skynyrd; Hank Williams Jr. with Travis Tritt, the Charlie Daniels Band and Jo Dee Messina; Sheryl Crow with Wilco; Aerosmith; and Barry Manilow.

A word to the wise: allow plenty of time when going to a Starwood show, as traffic for a major concert often backs up for miles on Interstate 24 as well as on Murfreesboro Road.

Also be aware that, with the 1999 bank merger of First American with AmSouth, the name of this venue may well change again.

### Riverfront Park
**100 First Ave. N. • (615) 862-8400**
**(Metro Parks office)**

Riverfront Park is the site of Dancin' in The District, a free concert series held each Thursday during the summer, as well as other seasonal concert events, some free and some with an admission charge. The 7.5-acre park, across the Cumberland River from the new stadium, includes a tiered, grassy hill that approximates an amphitheater. General capacity for concerts is 10,000.

### Ryman Auditorium
**116 Fifth Ave. N. • (615) 889-6611**

If any venue qualifies as Nashville's music Mecca, it is the Ryman, former home to the *Grand Ole Opry*. The historic, 2,085-seat former

tabernacle is now owned by Gaylord Entertainment, which also owns the Opryland property and The Wildhorse Saloon. Construction on the building began in 1889, with significant financial support from steamboat captain Thomas G. Ryman, who had recently "found" religion and banned drinking and gambling on his boats, and it opened in 1892 as the Union Gospel Tabernacle. The auditorium, though built for religious services, soon became well known for hosting lectures and theatrical performances. Through its early history, in addition to legendary preachers such as Dwight L. Moody and Billy Sunday, the stage was graced by speakers ranging from William Jennings Bryan and Helen Keller to Carrie Nation and Booker T. Washington, and by performers including Sarah Bernhardt, Enrico Caruso, Charlie Chaplin and Isadora Duncan.

After Thomas Ryman's death in 1904, the building was renamed in his honor. From 1943 to 1974 it was the home of the *Grand Ole Opry*. After the *Opry* moved to Opryland in 1974, the Ryman was neglected for years, but it reopened in June 1994 after a full restoration. Now it is noted for its excellent acoustics.

Today's Ryman is a fully functioning performing arts center that features concert-quality sound and lighting and has radio and TV broadcast capabilities. The main floor and balcony seat about 1,000 people each. The stage is 60 feet wide by 35 feet deep. It has been the site of TV specials and is also a popular spot for shooting videos.

In 1996 and 1997, it was the site of *Lost Highway: The Music & Legend of Hank Williams Sr.*, which ran Thursday through Saturday nights from May through October in both years. The big show for 1998 was *Bye Bye Love: The Everly Brothers Musical*. In 1999, the Ryman offered the musical *Pump Boys and Dinettes* and other smaller-scale productions. In addition, the *Grand Ole Opry* returned to the Ryman for a special, historic, one-weekend engagement. Other programs include Bluegrass Night each Tuesday during the summer and Sam's Place, a contemporary Christian music series held on select Sundays in the spring and fall.

The auditorium has featured concerts of a variety of musical genres and artists, including Merle Haggard, George Jones, Mary

Chapin Carpenter, Neil Young, Bruce Springsteen, Beck, Diamond Rio, Bryan White, Nanci Griffith, Elvis Costello, John Prine, Alison Krauss, John Fogerty, the Chieftains and Yo-Yo Ma. Neil Diamond recorded a TV special on the Ryman stage.

See the "Attractions" section of this chapter for information about Ryman exhibits and tours.

## Grand Ole Opry House
### 2804 Opryland Dr. • (615) 889-6611

The *Grand Ole Opry* is the show that started it all, and this is where it has happened since moving from the Ryman Auditorium in 1974. Since the *Opry* is only on Friday and Saturday nights, the Opry House is available for other concerts, awards shows and other special events during the week; it has recently played host to a series of shows by Ray Stevens, as well as single concerts by Sheryl Crow and others.

As for the *Opry* itself, it put the spotlight on country music and turned Nashville into Music City (see our History chapter). Since it made its debut in 1925 as the *WSM Barn Dance*, the *Opry* hasn't missed a broadcast. It is the world's longest-running radio show and has been drawing visitors to Nashville from around the world for decades. A recent listeners survey reported that more than 21,000 Nashvillians tune into the Saturday night broadcasts. Hundreds of thousands more tune in from 38 states and parts of Canada. The *Opry* had six homes, including the Ryman Auditorium, before it moved to the 4,400-seat Grand Ole Opry House at the Opryland complex in March 1974.

A typical *Opry* performance features a mix of country music legends, today's top stars and up-and-coming new artists. More than just traditional country, the *Opry* features bluegrass, gospel, Cajun, western swing, country rock and comedy. Opry legends such as Bill Anderson, Loretta Lynn and Porter Wagoner share the bill with today's favorites, including Garth Brooks, Vince Gill and Alison Krauss. Live broadcast performances (on WSM, 650 on the AM dial) each Friday and Saturday evening feature 20 to 25 performers. The two-hour Tuesday matinees in the summer feature eight to 10 artists. The lineup is released a couple of days before showtime. It's not unusual, however, for a special guest to drop by for a duet or surprise appearance during these unrehearsed performances.

The schedule of showtimes varies and is subject to change, so it's a good idea to call ahead before planning a visit. In 1999 the Saturday shows were at 6:30 and 9:30 PM; Friday shows were at 7:30 PM. Tickets are $20 for the main floor and mezzanine, $18 for the balcony. Tickets are sometimes still available just before showtime, but since shows often sell out, you might want to order them in advance if you're planning to visit on a specific day. Some ticket buyers cancel their reservations, so you can often get good seats at the last minute. To order tickets and check the schedule, call the listed number.

## Gaylord Entertainment Center
### 150 Second Ave. N. • (615) 770-2000

In August 1999, the name of the Nashville Arena changed to the Gaylord Entertainment Center, as the Gaylord Entertainment Company acquired the naming rights to this world-class, state-of-the-art entertainment venue. Although it features arena football and ice hockey games, along with other sporting events, it was designed primarily for concerts, so extra care went into the acoustical systems, and the sound is exceptional.

The arena, which contains more than a million square feet of total space, seats as many as 20,000 for an in-the-round concert and 18,500 using its 40-by-60-foot proscenium stage. It is also billed as "performer-friendly," with a number of amenities in the form of comfortable dressing rooms, a catering pantry and

## INSIDERS' TIP

**Kitty Wells, the first female country singer to become a major star, was also one of the rare country stars actually born in Nashville. She earned the title "Queen of Country Music."**

bath and shower facilities, so performers are likely to walk onto the stage in a good mood, which is good news for concertgoers.

Since its opening in 1996, this venue has hosted the likes of Tim McGraw, Faith Hill, ZZ Top with Kansas, The Artist, Jimmy Buffett, Metallica, Alan Jackson with LeAnn Rimes, Reba McEntire with Brooks & Dunn, and Mary J. Blige. Last-minute ticket buyers can take comfort in the fact that 20 box-office windows are available to speed the process.

## Nashville Municipal Auditorium
### 417 Fourth Ave. N. • (615) 862-6390

Municipal Auditorium, which opened in 1962, may have taken a back seat to some of the newer and larger venues around town, but it still plays host to a wide range of performers. Recent concerts have ranged from controversial shock-rockers Marilyn Manson to contemporary Christian artists dc Talk and Michael W. Smith. Other shows have included Bob Dylan, Soundgarden, Smashing Pumpkins, Reba McEntire and R. Kelly. Municipal Auditorium occasionally holds family shows such as *Sesame Street Live*.

## Tennessee Performing Arts Center (TPAC)
### 505 Deaderick St. • (615) 782-4000, (615) 255-9600 (Ticketmaster)

TPAC (pronounced "tee-pack") is mainly devoted to productions like its Broadway series and those of its resident groups (for information on such productions and more details about TPAC itself, see our Arts chapter). But it is occasionally the site of a pop or rock concert as well as some country events such as private shows and gatherings for artists' fan clubs during Fan Fair. TPAC contains three venues: 2,408-seat Jackson Hall, 1,003-seat Polk Theater and 288-seat Johnson Theater.

## Charles M. Murphy Athletic Center
### Tennessee Blvd., Murfreesboro • (615) 898-2103 (ticket information)

Elvis played here five times. The Judds' farewell tour in December 1991 made a stop. Major rock acts like Rod Stewart and AC/DC have played the Murphy Athletic Center, as have George Strait, Alan Jackson, Garth

Brooks, Pearl Jam, Kenny Rogers, Alabama, Billy Joel and Olivia Newton-John. Things have slowed down a bit, however, since the November 1996 opening of the Nashville Arena (now called the Gaylord Entertainment Center), and the preponderance of summer shows at First American Music Center also has had an impact. The university, which generally co-sponsors concerts with a promoter, hasn't given up on bringing in more big-time performers, but in the meantime it's primarily focusing more on smaller shows featuring local talent.

# Smaller Venues

## Barbara's
### 207 Printers Alley • (615) 259-BARB

Barbara's is a popular hangout for singers and songwriters, and don't be surprised if a genuine legend unexpectedly jumps on stage to join the house band.

## Bellevue Station
### 7490 Old Harding Pk., Bellevue • (615) 646-4667

Bellevue Station, in a former market, features live songwriters and bands Wednesday through Sunday nights.

## The Bluebird Cafe
### 4104 Hillsboro Rd. • (615) 383-1461

You can't talk about songwriter venues in Nashville without mentioning the Bluebird. And you can't talk at the Bluebird without someone hushing you. That may be an exaggeration, but only a slight one, because here the song is meant to be the focus, not background music for conversations. The cafe's brochures even say "Shhh!" on the front!

Owner Amy Kurland opened the Bluebird Cafe in 1982 as a restaurant with live music, and it wasn't long before the music moved to the forefront. A casual look around the 8-by-10-inch photographs covering the walls will tell you why: practically anybody who's anybody in new country and acoustic music has played here — Steve Earle, Mary Chapin Carpenter, Guy Clark, Townes Van Zandt, Janis Ian, Vince Gill, Maria Muldaur, John Prine, Bonnie Raitt . . . we could go on and on and on. Some, like Garth Brooks, played here as unknowns and went on to becoming super-star recording artists, while some have made their names as songwriters who pen hits for other people. Incidentally, the movie *The Thing Called Love*, which revolved around the Bluebird, was the last film River Phoenix made.

The songwriters in-the-round, in which four songwriters sit in a circle and take turns playing their own songs, was pioneered here by Fred Knobloch and Don Schlitz, and it's a tradition that continues most nights. If you haven't been to an in-the-round, you don't know what you're missing.

Reservations for Tuesday through Thursday shows are taken one week in advance; call (615) 383-1461. For Friday and Saturday shows, call Monday of the week of the show. Depending on who's playing, you might get in if you just show up for the evening show, which begins at 9:30 PM. But if it's a "big" show, don't count on it. The cover is generally $7 (though it can sometimes be $10 or even as much as $15 for special events), and each seat at a table also has a $7 food and drink minimum. You can avoid the minimum by sitting on the benches or sitting or standing at the bar; these positions are filled on a first-come, first-served basis. There's no cover for the early show, which starts at 6:30 PM and usually features up-and-coming songwriters.

The early show each Monday is open-microphone (for more info on that, see the "Open Microphones" section later in this chapter), typically followed by the blues music of The Bluebloods.

## Boardwalk Cafe
### 4114 Nolensville Rd. • (615) 832-5104

Boardwalk Cafe features live music seven nights, and charges a cover only on Saturday. Mondays, Tuesdays and Thursdays are writers/showcase nights.

## Bourbon Street Blues and Boogie Bar
### 220 Printers Alley • (615) 24-BLUES

Bourbon Street features live blues music seven nights a week in an appropriately dark, New Orleans–style atmosphere. The house band, Stacy Mitchhart & Blues U Can Use, typically plays Wednesday through Sunday, and the club also features frequent shows by

national acts like Kenny Neal. Cover is almost always $5, even when national acts are playing, with an occasional exception for a special engagement. The kitchen serves Cajun American cuisine.

## The Broken Spoke
### 1412 Brick Church Pk. • (615) 226-3230

The Broken Spoke, in the Ramada Inn North, is actually three separate bars: the Saloon, the Cafe and the Sports Grill. We'll focus on the first two. Country bands play in the Saloon, while the Cafe features both hit and up-and-coming songwriters. Hours vary.

## Courtyard Cafe
### 867 Bell Rd., Antioch
### • (615) 731-7228

This Italian restaurant near Hickory Hollow Mall is known not only for its pizza, but also for its live entertainment seven nights a week. Particularly strong are its songwriters nights. Hours vary.

## Davis-Kidd Booksellers
### 4007 Hillsboro Rd. • (615) 385-2645

Debi Champion is host of invitation-only writers night from 7:30 to 10 PM Friday at this hugely popular bookstore. To audition, send a tape to Champion at Davis-Kidd Booksellers, 4007 Hillsboro Road, Nashville, TN 37215.

## Douglas Corner Cafe
### 2106-A Eighth Ave. S. • (615) 298-1688

Douglas Corner is a funky little bar that showcases top Nashville songwriters, artists and bands. Songwriting legend Guy Clark ("Desperadoes Waiting for the Train") recorded his live *Keepers* album here in 1996. The Corner has open microphone Tuesday night (see the subsequent "Open Microphones" section for details). The cover charge varies but is generally just a few bucks for scheduled acts.

## Exit/In
### 2208 Elliston Pl. • (615) 321-4400

Exit/In, which opened in 1971, is one of the city's oldest clubs, and it still brings 'em in. It's essentially just a big room with a capacity of 500 people, a stage in the front and a bar in the back. Who needs anything more? The show schedule is inclined toward rock and

Photo: Cathy Summerlin

ASCAP, the American Society of Composers, Authors
and Publishers, has offices on Music Row.

alternative country, with a lot of artist-show-case concerts. At an NeA Extravaganza show-case headlined by Steve Earle in February 1995, people were packed in like the proverbial sardines. Other shows in recent years have included Sting, Hootie & the Blowfish, the Mavericks, Junior Brown, Robert Earl Keen, Social Distortion and Robbie Fulks. Jason and the Scorchers recorded a live album here over two nights in November 1997. At this writing, Exit/Inn was also home, on Tuesday nights, to Billy Block's Western Beat Roots Revival, a celebration of so-called alternative country music. The cover varies; it's generally $5 to $8 but sometimes can be $15 or more for prime shows.

### Gibson Cafe and Guitar Gallery
**318 Broadway • (615) 742-6343**
Gibson Cafe features writers nights, often

with hit writers, every Tuesday at 7 PM. It also has open mic nights every Tuesday and Sunday (see the next section in this chapter for more information).

### Gibson's Caffé Milano
**176 Third Ave. N. • (615) 255-0073**
This classy downtown restaurant (see Restaurants) and music club has been open only since July 1996 (Gibson Guitars bought it in 1998), but it has already gained recognition (and awards) as one of the top places to see and hear live music in Nashville. A series of weekly concerts by guitar legend Chet Atkins played a key role in launching Caffé Milano to greatness, and the momentum has continued with multiple concerts by Ronnie Milsap, occasional "cigar and martini" nights featuring Mavericks lead singer Raul Malo crooning Big Band and lounge standards, and other shows

### INSIDERS' TIP

In 1997, Anita Cochran became the first woman to write, produce, sing and play a lead instrument on a country album. The album, *Back to You*, was Cochran's first.

emphasizing jazz and Latin music. You'll hear anything from rock 'n' roll to Western swing from big-name acts at this venue, which also features an extensive Italian menu.

Gibson's Caffé Milano, which is in a building listed on the National Register of Historic Places, seats 250 in an open, intimate setting under a pitched roof. There's really not a bad seat in the house, and the acoustics are marvelous. Live music is featured every night except Sunday. Tickets range from about $8 to more than $20, depending on the artist. Reservations are strongly suggested as these shows tend to sell out quickly. Check the weekly ad in the *Nashville Scene* for a complete schedule, including pricing.

## Legends Corner
### 428 Broadway • (615) 248-6334

Legends, at Fifth and Broadway across from the former Nashville Arena (now called the Gaylord entertainment Center), features a variety of local talent and no cover charge.

## The Nashville Palace
### 2400 Music Valley Dr. • (615) 885-1540

It's become a part of modern country music lore that Randy Travis had a gig frying fish here and singing on the side when he was "discovered." The Nashville Palace features live country every night, with a $5 cover charge. From 8 to 10 AM Friday through Sunday the "Breakfast Club" features an all-you-can-eat buffet accompanied by the singing of Del Reeves or Jeannie Seely.

## Radio Café
### 1313 Woodland St. • (615) 262-1766

The name of this quaint little converted storefront in east Nashville comes from the collection of vintage radios on shelves lining the walls. Radio Café is essentially a coffee

shop serving soups, sandwiches and muffins, along with live music six nights a week. The cover is $4 or less. Catch Steve Key's free songwriter showcase on Thursday night (see Nightlife).

## Robert's Western World
### 416 Broadway • (615) 256-7937

You can buy a pair of cowboy boots while you listen to bluegrass and honky-tonk music at Robert's (also known as Robert's Western Wear). Even during the day, there's live entertainment during tourist season. The sign out front proudly proclaims the bar as home of BR5-49, the rowdy traditionalist honky-tonk group that served as house band for a while before signing a major-label record deal with Arista. There's a one-drink minimum but no cover charge.

## Station Inn
### 402 12th Ave. S. • (615) 255-3307

Station Inn features live bluegrass Tuesday through Sunday nights, with a different band each night from Tuesday through Saturday and an open jam session Sunday. Steve Earle has been known to sit in with the boys in the band, and he and the Del McCoury Band kicked off their 1999 joint tour with three sold-out shows here. Cover charge generally varies from $5 to $10, depending on the band, with no cover Sunday.

## Texas Troubadour Theatre
### 2416 Music Valley Dr., No. 108
### • (615) 885-0028

The 500-capacity Texas Troubadour Theatre takes evident pride in fact that it is an extension of the Ernest Tubb Record Shop — the legendary Tubb was known as "the Texas Troubadour" — and says that, like its namesake, it endeavors to always treat country mu-

Steve Earle and the Del McCoury Band celebrated the release of their bluegrass album with three packed performances at the Station Inn.

sic fans right. One example of this generosity is the continuation of the weekly "Midnight Jamboree" radio show, which Tubb started the night of May 3, 1947, the same date he opened his first record shop in downtown Nashville.

The *Midnight Jamboree*, which airs on WSM-AM 650 each Saturday after the *Grand Ole Opry*, is the second-longest-running radio show in history, taking a back seat only to the *Opry* itself. After 50 years of the show, it continues its tradition of free admission, even when a star such as Alan Jackson, Travis Tritt or Marty Stuart is in the lineup. That's the way Ernest Tubb, who started the show as way for new artists to get on the radio, always wanted it. The other regular program at the Troubadour is *Cowboy Church*, a free, nondenominational, come-as-you-are service every Sunday at 10 AM. That show, broadcast on World Wide Radio, features 45 minutes of music and 10 or 15 minutes of testimony in a laid-back but uplifting atmosphere. (See our Worship chapter for details.)

The Troubadour, which is in the Opryland area, also features theatrical productions such as *A Closer Walk With Patsy Cline*. For more information, see the Arts chapter.

### 3rd & Lindsley Bar and Grill
**818 Third Ave. S. • (615) 259-9891**

This club, a half-mile south of Broadway, boasts live blues and R&B seven nights a week. The cover charge varies according to the band but is rarely more than $8. "Nashville Sunday Nights," presented by WRLT FM 100.1 and broadcast live on that station, features a range of local and national acts.

### 328 Performance Hall
**328 Fourth Ave. S. • (615) 259-3288**

328 Performance Hall, named for its address, is one of Nashville's premier venues for cutting-edge music, from rock to pop to country. The former mattress and seed warehouse, which entered the concert scene in June 1990, is known as one of Nashville's best music venues. Capacity is about 800, and the seating situation varies, depending on the concert, from reserved to general admission to standing room only. A tiny sampling of recent concerts includes Lucinda Williams, Bruce

Cockburn, Los Lobos, Son Volt, World Party, the Wallflowers, Carl Perkins and Tracy Chapman. Ticket prices vary.

## Tootsie's Orchid Lounge
### 422 Broadway • (615) 726-0463

In the old days, Tootsie's was where legendary songwriters like Kris Kristofferson and Willie Nelson gathered to drink and write. Much of the lounge's history is reflected in the photos on the walls. There's a stage downstairs and another upstairs, where you can walk out into an alley to the side door to the Ryman Auditorium (you can't get in that way, but many legendary stars have been known to come out that door and into Tootsie's).

## 12th and Porter
### 114 12th Ave. • (615) 254-7236

12th and Porter, a favorite spot for artist showcases, features a wide variety of live music Monday through Saturday nights. The cover charge varies: usually $5 to $7; never more than $10. (See Restaurants for more information.)

## The Wildhorse Saloon
### 120 Second Ave. N. • (615) 251-1000

The Wildhorse, one of the top tourist attractions downtown in The District, is owned by Gaylord Entertainment, which also owns the Ryman Auditorium. This state-of-the-art country music club, which opened in June 1994, is host to a continuing parade of country music events. Concerts in the huge club have included Merle Haggard, Vince Gill, Billy Joe Shaver, Billy Ray Cyrus, Lee Roy Parnell and many more; the club recently announced that it would also begin featuring rock shows.

The Wildhorse presents house bands, booked from all over the United States, every night except during tapings. New country acts Lonestar and Ricochet have filled the house band slot in the past. Regular admission is $3 weekdays and $6 weekends. Concert tickets range from $6 to $15. (See also Nightlife.)

## Wolfy's
### 425 Broadway • (615) 251-1621

Wolfy's, "a grill and music room" downtown, has live music seven nights a week. There's never a cover, but often the band will pass a hat. Mark Aaron James hosts an in-the-round songwriters night Monday, and longtime session fiddle ace Buddy Spicher and his Nashville Swing Band keep the joint jumpin' Tuesday night. Original swing band BadaBing BadaBoom also appears here regularly on weekends. Wolfy's has a large selection of beers on tap.

## Zanies
### 2025 Eighth Ave. S. • (615) 269-0221

Zanies is a comedy club (see Nightlife), but it also has gotten into the music scene with concerts by such legendary artists as Roger McGuinn of the Byrds.

# Open Microphones

Here are some of the more highly regarded open-microphone venues in Nashville.

## The Bluebird Cafe
### 4104 Hillsboro Rd. • (615) 383-1461

Open-mic night at the legendary Bluebird, with host Barbara Cloyd, is Monday at 6 PM. If you're interested in playing, get there at 5:30, sign a slip of paper and put it in the basket. A drawing determines the order of performers, and unfortunately, not everybody generally gets a chance to play before time runs out at 9. If you do get on stage, you can play a maximum of two songs or 8 minutes, and your songs should be originals.

Now relax and play, keeping in mind that if you do screw up, nobody will boo you. Just about everybody else in the audience is, like you, a songwriter, and they know what it's like. And, while you should enjoy yourself, forget those dreams of being "discovered" at an open mic. It just doesn't happen that way anymore, but it's a great way to work on your

---

## INSIDERS' TIP

**A dead giveaway that you're not a Nashville Insider: pronouncing Demonbreun Street, "DEMON-brewin." The correct pronunciation is De-MON-bree-un.**

musical- and vocal-presentation skills. By the way, if you're one of the unlucky ones who don't get to play, you're guaranteed a spot the next open mic night you attend.

For more information about the Bluebird, see the listing earlier in "Small Venues" section of this chapter.

### Douglas Corner Cafe
**2106-A Eighth Ave. S. • (615) 292-2530 (recording to sign up)**
Ray Sisk hosts Douglas Corner's open mic, which starts at 8 PM Tuesday. You can reserve your spot in line by calling the listed number after 4 PM the same day you wish to attend. Calling Douglas Corner's main number won't do you any good. If you forget to call, just show up, and your name will be added to the end of the list. Depending on how many people are waiting to play, you'll get to do two or three songs.

### Gibson Cafe and Guitar Gallery
**318 Broadway • (615) 742-6343**
Gibson Cafe has open mic nights every Tuesday and Sunday. On Sunday, signup begins at 5:45 PM, with an 8 PM start; Tuesday, signup begins at 7 PM for a 10 PM start. Sunday also features a country song contest, with prizes awarded by music-industry judges.

# Support Organizations and Associations

Many support organizations are available to musicians, artists, songwriters, publishers and other members of the music industry. We have divided these into two broad groups: performance-rights organizations and other organizations.

## Performing Rights Organizations

The three performing rights organizations, or PROs — ASCAP, BMI and SESAC — are nonprofits that provide needed services such as royalty collection to songwriters and publishers. Their goal, in a nutshell, is to make sure songwriters and composers are paid

when their works are performed in public. Each organization accomplishes this by granting "blanket" licenses that permit users of copyrighted music to use any of the songs in its catalog, or repertoire, for an annual fee. Licensees fall into a wide range of categories, including radio and TV broadcasters, cable programmers, nightclubs, restaurants, theme parks, symphony orchestras, concert promoters, online service providers, skating rinks, jukebox operators and background-music providers.

While it is impossible for the PROs to monitor all broadcasts and public performances, they determine payment rates to writers and publishers through a random sampling process. They do not license the making of CDs, cassettes and phonograph records; those are administered by the music publishers, who are directly accountable to the writers and composers.

As a writer, you can affiliate with only one of the organizations, but publishers can register separate companies with all three if they desire, making it possible to sign publishing contracts with any songwriter they choose. All three organizations serve songwriters from every musical genre.

### American Society of Composers, Authors and Publishers (ASCAP)
**2 Music Sq. W. • (615) 742-5000**
When Congress added public performances to U.S. copyright law in 1897, it laid the groundwork for the founding of performing rights organizations. Encouraged by Italian opera composer Giacomo Puccini, a group of composers and songwriters including Victor Herbert, Irving Berlin and John Philip Sousa founded the American Society of Composers, Authors and Publishers in 1914, making it the first such organization. Meeting in New York with about 100 members of the music community, they sought an efficient way to ensure that creators of music would be properly compensated for public performances of their works.

Today, more than 75,000 composers, songwriters, lyricists and music publishers make up the membership of ASCAP. Dues, $10 for writers and $50 for publishers, have not changed since the start of the organization, which is governed by a Board of Directors consisting of 12 writers and 12 publishers, all elected by their peers.

ASCAP serves as a clearinghouse for creators and users of music. It simplifies the process by which users of music get permission to publicly perform ASCAP-licensed music, and by which member songwriters and publishers grant such permission. ASCAP has reciprocal international agreements with 54 foreign societies performing similar functions.

To become a writer member, you must have a commercially recorded music composition, a published composition available for sale or rental or written proof that your music was performed publicly in a venue licensed by ASCAP. Writers who do not meet any of those criteria are allowed to join as associate members, with the only requirement being proof of one music work registered with the U.S. Copyright Office. Publisher members must verify that their company is regularly engaged in the music publishing business or that they publish works that are publicly performed regularly by ASCAP licensees, and also demonstrate that they meet any of the requirements for writer members.

ASCAP, which provides such services as workshops, showcases and benefits packages to its members, also has offices in New York, Los Angeles, Chicago, London and Puerto Rico.

## Broadcast Music Inc. (BMI)
**10 Music Sq. E. • (615) 401-2000**

With more than 160,000 songwriter, composer and publisher members, Broadcast Music Inc. is the world's largest performing rights organization. A group of 600 broadcasters formed BMI in Chicago in 1939 as a more inclusive alternative to ASCAP, which at that time required five published hit songs for admission and, furthermore, did not represent such popular "roots music" forms as country, blues and R&B (remember, this was in the pre-rock 'n' roll days). The new organization's "open door" policy not only made it possible for more writers and publishers to collect royalties for performances of their works, but also made a much larger selection of music available to the public.

As the infant organization began building its catalog, it formed its own publishing company, which it later sold. Membership continued to grow as ASCAP became ensnared in a battle with broadcasting networks over its increasing fees. BMI still has the least restrictive admissions policy among the performing rights organizations: membership is open to any songwriter. In 1958, as BMI became more heavily involved in country music, it opened its Nashville office, which Frances Williams initially ran from her home. (Later, as Frances Preston, she became president of the entire organization and a highly influential force for the good of songwriters.)

BMI, which also has offices in New York, Los Angeles and London as well as agreements with 40 foreign PROs, charges no dues to writers. Publishers pay a one-time administrative fee of $100.

## SESAC
**55 Music Sq. E. • (615) 320-0055**

SESAC, established in 1930 as the Society of European Stage Authors and Composers (a moniker it no longer uses; it's just SESAC), is the second-oldest performing rights organization. It is also the smallest, although in recent years its membership has greatly expanded, attracting many former members of ASCAP and BMI in the process.

Paul Heinicke established the organization in 1930 to help foreign composers collect performance royalties for the public performance of their songs in the United States. SESAC began by licensing large amounts of jazz, gospel and other types of music that were largely neglected by ASCAP, and later by BMI. Since the 1970s, it has made major inroads into country music.

SESAC, which also has a New York office, remains the smallest PRO, largely by choice. Although there is no charge for writers or publishers to join, the organization has a selective admissions policy: prospective members submit a tape of their work, which is evaluated to determine whether a relationship would be mutually beneficial. The organization is the only PRO to provide a guaranteed royalty payment amount to its members. It also is a pioneer in the use of Broadcast Data Systems computer technology to monitor airplay of songs around the country; this system is more accurate than the random sampling methods used by ASCAP and BMI.

# Other Organizations

## American Federation of Musicians (AFM), Local 257
**Nashville Association of Musicians, 11 Music Cir. N. • (615) 244-9514**

Membership in the local chapter of the American Federation of Musicians, whose membership is now more than 150,000, provides a number of services aimed at performing musicians. Benefits include local job referral programs and a computerized service that can help members find work with traveling bands; legally binding contracts offering job and wage protection; established minimum wage scales and working conditions; free legal service for traveling musicians; and local and internationally recognized agreements providing protection in fields including studio and other recording work, TV, films, concerts and other performances.

Members also have access to toll-free phone lines that will put them in contact with various AFM divisions; they have opportunities to attend national conferences; and they can benefit from trust funds, pension plans, insurance plans, an emergency relief fund and more.

The American Federation of Musicians was founded in 1896. The Nashville Association of Musicians, Local 257 of the national group, was founded in 1902.

## Black Country Music Association (BCMA)
**629 Shady Ln. • (615) 227-5570**

Can you name an African-American country superstar besides Charley Pride? Didn't think so. And that's one of the reasons for the recent formation of this nonprofit organization, which aims to correct some unfortunately too-common misperceptions. Pride, CMA Entertainer of the Year in 1971 and 1972 and singer of hits including "Kiss an Angel Good Morning," is the only black country singer so far to have attained superstar status. But it's certainly not for a lack of talent in the genre, and the BCMA has already staged a series of successful local showcases featuring black country artists from across the country. The organization, whose members meet twice a month, is also working to find music-industry internships for students at Fisk and Meharry universities.

The relationship of blacks and country literally is almost as old as the hills from which the music sprang. Harmonica player DeFord Bailey became the first black to join the *Grand Ole Opry* in 1926, and he spent 15 years there, becoming one its most popular members. Countless artists before and since have grown up listening to, singing and being influenced by country instead of, or along with, blues and R&B. And, as many of the most enduring artists (Ray Charles comes immediately to mind, but there are many others) have ably demonstrated, all these American musical forms share roots. The BCMA sees its role as educational, reminding the public — and the record industry itself — of black contributions to country music. It also seeks to open doors on Music Row to black artists, songwriters, publishers, producers and executives.

The six-man group Wheels recently became the first black country band signed to a major label when it inked a contract with Asylum. Curb Records also recently signed a solo artist named Trini Triggs. And, of course, there have always been hits that, covered by different artists, have been hits on country and pop charts. Recent examples were "Nobody Knows," an R&B hit by the Tony Rich Project

---

**INSIDERS' TIP**

**Bobby's Idle Hour, a tiny beer bar at 1010 16th Avenue S., is a songwriters' hangout where a guitar is frequently passed around. Just down the street, at 26 Music Square E., is Sammy B's restaurant, a trendier spot that is excellent for music-industry people-watching.**

Photo: Cathy Summerlin

Hatch Show Print is best known for its early posters of *Grand Ole Opry* stars.

and a country smash by Kevin Sharp; and Dolly Parton's "I Will Always Love You," which Whitney Houston took to the top of the pop and R&B charts.

BCMA founder Frankie Staton and a growing number of believers are confident that, if Nashville's music industry will only throw its support behind black artists, the public will respond favorably. Stay tuned for further developments.

If you're interested in trying out for a BCMA showcase, send a tape, bio and photo to talent coordinator J.J. Jones, 235 Ross Avenue, Gallatin, TN 37066.

## Country Music Association
### 1 Music Cir. S. • (615) 244-2840

The Country Music Association was the first trade organization formed to promote a type of music. Founded in 1958, CMA works to guide and enhance the development of

country music worldwide, demonstrate country music as a viable medium to advertisers and provide an ongoing public relations initiative for the entire industry. Today the CMA has about than 7,000 members, including individuals and companies in 43 countries. Members must be directly involved in the industry to qualify for membership. CMA's Board of Directors consists of more than 60 industry leaders who volunteer their time. The CMA has a professional staff of 30 in its Nashville office and five international representatives.

To the general public, CMA is perhaps best known for its annual CMA Awards show, considered the most prestigious awards in country music. CMA's first awards were presented in 1967. The next year NBC taped the program for rebroadcast, and the show became the first such program to be carried on major network television. In 1969 the show was broadcast live. Today the CMA Awards, broadcast by CBS, are among the highest-rated entertainment specials on television.

CMA's Fan Fair, held each June at the Tennessee State Fairgrounds, draws as many as 24,000 country music fans, who come for the opportunity to meet their favorite performers and attend lots of concerts. Read more about it in our "Annual Events" section in this chapter.

CMA also serves the industry with its *Close Up* magazine, available to CMA members; the *Country Music Radio Directory*, available in a comprehensive published edition and on mailing labels; and a reference directory of CMA members, events and marketing initiatives. CMA established the Country Music Hall of Fame in 1961 to honor country music's greatest contributors and each year conducts the selection and induction into the prestigious institution.

## Gospel Music Association
**1205 Division St. • (615) 242-0303**

Since it was founded in 1964, the Gospel Music Association has continued to promote gospel music in all its many forms. The GMA has grown and diversified over the years, and today this umbrella organization offers a variety of programs, special projects and services for the burgeoning gospel music industry. The organization's premiere event is the annual Gospel Music Week (see our "Annual Events" section in this chapter), which attracts aspiring performers as well as seasoned professionals from throughout the music industry. The week of activities is capped by the Dove Awards show, a nationally televised program highlighted by live performances that show the diversity of gospel music; among the categories are pop, inspirational, rock, country, rap/hip-hop, urban, traditional gospel, instrumental and praise and worship.

In 1995, the GMA launched the Academy of Gospel Music Arts. This traveling educational program presented in as many as 10 cities nationwide is designed to educate, encourage and support the development of future generations of gospel music artists. The organization's other educational and public relations efforts include the publishing of industry networking guides and a membership newsletter.

The GMA formed the Gospel Music Hall of Fame in 1971 to honor the contributions of individuals who have played key roles in leading and developing the industry. While not set up for tours, the Hall of Fame is available as a resource center. Anyone wanting to research gospel music can make use of this facility; the 1,500-square-foot room contains CDs, cassettes, albums, photos and press kits of Hall of Fame members.

## Music City Blues Society
**(615) 297-1465, (615) 292-5222 (hotline)**

The Music City Blues Society aims to promote and preserve the tradition and heritage of blues music by educating the general public and schoolchildren about this uniquely American art form and providing opportunities for the live performance of blues music. The society offers resources such as archives and a library, CDs available through the public library, a newsletter and various concerts, performances and related programs. Annual membership is $15 per individual and $20 per family. Write to them at P.O. Box 22852, Nashville TN 37202.

## Nashville Entertainment Association (NeA)
**1105 16th Ave. S. • (615) 341-0097**

The NeA was founded in 1980 by a group of business executives who recognized Nashville's potential to become a major entertainment center for all types of music. Today this nonprofit trade organization is composed of representatives from all areas of the music industry: artists, record companies, promoters and many others. The NeA's mission is to unite, promote and serve all entertainment businesses in Nashville. Its profits go to music and arts education in area schools.

As part of the Nashville Area Chamber of Commerce's Arts, Entertainment and Music Department, NeA promotes every entertainment business in Nashville internationally. Here in Music City, NeA sponsors several events to promote budding talent. The NeA's annual Extravaganza showcase (see the "Annual Events" section in this chapter) spotlights some of the best noncountry talent in the region. The association also sponsors the Music City Music, a singer-songwriter showcase for artists in the country and Americana genres. This yearly event is an alternative to the traditional song-plugging process, offering songwriters direct access to those who are in a position to get their songs recorded. Garth Brooks obtained his record deal with Capitol after participating in one of NeA's showcases in 1988. In September NeA sponsors a celebrity golf tournament.

## Nashville Songwriters Association International (NSAI)
**1701 West End Ave. • (615) 256-3354**

NSAI, the world's largest not-for-profit songwriters organization, with membership approaching 3,000, is devoted to supporting songwriters through advocacy, education and networking opportunities. It was founded as the Nashville Songwriters Association (NSA) in 1967 by a group of about 40 songwriters — including Buddy Mize, Eddie Miller, Marijohn Wilkin, Kris Kristofferson and Felice and Boudleaux Bryant — concerned by the lack of credit and respect accorded members of the profession at that time.

Major accomplishments include the establishment of the annual Songwriter Achievement Awards in 1968; the printing of writers' names on record labels and sleeves, a practice that began in 1970; the establishment in 1970 of the Nashville Songwriters Hall of Fame; and the passing of an improved copyright law that took effect in 1978. The organization officially went worldwide in 1977, becoming the Nashville Songwriters Association International.

As a member, you can make use of the NSAI office facilities — the group moved in 1998 to new, larger offices on West End Avenue — whenever you're in town. You'll also have access to the association's toll-free number, which is especially useful for out-of-town members. At the office, you can make cassette dubs of your demos, type your lyrics, have photocopies made, make local phone calls while the receptionist takes any messages for you, use songwriting reference books and pick up plenty of other information. You can also submit one song at a time to the NSAI song-evaluation service, in which a songwriting pro provides an opinion on a song's readiness for the commercial market.

Workshops are held at 6:30 PM each Thursday at the Musicians Union building, 11 Music Square N. (see the previous entry for American Federation of Musicians, Local 257). The general schedule is: music-industry guest speakers the first Thursday of each month; song critiques by fellow NSAI members and moderators the second and any fifth Thursday; "pitch sessions," in which you can play your songs for publishers who are screening material, the third Thursday; and teaching sessions featuring pro songwriters and instructors the fourth Thursday. For out-of-town members, NSAI has a network of about 70 workshops around the country, and opportunities are available for starting new ones.

NSAI also sponsors several annual events. Song Camp 101, in April and July, and Song Camp 201, in October, are three-day songwriting retreats featuring pro songwriters teaching aspiring writers who are selected on the basis of a two-song demo. Spring Symposium is an educational conference and networking opportunity held each April during Tin Pan South, a week-long musical festival saluting songwriters, with nightly performances around town. The Songwriter Achievement Awards dinner, also during Tin Pan South, recognizes the achievements of Nashville's top writers in a variety of categories. Summer seminar is an educational conference and networking opportunity in July. The Nashville Songwriters Hall of Fame Dinner & Induction Ceremony is a "black tie optional" affair that each September or October adds three names to the Hall of Fame.

Active and associate membership is $100 a year. Office hours are 9 AM to 5 PM Monday through Friday.

## The Songwriters Guild of America (SGA)
**1222 16th Ave. S., Ste. 25**
**• (615) 329-1782**

The Songwriters Guild of America, founded in 1931 as the Songwriters Protective Agency, now has more than 5,000 members worldwide. It is a voluntary association run by songwriters. Services range from creative to administrative to financial and include reviewing of publishing contract offers and providing the Popular Songwriters Contract as an example of a fair agreement; collecting royalties and auditing music publishers; group medi-

# Q&A With a Leading Songwriter

Bob DiPiero is a highly successful Nashville songwriter. His numerous hits (13 No. 1 songs among them) include the Oak Ridge Boys' "American Made," Ricochet's "Daddy's Money," Shenandoah's "The Church on Cumberland Road," Pam Tillis's "It's Lonely Out There," George Strait's "Blue Clear Sky" and Neal McCoy's "Wink," BMI's 1995 Country Song of the Year. He talked with Insiders' Guide about being a songwriter in today's Nashville.

Close-up

INSIDERS' GUIDE: In what ways is a career as a songwriter different from a career as an artist?

BOB DiPIERO: It's different in that you don't have to sleep on a bus (laughs). Quite honestly, I think a songwriter — especially one fortunate enough to have had some success — has one of the best gigs going.

You work in your home or in your office, you set your own hours, you work at your own pace, you do what you love . . . and you get to go home at night. I've got nothing but great admiration and respect for the artists because their lives are so disrupted: traveling constantly, living out of a suitcase and on a bus, eating bad food, being on call 24 hours a day to do interviews, signings and the show itself. Being a songwriter is a great life.

IG: What was your first chart success — and when?

BD: I believe it was in the back half of 1980. It was a song called "I Can See Forever in Your Eyes" that I wrote by myself. It was recorded by this unknown singer from Oklahoma named Reba McEntire. I think it reached into the teens, was a Top-20 hit. At that time, I'm sure, most of the country had no idea who Reba McEntire was. I was grateful to anyone showing an interest in my work. That one's always been very special to me. Since then I have had two No. 1s with her, but that first one was a sweet one.

IG: What has been your biggest hit so far?

BD: That depends on what you mean by "big." One of the biggest was one of the first, "American Made" by the Oak Ridge Boys. To be on an album that sold gold back then was a major feat. If your album just goes gold today, you're in trouble. I think "American Made" was No. 1 for three or four weeks, and it became an anthem for the Miller Brewing Company. "Wink" was its own thing, Song of the Year for BMI, which was a tremendous honor.

IG: What is your opinion of the current state of affairs in Nashville?

Photo: Little Town Big Music

Bob DiPiero

— continued on next page

BD: I think the Nashville music scene, and the music business in 1997, is really healthy and will remain really healthy and vibrant for many years. I see the talent in the pipeline, the new people getting deals, and so forth.

Nashville fell victim to what every creative industry does — "OK, some guy with a hat sold a lot of records; I want a guy with a hat. Some girl with a ring in her navel sold a lot of records; I want a girl with a ring in her navel." We wound up with a lot of clones. You listen to the radio and you're not sure who it is singing. That makes the songwriter and the song more powerful. It ends up being the song driving the artist's career as much as it is the artist himself. What's going on now is not a downturn, just a correction. Some artists are being culled out like survival of the fittest.

But there's just some great talent out there waiting for a chance, so much product crying to come out. The Nashville music business is very healthy. There's more competition for people's entertainment dollars, and it makes the industry work that much harder to come out with good stuff that will give people their money's worth.

IG: What advice would you give to someone trying to break into the industry as a writer today?

BD: Have a tremendous amount of patience, be ready to have an even greater amount of perseverance and hope somewhere along the line that you're lucky. If you talk to any successful writer or artist, those three things will come up. They were totally persevering, they totally believed, they were willing to hang out through disappointments, and at some point things fell their way.

It's very competitive out there now; new writers should make no mistake about that. When they start working in the Nashville field, they're competing with the best in the world.

cal, life and disability insurance plans; a catalog administration program for members who control their publishing rights; copyright renewal; a songwriter collaboration service; and a nonprofit educational foundation that sponsors educational programs and annual university scholarship grants.

Weekly events at the SGA offices include song critiques, "ask-a-pro" sessions, instrumental clinics and analyses of hit songs. SGA, which has offices in New Jersey, Hollywood and New York in addition to Nashville, also lobbies for legislation favorable to songwriters and has played a major role in the passage of laws regarding copyright, copyright renewal and home recording.

# Annual Events

## February

### Nashville Entertainment Association Extravaganza
**Various local venues • (615) 341-0097**

Nashville may be synonymous with country music, but there has long been a strong rock and pop music scene here too. Music City is home to vibrant mix of talent spanning diverse musical genres that include pop, heavy metal, speed metal, gospel, world music, Americana, jazz, hip-hop and rap. Non-coun-

## INSIDERS' TIP

**Garth Brooks made his first trip to Nashville in 1985 but returned, discouraged, to his native Oklahoma less than a day later. He returned in 1987 with his wife Sandy, and the rest is history.**

try Nashville favorites in the past couple of decades have included Jason and the Scorchers, Walk The West, Intruder and Fleming & John.

For three days and four nights, usually during the third weekend in February, Music City celebrates non-country talent from Nashville and the Southeast during the Nashville Entertainment Association's Extravaganza. The event's mission is to showcase the best unsigned local, regional and national talent to the music industry and the public. As many as 500 music industry executives from New York and Los Angeles turn out in search of future hit-makers. Hundreds of acts perform each year. Since its inception in 1986, the Extravaganza has showcased many artists who have gone on to sign national recording contracts, song publishing contracts or management deals. BR5-49, Fleming & John, Gillian Welch, Edwin McCain, Jack Ingram, Jackyl and Better Than Ezra are among them.

The first few events were showcases for Nashville rock acts. Since then the Extravaganza has grown considerably, expanding its focus to include bands from around the Southeast and acquiring Apple Computer as a sponsor. A nationally known artist or two usually performs during the event as well. Most of the action takes place at night, but daytime activities include the Musicians' Power Lunch, music seminars and a trade show. Most of the downtown-area clubs get in on the action, opening their doors to the music biz crowd and the public.

Tickets range from about $5 to $20, depending on the venue and artist performing. Four-day passes are available from the NeA. Shows usually begin at 8 PM.

# April

## Tin Pan South
### Ryman Auditorium and various Nashville venues • (615) 256-3354
One of our city's treasures is its talented songwriting community. Nashville songwriters pen hits that are heard and loved by millions around the world. Eric Clapton's Grammy-winning song "Change the World" was written by Music City's Gordon Kennedy, Wayne

Kirkpatrick and Tommy Simms. Country hits like "The Gambler" and "Elvira" came out of Nashville, as have pop hits such as "Butterfly Kisses," the huge hit by Nashvillian and contemporary Christian artist Bob Carlisle. We are fortunate that on just about any night of the week, we can head out to a club like the Bluebird Cafe or Douglas Corner and hear great songs performed by the talented individuals who wrote them.

For about six days in mid-April, Tin Pan South offers the chance to catch a bunch of top songwriters performing their hits acoustically in an intimate club setting. The Nashville Songwriters Association International sponsors this event, the nation's only festival celebrating the songwriter and the song, and writers from around the country join in. Tin Pan South takes its name from Nashville's songwriting predecessor, the famous Tin Pan Alley in New York. Among the activities are the Songwriters Achievement Awards at the Ryman Auditorium; Tin Pan Jam Night, featuring legendary songwriters; the Tin Pan South Golf Tournament for members of the corporate community, music executives and songwriters; and a two-day symposium offering songwriting workshops, song evaluations with writers and publishers, and guest lectures.

A highlight of the event is the Tin Pan South Legendary Songwriters' Acoustic Concert at the Ryman Auditorium, which features four or five legendary songwriters. Past performers at this concert have included Steve Winwood ("Higher Love"), Alan and Marylin Bergman ("You Don't Send Me Flowers"), Michael McDonald ("Minute By Minute"), Jimmy Webb ("Up, Up and Away"), Christopher Cross ("Sailing"), Janis Ian ("At Seventeen"), John Phillips ("Do You Believe In Magic"), Cy Coleman ("Big Spender"), Barrett Strong ("I Heard It Through The Grapevine") and Dennis Morgan ("I Knew You Were Waiting (For Me)"). Tickets are available through Ticketmaster, (615) 255-9600, and at the door if tickets aren't sold out. Ticket prices vary. Shows usually begin at 7 and 9:30 PM.

## Nashville River Stages
### Riverfront Park • (615) 641-5800
This music festival debuted in 1998, more or less replacing Nashville's Summer Lights

music and arts festival that was held in the '80s and '90s. River Stages is a three-day music festival that features as many as 60 bands on five stages. The focus is on rock music. Past performers have included Hootie & The Blowfish, Steve Earle, Indigo Girls, Bonnie Raitt, George Thorogood & The Destroyers, Hole, Paula Cole and Wilco. Tickets are available through Ticketmaster, (615) 255-9600. In 1999 tickets were $17.50 in advance and $20 the day of the show; a three-day pass was $35.

## Gospel Music Week
**Renaissance Nashville Hotel, Nashville Convention Center and various venues • (615) 242-0303**

If you think gospel music is just something you hear in church, you've obviously never been near the Renaissance Nashville Hotel and Nashville Convention Center in late April. That's when 2,000 or more gospel artists, radio station executives and music industry types from around the world arrive for the Gospel Music Association's annual Gospel Music Week.

It looks more like a rock music convention than a choir meeting. Nashville being the headquarters of the thriving Christian music scene, all the players who don't live in Music City come here for a yearly dose of seminars, showcases, parties and networking opportunities. Seminars covering such topics as artist development, concert promotion, marketing and getting a record deal take place Monday through Thursday at the convention center. There's also a trade show with 70 or more exhibitors. Showcase luncheons and worship services are scheduled throughout the week. These events are for convention registrants, but the nighttime showcases held in various local venues are open to the public. The schedule and ticket prices vary, so check the newspapers for up-to-date information.

All genres of Christian music are represented — from Christian rock to Southern gospel to traditional black gospel. Among the hundreds of past performers are Steven Curtis Chapman, Michael W. Smith, DC Talk, 4HIM, Petra, Amy Grant, Sandi Patty, Point of Grace and Jars of Clay. The convention traditionally culminates Thursday evening with the presentation of the Dove Awards, when awards in more than 35 categories are bestowed upon the industry's best. The show takes place at the Grand Ole Opry House and is televised nationally. Some tickets are available to the public; contact the GMA at the number above for more information.

# May

## Tennessee Jazz & Blues Society Concert Series
**Belle Meade Plantation, 5025 Harding Rd. • (615) 356-0501**
**The Hermitage, 4580 Rachel's Ln., Hermitage • (615) 889-2941**

Picture this: it's a warm summer evening, a gentle breeze is blowing, and you're kicking back on the lawn of a magnificent mansion as the sounds of jazz and blues music waft by and the stars twinkle overhead. You can have that experience, thanks to the Tennessee Jazz & Blues Society, which has been sponsoring a summer concert series for more than a dozen years.

From late May through early August, on Sunday evenings from 6 to 8 PM, the society presents concerts under the stars, alternating between Belle Meade Plantation and The Hermitage. Bring a blanket or folding chairs and pack a cooler with your favorite picnic fare. Everyone is welcome — you can even bring the dog. Admission is $10 at the gate or through Ticketmaster, (615) 255-9600; children 12 and under are admitted free. Members of the Tennessee Jazz & Blues Society can purchase tickets for half-price. Group rates are available by calling either location in advance. For more info, call the Tennessee Jazz & Blues Society Hotline at (615) 386-7500.

# June

## International Country Music Fan Fair
**Tennessee State Fairgrounds, Wedgewood Ave. at Rains Ave. • (615) 889-7503**

Country music fans have traditionally been a loyal bunch, and country artists bend over

# Eating and Playing With the Stars

If you haven't figured it out by now, we're big fans of Music City. We can't help it — there is just so much to like. We like the fact that Nashville serves up the conveniences

and amenities of big-city life with a friendly smile and a laid-back attitude. We like our parks, lakes and green, rolling hills. We like our little secret out-of-the-way restaurants — the ones most tourists overlook. We like our cool songwriters' clubs. And, of course, we like Nashville's music.

We asked some of Nashville's performers and songwriters what they like about our city and found out they are not so different from you and me. Before we get to the answers, let's briefly introduce you to our panel of stars.

Nashville native **Lorrie Morgan** has been performing country music for more than 25 years and has grown up in the industry to become one of country music's hottest stars.

**Steven Curtis Chapman** is one of contemporary Christian music's most recognizable names. A Franklin resident, Chapman has earned three Grammy awards, three gold records, 28 Dove awards and 22 No. 1 singles.

**Charlie Daniels** is known throughout the musical worlds of rock, country, bluegrass and gospel. The legendary performer has been singing, writing songs and playing for more than 30 years, and he still performs 175 to 200 concerts a year. He's perhaps best identified with his huge 1979 pop and country hit "The Devil Went Down to Georgia."

Since his debut album, *A Thousand Winding Roads,* was released on Epic Records in 1990, **Joe Diffie** has emerged as one of the hottest

Steven Curtis Chapman is a contemporary Christian superstar.

artists in country music. Diffie's fourth album, *Third Rock From the Sun*, was a huge hit, reaching platinum status and producing three No. 1 singles. The title cut from his 1999 album, *A Night to Remember*, was a big hit that year.

**Bob DiPiero** is a successful Nashville songwriter. His numerous hits include the Oak Ridge Boys' "American Made," Shenandoah's "The Church on Cumberland Road," Pam Tillis's "It's Lonely Out There" and Neal McCoy's "Wink," BMI's 1995 Country Song of the Year.

BNA recording group **Lonestar** burst onto the country music scene in 1995 with their eponymous debut album. The gold-selling album produced four hit singles, including the smash "No News." Lonestar's single, "Amazed," from their 1999 release *Lonely Girl*, was No. 1 on the country chart for several weeks in the summer of 1999.

*Where would you go if you had a day to spend alone in or around Nashville?*

**Charlie Daniels**: I would probably stay at home and ride my horses (on his 400-acre ranch near Mt. Juliet).

**Lorrie Morgan**: I would spend it on Old Hickory Lake.

— continued on next page

**Steven Curtis Chapman**: Ride my Harley on the Natchez Trace Parkway.

**Joe Diffie**: Any of the great golf courses.

**Michael Britt** (Lonestar): I would look for a good writers night or live act, or shop at one of the many music stores. **Keech Rainwater** (Lonestar): Fishing at Percy Priest Lake.

*Where would you take your family for a day of fun in or around Nashville?*

**Joe Diffie**: Touring up and down Music Row, Opryland Hotel or perhaps a mall.

**Lorrie Morgan**: Old Hickory Lake.

**Michael Britt** (Lonestar): Hickory Hollow Mall, Percy Priest Lake or one of the many state parks within driving distance. **Richie McDonald** (Lonestar): Center Hill Lake. **Keech Rainwater** (Lonestar): Fishing at Percy Priest Lake.

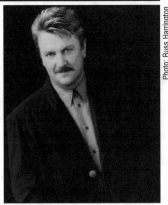

Photo: Russ Harrington

Joe Diffie is an established country chart-topper.

---

*Where might you take visiting relatives and friends to show them a good time in Nashville?*

**Lorrie Morgan**: Bluebird Cafe for writers' night.

**Joe Diffie**: Lower Broadway (Planet Hollywood, Hard Rock Cafe, Wildhorse Saloon, etc.).

**Charlie Daniels**: If they had kids, I would take them to Opryland. If they had Civil War interests, I'd take them to Stones River. If they were into country music, I'd take them to the *Grand Ole Opry*. Downtown is good too.

Photo: Lorrie Morgan Entertainment

Songstress Lorrie Morgan grew up in the industry.

**Michael Britt** (Lonestar): Opryland Hotel, Second Avenue, Music Row. **Richie McDonald** (Lonestar): Centennial Park. **Dean Sams** (Lonestar): The Riverfront area. There are lots of clubs and places to eat and usually a good time. You have the Hard Rock Cafe and Wildhorse Saloon, to name a couple.

*Where would you go for a good breakfast in or around Nashville?*

**Lorrie Morgan**: Mason Jar (W. Main Street in Hendersonville).

**Joe Diffie**: Any Cracker Barrel.

**Bob DiPiero**: Obviously I love Pancake Pantry, but it's so well known and so packed that it's hard to get in. I've become a fan of Waffle House — there's one near my house, and you can get in and out quickly.

**Michael Britt** (Lonestar): The Pancake Pantry near Vandy or any Cracker Barrel. **Richie McDonald** (Lonestar): Waffle House. **Dean Sams** (Lonestar): Sunday brunch at the Opryland Hotel is great.

*What is one of your favorite Nashville lunch spots?*
**Steven Curtis Chapman**: The Orchid or The East India Club (Brentwood).
**Bob DiPiero**: Being Italian, I'm kind of picky when it comes to Italian food. Nick's Italian Deli, downtown in the workers' district, is only open for lunch. But it has great sandwiches and mainstays like spaghetti and meatballs and ravioli and lasagna. It's cheap and fast, kind of cafeteria style.
**Lorrie Morgan**: Prince's Chicken Shack.
**Joe Diffie**: Green Hills Grille.
**Charlie Daniels**: Swett's is a really good place. For dinner, Morton's Steakhouse.
**Michael Britt** (Lonestar): Mack's Cafe. **Richie McDonald** (Lonestar): Rosko's.

*What do you like about Nashville?*
**Lorrie Morgan**: It has the community closeness, yet a sophisticated atmosphere. I visit a lot of big cities, and Nashville is homey and just big enough for me.
**Joe Diffie**: It's a big city with a small-town atmosphere. It's a great place to raise a family.
**Charlie Daniels**: I like how centrally located it is. We spend a lot more time at home than we would if we lived, say, in Dallas. I feel I've really found a home in Tennessee.
**Michael Britt** (Lonestar): I like the size, the ability to do a lot of things without having to drive hours to get there. Also, the whole music business. I like the small-town feel of Nashville. I wouldn't want to see it grow into a Dallas or Atlanta. **Dean Sams** (Lonestar): It's a big town that has all the charm of a small town!

Photo: BNA Records

*What's your favorite place to play live?*
**Bob DiPiero**: My favorite is the Blue-bird. It's kind of my home turf, my home base. I've been playing there in one incarnation or another since it opened. I played in a band called Wolves in Sheep's Clothing in the early days. For years I've been doing those in-the-rounds that the Blue-bird has made world-famous. That's like home to me. It's a great place to see great music.

Lonestar helps carry the city's "young country" banner.

backward to show their gratitude during Fan Fair, the annual celebration designed to honor music fans. The bond between country fans and their favorite artists is a unique one in the music industry. You probably wouldn't find many famous rock bands standing in a booth all day to sign autographs for their fans, but country artists do just that. In 1996, Garth Brooks made a surprise visit to the 25th annual Fan Fair and signed autographs for 23 consecutive hours — reportedly without a bathroom break! Another year, Kathy Mattea, under strict orders from her doctor not to speak because of vocal cord injuries, managed to communicate with her fans via personal computer.

Since its inception in 1972, Fan Fair, organized and sponsored by the Country Music Association and *Grand Ole Opry*, has become a tradition for country fans and Nashville's music industry. The first event drew 5,000 to the Municipal Auditorium. In 1982, the event was moved to the Tennessee State Fairgrounds, where it could accommodate more fans. By the 1990s, Fan Fair was drawing as many as 24,000, garnering worldwide media attention and selling out months in advance. In 1999, its economic impact on Nashville was estimated at $11.4 million.

Today, Fan Fair offers nearly a full week of events, including some 35 hours of concerts at the fairgrounds' grandstand, photograph and autograph sessions and various fan club events. Typically, more than 200 country music artists participate, making scheduled appearances at booths in the exhibit buildings. Devoted fans stand in line for hours to have their picture taken with their favorite stars, and the artists put in long days to accommodate as many fans as possible.

Most major artists participate in Fan Fair, although not all stars attend each year. Among the artists who have participated are Bill Monroe, Billy Ray Cyrus, Randy Travis, Roy Acuff, Tim McGraw, Alan Jackson, Doug Stone, Lorrie Morgan, Pam Tillis, Loretta Lynn, Reba McEntire, Ernest Tubb, Deana Carter and Vince Gill. In 1974, Paul McCartney made a surprise visit, and in 1993 pop star Bryan Adams showed up.

Net proceeds from Fan Fair are used to advance the growth and popularity of country music. CMA earmarks the money for such entities as the Country Music Retirement Center Initiative, International Development for Country Music, the Hall of Fame Building and industry research.

If you're planning to attend, plan early. Purchase your tickets well in advance. In recent years, Fan Fair has sold out four months in advance. Wear cool clothing, as it's pretty hot and humid here this time of year; wear comfortable shoes (you'll do a lot of walking); and bring along plenty of patience (you'll do a lot of waiting). A $90 ticket is good for admission to all Fan Fair events as well as the Country Music Hall of Fame and Museum and the Ryman Auditorium. It also entitles you to two barbecue meals cooked by the Odessa Chuck Wagon Gang of Odessa, Texas. For more information, or to register, call the number listed.

# August

## Franklin Jazz Festival
**Franklin town sq. • (615) 791-9924**

Music City U.S.A. jazzes its way to neighboring Franklin for this event, which is traditionally held the first full weekend in August (though 1999's festival was scheduled for September). Traditional jazz, Dixieland and Big Band music fill the town square of Franklin, 15 miles south of downtown Nashville. The festival is listed as one of the top 20 events in the Southeast. It's sponsored by the Downtown Franklin Association and Williamson County Arts Council. The music begins Saturday morning with a New Orleans–style parade, and the community is invited to get in the spirit by showing up in their most outlandish costumes. Restrooms, free bus parking and food and drink are available. A fireworks display caps off the activities. Admission is free. Franklin's town square is 3 miles west of I-65 at the Highway 96 exit.

## Bell Witch Bluegrass Festival
**Old Bell School, Adams**
**• (615) 696-2589**

Bluegrass musicians and fans alike enjoy this festival, which features competitions in harmonica, bluegrass banjo, mandolin, guitar, clogging and square dancing. It's organized by a local bluegrass musician and sponsored by the Adams Community Men's Club. Amateur musicians from Tennessee and surrounding states compete for more than $3,000 in prize money. It takes place the first or second weekend in August in Adams, 40 miles north of downtown Nashville.

The pickin' starts Friday evening and continues all day Saturday. All final prize money and a trophy for best overall fiddle player are

## INSIDERS' TIP

**Elvis Presley made his first Nashville recordings January 10, 1956.**

## It's A Grand Ole Cast

How many of these names do you recognize? Those of you who are diehard country music fans probably know them all. As of July 1999, this was the cast of the *Grand Ole Opry*; the names are followed by the year they joined. The cast changes from time to time, as new members are added and others choose to drop out for a while. The invitation to join the *Opry* is extended by Grand Ole Opry President and general Manager Bob Whittaker. New members are invited on the basis of their contributions to country music and whether they are available to perform from time to time during the live radio broadcast.

Bill Anderson, 1961; Ernie Ashworth, 1964; Clint Black, 1991; Garth Brooks, 1990; Jim Ed Brown, 1963; Jumpin' Bill Carlisle, 1953; Roy Clark, 1987; John Conlee, 1981; Wilma Lee Cooper, 1957; Skeeter Davis, 1959; Diamond Rio, 1998; Little Jimmy Dickens, 1948; Joe Diffie, 1993; Roy Drusky, 1958; Holly Dunn, 1989; The 4 Guys, 1967; The Gatlins, 1976; Don Gibson, 1958; Vince Gill, 1991; Billy Grammer, 1959; Jack Greene, 1967; Tom T. Hall, 1980; George Hamilton IV, 1960; Emmylou Harris, 1992; Jan Howard, 1971; Alan Jackson, 1991; Stonewall Jackson, 1956; Jim & Jesse, 1964; George Jones, 1969; Hal Ketchum, 1994; Alison Krauss, 1993; Hank Locklin, 1960; Charlie Louvin, 1955; Patty Loveless, 1988; Loretta Lynn, 1962; Barbara Mandrell, 1972; Martina McBride, 1995; Mel McDaniel, 1986; Reba McEntire, 1986; Ronnie Milsap, 1976; Lorrie Morgan, 1984; Jimmy C. Newman, 1956; The Osborne Brothers, 1964; Bashful Brother Oswald, 1995; Dolly Parton, 1969; Johnny PayCheck, 1997; Stu Phillips, 1967; Ray Pillow, 1966; Charley Pride, 1993; Jeanne Pruett, 1973; Del Reeves, 1966; Riders In The Sky, 1982; Johnny Russell, 1985; Jeannie Seely, 1967; Ricky Van Shelton, 1988; Jean Shepard, 1955; Ricky Skaggs, 1982; Melvin Sloan Dancers, 1957; Connie Smith, 1971; Mike Snider, 1990; Hank Snow, 1950; Marty Stuart, 1992; Randy Travis, 1986; Travis Tritt, 1992; Porter Wagoner, 1957; Billy Walker, 1960; Charlie Walker, 1967; Steve Wariner, 1996; The Whites, 1984; Teddy Wilburn, 1953; Trisha Yearwood, 1999.

presented Saturday night. Bring your lawn chairs or blankets and kick back under a shady tree. Concessions and restrooms are available. This is a no-alcohol event. Admission is $4 for anyone 12 and over on Friday, $5 on Saturday. There are no fees for entering the competition. In addition to the music, there is also an arts and crafts show. Rough campsites are available, and parking is free.

## October

### Chet Atkins Musician Days
**Various indoor and outdoor venues**
**• (615) 256-9596, (615) 256-6414**

Chet Atkins Musician Days was held for the first time in 1997, during the last full week of June. In 1999, it moved to the first week in October. This event is all about celebrating

musicians. Past events have been citywide, with as many as 50 to 100 informal acoustic stages set up everywhere from department stores to the Metro Courthouse. The program changed in 1999, but there are still free concerts, master classes and other activities featured throughout the week, which is capped off by a concert at the Ryman Auditorium (ticket required).

### Country Music Week
**various Nashville locations**

For one week each fall, Nashville's music industry participates in a dizzying array of parties, showcases, seminars and awards presentations. It's schmooze city, as industry executives, songwriters, performers, media and wannabes attend these events at various venues around the city. Most events are invitation-only, but those who are determined will

# Country Music Fast Facts

• In 1998, country music was the second-most popular music genre, claiming 14.1 percent of the $13.7 billion in total U.S. record sales. (Rock music was No. 1, with 25.7 percent of the market.)

• Country music sales revenue more than quadrupled in the 1990s. 1997's volume was $1.8 billion, up from $724 million in 1990.

• Country remains the leading radio station format in the U.S. As of November 1998 there were 2,368 country radio stations, followed by news/talk with 1,131 and adult contemporary with 844.

• The top-grossing country music concert in 1998 was Garth Brooks's nine sellouts at the Target Center in Minneapolis, which grossed $3,500,609. Trisha Yearwood opened the shows.

• Garth Brooks was the most popular country artist on tour in 1996, 1997 and 1998. In 1998, he had at least 98 sellouts, which were attended by more than 1.3 million fans, and grossed nearly $24.2 million from ticket sales.

• Recent data show that 73 percent of country music record buyers own their homes and 41 percent have household incomes exceeding $50,000.

• More than 36 million U.S. residents listen to country radio stations each week.

• The Country Music Association's awards are televised around the world. In recent years, music fans from the United States, Australia, Austria, Canada, Denmark and Germany could tune in.

• The country music audience is growing. In the past few years, several artists, including Shania Twain ("You're Still The One"), Faith Hill ("This Kiss"), LeAnn Rimes ("How Do I Live"), Garth Brooks ("To Make You Feel My Love") and Martina McBride ("Valentine"), have received airplay on noncountry stations, exposing country music to new audiences.

• The number of country music albums that were certified for gold, platinum and multiplatinum sales increased from 39 in 1990 to 121 in 1997.

(Sources: Country Music Association, Recording Industry Association of America, *Amusement Business*)

find that it's not too difficult to track down someone with a ticket or invitation to spare.

Country Music Week usually takes place in October, but sometimes it's held in late September and early October. The highlight of the week is the Country Music Association's nationally televised awards show (read more about that in the Support Organizations section of this chapter). Performing rights organizations ASCAP, BMI and SESAC each host galas, presenting awards to the year's top songwriters.

## Grand Ole Opry Birthday Celebration
**Grand Ole Opry House,**
**2802 Opryland Dr. • (615) 889-3060**

WSM radio station was launched October 5, 1925, and soon began broadcasting old-time country fiddling, banjo and string band

---

**INSIDERS' TIP**

**The first Nashville publishing company, Acuff-Rose, was formed by Roy Acuff and Fred Rose in 1942.**

music. The old-time music program was originally called the *WSM Barn Dance*, but the name was changed to the *Grand Ole Opry* in December 1927. For more than 70 years since, *Opry* fans have been gathering each October to celebrate the birthday of the *Grand Ole Opry*, America's longest-running radio program. The three-day party is held in mid-October and includes concerts, a *Grand Ole Opry* performance, and autograph and photo sessions with the stars.

A package that includes reserved seats at an *Opry* show, a show at the Ryman Auditorium, a bluegrass show and other events is $50 for everyone age 4 and up. There are also special ticket packages that include accommodations at the Opryland Hotel. Group rates are available. Call the Opryland USA reservations and ticketing office at the number listed for more information.

## Fall Music Festival
**Moss-Wright Park at Caldwell Rd.,
Goodlettsville • (615) 859-7979**

In mid-October, Goodlettsville's Moss-Wright Park is the place to go for some great live music, dancing and delicious barbecue. Local bands perform country, jazz, gospel and bluegrass music at the Friday and Saturday Fall Music Festival. Bring your lawn chairs and blankets and make a day of it. A craft show features handmade items from 50 or more crafters. You can fill up on barbecue from one or more of the 20-plus contestants in a barbecue cook-off sanctioned by the Kansas City Barbeque Society. There's also an amateur chili cook-off. The kids can enjoy pint-sized games and carnival rides. Admission is free. Hours are 5 to 8 PM Friday, 9 AM to 4 PM Saturday.

From antiques to
cowboy boots, and toys
to Italian-made suits,
Nashville has it all.

# Shopping

Shopping. It's a favorite pastime for some, a dreaded inconvenience for others. But whether you view shopping as a fun activity or a necessary evil, Nashville has the stores that will make your shopping experiences pleasant. From antiques to cowboy boots, and toys to Italian-made suits, Nashville has it all. There are so many shopping districts in and around Nashville that it could take years to discover them all. Major malls are in just about any direction, and you can't go wrong shopping at any of these. Shopping meccas like Rivergate and Hickory Hollow are always jam-packed and offer almost any merchandise you want, from pet supplies to automobiles.

There are also many neighborhood-type shopping districts, such as Hillsboro Village, White Bridge Road, Nolensville Road and Eighth Avenue S., that make shopping super convenient. You'll often find some interesting stores and merchandise in these areas. Nashville is a top tourist destination, and naturally we also have tons of country music souvenirs. You'll find most of those in shops and attractions on or near Second Avenue, Demonbreun Street and in the Music Valley area across from the Opryland Hotel. We list some of those shops along with music stores in our Music City U.S.A. chapter. For information on even more shopping opportunities, see our Arts, Attractions and Annual Events chapters.

We have arranged this chapter by category of goods. This is definitely not a comprehensive list of stores and shops in Nashville, just a guide to some of the local hot spots and favorites. If we have overlooked your favorite shop, let us know and we'll try to include it in a future edition. We're always interested in other Insiders' perspectives. The categories in this chapter include Western clothing, antiques, gardening supplies, sporting goods, books, gifts and more. Keep this book handy so the next time a gift-giving occasion comes around (or if you just want to treat yourself to some-

thing nice) you can glance through our listings. You might find a neat shop, an unusual gift or a great deal you might have otherwise missed. A note to shopaholics and borderline shopaholics: we take no responsibility for shopping binges this chapter may inspire.

## Malls

### Bellevue Center
**7620 U.S. Hwy. 70 S. • (615) 646-8690**

When this upscale west Nashville mall opened in 1990, it brought several new names to the city's retail offerings. Encompassing 940,000 square feet on two levels, Bellevue Center has nearly 100 stores, including Nashville's only Abercrombie & Fitch, Everything But Water, Charter Club, Franklin Covey and Godiva Chocolatier. You can also shop 'til you drop at such favorites as Ann Taylor, Eddie Bauer, The Disney Store, Gap, Gap Kids, Banana Republic, Williams-Sonoma, Johnston & Murphy, Nine West, Jones New York Footwear and Tennessee Museum Store. Bellevue Center's anchors are Dillard's, Proffitt's and Sears. Rarely crowded, Bellevue Center offers a relaxing shopping experience, avoiding the three-ring circus atmosphere of some of the larger suburban malls. At the top of the mall's food court is a colorful play area that's a big hit with kids. Benches and tiered, carpeted steps offer plenty of space for parents to relax while keeping an eye on their youngsters. A Ruby Tuesday anchors the food court. There is plenty of free parking. Bellevue Center is just off I-40 west at Exit 196.

### CoolSprings Galleria
**1800 Galleria Blvd., off I-65 S. at Moores Ln., Franklin • (615) 771-2128**

CoolSprings Galleria, about 14 miles south of Nashville, is the area's newest and largest major mall. Anchored by five major department stores —Proffitt's, Dillard's, JCPenney, Parisian and Sears — this 1.3 million-square-foot upscale mall has 165 stores, plus the 500-seat Oasis Food Court. Specialty stores include Ann Taylor, Gap, Gap Kids, The Limited Stores, Eddie Bauer, American Eagle Outfitters, US Male, The Disney Store and Talbots. Surrounding the mall are a number of stores, including Pier 1, Target, Service Merchandise, Uptons and Toys-R-Us, plus several restaurants and a movie theater. There is plenty of free parking and lots of other stores nearby in each direction.

www.insiders.com

See this and many other
**Insiders' Guide®**
destinations online.

Visit us today!

## Factory Stores of America
**2434 Music Valley Dr.**
• **(615) 885-5140, (800) SHOP-USA**
You had better allow plenty of time to shop at this outlet mall, because once you arrive, you're going to want to snap up as many bargains as you can. Factory Stores of America, opened in 1993, is right across from the Opryland Hotel. The mall has more than 70 factory stores offering savings of 30 to 70 percent off regular retail prices. Head here first for great deals on everything from clothes to kitchenware. Among the stores are Levi's, Gap, Geoffrey Beene, Van-Heusen, adidas, Casual Corner, London Fog, Oneida and L'eggs/Hanes/Bali/Playtex.
You can get to the mall from McGavock Pike or Music Valley Drive (main entrance).

## Harding Mall
**Harding Pl. and Nolensville Pk.**
• **(615) 833-6327**
You can't tell by looking at it, but Harding Mall is one of Nashville's oldest malls. Opened in 1962, it underwent an approximately $16 million overhaul in 1989. The mall, near I-24, I-65 and I-40, is an easy-to-get-to shopping destination for many Nashvillians. A lunchtime visit isn't out of the question for workers from Music Row or downtown, for instance. Anchored by Dillard's and Marshall's, Harding Mall encompasses 300,000 square feet of space. Among its approximately 43 stores are Shindigs and Celebrations party supply store

and Rack Room Shoes. Gift wrapping, laminating, faxing and other services are available at the customer service center, across from Luby's Cafeteria, the largest of the mall's handful of restaurants. Mr. Gatti's has a Gattiland gameroom where kids can entertain themselves before their pizza arrives. There are several other restaurant options nearby, including an International House of Pancakes and a Fuddruckers in the parking lot. In back of the mall is the Carmike 6 movie theater.

## Hickory Hollow Mall
**5252 Hickory Hollow Pkwy., Antioch**
• **(615) 731-MALL**
Encompassing 1.2 million square feet, Hickory Hollow Mall is the second-largest mall in the Nashville area. It opened in the late 1970s and since then, the area around the mall has grown tremendously. Retail stores, restaurants, car dealerships and businesses of every sort surround the mall, making this a major shopping destination but also making for constant traffic jams. Don't expect to zip in and out of here quickly. Hickory Hollow has about 180 stores on two levels, including anchors Proffitt's, Dillard's, JCPenney and Sears. There is also a full-service gym, Power House Gym Aerobics & Fitness, inside the mall. The mall has about 20 restaurants, including a Ruby Tuesday. Hickory Hollow mall is off I-24 east at Exit 60.

## The Mall at Green Hills
**Hillsboro and Abbott Martin rds.**
• **(615) 298-5478**
Perhaps Nashville's most fashionable mall, The Mall at Green Hills, or Green Hills Mall as we usually call it, has lots of nice specialty stores in an attractive, upscale environment. Remodeled just a few years ago, the 24-acre mall won a major design award from the International Council of Shopping Centers. A series of skylights, marble and brass touches, loads of flowering plants and lots of open spaces contribute to the elegant and pleasant-to-shop atmosphere. Among the stores are Pottery Barn, Restoration Hardware, Ann Tay-

Charles Elder and son Randy stand outside Elder's Bookstore on Elliston Place.

lor, Bachrach Clothing, Banana Republic, Brooks Brothers, Brookstone, Crabtree and Evelyn, The Disney Store, Harold's, Laura Ashley, The Museum Company, The Nature Company, Nine West, Wentworth Gallery and Williams-Sonoma. Anchors are Proffitt's and Dillard's. Restaurants include Cheeseburger Charley's. There is plenty of parking all around, including garage parking. After an afternoon of shopping, you might want to head over to the adjacent Regal Cinemas Green Hills 16 to catch a movie or the adjacent Funscape, where you can ride a virtual roller coaster or bumper cars, play in a high-tech arcade or let the kids work off some steam at the children's interactive play area (see our Kidstuff chapter for more details)

## 100 Oaks Mall
**719 Thompson Ln. at Powell Ave.**
**• (615) 383-6002**

In the mid-1990s, 100 Oaks underwent a multimillion-dollar renovation that turned it into a 750,000-square-foot, two-level, value-oriented shopping mall. It was a much-needed overhaul for the property, which originally opened in 1967 as the first shopping mall in the state of Tennessee. It was only the second enclosed mall in the entire Southeast. Today, 100 Oaks has some 40 stores, anchored by Burlington Coat Factory, JCPenney Catalog Outlet Store, OFF 5th – Saks Fifth Avenue Outlet and Reebok. Other favorite stores here include T.J. Maxx, CompUSA, Luxury Linens, MediaPlay, Totally 4 Kids, PetSmart and Michaels. The mall is right off I-65 at the Armory Drive exit, in between Thompson Lane and Powell Avenue.

## Rivergate Mall
**1000 Two-Mile Pkwy., Goodlettsville**
**• (615) 859-3456**

This enormous, sprawling mall covers 1,108,000 square feet of space, and has 155 specialty stores, including Eddie Bauer, American Eagle, Carlyle & Co., The Disney Store,

Gap, Bath & Body Works and Blockbuster Music. Anchors are Proffitt's, Dillard's, JCPenney and Sears. Rivergate Mall, open since 1971, is one of Nashville's favorite places to shop. If you can't find what you're looking for in the mall, however, there's a good chance you'll find it in one of the retail areas surrounding it. Nearby stores include Pier 1 Imports, Target, Michaels, and just too many others to mention. If you're shopping with little ones, stop by the mall's Fox 17 Clubhouse and let them play while you recharge. The mall's 500-seat food court is anchored by three full-service restaurants, and there are all kinds of restaurants on Gallatin Pike and the other streets around the mall. Rivergate Mall is at Two-Mile Parkway and Gallatin Road; take I-65 north from downtown to Exit 96.

# Department Stores

## Proffitt's
**CoolSprings Galleria, 1800 Galleria Blvd., Franklin • (615) 771-2100
Bellevue Center, 7616 U.S. Hwy. 70 S. • (615) 646-5500
The Mall at Green Hills, Hillsboro and Abbott Martin rds. • (615) 383-3300
Hickory Hollow Mall, 5252 Hickory Hollow Pkwy., Antioch • (615)731-5050
Rivergate Mall, 1000 Two-Mile Pkwy., Goodlettsville • (615) 859-5251**

Proffitt's entered the Nashville market in late 1998. After century-old Nashville retailer Castner Knott was purchased by Dillard's, Proffitt's purchased five of the former Castner Knott locations. Proffitt's stores offer a nice selection of men's, women's and children's clothing and shoes, plus home furnishings, housewares, cosmetics, accessories and more. They have some great sales, too. Based in Alcoa, Tennessee, the company also owns Saks Fifth Avenue, Parisian, Younkers, McRaie's and Herberger's department stores.

## Dillard's
**Bellevue Center, 7624 U.S. Hwy. 70 S. • (615) 662-1515
CoolSprings Galleria, 1800 Galleria Blvd., Franklin • (615) 771-7101**
**The Mall at Green Hills, Hillsboro and Abbott Martin rds. • (615) 297-0971
Harding Mall, 4070 Nolensville Rd. • (615) 832-6890
Hickory Hollow Mall, 5252 Hickory Hollow Pkwy., Antioch • (615) 731-6600
Rivergate Mall, 1000 Two-Mile Pkwy., Goodlettsville • (615) 859-2811**

This full-service department store is similar to Proffitt's. Little Rock, Arkansas–based Dillard's purchased the locally owned Cain-Sloan department stores, which had been a Nashville favorite for years. Today, Dillard's has stores at all the major area malls. In addition to large men's, women's and children's clothing departments, Dillard's has accessories, cosmetics, housewares, home furnishings and more. You can even book a vacation at some stores: the Bellevue, Hickory Hollow, Green Hills and CoolSprings locations have Dillard's Travel offices.

## McClure's
**6000 Tenn. Hwy. 100 • (615) 356-8822**

This family-owned specialty store is a favorite among tastefully dressed Nashvillians. Whether you're in need of a spangled cocktail dress or evening gown, an Armani suit, a spiffy pair of shoes or a spectacular swimsuit, McClure's carries it. Such lines as DKNY, Dana Buchman, Giorgio Armani and Nicole Miller are in plentiful supply, and on top of that, the sales staff is friendly and customer-service-oriented. In addition to clothing, accessories and a great shoe department, McClure's has an interesting and creative selection of gifts and nice things for the home. McClure's has several good sales throughout the year, so if the regular prices are a little beyond your budget, come by during a sale and you might find a bargain. This store is a fun place to shop during the holidays. As you browse for neat gifts, unusual ornaments and designer wrapping paper, a tuxedoed pianist plays seasonal tunes on a grand piano to put you in the holiday spirit. Specially designed holiday boxes are another McClure's tradition. The store also has spectacular gift wrapping. An interesting tidbit of McClure's history: it was founded in 1936 and for many years operated as a clothing store in very small towns in Middle Tennessee and Northern Alabama. The store moved to Nashville in the '60s and changed its focus to upscale merchandise in the '70s, after opening the Belle Meade store. The store sits right in the "V" where Harding Road forks and becomes U.S. 70 and Tenn. 100.

# Western-wear Stores

## Boot Country
**2416 Music Valley Dr. • (615) 883-2661**
**304 Broadway • (615) 259-1691**
**2327 Tenn. Hwy. 46 S., Dickson**
**• (615) 446-0634**

A lot of locals consider Boot Country to be the best place to buy Western-style boots. The stores are owned by Nashville- and Lebanon-based Texas Boot, which has about 100 Boot Country and Boot Factory stores around the country. In addition to boots, the stores have a large selection of clothing. Brands include Wrangler Western apparel; Acme, Texas, J. Chisholm and Abilene boots; and Stetson and Resistol hats.

## Boot Factory/Boot Country USA
**1415 Murfreesboro Rd. • (615) 360-3866**
**2434 Music Valley Dr. • (615) 871-9953**

Boot Factory/Boot Country USA has plenty of boots, including Dan Post, Code West and Laredo brands, at discount prices. The store also sells Timberland hiking boots. You'll also find some cowboy hats here, as well as men's and women's shirts and a limited selection of jeans. The Murfreesboro Road store is in Genesco Park, while the Music Valley store is in the Factory Stores of America outlet mall.

## Circle S Western Store
**6013 Charlotte Pk. • (615) 356-9783**

Cowboys and cowgirls can get everything from jeans to horse trailers at Circle S Western Store, the only Western store around that carries a full line of tack. This store, about a half mile west of White Bridge Road, carries everything for the horse person except boots. Open since 1991, Circle S sells such Western wear favorites as Panhandle Slim shirts, Wrangler shirts and jeans, Rocky Mountain jeans, Hobby Horse show clothing, Stetson and Resistol hats and Sundowner horse trailers. Urban cowboys and cowgirls are welcome.

## Dangerous Threads
**105 Second Ave. N. • (615) 256-1033**

Dangerous Threads technically isn't a Western wear store, but this unique boutique does have some Western-style jackets and other items that might complement a cowboy or cowgirl look. Dangerous Threads has been selling original, cutting-edge clothing and accessories since 1988. Items range from rock 'n' roll–inspired fashions to high-fashion dress shirts and suits for men and unique dresses and evening wear for women. Many pieces are one-of-a-kind. All kinds of customers shop here — from hip business people to the night-club crowd to performers such as Aerosmith, ZZ Top, Sheryl Crow, Lynyrd Skynyrd and George Jones.

## Katy K's Ranch Dressing
**113 17th Ave. S. • (615) 259-4163**

We love the name of this Western wear store: Ranch Dressing. Get it? This tiny store is packed with all sorts of interesting clothing, shoes and accessories. Actually, Ranch Dressing carries more than Western wear. The store has a lot of vintage clothing, including '40s and '50s dresses and vintage Western outfits for rent and for sale, and reproductions with an antique look. Whether you're looking for a neat $25 shirt or an original Nudies of Hollywood creation for $2,000, you'll have lots to choose from. Ranch Dressing also carries all sorts of kitschy gift items and accessories. Since it opened in 1994, the store has developed a following among music-video stylists, recording artists, musicians and others who want to look like a star.

## Manuel Exclusive Clothier
**1922 Broadway • (615) 321-5444**

Manuel is best known for the flashy rhinestone garb worn by some country music performers, but the store also designs high-quality one-of-a-kind pieces for business people worldwide. Originally founded in Los Angeles in 1972, Manuel today is based in Nashville. Most of the store's business is custom costumes for performers, among them Linda Ronstadt and Bob Dylan. The prices are steep — a custom coat starts at around $1,250 and shirts start at $200 to $350 — but browsing is free. The store welcomes the curious to come

Photo: Cathy Summerlin

The Nashville Arcade has been a landmark for Nashville shoppers since 1903.

in and check out the showroom. Manuel himself is usually there from 9 AM to 6 PM Monday through Friday.

## Scooters
**121 2nd Ave. N. • (615)254-6672**

Convenient for downtown shoppers, this Texas Boot–owned store offers boots and Western wear. Even if you're not in the market for boots, you might want to stop by and check out the 1959 pink Cadillac.

## Trail West
**1183 W. Main St., Hendersonville**
**• (615) 264-2955**
**7114 Moores Ln. • (615) 370-1737**
**2416 Music Valley Dr. • (615) 883-5933**
**989 Murfreesboro Rd. • (615) 367-1948**
**127 River Rock Blvd., Murfreesboro**
**• (615) 896-5212**
**219 Broadway • (615) 255-7030**

Since its first store opened in 1992 in Hendersonville, Trail West has continued to expand and build new stores. It now has six locations in the Nashville area. Trail West offers clothing and accessories for men, women and children. The stores are huge and they're stocked with all the favorite Western wear brands, including Wrangler, Larry Mahan, Roper, Laredo, Durango, Panhandle Slim, Crumrine, Nocona, Resistol, Stetson and Charlie 1 Horse. The Murfreesboro location also carries tack and supplies.

## Western Outlet #3 Inc.
**323 Broadway • (615) 259-2370**

Western Outlet #3 has been here since the early 1990s. Friendly proprietor Louise Odum, a retired buyer for Harvey's department store, also operates stores in Lebanon, Tennessee and East Tennessee. Western Outlet is a favorite with tourists, especially international tourists who come in looking for vintage Nashville styles. Odum sees lots of repeat customers from as far away as Iceland, Wales and Sweden. She sells Western shirts, boots, jackets, leather goods, hats and jewelry, and offers a discount special each month.

# Clothing and Accessories . . .

## . . . for Women

### Coco
**4239 Harding Rd. • (615) 292-0362**

A favorite of mostly upscale baby boomers, this women's specialty store in Belle Meade has an extensive collection of designer clothing for all occasions. From sophisticated chic to career classics and contemporary, cutting-edge styles, labels include Anne Klein II, Dana Buchman, Ellen Tracy, CK Calvin Klein, Emanuel, Jenne Maag, Body Action, French Connection, Ghost, A-line, Company, 5.2.5, Ballinger, Belford, CP Shades, Fitigues, M.A.G., Joan Vass and more. Coco also sells cosmetics and gift items. Expect to pay full price at this shop. There are only a couple of times a year when you can buy something on sale, usually once after the first of the year and once at the end of summer.

### Jamie Inc.
**4317 Harding Rd. • (615) 292-4188**

This Belle Meade boutique carries mainly American designers, such as Calvin Klein, Donna Karan and Bill Blass. A contemporary department in the back caters to the young and fashionable. Jamie also has Cindi Earl Fine Jewelry, which offers creations by well-known national and international jewelry artists and also sells estate pieces. After a tough day of shopping for clothes, shoes and jewelry, you can treat yourself to a manicure and a facial here too.

### The French Shoppe
**5423 Harding Rd. • (615) 352-9296**
**2817 West End Ave. • (615) 327-8132**
**4010 Hillsboro Cir. • (615) 297-1880**

Known for its selection of good-quality career wear and casual weekend clothes at affordable prices, The French Shoppe has been outfitting fashion-minded Middle Tennessee women since 1968, when the store first opened in Murfreesboro. The family-owned business moved to Nashville in 1978 and today has three stores, in addition to the "traveling store," which presents about 250 trunk shows a year all over the country. Among the lines the store carries are Adolfo, Taiga, Focus 2000, Silkland, Joseph A. and Brighton. Merchandise varies somewhat by store. The West End shop caters more to young career women, and offers alterations. A makeup artist and manicurist at that location can help you put the finishing touches on your look. (You deserve some pampering, *non*?) The Belle Meade (Harding Road) and Green Hills (Hillsboro Circle) shops pick up where the West End store leaves off. The Belle Meade shop has also introduced antiques and specialty gifts. Browse while you sip a complimentary espresso, coffee, café mocha or hot chocolate.

## INSIDERS' TIP

The Nashville Arcade, connecting Fourth and Fifth avenues N. between Union and Church streets, is one of Music City's oldest shopping centers. This two-level, glass-covered mall opened in 1903 and was modeled after a mall in Milan, Italy, and others in northern U.S. cities. It is one of only four such structures left in the United States. Inside, The Peanut Shop Inc. fills the air with the scent of its freshly roasted nuts as it has since 1927. Other stores include Percy's Shoe Shine, the Arcade Smoke Shop, Arcade Fruit Stand, Arcade Barber Shop, Jimbo's ("world class hot dogs and taters") and Las Brisas Cantina Mexicana. For more information, call (615) 255-1034.

## Gill & Arnold
### 334 Main St., Franklin • (615) 791-1207

Sisters Janis Gill and Kristine Arnold perform together in the bluegrass and country duo Sweethearts of the Rodeo, but when they're not on the road, they can often be found at their boutique, Gill & Arnold, which they opened in 1995. The store specializes in upscale but affordable clothing, accessories and gifts.

## Off Broadway Shoe Warehouse
### 118 16th Ave. S. • (615) 254-6242
### 1648 Westgate Cir., Brentwood (Cool Springs area) • (615) 309-8939

SHOES! With 35,000 to 45,000 pairs of designer shoes in what seems like acres of space, Off Broadway Shoe Warehouse is shoe heaven. You can find the latest trendy styles as well as the classics — from penny loafers and must-have sandals to hiking boots and towering stiletto heels — at substantial savings. Women's sizes range from 5 to 12; there are lots of narrows and a few wide widths too. Expect to pay 25 to 70 percent less than you would at most retail stores. It's hard to leave here with only one box.

# . . . for Men

## R. Joseph Menswear
### 2010 Glen Echo Rd. • (615) 298-2100

Contemporary Italian clothing with an emphasis on fabrics is the specialty of R. Joseph Menswear in Green Hills. One touch and you'll be hooked. Silk, silk gabardine, merino wool, cashmere-merino wool mix and all-cotton dress shirts — fabric and texture add a definite upscale feel to these clothes, which bear such names as Stefano Milano, Format, Hubert and Serica. This shop is a favorite among pro-

fessionals, Music Row's power brokers and entertainers. Looking for an interesting tie? R. Joseph also has a fantastic selection — up to 700 to choose from. And the store stocks only up to three of each design, so it's not likely you'll run into someone wearing your tie at that big social event. While the merchandise is pricey, the store has good sales twice a year, when prices start off slashed by a third. This store is on the Glen Echo Road side of The Glendale Center.

## Levy's
### 3900 Hillsboro Pk. • (615) 383-2800

Levy's has been dressing Nashville men since 1855 and is one of the few remaining individually owned clothing stores around. This family-owned store is in the Hillsboro Plaza shopping center in Green Hills. Upscale men's business clothing and sportswear is the specialty. Levy's lines include Hart Marks, Hickey-Freeman, Oxford, Tallia, Brioni, St. Croix and Italian-made Canali, Ermenegildo Zegna and Boss. The store also carries some of the finest leather in town, including the Bruno Magli, Torras and Crown labels. Many of Levy's knowledgeable sales employees have been with the store for decades, and they'll help you put together all the right pieces, whether you're looking for dressy casual wear for "casual Fridays" or a high-power suit fit for the corner office. Levy's has been named the "best men's clothing store" by readers of the *Nashville Scene*.

## Off Broadway Shoe Warehouse
### 118 16th Ave. S. • (615) 254-6242
### 1648 Westgate Cir., Brentwood (Cool Springs area) • (615) 309-8939

Althouth these enormous stores devote most of their space to women's shoes, each has a good selection of men's footwear too.

This is a great place for shoes — you can expect to pay 25 to 70 percent less than you would at department stores.

## The Oxford Shop
**4001 Hillsboro Pk. • (615) 383-4442**

The Oxford Shop, three doors down from Davis-Kid Booksellers in Green Hills, carries high-end suits and casual wear for men, including such lines as Samuelsohn, Southwick and Corbin. The locally owned store, in business since 1961, also offers expert tailoring and free lifetime alterations on every garment. The Oxford Shop has two sales a year — one after the holidays and another at the end of summer. The store also does two trunk shows every year.

## . . . for Children

## Chocolate Soup
**3900 Hillsboro Pk. • (615) 297-1713**

The Chocolate Soup designer line of kids clothing is sold in the Missouri-based company's 14 stores, including this one in Green Hills. Prices can be high, but there is always a sale going on here. In addition to its own line, the store carries other popular children's brands, from newborn to size 7 for boys and from newborn to 16 for girls. You'll find nice accessories here too, including bows, backpacks and socks, as well as puzzles, stuffed animals and other toys.

## Especially Baby
**2164 Bandywood Dr. • (615) 298-2323**

This store caters to babies, from newborns to toddlers — and the mommies, daddies, relatives and friends who want to get them lots of neat stuff. In Green Hills, Especially Baby sells fine-quality clothing, bedding, furniture, accessories, stuffed animals and lots of personalized items. The staff can help you design your nursery too. There are occasional markdowns, and clothing sales take place in January and June. Free gift wrap is a nice extra.

## Just 4 Kids
**5133 Harding Rd. • (615) 356-7292**

Just 4 Kids, in the Belle Meade Galleria, sells custom-made and custom-painted children's furniture, specialty gift items, clothes and all kinds of fun things that kids like.

# Specialty and Miscellaneous

## Old Negro League Sports Shop
**1213 Jefferson St. • (615) 321-3186**

This store, in business since 1993, sells Negro League sportswear and memorabilia, including T-shirts, baseball jerseys, books, calendars, posters, baseball cards, logo baseballs, caps, photos, and autographed balls and bats. There's a good chance you'll run into a player from the league here too, so come prepared to chat and learn a bit about baseball history.

## Pangea
**1721 21st Ave. S. • (615) 269-9665**

This Hillsboro Village store has lots of funky and fun clothing and home decor items. Mexican folk art is the main feel at Pangea, and there is a lot of primitive- or antique-style, natural fiber clothing from Mexico and India, as well as unique and interesting tabletop items. The store has a good selection of candles and candle holders, as well as Mexican mirrors, jewelry and even bedding.

# Antiques

There are numerous antique malls and shops in and around Nashville. Nashville's Eighth Avenue S., Franklin, Goodlettsville and Lebanon are some of the best-known antique hot spots, but you can find shops almost anywhere. Take a drive out in the country and you're bound to come across several charming little stores filled with all sorts of antiques, collectibles and other knickknacks from years gone by. We've highlighted a few locations, enough to keep weekend treasure seekers busy. Most of the malls are open daily, but hours vary, so it's a good idea to call before visiting. For other information on antiques, see our Annual Events chapter. FYI: an "antique," in the strictest sense, is something more than 100 years old, while a "collectible" is usually at least 20 years old but may be older.

In her book *The Treasure Hunter's Guide to Historic Middle Tennessee and South Central Kentucky Antiques, Flea Markets, Junk Stores & More* (Gold-Kiser Co., Nashville, 1995), Maude Gold Kiser offers tips on successful antiquing. Here are some of her ideas:

• If you're a first-timer, go with someone who is experienced and who enjoys it.

•Cash sometimes can improve your negotiating power. Don't expect prices to be dirt cheap in small towns.

•Take along notes about what you're looking for — size, color, etc. Keep room and specific area measurements with you at all times, as well as a tape measure, a magnet that will not stick to sterling silver or solid brass, and a magnifying glass.

•These goods are bought as-is. Check items carefully for cracks, chips, inadequate repairs or missing pieces.

•Clean out your car, truck or van so you'll have maximum room for treasures you find.

•All dealers are on the lookout for merchandise. They will usually be willing to pay you only the wholesale value (but that's still better than what you'll get at a garage sale). And don't expect to get free appraisals.

•Do your gift buying at antique stores. Antiques or old collectibles will increase in value.

•Give a gift certificate to an antique mall or shop.

•Don't be afraid to ask questions. Most dealers are in the business because they love antiques and will talk your ear off about their field of expertise.

•Wear comfortable shoes.

# Nashville's Eighth Avenue S. District

## Antique Merchants Mall
### 2015 Eighth Ave. S. • (615) 292-7811

This 8,000-square-foot mall features merchandise from 40 dealers, including lots of silver and porcelain, some furniture, paintings, lamps, rugs and other household items.

## Art Deco Shoppe and Antique Mall
### 2210 Eighth Ave. S. • (615) 386-9373

If you're a fan of art deco style, you'll enjoy this shop. There are 10 to 12 dealers here with lots of furniture, lamps, wall decorations, glassware and jewelry, all in the hip retro modern look. There's lots of cool '50s stuff too.

## Cane-ery Antique Mall
### 2112 Eighth Ave. S. • (615) 269-4780

Cane-ery Antique Mall has lots of furniture, cane repair and reproduction hardware.

## Dealer's Choice Antiques and Auction
### 2109 Eighth Ave. S. • (615) 383-7030

Antique auctions take place here every other Friday night and draw about 150 dealers and individual antiquers. Dealer's Choice also sells off the floor, but store hours vary. You might want to call before visiting since the owner often closes in order to pick up new shipments. You'll find everything from decorator items to fine furnishings here, including Victorian, French, country and mahogany furniture.

## Downtown Antique Mall
### 612 Eighth Ave. S. • (615) 256-6616

This 13,000-square-foot mall is fun to visit. It's in an old warehouse building beside the railroad tracks. The mall features all sorts of neat stuff, including lots of furniture and collectibles, from 42 dealers.

## Estelle's Antiques and Consignment Furniture
### 601 Eighth Ave. S. • (615) 259-2630

This shop has a varying collection of antique and collectible furniture and accessories.

## Tennessee Antique Mall
### 654 Wedgewood Ave. • (615) 259-4077

Furniture, glassware, paintings and prints, mirrors, jewelry and all sorts of treasures from 100 dealers are tucked into this 25,000-square-foot mall.

## Wedgewood Station Antique Mall
### 657 Wedgewood Ave. • (615) 259-0939

Wedgewood Station Antique Mall has 40 dealers offering a wide variety of antiques and collectibles.

## Whiteway Antique Mall
**1200 Villa Pl. • (615) 327-1098**

This mall, off Edgehill, is one of the older malls in town. It was named the best in Nashville in one of the local publications. Its 9,000-square-foot space is filled with American primitive furniture, folk art, vintage clothing, jewelry, and more.

# Also In Nashville

## Garden Park Antiques by Herndon & Merry
**515 W. Thompson Ln. • (615) 254-1996**

This store specializes in antique iron work — fences, gates, window panels, urns, fountains and statuary.

## Green Hills Antique Mall
**4108 Hillsboro Pk. • (615) 383-9851 (upstairs), (615) 383-4999 (downstairs)**

Green Hills Antique Mall has 22,000 square feet and 100 dealers. Lots of furniture, both antiques and quality reproductions, is beautifully displayed upstairs. Downstairs there is

an assortment of antique and collectible furniture and accessories.

## Maude's Junk Store
**2823 Bransford Ave. • (615) 383-3411**

This store is owned by Maude Gold Kiser, author of *The Treasure Hunter's Guide to Historic Middle Tennessee and South Central Kentucky Antiques, Flea Markets, Junk Stores & More*. You'll find an eclectic collection of old and other wonderful things here, including textiles, furniture restoration supplies and vintage-style lamp parts. The store is across Thompson Lane from 100 Oaks Mall.

## Pembroke Antiques
**6610 Tenn. Hwy. 100 • (615) 353-0889**

Pembroke Antiques specializes in American and Continental furniture "with a sophisticated look but a warm country feel." This is a good place to find majolica pottery too. The store also has decorative garden items.

## Polk Place Antiques
**6614 Tenn. Hwy. 100 • (615) 353-1324**

Polk Place specializes in items from the

Photo: Cindy Stooksbury Guier

From pumpkins to perennials, the Farmer's Market has it all.

American Federal period (1790-1840), which includes late Chippendale, Hepplewhite, Sheraton and Early Empire. The store also offers a selection of porcelains, coin silver, copper, pewter, brass, oil paintings and custom-made lamps.

# Franklin

There are two concentrated areas of shops and several others scattered about in Franklin. One concentration is on and near Second Avenue while the other is on Bridge Street, which runs parallel to Main Street.

## Battleground Antique Mall
**232 Franklin Rd., Franklin**
**• (615) 794-9444**

This 13,000-square-foot mall is filled with French, English and American furniture, Civil War artifacts, glassware and linens. Insiders say the store has especially good prices on furniture.

## Country Charm Antique Mall
**301 Lewisburg Pk., Franklin**
**• (615) 790-8908**

You'll love browsing through this mall's hodgepodge of antiques and collectibles — lots of furniture, glassware, and garden items such as benches, obelisks and other decorative pieces.

## Franklin Antique Mall
**251 Second Ave. S., Franklin**
**• (615) 790-8593**

Housed in the historic handmade brick ice house building, Franklin Antique Mall has 100 booths. There is a good selection of furniture and glassware, lamp parts and glass replacement shades, as well as collectible magazines and prints.

## Harpeth Antique Mall
**529 Alexander Plaza, Franklin**
**• (615) 790-7965**

Harpeth Antique Mall is in a strip shopping center off Highway 96 near I-65. It's easy to spot: the plate glass windows across the front are filled with brilliantly colored glassware. The mall has 80 booths, with lots of art, glass, furniture, prints and maps, books and linens.

## Rustic House Antiques
**111 Bridge St., Franklin • (615) 794-7779**

If you're looking for real antique furniture, you'll find it here. Rustic House Antiques has lots of big, true antique pieces, and, as you might guess from the name of the store, items are in varying conditions.

## Winchester Antique Mall
**113 Bridge St., Franklin • (615) 791-5846**

There are about 30 booths in this mall. They're filled with furniture, linens, glassware, vintage clothing, books and jewelry.

# Goodlettsville

Goodlettsville's antique district stretches along the historic Main Street. To get there, take I-65 N to Exit 97 and go west to Dickerson Pike..

## Antique Corner Mall
**128 N. Main St., Goodlettsville**
**• (615) 859-7673**

Antique Corner Mall has a mix of antiques, collectibles and costume jewelry.

## Goodlettsville Antique Mall
**213 N. Main St., Goodlettsville**
**• (615) 859-7002**

You can spend hours treasure hunting in this enormous mall. There are 123 booths filled with lots of furniture, glassware, antiques and collectibles and toys. About 15 crafts booths are mixed in.

## Rare Bird Antique Mall
**212 S. Main St., Goodlettsville**
**• (615) 851-2635**

Scout for furniture, toys, gas station memorabilia, linens and glassware in more than 70 booths here.

# Lebanon

Lebanon, about a 30-minute drive east of Nashville on I-40, is a major antique hot spot. The town square is filled with antique shops on three sides. The names and locations change from time to time, but some of the shops here have been around for years. We've included just a sampling.

## Cuz's Antiques Center
140 Public Sq., Lebanon
• (615) 444-8070

If you ever travel along I-40, you've probably noticed the billboards advertising Cuz's. You'll want to allow plenty of time to explore this huge mall — it spreads into two or three buildings. Cuz's is filled with American, French and English antiques and reproductions, bronze statues and fountains, stained glass, lamps, paintings and lots of Victorian pieces. Cuz's also has a good selection of estate jewelry.

## The Crown & The Rose
147 Public Sq., Lebanon
• (615) 443-4996

Tea is the focus of this Victorian-inspired gift shop, which has antique furniture and many reproduction pieces, including china, teapots and silverplated tea accessories. There's a nice tea room in the back.

## The Emporium
109 Public Sq., Lebanon
• (615) 449-9601

The Emporium has three floors of furniture, glassware, antiques and collectibles, including children's blue willow.

## Heartbreak Ridge General Store
108 Public Sq., Lebanon
• (615) 449-5993

Heartbreak Ridge has a mixture of glassware, furniture, antiques and collectibles. It also has Beanie Babies.

## Caroline's Antiques
107 Public Sq., Lebanon
• (615) 443-0783

Caroline's has several dealers on two floors selling antique glassware, oak and handmade and handpainted furniture and ornaments.

# Consignment Stores

## Bargain Boutique
4004 Hillsboro Pk. • (615) 297-7900

Bargain Boutique is in the Green Hills Court shopping center, across from Davis-Kidd Booksellers. The store first opened in 1970 and has built a good reputation among consignment shoppers. The store sells women's clothing, but no accessories or shoes. Fashion-savvy bargain hunters will find such names as Ellen Tracey, Dana Buchman, Chanel and Valentino here. The store is open Monday through Saturday.

## Designer Renaissance
3706 Hillsboro Pk. • (615) 297-8822

Owner Jodi Miller opened this store in 1988. It's behind Kinko's in Green Hills. Location is a big plus for Designer Renaissance. Since the store is near the homes of some of Music City's best dressed, it has lots of better-quality clothing. The store stays busy with shoppers looking for a bargain. As its name suggests, Designer Renaissance carries designer clothes (but not exclusively designer) as well as high-end secondhand clothing from stores such as Ann Taylor. Miller also stocks accessories. The store's bridal section has 30 to 40 wedding gowns plus bridal accessories. Open Monday through Saturday, the store closes on all major (and some minor) holidays. If this store isn't in or near your neighborhood, you might want to call before you come because it sometimes closes on special occasions.

## Fashion Connection
5115 Nolensville Rd. • (615) 333-2632
4734 Old Hickory Blvd., Old Hickory
• (615) 872-9746

Fashion Connection sells upscale women's

and men's clothing and accessories. Owner
Jo Jackson opened Fashion Connection in
1990. The store on Nolensville Road is in the
Tusculum Square Shopping Center. The Old
Hickory store is in the Hermitage Crossings
center, near Hermitage. The stores are open
Monday through Saturday.

### The Pink House
**2822 Bransford Ave. • (615) 292-2195**

Close to 100 Oaks Mall, The Pink House is
stocked with all sorts of furniture and household accessories. Items are arranged according to function — kitchen items are in the
kitchen, living room items are in the living room,
etc. This is a fun place to explore, with an
always-changing selection of merchandise.
There's something for every budget. The Pink
House is open Monday through Saturday.

### Play It Again M'aM
**158 Belle Forest Cir. • (615) 646-7910**

Play It Again M'aM is a cozy and friendly
store in a small strip center in Bellevue, right
off Old Hickory Boulevard. The store sells
women's clothing from hundreds of consign-
ors. It has a formal section, and also sells jewelry and other accessories and shoes. You
can find a variety of household items here too.
The store is open Tuesday through Saturday.

### Second Time Around
**235 E. Main St., Hendersonville**
**• (615) 822-6961**

The friendly staff at this store makes shopping here a pleasure. Second Time Around, in
Hendersonville's Kmart Shopping Center, has
a boutique atmosphere. If you like, the staff
will help you put together a whole look. The
store sells women's clothing, including such
lines as Dana Buchman, Anne Klein and Ellen
Tracy. The store emphasizes that it is very
particular regarding the clothing it accepts, so
you can count on good quality items here.
The store has a bridal room, an "after 5" room

and a good selection of well-cared-for shoes
and accessories. The store is open Tuesday
through Saturday.

# Toys

### The Games Store
**2104 Crestmoor Rd. • (615) 383-4104**

The Games Store in Green Hills has plenty
of quality toys and other fun goodies for in-
fants, children and grown-ups. The store
stocks a variety of fine toys, and has an extensive selection of board games for kids of all
ages. You'll also find bunches of stuffed animals here — the usual teddy bears as well as
some more out-of-the-ordinary critters — plus
puzzles, chess, gaming supplies, arts and
crafts, dolls, doll clothes and furniture.

### Imagination Crossroads
**3900 Hillsboro Pk. • (615) 297-0637**

This Green Hills store, owned by early
childhood educators, sells "educational and
specialty toys for the thinking child." You won't
find Barbies or toy guns here, but you will find
an excellent collection of puzzles, books, craft
kits, wooden toys, games and other interesting and fun things to stimulate your little one's
mind. Play stations are set up around the store,
so children can try out the toys. Monday and
Tuesday morning preschool workshops and
Saturday morning play days are a hit with parents and children. You can book birthday parties here too. What kid wouldn't like to have a
birthday party in a toy paradise? Imagination
Crossroads is in Hillsboro Plaza, across from
the Mall at Green Hills.

### Phillips Toy Mart
**5207 Harding Rd. • (615) 352-5363**

In business for more than 50 years, Phillips
Toy Mart has been at this Belle Meade address for nearly 40 years. An old-timey kind of
toy store, Phillips sells all sorts of toys, includ-

**INSIDERS' TIP**

Nashville's many craft fairs offer a variety of creative items that
make wonderful gifts. See our Annual Events chapter for more
information on these events.

ing games for kids and adults and a large selection of imported educational toys. The store also sells a variety of collector dolls and has one of the largest model selections in the South, including tools and hobby supplies.

### Real Toys
#### 127 Franklin Pk. • (615) 370-8910
This specialty toy store stocks a good selection of quality toys — everything from BRIO trains, Playmobil sets and Kettcar pedal cars and bikes to Beanie Babies, books and puzzles. Most toys are geared to children younger than 12, but the store also carries games and other fun things that are suitable for the whole family. Nostalgic baby boomers can pick up a traditional Radio Flyer wagon here for their little ones. The store is in the Brentwood House Shopping Center, about a block south of the Franklin Pike and Old Hickory Boulevard intersection.

# Gift Shops

### The American Artisan
#### 4231 Harding Rd. • (615) 298-4691
Colorful and attention-grabbing glass objects line the large windows of this crafts store in Belle Meade, catching the light and beckoning you to come in to treasure-hunt. The American Artisan is a fabulous store filled with crafts handmade by artists all over the United States. This is just the right place to find that special gift or one-of-a-kind item for the person who has everything — or the person who appreciates "designer" crafts. The American Artisan carries many clay and wood crafts, as well as hand-blown glass, metal and leather items. Beautiful bowls, stemware, wood boxes, jewelry and quirky objets d'art plus unusual pieces of furniture fill the various rooms in the store. Each year on Father's Day weekend, The American Artisan sponsors The American Artisan Festival in Centennial Park. (See our Annual Events chapter for details.)

### Crystal's
#### 4550 Harding Rd. • (615) 292-4300, (800) 525-7757
Country singer Crystal Gayle opened this store in 1987 with the goal of providing top-quality crystal and other gift items in a friendly, relaxed atmosphere. While there are some spectacular high-end items here, the store stocks plenty of affordable items, so whether you want to spend less than $20 or more than $1,000, you'll be able to find something that suits your budget. If it's crystal you want, this is the place. Crystal's carries Waterford, Lalique, Baccarat and Lladro crystal. Herend porcelain and Gail Pittman handpainted ceramics are among the other notable lines in the store. Fine jewelry in sterling silver, gold and precious and semiprecious stones is available. The store also has a baby gift section, stocked with Gund stuffed animals, silver spoons, porcelain dolls and other keepsakes. Gifts for men include bookends, paperweights and humidors. The store also offers a gift registry and does a lot of corporate business. It offers free gift wrapping too.

### Tanner & Company
#### 2109 Abbott Martin Rd.
#### • (615) 269-4599
#### Bellevue Center, 7620 U.S. Hwy. 70 S.
#### • (615) 662-2178 (seasonal)
Readers of the *Nashville Scene* voted this store the "best place to shop for the person who has everything." Tanner & Company specializes in high-design items for the home. You can always count on finding an excellent assortment of out-of-the-ordinary items here, from colorful, artistic glassware to whimsical doormats to unusual picture frames. It's a sort of "urban outfitters" for those with contemporary taste. Tanner & Company's store in Bellevue Center is open from October through December. If you find the items a bit pricey, visit around Valentine's Day, when the big sale is taking place.

### Tennessee Memories
#### 2182 Bandywood Dr. • (615) 298-3253
Tennessee Memories is a delightful and cozy store brimming with lovely pottery, woodwork, pewter, all sorts of neat collectibles and other good stuff. When you walk in the door, owner Lorena Bass or a friendly salesperson will offer you a complimentary cup of hot spiced tea to sip as you make your way around the store. Tennessee Memories focuses on high-quality "antiquey," old-fashioned and Vic-

torian-style items; 85 percent of the merchandise is handmade by Tennessee artisans. The food pantry in the back corner is stocked with an assortment of delicious treats — teas, coffees, cocoas, jams and jellies, spices and other goodies. If you enjoy the spiced tea, you'll want to take home a jar so you can make a pot to sip by the fire on cold winter nights. The store creates breakfast or dinner gift baskets from items stocked in the pantry. During the holidays, the store has an assortment of holiday decorations. We stop here at least once during the season to pick a few ornaments off the Christmas trees to give as gifts. Lorena and her husband George designed and copyrighted the "Tennessee Afghan," an afghan adorned with symbols representing every area of the state, such as the iris, a raccoon, a riverboat, Ryman Auditorium, The Hermitage and a black bear.

# Gardening Stores

## Bates Nursery & Garden Center
**3810 Whites Creek Pk. · (615) 876-1014.**

This garden center has been in business since 1932. It began during the Great Depression, when Bessie Bates, grandmother of the current owner, David Bates, started selling flowers and shrubs from her backyard greenhouse on Charlotte Pike. Today, Bates Nursery has a huge selection of flowers, herbs, trees, shrubs, fountains, statuary and accessories — anything you need for your garden. The store offers free landscaping design services (call for an appointment) and, for a fee, will come to your home and design a more detailed plan for you.

## Mark Bates Landscaping & Garden Center
**1608 Franklin Pk., Brentwood**
**· (615) 370-9222**

This full-service landscaping center has everything you need to build your garden or landscape your property: annuals, perennials, trees, shrubs, mulch and more. The shop has a large selection of stone statuary items, gifts and accessories too. If you don't like digging in the dirt, or if you have a brown thumb, let

the store's on-staff specialist design and install everything for you. This store is near CoolSprings Galleria, two blocks north of the Franklin Pike and Moores Lane intersection. We recommend taking the scenic route: Franklin Pike.

## Flower Mart
**4002 Hillsboro Pk. · (615) 269-5733**

This Green Hills shop, in business since 1976, has tons of loyal customers who come in from as far away as Bowling Green, Kentucky. Loaded with flowers, plants and supplies, with new shipments arriving daily, the Flower Mart is a great place for spring bedding plants, fall mums, Christmas trees and other holiday greenery. The shop keeps a variety of tropicals in stock in its two greenhouses. You can always find plenty of ferns, cacti, orchids, houseplants and hanging baskets here. The store is also a full-service florist and has a huge selection of clay pots and concrete garden statuaries. There is also a large assortment of ceramics, ribbons, candles, silk and dried flowers, and a room full of baskets.

## Moore & Moore Garden Center
**106 Harding Pl. · (615) 353-0251**
**8216 Highway 100 · (615) 662-8849**

Moore & Moore has been voted Nashville's best garden center by readers of the *Nashville Scene*. This friendly, full-service garden store's original location is in Belle Meade is near the intersection of Harding Place and Harding Road, behind the Nashville Humane Association. The second store is out Highway 100, near Chaffin's Barn. Open since 1980, Moore & Moore specializes in native plants and wildflowers. If you don't know what to plant, or don't know how to plant it, you're in luck, because the store offers landscaping and design services. If you have an herb garden, this is the place to restock in the spring. If you don't have one, once you walk past the fragrant lemon thyme, sage, cilantro and basil, you'll probably be tempted to start one right away. The store also has one of the best selections of bulbs around. Don't miss the garden accessories, especially the designer pottery, which any gardener would no doubt love

Photo: Archer/Malmo Advertising

Nashville has outlet stores and other value-oriented shopping.

to receive as a gift. The knowledgeable staff is always a good source of free, friendly advice on everything from orchids to garden tools.

### Betty Smith Nursery
**900 Eighth Ave. N. • (615) 256-2060**

Betty Smith has been in business at the Farmers Market since 1988. A fun place for gardeners, Smith's nursery has beautiful things in bloom year-round. In addition to a well-stocked supply of annuals, perennials, trees, shrubs and tropicals, the nursery sells lots of special seasonal items — pumpkins and hay bales in the fall, and Christmas trees, magnolia wreaths and 500 different Santa Clauses during the holidays. The store also sells a variety of painted gourds, souvenirs, birdhouses, garden tools and accessories, and grows as many as 3,000 hanging baskets on site.

## A Newsstand

### Rosko's & The Muncheonette
**2204 Elliston Pl. • (615) 327-2658**

Rosko's (formerly Mosko's) is so cool. The store's motto is "Eat It, Read It, Smoke It," so as you might guess, Rosko's has good eats, reading material and smokable things. The

store sells several out-of-town newspapers and has a great selection of magazines. There is a huge selection of offbeat greeting cards for every occasion too, plus some funny gag gifts. The store's walk-in cigar humidor makes it a popular stop with the cigar crowd, and everyone likes the yummy sandwiches at the Muncheonette (we'll tell you about those in our Restaurants chapter).

## Bookstores

### Alkebu-Lan Images
**2721 Jefferson St. • (615) 321-4111**

Translated from Moorish-Arabic, the name of this store means "land of the blacks." Alkebu-Lan Images carries a variety of African-American books and gifts. Among the mostly Afrocentric items are greeting cards, figurines, note cards, body oils, incense, jewelry and imported African carvings. Many of the store's products are educationally focused.

### LifeWay Christian Store
**1010 Broadway • (615) 251-2500**

This spacious store has a large selection of Christian books, from Bibles to self-help and fiction, often at good prices. The store also sells church resources as well as cards, gifts and collectibles. There is a good selection of all sorts of Christian and gospel music on CD, cassette and video. They also carry children's books and videos too.

## Barnes & Noble Booksellers
**1701 Mallory Ln., Franklin**
**• (615) 377-9979**

Not only is this a fantastic bookstore, but it's the only place around (at least at this writing) where you can buy a cup of delicious Starbucks coffee. It's hard to pass by the Barnes & Noble Café in front of the store without stopping for a flavorful cup of hot coffee, a yummy mocha or an icy cold Frappuccino. You Starbucks aficionados will be glad to know you can buy bags of coffee here too. But enough about coffee — back to the books. The spacious Barnes & Noble, across from CoolSprings Galleria, has about 150,000 books in stock plus some strategically positioned, big comfy chairs where you can settle in and peruse a few. They offer a 10 percent discount on most hardcover books, 20 percent off current *New York Times* paperback bestsellers, 30 percent off hardback bestsellers and 30 percent off the current staff-recommended books. There's also a music department with a good selection of classical, opera and jazz CDs. At least a couple of book clubs meet here every month, and their books are discounted 30 percent. Each month the store has author signings and presents workshops on topics as varied as writing resumes and wintering your houseplants. Live music is presented occasionally. On Monday and Saturday mornings at 11, kids are treated to storytime readings, crafts and refreshments and entertained by costumed characters. Barnes & Noble also owns Bookstar in Belle Meade;

Doubleday Book Shop, in Bellevue Center; and B. Dalton Bookseller.

## Books-A-Million
**1789 Gallatin Pk. N. • (615) 860-3133**

A million books? We didn't have time to count them, but there is definitely a huge selection here. This roomy store is housed in a former Wal-Mart building across from the Olive Garden near Rivergate Mall. One of about 160 stores nationwide, it has a nice section of books by Southern writers, as well as everything from Hallmark cards and out-of-town newspapers to Bibles and toys. The store can order any in-print book for you if you can't find it in the store. Books-A-Million's Club Card is free and offers 10 percent off everything in the stock, 40 percent off the store's list of top 10 hardback bestsellers and 25 percent off its top 10 paperback bestsellers. The store's Joe Muggs coffee shop sells specialty coffees and baked goods. Poets and the poetically inclined are invited to participate in the Friday evening poetry readings.

## Bookstar
**4301 Harding Rd. • (615) 292-7895**

We hated to see the famous Belle Meade Theater close its doors and undergo renovation, but we love the building's new incarnation as Bookstar. Since the store opened in 1991, it has become a favorite of many Nashvillians. Owned by Barnes & Noble, this approximately 15,000-square-foot store is stocked with some 100,000 books on two levels. The upstairs children's section is quite nice, and that's where you'll find lots of mementos of the building's past — photos and autographs of movie stars and other celebrities. Downstairs are rows and rows of books where you can while away the day. Bookstar has a

---

**INSIDERS' TIP**

McClure's is known for its special holiday boxes, which feature a new design each year. The store has even based advertising campaigns around these sought-after sturdy cardboard containers. They're free with the purchase of store merchandise and are usually so pretty you could get by without wrapping them. After the gifts have been opened, they make attractive storage containers for ornaments, holiday cards or other keepsakes.

# Steven Womack Puts the Mystery in Nashville

Raymond Chandler had his Los Angeles, Dashiell Hammett his San Francisco. Many subsequent detective novelists have concentrated on these locales, or other big cities such as Chicago or New York. But, thanks to Steven Womack, the current "hot spot" for crime fiction just may be Nashville.

Womack, whose *Dead Folks' Blues* (1992) received the Edgar Award for best original paperback mystery novel, may have started a trend with his series of Harry James Denton mysteries set in Music City. Other Nashville-based mysteries have recently hit the bookstores.

"Living in Nashville and being a Nashville native, I know the city pretty well," Womack says. "Nashville is a *fascinating* city, on a lot of different levels. There's a lot more to it than country music. There's old money, there's politics, there's corruption. We had Sheriff Fate Thomas, who eventually went to prison. Gov. Ray Blanton, who literally padlocked the door to the State Capitol a few hours before Lamar Alexander was inaugurated (laughs), went to prison. A lot of our politicians ultimately graduate to the penitentiary.

"This is a tough city, in many ways. I love Nashville, and it's a very friendly, very warm place, but there's a dark underside to it. As I put in one of my books, we have more churches here, per capita, than any place in the world. We also have more nude dance clubs, sex bars, escort services than anyplace I've ever seen. It's amazing; it's a weird, curious kind of dichotomy. If you're a writer, it's a gold mine."

In many ways, but not all, Harry Denton is like his creator.

"Harry says a lot of things that I would be afraid to say to anybody. He's a wise guy," Womack says. "Fortunately, that seems to be part of his appeal for readers, this very dry sense of humor. But he loves the city very much. As do I. Hell, I've been here for 14 years nonstop."

Despite his sarcasm, Denton comes across as a sensitive guy, sometimes bordering (almost) on politically correct.

"I wanted to avoid some of the stereotypes of the hard-boiled, bourbon-swilling, gat-carrying, cigarette-smoking gumshoe. I've been influenced a lot by the women mystery writers who have come to the forefront of the genre in the last 12 or 15 years. Women have redefined how mysteries work and the kinds of characters you can write about. When I started writing about Harry, I wanted to create a character who had a real life. Which meant that he struggled with money, he struggled with the opposite sex in relationships, he struggled with self-image — all of that stuff. To that

Photo: Courtesy of Steven Womack

Nashville native Steven Womack lived in New Orleans and other major cities for a while, but now he's back at home, writing Harry James Denton detective novels set in Music City.

— continued on next page

extent, I guess he's kind of autobiographical."

Womack says that most of his readers are women. "Women seem to really like Harry. I don't get too many complaints about him," he says.

Although one book, *Chain of Fools*, revolved around the sex industry, it didn't get overly explicit. "*Chain of Fools* was a weird book because it really was darker than the other three," he says, then explains that book's genesis. "I had my bachelor party at Brown's Diner. But several of the guys had conspired to take me to Deja Vu (a strip club) at the end of the evening, and I didn't know that. First time I'd ever been in the place, and I was profoundly uncomfortable. I got out of there as soon as I could. But ever since then, I've been intrigued by that scene, and I wanted to set a story in that arena. I started hanging around in these places, doing research, mostly trying to meet the people who worked there. It was very depressing. I haven't been back to one of these places since — don't intend to."

Whether by coincidence or by imitation, several other mystery writers have since set novels in Nashville. Asked whether he sees himself as a trend-setter, Womack says with a laugh: "I didn't mean to be! I don't even know if all these people read my books and then decided to do this. But at least it's opened up Nashville as a place of intrigue and interest and the kind of convoluted, mysterious setting that you need for a good crime novel. People are trying to get away from setting every crime novel in LA, Chicago or New York."

Like his detective, Womack isn't particularly fond of today's country music. A "struggling clarinet player," he prefers traditional jazz and swing, citing Louis Armstrong, Sidney Bechet and Johnny Dodd as favorites. He adds: "I also listen to a lot of alternative. There's a huge alternative scene here in Nashville."

Interestingly, after the 1998 paperback, *Murder Manual*, Womack and Denton took a break from Nashville. As the novel ends, the detective is headed for Reno, Nevada (in his acknowledgments, the author thanks a friend who "left Nashville for Reno and talked me into setting my next book there so I could visit him").

Womack doesn't drink and rarely hangs out in bars, though he likes Jonathan's Village Cafe in Hillsboro Village. He also recently discovered Radio Café in east Nashville. He enjoys catching movies at Vanderbilt's Sarratt Cinema. The Harry James Denton mysteries are, in chronological order, *Dead Folks Blues*, *Torch Town Boogie*, *Way Past Dead*, *Chain of Fools* and *Murder Manual*.

---

variety of magazines as well as some nice journals and address books.

Those who love a good mystery will enjoy the large selection of mystery books here. The local chapter of Sisters in Crime, a mystery interest group, meets here regularly. The store sponsors three book groups that meet monthly. Bookstar schedules lots of events, including book signings, a monthly open mic poetry night, Tuesday morning and Sunday afternoon story hours for kids, and occasional children's parties. You can pick up a copy of the store's calendar of events at the cash register.

Bookstar discounts all hardcovers 10 percent. The current *New York Times* hardcover

bestsellers are 30 percent off, and the paperbacks are 20 percent off. The store's staff-recommended books are discounted 30 percent. Special orders usually arrive within seven days. Open until 11 PM Monday through Saturday, and until 9 PM Sunday. Bookstar has plenty of parking, and a rear entrance.

## Brentanos
**Bellevue Center, 7620 U.S. Hwy. 70 S.**
**• (615) 662-1913**

Brentanos, a Waldenbooks store, is on the first floor of Bellevue Center, near Proffitt's. This store has good local and Civil War sections. The Preferred Reader program, which costs $10 to join, offers a 10 percent discount on all Brentanos or Waldenbooks purchases and earns participants a $5 gift certificate after they spend $100 (the first purchase is doubled).

## Davis-Kidd Booksellers Inc.
**4007 Hillsboro Pk. • (615) 385-2645, (615) 292-1404 (hours and events hotline)**

Davis-Kidd is Nashville's favorite bookstore. With more than 100,000 books filling the store's two-story, 27,000-square-foot space in Green Hills, this store is not only a book lover's paradise, but a popular and comfortable gathering place too. Benches are positioned among the rows of books, inviting shoppers to linger and browse as long as they like. The store's Second Story Café, (615) 385-0043, serves a variety of tasty munchies, coffees and desserts, and is a nice spot to relax any time of day (see our Restaurants chapter for the details). Davis-Kidd was founded by Nashville's Thelma Kidd and Karen Davis in 1980. The two later opened similarly successful stores in Knoxville, Memphis and Jackson, Tennessee. In 1997 they sold the stores to Neil and Mary Beth Van Uum, founders of Joseph-Beth Booksellers.

Davis-Kidd offers 25 percent off the store's list of hardcover fiction and nonfiction best sellers. In addition to stocking plenty of current favorites, the store has many backlist titles, including a lot of hard-to-find books. The store's customer service is excellent. Most special orders arrive within a couple of days. Davis-Kidd also has a large magazine and newspaper section, including foreign publications, and a nice selection of greeting cards, stationery, calendars and gift items. During the holidays, the store has a fantastic selection of boxed greeting cards in all styles — from humorous and unusual cards to traditional greetings to artsy handmade cards. The children's area has a variety of educational toys as well as books, and is a big hit with the little ones.

The store has occasional nighttime poetry readings, and every Friday night is songwriters' night in the upstairs cafe. Davis-Kidd has as many as 30 in-store author signings each month, and sponsors three book clubs, which meet several times a month. On Saturday and Monday mornings, the store has a program for children (see our Kidstuff chapter for more about that).

## Doubleday Book Shop
**Bellevue Center, 7620 U.S. Hwy. 70 S.**
**• (615) 646-7195**

You'll find Doubleday Book Shop on the upper level of Bellevue Center, near Dillard's. This store keeps about 50,000 books in stock, including gift books and children's books. There are select gift items too.

## Logos Bookstore
**4012 Hillsboro Pk. • (615) 297-5388**

Logos is a cozy and friendly Christian bookstore in Green Hills. It sits off the main road a bit in a brown brick building adjacent to the Green Hills Court shopping center. The store carries a variety of Bibles and religious books, including an extensive selection of Reformed theology literature. You can also find home-schooling books here. There's a good selection of CDs, greeting cards, Beanie Babies and gift items too. Logos also buys and sells used books and CDs. The knowledgeable staff is always happy to place special orders. Logos's Decent But Not Dull video club has 1,300 family-oriented videos in stock. You can rent 3 videos for $5 and keep them for a week.

## Magical Journey
**212 Louise Ave. • (615) 327-0327**

This New Age bookstore, in a renovated house behind Elliston Place, carries all sorts of metaphysical books and welcomes people of all religious beliefs. Included in the selection of 5,000 books are works on Buddhism, Hinduism, Native American beliefs and practices, Christianity and more. The store also carries a large selection of candles as well as incense, crystals, cards, meditation tools, aromatherapy lines, jewelry, music and other items. The store holds a monthly psychic reading fair and other events.

## MediaPlay
**100 Oaks Mall, 719 Thompson Ln.**
**• (615) 383-5114**
**5434 Bell Forge Ln. E., Antioch**
**• (615) 731-4345**
**2101 Gallatin Pk. N. • (615) 851-1586**

These massive stores provide one-stop

shopping for your book, video, video game, music and computer software needs. MediaPlay has about 60,000 book titles in stock and discounts its top 15 hardcovers 35 percent and its top 10 paperbacks 25 percent. The stores hold occasional author signings, but the merchandise, not special events, is really the focus here. With rows and rows of software, books and music, to some, shopping at MediaPlay is almost as much of an entertainment experience as a shopping experience.

### St. Mary's Book Store & Church Supplies
**1909 West End Ave. • (615) 329-1835**

St. Mary's Book Store & Church Supplies has been in business for more than 50 years. It is a full-line, Christian bookstore, with Bibles, liturgy aids, hymnals and sheet music, gifts, CDs and cassettes.

### Tennessee Museum Store
**Bellevue Center, 7620 U.S. Hwy. 70 S. • (615) 662-2922**

This is a nonprofit store owned by the Tennessee State Museum downtown. Though technically not a bookstore, the Tennessee Museum Store has a good selection of books relating to Tennessee — everything from Civil War history to Tennessee recipes and travel. The store also sells food, pottery, art and other items related to Tennessee and created by Tennessee artists.

### Tower Books
**2404 West End Ave. • (615) 327-8085**

You may have to circle the block a time or two to find a parking space, but Tower Books is worth the trouble. The store has about 80,000 books in stock and is known for having one of the largest pop culture sections around. In fact, the store calls itself "Nashville's literary alternative." In addition to alternative books and underground magazines, Tower stocks all the

traditional categories. If you don't find what you're looking for, the store will order it for you at no extra charge. Open 365 days a year, Tower Books discounts its hardcover and paperback bestsellers 30 percent and new release hardcovers 20 percent. The store has a couple of signings a month, and also schedules readings and poetry events. This store is open until midnight on Friday and Saturday.

### Waldenbooks
**Rivergate Mall, 1000 Two-Mile Pkwy., Goodlettsville • (615) 859-3387**
**Hickory Hollow Mall, 5252 Hickory Hollow Pkwy. • (615) 731-2159**
**Stadium Sq., 386 W. Main St., Hendersonville • (615) 824-9044**

The Hickory Hollow store, in the lower level of Hickory Hollow Mall, near Sears, is the largest of the three area Waldenbooks. It has an especially large kids' section. The Rivergate Store is near Proffitt's, and the Hendersonville store is in the Stadium Square strip center. Participants in Waldenbooks' Preferred Reader program earn a $5 gift certificate for every $100 they spend in Waldenbooks or Brentanos stores, and their first purchase is counted double toward the $100; they also get a 10 percent discount on any purchase. It costs $10 to join the club. Waldenbooks discounts its top 10 bestsellers at 15 percent. The store also has a large selection of bargain coffee-table books priced from 99¢ to $25. From November to early January, the store operates the Day by Day calendar stores at the Hickory Hollow and Rivergate malls.

# Used Books

### Bookman Rare and Used Books
**1713 21st Ave. S. • (615) 383-6555**

This book store opened in fall 1995 in Hillsboro Village. Bookman has 80,000 books, including lots of modern first editions. The store has a large mystery collection, as well as good selection of science fiction, art and photography, history and children's books. The store also has many signed editions. Serious collectors with money to spend might want to check out the store's original first edition *Frankenstein*, which was recently appraised for $90,000.

### Dad's Old Book Store
**4004 Hillsboro Pk. • (615) 298-5880**

Dad's Old Book Store specializes in old and rare hardcover books and autographs. The store has a stock of about 50,000 books, including first-edition, rare and out-of-print books, lots of books by Southern authors, many history books and leather-bound books. The store also has thousands of autographs from such figures as Winston Churchill, Abraham Lincoln, Vivian Leigh and Robert Frost.

### Elder's Bookstore
**2115 Elliston Pl. • (615) 327-1867**

Elder's Bookstore is one of Nashville's oldest used and rare book stores. The store was founded by Charles Elder, who can still be found here almost daily, but it is now owned and managed by his son Randy. Elder's is known for its tremendous collection of regional, Southern and Civil War books. Tennessee history buffs will find plenty to occupy them. Elder's also has a good collection of Native American books, rare and out-of-print books, children's books, cookbooks, art reference books, books on genealogy, late-edition encyclopedias and more. They have done reissues of important titles through the years. Each shelf is themed somewhat, but things are usually in a pleasant disarray here, so you might have to do some searching to find what you're looking for. A wonderful place to browse on a rainy afternoon, Elder's is across from Baptist hospital at 22nd and Church, next to the Elliston Place Soda Shop.

### The Great Escape
**1925 Broadway • (615) 327-0646**
**111 N. Gallatin Pk., Madison**
**• (615) 865-8052**

If you're looking for comic books, the Great Escape is the place to go. The Great Escape has more than 100,000 comics in stock, a huge selection of back issues and receives weekly shipments of the latest books. Collectors will find collectible comics here that range in price from 50¢ to $500 or more. The Great Escape also has used paperbacks, mostly fiction, with an emphasis on pop culture. The store has a large selection of used CDs, tapes and records, as well as videos, used video games, gaming cards and baseball cards.

# Sporting Goods/
# Outdoor Gear

### Bike Pedlar
**2910 West End Ave. • (615) 329-BIKE**

Rows and rows of Trek and Schwinn bikes of all shapes and sizes fill the Bike Pedlar, a full-service bike shop on West End. In addition to a complete line of bicycles (more than 400 on display), this store carries all the biking accessories you'll need. The store's pro shop does custom frames, including Colnago, Look, Eddy Merkx and Pinarello.

### Blue Ridge Mountain Sports
**108 Page Rd. • (615) 356-2300**
**7090-B Bakers Bridge Ave., Franklin (Cool Springs) • (615) 771-5650**

This store carries backpacking, climbing and camping gear, plus the right clothing to wear while you're doing it. They also have a good assortment of travel gear.

### Bluewater Scuba
**103 White Bridge Rd. • (615) 356-9340**

Bluewater Scuba offers complete instruction in scuba diving. You can learn it all at their indoor pool and then take a diving trip to Florida or a number of more exotic locations with your classmates. The shop is also a full-service travel agency and it specializes in trips to the Red Sea (Egypt), Costa Rica and Thailand. They make one or two trips per month to these and other locations around the world, plus two trips to Florida each month. Bluewater Scuba also teaches P.A.D.I. (Professional Association of Diving Instructors) courses and sells the top lines of scuba equipment.

## Cumberland Cycles
**2807 West End Ave. • (615) 327-4093**

This huge full-service bike shop is next door to the Cumberland Transit outdoor sports shop. You can usually find a parking space behind the stores, and enter through the back door. Cumberland Cycles has been voted Nashville's best bike shop by *Nashville Scene* readers year after year. It's one of the largest, if not *the* largest, shops in the state and specializes in all aspects of biking. The store has a large stock of mountain bikes, road bikes, hybrids and BMX bikes in its warehouse and has around 100 on display at any one time. The store also carries a complete line of in-line skates and skateboards. Vandy grad John Carnes founded the store in 1971 after using cycling to recover from injuries he sustained in a car accident. He sold the business in 1978, but repurchased the cycling side of Cumberland Transit in 1996. In addition to selling bicycles, Cumberland Cycles works to promote the sport of biking. The knowledgeable staff provides instructions in all types of cycling and offers safety tips. The store's large cycling team participates in hundreds of events each year and presents safe-cycling programs to youngsters. Custom frame fitting and 48-hour repair service are available.

## Cumberland Transit
**2807 West End Ave. • (615) 321-4069**

Adventure-minded outdoor types will find all sorts of clothing and equipment at Cumberland Transit, across the street from Centennial Park. In business since 1972, this store has gear for backpacking, camping, rock climbing and rappelling, canoeing, fly fishing and about every other outdoor activity you can think of. In addition to sporting equipment, the store has men's and women's clothing, travel gear and luggage. If you need to brush up on your outdoor skills, sign up for one of Cumberland Transit's classes in rock climbing, rappelling, fly fishing, flytying or backpack-

ing. Courses are usually offered in the spring and fall.

## Jumbosports
**5035 Harding Pl. • (615) 331-1800**

Offering everything from mountain bikes to free weights to clothing, Jumbosports is a favorite for its wide selection and good prices. Jumbosports is near Sam's Club on Harding Place, not far from Harding Mall.

## Nevada Bob's Discount Golf & Tennis
**1305 Antioch Pk. • (615) 833-6440**

This store, one among a few hundred Nevada Bob's franchises nationwide, has a strong local following among Nashville golfers. Competitive prices and an emphasis on customer service keep them coming back again and again. Across from Sam's near I-24 and Harding Place, Nevada Bob's has 10,000 square feet of space, 90 percent of which is filled with all sorts of golfing gear; the rest is devoted to tennis. The store carries all the major lines of equipment, apparel and accessories. During the holidays, this is a good spot to find a gift for the golfer in your life.

## Play It Again Sports
**5354 Mt. View Rd. • (615) 731-9077**
**1745 Galleria Blvd., Franklin**
**• (615) 771-8811**
**2107 Gallatin Pk. N., Madison**
**• (615) 851-6190**
**155 Mall Circle Dr., Murfreesboro**
**• (615) 895-7529**

Play It Again Sports is a national chain that offers new and used sporting equipment at great prices. These stores are the first stop for many Nashvillians looking for a deal on golf equipment, softball and football gear, roller-hockey equipment, in-line skates or exercise machines.

If you have equipment to sell, the store will either buy it from you or sell it for you on

---

**INSIDERS' TIP**

**For more information on consignment shopping in Nashville (as well as other tips on living on a budget), check out *Ms. Cheap's Guide To Nashville* by Mary Hance (Rutledge Hill Press, 1998).**

# Monthly "Flea" Treatment

Nashvillians love to shop at the Tennessee State Fairgrounds Flea Market. It's held the fourth weekend of every month from January through November and the third weekend in December. The flea market draws anywhere from 100,000 to 250,000 people from Nashville and neighboring states in a two-day period. In October 1997 the flea market had 2,970 booths. Most other months, you'll find about 2,200 indoor and

outdoor booths. Traders, craftspeople and antique dealers from about 17 states exhibit antiques, crafts and new products. There's something to fit every budget — from knickknacks for less than $1 to the priciest antique furniture. You can bargain with some of the dealers.

The flea market is open from 6 AM to 6 PM Saturday and from 7 AM to 5 PM Sunday. Hint: come early. Some months, traffic is backed up all the way to the interstate as early as 6 AM, so allow time to sit in traffic. Finding a parking spot can also be a challenge. A free shuttle will transport you to the top of the hill at the fairgrounds, but it's not too far to walk. Admission and parking are free.

The Tennessee State Fairgrounds is at Wedgewood Avenue and Rains Avenue. For more information, call (615) 862-5016.

The October flea market is one of the largest and a good place to find Christmas-themed items.

consignment (you'll get 60 percent of the sales price), or you can trade it for something in the store.

### Tee To Green Golf Shop
**68 White Bridge Rd. • (615) 353-1330**
This locally owned store opened in 1987 and has become a favorite of many Nashville golfers. Owner Craig Parrish says the secret to his success is that the store is super nice, with the look of a pro shop. In the Lions Head Shopping Center, the store has everything the golfer needs: clothing, shoes, bags and all name-brand clubs. This is also a good place

to pick up a gift for the golfer in the family. The store carries a number of golf-themed gift items and art work.

## Wilderness Sports Outfitters
**73 White Bridge Rd. • (615) 356-5230**

This full retail outfitter has everything you need for backpacking and hiking, canoeing and kayaking, and climbing and rappelling. If you aren't into these activities, a visit to this store will probably inspire you to take up at least one of them. You'll find canoes, kayaks, backpacks, clothing, shoes, car racks and much more. The store also has a good selection of literature on climbing, hiking, paddling and other fun outdoor sports. Wilderness Sports is in the Paddock Place shopping center across from Target on White Bridge Road.

# Pets and Pet Supplies

## Aquatic Critter
**5009 Nolensville Rd. • (615) 832-4541**

If you have an aquarium, you'll want to check out this store. It has an excellent selection of fish, plants, corals and reptiles. There's plenty for both the freshwater and marine aquarist. The fish are healthy and the store guarantees them for a week. The staff is knowledgeable and helpful too, and the store provides a variety of services.

## Nashville Pet Products Center
**2621 Cruzen St. • (615) 242-2223**
**7078 Old Harding Pk. • (615) 662-2525**
**4066 Andrew Jackson Pkwy., Hermitage**
**• (615) 885-4458**

Nashville Pet Products Center is a locally owned chain of stores that sells pet supplies only. The stores stock a variety of premium diets pet foods, vitamins, shampoos and conditioners, toys and collars, as well as kennels, carrying cages and doggie sweaters. The stores also have bird cages and supplies and fish supplies, mainly for tropical fish..

## PetSmart
**100 Oaks Mall, 719 Thompson Ln.**
**• (615) 386-0105**
**2201 Gallatin Pk. N., Madison**
**• (615) 859-5100**

**8105 Moores Ln., Brentwood**
**• (615) 371-8890**
**135 Mall Circle Rd., Murfreesboro**
**• (615) 890-4344**

PetSmart, a Phoenix-based chain with hundreds of stores in the United States and United Kingdom, has a huge selection of pet supplies. The stores have a grooming department and offer veterinary clinics about every other weekend. PetSmart sells fish, birds and a few small reptiles, but not cats or dogs. The store recommends adopting cats and dogs from local animal shelters.

## Wet Pets
**7053 U.S. Hwy. 70 S. • (615) 646-8950**

Wet Pets is a favorite among Nashvillians who have aquariums. Located in Bellevue's Kroger shopping center, the store stocks all sorts of fish, aquariums and supplies, as well as indoor and outdoor ponds and supplies, and reptiles and other small animals. Wet Pets is one of the few saltwater dealers in the area and has aquariums full of saltwater creatures. The store also has a good freshwater selection. You can special order a fish or other wet pet if the store doesn't have it in stock. The staff can offer advice in setting up and maintaining an aquarium, and the store also does saltwater and freshwater testing. For those who want to enjoy an aquarium without the hassle of maintaining it, Wet Pets offers home aquarium maintenance programs that include cleaning, water changes, and testing and analyzing water. The fish doctor can even test and diagnose ailing wet pets and suggest treatments.

# Fresh Produce

## The Corner Market
**6051 Tenn. Hwy. 100 • (615) 352-6772**

The Corner Market has a lovely produce section, with fresh, local produce as well as specialties flown in from around the world. While prices are higher than the downtown Farmer's Market, The Corner Market is more convenient for many on the west side of town. It is also just a great place to visit. In addition to fresh produce, The Corner Market has a variety of gourmet food items. Imported olive oils, artisan cheeses, delectable homemade cookies and focaccia, plus baked goods from the best bakeries in town are among the specialties here. Of course, The Corner Market is also known for its breakfasts, lunches and gourmet take-out. Read more about that in our Restaurants chapter.

## Farmer's Market
### 900 Eighth Ave. N. • (615) 880-2001

The Farmer's Market, at the corner of 8th and Jefferson across from the Bicentennial Mall, is a favorite spot for buying fresh produce. The indoor/outdoor market is packed with farmers and re-sellers offering some of the tastiest vegetables you can buy, and at very good prices. Indoors, there are a few international markets, including a Hispanic and an Asian market, as well as a meat shop and fresh seafood shop. Other specialty shops include a fudge counter, JB's Hot Stuff (he sells hundreds of hot sauces and other spicy stuff), and the Tennessee Stinking Rose (a garlic shop). The Farmer's Market does a brisk lunchtime business. Swett's, a meat-and-three restaurant (see Restaurants) that has been in business since 1954, has a location here, and is always a favorite. There is also an Asian restaurant, Chicago Style Gyros, Parco Cafe, Lady J's Bakery and C.D. Concessions. At one end of the market is Betty Smith's Nursery, where you can find all sorts of plants and garden supplies. The Farmer's Market is open every day except Christmas Day.

## Produce Place
### 4000 Murphy Rd. • (615) 383-2664
### 7107 U.S. Hwy. 70 S. • (615) 662-1184

The Produce Place is a natural food grocery store that caters to customers who want organic produce. The store opened in 1988 in the Sylvan Park neighborhood and in 1994 the owner opened a second, larger store in Bellevue. In addition to fresh fruits and veg-

etables, the Produce Place carries some gourmet food items, health and beauty items and vitamin supplements and has a reverse-osmosis water-filtering system. The Murphy Road store has fresh breads from Bread & Company, while the Bellevue location carries breads by Provence Breads & Café and Great Harvest.

## Sunshine Grocery
### 3201 Belmont Blvd. • (615) 297-5100

The Sunshine Grocery natural food store is a favorite with many health-conscious Nashvillians. The store has a variety of natural and organic groceries and is very discriminating in the types of foods it sells — no artificial flavors, colors and unnecessary preservatives here. Sunshine Grocery also has a bulk food section with lots of pastas, beans, nuts and grains; plus a dairy section; frozen foods; and soy-based and wheat-based meat substitutes. The store also carries a full line of supplements, including herbal remedies, homeopathic remedies and vitamins, and offers customer assistance in this area. You'll also find natural cleaning supplies, pet foods and baby foods here. You can fill up your water jugs for pennies with pure water filtered by the store's state-of-the-art reverse-osmosis system. Sunshine Grocery's carry-out deli serves baked goods, soups and hot lunch items cooked from scratch.

# Bakeries

## Bread & Company
### 106 Page Rd. • (615) 352-7323
### 4105 Hillsboro Pk. • (615) 292-7323
### 18 Cadillac Dr., Brentwood
### • (615) 309-8330

Bread & Company specializes in hearthbaked European-style crusty breads and traditional pastries. Owner Anne Clay and her

son John Clay III opened for business in November 1992 and quickly found a devoted following. The Page Road location near Belle Meade did so well that they opened a second store in Green Hills, and a third store in Brentwood. Bread & Company bakes about 18 different breads. The light sourdough farm bread, good for sandwiches or with dinner, is the best seller. The pane bello, a traditional rustic loaf, and pane paisano, a beautiful round bread perfect for dipping into olive oil and sauces, are also favorites. And no one can turn down the delicious, dense and chewy raisin pecan, a sourdough loaf containing a half pound of raisins and a half pound of pecans. They also make fantastic focaccia daily. Take home a few loaves, but ask for instructions on how to keep them fresh if it's your first visit.

There is a tantalizing selection of beautiful gourmet foods for sale too. The imported olive oils and mouth-watering jams, jellies, marmalades, and green olive tapenade are guaranteed to bring out the gourmet in you. A se-

lection of these treats makes a wonderful gift, and Bread & Company prepares lots of holiday and hostess gift baskets. Bread & Company also sells delicious sandwiches, smoothies and Hubbard & Cravens coffees. Read more about that in our Restaurants chapter.

### The Great Harvest Bread Company
**3900 Hillsboro Pk. • (615) 298-1032**

This Green Hills bakery has been in business for years. Great Harvest specializes in soft-crust sandwich breads. The best seller is the honey whole wheat loaf. The store also sells a variety of cookies and muffins and other baked goods such as cinnamon rolls and banana bread, and prepares special breads, such as spinach-feta, on certain days of the week.

### Provence Breads & Café
**1705 21st Ave. S. • (615) 386-0363**

Provence sells wonderful artisan breads, fine French pastries and a variety of foods that make it popular with the lunch crowd. Owner Terry Carr-Hall opened this store in spring of 1996. The breads and pastries here are the traditional French style, so that's probably why Provence Breads & Café has a large European clientele. San Francisco native Carr-Hall studied baking in France, purchased all his equipment in France and does everything here the traditional French way. His goal was to take the best of Provence, a region known for its food, and bring it to Nashville. Provence Breads & Café has a 12-foot cheese showcase that features trendy artisan cheeses, cheeses that are made by hand on small farms, some imported from France. Anything from Provence is a treat. Read more about its delicious lunch and takeout items in our Restaurants chapter.

Call 931-759-6180 for tour infomation. Or visit us online at http://www.jackdaniels.com

BEING A TOUR GUIDE at Jack Daniel Distillery is a job for Sammy Gulley, but it's no chore.

We have a number of gentlemen like Sammy here, who will gladly take you down a quiet lane Jack Daniel himself once walked...past

a limestone cave where pure, ironfree water flows... and finally, up to a room where every drop of Jack Daniel's is gentled through ten feet of charcoal. If you ever visit this part of Tennessee, we hope you'll drop by. Nothing would make our guides happier than to stroll you around our oldtime distillery.

SMOOTH SIPPIN'
TENNESSEE WHISKEY

*We're glad you like our whiskey. Please enjoy it responsibly.*

Tennessee Whiskey • 40-43% alcohol by volume (80-86 proof) • Distilled and Bottled by
Jack Daniel Distillery, Lem Motlow, Proprietor, Route 1, Lynchburg (Pop. 361), Tennessee 37352
*Placed in the National Register of Historic Places by the United States Government.*

# Attractions

There is a lot more to Nashville than music, as you'll see in this chapter. Whether you are a longtime resident, a frequent visitor or a first-timer, Nashville has a great mix of attractions to entertain and enlighten. In fact, we have so many great places to visit and so many fun things to do, we can't possibly list them all here. For that reason, we're highlighting some of the Nashville area's most popular attractions — the ones residents and tourists alike visit year after year.

In this chapter, we arrange attractions by the following categories: Historic Sites, Museums, Amusements & Zoos and Fun Transportation Attractions. If you're planning an itinerary filled with country music-related locales, you'll find all the information you need in our Music City U.S.A. chapter. We list all the music attractions there — everything from country music museums to the hottest nightspots to annual music festivals. Also, be sure to look in our Parks, Recreation, The Arts, Daytrips & Weekend Getaways, Annual Events and Shopping chapters for other fun and interesting places to visit in and around Nashville.

Most attractions charge an admission fee. We provide prices and list hours of operation. If an admission price isn't listed for very young children, that's because they are admitted free. Since fees and hours are subject to change, it's a good idea to call first to verify rates and hours.

## Historic Sites

### Belle Meade Plantation
**5025 Harding Rd. • (615) 356-0501, (800) 270-3991**

Relive a bit of the Old South at Belle Meade Plantation, the 1853 mansion known as the "Queen of the Tennessee Plantations." The Greek Revival mansion was once the centerpiece of a 5,400-acre plantation known the world over in the 19th century as a thoroughbred farm and nursery. In 1807, John Harding purchased a log cabin and 250 acres of land adjacent to the Natchez Trace from the family of Daniel Dunham. Harding and his wife Susannah enlarged the cabin as their family grew. In the 1820s, they began construction of the present-day Belle Meade (a French term meaning "beautiful meadow") mansion, originally a two-story, Federal-style farmhouse.

Harding, who built a successful business boarding and breeding horses, continued to add to his estate. In 1836, his son, William Giles Harding, established the Belle Meade Thoroughbred Stud. William Giles Harding made additions to the mansion in the 1840s and in 1853. The Hardings also maintained a wild deer park on the property and sold ponies, Alderney cattle, Cotswold sheep and Cashmere goats. During the Civil War, the Federal government took the horses for the army's use and removed the plantation's stone fences. Loyal slaves are said to have hidden the most prized thoroughbreds. The mansion was riddled with bullets during the Battle of Nashville (see our History chapter).

After the war, William Giles Harding and his son-in-law, Gen. William H. Jackson, expanded the farm. It enjoyed international prominence until 1904, when the land and horses were auctioned. The financial crisis of 1893, an excessive lifestyle and the mishandling of family funds led to the downfall of Belle Meade, which in the early 1900s was the oldest and largest thoroughbred farm in America. The stables housed many great horses, including Iroquois, winner of the English Derby in 1881. The mansion and 24 remaining acres were opened to the public in 1953, under the management of the Nashville

Chapter of the Association for the Preservation of Tennessee Antiquities. For more information on Belle Meade, take a look at *The History of Belle Mead: Mansion, Plantation and Stud* by Ridley Wills II (Vanderbilt University Press, 1991). Wills is the great-great-grandson of William Giles Harding and great-grandson of Judge Howell E. Jackson.

The beautifully restored mansion is listed in the National Register of Historic Places. It is elegantly furnished with 19th-century antiques and art of the period. The site also includes the 1890 carriage house and stable filled with antique carriages; the 1790 log cabin (one of the oldest log structures in the state); and several other original outbuildings, such as the garden house, smokehouse and mausoleum. Guides in period dress lead tours of the property, offering a look back at the lifestyles of early Nashville's rich and famous. The shaded lawn is a popular site for festivals (see our Annual Events chapter). Admission is $8 for adults, $3 for children ages 6 to 12, and $6 per person for groups of 15 or more. Belle Meade Plantation is open year round except Thanksgiving, Christmas and New Year's Day. Hours are 9 AM to 5 PM Monday through Saturday and 1 to 5 PM Sunday.

## Belmont Mansion
### 1900 Wedgewood Ave. • (615) 460-5459

This magnificent mansion was built in 1850 as the summer home of Joseph and Adelicia Acklen. The beautiful and aristocratic Adelicia was said to have been the wealthiest woman in America during the mid-1800s. She owned 8,800 acres of cotton plantations in Louisiana, 40,000 to 50,000 acres of land in Texas and 2,000 acres in Tennessee, all of which she inherited after her first husband, wealthy businessman Isaac Franklin, who died in 1846. Her wealth placed her in the top one-half of 1 percent of antebellum society.

The Italianate villa is furnished in original and period pieces, including gilded mirrors, marble statues and art that Adelicia Acklen collected as she traveled the world. The

Acklens enlarged and remodeled the mansion in 1859. After the expansion, Belmont boasted 36 rooms with nearly 11,000 square feet of living space and another 8,400 square feet of service area in the basement. The Grand Salon is the most elaborate domestic space built in antebellum Tennessee. The property also boasted extensive gardens and numerous outbuildings. A 105-foot water tower, which still stands, irrigated the gardens and provided water for the fountains. Also on the property were a 200-foot-long greenhouse and conservatory, an art gallery, gazebos, a bowling alley, a bear house, a deer park and a zoo. Adelicia Acklen opened the gardens as a public park.

Visitors to Belmont Mansion will hear the fascinating story of Adelicia, an extraordinary woman who led an interesting life. When her second husband died during the Civil War, she was left with 2,800 bales of cotton. She traveled to Louisiana and cunningly "negotiated" the illegal sale of her cotton to England for $960,000 in gold. She later remarried but eventually moved to the Washington, D.C., area to spend time with her only surviving daughter, Pauline. In 1887, she sold Belmont to a land development company.

Two women from Philadelphia purchased the mansion in 1890 and opened a women's school, which later merged with Nashville's Ward School to become Ward-Belmont, an academy and junior college for women. In 1951, the Tennessee Baptist Convention purchased the school, which has become Belmont University, a coeducational, liberal arts school offering undergraduate and graduate degrees (see our Education and Child Care chapter).

Admission is $6 for adults and teens, $2 for children ages 6 through 12, free for young children and $5.50 for groups of 15 or more and senior citizens. From September through May, the hours are 10 AM to 4 PM Tuesday through Saturday. From June through August, the mansion is also open Mondays and Sundays 2 to 5 PM.

Photo: Nashville CVB/Robin Hood

The Belmont Mansion was once the home of the wealthiest woman in America. Later it was a women's college. Today it's a museum.

## Bicentennial Capitol Mall State Park
**James Robertson Pkwy.**
• **(615) 741-5280, (888) TNPARKS**

This 19-acre downtown attraction offers a trip through Tennessee history. It opened in 1996 to commemorate the state's bicentennial. A 200-foot granite map of the state, 31 fountains designating Tennessee's major rivers and a Pathway of History are among the attractions. The mall also offers a great view of the Tennessee State Capitol. Admission is free. Hours are 7 AM to sunset. (See our Parks and Kidstuff chapters for more information.)

## Cannonsburgh Village
**312 S. Front St., Murfreesboro**
• **(615) 890-0355**

Get a glimpse of what life was like in the pioneer days at this attraction, an American bicentennial project. The village features restored original buildings such as a church, general store, guest house, and gristmill from Rutherford and other Middle Tennessee counties. There is also an art league exhibit, a his-

torical Murfreesboro exhibit and displays of antique farm equipment and automobiles. You should allow at least 45 minutes to tour this attraction. Restrooms and a gift shop are on site. Admission is free, but guided tours cost $2.50 per adult and $1.50 for children ages 7 through 13. The buildings are open from May 1 to 13. The buildings are open from May 1 through January 1; the grounds are open year-round. Hours are 10 AM to 5 PM Tuesday through Saturday and 1 to 5 PM Sunday.

## Carnton Plantation
**1345 Carnton Ln., Franklin**
• **(615) 794-0903**

This 1826 antebellum plantation was built by Randal McGavock, who was Nashville's mayor in 1824 and 1825. The late-neoclassical plantation house is considered architecturally and historically one of the most important buildings in the area. In its early years, the mansion was a social and political center. Among the prominent visitors attending the many social events there were Andrew Jackson, Sam Houston and James K. Polk.

On November 30, 1864, after the bloody

Historic Fort Nashborough was built near the area called French Lick in 1779 as a new settlement for colonists from North Carolina.

Battle of Franklin, in which some 1,600 Confederate soldiers were killed, the home was used as a hospital. Wounded and dead soldiers filled the house and the yard. The Confederates lost 12 generals during the battle. The bodies of four of the generals were laid out on the mansion's back porch. At that time, Carnton was the home of McGavock's son, Col. John McGavock, and his wife, Carrie Winder McGavock. In 1866, the McGavock family donated 2 acres adjacent to their family cemetery for the burial of some 1,500 Southern solders. The McGavock Confederate Cemetery is the country's largest private Confederate cemetery.

A guided tour of the house costs $6 for adults and teens, $4 for seniors and $2 for children ages 6 through 12. Groups of 20 or more pay 2 per person. Admission to the grounds and cemetery is free. From April through October, hours are 9 AM to 5 PM Monday through Saturday and 1 to 5 PM Sunday. November through March, hours are 9 AM to 4 PM Monday through Saturday and 1 to 4 PM Sunday.

## Carter House
### 1140 Columbia Ave., Franklin
### • (615) 791-1861

This 1830 brick house was the center of fighting in the Battle of Franklin in 1864, one of the bloodiest battles of the Civil War. The house, built by Fountain Branch Carter, was used as a Federal command post while the Carter family, their friends and neighbors hid in the cellar during the battle. More than 2,000 Federal soldiers and more than 6,000 Confederates were killed in the battle. Among the dead were 12 Confederate generals, including Capt. Tod Carter, the youngest son of the Carter family, who died at the home 48 hours after being wounded in battle.

The Carter House is a registered National Historic Landmark. A video presentation, a visit to the museum in the visitors center — it features Confederate artifacts and photos of soldiers — and a guided tour of the house and grounds are included with admission to the attraction. Admission is $7 for adults and teens, $5 for seniors 65 and over, $4 for children ages 6 to 12 and $4 a person for groups of 25 or more. From April through October, hours are 9 AM to 5 PM Monday through Saturday, 1 to 5 PM Sunday. November through March, hours are 9 AM to 4 PM Monday through Saturday, 1 to 4 PM Sunday.

### Fort Nashborough
**170 First Ave. N. • (615) 862-8400**

On the banks of the Cumberland River at Riverfront Park stands the reconstruction of the original settlement of Nashville. The original log fort was built slightly north of here by James Robertson when he and his party first settled in the area in 1779 (see our History chapter). It occupied about 2 acres of land on a bluff overlooking the river and protected settlers from Indian attacks.

Named in honor of Gen. Francis Nash, who was killed during the Revolutionary War, the fort is where early Nashvillians met and adopted the Cumberland Compact for government of the new settlement. In 1930 the

Daughters of the American Revolution sponsored the construction of a replica of the original structure near the site of Fort Nashborough. The current fort, built in 1962, consists of five reproductions of the early cabins; it is smaller than the original and contains fewer cabins. It was restored and renovated by Metropolitan Nashville and Davidson County government. The reconstruction is authentic in many details. Exhibits of pioneer furniture, tools and other items are featured, allowing visitors a glimpse at the lifestyle of Nashville's first settlers. Admission is free. The fort is open to the public for self-guided tours from 9 AM to 5 PM Tuesday through Sunday, weather permitting.

### Hatch Show Print
**316 Broadway • (615) 256-2805**

Founded in 1879 in downtown Nashville, Hatch Show Print is the oldest working letterpress print shop in America. For years, the shop produced promotional handbills and posters for vaudeville acts, circuses, sporting events and minstrel shows throughout the Southeast, but it is best known for its posters of *Grand Ole Opry* stars. From 1925 to 1991, it was on Fourth Avenue N., near the Ryman Auditorium; it relocated a few times before settling at its current site, a 100-year-old building between Third and Fourth avenues. In 1985 Opryland USA purchased the business, which is managed by the Country Music Foundation.

Today, Hatch finds its letterpress posters and designs in constant demand. The shop

---

**INSIDERS' TIP**

Take a 2-mile walk through 200 years of history on the Nashville CityWalk. The Metro Historical Commission has planned this self-guided tour to teach you about some of the city's historic sites. Starting at Fort Nashborough, you'll see and learn about 15 historic downtown sites, tracing Nashville's history from frontier settlement to modern-day Music City. Follow the green painted line. Among the points of interest are historic Market Street (Second Avenue), Printers Alley, Davidson County Courthouse, the Tennessee State Capitol, Ryman Auditorium, the historic black business district and Hermitage Hotel. Most of the sites are open to the public and offer free admission. Stop by the Historical Commission office at 209 10th Avenue S. to pick up a brochure, or call (615) 862-7970 for more information.

continues to create posters and art for such clients as Nike, the Jack Daniel Distillery, local bands and national recording artists. One wall of the tiny space is lined with thousands of wood and metal blocks of type used to produce posters. With its original tin ceilings, wooden floors, metal windows, shelves and composing tables, the shop appears today much as it did in the early 1900s. Take a peek inside the next time you're downtown. Though formal tours aren't offered, some 10,000 visitors stop by each year. You can even take home a sample of Hatch's product. Posters are available and range in price from $3 to $300. Admission is free. Hours are 10 AM to 6 PM Monday through Saturday.

## The Hermitage: Home of President Andrew Jackson
**4580 Rachel's Ln., Hermitage**
• **(615) 889-2941**

More than 250,000 people visit this attraction each year, making it the fourth most-visited presidential home in America, behind only the White House, George Washington's Mount Vernon and Thomas Jefferson's Monticello. A tour of the Hermitage offers insight into one of America's most interesting presidents, as well as a look at life on a 19th-century plantation (see our History chapter).

Andrew Jackson, seventh president of the United States and hero of the Battle of New Orleans, lived and died here, and is buried next to his wife Rachel on the grounds. The Hermitage was first built in 1821 as a Federal-style brick home. It was enlarged in 1831 then rebuilt in Greek Revival style as it appears today after a fire destroyed part of the upper floor. Today a National Historic Landmark, managed since 1889 by the Ladies' Hermitage Association, the mansion has been restored to the period of Jackson's retirement in

1837. It contains a large collection of original furnishings and personal belongings, including furniture, porcelain, silver and rare French wallpaper. The scenic wallpaper in the entry hall portrays Greek hero Telemachus's search for his father, Odysseus. Jackson filled the house with elegant and sophisticated pieces from the same dealers who supplied the White House.

Among the many notables Jackson welcomed to the Hermitage were Revolutionary War leader Marquis de Lafayette; Sam Houston, former Tennessee governor, hero of the Alamo and Texas' first governor; and Jackson's presidential successors, Martin Van Buren and James K. Polk. The Hermitage is surrounded by 650 acres of rolling woodlands. On the east side of the house is Rachel's Garden, designed in 1819 by English gardener William Frost. The garden has been maintained as it was then, and the flowers and shrubs you see here are typical of the early 19th century. The central flower beds feature a formal geometric design and are bordered by bricks made at the property's kiln. Among the many varieties of trees, shrubs and groundcovers are English boxwood, crepe myrtle, chestnut rose, lilac, honeysuckle, Southern magnolia, weeping willow, crocus, tulip, narcissus, daylily and various herbs.

At the north border is the original "necessary house." The southeast corner of the garden contains the Jacksons' tomb. Rachel died December 22, 1828, weeks before Jackson was inaugurated as president. Jackson is said to have visited the tomb every evening while he lived at the Hermitage. Jackson died in his bedroom on June 8, 1845. Per his directions, he was buried next to his wife. Other members of his family are buried next to the Jackson Tomb. On the other side of the tomb is the grave of Alfred, a slave who lived at the

## INSIDERS' TIP

In 1904, the One-Cent Savings Bank became the first minority-owned bank in Tennessee. The bank was founded by distinguished community leaders including James C. Napier, the Rev. Richard Henry Boyd and Preston Taylor. Now called Citizens Bank, it is the oldest continuously operating minority-owned bank in the country.

Robert's Western World may be the only place in the country where you can listen to bluegrass and honky-tonk music while trying on cowboy boots.

property all his life and was Jackson's devoted servant. Be sure to visit the other historic structures on the grounds, including the original cabins where the Jacksons lived from 1804 to 1821; the Old Hermitage Church; an original slave cabin, smokehouse, springhouse and kitchen; and Tulip Grove mansion, the home of Andrew Jackson Donelson, Rachel's nephew and the president's secretary.

The Hermitage has occasional special events. Each summer, Dr. Larry McKee, Hermitage director of archaeology, leads a 10-week excavation of the property. His work has unearthed thousands of artifacts yielding insights into the lives of the slaves who worked here. (For more information on yearly events at the Hermitage, see our Annual Events chapter.)

Your tour of the Hermitage will begin with a short orientation film, followed by live and audiotaped tours of the mansion and grounds. At the visitors center, you can get a quick bite at Rachel's Cafe and browse for gifts at the Hermitage Museum Store. The Hermitage is open 9 AM to 5 PM daily. It is closed on Thanksgiving, Christmas and the third week of January. Admission is $9.50 for adults and teens, $8.50 for seniors 62 and older and $4.50 for children ages 6 through 12. Groups of 20 or more receive a discount. Admission is free on January 8, which is the anniversary of the Battle of New Orleans. On Jackson's birthday, March 15, admission is reduced.

### Historic Mansker's Station Frontier Life Center
**Moss-Wright Park at Caldwell Rd., Goodlettsville • (615) 859-FORT**

Bowen Plantation House and Mansker's Station are at this site. The two-story, Federal-style house built in 1787 is the oldest brick home in Middle Tennessee. It was built by Revolutionary War veteran and Indian fighter William Bowen, who brought his family to the area in 1785. He received the land as partial compensation for his military service and later expanded the plantation from 640 acres to more than 4,000. In 1807, William Bowen Campbell was born here. He fought in the Seminole War and the Mexican War, and served as Tennessee's 15th governor from 1851 to 1853 and a member of Congress in 1855. The restored house was listed on the National Register of Historic Places in 1976.

About 200 yards away is Mansker's Station, a reconstruction of a 1779 frontier fort where Kasper Mansker lived. Mansker is considered Goodlettsville's first citizen. The fort is near Mansker's Lick, one of the area's salt licks where long hunters came to hunt and trap. John Donelson, one of the founders of Nashville, moved his family here after abandoning his Clover Bottom Station following an Indian attack in 1780. Visitors get a look at pioneer life in Tennessee. Living history encampments held six weekends a year offer demonstrations of frontier skills such as hide-tanning, soapmaking, blacksmithing, candle-dipping, butter-churning, natural dyeing and fireside cookery. The three largest events are Yulefest, the fall encampment and the Colonial Fair (see our Annual Events chapter). Historic interpreters in period clothing provide tours Tuesday through Saturday 9 AM to 4 PM from March through December. The attraction is closed January and February. Admission is $5 for adults, $3 for students.

## Historic Rock Castle
### 139 Rock Castle Ln., Hendersonville
### • (615) 824-0502

The late-18th-century house on the shores of Old Hickory Lake was at one time the center of a 3,140-acre plantation, home of senator and Revolutionary War veteran Daniel Smith and his family. Today the property occupies 18 acres and includes the furnished, seven-level limestone house, a smokehouse and the family cemetery. Other buildings were claimed by the creation of Old Hickory Lake in the 1950s.

The original two-room structure was built in the mid-1780s. The multilevel stone house was completed in 1796; it had four rooms downstairs and three upstairs. The large limestone blocks used in the home's construction

were quarried nearby, and the wood for the house came from trees on the property. Floor-to-ceiling black walnut cupboards were built into the fireplace walls in some rooms. Smith, a well-known surveyor of the North Carolina (now Tennessee) boundaries and of Davidson County, made the first map of the area. Some say he gave the state its name as well, adopting the Cherokee word "Tanasie," which may have meant "where the rivers tangle together." (However, accounts of who named the state, and the meaning of the Cherokee word from which the name was taken, vary quite a bit.) Smith and his wife, Sarah, are buried in the family cemetery.

You can learn more about the family and the property on a guided tour. Stop first at the visitors center for an orientation to the property. There's a gift shop there that sells souvenirs and items representative of the period, such as lye soap, traditional games and toys and reproductions of Smith's early maps. The visitors center also houses staff offices and a meeting room. Rock Castle is 2 miles south of Gallatin Road off Indian Lake Road. Admission is $3 for adults and teens, $2.50 for seniors and $1.50 for children 6 through 12. Call for group rates. This attraction is open February through December. Hours are 10 AM to 4 PM Wednesday through Saturday and 1 to 4 PM Sunday. During daylight-saving time, weekend hours are extended until 5 PM.

## Jack Daniel Distillery
### Tenn. Hwy. 55, Lynchburg
### • (931) 759-6180

Founded in 1866, the Jack Daniel Distillery is the oldest registered distillery in the United States and is on the National Register of Historic Places. This is where the famous Jack Daniel's "smooth sippin' Tennessee whiskey" is made. You can learn all about how this sour mash Tennessee whiskey is made during a personally guided tour of the facility, after which you'll be served a complimentary lemonade. You can't sample the whiskey because the county is dry, but you can purchase a specially designed decanter of it in the distillery's visitor center. Admission is free. Tours are conducted daily from 8 AM to 4 PM except Thanksgiving, Christmas and New Year's Day. Plan to spend about 90 minutes on the tour. The distillery is about 80 miles south of Nashville, about 26 miles off Interstate 24.

## Nashville City Cemetery
### 1001 Fourth Ave. S. at Oak St.

This cemetery was opened January 1, 1822, making it Nashville's oldest remaining public cemetery. It's also one of the few cemeteries in the state listed as an individual property on the National Register of Historic Places. There are some 23,000 graves here, including the graves of many early settlers, whose remains were brought here for permanent burial. Many graves are unmarked. Among the notables buried here are Nashville founder Gen. James Robertson (1742–1814); Capt. William Driver (1803–1886), who named the American flag "Old Glory"; and Gov. William Carroll (1788–1844), who served as governor from 1821 to 1827 and from 1829 to 1835. Three Civil War generals are also buried here: Major Gen. Bushrod Johnson (1817–1880), hero of the Battle of Chickamauga; Lt. Gen. Richard S. Ewell (1817–1872), a commander at the Battle of Gettysburg; and Gen. Felix Zollicoffer (1812–1862), editor of the city's first daily newspaper, killed at the Battle of Fishing Creek, in Kentucky.

In 1878 city officials voted to allow only descendants of owners with unfilled plots to be buried here. This policy is still in place; only about one burial a year takes place. The property is administered by the Metro Historical Commission, (615) 862-7970, and maintained by Metro Parks. Many of the grave markers and monuments have deteriorated and are no longer legible. Metal markers containing historical information are located throughout the grounds. In 1997 a restoration project began to repair some of the structures. The cemetery is open daily from about 7:30 AM until dusk. Cemetery records are in the Tennessee State Library and Archives at 403 Seventh Avenue N., (615) 741-2764.

## Oaklands Historic House Museum
### 900 N. Maney Ave., Murfreesboro
### • (615) 893-0022

One of the most elegant antebellum homes in Middle Tennessee, this house began around 1815 as a one-story brick home built by the Maney family. The family enlarged the house with a Federal-style addition in the early 1820s and made additional changes in the 1830s. The last addition was the ornate Italianate facade, completed in the 1850s.

Oaklands was the center of a 1,500-acre plantation. Union and Confederate armies alternately occupied the house during the Civil War. On July 13, 1862, Confederate Gen. Nathan Bedford Forrest led a raid here, surprising the Union commander at Oaklands. The surrender was negotiated here. In December 1862, Confederate President Jefferson Davis boarded at Oaklands while visiting nearby troops. There is a gift shop on the property. Admission is $5 for adults, $4 for seniors 65 and up and $2 for children 6 through 16. Groups of 15 or more receive a $1 discount per person. Hours are 10 AM to 4 PM Tuesday through Saturday, 1 to 4 PM Sunday.

## Printers Alley
### Between Church and Union and Third and Fourth aves.

Printers Alley was originally the center of Nashville's publishing and printing industry. Speakeasies sprang up here during Prohibition. During the 1940s, nightclubs opened and Printers Alley became the center of the city's nightlife. You could come here to catch performances by such stars as Boots Randolph, Chet Atkins, Dottie West and Hank Williams.

Today, you'll find several nightspots here, including honky-tonks like Barbara's and the Bourbon Street Blues & Boogie Bar. Printers Alley is really more a tourist destination than a local nightlife hot spot.

## Ryman Auditorium
### 116 Fifth Ave. N. • (615) 254-1445, (615) 889-7070

The legendary Ryman Auditorium (see also our History, Music City U.S.A. and Arts chapters), home of the *Grand Ole Opry* from 1943 to 1974, has enjoyed a sort of rebirth in recent years. After an $8.5 million renovation, the 2,100-seat landmark venue reopened in 1994, restored to its original splendor. Today the Ryman hosts musical productions such as *Lost Highway – The Music & Legend of Hank Williams* and *Always . . . Patsy Cline* as well as concerts by country, bluegrass, pop, classical and gospel artists. Its excellent acoustics have made it a popular spot among recording artists such as Bruce Springsteen, Merle Haggard, Bob Dylan and Sheryl Crow.

The building was originally called the Union Gospel Tabernacle. Riverboat captain Thomas Ryman, inspired by the preaching of evangelist Sam Jones, built the facility in 1892 as a site for Jones's revivals and other religious gatherings. It soon became a popular venue for theatrical and musical performances and political rallies. The building was renamed to honor Ryman after his death in 1904.

Though it wasn't the first home of the *Grand Ole Opry*, which began in 1925, the Ryman earned the nickname "the Mother Church of Country Music." For 31 years, the live *Opry* radio show originated from this building. Country legends such as Hank Williams, Roy Acuff and Patsy Cline performed on the stage. While fans packed the wooden pews, others tuned in to their radios to hear the live broadcast. When the *Opry* moved to the new Grand Ole Opry House at Opryland USA, the Ryman became a tourist attraction, and the building was used as a backdrop in such films as *Nashville*, *Coal Miner's Daughter* and *Sweet Dreams*. An exterior renovation began in 1989 to prepare for the facility's 100th anniversary in 1992. It was closed from fall 1993 to June 1994 for the major renovation that allowed the historic, much-loved attraction to open its doors to a new generation of performers and music fans.

The Ryman remains a top tourist destination. Individuals and groups stop here daily to tour the building and travel back to the early days of country music. Inside, various exhibits and displays tell about the Ryman and country music history. Audiovisual displays on the main floor feature a variety of memorabilia. An interactive unit downstairs is popular with kids. Self-guided tours are available seven days a week from 8:30 AM to 4 PM for $6 for adults and $2.50 for children 4 to 11. A concession stand and gift shop are on site.

## Sam Davis Home Historic Site
### 1399 Sam Davis Rd., Smyrna
### • (615) 459-2341

This Greek Revival home, built around 1820 and enlarged around 1850, sits on 169 acres of the original 1,000-acre farm that was the home of Sam Davis. Davis, called the "Boy Hero of the Confederacy," enlisted in the Confederate Army at the age of 19. He served as a courier, and while transporting secret papers to Gen. Braxton Bragg in Chattanooga, he was captured by Union forces, tried as a spy and sentenced to hang. The trial officer was so impressed with Davis' honesty and sense of honor that he offered him freedom if he would reveal the source of military information he was caught carrying. Davis is reported to have responded, "If I had a thousand lives I would give them all gladly rather than betray a friend." He was hanged in Pulaski, Tennessee, on November 27, 1863.

The home is a typical upper-middle class farmhouse of the period. A tour of the property also includes outbuildings. Several annual events take place here (see our Annual Events chapter). Admission is $5 for adults and teens, $4 for seniors 65 and older and $2.50 for children 6 to 12. Group discounts are available. From June through August, hours are 9 AM to 5 PM Monday through Saturday and 1 to 5 PM Sunday. September through May, hours are 10 AM to 4 PM Monday through Saturday, 1 to 4 PM Sunday.

## Stones River National Battlefield
### 3501 Old Nashville Hwy., Murfreesboro
### • (615) 893-9501

One of the bloodiest Civil War battles took place at this site between December 31, 1862, and January 2, 1863. More than 83,000 men fought in the battle; nearly 28,000 were killed or wounded. Both the Union army, led by Gen. William S. Rosecrans, and the Confederate army, led by Gen. Braxton Bragg, claimed victory. However, on January 3, 1863, Bragg retreated 40 miles to Tullahoma, Tennessee, and Rosecrans took control of Murfreesboro.

The Union constructed a huge supply base within Fortress Rosecrans, the largest enclosed earthen fortification built during the war. The battlefield today appears much as it did during the Battle of Stones River. Most of the points of interest can be reached on the self-guided auto tour. Numbered markers identify the stops, and short trails and exhibits explain the events at each site. Plan to spend at least two hours to get the most out of your visit, and stop first at the visitor center. An audiovisual

# Take A Colorful Spin Through Tennessee History

The Tennessee Fox Trot Carousel is one of Nashville's more unusual attractions. Located in Riverfront Park, the $1.75 million carousel was created by internationally renowned artist and Nashville native Red Grooms. It opened in November 1998.

The carousel features 36 figures and 28 panels relating to Tennessee history and cultural life. Instead of the usual carousel horses, the "rides" on the Tennessee Fox Trot Carousel include colorful and animated "sculpto-pictoramas" of such figures as Andrew Jackson, Davy Crockett, *Opry* star Kitty Wells, Captain Ryman (of Ryman Auditorium fame), Olympic medalist Wilma Rudolph, the Purity Milk Truck and even the pesky Tennessee Chigger. Grooms is known for his wit and humor, and the carousel's cast of characters are cleverly and often humorously portrayed.

Standing 30 feet high and measuring 42 feet in diameter, the carousel is Grooms's largest work to date. It's something he dreamed of creating for 20 years. The carousel was created in sculptural tableaux, one of the artist's favorite mediums. It took five years of planning and about two years to construct. The piece has been called one of the country's best public art projects by one of the country's most important artists working today.

Grooms, who grew up in Nashville and now lives in New York, has exhibited extensively at galleries and museums around the world. His works can be found in New York's Metropolitan Museum of Art, Museum of Modern Art, Solomon R. Guggenheim Museum and Whitney Museum of Art as well as the Art Institute of Chicago and Washington, D.C.'s Hirshhorn Museum and Sculpture Garden. In 1996 Grooms was commissioned by the city of Nagoya, Japan, to create a permanent outdoor sculpture in the city's entertainment district.

The Tennessee Fox Trot Carousel was funded through contributions and grants from individuals and families, corporate sponsorships, foundations and public support. It is expected to earn $225,000 per year, at least $100,000 of which will be dedicated to the arts.

The carousel is open daily except Christmas. Tickets are sold at the adjacent ticket booth and cost $2 each, or you can buy six tickets for $10; groups of 15 or more can purchase tickets for $1.60 apiece.

For more information, call the ticket booth at (615) 254-7020 or the Nashville Visitor Center at (615) 259-4747.

Photo: Cindy Stooksbury Guier

Kitty Wells is the character on this carousel figure.

Marty Stuart knows the Country Music Hall of Fame contains exhibits relating to country music superstars like Hank Williams as well as Elvis's "solid gold Cadillac."

program and museum will introduce you to the battle. A captioned slide program is available too. Pick up a brochure or recorded guide to use on the self-guided auto tour.

During summer, artillery and infantry demonstrations and talks about the battle are scheduled. The park is administered by the National Park Service. Stones River National Battlefield is open daily except Christmas. Hours are 8 AM to 5 PM. Admission is free.

## Tennessee State Capitol
**Charlotte Ave., between Sixth and Seventh aves. • (615) 741-1621, (615) 741-0830 (reservations for groups of 10 or more)**

The Greek Revival-style building was begun in 1845 and completed in 1859 (see our History chapter). Its architect, William Strickland of Philadelphia, began his career as an apprentice to Benjamin Latrobe, architect of the U.S. Capitol in Washington, D.C.

Strickland died before the Tennessee State Capitol was completed and, per his wishes, was buried in the northeast wall of the building, near the north entrance. Strickland's son, Francis Strickland, supervised construction until 1857, when Englishman Harvey Akeroyd designed the state library, the final portion of the building.

The capitol stands 170 feet above the highest hill in downtown Nashville. On the eastern slope of the grounds is the tomb of President and Mrs. James K. Polk and a bronze equestrian statue of President Andrew Jackson. During the Civil War, the capitol was used as a Union fortress. In the 1930s, the murals in the governor's office were added. Various restoration projects have taken place over the years. In 1996, a bronze statue of Andrew Johnson was erected so that all three U.S. presidents from Tennessee are commemorated on the capitol grounds.

The building is open Monday through Friday from 9 AM to 4 PM; guided tours are conducted from 9 AM to 3 PM. A brochure is available for self-guided tours. Admission is free. The building is closed on weekends and state holidays.

## Historic Travellers Rest Plantation House and Grounds
**636 Farrell Pkwy. • (615) 832-8197**

Travellers Rest was built in 1799 by Judge John Overton, a land speculator, lawyer, cofounder of Memphis and presidential campaign manager for lifelong friend Andrew Jackson. The Federal-style clapboard farmhouse offers a glimpse of how wealthy Nashvillians lived in the early 19th century. The well-maintained grounds feature magnolia trees, gardens and outbuildings. The house began as a two-story, four-room house, but additions throughout the 1800s increased its size. Changes in architectural styles are evident in the expansions. It has been restored to reflect the period of the original owner and features a large collection of early 19th-century Tennessee furniture.

The home served as headquarters for Confederate Gen. John B. Hood just before the 1864 Battle of Nashville. Overton's son John had financed a Confederate regiment during the war. The Overton family owned the house until 1948. Its last owner, the Nashville Railroad Company, gave the home to the Colonial Dames of America in Tennessee, which manages it as a historic site. Today, Travellers Rest is listed on the National Register of Historic Places. Special events are held on the grounds (see our Annual Events chapter). Admission is $7 for adults and teens, $6 for seniors 65 and older and $3 for children 6 to 12. Groups of 15 or more pay $6 a person.

# Museums

## Oscar Farris Agricultural Museum
**Ellington Agricultural Center,**
**440 Hogan Rd. • (615) 837-5197**

This attraction is about seven minutes south of downtown Nashville, at the beautiful 207-acre Ellington Agricultural Center. It operates under the umbrella of the Tennessee Department of Agriculture and is the department's headquarters. Labeled perennial gardens greet visitors at the front entrance.

The museum, a 14,000-square-foot, two-story horse barn built in 1920, houses an extensive collection of home and farm artifacts from the 1800s and early 1900s, a blacksmith shop and the Tennessee Agriculture Hall of Fame exhibit. A log cabin area, near the main barn, features five cabins with exhibits relating to early farm life in Tennessee. An interpretive herb garden is next to the cabins, and a nature trail from the cabin area leads to an iris garden, pond and gazebo. The property is also designated as an arboretum, featuring 80 tree species. Special events held here include the Rural Life Festival in early May and the Music and Molasses Festival the third weekend in October. Hours are 9 AM to 4 PM Monday through Friday. Admission is free, but there is a $1-a-person activity fee for large groups. Reservations are required for large groups of 15 or more. Each year, 13,000 area students take part in the center's programs. Special events are held on the property throughout the year.

## Cheekwood — Nashville's Home of Art and Gardens
**1200 Forrest Park Dr. • (615) 356-8000**

This magnificent 1929 mansion surrounded by 55 acres of botanical gardens, lawns and fountains is one of Nashville's favorite attractions. It was once the private estate of the Leslie Cheek family. Cheek was the cousin and business associate of Joel Cheek, founder of Maxwell House Coffee. In 1960, the family gave the estate to the nonprofit Tennessee Botanical Gardens and Fine Arts Center. Today the mansion houses a prestigious collection of 19th- and 20th-century American art as well as items from around the world and major traveling art exhibits (see our chapter on The Arts).

The three-story, neo-Georgian mansion was built with Tennessee limestone quarried on the property. The Cheeks and their architect, Bryant Fleming, selected such opulent appointments as towering mahogany doors, a lapis lazuli mantel, 19th-century English crystal chandeliers, a fine wrought-iron stair railing from Queen Charlotte's Palace at Kew and *trompe l'oeil* paintings on the walls. The house sits atop a hill, surrounded by formal gardens designed by Fleming. A walk through these lovely gardens is a must. They feature marble sculptures, water gardens and bubbling streams. The design includes an award-winning wildflower garden, an herb garden, perennial garden, traditional Japanese garden and a dogwood trail. Along the border of the property is the Woodland Sculpture Trail, a mile-long trail featuring more than a dozen sculptures by artists from around the world.

The Botanic Hall is on the grounds and features horticultural exhibits, flower shows and the annual Trees of Christmas exhibit. Greenhouses are open to the public as well. Inside the main gate are the Pineapple Room Restaurant, offering regional cuisine (see our Restaurants chapter), and the Cheekwood Museum Gift Shop, where you'll find a selection of books, Tennessee crafts and nice gift items. Cheekwood's Learning Center offers classes, lectures, workshops and special events relating to horticulture and art for all ages.

Cheekwood is 8 miles southwest of downtown, off Belle Meade Boulevard and Tenn. Highway 100. Admission is $8 for adults, $7 for senior citizens and college students and $5 for children 6 to 17. Group rates are available. Cheekwood is open daily except Thanksgiving, Christmas, New Year's Day and the third Saturday in April. Hours are 9 AM to 5 PM Monday through Saturday, 11 AM to 5 PM Sunday. From April 15 to September 1, Cheekwood is open evenings until 8 PM Monday through Thursday.

## Cumberland Science Museum & Sudekum Planetarium
**800 Fort Negley Blvd. • (615) 862-5160**

A fun place to learn and explore, this museum features exhibits on nature, the universe, health and more. Since the museum opened in 1973, it has been entertaining and educating children and adults with more than 100 hands-on exhibits, live animal shows, science demonstrations, a planetarium and traveling exhibits. Nine permanent exhibits include the Sudekum Planetarium, Kinetic Coaster, Micro Lab, Curiosity Corner and Deep Sea Adventure. For more information, including operating hours and prices, see the listing in our Kidstuff chapter under "Amuseums."

## Hartzler-Towner Multicultural Museum
**1104 19th Ave. S. • (615) 340-7481, (615) 340-7500 (Scarritt-Bennett Center)**

This museum is on the second floor of the library at the Scarritt-Bennett Center. It features 4,000 items from around the world, with an emphasis on pieces from Africa and Asia. Objects relating to religion, social organization and arts and crafts are featured. Included is a collection of 700 international dolls. Three or four temporary exhibits are featured annually. Admission is free. Hours are 8 AM to 9 PM Monday through Friday, 8 AM to 5 PM Saturday and 1 to 6 PM Sunday.

## The Museum of Beverage Containers and Advertising
**1055 Ridgecrest Dr., Millersville • (615) 859-5236**

One of the Nashville area's quirkier attractions, this museum boasts the world's largest collection of beverage containers. More than 30,000 different beer and soda cans, thousands of antique soda bottles and antique soda and beer advertisements are on display. Other displays focus on major soft drink brands and Tennessee's brewery history. A well-stocked gift shop features more than 250,000 signs, mini drink bottles, trays, glasses, key chains and reproduction collectibles. The museum is about 10 minutes north of Rivergate Mall, about 1.5 miles off Interstate 65; take the Millersville exit. Admission is $4 for adults, free for children younger than 12. Call for group rates. Hours are 9 AM to 5 PM Monday through Saturday and 1 to 5 PM Sunday.

## Music Valley Car Museum
**2611 McGavock Pk. • (615) 885-7400**

Car enthusiasts and country music fans will get a kick out of this museum. Located across from the Opryland Hotel in the Music Valley area, it features approximately 50 vehicles, many owned by country music stars.

The gift shop offers typical Nashville souvenirs plus NASCAR merchandise, model cars and other auto-related items. (For more information, including hours, admission fees and details about country music celebrities represented here, see the related entry in our Music City U.S.A. chapter.)

## Nashville Toy Museum
**2613 McGavock Pk. • (615) 883-8870**

Both kids and adults enjoy this museum, which showcases a collection of European and American toys of the past 150 years. A model train travels through the museum, running through 7-foot mountains; another giant layout features a wind-up train. Other attractions include 1,000 lead soldiers in battle dioramas, toy guns, toy tractors, automotive toys and toy boats. Guided tours are available. The gift shop features a mix of toys, including a large selection of reproduction European tin toys, and souvenir items. Admission is $3 for folks 12 and older, $1.50 for children ages 6 to 11 and free for those 5 and younger. Group discounts are available. The museum is open 9:30 AM to 5 PM Monday through Saturday and noon to 5 PM Sunday. It's closed Thanksgiving and Christmas. (See our Kidstuff chapter for more information.)

## The Parthenon
**Centennial Park, West End Ave. and 25th Ave. • (615) 862-8431**

One of Nashville's most dramatic and most recognized attractions, this is the world's only full-size reproduction of the ancient Greek temple. Nashville's magnificent Parthenon, listed on the National Register of Historic Places, mirrors the dimensions of the original to an eighth of an inch. Our first Parthenon was built between 1895 and 1897 as the centerpiece for the state's Centennial Exposition. It was a symbol of our city's reputation as the Athens of the South. Like the other exposition buildings, the Parthenon was created of plaster and wood.

While the other buildings were demolished after the expo, the Parthenon was so popular that Nashville kept it, and Centennial Park was created around it in the early 1900s. After it had begun to deteriorate, it was rebuilt with concrete from 1920 to 1931. Nashville architect Russell E. Hart and New York architect and archaeologist William B. Dinsmoor worked on the plans. After studying the ruins of the original Parthenon in Greece, Dinsmoor designed the interior, which is accepted by scholars as true to the original.

A $2 million renovation was completed in 1988, and today, work continues to preserve the historic structure. Encircling the Parthenon are 46 Doric columns. Two pairs of bronze doors — the largest in the world, weighing 7.5 tons each — mark entrances on two sides of the building. Inside, the floors are made of Tennessee marble and the ceiling of cypress from the Florida Everglades. Just as it was in ancient Greece, the focus of our Parthenon is a 42-foot statue of the goddess Athena, created by Nashville sculptor Alan LeQuire. It is the tallest indoor sculpture in the Western world. A 6-foot statue of Nike, the Greek goddess of victory, rests in Athena's right hand.

The Parthenon is also the city's art museum and boasts an impressive collection of art, including the Cowan Collection, which features more than 60 works by 19th- and 20th-century American painters. Other gallery spaces showcase temporary art shows and exhibits. There are more than 25 trained docents who provide information about the art collection as well as mythology and Nashville history. A gift shop in the main lobby of the gallery-level entrance offers a moderately priced and interesting selection of clothing, games, jewelry, stationery, original art, reproductions of Greek antiquities and other items. A visit to the Parthenon is a must. Hours are 9 AM to 4:30 PM Tuesday through Saturday. From April through September, it is also open Sundays from 12:30 to 4:30 PM. Admission is $2.50 for adults 18 to 61, $1.25 for seniors and students. Group rates are available.

## Tennessee State Museum
**505 Deaderick St. (Fifth Ave., between Union and Deaderick) • (615) 741-2692**

This museum offers a fascinating look at the history of Tennessee, from prehistoric times through the 20th century. Displays include collections of prehistoric Indian artifacts, firearms, silver, quilts, paintings and pottery. There is

## INSIDERS' TIP

Some attractions offer occasional free or reduced admission. Call to inquire.

# Hotel's Indoor Gardens Grow Into Bona-fide Attraction

A favorite among Nashvillians and visitors, the massive Opryland Hotel is as much an attraction as it is a hotel. There are 9 acres of impressive indoor gardens, 2,884 guest rooms, 15 restaurants, 30 retail shops and much more.

## Close-up

The Conservatory, a 2-acre bilevel space filled with tropical plants, was the hotel's first indoor garden; it opened in 1983. Wander along the winding path, then walk upstairs and check out the view of the 10,000 tropical plants from above. The 1988 expansion featured The Cascades, another 2-acre indoor area. The Cascades' three waterfalls, ranging in height from 23 feet to 35 feet, splash down from the top of a 40-foot mountain into a 12,500-square-foot lake. You can linger here at the tropical Cascades Restaurant or enjoy drinks and appetizers at the revolving Cascades Terrace lounge. Each night, visitors crowd around the Cascades' Dancing Waters fountains, which are the focus of a laser show performed to the music of a pianist perched on a stage overlooking the room.

Photo: Nashville CVB/Donnie Beauchamp

The newest indoor "garden," The Delta, opened in 1996. When you step into this 4.5-acre area, you'll be transported to a Mississippi Delta town — complete with a river and flatboats that carry guests through the area. The Delta's glass roof peaks at 150 feet (15 stories). Two- and three-story

Flatboats carry guests through Opryland Hotel's 4.5-acre Delta area.

buildings house a variety of interesting gift shops, meeting rooms and lounges. The Delta Food Court is the place to find drinks, New Orleans beignets and other goodies.

For more information, contact Opryland Hotel Indoor Garden & Collections, 2800 Opryland Drive, (615) 889-1000. Also, see our Accommodations and Annual Events chapters for more on lodging options and yearly happenings at this Nashville showplace. Admission to the hotel gardens is free; parking at the Opryland Hotel costs $5.

an extensive collection of Civil War uniforms, battle flags and weapons. You can learn about the long hunters such as Daniel Boone, who hunted in the area beginning in the 1760s, as well as interesting political figures such as Andrew Jackson and Sam Houston.

Other exhibits relate to African Americans, Prohibition, women's suffrage and important events that shaped the history of the Volun-

teer State. Replicas of building facades and period rooms are featured too. A temporary exhibit gallery presents four exhibits each year that relate to art and/or historical subjects of regional and national interest. Allow at least an hour to tour the museum, but be prepared to spend an entire afternoon. The museum is below the Tennessee Performing Arts Center (see Arts). There are restrooms and a gift shop.

The museum's Military History Branch is in the War Memorial Building one block away. There you'll find exhibits on America's involvement in foreign wars, from the Spanish-American War through World War II. Displays feature weapons, uniforms and battle histories. Admission is free at both museums. Hours are 10 AM to 5 PM Tuesday through Saturday, 1 to 5 PM Sunday. The museums are closed Mondays and major holidays.

## The Upper Room Chapel and Museum
**1908 Grand Ave. • (615) 340-7207**

An interesting attraction here is the chapel's 8- by 17-foot wood carving of *The Last Supper*, based on da Vinci's painting. It was created by Italian sculptor Ernest Pellegrini in 1953 for the Upper Room, an interdenominational ministry of the United Methodist Church. A short presentation on this piece and the chapel's 8- by 20-foot stained glass window is given on the hour and half-hour inside the chapel.

The museum contains religious artifacts, paintings of religious subjects made from 1300 through 1990, manuscripts, books and seasonal displays of 100 nativity scenes and 73 Ukranian eggs. In between the wings of the building is the Agape Garden, featuring statues, fountains and symbols relating to the garden of Gethsemane. Admission is free, but a $2 donation is encouraged. Hours are 8 AM to 4:30 PM Monday through Friday.

# Amusements & Zoos

## Nashville Zoo at Grassmere
**3777 Nolensville Rd. • (615) 833-1534**

Nolensville Road between Harding Mall and Thompson Lane is a busy area filled with fast-food restaurants, a shopping mall, all types of stores and lots of traffic. It's an unlikely spot for a wildlife sanctuary, yet just off this road is a 200-acre zoo that is home to animals from all around the world.

Until 1998, the Nashville Zoo was located in Joelton. Now, the zoo and Grassmere are consolidating. Animals will be relocated in phases to the Grassmere site over the next three to five years or so. When the transition is completed, the zoo will cover more than twice the area as the Joelton location, which will be used as a breeding facility for endangered species and as a "retirement home" for older animals. Formerly known as Grassmere Wildlife Park, and home to animals indigenous to North America, this attraction opened in 1990 on land donated by the estate of sisters Elise and Margaret Croft for the protection of natural areas and wildlife. (The Grassmere name comes from the c. 1815 residence on the property, one of the earliest brick homes in Davidson County. It was built by Michael C. Dunn, an early Nashville sheriff, from whom the Crofts descended.) At the entrance to the park is the Croft Center, a two-story educational facility with lecture rooms, an aviary, an aquarium, reptile and aquatic exhibits and an amphitheater. Lecture sessions offer up-close visits with (and a chance to touch some) animals and are popular with the kids.

Attractions include the African Species Yard, where you can observe such species as ostrich, zebra and springbok in naturalistic environments, and an elephant exhibit. The Australian Walkabout, featuring animals from the Outback, is the first phase of the Mae Boren Axton Children's Zoo, scheduled to be completed in spring 2000. Africa and Asia exhibits are scheduled to open between 2001 and 2002.

Admission is $6 for adults, $4 for seniors and for children ages 3 to 12. From April through September, hours are 9 AM to 6 PM daily. From October through March, hours are 9 AM to 4 PM daily.

## Wave Country
**2320 Two Rivers Pkwy. • (615) 885-1052**

The closest beach is at least a seven-hour drive away, but this water park will do in a pinch. It's a fun place to cool off on one of our hot, humid summer days. Catch a wave, zoom down a slippery slide or play in the surf. Wave Country has a wave pool, two adult slides, one kiddie slide, a playground and two sand volleyball courts. Inflatable rafts are available for rent. It's at Two Rivers Park, just off Briley Parkway near Opryland. Wave Country is open daily from 10 AM to 7 PM from Memorial Day weekend to Labor Day weekend. Admission is $6 for adults and teens, $5 for children 4 to 12. Admission is half-price after 4 PM. Discounts are available for large groups. All children must be accompanied by an adult 18 or older. (For more on Wave Country, see our Kidstuff chapter.)

# Fun Transportation Attractions

## General Jackson
**2812 Opryland Dr. • (615) 871-6100, (615) 871-7817 (group bookings)**

March 1819 marked the arrival of the first steamboat in Nashville — the $16,000 *General Jackson*. By the mid-1800s, Nashvillians traveled to such cities as New Orleans, Memphis and St. Louis aboard steamboats outfitted with entertainment. Today you can experience a bit of that bygone era aboard Opryland's *General Jackson*. The $12 million, 300-foot-long, four-deck paddlewheel showboat takes guests on sightseeing, dining and entertainment cruises along the Cumberland River. It carries up to 1,200 passengers. A highlight of the boat is the ornate Victorian Theater, which can accommodate 620 people for banquets and 1,000 for theater presentations.

Cruises depart from outside the front gate area at Opryland. Except during the winter, an optional lunch buffet is offered on midday cruises Friday through Sunday (Thursdays too, during the summer). Music and comedy shows are featured during the trip. The evening dinner cruise includes a three-course prime rib dinner served in the theater. You can step outside to see the nighttime Nashville skyline and enjoy the sounds of the onboard orchestra. Entertainment includes a well-produced stage show and a comedy break.

From June through September you can take a Southern Nights Cruise, which features dancing under the stars to the music of a live band, plus hors d'oeuvres. Day cruises that include meals are $35 for adults, $25 for children 4 to 11. Evening cruises, including meals, are approximately $48 to $52 for adults and $40 to $43 for children, depending on the night of the week. Group discounts are available. For other prices and discounts, call the numbers above. The *General Jackson* operates year-round.

## Nashville Carriage Service
**Riverfront Park • (615) 758-8629**

A carriage ride through downtown Nashville offers a different view of the city. It might be a nice way to end a romantic summer evening, or it might be a fun diversion for Mom, Dad and the kids. Each year some 20,000 people board the vis-à-vis-style carriages, pulled by large Percheron or Belgian draft horses. Nashville Carriage Service, a family-owned business that opened in 1988, operates seven carriages on weekends and two to four during the week. Hours are 7 PM to 2 AM Friday and Saturday, 7 PM to midnight Monday through Thursday. The business is usually closed Sunday, but you might be able to make special arrangements for a ride if you call in advance. The basic ride costs $25 for up to four people, and $5 per extra person. The 20- to 25-minute ride departs from Riverfront Park, travels down Broadway and past the Ryman, Printers Alley and other down-

**INSIDERS' TIP**

If you're planning a day of sightseeing, you might want to make your first stop the Visitor Information Center at the base of the Gaylord Entertainment Center's glass tower. You'll find maps and brochures about places featured in this book as well as other area attractions, shops and restaurants. Souvenirs are for sale and helpful advice is available from the friendly Nashville experts at the desk. The Center (formerly known as the Nashville Arena) is at 501 Broadway. The Visitor Information Center is open daily 9 AM to 5 PM with hours extended to 8 AM to 8 PM in summer.

town attractions. Reservations aren't necessary, but if you have a special evening planned or a different route in mind, they are suggested.

## Nashville Trolley Co.
### 130 Nestor St. • (615) 862-5950

The Metropolitan Transit Authority operates about 13 trolleys that make circular routes downtown and also run along Music Row and Music Valley Drive. The one-way fare is $1 a person. Contact MTA at the listed number for information about routes and schedules.

## Opryland USA River Taxis
### Departs from 2812 Opryland Dr. and from Riverfront Park • (615) 871-6100

Traveling between Opryland and downtown Nashville? Forget traffic and parking hassles and take a river taxi. Opryland USA's two river taxis offer a scenic connection between Music City's most popular attractions. The red, white and blue taxis are named *Miss Minnie* and *Mister Roy*, in honor of *Grand Ole Opry* legends Minnie Pearl and Roy Acuff. A taxi departs from the Opryland Hotel area on every even hour and from downtown every odd hour. The 7-mile trip takes about 45 minutes.

Each enclosed, climate-controlled taxi seats about 100 in the main deck cabin. An open-air second deck provides room for a few more passengers. Operating April through October, the taxis run daily 9 AM to 11 PM. Roundtrip tickets are $13 for adults, $10 for children ages 4 to 11. Group rates and special package discounts are available.

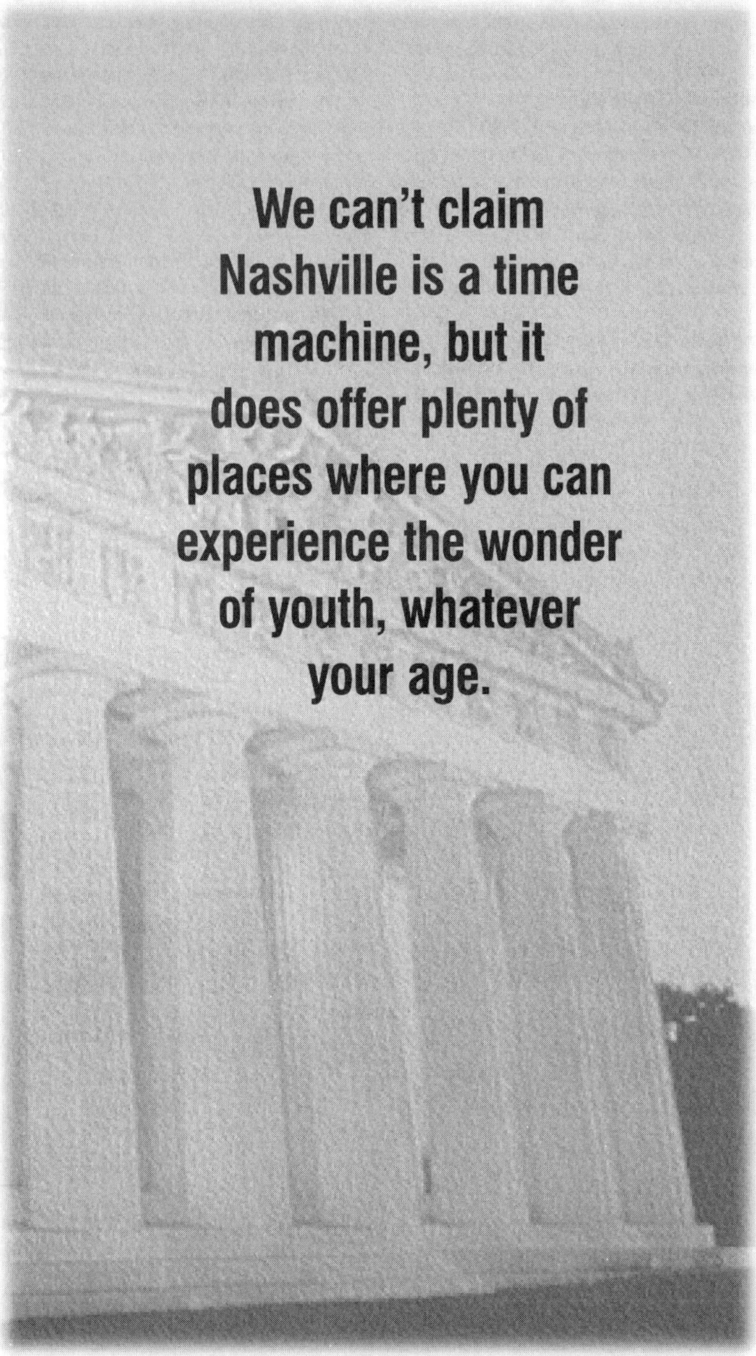

We can't claim
Nashville is a time
machine, but it
does offer plenty of
places where you can
experience the wonder
of youth, whatever
your age.

# Kidstuff

When Billy Dean sings, "I miss Billy the Kid," he is yearning not for the notorious outlaw but for his own lost childhood. "Ain't it funny how time slips away" is how another song puts it.

Now, we can't claim Nashville is a time machine, but it does offer plenty of places where you can experience the wonder of youth, whatever your age. And that's a good thing, in our opinion, because this is a town obsessed with youth. (If you have any doubt about that, just watch an hour or so of Country Music Television videos.) From a songwriter's point of view, music presents the alluring prospect of achieving immortality by stating a universal, heartfelt truth in a fresh new way — or at least spawning a line dance or two. And how do we court immortality but by seeking eternal youth. By refusing to grow old. By retaining a healthy sense of humor. By taking time to sing and dance and shout and run and play. By remaining curious and excited and questioning and open to all the wondrous possibilities. In Nashville, dear friend, those possibilities are nearly as endless as the big belt buckles and Stetsons at the Wildhorse Saloon.

So pack up the kids and/or grandkids — or just get out there on your own, for that matter — and have some fun! Many of the attractions in this chapter can be found elsewhere in the book (several, for example, are in the Attractions chapter), and they are cross-referenced. Please note that prices and hours, though current at press time, are subject to change.

## "Amuseums"

"Museums" is kind of a stuffy word that turns a lot of people off right from the start. We prefer the term "amuseums" because, as the places listed prove, there's no rule that says you can't be amused and educated at the same time.

### Cumberland Science Museum & Sudekum Planetarium
**800 Fort Negley Blvd. • (615) 862-5160**

Science is fun at Cumberland Science Museum, which offers a world of hands-on activities geared toward exploration and discovery. On one visit, we stood transfixed for a good 10 minutes as we watched the Kinetic Coaster, a Rube Goldberg-like contraption that makes a number of complex physics concepts understandable. A "yellow submarine" will take you on a simulated Deep Sea Adventure to study the effects of pollution on Pelican Bay. Health Hall is filled with interactive exhibits about the way our bodies function (and how to keep them functioning properly). Permanent exhibits explore topics like computers, chemistry and other cultures. In addition, the museum plays host to a variety of changing temporary exhibits. It's available for birthday parties, and it has its own summer camp from June through August.

Sudekum Planetarium lets visitors "experience the universe and beyond" through a changing lineup of informative and entertaining shows. When comet Hale-Bopp was visiting during the winter and spring of 1997, for example, the planetarium featured an exploration of the comet phenomenon. An in-depth look (and listen) at how music is made was here during spring and summer 1997.

The museum and planetarium are open year round from 10 AM to 5 PM Monday through Saturday and 12:30 to 5:30 PM Sunday. It is closed Easter, Thanksgiving, Christmas and New Year's Day. Admission is $6 for teens and adults, $4.50 for children 3 to 12 and seniors, and free for children 2 and younger. For just $1.25 more, you also get a planetarium show, which will cost you $3 by itself. And on

Tuesday, admission is half price from noon to 5 PM.

## Nashville Toy Museum
### 2613 McGavock Pk. • (615) 883-8870

An extensive collection of electric, steam and model trains — including a huge layout with one continuously running train — is the most popular attraction at Nashville Toy Museum, across from Opryland Hotel. But there's a lot more, including many antiques. Bears, dolls (including china dolls dating to 1850), boats and toy soldiers, some arranged in battle dioramas, are among the other highlights. Old-timers will feel nostalgic, and young ones will gain some needed insight into life before Nintendo. Hours are 9:30 AM to 5 PM Monday through Saturday and noon to 5 PM Sunday. The museum is open every day except Thanksgiving and Christmas. Admission is $3 for anyone 12 and older, $1.50 for kids ages 6 to 11 and free for those 5 and younger. (See our Attractions chapter for more information.)

# Parks, Playgrounds and All-around Action and Adventure

## Centennial Park
### West End Ave.

The centerpiece of Centennial Park, built to celebrate Tennessee's 100th birthday in 1897, is a full-size replica of the Greek Parthenon that houses an art gallery. Children, however, are more likely to be interested in the abundant outdoor activities at the park. There's a small lake populated with ducks and (in season) paddle boats, and you'll also find a band shell, picnic tables, a steam engine and fighter plane and lots of green grass. One child close to our hearts is particularly fond of the relaxing two-person swings with foot rests. Centennial Park is the site of the Nashville Shakespeare Festival, concerts by the Nashville Symphony, various arts and crafts fairs and other annual events. For more information on the Parthenon and yearly activities, see our Attractions and Annual Events chapters.

## Discovery Zone
### 5314 Mountain View Rd.
### • (615) 731-8449
### 2088 Gallatin Pk. N., Madison
### • (615) 859-9952

Here's a twist: it's the adults who get in free (when accompanied by a child) at Discovery Zone, an indoor playground featuring tunnels, slides, rope bridges, a sea of colored balls to dive in and much more. Children ages 3 through 12 can get unlimited play time: $4.99 for those shorter than 38 inches and $7.99 for those 38 inches and taller. Adults get in free, as do children younger than 12 months with one paid admission And yes, everyone who wants to can play. Hours Monday through Thursday are 11 AM to 7:30 PM at the Mountain View location and 11 AM to 8 PM in Madison; the rest of the week, both Zones are open 10 AM to 9 PM Friday and Saturday and 11 AM to 7 PM Sunday.

## The Dragon Park
### Blakemore and 24th Ave. S.

Its official name is Fannie Mae Dees Park, but this highly popular area just off the Vandy campus is usually identified by its dominant feature: a huge sea dragon or serpent covered with brightly colored tile mosaic. The recently refurbished dragon, which seemingly snakes above and below the "surface," is

Known locally as "Dragon Park," Fannie Mae Dees Park is
a popular gathering spot for Hillsboro/Vandy residents.

Photo: Cathy Summerlin

decorated with animals, flowers, rainbows, musical instruments, historical figures and countless other fanciful scenes; its tail doubles as a bench where parents can sit while their children play. In addition to the dragon, there's a tunnel through a "mountain" of rocks topped by a sandy "mesa," with a swinging bridge connecting the mountain to a fort with a slide. The park also contains three tennis courts, swings and other playground equipment, wooden benches, picnic tables, a shelter and two covered tables inlaid with chess/checker boards.

## Elmington Park
### West End Ave., near West End Middle School

The colorful, modern playground at Elmington Park, a gift from the Junior League, represents dozens of opportunities for swinging and swaying, climbing and crawling, sliding and hiding. Relax while the kids wear themselves out.

## Funscape
### The Mall at Green Hills, Hillsboro and Abbott Martin rds. • (615) 386-9535

Funscape provides a bunch of flashy fun for kids of all ages. Activities for the whole family (priced separately) include a virtual roller coaster, a high-tech arcade and a 3-D motion-simulator theater. Kids can also enjoy a foam "fun machine" and an interactive play area. There's a food court featuring Pizza Hut, Taco Bell and Orange Julius. Birthday parties and group packages are available. Hours are 10 AM to 9 PM Monday through Thursday, 10 AM to 11 PM Friday and Saturday, and noon to 9 PM Sunday.

## Laser Quest
### 166 Second Ave. N. • (615) 256-2560
## Q-Zar Centre of Rivergate
### 1699 Gallatin Pk. N. • (615) 865-6662

You've seen all the *Star Wars* movies. Now it's your turn to be Luke Skywalker. Laser Quest and Q-Zar, which are similar in concept but

Many of Nashville's kid-friendly attractions let kids (and adults) learn and play at the same time.

parts of different chains, fit you with a laser gun and sensor pack and turns you loose in a dark maze for a game of high-tech shoot-'em-up. Points are gained or lost depending on number of foes hit and number of times hit by foes. It's kind of like cowboys and Indians in outer space, and it's a harmless way for the kids to release some energy. Laser Quest's hours vary according to the season and the day, generally opening in the afternoon and closing somewhere between 10 PM and midnight. It's closed Mondays in the summertime. A 20-minute game there is $6.50, and group rates and birthday packages are available. Q-Zar, open from 3 to 10 PM Sunday through Thursday and 3 PM to midnight Saturday and Sunday, costs $6 a game or $10 for two games.

## Fountains of Youth

There's nothing like a good dose of wa-tery fun to bring out the kid in you, as these attractions attest.

### Bicentennial Capitol Mall State Park
**James Robertson Pkwy.**
• **(615) 741-5280, (888) TNPARKS**

There aren't too many places where you can get soaking wet while absorbing some fascinating lessons in state history, geography and culture. But Bicentennial Capitol Mall is just such a place.

This 19-acre park just north of the Tennessee State Capitol opened in 1996, and its fountains — 31 of them designating major state rivers — quickly became a cool place to play during a sultry summer. Nearby on the plaza, a 200-foot granite map of Tennessee lets you walk from Memphis to Knoxville in record time; smaller maps provide details about various facets of the state. There's much more, including clean restrooms and a visitors center.

Visit the adjacent Farmer's Market, along with the State Capitol, and you've got one nice (and cheap) afternoon. (For more information on the Bicentennial Capitol Mall State Park, see our Attractions and Parks chapters.)

## Metro and YMCA Pools
**YMCA corporate office, 900 Church St.**
**• (615) 259-9622**
**Metro Parks aquatics office, 222 25th**
**Ave. N. • (615) 862-8480**

Nashville YMCAs operate a total of 23 pools: eight outdoor and 15 indoor. The Metro Parks department operates more than a dozen pools, including Wave Country (see below). For more information, see our Recreation chapter.

## Shelby Park
**Shelby Ave. and S. 20th St.**
**• (615) 862-8467**

This park in east Nashville is known for its golf course (see our Golf chapter), but its lake is also a popular fishing spot for kids as well as senior citizens. Each May, it's the site of County Clerk Bill Covington's Junior Fishing Rodeo, which is free for kids and lets everyone take home a prize.

## Wave Country
**2320 Two Rivers Pkwy. • (615) 885-1052**

Wave Country, just off Briley Parkway, lets you visit the ocean without leaving Nashville. Hold on tight as you ride the wave pool's simulated surf. There are also two water slides and one kiddie slide. Hours are 10 AM to 7 PM daily from Memorial Day weekend through Labor Day. Admission is $6 for adults and teens, $5 for folks ages 5 through 12 and free for kids 4 and younger. (For more on Wave Country, see our Attractions chapter.)

# Where the Wild Things Are

## Bobby Bare Trap
**2416 Music Valley Dr. • (615) 872-8440**
**325 Broadway • (615) 242-8337**

More than 5,000 teddy bears, including one billed as the world's largest, are on dis-

play at these stores owned and operated by singer Bobby Bare and his wife, Jeannie. Admission is free seven days a week, and there's a gift shop. Hours are 9 AM (10 AM January through March) to 8 PM Monday through Saturday and noon to 6 PM Sundays.

## Nashville Zoo at Grassmere
**3777 Nolensville Rd. • (615) 833-1534**

Nashville Zoo at Grassmere is a habitat for more than 500 animals from around the Americas and the world. You'll see rare white Bengal tigers and other endangered species, bison and much more. The zoo, open 9 AM to 6 PM daily, also includes a large playground and water play area and a 24-foot-tall tree house. Admission is $6 for adults, $4 for children and free for 2 and younger, and parking is $2 extra. For more information, see our Attractions chapter.

## Warner Parks
**7311 Tenn. Hwy. 100**
**• (615) 370-8051 (headquarters),**
**(615) 352-6299 (nature center)**

On a recent late-afternoon summer drive through Percy Warner Park, we saw three deer and two rabbits within minutes, and we weren't even looking for them. Percy Warner Park, the largest municipal park in Tennessee, and its neighbor, Edwin Warner Park, total 2,681 acres, much of which is rugged, scenic woodland. There's a nature center, picnic areas, playground equipment, hiking trails, bridle trails and a steeplechase area, as well as two golf courses. Note: before or after visiting Warner Parks, take time to drive through nearby Belle Meade, one of Nashville's most exclusive areas; these houses will produce lots of "oohs" and "ahhs." The parks are open daily from sunrise until 11 PM, and the nature center is open from 8:30 AM to 4:30 PM Monday through Saturday. (For more information, see our Parks chapter.)

# Grandpa, Tell Me 'bout the Good Ol' Days

History is a funny thing. Depending on your outlook, it can make you feel old or make you

Photo: Cindy Stooksbury Guier

Some shopping malls have indoor playgrounds.

feel young. Here's hoping these selected historic sites will bring out the inquisitive little kid in you and other members of your family.

## CityWalk

We said earlier that Nashville is not a time machine, but we may have lied. CityWalk is a 2-mile journey through downtown that will transport you back through two centuries of history. Beginning at Fort Nashborough and following the painted green line, you'll visit 14 sites including historic Second Avenue (formerly Market Street), Printers Alley, the Tennessee State Museum, the State Capitol and the Ryman Auditorium. Most sites are free. For a self-guided tour, pick up one of the informative brochures at one of the many tourist-information racks around town, or call the Metropolitan Historical Commission at (615) 862-7970 for more information.

## Fort Nashborough
**170 First Ave. N. • (615) 862-8400
(Parks Dept.)**

This is where it all got started in 1779, when James Robertson and his fellow settlers established a settlement on the west bank of the Cumberland River. This reproduction of the original log fort, which withstood attacks from natives, is open 8 AM to 4 PM daily, except Thanksgiving and Christmas, for a free self-guided tour. (See our Attractions chapter for more information.)

## The Hermitage: Home of President Andrew Jackson
**4580 Rachel's Ln., Hermitage
• (615) 889-2941**

Andrew Jackson was a brave and adventurous man who was influential in the early expansion of our country. In addition to being seventh president of the United States, he was a military hero, lawyer, planter, statesman and true romantic (he once shot a man who said bad things about his wife).

The Hermitage, 12 miles east of Nashville off Old Hickory Boulevard, is where he made his home. The 1800s mansion, a mixture of Federal and Greek Revival styles, is open 9 AM to 5 PM daily (closed Thanksgiving, Christmas

## INSIDERS' TIP

**Nashville's public libraries present a variety of story hours and other special programs for children.**

# Goo Goo

If there were a candy hall of fame, Nashville would have a place in it. Music City is where the first combination candy bar was invented, and it's still made right here at the Standard Candy Company.

The historic candy — the Goo Goo — has been satisfying sweet tooths for more than eight decades. As they say on the *Grand Ole Opry* radio show, which Standard has sponsored since the early 1960s, "Generations of Southerners have grown up on them." Dozens of people — Southerners as well as non-Southerners — from as far

away as California and Canada are gaga over Goo Goos. They write the company each week requesting orders of the chewy, gooey candy. But you don't have to write for it; you can find Goo Goos in just about every part of the country, in stores like Walgreen, Wal-Mart, Eckerd, Kroger and Safeway. They're most plentiful in Music City, however, and tourist attractions and gift stores here usually keep a good supply on hand for visitors who want to take home a taste of Nashville.

Standard, today operated by Jim Spradley and son Jimmy, sells about 25 million Goo Goos (approximately $8.5 million-worth) each year. The candy bar has come a long way since its premiere in 1912. The Goo Goo was invented by Howell Campbell who, in 1901 at the age of 19, founded the Standard Candy Company. The company's first products were hard candies and chocolates, but Howell and original plant superintendent Porter Moore developed a recipe combining fresh roasted peanuts, caramel, marshmallow and milk chocolate, and the recipe became a classic. Today, the Goo Goo comes in three varieties — the original Goo Goo Cluster, the Peanut Butter Goo Goo and the Goo Goo Supreme.

The candy bar didn't have a name at first because no one could decide what to call it. Stories of how the candy got its name vary. Campbell's son, Howell Campbell Jr., says his father took the streetcar to work each morning and would discuss the matter with fellow passengers. One passenger, a schoolteacher, suggested the name Goo Goo. But some people say the candy was named Goo Goo because it's the first thing a baby says.

In its early days, the candy bar's circular shape made it difficult to wrap, so it was sold unwrapped from glass containers. Later, the Goo Goo was hand-wrapped in foil and advertised as a "Nourishing Lunch for A Nickel." While it wouldn't pass for a nourishing lunch today (the Goo Goo Cluster in the silver package has 240 calories, 11 grams of fat and just a smidgen of calcium, protein and iron), Nashville's Goo Goo is still a delicious treat.

Photo: Standard Candy Company

Nashvillians have enjoyed Goo Goo candies for more than 85 years.

and the third week of January). Admission is $9.50 for adults and teens, $8.50 for seniors 62 and older, $4.50 for children ages 6 through 12 and free for those 5 and younger. For much more information, see our Attractions chapter.

### Historic Mansker's Station
### Frontier Life Center
**Moss-Wright Park at Caldwell Rd.,**
**Goodlettsville • (615) 859-FORT**

The Frontier Life Center at Historic Mansker's Station offers a look at the lifestyles of the area's early settlers through a reconstructed 1779 forted station. You'll see and listen to people in period costumes as they perform activities such as cooking, spinning and blacksmithing. For more information, including hours and prices, see our Attractions chapter.

### Tennessee State Museum
**505 Deaderick St. • (615) 741-2692**

Tennessee State Museum, at the corner of Fifth and Deaderick streets, offers exhibits ranging from prehistoric Nashville through the early 1900s, with a large Civil War display. Popular artifacts include a Conestoga wagon and an Egyptian mummy that a Tennessee explorer brought back from overseas several decades ago. Hours are 10 AM to 5 PM Tuesday through Saturday and 1 to 5 PM Sunday; the museum is closed on Monday. Admission is free. (See Attractions for more information.)

# Fun Food

### Elliston Place Soda Shop
**2111 Elliston Pl. • (615) 327-1090**

OK, so your kids are now watching reruns of *Happy Days*. But have they ever been in a good old-fashioned diner a la Arnold's? Elliston Place Soda Shop is the real deal, from its tile floor and Formica tabletops to its fare: thick chocolate milk shakes (one is easily enough for two people); root beer floats, banana splits and sundaes; burgers, fries and onion rings; and daily "meat and three" specials. Elliston Place Soda Shop was established in 1939 by J. Lynn Chandler, and it still packs 'em in. The mini-jukeboxes in the booths will make you nostalgic, though they don't work; to compen-

sate, there's a Wurlitzer in the back of the room with actual 45-rpm records (remember those?) of pop and country hits.

### Hard Rock Café
**100 Broadway • (615) 742-9900**

Guitars, stage costumes and other memorabilia from your favorite rock 'n' roll musicians are the main attractions at the local installment of this popular chain. Display items include a priceless brown suede hand-painted jacket worn by Jimi Hendrix at Woodstock and a Fender Stratocaster guitar autographed by Eric Clapton. There's food too, of course, but you don't have to eat to check it all out. Visitors are welcome to browse for free; after all, a lot of them end up buying T-shirts.

### Planet Hollywood
**322 Broadway • (615) 313-STAR**

With its revolving planet outside, this growing chain restaurant is hard for downtown visitors to miss. Arnold Schwarzenegger, Sylvester Stallone, Bruce Willis and Demi Moore and numerous other celebrities attended the gala 1996 grand opening in Nashville, and they left their handprints embedded in the exterior wall. Inside you'll find loads of costumes, props and other movie memorabilia, mostly from recent Tinseltown blockbusters. As at Hard Rock Café, you're welcome to enter and browse.

# Story and Showtime

### Davis-Kidd Booksellers
**4007 Hillsboro Rd. • (615) 385-2645**

Davis-Kidd has an outstanding children's section that includes a toy train, and every Saturday and Monday morning at 11 AM is the Kidd's Corner storytime.

### Ben West Downtown Public Library
**225 Polk Ave. • (615) 862-5785**
**(children's department)**

One library card allows you access to all 18 locations of the Public Library of Nashville and Davidson County. That means you'll have the key to more than 700,000 books, audio recordings and more. All of Nashville's libraries hold special story hours and other programs especially appropriate for preschoolers.

The downtown Ben West location, which is the main library, often features storytelling with hand puppets and sometimes with marionettes. For information about these and other programs, call your neighborhood branch or (615) 862-5800, the central library information number.

### Nashville Children's Theater
**724 Second Ave. S. • (615) 254-9103**

The acclaimed Nashville Children's Theater offers a variety of productions and programs for children of all ages. It puts on about six shows a year, each recommended for a certain age group. Recent productions have included *Wind in the Wood, Pinocchio, Bambi: A Life in the Woods, Goldilocks and the Three Bears, Little House Christmas, Anne of Green Gables* and *The Hobbit*. Nashville Children's Theater also offers summer camps and creative drama classes throughout the year for kids in grades 2 through 9. (See our Arts chapter for more information.)

# Sing Me a Song

This is Music City, after all, and music has the power to make everyone feel young. These attractions are selected for their kid-friendliness; for more information, see our Music City U.S.A. chapter. (Many downtown nightspots are open to children before a certain hour and closed to them afterward, and many have no cover charge. Just ask.)

### Country Music Hall of Fame and Museum
**4 Music Sq. E. • (615) 256-1639**

Elvis's gold piano is just one highlight among the scores of automobiles, stage costumes, instruments and other artifacts from throughout the history of country music. Admission — $10.75 for adults, $6.75 for children ages 6 to 11 and free for children younger than 6 — includes a Music Row trolley tour and a visit to the legendary Studio B. The Country Music Hall of Fame and Museum, which plans to move into a new downtown location in 2001, is open daily from 9 AM to 5 PM, except for major holidays.

### Wildhorse Saloon
**120 Second Ave. N. • (615) 256-WILD**

Children are welcome here, although anyone younger than 21 must be accompanied by a parent. Line-dance lessons are available some nights. Nightly cover charge varies, but it's usually $3 except for special events, like

Photo: Cindy Stooksbury Guier

Neighborhood playgrounds can be found all over town.

when the Wildhorse presents concerts by today's top stars. The saloon opens at 11 AM for lunch, and dinner is served until 10 PM. For more information, see our Nightlife chapter.

## Wolfy's
### 425 Broadway • (615) 251-1621

Wolfy's is a bar, but it's also a restaurant, and kids are welcome with their parents. Best of all, there's generally no cover charge to enjoy the nightly music, which might include the red-hot fiddle of session ace Buddy Spicher and his band.

## You're the Star Recording Studio
### 172 Second Ave. N. • (615) 742-9942

Want to record a song but without paying demo-studio prices? Test the musical waters at You're the Star, where you can choose from more than 500 modern and classic songs in a variety of styles. You can also make your own video, complete with costumes and props. You're the Star is open 10 AM to 10 PM Monday through Thursday, 10 AM to midnight Friday and Saturday and 1 to 6 PM Sunday. Cost is $18.35 for audio, $27 for video, with discounts for groups or multiple recordings.

# Summer Camps

## Camp Biota
### Biota Tr., Joelton • (615) 876-6062

"Biota" comes from the Greek word for life, and there's lots of it at this 750-acre nature preserve. Wading in a creek, pony and hay rides, canoeing on a 14-acre lake and general exploration of the great outdoors are just a few of the activities available. The family-owned camp, accredited by the American Camping Association and directed by Curtis Evans, was founded in 1956 as a boys' summer science camp, but now it's open to boys and girls ages 5 to 16.

Camp Biota offers year-round activities, but it's at its busiest during the summer, with 150 to 200 children at a time attending two-week sessions. The owners are proud of their counselor-in-training program, which provides at least one counselor for every six 5- and 6-year-old summer campers, and one for every eight older kids. Moms and dads are invited for a parent-camper day at the end of every two-week session, so they can get a taste of what their child has been experiencing (they'll have opportunities to cook out and go camping too). And a special camp for younger children allows 3- and 4-year-olds to feed goats and pigs and participate in other camp activities with their parents. The camp also has trail rides for the public, saddlebag luncheons, environmental education programs in the spring and fall and horse camp for kids ages 10 to 16.

A new addition to the schedule last year is a one-week, residential "adventure camp," with two sessions available for kids ages 11 through 14. The cost is $495. Day camp for kids ages 5 through 12 runs in two-week sessions and costs $350. The counselor-in-training program, for ages 13 through 15, is also $350. The two-week horse camp, also known as the Biota Saddle Club, is for kids ages 10 through 16 and costs $450. All costs include transportation, lunch, snacks and refreshments. Discounts and financial aid are available.

## Whippoorwill Farm Day Camp
### 7840 Whippoorwill Ln., Fairview
### • (615) 799-9925

Owner/operator Sidney Wooten has B.S. and M.S. degrees in education, plus more than 25 years of experience working with camping and children. At 50-acre Whippoorwill Farm Day Camp, children ages 6 to 12 sign up twice a day for activities that interest them. There's plenty to choose from: canoeing, hiking, guitar lessons, swimming (lessons as well as "free" swim), horseback riding, horse care, crafts, folk arts, woodland lore, pottery, weaving, rappelling, soccer, photography, archery, drawing and painting, outdoor cooking, pioneer skills . . . even root beer making. There's one counselor for every eight campers, and older kids can enroll in the counselor-in-training program. The camp is open from 9 AM to 3 PM daily, but working parents can take advantage of a van service that picks up kids in the morning at central points in west Nashville and Franklin, then drops them off around 5:15 PM. The cost is $300 for a two-week session and $155 for a one-week session.

### Youth Inc. Circle YI Ranch
**312 Plaza Professional Bldg., Madison**
**• (615) 865-0003**

This two-week residential camp on Percy Priest Lake helps boys and girls ages 7 to 13 develop skills like water skiing, canoeing, fishing, swimming, horseback riding and crafts as well as "the everyday living skills of cooperation, respect and responsibility." There's also a low-ropes course. Campers stay in rustic cabins in groups of nine with a counselor. An open house is held each May for prospective or registered campers and their parents. The camp, established in 1945, is ACA accredited. The cost is $395.

### St. Andrews-Sewanee School: ASCENT
**290 Quintard Rd., St. Andrews**
**• (931) 598-5651**

The St. Andrews-Sewanee School's ASCENT program is a five-week intensive summer academic program that also incorporates rigorous outdoor and wilderness activities. Students in grades 8 through 11 can earn one full credit or two semester credits in math, science, language, art or writing. While much of the day is spent in classes, afternoons and weekends allow free time for activities such as rock climbing, canoeing, kayaking and community service.

The school itself, one of the oldest Episcopal boarding schools in the nation, is accredited by the Southern Association of Colleges and Schools. The campus comprises 450 acres adjoining the University of the South (Sewanee) in Franklin County, about 90 miles from Nashville by way of Interstate 24. Sixty to 70 students participate each year in the AS-CENT program. The cost is $3,200 for residential students and $1,250 for commuters.

### YMCA Camp Ocoee
**301 W. Sixth St., Chattanooga**
**• (423) 265-0455**

Camp Ocoee, a coed camp for ages 6 to 17, offers a traditional resident program plus adventure camps emphasizing canoeing, kayaking, climbing and backpacking. Costs range from $395 for a regular one-week ranger camp to $460 for the one-week adventure camp (either kayaking or climbing) to $795 for the two-week explorers camp. Camp Ocoee's offices are in Chattanooga, but the camp is in Ocoee, on the North Carolina border about 3½ hours from Nashville. Take Interstate 24 to Chattanooga, then I-75 to Ocoee.

# Parent/Child Programs

### Gymboree Play Programs
**The Mall at Green Hills, 2126 Abbott Martin Rd. • (615) 386-0062**

Gymboree, which is upstairs near Dillard's in the mall, describes itself as a "developmental parent-child play program." What this means, basically, is that it helps little ones from three months to 4 years learn through fun. Instructors and parents engage in "age appropriate" physical play with the children, and there's a different lesson plan each week for each age level. About 40 pieces of play equipment are set up in new ways each week. Kids arrive once a week for 45-minute sessions.

One popular feature is "parachute time," which involves a large, multicolored parachute that children first sit on and later gather under as parents grasp the edges and make it billow above them. On Monday mornings, the program offers Kindermusik, a 30-minute class in which children play rhythm instruments, move to music and develop their listening skills. Birthday parties are held Saturday afternoons. Gymboree is open mornings and afternoons Monday through Saturday (hours vary).

Just about any weekend — January through December — you can find at least one special event taking place in or around Nashville.

# Annual Events

Want to have some fun? Learn something new? Mingle with a crowd? Maybe just get out of the house? Check out some of Nashville's annual events. Music City's calendar is full of festivals, celebrations, seminars, shows and other fun and interesting happenings — enough to keep you busy year round.

Just about any weekend — January through December — you can find at least one special event taking place in or around Nashville. What's your pleasure? From crafts to carnivals, balloons to books, and mules to Moon Pies, there's something for everyone.

Music, of course, is the focus of many of our biggest and best events. Nashville is Music City, and we like to think we have some of the best music events you'll find anywhere. Among them are country and jazz festivals, rock 'n' roll showcases and special symphony performances in the park. You can find those events in this chapter, but see our Music City U.S.A. chapter for more information.

Even the events that focus on topics other than music usually include top-notch musical entertainment in their programming. There's plenty to eat and drink too. Depending on the event, you can indulge in all kinds of international fare, country cookin', local restaurants' specialties, wines or just plain fun food like funnel cakes and cotton candy.

In this chapter, we list some of Nashville's favorite events (plus a few that aren't so well-known) by month, roughly in the order they occur. Schedules are subject to change, so before making plans, it's a good idea to check *The Tennessean* or the alternative weekly *Nashville Scene* for up-to-date information on events, dates and admission prices. We also provide the sponsoring organization's phone number in case you would like to call for more information.

Most annual events have a gate charge, but you'll find a few that offer free admission. Children's admission is usually a few dollars less than adult admission. We list both rates. If a rate is not given for very young children, assume that they are admitted free. Most events also offer discounts for senior citizens and groups. Some have special rates during designated days or hours, and some offer discounts if you bring a coupon. We list that information whenever possible.

Keep your *Insiders' Guide® to Nashville* handy all year. The next time you're looking for something to do, check our listing of annual events, then go out and have some fun!

## January

### Nashville Boat and Sport Show
**Nashville Convention Center, 601 Commerce St. • (314) 567-0020**

The holidays are over, it's cold outside, the sky is gray, daylight hours are short, and Old Man Winter isn't going anywhere for two or three more months. Why not come out to the National Marine Manufacturers Association's five-day Nashville Boat and Sport Show, and get your mind on sunny days and warm-weather fun? This popular show, held the second or third week of January, is sure to put you in a summer state of mind. You'll find a wide variety of boats and marine recreation products — everything from fishing lures to houseboats — plus information on vacation destinations, which are exactly what many of us are dreaming about this time of year. Fishing, water-skiing and hunting seminars and other outdoor sports-oriented attractions also are offered. Entertainment at previous seminars has included a live shark tank, virtual reality sport-fishing simulator and watercraft simulator.

Admission is $6 for adults and teens, $2 for children ages 6 through 12. Admission discounts are usually available, so watch for coupons and announcements of promotions.

### Celebration of Martin Luther King's Life & Ministry
**Scarritt-Bennett Center, 1008 19th Ave. S. • (615) 340-7500**

This event celebrates the life and heritage of civil rights leader Martin Luther King Jr. Each January, on the Wednesday closest to January 15, King's birth date, the Scarritt-Bennett Center's Wightman Chapel hosts a morning worship service in conjunction with the United Methodist Church's Upper Room and General Board of Higher Education and Ministry. The service also features a gospel singing group. Anyone is welcome to attend.

The Scarritt-Bennett Center is an interfaith, international conference and retreat center on property owned by the women's division of the United Methodist Church.

# February

### Americana Spring Sampler Craft, Folk Art & Antique Show
**Tennessee State Fairgrounds, Wedgewood Ave. at Rains Ave. • (615) 227-2080**

If you like crafts, art or antiques, this four-day event is a must. It's one of the country's top wholesale and retail folk art shows and is one of four Americana Sampler events held at the fairgrounds each year. The others are held in April, August and November. Each event attracts 4,000 to 7,000 attendees. At the February show, usually held the second weekend of the month, you'll find more than 200 country-craft, folk- and fine-art professionals and antique dealers from 30 states selling high-quality hand-crafted goods. It's a good place for gift shopping, and there is something to fit every budget. Be sure to check out the gourmet food exhibit too.

In addition to the exhibits, the show offers a chance to learn from the experts, who lecture on a variety of topics. Strolling folk-style musical entertainment adds to the fun. It all takes place indoors at the fairgrounds. Admission for the entire weekend is $5 for adults and teens, $1.50 for children ages 6 through 12.

### Antiques & Garden Show of Nashville
**Nashville Convention Center, 601 Commerce St. • (615) 352-1282**

This event has been named one of the Top 20 Events in the Southeast by the Southeast Tourism Society. Founded in 1991, it draws approximately 30,000 visitors each year in mid-February. More than 70 antique dealers from the United States, United Kingdom and France and 80 eastern U.S. horticulturists fill the convention center's trade show floor.

The show focuses on high-end items and features a wide range of goods; you'll find furniture, paintings, antique jewelry, rare books, porcelain and more, and you can spend anywhere from $10 to $100,000. Surrounding the antiques are beautifully landscaped gardens. You'll also find booths filled with flowers, herbs and other garden necessities for sale.

Learn something new at lectures by high-profile furniture and gardening experts. A Saturday seminar series offers the chance to chat informally with gardeners. The Garden Café, on the trade show floor, sells reasonably priced lunch items and serves afternoon tea daily. A Thursday night preview party offers the first chance to view the antiques. Admission is $12 at the gate, $10 in advance; children 12 and younger are admitted free.

## Nashville Entertainment Association Extravaganza
**Various local venues • (615) 327-4308**

This annual event puts the spotlight on non-country talent. The best local and regional acts showcase at clubs and other venues throughout Nashville, drawing record company executives from around the country in search of new talent. (Read more about it in our Music City U.S.A. chapter.)

## All American Heart of Country Antiques Show
**Opryland Hotel, 2800 Opryland Dr. • (800) 862-1090**

Held in mid-February and again in mid-October, this award-winning event features more than 200 top antique dealers from around the United States and Canada. Some 20,000 antique lovers attend the show. You're bound to find something you like among the exhibits of unique furniture, paintings, folk art, textiles and 18th- and 19th-century Americana. Prices run the gamut — from $1 to $50,000. The "Under $200 Booth" features some of the lower-priced items. There are always special exhibits — Amish quilts, game boards and late 19th-century/early 20th-century handmade signs, for example — as well as educational seminars and lectures. A Thursday preview party precedes the three-day show.

The show is produced by Richard E. Kramer & Associates of St. Louis. Party tickets are $60 in advance and $65 at the door, and include admission throughout the weekend. Daily admission is $8; children 14 and younger are admitted free. Special rates at the Opryland Hotel are available for show attendees.

## Nashville Lawn & Garden Show
**Tennessee State Fairgrounds, Wedgewood Ave. at Rains Ave. • (615) 352-3863**

Gardeners and would-be gardeners can find inspiration, products and practical advice at this four-day event, held in late February or early March. Landscape contractors and plant societies prepare more than 20 garden displays; study them and take home ideas for your garden — free! The show, presented by the Horticultural Association of Tennessee, also features lectures on gardening-related topics and some 180 exhibits of products, services and equipment for show and sale. Allow at least two hours to take it all in. Admission is $6 for adults and teens, $5 for seniors and $1 for children 12 and younger. Groups of 15 or more adults get a $1 discount per ticket.

# March

## Arbor Day
**Scarritt-Bennett Center, 1008 19th Ave. S. • (615) 340-7500**

Scarritt-Bennett Center campus is a designated arboretum, so this is an appropriate place to celebrate Arbor Day. Events include guided tree trails. Admission is free.

## Women's History Month
**Margaret Cuninggim Women's Center, Vanderbilt Univ., 316 West Side Row • (615) 322-4843**
**Nashville State Technical Institute, 120 White Bridge Rd. • (615) 353-3233**

Vanderbilt and Nashville Tech each sponsor their own events celebrating women's history and spotlighting women's achievements. The community is invited to attend. Nashville Tech usually holds a brown-bag luncheon with a speaker or focus groups addressing the topic of women in nontraditional roles. Admission is free.

## Dove Awards
**Nashville Arena, 501 Broadway • (615) 242-0303**

The Gospel Music Association presents its annual Dove Awards show each spring. Read more about it in our Music City chapter.

# April

## Cheekwood Spring Art Hop
**Cheekwood — Nashville's Home of Art and Gardens, 1200 Forrest Park Dr. • (615) 356-8000.**

Held the Saturday before Easter, this event

Photo: Cheekwood

Trees of Christmas has been a tradition for more than three decades.

features egg hunts for kids, Victorian games, music, storytelling, art activities, an antique Easter train, and, of course, the Easter Bunny. Admission for nonmembers is $8 for adults and children; admission for members is free, but there's a $4 program fee per child.

## Mule Day
**Maury County Park, 1018 Maury County Park Dr., Columbia • (931) 381-9557**

Mule lovers take note! Mule Day, your chance to see 500 or more mules, is held the first or second weekend (Thursday through Sunday) in April. Even if you're not particularly interested in mules, you're bound to enjoy this old-time festival, held at Maury County Park in Columbia, about 43 miles south of downtown Nashville.

The Mule Day tradition began in 1934. Farmers used to bring their livestock to town once a year, and the festival grew around this annual happening. Around 1950, the event faded away, but it was brought back in 1973 by the Maury County Bridle & Saddle Club. Today, the festival features a mule parade, mule show, mule-pulling, arts and crafts, a flea market, square dancing, clogging contest, liars' contest and even a "donkey softball game," featuring players mounted on donkeys. You can enjoy "pioneer foods" such as roasted corn, fried pies and apple fritters as well as more modern fare like hamburgers, hot dogs and soft drinks.

This event generates interest from across the country; apparently there are many mule fans out there. While attending Mule Day, impress your friends by informing them that a mule, as defined by the *Random House Webster's Dictionary*, is "the sterile offspring of a female horse and a male donkey."

To get to Maury County Park from Nashville, take I-65 south to the first Columbia exit and turn right. Follow the signs about 10 miles to the park. Admission is $5 for adults and teens, $4 for children 12 and younger.

## Al Menah Temple Shrine Circus
**Nashville Municipal Auditorium, 417 Fourth Ave. N. • (615) 226-7766**

This three-ring circus has been entertaining Nashvillians every year since the early 1940s. Usually held in April or March, it's a family show featuring top performers and a variety of animal acts. Evening shows are presented Thursday through Saturday; matinees are presented Saturday and Sunday. Tickets cost $6 ($9 for reserved seats) and are available at Al Menah Temple, 1354 Brick Church Pike, or by phone (use your credit card); call the listed number. Some tickets might be available at the auditorium box office; call to inquire.

## Southern Women's Show
**Nashville Convention Center, 601 Commerce St. • (704) 376-6594, (800) 849-0248 (for tickets)**

This early April event focuses on areas of interest to women. You'll find more than 400 exhibits and demonstrations on everything from fashion to finance, sports to careers. Fashion shows, a celebrity kitchen and seminars round out the activities. Admission is $7 for adults and teens, $4 for children ages 6 through 12.

## Cheekwood's Wildflower Fair
**Cheekwood — Nashville's Home of Art and Gardens, 1200 Forrest Park Dr. • (615) 356-8000.**

One of Cheekwood's most popular events, the Wildflower Fair features more than 100 species of wildflowers for sale, as well as garden ornaments and accessories. Drinks, homemade foods and tours of the wildflower garden and sculpture trail are available. Admission is $8 for adults, $7 for seniors and college students and $5 for children ages 7 through 18.

## The Junior League Decorator's Show House
**Nashville home to be announced • (615) 269-9393**

Each year the Junior League of Nashville selects a landmark Nashville home and brings in top decorators, interior designers, landscape architects and gardeners, who donate their time and services to turn the property into a showplace. The Show House is usually open

the second and third weeks of April. It's a popular event, usually attended by about 20,000. Previous Decorators' Show houses have included the West Meade Plantation at Old Harding Road and U.S. Highway 70 W., and the H.G. Hill Home on Post Road.

In addition to touring the house, you can browse for gifts at the on-site gift shop and enjoy lunch, afternoon tea and dessert at the tea room. A lecture series features locally and nationally known gardening and design experts. There also may be a live auction of antiques and collectibles, and a dinner series featuring local restaurants. A shuttle service usually operates out of the nearest large church's parking lot. Reservations aren't necessary, but allow about 1½ hours to park, catch the shuttle and tour the house; allow more time if you plan to visit the gift shop or tea room. Then, catch the next available shuttle back to the parking lot.

Tickets are $10 in advance, $15 at the door. Be sure to arrange for a babysitter if you have young children; kids younger than 8 are not allowed — there are too many breakable items in the house! All proceeds from the Decorators' Show House go back to the community in the form of Junior League grants. The event typically raises $450,000. In case you're wondering, all those fabulous furnishings and decorations, right down to the wallpaper, are removed after the event takes place, unless the owner has negotiated with the suppliers in advance.

## Tin Pan South
**Various Nashville venues • (615) 251-3472**

The Nashville Songwriters Association International (NSAI) sponsors this annual music festival that celebrates songwriters and songwriting. Concerts, awards and a golf tournament are held during the week. (See our Music City U.S.A. chapter for information.)

**INSIDERS' TIP**

Looking for a unique gift for that special someone? Check out one of Nashville's craft fairs. Centennial Park and the state fairgrounds host several such events each year. You'll find everything from modern art to old-fashioned country crafts.

## Gospel Music Week
**Renaissance Nashville Hotel, Nashville Convention Center and other venues**
**• (615) 242-0303**

This industry event attracts artists, record company personnel, radio representatives, concert promoters and others who work in the gospel music industry. (Read more about it in our Music City U.S.A. chapter.)

## Earth Day
**Scarritt-Bennett Center, 1008 19th Ave. S. • (615) 340-7500**

Learn about Earth-friendly ways of gardening at this event, held on the Saturday closest to Earth Day. There are organic gardening demonstrations and free composting kits. Admission is free.

## Main Street Festival
**Downtown Franklin • (615) 791-9924**

This two-day, free-admission event held during the last full weekend in April averages an attendance of 100,000. The Southeast Tourism Society has listed it as one of the top 20 events in the Southeast. It's a fun time and definitely worth the short drive to Franklin.

The festival takes place on five city blocks in the historic downtown area, from First Avenue to Fifth Avenue, and encompasses the town square. Crafts and food booths line the streets. More than 200 artists and craftspeople from across the United States exhibit their works. This isn't the place for country crafts, but you'll find a wide selection of other handcrafted items — everything from stained glass to sculpture to baskets. Approximately 20 food vendors offer such items as barbecue, roasted corn and Greek, Italian, Mexican and Asian fare; you'll also find burgers and hot dogs. A children's area on Third Avenue off Main Street caters to kids 8 and younger. Bring the youngsters here for face painting, pony rides, games, a jump on the Moon Bounce and a ride on the Ferris wheel.

Two stages of entertainment — one at City Hall in the square and one on Fourth Avenue — offer continuous entertainment including music, dance and storytelling. At 6:30 PM Saturday, a locally popular musical act performs rock, pop, oldies and country tunes during Dancin' in the Street. It's a family-oriented fun evening. You can find parking along nearby streets and in downtown lots.

## Americana April Sampler Craft, Folk Art and Antique Show
**Tennessee State Fairgrounds, Wedgewood Ave. at Rains Ave.**
**• (615) 227-2080**

This is one of four annual Americana Sampler shows presented indoors in the air-conditioned buildings at the fairgrounds. See the listing in the "February" section for a description of the show.

## Nashville Music Festival
**Ryman Auditorium, 116 5th Ave. N.**
**• (615) 868-4468**

This annual benefit concert features some of Nashville's top performers. See the Music City U.S.A. chapter for more information.

## Nashville River Stages
**Downtown, Riverfront Park**
**• (615) 641-5800**

River Stages is a three-day music festival featuring as many as 60 bands on five stages. See the Music City U.S.A. chapter for more information.

# May

## Dancin' in The District
**Riverfront Park, First Ave. N.**
**• (615) 256-9596**

Every Thursday night from May through July or August, Riverfront Park is the site of a big street party featuring top-name musical entertainment. It's a lot of fun, and it's free! Read more about it in our Music City U.S.A. chapter.

## Colonial Fair
**Historic Mansker's Station, Moss-Wright Park at Caldwell Rd., Goodlettsville**
**• (615) 859-FORT, (615) 859-7979**

This re-creation of an 18th-century market draws some 5,000 to 6,000 attendees during the first weekend in May. Crafters and merchants sell reproductions of 18th-century goods such as clothing, baskets, copper ware, flint-rock firearms and knives. Native Ameri-

Photo:Cindy Stooksbury Guier

The RC and Moon Pie Festival takes place in the quaint little town of Bell Buckle each June.

cans display and sell skins and other items typical of the period. The juried craft show requires that every artist, merchant and costumed participant adhere to the 1750–1790 time period. Re-enactors take on such characters as beggars, trollops and other people you might find at an 18th-century fair. Musical entertainment, jugglers, sword swallowers and other entertainment from the period are scheduled. Admission is $5 for adults, $3 for students.

## Tennessee Crafts Fair
### Centennial Park, West End Ave. and 25th Ave. N. • (615) 665-0502

It seems like there's a crafts fair at Centennial Park every other weekend. They're popular events and draw thousands of people. This one, a juried crafts festival produced by the Tennessee Association of Craft Artists, is the largest market of Tennessee crafts you'll find anywhere. Some 170 contemporary and traditional artisans, all from the Volunteer State, set up on the lawn of Centennial Park, and as many as 50,000 visitors stop by during the three-day show, held the first weekend in May. You can find affordable gifts for around $25 as well as collectible items costing thousands of

dollars. Children's craft activities, live music, demonstrations and food will keep you in the park for hours. Admission is free. TACA also hosts the Fall Crafts Fair here on the last weekend of September (see that month's section for details).

## Tennessee Renaissance Festival
### Near Castle Gwynn, Triune
### • (615) 395-9950

Ready for some medieval entertainment? Weekends in May, ending on Memorial Day, the wooded grounds across from the Castle Gwynn turn into a medieval village, where you'll find jousting knights, fair maidens, fortune tellers, gypsy jugglers and entertainers plus medieval-themed arts and crafts. Twice daily, knights in full armor mount large Percherons and engage in combat. In addition to jousting exhibitions, you can enjoy drama and comedy (presented in Old English) at two stages on the grounds as well as Renaissance music.

All vendors, entertainers and some 150 volunteer greeters wear period costumes. Fifty-plus crafts vendors and artisans offer such items as clothing, glass, candles, wood crafts, pewter jewelry, silver crafts and weaponry.

Food takes on a medieval flavor too — you can gnaw on a roasted turkey leg if you like; you can also order sandwiches, salads, fresh fruit and vegetables. Free children's activities include storytelling, games and coloring. For an extra charge, adults can try their luck at such games of skill as archery and ax-throwing. A huge, human-powered Dragon Swing ride is a popular attraction. Tours of the main floor and gardens of Castle Gwynn, a replica of a Welsh Castle, are available.

Triune is about 20 miles south of downtown Nashville. The castle is 8 miles from I-24, off the Tenn. Highway 96 exit, or 6 miles from I-65. Admission is $12 for adults and teens, $5 for children ages 4 to 12. Parking is free.

### Sara Lee Classic LPGA Golf Tournament
**Hermitage Golf Course, 3939 Old Hickory Blvd., Old Hickory**
**• (615) 847-5017**

This Ladies Professional Golf Association event features 144 of the world's top women players. Scheduled to get a new sponsor in 2000, it is held during the last week of April or the first or second week of May at Hermitage Golf Course, about 10 miles east of downtown Nashville. In 1999 the Classic had a purse of $750,000, ranking it among the top 12 LPGA tournaments in America. The event features the Vince Gill Pro-Celebrity Skins Game, a six-hole match in which the pros vie for a prize of $30,000; a Junior Clinic, in which LPGA touring professionals work with junior golfers; a two-day Pro-Am Tournament, offering sponsors and amateurs from around the country the chance to play with the pros; and the Iris Classic, a women's-only pro-am event. Approximately 55,000 attend the week-long lineup of events.

The Classic donates some $100,000 to charities each year. Daily tickets range from $5 to $12; weekly badges are $30. Concessions are available on the course. Tickets are available by mail or at the course.

### Iroquois Steeplechase
**Percy Warner Park, off Old Hickory Blvd.**
**• (615) 322-7284**

Mark your calendar for the second Saturday in May. That's when the Iroquois Steeplechase takes place. One of Nashville's most

popular sporting and social events, this is the nation's oldest continually run weight-for-age steeplechase. Some 30,000 attend every year. Various parties and gala events precede the running of the Iroquois Steeplechase, which was first held in 1941. If you come, plan to make a day of it. You can picnic or have a tailgate party. Thousands take blankets, lawn chairs and their favorite food and drink to a spot on the grassy hillside overlooking the course.

The seven-race card culminates with the featured Iroquois Memorial at 4 PM. Admission is $10 in advance, $12 at the gate; admission for a family of four is $25. Children ages 6 and under are admitted free. The event benefits Vanderbilt Children's Hospital.

### Tennessee Jazz & Blues Society Concert Series
**Belle Meade Plantation, 5025 Harding Rd. • (615) 356-0501**
**The Hermitage, 4580 Rachel's Ln., Hermitage • (615) 889-2941**

Weekends from mid-May through early August, the Tennessee Jazz & Blues Society sponsors concerts under the stars at Belle Meade Plantation and the Hermitage. Call the Tennessee Jazz & Blues Hotline at (615) 386-7500. (For more information, see our Music City U.S.A. chapter.)

# June

### Dancin' in The District
**Riverfront Park, First Ave. N.**
**• (615) 256-9596**

See the "May" listing or read more about this event in the Music City U.S.A. chapter.

### Performing Arts Series
**Centennial Park, Riverfront Park and other area parks • (615) 862-8424**

Looking for some inexpensive entertainment? You can't find anything more affordable than Metropolitan Nashville Parks and Recreation's free summer schedule of concerts, dance and theater performances. Events are held at parks throughout the city. Contact the parks department or check the entertainment listings in local daily and weekly publications for more information.

## BellSouth Senior Classic
**Springhouse Golf Club, 18 Springhouse Ln. • (615) 871-PUTT**

Catch the top players on the PGA Senior Tour at the BellSouth Senior Classic, usually held the first or second week of June. Lee Trevino won the inaugural tournament in 1994; Jim Dent won in 1995; Isao Aoki in 1996 and 1998; and Dr. Gil Morgan in 1997. Net proceeds, which in 1998 exceeded $200,000 , go to local charities. Tickets are $15 a day, $35 for the week; spectators 18 and younger are admitted free. (See our Golf chapter for more information on Springhouse Golf Club.)

## American Artisan Festival
**Centennial Park, West End Ave. and 25th Ave. N. • (615) 298-4691**

This invitational festival, held mid-June during Father's Day weekend, features craftspeople from 35 states. It's sponsored by The American Artisan Inc., the upscale crafts gallery on Harding Road in west Nashville (see Shopping). The event is attended by thousands. You'll find pottery, wood, blown glass, leather, photography, metal, furniture, quilts and more. It's a great place to find unique jewelry — there are usually about 24 jewelry booths at this festival. Prices range from about $15 to $1,500 or more. There's good food too, with an emphasis on healthy items. You can choose from Thai specialties, fajitas, gyros and more. A children's art booth and musical entertainment round out the offerings.

If you're not in the market for crafts, it's still a fun event. This is a great place to people-watch. Adults of all ages, children, babies in strollers and dogs wearing brightly colored bandanas wander through the rows of crafts booths and relax in the picnic area. If you're planning to come here, be sure to wear comfortable clothing; it can be pretty hot and humid in Nashville this time of year. And the park grounds can be muddy in places, so choose appropriate footwear. Admission is free.

## Balloon Classic
**Edwin Warner Park, off Old Hickory Blvd. at Vaughan Rd. • (615) 329-7807**

Although this event took the year off in 1999, plans called for it to return in 2000. Traditionally held the third weekend in June, the Balloon Classic may move to a different month,

and possibly a different location, in 2000. For 14 years, this was one of Nashville's favorite June events. It featured more than 50 hot-air balloons of various shapes, sizes and colors. Events included the Friday night balloon glow, balloon races and tests of skill, children's activities, balloon rides and musical entertainment.

## International Country Music Fan Fair
**Tennessee State Fairgrounds, Wedgewood Ave. at Rains Ave. • (615) 889-7503**

Imagine 24,000 hard-core country music fans, more than 35 hours of concerts and long lines of autograph-seekers. That's Fan Fair in a nutshell. This mid-June event is like none you've seen before. (Read more about it in the Music City U.S.A. chapter.)

## Nashville Independent Film Festival
**Regal Green Hills 16 and other venues • (615) 322-4234**

Formerly known as the Sinking Creek Film/Video Festival, this mid-June event features several days of film and video screenings from renowned and up-and-coming filmmakers from around the world, including Tennessee. More than 120 films are featured, along with 15 workshops, film analyses, forums and other events. Admission ranges from $4 to $6 for a single film to about $200 for an all-festival pass. Call for a schedule of daily and evening shows, or watch for a listing in local publications.

## RC and Moon Pie Festival
**Bell Buckle town Sq. • (931) 389-9371**

An RC Cola and a Moon Pie—if you have to ask, you're probably not a Southerner. The RC–Moon Pie combo is a classic. The tiny, charming town of Bell Buckle celebrates the big round chocolate-and-graham cracker-covered marshmallow treat the third Saturday in June. It all started in 1995, when the town wanted to celebrate the 75th birthday of the Moon Pie, which is made in nearby Chattanooga. RC Cola got involved as a sponsor, and the festival was born.

As you might guess, this event doesn't take anything too seriously. It's purely for fun. Festival activities include a Moon Pie toss, Moon Pie hockey, synchronized wading, a Moon Pie dessert recipe contest, a Moon Pie song contest and a Moon Pie/RC story contest. A parade featuring Moon Pie–themed vehicles and passengers marches through the town square. You wouldn't want to miss the crowning of the Moon Pie King and RC Cola Queen. Country and bluegrass music, clogging demonstrations and Tennessee Walking Horses add to the fun. The event is held in conjunction with the Country Fair, featuring arts and crafts booths and home demonstration (canning, baking, etc.) exhibits.

Bell Buckle is about an hour's drive from Nashville, off I-24 between Murfreesboro and Shelbyville. The historic town has been a sort of magnet for the arts community, attracting sculptors, potters and other artisans. While you're here, you might want to check out the Bell Buckle Café, a popular spot with musicians. Admission is free.

## Celtic Music Festival and Summer Solstice Picnic
**Travellers Rest Historic House Museum, 636 Farrell Pkwy. • (615) 832-8197**
How about celebrating Father's Day with an evening of Celtic music, dance and culture? Bring a picnic, blankets or lawn chairs and be entertained by Irish step dancers, bagpipes, highland dancers and contemporary and traditional Celtic music. You can also tour historic Travellers Rest. Admission is $8 for adults, $5 for children ages 6 through 12.

## Chet Atkins Musician Days
**Various indoor and outdoor venues around town • (615) 256-9596**
This event, named after guitarist extraordinaire Atkins, is all about celebrating musicians. The first event was held in June 1997. Musicians present free workshops and concerts at parks, clubs and other venues. The event also features a ticketed concert by Atkins and friends. (See our Music City U.S.A. chapter.)

# July

## Dancin' in The District
**Riverfront Park, First Ave. N.**
**• (615) 256-9596**
See the related listing in "May," or read more about this event in our Music City U.S.A. chapter.

## Independence Day Celebration
**Riverfront Park, First Ave. N.**
**• (615) 862-8400**
This is Nashville's largest one-day event, drawing 100,000 to the riverfront to celebrate the Fourth of July. It's a free afternoon and evening of music and fireworks, sponsored by the mayor's office and Metro Parks and Recreation. There are food and alcohol-free drinks too, but you'll have to pay for that (*everything* can't be free). The family-oriented celebration usually kicks off around 4 PM; a variety of locally popular bands and the Nashville Symphony perform at the riverfront stage. If you come early, you can find a spot to sit and relax on the tiered hillside facing the Cumberland River; it's a great place to listen to the bands while watching boats travel up and down the Cumberland. If you prefer, you can walk along First Avenue while sampling festival food and people-watching. The fireworks display begins around 9 PM.

## Celebration of Cultures
**Scarritt-Bennett Center, 1008 19th Ave. S. • (615) 340-7500**
This one-day international festival began in 1996 as a way to celebrate the cultural diversity in Nashville and Middle Tennessee. Japanese, Korean, African-American, Chinese, Greek, Kurdish and rural Appalachian are among the more than 40 cultures represented. Dancers, musicians, storytellers and exhibits provide the entertainment. Bring your appetite and sample a variety of ethnic food offerings, including Ethiopian, Indian, Mediterranean and Japanese. A family activity area fea-

## INSIDERS' TIP

**Christian/Pop singer Amy Grant is a Nashville native.**

Amy Grant's annual Christmas concerts with the Nashville Symphony were such a success that, in 1997, Grant took the symphony with her on a 19-city U.S. tour.

tures storytelling and international games and crafts such as origami, Guatemalan worry dolls and Muslim hand-painting.

It's usually held the second Saturday in July. Admission is $5 for folks 12 and older, $2 for children 11 and younger. A $10 family ticket is available, and there are special rates for groups of 10 or more.

## Uncle Dave Macon Days
**Cannonsburgh Village, 312 S. Front St., Murfreesboro • (615) 893-2369, (800) 716-7560**

This nationally recognized old-time music and dance festival is named for Uncle Dave Macon, a pioneer of the *Grand Ole Opry*. The four-day event, which begins the Thursday following July 4th, offers national championship competitions in old-time clogging, old-time buck dancing and old-time banjo. There's plenty of fiddling too. Musicians of all ages bring their instruments and get together for impromptu concerts throughout the event. The motorless parade on Saturday features mules, horses and wagons. A gospel celebration is held on Sunday. The festival also features a juried crafts show, a variety of food vendors and historical photo displays, all set against the backdrop of Cannonsburgh Village, a re-creation of a pioneer village. The village is off Broad Street on Front Street. Admission is free.

### Tennessee-Kentucky Threshermen's Association Show
**Old Bell School, U.S. Hwy. 41, Adams**
**• (615) 696-8179**

This old-time country show is held the third weekend in July. Every year locals plant 10 acres of wheat, harvest it with an old-time com-bine, cure it, load it on wagons and bring it in for wheat threshing demonstrations during the three-day show — rain or shine. There is also a display of antique tractors, steam engines and other antique machinery, plus tractor pulls, mule pulls, live country music, square danc-ing, storytelling, a Civil War encampment, a Sunday morning worship service, balloon rides and more. Restrooms and food and drink are available. Admission is $4 for adults, free for children under 12; group rates are available. Adams is 13 miles north of Springfield.

# August

### Dancin' in The District
**Riverfront Park, First Ave. N.**
**• (615) 256-9596**

See the listing in "May" or check out our Music City U.S.A. chapter for more informa-tion.

### The Vinny
**Golf Club of Tennessee, Kingston Springs • (615) 790-7755**

Although he's best known for his fantastic voice, country music's Vince Gill is also a great golfer. Each August, he stars in his own pro-celebrity invitational. The Vinny features tour professionals on Monday and celebrities on Tuesday. It's held in Kingston Springs, just a few miles west of Nashville. Two-day admis-sion passes are $12 for adults ages 18 and older.

### Franklin Jazz Festival
**Franklin town sq. • (615) 791-9924**

Head to Franklin, 15 miles south of down-town Nashville, for a good dose of jazz the first full weekend in August. You'll hear tradi-tional jazz, Dixieland and Big Band music. The event has been listed by the Southeast Tour-ism Society as one of the top 20 events in the Southeast. Admission is free. (See our Music City U.S.A. chapter for more information.)

### Americana Summer Sampler Craft, Folk Art & Antique Show
**Tennessee State Fairgrounds, Wedgewood Ave. at Rains Ave.**
**• (615) 227-2080**

Some 250 to 300 country-craft, folk- and fine-art professionals and antique dealers from 25 states exhibit at this popular show. It's one of four that Americana Sampler Inc. presents at the fairgrounds each year, and it likely will be held the second weekend of August. You'll find seasonal decorations, antiques and col-lectibles, fine art, home and garden furnish-ings, clothing and gourmet foods. Also in-cluded are a Decorator Showcase, seminars and craft demonstrations.

In the past, the event has featured presen-tations by experts on herb gardening, herbal cooking and herbal skin care, tin and metal working, and woodworking and furniture de-signing. (See the "February" section for re-lated entries on Americana Sampler shows.)

### BellWitch Bluegrass Festival
**Old Bell School, U.S. Hwy. 41, Adams**
**• (615) 696-2589, (615) 696-2469**

This event is popular with bluegrass-mu-sic musicians and fans. Held the second week-end in August, it features mainly amateur mu-sicians from Tennessee and surrounding states. (Read more about it in our Music City U.S.A. chapter.)

### Tennessee Walking Horse National Celebration
**Celebration Grounds, Shelbyville**
**• (931) 684-5915**

This event, the World Grand Champion-ships for the high-stepping Tennessee Walk-ing Horse, has been called "the world's great-est horse show." The 10-day celebration is held in late August. When you're not watching the action in the show ring, you can enjoy the trade fairs, dog shows and the elaborately decorated barn area. Shows run three to four hours, so you'll want to allow plenty of time

here. Ticket prices are $7 to $15 for reserved seats, $5 to $10 general admission. Groups of 30 or more receive discounts of approximately 30 percent. Shows begin at 7:30 PM Sunday and at 7 PM all other evenings, but the grounds are open all day.

Shelbyville is 40 miles southeast of downtown Nashville. The show site is a mile off U.S. Highway 231 S., or 25 miles from I-24.

### Miss Martha's Old Fashioned Ice Cream Crankin'
**First Presbyterian Church, 4815 Franklin Rd. • (615) 254-1791**

Who can pass up an opportunity to dig into some delicious homemade ice cream on a hot August day? Every year on the first Sunday in August, from 3 to 5 PM, 250 to 300 ice cream makers crank out dozens of their favorite frozen concoctions for you to sample. Categories are vanilla/vanilla base, chocolate, specialties (sorbets, yogurts, sherbets) and fruit. Find a comfortable spot on the lawn, kick back and enjoy every rich and creamy spoonful. You can listen to music from the Nashville Community Concert Band, and the kids can participate in games planned especially for them. A stacking contest features area ministers in a two-minute race to see who can stack the most scoops of ice cream on a cone. While you're enjoying the tasty treats, volunteer judges are choosing the best in each category.

Held for years on the lawn of Trinity Presbyterian Church near Green Hills, the event moved in 1999 to First Presbyterian. For a $5 donation per adult, or $15 for a family of three or more, you can sample all the ice cream you want. Proceeds benefit the Martha O'Bryan Center, a family-services center serving the James A. Cayce Homes and surrounding East Nashville communities.

## September

### Italian Street Fair
**Centennial Park, West End Ave. and 25th Ave. N. • (615) 255-5600**

Nashville takes on an Italian flavor during this festival, one of the city's favorite events. It's a four-day celebration featuring delicious Italian foods plus art and crafts, games and more. The event ends on Labor Day. The Italian Street Fair was founded in 1955 as a fundraiser for the Nashville Symphony. Today, it is presented by the Symphony Guild and is the largest continuous fund-raising special event in the United States to benefit a symphony. It typically raises $200,000. Through the years it has had 10 different homes, including Riverfront Park and Brentwood's Maryland Farms, but in 1997 it moved to Centennial Park.

The Nashville Symphony performs twice during the festival, usually on Friday and Sunday nights. The Sunday show features a headline performer; past headliners include Johnny Cash and Steve Wariner. A big attraction is the children's area, where you'll find 15 or more carnival rides, several children's games and arts and crafts especially for kids. The boccie game is always busy.

Admission is $5 for adults, $3 for children ages 11 to 16.

## Fall Music Festival
**Moss-Wright Park, 745 Caldwell Rd., Goodlettsville • (615) 859-7979**

All kinds of music plus dancing, food and a barbecue cook-off are featured at this event, which takes place the Saturday after Labor Day. (See our Music City U.S.A. chapter for more information.)

## Tennessee State Fair
**Tennessee State Fairgrounds, Wedgewood Ave. at Rains Ave.
• (615) 862-8980**

The educational and fun state fair is a huge livestock and agricultural fair, featuring 4-H Club and Future Farmers and their projects in the Agriculture Hall, along with crafts and antiques. The carnival midway, open until midnight, features all your favorite adult and kiddie rides and games. Save a bundle here by taking advantage of promotions and ride specials. Hoot Owl Junction is the place to see demonstrations of how everyday tasks were accomplished in the days before modern technology. There's usually a circus attraction, petting zoo and maybe a sideshow or two, and there's plenty of fair food too — sausage and peppers, hot dogs, cotton candy, funnel cakes, lemonade and more.

The fairgrounds is four blocks off I-65. Admission is $4 for adults and teens, $2 for children ages 6 through 12.

## Ted Rhodes Golf Classic
**Ted Rhodes Golf Course, 1901 Ed Temple Blvd. • (773) 785-9009**

This pro-am golf tournament, held Friday through Sunday in early September, is a fundraiser for the Ted Rhodes Foundation to help urban programs for up-and-coming young golfers. Rhodes was the first African American to play in a Professional Golfers' Association event. The tournament offers a pro purse of

$28,000 and a hole-in-one event plus lots of prizes and gifts. Food and drink are available. For fees and more information, contact the Ted Rhodes Foundation Inc. at the number above.

## African Street Festival
**Tennessee State University main campus, 28th Ave. N. • (615) 299-0412**

Merchants from 20 or more states, exotic food concessions and eight hours of daily entertainment are featured at this three-day festival. It's an ethnic celebration for the whole family. The stage show features lots of music — blues, gospel, jazz, rap and reggae — as well as poetry and drama. Other attractions are African dance lessons, children's storytelling, a teen tent, art show, fashion show and lectures. Day-care assistance is provided on site. It's held the third weekend in September at the TSU Barn, a mile from downtown, at the 28th Avenue N. exit off I-40. Admission and parking are free.

## Belle Meade Fall Fest
**Belle Meade Plantation, 5025 Harding Rd. • (615) 356-0501, (800) 270-3991**

Leaves have begun changing from green to red, orange and gold, and the unmistakable feeling of fall is in the air — a perfect time to celebrate the changing of the seasons at a fun outdoor event. This mid-September festival features antiques, crafts by noted artisans, local retail merchandise, food by local restaurants, a children's festival and music. A tour of the Greek Revival mansion is included in the $8 admission fee. (See our Attractions chapter for more information on Belle Meade Plantation.)

## Home Decorating & Remodeling Show
**Nashville Convention Center, 601 Commerce St. • (615) 748-9980**

If you're considering a decorating or remodeling project, you'll find just about everything you need and then some at this four-day show held in mid-September. Even if you're not into home improvement, you'll probably come away from this show with lots of good ideas and knowledge of new products. More than 650 booths fill the trade show floor, offering everything from landscaping and building

# Nashville: A City for All Seasons

Although its climate isn't perfect, Nashville is a city for all seasons. While each season has its advantages and disadvantages, you'll generally find that the benefits far outweigh the downsides.

The year-round climate here often is referred to as "mild." That doesn't mean there aren't some extremes. You'll have no trouble telling the seasons apart, even if you've just awakened from a long hibernation. And we'll warn you allergy sufferers up front: this area is one of the worst in the country for pollen and mold counts, which is unfortunate for singers. (On the other hand, maybe that explains the "twang.")

As for the seasons, spring tends to be pleasantly mild, with temperatures ranging from the high 30s in early March on up into the high 70s or low 80s just before summer. Evenings can be a bit nippy at times, even in late spring. It's a beautiful time, as the magnolia blossoms and other flowering plants begin to appear throughout the area.

Summer is hot and, like much of the Southeast, quite humid. Temperatures range from the mid-60s to average highs around 90 (note the word "average," because the temperature will occasionally approach or even reach 100). You'll probably find yourself breaking a sweat with little effort, so dress as coolly as you can if you're spending time outdoors. And be sure to take advantage of Nashville's swimming pools and lakes.

Fall can be unpredictable, though days are usually warm and nights cool. It's wise to have a jacket or sweater on hand because evening temperatures can dip down into the 30s. You'll enjoy the vivid oranges, golds and browns that cover Tennessee when the leaves change.

Winter is mild, for the most part, with temperatures ranging from the mid-20s to around 50. It can get colder sometimes, but not often. Occasional snowfalls in January and February typically total less than 11 inches. With or without snow, the holiday season here is festive and bright; the zillions of lights that decorate the Opryland Hotel, for example, will make all but the Grinch feel warm inside.

The average annual precipitation in Nashville is around 47 inches.

Photo: Richard Cheek

Cheekwood's gardens are beautiful in the spring.

supplies to appliances and satellite dishes. Admission is $7 for adults and teens, but you can get in for $5 if you bring a discount coupon from the newspaper. Children 12 and younger are admitted free. Senior citizens are admitted free on Thursday and Friday. Food and drink are available.

### Tennessee Aviation Days
**Smyrna Airport, 660 Fitzhugh Blvd., Smyrna • (615) 443-3279**

Come to this mid-September weekend event to stare in awe at aerobatic maneuvers and check out the displays on the ground. Past participants (squadrons and aircraft) include The Blue Angels, The Canadian Snowbirds, the Harrier, the Navy F-14, the Stealth Fighter and Bomber, The United States Air Force Thunderbirds, the U2 Spy Plane and World War II aircraft.

The Smyrna Airport is about 20 miles southeast of Nashville. Take I-24 east to Exit 66B and follow the signs to the airport, about 5 miles away. Admission at the gate is $10 for adults (16 and older), $5 for children ages 6 through 15. Groups of 20 or more can order tickets in advance at a special rate of $7 per person. Tickets also are sold at all Tennessee Kroger Food Stores. Food and drink are available on site.

### TACA Fall Crafts Fair
**Centennial Park, West End Ave. and 25th Ave. N. • (615) 665-0502**

Crafters from around the country, selected for the quality of their work, exhibit at this juried market of fine crafts, held the last weekend in September. Stop and check out one of the many interesting craft demonstrations. Food and picnic facilities are available. You'll want to allow a minimum of one hour to enjoy this fun event, but it's easy to spend a whole afternoon here. Admission is free. The fair is presented by the Tennessee Association of Craft Artists, which also presents the Tennessee

Crafts Fair here the first weekend in May (see that section's related entry).

### Downtown Progressive Party
**Broadway, Second Ave. and Printers Alley • (615) 259-4763**

This late September or early October traveling party features live entertainment from some of Nashville's favorite performers plus plenty of delicious food and a look inside the newest hot spots in the downtown historic district. Join the 500 partiers and visit new restaurants, nightclubs, retail stores and other interesting new spots along lower Broadway, Second Avenue and Printers Alley. The fun begins around 5:30 PM and continues until the wee hours. Admission is $50 per person.

# October

### Music City Hog Jam
**Riverfront Park, First Ave. N.**
**• (615) 834-4079**

Live music, barbecue, a chili cookoff, hog calling — this two-day event has a little something for most everyone. The cook-off raises money for a nonprofit organization devoted to art, entertainment, medicine, research, education or military service. Previous beneficiaries have included Vanderbilt Children's Hospital and Child Abuse Prevention of Tennessee. Admission is $3 to $5, and everyone is encouraged to bring a couple of canned goods to benefit Second Harvest Food Bank.

### Heritage Days
**Sam Davis Home Historic Site, 1399 Sam Davis Rd., Smyrna • (615) 459-2341**

This event is a living-history celebration featuring such activities as lye soap making and blacksmithing. It's held on the Thursday and Friday closest to October 6 at the Sam Davis Home. (See our Attractions chapter for more information on the Sam Davis Home Historic

*Photo: Cathy Summerlin*

Fan Fair welcomes country music fans from the world over.

Site.) Admission is $4 for everyone ages 4 and up. Smyrna is 20 miles southeast of Nashville. The Sam Davis Home is off I-24 E.

## Southern Festival of Books
### War Memorial Plaza, Downtown between Charlotte and Union, and 6th and 7th aves. • (615) 320-7001

More than 30,000 book lovers attend this annual three-day event sponsored by the Tennessee Humanities Council. Some 200 authors from around the country, with an emphasis on the Southeast, gather for readings, panel discussions, book signings and sales. A children's area features children's authors and activities. Admission is free. Tickets to the Friday night dinner and awards presentation are approximately $40 a person. The festival is usually held the second weekend of October.

## Oktoberfest
### Throughout historic Germantown
### • (615) 256-2729

Live German music, German food and drink plus more than 80 booths full of German and American arts and crafts are featured at this annual event, which is attended by 5,000 to 6,000. It's held on the second Saturday in October in historic Germantown, at the corner of Eighth Avenue N. and Monroe Street.

The festival opens with worship services at the Church of the Assumption Catholic Church and the Monroe Street United Methodist Church, which co-sponsor the event. Admission is free. To get there, take I-265 to the MetroCenter exit and proceed to Eighth Avenue. The festival site is two blocks north of the Bicentennial Mall.

## Grand Ole Opry Birthday Celebration
### Grand Ole Opry House, 2804 Opryland Dr. • (615) 889-3060

For more than 70 years, *Grand Ole Opry* fans have been gathering each October to celebrate the birthday of the *Grand Ole Opry*, America's longest-running radio program. The three-day party is held in mid-October and includes concerts, a *Grand Ole Opry* performance and autograph and photo sessions with the stars. (See our Music City U.S.A. chapter for more information about the event, and our History chapter for more on the *Opry*.)

## NAIA Pow Wow
### Nashville Shores, 4001 Bell Rd., Hermitage • (615) 726-0806

The Native American Indian Association sponsors this annual event that brings together Native Americans from throughout North America. It's held during three days in mid-October. Competitive dancing, arts and crafts, storytelling, demonstrations and fine-art displays are among the festivities. Food booths feature traditional foods from various tribes. Admission is $5 for adults and teens, $2 for children ages 6 through 12. There's lots to see and do, so allow a minimum of three hours to enjoy this event.

## Hands on Nashville Day
### Throughout Nashville • (615) 298-1108

One day a year, usually in October but sometimes in September, Nashville's volunteer-services organizations plus thousands of volunteers get together to provide community service at nonprofit agencies and schools. While some paint and clean schools, clean up parks, landscape school grounds and build small play areas at schools and community centers, others organize intergenerational parties for senior citizens and walk dogs at the humane society. In addition to providing needed services, the event raises the community's awareness of Nashville's nonprofit organizations.

# November

## Americana Christmas Sampler Craft, Folk Art & Antique Show
### Tennessee State Fairgrounds, Wedgewood Ave. at Rains Ave.
### • (615) 227-2080

Don't wait until the last minute to do your holiday shopping. You can find lots of nifty gifts at this show, and you might even find a thing or two for yourself. This is one of four annual events presented by Americana Samplers at the fairgrounds. This one, usually held the first weekend in November, is the largest, featuring hundreds of exhibits by country- and traditional-craft, folk- and fine-art professionals as well as antique dealers from around the country. The Christmas Sampler Showcase, designer room settings, lectures, demonstrations and entertainment keep you busy. Weekend admission is $5 for adults and teens, $1.50 for children ages 6 through 12.

## Longhorn FINALS Rodeo
### Gaylord Entertainment Center, 501 Broadway • (615) 876-1016, (800) 357-6336

Every year in mid-November, the Nashville-based Longhorn Rodeo wraps up its national tour in Music City with a two- to three-day engagement. This event features the top 72 contestants from the over 1,200 who compete nationally. The purse and awards total more than $175,000. It's a fun event for all ages, complete with bull riders, bronco busting, team roping, pageantry and rodeo clowns. Tickets are $12 for all seats Friday night and $20, $16 and $14 Saturday; at Saturday's matinee, children 12 and under and senior citizens can buy tickets for half-price.

## Christmas Village
### Tennessee State Fairgrounds, Wedgewood Ave. at Rains Ave.
### • (615) 320-5353

The fairgrounds is the site of lots of holiday exhibits and sales at this time of year. The Christmas Village offers more than 275 merchants with seasonal and gift items. You'll find Christmas ornaments, hand-painted and personalized items, clothing, pottery, jewelry, toys and food items. Kids can also visit with Santa. This three-day mid-November event benefits the Bill Wilkerson Hearing & Speech Center and Pi Beta Phi philanthropies. Admission is $6 for anyone 10 and older; children 9 and younger get in free. Advance tickets are available for $5 from any Pi Beta Phi alumna, at the Bill Wilkerson Center or by mail. Write to Christmas Village, P.O. Box 158826, Nashville TN 37215.

## A Turn of the Century Holiday
### Belle Meade Plantation, 5025 Harding Rd. • (615) 356-0501, (800) 270-3991

Belle Meade Plantation decks the halls the

way they did it in the late 1890s, offering a look at how Nashvillians — at least some of them — celebrated Christmas a century ago. Admission is $7 per person. Wassail tours are available by reservation.

## Country Christmas
**Opryland Hotel, 2800 Opryland Dr.**
**• (615) 889-1000**

A holiday outing to the Opryland Hotel during the holidays has become a tradition among Nashvillians, and the hotel is a popular place to take visiting friends and relatives this time of year. Wide-eyed visitors marvel at the hotel's outdoor lights display of more than 2 million bulbs. The decorations indoors are spectacular as well.

If you wait until late in the season to visit, you'll probably end up in a major traffic jam (often extending for miles down Briley Parkway), and once inside the hotel, you'll find it jam-packed as well. To avoid the crowds, get it the spirit early and come in November — the earlier the better. If you plan to visit only the hotel, you'll have to pay only for parking (about $5). Of course, once inside, you're bound to want to stop in one of the many food and drink spots for a holiday treat.

Country Christmas includes everything from a breakfast with Santa for the kids to a musical stage show to an art, antique and craft fair. Several events, such as the Yule Log lighting ceremony and nightly Dancing Waters fountain shows, are free.

## Christmas at Belmont
**Belmont Mansion, 1900 Wedgewood Ave. • (615) 460-5459**

Belmont Mansion, on the campus of Belmont University near Music Row, is decorated in Victorian style during the holidays, trimmed with hundreds of yards of garland, fruit and dried flowers. Ribboned swags adorn the Grand Salon, extending from the corners of the vaulted ceilings to the center chandelier. The grand staircase is trimmed with garlands, fancy tussie-mussies and Victorian paper flowers. You can browse for gifts at the mansion's Victorian Gift Shop. Christmas at Belmont begins around the third weekend in November and lasts about four weeks. Tours of the 1853 mansion are available Tuesday through Saturday. Private group tours and food functions may be arranged.

Admission is $6 for adults and teens, $2 for kids ages 6 through 12. Groups of 15 or more pay $5.50 a person. (For more information on Belmont Mansion, see our Attractions chapter.)

## Goodlettsville Antique Festival
**Goodlettsville Antique Community, Main St., Goodlettsville • (615) 859-7979**

An antique lover's paradise, Goodlettsville's numerous antique malls and shops have a Christmas Open House with special decorations, refreshments and sales. It takes place usually the last weekend in November. From downtown take I-65 north to Exit 97, then go west to Dickerson Pike. The malls are on Main Street. (For more information on these shops, see the "Antiques" section of our Shopping chapter.)

## Trees of Christmas
**Cheekwood — Nashville's Home of Art and Gardens, 1200 Forrest Park Dr.**
**• (615) 353-2150**

Since it began in the 1960s, this has become one of Nashville's favorite holiday events, attracting as many as 15,000 visitors from late November to early January. Each year the event has a theme, and 15 giant Christmas trees, each elaborately trimmed and themed, deck the Botanic Hall of the 1920s Cheekwood mansion. (See our Attractions chapter for more on Cheekwood.) Themes in previous years include "Christmas Around the World," with each tree featuring decorations relating to a specific country, and "Storybook Christmas," with each tree trimmed to a different Christmas story. It's a fun event for kids and grownups alike.

While at Cheekwood, you can tour the beautifully landscaped grounds (although they are much lovelier in spring and summer) and have lunch at the Pineapple Room. Stop by the Holiday Shoppe to browse for ornaments and baked goods.

Trees of Christmas is presented by the Horticultural Society of Middle Tennessee. Admission is $7 for adults; children ages 6 through 17 get in free. Groups of 15 or more pay $5 a ticket.

# December

## Twelfth Night Celebration
### Travellers Rest, 636 Farrell Pkwy.
### • (615) 832-8197

Historic Traveller's Rest celebrates the holidays with special decorations and music of the 1830s throughout December and early January. The celebration culminates January 6 with observance of the Epiphany, or Twelfth Day of Christmas, a traditional Christian celebration. Activities include storytelling, candlelight tours and musical performances. Special holiday events, refreshments and activities for children take place on weekends.

Traveller's Rest, built in 1799 by John Overton, a land speculator, lawyer, judge, longtime friend of Andrew Jackson and co-founder of the city of Memphis, is open throughout the year for daily tours (see our Attractions chap-

ter). Admission is approximately $6 for adults and teens, $5 for seniors and $3 for kids ages 6 through 12. Reservations are required for candlelight tours; admission is $8, $7 and $5 respectively.

## Yulefest
### Historic Mansker's Station, Moss-Wright Park at Caldwell Rd., Goodlettsville
### • (615) 859-FORT, (615) 859-7979

Christmas of the 1770s is the theme of Yulefest, held the first weekend in December. Guides in period dress re-enact Colonial Christmas customs at this historic site, which features a reconstruction of a 1779 frontier fort, Mansker's Station. There are refreshments, music and decorations too. The historic brick structure on the site is Bowen Plantation House; built in 1787, it was the first brick home in Middle Tennessee and is listed on the National Register of Historic Places.

Admission is free. Mansker's Station and Bowen Plantation House are at Moss-Wright Park at Caldwell Road, between Longhollow Pike and Gallatin Road. (For more info about Mansker's Station and Bowen Plantation House, see our Attractions chapter.)

## Tribute to African Americans in the Battle of Nashville
### National Cemetery and area sites
### • (615) 299-0412

A lecture, tour and wreath-laying are highlights of this event, which is presented by the African-American Cultural Alliance. The activities take place over three days in mid-December. The tour includes stops at locally significant sites such as Fort Negley and Shy's Hill. National Cemetery is near Kmart on Gallatin Road. Admission is free.

## Rudolph's Red Nose Run and Nashville Gas Christmas Parade
### Downtown Nashville • (615) 734-1754, (615) 734-1702

As many as 100,000 spectators turn out

for the annual Christmas parade, which features more than 100 floats, bands, clowns and other attractions — Santa too. The parade starts at Ninth Avenue and Broadway and marches to 25th Avenue S. The event is broadcast live by WKRN-TV Channel 2. Before the parade are a 5K race and 1-mile fun run. Participants vie for prizes for best costumes and best time. It all takes place the first Sunday in December. The fun usually starts just before noon. Admission is free.

## Dickens of a Christmas
**Downtown Franklin • (615) 791-9924**

You'll feel like you've stepped back in time to a Charles Dickens Christmas during this event, held the second full weekend in December in historic downtown Franklin. For those two days, two blocks of Main Street are themed to the 1800s. You'll see carolers in Victorian costumes as well as characters such as Scrooge and the ghosts of Christmases past, present and future. In the store windows, artisans dressed in period clothing demonstrate crafts of the 1800s. Shopkeepers dress in period clothing too. Take a free ride in a horse-drawn carriage, then visit a street vendor for some sugar plums, plum pudding, tea or hot cider. An "Opera House" offers musical and dramatic performances each day.

Dickens of a Christmas is gaining national attention. It attracts thousands from several different states and has been covered by national magazines. Admission is free.

## Nashville Ballet's Nutcracker
**Jackson Hall, Tennessee Performing Arts Center, 505 Deaderick St.**
**• (615) 244-7233**

You'll see sugar plum fairies, toy solders, the Dance of the Snowflakes and more. . . . Drama, fantasy, music and dance meld beautifully in this traditional holiday production. The Nashville Ballet's version of *The Nutcracker* was an immediate hit when it opened in the late 1980s, and it has become a holiday tradition for many Nashvillians. In addition to the Nashville Ballet, the production features local children and the Nashville Symphony. Tickets range from about $15 to $35.

## Music City Bowl
**Adelphia Coliseum, downtown**
**• (615) 880-1900**

Founded in 1998, the Music City Bowl is an annual post-season college football game that pits a Southeastern Conference school against an at-large rival. Tickets range from about $20 to $55.

If you're a serious aficionado of symphony or theater, don't forget that the season tickets or subscription packages offered by many groups can be much more affordable than purchasing tickets by the event.

# The Arts

Ballet. Symphony. Shakespeare. Broadway musicals. Opera. Visual arts. Nashville has it all . . . and more. These are essential elements of a thriving arts scene befitting a city with the nickname "Athens of the South."

Recent years have seen a steady growth in the number of arts groups busily creating new works or new interpretations of old favorites. That's not surprising because Nashville has long been a magnet for creative, energetic people. If there's a downside to all the activity, it may well be that the abundance of artistic and cultural opportunities can lead to difficulty in making a decision.

Of course, we're not about to say that all of the creative people in Nashville are getting filthy rich. That's obviously not the way things work, which is why "starving" is one of the more common adjectives used to modify "artist." Musicians and actors and dancers and painters need your support — and you owe it to them and to yourself to turn off the TV, get out there and sample what they have to offer.

Yes, you'll still see empty seats at concerts and plays, a fact that can be frustrating to performers as well as to those who actively support such events (although it can be a boon to the casual arts patron in search of tickets). But, while it's not uncommon to hear people complaining about a lack of support for the arts, support actually appears to be growing. The Metro Nashville Arts Commission and the Nashville Area Chamber of Commerce released a report in July 1997 based on a study of 66 local arts groups. Those groups reported a total attendance of 2.4 million people during the past year — a 14.9 increase over the previous two years.

Going back a few years further, it was support for the arts that helped rescue from bankruptcy a symphony orchestra that has since gone on to earn favorable national notices. It is support for the arts that allows the Tennessee Performing Arts Center and various groups to provide Middle Tennessee with high-quality shows that rival those you'll see in any major city.

In general, Nashville's arts groups are seeing the value of cooperation and collaboration, even (or perhaps especially) across disciplines. One shining recent example was "An Evening With the Arts" in April 1999 at the Tennessee Performing Arts Center. This event, which we hope becomes an annual event, featured performances by Nashville Symphony, Nashville Opera Association, Nashville Ballet and Tennessee Repertory Theatre, along with a reception.

Another positive development is ArtSynergy, a coalition formed by three influential performing arts organizations and described in further detail at the end of this chapter.

Local artists, gallery owners and art lovers are excited about the coming of the Frist Center for the Visual Arts in the spring of 2001. The $45 million center, in a renovated Art Deco post office building at 901 Broadway, is expected to play host to major traveling exhibitions while also providing visibility for important local collections that have been in storage because of a lack of display space. Director Chase Rynd says Frist Center will help "give Nashville a national presence" on the visual arts scene.

Meanwhile, there are plenty of arts opportunities in Nashville. If you're a serious aficionado of symphony or theater, don't forget that the season tickets or subscription packages offered by many groups can be much more affordable than purchasing tickets by the event.

## Tickets

### Ticketmaster
505 Deaderick St. • (615) 255-ARTS, (615) 255-9600 (charge by phone)

Ticketmaster, a nationwide service, handles ticket sales for a number of local concerts, plays and other productions at a variety of venues. If you're going to order tickets by phone, have your credit card ready — and be aware that Ticketmaster always adds a surcharge (generally $3 or more) to the price of each ticket.

# TPAC

## Tennessee Performing Arts Center
### 505 Deaderick St. • (615) 782-4000

The Tennessee Performing Arts Center, commonly known as TPAC (pronounced "tee-pack") merits its own special category for the sheer breadth of artistic and cultural events it presents or otherwise helps make available. TPAC, a private, nonprofit corporation in a huge downtown office building, has three stages: 2,408-seat Jackson Hall, 1,003-seat Polk Theater and 288-seat Johnson Theater. These stages are home to five local resident groups: the Nashville Symphony, Tennessee Repertory Theatre, Nashville Opera, Nashville Ballet and Circle Players.

TPAC's First American Broadway Series brings touring hit Broadway musicals to town. Recent productions have included the Pulitzer- and Tony-winning smash *Rent,* and *Cats,* Broadway's longest-running hit. The New Directions Series, launched in 1995, presents cutting-edge performances ranging from contemporary music concerts and dance to performance art, all chosen for their uniqueness and appeal to diverse audiences. Both series' seasons run September through June. (For more information on these series, see the "Theater," "Dance," and "Classical Music and Opera" sections of this chapter.) The phenomenally successful dance production *Riverdance the Show* was another TPAC highlight in 1999.

The center serves area schools with its Humanities Outreach in Tennessee program, which includes live performances at TPAC, arts workshops, in-school visits and more.

Call (615) 782-6560 for season ticket information, or Ticketmaster's arts line at (615) 255-ARTS for single tickets to TPAC events.

# Dance

## Nashville Ballet
### 2976 Sidco Dr. • (615) 244-7233, (615) 782-6560 (subscriptions)

Nashville Ballet, founded in 1981 as a nonprofit civic dance company, became a professional company in 1986. Each year it presents a four-program series, accompanied by The Nashville Symphony, at the Tennessee Performing Arts Center's Polk Theater and Jackson Hall. The company's classically based repertoire is balanced with modern, neoclassical and contemporary works.

Under the leadership of artistic director Paul Vasterling and managing director Jane Fabian, Nashville Ballet employs 14 company dancers and five trainees in presenting about 20 subscription-series performances. Recent performances have included *Swan Lake*, *The Nutcracker* (which draws more than 14,000 to its annual holiday performances), *Robin Hood* and the Spring Repertory Series. Tickets range from $15 to $36. Contact Ticketmaster at (615) 255-ARTS for single tickets.

Nashville Ballet, which has an affiliated School of Nashville Ballet, serves the community with varied educational programs. It regularly performs as part of Humanities Outreach Tennessee and prepares and manages the dance program each year for The Governor's School for the Arts. The company also has helped develop dance badge programs for area Girl Scouts and, through the Edgehill Center Program, serves the predominantly low-income Edgehill community with dance instruction, attire, equipment and tickets to select performances.

## Sarratt Performing Arts
### Great Performances at Vanderbilt series, 402 Sarratt Student Center, Vanderbilt Univ. • (615) 322-2471

The Great Performances at Vanderbilt series, sponsored by Sarratt Performing Arts, includes performances by some of the top dance troupes in the world. Many performances are

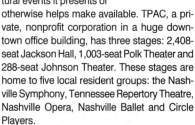

held at Vandy's Langford Auditorium; others are co-sponsored by TPAC's New Directions Series (see subsequent entry) and held at Jackson Hall and Polk Theater. Public tickets for Langford performances are $24, $22 and $20. Various subscription packages are available.

The Sarratt Student Center is on 24th Avenue S. near Vanderbilt Place.

### Tennessee Dance Theatre
**(615) 248-3262**

The award-winning Tennessee Dance Theatre, which presents a modern repertoire under the artistic direction of Donna Rizzo and Andrew Krichels, performs at various indoor and outdoor locations around town. The company has distinguished itself with a number of original works that capture the unique flavor of the South. Live music also plays a vital role, and the company has collaborated with such stars as Chet Atkins, Mike Reid, Riders in the Sky and Mark O'Connor as well as the Nashville Symphony and Blair School of Music faculty. It all adds up to great fun. Ticket prices range from free — annual performances at Centennial Park — to $20, and various discounts available for students and seniors. Write Tennessee Dance Theatre at P.O. Box 121884, Nashville TN 37212.

### TPAC's New Directions Series
**505 Deaderick St.**
**• (615) 782-6560 (subscriptions)**

The New Directions Series has included performances by the Alvin Ailey Dance Theater, The Parsons Dance Company, Tap Dogs and other leading dance groups. Performances are held at TPAC's Jackson Hall and Polk Theater and other venues. Ticket prices typically range from $10 to $37. Contact Ticketmaster for single tickets.

### Uhuru Dance Company
**(615) 227-0400**

The children and adults in Uhuru Dance Company perform, teach and document African cultural traditions in the form of dance, music, theater and storytelling. They present concerts, dance and drum workshops, lecture demonstrations and slide/film presentations about West African, Brazilian and Haitian cul-

tures, modern jazz and liturgical dance. Write to them at P.O. Box 41686, Nashville TN 37204.

# Classical Music and Opera

### Belmont University School of Music
**1900 Belmont Blvd. • (615) 460-6408**

Belmont's comprehensive music program offers studies in diverse music styles, and its free solo and group concerts cover a wide range as well, from classical and jazz to bluegrass and rock. Camerata Musicale, a chamber music ensemble that celebrated its 12th anniversary in 1999, performs several times a year in the Belmont Mansion. Other groups, including the Belmont Concert Band and the University Orchestra, perform at various locations on campus. The Faculty Concert Series features a variety of music performed by the school faculty.

### Blair School of Music
**2400 Blakemore Ave. • (615) 322-7651**

The Blair School of Music at Vanderbilt University presents about 140 free concerts each year by groups including the Vanderbilt Orchestra, Symphonic Choir, Symphonic Wind Ensemble, Opera Theatre and Jazz Band as well as the Nashville Youth Symphony, a precollege orchestra of community youth. Performances are held at Blair Recital Hall and Langford Auditorium campus.

In addition, the highly respected Blair Concert Series features about 15 concerts and recitals a year, including shows by special guests such as fiddler/multi-instrumentalist extraordinaire Mark O'Connor. Tickets are $8 for adults, $6 for Vanderbilt faculty and staff and $4 for students and seniors, and season tickets are available.

### Nashville Chamber Orchestra
**404 Greenway Ave. • (615) 292-7815**

The Nashville Chamber Orchestra, formerly the Cumberland Chamber Orchestra, presents a broad mix of new music and traditional classics within a chamber music format. Though primarily a string orchestra, the flexible group, led by music director and conductor Paul Gambill, adds brass, winds and percussion when at its full size of about 35 members. The orchestra's growing acceptance has resulted in new opportunities, such as the recording of a CD for the Warner Brothers label (at this writing, plans were being made for a second CD on Angel Classical Records); the recording by National Public Radio of two NCO concerts; and a date to play at Carnegie Hall in the spring of 2000. The 1999 season included a pair of dates with the acclaimed Eroica Trio. A study by the Metro Nashville Arts Commission found that, for the last four years, the orchestra was the city's fastest-growing arts organization, with an annual budget that has more than doubled over the last two seasons. Ticket prices vary, but most are $15 or $20, with discounts for students and seniors.

## David Lipscomb University Department of Music
**3901 Granny White Pk. • 279-5932**

Lipscomb's Department of Music, headed by Larry Griffith, presents concerts by soloists and groups, including the University Concert Band, University Jazz Band, University Singers and A Capella Singers, at various campus locations. Tickets for Artist Series events are $7, but others are free.

## Nashville Opera
**719 Thompson Ln., Ste. 401**
**• (615) 292-5710**

Artistic director John Hoomes, who joined the Nashville Opera in February 1995, and executive director Carol Penterman have been credited with not only significantly improving the quality of the company's productions, but also expanding its audience through innovative marketing and education programs. As a result, attendance rose from 3,200 during the 1995-96 season to 8,000 in 1996-97.

Nashville Opera, founded in 1980, merged with Tennessee Opera Theatre in September 1996 to form the Nashville Opera Association. That umbrella group now consists of the Nashville Opera, which produces professional, full-scale operas; Tennessee Opera Theatre, an education division that trains young singers and promotes local talent; and the Nashville Opera Guild, a group of 400 fund-raising and promotional volunteers.

Recent productions have included, *Aida*, *The Turn of the Screw*, *H.M.S. Pinafore*, Mozart's *Cosi Fan Tutte* and Strauss's *Der Rosenkavalier*. Single tickets range from $10 to $44, and season subscriptions range from $46 to $152.

## The Nashville Symphony
**209 10th Ave. S. • (615) 255-5600**

The Nashville Symphony, the largest performing arts organization in Tennessee, puts on more than 200 concerts — ranging from classical and pops series to children's concerts and special events — during its 37-week season. It also performs with the Nashville Ballet and the Nashville Opera (see previous entries).

The resurgence of the symphony after filing for bankruptcy in February 1988 is a testimony to the Nashville community's support. A reorganization plan developed by the Chamber of Commerce, local government, volunteers and business leaders had the symphony back on track by fall 1988. Since then The Nashville Symphony has garnered acclaim, releasing a well-received recording of Beethoven's *Symphony No. 7* to mark its 50th anniversary in 1996 and attracting such prominent guest artists as Van Cliburn, Isaac Stern, Doc Severinsen and Rosemary Clooney. Scheduled guests for the 1999-2000 season include Itzhak Perlman, Melissa Manchester and Marvin Hamlisch.

You can catch The Nashville Symphony, which has been under the direction of Maestro Kenneth Schermerhorn since 1983, at the Tennessee Performing Arts Center's Jackson Hall, Ryman Auditorium, the Grand Ole Opry House, outdoor venues like Centennial Park and Cheekwood, and other sites throughout Middle Tennessee and in adjacent states. Many of these performances are free.

## Sarratt Performing Arts
**Great Performances at Vanderbilt series, 402 Sarratt Student Center, Vanderbilt Univ, • (615) 322-2471**

The Great Performances at Vanderbilt series, sponsored by Sarratt Performing Arts, includes musical performances by instrumental and vocal groups from around the world. Many performances are held at Vandy's Langford Auditorium; others are co-sponsored by

TPAC's New Directions Series (see previous entry) and held at Jackson Hall and Polk Theater. Public tickets for Langford performances are $24, $22 and $20. Various subscription packages are available.

## Scarritt-Bennett Center Concert Series
**1008 19th Ave. S. • (615) 320-4657**

The Scarritt-Bennett Center, a conference retreat and education center on a former college campus, presents 10 to 12 vespers concerts a year in the beautiful Wightman Chapel on campus. Many musicians say the chapel is a perfect place acoustically for solo performances by such instruments as viola, cello, organ, flute, oboe and harp. Most of the concerts are solo, although some are duets or combinations like voice and harp. Vocal highlights include the Scarritt-Bennett A Capella Singers, who have a varied multicultural repertoire, and, in the last couple of years, an annual performance by the famed Fisk Jubilee Singers. Scarritt-Bennett also presents occasional concerts on the lawn, such as a recent performance by bluegrass music's Mclain Brothers Band. All performances are free.

# Theater

You'll find an abundance of theatrical opportunities in Nashville, ranging from professional companies to amateur and dinner theater to children's shows. We've included some of the more visible groups, but independents are always popping up, so keep your eyes open.

## A.C.T. I
**4210 Georgia Ave. • (615) 726-2281**

A.C.T. I, a group of local artists — the acronym stands for Artists Cooperative Theater — performs a varied selection of plays at local venues, including the Darkhorse and Z. Alexander Looby theaters. ACT I's season runs from September through May.

Recent productions have included Molière's *The School for* Wives, Thornton Wilder's *Our Town* and Noel Coward's *Private* Lives. Tickets are $10. Season tickets, which allow you to see all five plays for the price of four, are $40 for adults, $32 for students.

## Actors Bridge Ensemble
**2141 Acklen Ave. • (615) 460-9439**

In its 2½ years of existence, Actors Bridge, based in St. Augustine's Chapel on the Vanderbilt campus, has pursued a mission statement centered on strong ensemble acting and works that reflect social issues of the time. In 1999, the group presented *American Duet*, a new musical written by artistic director Bill Feheely with music and lyrics by hit Nashville songwriter Marcus Hummon. The thought-provoking production garnered national interest for its portrayal of the cultural stereotypes and boundaries faced by a black country singer and a white rock 'n' roller who grew up in Africa. "We don't necessarily choose what we're drawn to; it's something inside of us," Feheely said in describing the show's appeal.

Other recent performances have included the Molière comedy *Tartuffe* and the dramas *Holy Ghosts*, about snake handlers, and *Two Rooms*, about a professor kidnapped in Beirut. Feheely and Hummon are also "planting seeds" for another musical that would focus on Spanish Revolution. Ticket prices to Actors Bridge events are generally $10.

Photo: The Nashville Symphony

Kenneth Schermerhorn has directed The Nashville Symphony, which maintains a full-time orchestra of 73 musicians, since 1983.

In addition to its ensemble theater, Actors Bridge offers an ongoing training program.

## American Negro Playwright Theater
### (615) 871-4283

This theater, founded by local actor and playwright Barry Scott, who serves as producing artistic director, mounts productions by black writers at different local theaters. While productions are targeted primarily at acquainting children of all races with the black experience, the theater also has branched out into other areas, including Shakespeare. Scott, who played the role of Tee-Tot in the Ryman Auditorium's 1997 production of *Lost Highway: The Music & Legend of Hank Williams Sr.*, also has produced two of his own plays: *Harlem Voices* and *A Joyful Noise*, which tells the story of Fisk University's Jubilee Singers.

The American Negro Playwright Theater generally mounts a spring production and a fall production in addition to running a 10- to 12- week summer stock program for all ages through Tennessee State University. You can write the theater at P.O. Box 24976, Nashville TN 37202.

## Belmont University Little Theatre
### 1900 Belmont Blvd. • (615) 460-5503

The Belmont Little Theatre is an intimate, on-campus performance space with maximum seating capacity of 100. It is managed by the faculty and students in the university's theater and drama degree program. The annual season of shows, which range from classical to contemporary and include works written and directed by Belmont students, is open to the public.

## Blue Wave/Black Taffeta & Burlap
### (615) 361-9678

This group, the theatrical branch of Blue Wave Productions, is primarily devoted to plays with an African-American theme, which it presents at different area theaters.

## Chaffin's Barn Dinner Theatre
### 8204 Tenn. Hwy. 100 • (615) 646-9977

Opened in 1967, Chaffin's Barn is Nashville's oldest professional theater. For one price, you can enjoy an all-you-can-eat country buffet followed by a stage production. It could be Shakespeare, a musical, a mystery or a comedy. Chaffin's has two theaters running simultaneously: the 300-seat MainStage theater, with its stage that "magically" descends from the ceiling at showtime, and the more intimate 60-seat BackStage theater. The two theaters share the buffet line and starting times. (See also our Nightlife chapter.)

Chaffin's, which uses local and out-of-town actors and holds open auditions, presents 16 productions each year, including one Shakespeare work. You'll generally find a musical or comedy on MainStage. BackStage, which usually has a mystery or comedy, also presents the Bard's works. Highlights in 1999 included *Fiddler on the Roof*, the musical *Bob She Bops* and a Sherlock Holmes trilogy. Chaffin's also offers a special children's Christmas matinee throughout each December.

Performances are held Tuesday through Saturday year round, with dinner served from 6 PM to 7:30 PM and showtime at 8 PM. One Sunday matinee is presented sometime during each production's run. Two reduced-rate senior matinees are also held for each show; call for details. The cost for the dinner buffet and show during the week is $30 for adults and teens and $15 for children 12 and younger; on Friday and Saturday, it's $32 and $16, respectively. Show-only pricing is $20 a person. Reservations are required.

## Circle Players
### 505 Deaderick St. • (615) 254-0113 (information), (615) 255-ARTS (Ticketmaster)

Circle Players, Nashville's longest-running theater group, are celebrating their 50th anniversary in 1999-2000. They've been one of the

---

**INSIDERS' TIP**

Thomas Hart Benton's final painting, *The Sources of Country Music*, on permanent display at the Country Music Hall of Fame and Museum, poignantly illustrates the influence of blues, Appalachian, gospel and Western music on country.

Tennessee Performing Arts Center's resident groups since 1980. They stage six to seven productions a season, which typically runs from early September through mid-May. The Players present a wide range of theater — musicals, comedies and drama — in TPAC's 288-seat Johnson Theater. Recent performances have included the bawdy comedy *Sylvia*, the social commentary of *The Song of Jacob Zulu*, the song-and-dance gay comedy *La Cage Aux Folles* and Cole Porter's musical *Anything Goes*. Performances are generally at 8 PM Friday and Saturday and 2:30 PM Sunday. Tickets for plays are $12 for adults, $9 for seniors and $7 for folks 17 and younger; musicals are $2 more. Season tickets are a bargain, averaging out at $7.50 a show.

### Darkhorse Theater
**4610 Charlotte Ave. • (615) 297-7113**

Darkhorse Theater, a popular venue for a range of local and touring theater companies, is a warm and intimate space seating 136 people in a renovated church. It's home to several independent, not-for-profit theatrical companies, including A.C.T. I and Mockingbird Public Theatre (see this chapter's entries). Tickets are usually $10.

### Lakewood Theatre Company Inc.
**2211 Hadley Ave., Old Hickory**
**• (615) 847-0934, (615) 847-2585**
**(reservations)**

Lakewood Theatre Company is a community theater group that maintains its own venue in a historic former bakery just down the street from Andrew Jackson's home, The Hermitage (see Attractions). Before renovating the building, one of Davidson County's oldest, in 1983, the group performed in several other locations — its first play, *Our Town*, was actually performed on the banks of the Cumberland River.

The company, begun for children in the community, continues to offer a children's workshop each June. It also continues to offer a variety of productions; the recent and current productions include *Bus Stop*, *Nunsense*, Neil Simon's *Plaza Suite*, the horror spoof *It's a Scream* and a special holiday presentation of *Hansel and Gretel*.

Most productions run for three weekends except in cases of special holdovers. Plays are at 8 PM Friday and Saturday nights and 2:30 PM Sunday. Tickets are $8 for adults and $6 for children and seniors, with group rates available. Reservations are strongly suggested.

### Lipscomb University Theater
**3901 Granny White Pk. • (615) 279-5715**

Lipscomb University Theater, under the direction of Dr. Larry Brown, stages three or four productions a year. They can vary from Shakespeare or other classics to musicals and mysteries. Most productions are presented in the university's intimate 128-seat Arena Theater, with one show a year at the 1,300-seat Collins Auditorium on campus. Recent shows have included *Guys and Dolls*, *Man of La Mancha* and *The Importance of Being Earnest*.

The group, which includes theater majors as well as other interested students, also presents an occasional dinner theater, usually an original murder mystery, at Avalon Hall, the former home of university founder David Lipscomb. But you'll have to be lucky to snare a seat for the dinner theater; it is usually a limited run not advertised off-campus.

Everything the group does is free to the public.

### Mockingbird Public Theatre
**(615) 463-0071**

Mockingbird Public Theatre, a nonprofit professional group formed in 1994, is dedicated to the advancement of Southern writers and themes. It uses only local and regional actors in its intimate productions, which include original plays (submissions are accepted) as well as classics. The group stages four to five productions a year, generally for a four-week run. Recent works include *Hamlet*; "A Classic Mismatch" featuring two one-act comedies by Anton Chekhov and George Bernard Shaw; and NeST '99, the New Southern Theatre Project showcasing new Southern plays.

Tickets generally range from $10 to $15 for Mockingbird productions, which usually are staged at Darkhorse Theater, but the group occasionally performs at TPAC's Johnson Theater or Polk Theater. Write to Mockingbird Public Theatre at P.O. Box 24002, Nashville TN 37202.

## Nashville Children's Theatre
### 724 Second Ave. S. • (615) 254-9103

Nashville Children's Theatre, officially known as Nashville Academy Theatre for 17 years, changed its name back to the more descriptive title in 1996 because that's what most people called it anyway. Whatever you call it, it's well worth your and your kids' time.

The 1999-2000 season is the theater's 68th, making it the country's longest-running children's theater group. The not-for-profit group has been recognized internationally as a model for excellence in the field of theater for young audiences and has received numerous awards. The theater holds after-school and in-school workshops and a summer drama day camp.

Nashville Children's Theatre produces a six-show season featuring shows at 10 and 11:30 AM each weekday and a weekend family series from September through May. Recent productions have included *Most Valuable Player*, a drama about baseball player Jackie Robinson, who broke the sport's "color barrier"; *And Then They Came for Me: Remembering the World of Anne Frank*; *The Reluctant Dragon*; and an adaptation of Rudyard Kipling's *The Jungle Book*, Tickets are $4.50 a person during the week and, on the weekends, $8.50 for adults and $6.50 for children. Teachers are admitted free with groups of 10 or more.

## The Nashville Shakespeare Festival
### 615 5th Ave. S. • (615) 255-2273

The Nashville Shakespeare Festival is dedicated to producing the plays of the Bard as well as works by other classical, modern and emerging playwrights. It is best known for its free "Shakespeare in the Park" productions, which since 1988 have drawn thousands of Nashvillians to Centennial Park. Recent performances have included *Twelfth Night* in 1998 and *The Tempest* in 1999; other years have

brought *A Midsummer Night's Dream*, *Macbeth* and *Julius Caesar*.

In summer 1997, the Shakespeare Festival expanded to offer two different productions during its run. In addition, the festival takes its "Shakespeare sampler," a combination of 50-minute condensed versions of the Bard's classics with a workshop, on tour to high school students throughout Tennessee. It also works with the Nashville Institute for the Arts and TPAC's Humanities Outreach in Tennessee to produce shows for schoolchildren. And in 1999, the festival kicked off an apprentice program for children 13 and older, with 12 students receiving 30 hours of Shakespeare training as well as a role in the play.

## Pull-Tight Players
### Pull-Tight Theater, 112 Second Ave. S., Franklin • (615) 790-6782 (reservations), (615) 790-3204 (information)

This local company stages classic and contemporary plays and musicals. Recent productions include *Arsenic and Old Lace*, *Camelot* and *To Kill a Mockingbird*. Tickets are generally $10 for adults, $8 for folks 17 and younger. Season tickets are available. Box office hours are 6 to 7:30 PM Monday through Friday and 10 AM to noon Saturday.

## Ryman Auditorium
### 116 Fifth Ave. N. • (615) 254-1445 (administrative offices), (615) 889-6611 (information)

In addition to the Ryman's constant stream of concerts, weekly concert series and television tapings, the venerable auditorium has in recent years presented major theatrical productions with a musical/biographical theme. In 1994 and 1995, *Always . . . Patsy Cline* drew widespread acclaim, and it later toured as a Broadway production. The award-winning *Lost Highway: The Music & Legend of Hank Williams Sr.* filled the slot in 1996 and 1997, fol-

---

**INSIDERS' TIP**

The seasons of many concert and theater groups in Nashville run from September to April or May — roughly in line with school schedules.

Photo: Donnie Beauchamp

A trip to the *Grand Ole Opry* is a must,
whether you're just visiting Nashville or are a Music City resident.

lowed by *Bye Bye Love: The Everly Brothers Musical* in 1998. These productions ran Thursday, Friday and Saturday nights from May through October. In 1999, productions included a run of the off-Broadway musical *Pump Boys & Dinettes*, which was scheduled to run from mid-June through mid-August.

## Sarratt Performing Arts
### Great Performances at Vanderbilt series, 402 Sarratt Student Center, Vanderbilt Univ. • (615) 322-2471

The Great Performances at Vanderbilt series, sponsored by Sarratt Performing Arts, includes touring theatrical performances. Many are held at Vandy's Langford Auditorium; others are co-sponsored by TPAC's New Directions Series (see this chapter's previous entry) and held at Jackson Hall and Polk Theater. Public tickets for Langford performances are $24, $22 and $20. Various subscription packages are available.

## Tennessee Performing Arts Center
### 505 Deaderick St. • (615) 782-4000 (administrative offices), (615) 255-ARTS (Ticketmaster)

TPAC's Broadway Series features performances in Jackson Hall and Polk Theater. Recent shows have included the smash hits *Rent* and *Cats*. The 1999-2000 schedule includes six Broadway Series productions: *The Sound of Music* starring Richard Chamberlain; Disney's *Beauty and the Beast; Sunset Boulevard; Ragtime; The Civil War; Red, White and Tuna;* and *The Scarlet Pimpernel,* as well as special non-series return engagements of *Chicago* and *Annie.*

Individual tickets for the Broadway Series are sold through Ticketmaster and are priced, depending on the show, from $15 to $60. Subscriptions for the entire series range from $110 to $312.

TPAC's New Directions Series, which includes performances in a variety of disciplines from dance to theater, has featured recent performances by Manhattan Transfer, Tony Bennett, and John Davidson as Theodore Roosevelt in *Bully*. Individual ticket prices for this series, available through Ticketmaster, typically range from $10 to $37.

### Tennessee Repertory Theatre
#### 427 Chestnut St. • (615) 244-4878

Tennessee Repertory Theatre, the state's largest professional theater company, was established in 1985. Its programs, staged in TPAC's Polk Theater, range from blockbuster musicals to Pulitzer Prize-winning plays to original productions.

The Rep uses professional actors, mainly Equity actors from New York, for all its productions. It creates all costumes and set designs and conducts all rehearsals at its offices and studios at 427 Chestnut Street.

Individual tickets are priced from $7 to $35. Subscriptions are available. Contact Ticketmaster, (615) 255-ARTS, for reservations.

### Texas Troubadour Theatre
#### 2416 Music Valley Dr., No. 108
#### • (615) 885-0028

*A Closer Walk With Patsy Cline*, a musical based on the life of the country legend, began its third straight season at the Troubadour in 1999. The show, with Lisa Layne in the title role and Alan Barnes as her husband, Charlie Dick, features Layne's impressive renditions of 22 Patsy classics. Regular performances are at 7 PM every night except Tuesday and Saturday, with periodic matinees and Saturday shows. Tickets are $17, $14 for those 60 and older, and $5 for children 6 to 12. Group rates are also available.

The Troubadour is also home to the long-running "Midnite Jamboree" each Saturday at, yes, midnight and "Cowboy Church" at 10 AM each Sunday. Both are free. For more information, see the Music City chapter.

### Vanderbilt University Theater Department
#### Neely Theatre, West End at 21st Ave. S.
#### • (615) 322-2404

Vandy's Theater Department, under the long-time direction of husband-and-wife team John and Terryl Hallquist, stages four major productions a year representing a range of time periods and genres. Productions in 1999 included Edward Albee's *Three Tall Women* and Tony Kushner's *Angels in America: Millennium Approaches,*.

Neely Auditorium is a flexible black-box theater that seats about 300. Ticket prices are $7 general admission and $4 for graduate students and those in groups of 10 or more. Undergraduates are admitted free with student ID.

### Z. Alexander Looby Theater
#### 2301 MetroCenter Blvd.
#### • (615) 862-8456

Looby Theater, run by the Metro Board of Parks and Recreation, holds an average of 12 to 14 productions a year by local groups including Black Taffeta & Burlap, Tennessee Dance Theater, Nashville Shakespeare Festival (see previous entries) and various independent groups. Tickets range from free to $15.

The theater, which seats about 200, features a proscenium stage with wing space. Looby, which holds a summer theater camp for teens and children, also offers theater classes for children, teens and adults; all instruction is free. Looby is also available for public rental.

# Art Galleries and Museums

Art is practically everywhere you look in Nashville — from the architecture of the famed skyline to the public parks. The city is home to several public art collections as well as many privately owned galleries that display works from local, regional, national and international artists. Admission is free to most public museums, though a few charge a fee and others accept donations. There's no charge to visit the private galleries, which display and sell artwork on consignment and are probably hoping you'll buy something.

You'll also find changing displays at a variety of alternative exhibit spaces, including banks, restaurants, bookstores, coffeehouses, schools and, periodically, at places like the Country Music Hall of Fame, the Cumberland Science Museum and the Ryman Auditorium.

See the "Listings" section each week in the *Nashville Scene* for details.

After you've checked out some of the art in Nashville, you might want to find a quiet country scene or a spectacular view of the skyline and create your own masterpiece.

## Aaron Douglas Gallery
**Fisk University, Jackson St. and 17th Ave. N. • (615) 329-8720**

Aaron Douglas Gallery has a huge collection of African and African-American art, which it features in changing displays. Among the highlights are Cyrus Baldridge's illustrations of African people and scenes. The gallery, in the university library, is open 11 AM to 1 PM Tuesday through Friday. Admission is free, but donations are accepted.

## The Arts Company/Nashville
**215 Fifth Ave. N. • (615) 254-2040**

The personal collection of *LIFE* magazine photographer Ed Clark is one of the highlights at this eclectic gallery. Other photographers are also featured, along with "outsider art," paintings and sculpture. Hours are 10 AM to 5:30 PM Monday through Saturday, with an art matinee from 1 to 5 PM on the third Sunday of each month.

## Arts in the Airport Foundation
**1 Terminal Dr., Ste. 501 • (615) 275-1614**

The Arts in the Airport program brings a variety of changing visual arts exhibits as well as musical performances to all three levels at Metro Nashville International Airport. For information on the Airport Sun Project light sculpture, see our Getting Around chapter.

## Auld Alliance Gallery
**6019 Tenn. Hwy. 100 • (615) 352-5522**

Auld Alliance displays traditional and contemporary paintings and sculpture by artists from all over. Hours are 10 AM to 5 PM Monday through Saturday.

## Belmont University Art Department – Leu Gallery
**1900 Belmont Blvd. • (615) 460-5577**

Leu Gallery features changing individual and group exhibits by faculty members and students and some regional and national artists as well as traveling exhibits. Hours are 8 AM to 4:30 PM Monday through Friday, 9 AM to 4:30 PM Saturday and 2 to 5 PM Sunday.

## The Carl Van Vechten Gallery
**Fisk University, Jackson St. and Dr. D.B. Todd Jr. Blvd. • (615) 329-8720**

Fisk University's Carl Van Vechten Gallery is noted for its Alfred Stieglitz Collection of Modern Art, which includes works by photographer Stieglitz, Georgia O'Keeffe (who was married to Stieglitz) and others. Permanent exhibits also include paintings by Picasso, Renoir, Cezanne and Toulouse-Lautrec and other renowned artists as well as some African sculpture. Hours are 9 AM to 5 PM Tuesday through Friday and 1 to 5 PM Saturday and Sunday. Admission is free, but donations are accepted.

## Centennial Arts Center
**25th Ave. N. • (615) 862-8442**

Centennial Arts Center, run by Metro Parks and Recreation, presents nine monthly shows a year. Exhibits include photography, sculpture, paintings and mixed media. The center also offers classes in painting, drawing, sculpture and pottery here and throughout the city. Hours are 9:30 AM to 4:30 PM Monday through Friday. There are nine shows a year, changing monthly.

## The Collector's Gallery
**6602 Tenn. Hwy. 100 • (615) 356-0699**

The Collector's Gallery, founded more than 25 years ago, emphasizes well-known 20th century Southeastern artists. It is the only gallery that shows the works of Tennessean Carl Sublett. Hours are 10 AM to 4 PM Tuesday through Thursday and Saturday, and by appointment Monday and Friday. Admission is free.

## Cumberland Gallery
**4107 Hillsboro Cir. • (615) 297-0296**

Carol Stein's Cumberland Gallery, founded in 1980, focuses on paintings, photography and sculpture by established and up-and-coming state and regional artists. Hours are 10 AM to 5 PM Tuesday through Saturday and by appointment Sundays and evenings.

## Cheekwood — Nashville's Home of Art and Gardens
**Museum of Art, 1200 Forrest Park Dr.**
• **(615) 356-8000**

The Cheekwood estate, formerly owned by the Leslie Cheek family, which made a fortune with Maxwell House coffee, is a feast for lovers of architecture, gardens and art. At this writing, Cheekwood was in the midst of a $16 million restoration, with many changes taking place, among them the temporary closing of the Cheekwood Museum of Art (more on that in a moment). But even with that temporary closing, which was scheduled to end in August 1999, art abounds here.

The 55-acre estate includes a three-story neo-Georgian mansion and 11 lush garden areas filled with streams, water gardens and marble sculpture. The mansion itself has been turned into the prestigious Cheekwood Museum of Art, the renovation of which consolidates all the art galleries on the third floor, gives the first two floors more of a "home" feel, as it was when the Cheeks lived here, and adds a small cafe and gift shop. The mansion is packed with European architectural treasures; 19th- and 20th-century American artwork; and a world-famous collection of Worcester porcelain, European and American silver and Asian snuff bottles. The Stallworth galleries host a variety of traveling exhibits. The contemporary galleries, along with the seven installation galleries (converted horse stalls) are housed in the mansion's renovated carriage houses

The Monroe Carell Woodland Sculpture Trail is a mile-long path featuring 15 interactive pieces by modern sculptors. New gardens have also been added, one of them designed by landscape architect Michael Van Valkenburgh, who has overseen the site renovation.

Cheekwood's hours are 9 AM to 5 PM Monday through Saturday, 11 AM to 5 PM Sunday. From April 15 through September 1, Cheekwood stays open until 8 PM Monday through Thursday. It's closed Thanksgiving, Christmas Day, New Year's Day and the third Saturday in April. Admission is $8 for adults, $7 for seniors and college students with ID, $5 for folks ages 6 through 17 and free for kids 5 and younger.

For more information about Cheekwood, see our Attractions chapter.

## Finer Things
**1898 Nolensville Rd. • (615) 244-3003**

Finer Things, which specializes in one-of-a-kind furniture, has a contemporary gallery of two- and three-dimensional works, a "wearable art" gallery and an outdoor sculpture park. Hours are 10 AM to 6 PM Tuesday through Saturday

## Hartzler-Towner Multicultural Museum
**Scarritt-Bennett Center,**
**1008 19th Ave. S. • (615) 340-7481**

Arts and crafts exhibits at this educational museum aimed at promoting tolerance and diversity include Chinese porcelain and textiles, Indian temple hangings, African musical instruments and baskets, Mexican ceramics and 700 dolls from all around the world. The museum also displays three temporary exhibits yearly. Hours are 9 AM to 7 PM Monday through Friday, 9 AM to 5 PM Saturday and noon to 4 PM Sunday.

## In the Gallery
**624-A Jefferson St. • (615) 255-0705**

In the Gallery, across from Bicentennial Mall, specializes in changing exhibits and special collections of African, African-American and other art. Hours are noon to 5 PM Tuesday through Saturday or by appointment.

## INSIDERS' TIP

To keep track of concerts, theater, exhibits and other arts events in Nashville, be sure to pick up a copy of the *Nashville Scene* each week. The *Scene*, available free at locations all over town, comes out Wednesday afternoon; listings cover an eight-day period, from Thursday to Thursday.

## Local Color Gallery
**1912 Broadway • (615) 321-3141**

Local Color, one of Nashville's popular galleries since 1990, features works from more than 60 local artists in a variety of media and styles. Hours are 10 AM to 5 PM Tuesday through Saturday.

## Margaret Cuninggim Women's Center
**Vanderbilt Univ., Franklin Bldg.,
316 West Side Row • (615) 322-4843**

The Cuninggim gallery is devoted to promoting area women in art. In addition to four exhibits a year, the center offers programs, workshops and seminars to promote equality in art, the center also has an excellent resource library. Hours are 8:30 AM to 5 PM Monday through Friday

## Midtown Gallery
**1912 Broadway • (615) 322-9966**

Midtown Gallery represents more than 60 regional, national and international artists. While the emphasis is on contemporary oil, acrylic and watercolor painting, you'll also find pastels, mixed media, photography and wood, metal and stone sculpture. Exhibits change every six weeks. Hours are 10 AM to 5 PM Tuesday through Saturday.

## Parthenon Museum
**Centennial Park, West End Ave.
• (615) 862-8431**

A 42-foot-high sculpture of the Greek goddess Athena guards the interior of the Parthenon, which houses the city of Nashville's permanent art collection. The full-size replica of Athena's temple is also host to a variety of changing exhibits throughout the year. Hours are 9 AM to 4:30 PM Tuesday through Saturday. From April through September, the museum is also open from 12:30 to 4:30 PM Sunday. Admission is $2.50 for adults, $1.25 for seniors and students and free for children 4 and younger. See our Attractions chapter for more information on the Parthenon Museum.

## Sarratt Gallery
**Sarratt Student Center, Vanderbilt Univ.,
24th Ave. S. near Vanderbilt Pl.
• (615) 322-2471**

Sarratt Gallery, in the main lobby of the Sarratt Student Center, has about 10 major exhibits and a student show each year featuring national and regional contemporary artists. The gallery is open, subject to the school calendar, from 9 AM to 9 PM Monday through Saturday and 11 AM to 9 PM Sunday. During the summer and holiday and semester breaks, it closes at 4:30 PM weekdays and is closed weekends. Admission is free.

## Shelton Gallery
**4239 Harding Rd. • (615) 298-9935**

This gallery in Stanford Square features changing exhibits of African and Haitian works as well as American and Southern folk art. Hours are 10 AM to 6 PM Monday through Saturday.

## Stanford Fine Art
**102 Woodmont Blvd., Ste. LL120
• (615) 383-1664**

Stanford Fine Art displays changing exhibits of American and European painting from the 19th and early 20th centuries. Hours are 9 AM to 6 PM or by appointment.

## Tennessee Art League Gallery
**3011 Poston Ave. • (615) 298-4072**

This gallery displays two- and three-dimensional works by local member artists. Exhibits change monthly, with receptions generally open to the public. The Tennessee Art League also produces the Central South exhibition, one of the largest in the country, every June. Hours are noon to 4 PM Tuesday through Sunday.

## Tennessee Arts Commission Gallery
**401 Charlotte Ave.• (615) 741-1701**

The Tennessee Arts Commission Gallery displays only work by Tennessee residents, with six to eight exhibits a year. A professional panel juries the competition, which takes place every two years. The commission offers annual fellowships in crafts, photography and visual arts to the state's top artists. Hours are 8 AM to 4:30 PM Monday through Friday.

## Tennessee State Museum
**505 Deaderick St. • (615) 741-2692**

This museum, which is dedicated to exhibits related to various aspects of Tennessee history, sometimes features art displays that are complementary to its mission. For example, during summer and fall 1997, it included the widely acclaimed *Visions of My People: African-American Art in Tennessee*. Tennessee State Museum is open 10 AM to 5 PM Tuesday through Thursday and Saturday, 10 AM to 9 PM Friday and 1 to 5 PM Sunday. Admission is free, but donations are accepted. (Also see the Attractions chapter.)

## Hiram Van Gordon Memorial Gallery
**Tennessee State Univ., 3500 John Merritt Blvd. • (615) 963-7509**

TSU's Hiram Van Gordon Memorial Gallery features permanent, changing and traveling exhibits of both individual artists and groups. Hours are 9 AM to noon and 1 to 3 PM Monday through Friday; special weekend tours are available by appointment.

## The Upper Room Chapel & Museum
**1908 Grand Ave. • (615) 340-7207**

The Upper Room's collection of religious art and artifacts includes an Old Masters gallery featuring paintings from 1300 to 1900, including copies of Raphael paintings. Rare books and antique English porcelains are also on display. Seasonal events include a collection of 100 Nativity scenes in November and December and a Lenten Easter display of 75 Ukrainian eggs. The focal point of the chapel is a nearly life-size woodcarving of da Vinci's painting *The Last Supper*. Hours are 8 AM to 4:30 PM Monday through Friday. A $2 contribution is recommended.

## Vanderbilt University Fine Arts Gallery
**23rd and West End aves.**
**• (615) 343-1704, (615) 322-0605 (current exhibit information)**

Vandy's art gallery features a range of Eastern and Western art, from ancient through contemporary. The Samuel H. Kress collection of Renaissance paintings is a highlight. Hours, subject to the school calendar, are noon to 4 PM Monday through Friday and 1 to 5 PM Saturday and Sunday. It is closed Sunday and Monday during the summer break.

Photo: Nashville CVB/Donnie Beauchamp

The historic Ryman Auditorium hosts concerts and theatrical productions with a musical theme.

## Zeitgeist Gallery
**1819 21st Ave. S. • (615) 256-4805**

Zeitgeist, which moved from Cummins Station to its current Hillsboro Village location in 1999, exhibits works by contemporary regional mixed-media artists, emphasizing conceptual and design-oriented works in formats such as three-dimensional, furniture and lighting. Hours are 10 AM to 5 PM Tuesday through Friday, noon to 3 PM Saturday and by appointment.

# General Instruction and Awareness

## ArtSynergy
**(615) 256-9001**

Described by its charter members as an "arts incubator," ArtSynergy is a coalition formed by three performing arts organizations: Tennessee Dance Theatre, Nashville Shakespeare Festival and Nashville Chamber Orchestra. Paul Gambill, music director of the orchestra, founded the group; Ellen Zisholtz is executive director.

ArtSynergy, launched with the aid of a three-year, $215,000 "collaboration grant" from the Frist Foundation, provides the proverbial strength in numbers for smaller local arts groups. As a coalition, these diverse groups can qualify for larger grants from local, state and federal sources, therefore growing artistically as well as financially.

## The Leonard Bernstein Center for Education Through the Arts
**3017 Poston Ave. • (615) 292-9444**

The Bernstein Center, founded in 1992, is a national education center with programs in New York; Boston; Dallas; Miami; Atlanta; Portland, Oregon; and Indianapolis, as well as its home base of Nashville. The center honors the famed conductor's legacy and commitment to arts and education through a comprehensive school design it has developed that uses the arts to improve student achievement and create a love of learning.

## Metro Parks and Recreation Arts Programs
**Centennial Park Office, 511 Oman St.**
**• (615) 862-8424**

Metro Parks and Recreation provides a variety of activities in music, dance, visual arts, crafts and theater for all ages from children through seniors. Offerings include instruction; concerts, festivals and other performances (such as Jazz on the Porch on September Sunday evenings at Two Rivers Mansion, for example, and Shakespeare in the Park); and resources and services. Activities take place at various venues, including the Centennial Arts Center Courtyard, the Parthenon, the Centennial Park Bandshell, Z. Alexander Looby Theater and Shelby Park.

## Metro Nashville Arts Commission
**Cummins Station, 209 10th Ave. S.,**
**Ste. 416 • (615) 862-6720**
**• www.nashville.net/~metroart/**

The Metro Nashville Arts Commission, on the fourth floor of Cummins Station, works hard to connect various arts organizations with the community, providing leadership and resources to all forms of the arts. The commission assembles an annual Arts Directory and other information to help make the arts more accessible to all. The commission's web site contains the *Artist Registry*, an illustrated catalog of Nashville-area artists; the *Arts Directory*, a guide to Nashville-area arts organization; the commission's mission statement; a billboard with announcements, links to other arts-related sites; and a grant application for not-for-profit arts organizations.

## Nashville Institute for the Arts
**Cummins Station, 209 10th Ave. S.,**
**Ste. 504 • (615) 244-6930**

The Nashville Institute for the Arts, on the fifth floor of Cummins Station, works with various local arts groups to develop cultural literacy, stimulate learning and teach students how to perceive and understand the arts. It does this through classes, concerts, exhibits and other programs.

As of early 1999, the Metropolitan Board of Parks and Recreation operated 84 parks totaling over 9,300 acres — more parkland per capita than any other major city in the country.

# Parks

Nashville is known worldwide as Music City U.S.A., and no doubt you've heard the nicknames Athens of the South, Twangtown and Third Coast. But did you know Nashville is also called the City of Parks? That's because of the abundance of parks and greenways here. You never have to travel far in Nashville to find green spaces.

As of early 1999, the Metropolitan Board of Parks and Recreation operated 84 parks totaling over 9,300 acres — more parkland per capita than any other major city in the country. The 2,058-acre Percy Warner Park is the largest; it's about three times larger than New York City's Central Park. The smallest is the nearly quarter-acre Bass Park, a playground in east Nashville. Metro Parks maintains 20 community centers, more than 60 ball fields, seven golf courses, more than 50 picnic shelters, more than 50 playgrounds and several indoor and outdoor swimming pools. Add to that the attractions at the numerous state parks and natural areas in and around Nashville, and you can see that Nashvillians rarely have an excuse for staying indoors. Not that we do stay in. Nashvillians love their parks, and can be found enjoying the great outdoors seven days a week year round.

Nashville-area parks offer a variety of opportunities for recreation and relaxation. Whether you're looking for a quiet spot to commune with nature, a curvy paved in-line-skating route, a lake for water-skiing or fishing, a wide-open field for flying a kite or playing Frisbee, a cozy picnicking spot, or trails for hiking and biking, there is a place for you. (Check out the Recreation chapter for a more in-depth look at recreation options at parks.) Nashville's parks also offer a variety of cultural experiences — from drama and symphony performances to rock concerts to art fairs. It's a truly diverse park system, offering something for everyone.

In the late 1800s, Nashville had several small city parks and privately owned "trolley parks" — amusement parks along the trolley lines — but there wasn't a city-owned and -managed public park system until after the turn of the century. Nashville's park system was founded in 1901, with no parks, personnel or funds. Despite the lack of resources, the board managed to open the city's first park that year. Many think Centennial Park was Nashville's first park, but the board didn't acquire that property until 1902. Nashville's first park public park was actually the 8.2-acre Watkins Park, at Jo Johnston Avenue and 17th Avenue N. Watkins Park was given to the city by brick manufacturer and construction contractor Samuel Watkins in 1870. The property had served as an unofficial park known as Watkins Grove in the 1850s only to be ravaged in the early 1860s by the Civil War. Around the turn of the century, area residents were using the then-treeless and barren lot as a pasture and unofficial dump. With donated materials and some city funds, the park board stepped in and built an entrance and walkways, planted flowers, installed water and lighting systems and placed benches on the property. In 1906 the Centennial Club took over and added the city's first playground, including swings, a skating area and a merry-go-round. It was such a success that in 1909 the board opened children's playgrounds on vacant lots throughout Nashville. Watkins Park, by the way, is still there. Today it has a community center, tennis courts, a basketball court and picnic shelter.

In recent years there has been an effort to establish greenways in Nashville. Metro Parks' Greenways Commission describes greenways as "corridors of protected open space that are managed for conservation and/or recreation, often including urban bike paths, hiking trails, scenic roads, river floodplains, waterways, old railroad tracks and wildlife linkages." The commission is involved in the development of numerous projects throughout the county, a few of which are partially complete. A long-term plan calls for a regional greenway that will connect Murfreesboro to Clarksville.

In this chapter, we've chosen to list only a portion of Nashville's many parks and green spaces — just enough to get you in the mood for getting out and about. There isn't enough space to describe every location, so we have listed some of the most popular ones. Besides, we wouldn't want to spoil the fun of making your own discoveries!

To ensure your park excursions are safe and enjoyable, take note of the rules and hours of operation. Many parks are open from sunrise to sunset, and unless otherwise noted, you can assume those are the operating hours. Be aware that even in a friendly city like Nashville, unless there is a park event taking place, it isn't a good idea to be in most parks after dark. Similarly, cars parked in an area where the activities nearby — fishing, golfing, etc. — would keep their owners absent for a prolonged time may be especially vulnerable.

Most parks offer wheelchair-accessible attractions and barrier-free access. Some are more accessible than others, so if accessibility is a concern, it's a good idea to contact Metro Parks, Tennessee State Parks or the individual park for more information. Metro Parks' Special Recreation Program serves children and adults with disabilities. The programs are held in community centers, schools and various spots around town.

Admission is free at area parks, but special activities or programs might require a fee.

You might want to pick up a copy of Metro Parks' great map that lists and describes Nash-ville parks. You can reach the Metro Parks at (615) 862-8400. For information on Tennessee's state parks and natural areas, call (615) 532-0001 or, toll-free, (888) TN PARKS.

Are you ready for a day at the park? Grab your sunglasses, some sunscreen, a bottle of water and your favorite fun accessories and get going!

# State Parks and Natural Areas

## Bicentennial Capitol Mall State Park
**James Robertson Pkwy. (Jefferson St. between Eighth and Sixth aves.)**
• **(615) 741-5280**

Don't let the word "mall" throw you off: This is not a shopping mall, but rather a mall similar to the National Mall in Washington, D.C. This 19-acre downtown attraction, Tennessee's 51st state park, is part park and part outdoor history lesson. It opened in 1996 on the north side of the Tennessee State Capitol to commemorate the state's 200th birthday celebration and preserve the last unobstructed view of the capitol. The park is at the site of the French Lick, a salt lick and sulfur spring that drew wildlife, Indians, trappers and, eventually, settlers. French-Canadian traders and hunters such as Jean de Charleville and Jacques-Timothe De Montbrun set up trading posts here beginning in the late 1600s. The spring still flows underground. (See our History chapter for more information.)

---

**INSIDERS' TIP**

For about $1,590, you can sponsor a historical marker and post to erect at a historically significant site in Tennessee. The Tennessee Historical Commission can purchase only a few of the signs each year, so most of the new markers must be paid for by sponsors. If you or your group are interested in sponsoring a new marker, contact the Tennessee Historical Commission, 2941 Lebanon Road, Nashville, (615) 532-1550.

For an overview of the entire mall, head to the State Capitol grounds (the capitol is at Charlotte Avenue between Sixth and Seventh avenues). Across James Robertson Parkway, in the mall's concrete plaza entrance, a 200-foot granite map will take you on a walking trip through Tennessee. The map, believed to be the largest granite map in the world, highlights major roads, rivers and other details of the state's 95 counties. At night, the county seats light up. A variety of other granite maps detail topics such as the state's geography, musical diversity and topography. Straight ahead of the Tennessee map, just past the railroad trestle, is the Rivers of Tennessee Fountains, with 31 fountains of varying heights, each representing one of the state's major rivers. The Walk of Counties on the east side represents the topographical features and diverse vegetation of East, Middle and West Tennessee. This is also where time capsules from the 95 counties are buried; they will be opened during Tennessee's tercentennial celebration in 2096. The Walk of Counties starts out in Shelby County and travels to West, Middle then East Tennessee.

At the northern end near Jefferson Street is the focal point of the mall: the Court of Three Stars, a red, white and blue granite map representing the three divisions of the state. For an excellent view of the capitol, head here. The Pathway of History starting at the west side of the mall features marble columns that divide state history into 10-year increments.

A World War II memorial, paid for by veterans of the war, takes the shape of an 18,000-pound granite globe supported by a constant stream of water; visitors can rotate the globe to view areas of the world as it was from 1939 to 1945 and see Tennessee's ties to the war's major battlefields. The Centennial Memorial features granite carvings of the buildings used in the state's 1897 centennial celebration, which was held one year late. Other features of the mall include the McNairy Spring Fountains — atop the sulfur spring that created the French Lick. Placards in the mall recount history of the French Lick and of Sulphur Dell, the historic ballpark where professional baseball was played from 1885 to 1963. The mall also has a visitors center and 2,000-seat amphitheater. Guided group tours are available.

Restrooms are near Seventh Avenue, and a gift shop is near Sixth, at opposite ends of the railroad trestle. Mall-designated parking is available along Sixth and Seventh avenues. On weekends, holidays and Monday through Friday after 4:30 PM, parking is available at state employee parking areas. Handicapped parking is at the corner of Sixth and Harrison. Buses and RVs can park at Eighth and Jefferson. The mall hours are 6 AM to midnight, but you can drive through the area at any time; the visitors center is open 8 AM to 7 PM daily. The park is patrolled 24 hours a day.

## Bledsoe Creek State Park
**400 Zieglers Fort Rd., Gallatin**
**• (615) 452-3706**

An environmental education area, this 164-acre park is 6 miles east of Gallatin off Tenn. Highway 25, on the Bledsoe Creek embayment of Old Hickory Lake in Sumner County. More than 200,000 people visit every year, lured by the park's 114 campsites (102 with water and electricity), two boat-launching ramps, waterskiing, five hiking trails (the Mayo Wix is a paved, wheelchair-accessible trail), a regulation-size volleyball court, three playgrounds, fishing, picnic areas and wildlife viewing opportunities. Deer, wild turkey, birds and even snakes are protected in this sanctuary.

To make your trip to the park educational as well as recreational, check out some of the nearby historic sites. Bledsoe Creek State Park, named for long hunter and Revolutionary War veteran Isaac Bledsoe, who came to the area in the 1770s, is in an area rich in history. The settlement of Cairo in Sumner County occupied an area near here in the 1780s. Also nearby are the historic sites of Wynnewood, Cragfont, Rock Castle and Bledsoe's Fort. The latter, on Tenn. Highway 25, 5 miles east of Gallatin, was built by Bledsoe in 1783 to protect settlers from Indian attacks. Isaac and brother Anthony were killed not far from there by Indians and are buried at the Bledsoe Monument. Cragfont is the rock house that sits on a bluff about 3.5 miles north of the park entrance. It was the home of Gen. James Winchester, veteran of the American Revolution and the War of 1812.

The park is open 8 AM to 7 PM in the summer and until 5 PM in the winter. At closing time, the main gate is shut and locked, but registered campers receive the combination for the gate.

## Cedars of Lebanon State Park
**328 Cedar Forest Rd., Lebanon**
**• (615) 443-2769**

This park, the largest red cedar forest in the United States, is about 31 miles east of Nashville in Wilson County, 6 miles south of Interstate 40 on U.S. Highway 231. Only 950 of the total 9,000 acres are used for recreation. The remaining acreage is operated as a natural area by the Parks Division and as a state forest by the Forestry Division.

Approximately 600,000 people visit this popular state park every year. It is named for the cedar forests in the biblical lands of Lebanon. The cedar trees here, however, are actually eastern juniper, a coniferous cousin of the fragrant-wooded cedar. By 1900, the junipers had been cut down, used for making pencils, cross-ties and cedar oil. In the 1930s the area was replanted by the Civilian Conservation Corps.

Numerous wildflowers and other native plants can be found in the open limestone glades. Accommodations include 117 campsites, nine modern two-bedroom cabins (each sleeps six people), one small two-person cabin and an 80-person–capacity group lodge with separate sleeping facilities. Among the other attractions are 125 picnic tables, 11 picnic pavilions, an "Olympic-plus-size" swimming pool, 8 miles of hiking trails through the cedar forests and glades, 12 miles of horseback-riding trails (the park doesn't rent horses, though), fully equipped playgrounds, a volleyball court, horseshoe pits, a lighted softball field, archery range and disc golf.

The Dixon Merritt Nature Center is a popular spot, offering exhibits plus a recreation director and a naturalist who conduct daily programs during the summer. Visitors can participate in such activities as guided tours, arts and crafts, and hayrides during the warm-weather months. The cabins, lodge, campground and assembly hall are available by reservation year round. If you're interested in reserving the group lodge, make your plans well in advance.

The park is open 8 AM to 10 PM in summer, until 8 PM in winter.

## Harpeth Scenic River and Narrows of the Harpeth State Historic Area
**Off U.S. Hwy. 70 at Cedar Hill Rd.,**
**Kingston Springs • (615) 797-9052**

This enjoyable and well-attended park, considered a satellite area of Montgomery Bell State Resort Park about 11 miles west, offers recreation on the river, hiking and a bit of education too. The state acquired the property in July 1979, and in winter 1996-97, another 30 acres, for a total of 133 acres.

The Harpeth Scenic River Complex offers canoe-access points at the Tenn. Highway 100 bridge just past the Warner Parks, at the 1862 Newsoms Mill ruins and at Kingston Springs. The Narrows of the Harpeth provides upstream and downstream access. One nice thing about canoeing the Harpeth is that the Bell's Bend 5-mile loop allows you to put in and take out at the same area. Be sure to see the Recreation chapter for more information on canoeing the Harpeth — it's a fun (and easy) excursion you don't want to miss!

While you're at the Narrows site, be sure to check out the historic 100-yard tunnel, hand-cut through solid rock; it is an industrial landmark listed on the National Register of Historic Places. Officials say it is the oldest existing man-made tunnel in the nation. Montgomery Bell, an early iron industrialist, built the tunnel to supply water power to his iron forge on the river. Bell is buried on a hillside across the river. The wooden walkway leading from the parking area will take you to the front of the tunnel. If hiking is on your itinerary, the trails begin about 150 yards from the parking lot. The trail to the top of the bluff over the tunnel (it's steep, but short — the three trails combined total only about 1.5 miles) offers a fantastic view of the Harpeth River valley. Take your camera — it's a nice spot for a photo. If you have a fear of heights, stay close to the trail — some of the drop-offs can be a little scary.

A historical marker at Scott Cemetery on Cedar Hill Road tells about Mound Bottom, an ancient Indian ceremonial site along the river. Indians of the Mississippian period were be-

Photo: Cindy Stooksbury Guier

Narrows of the Harpeth State Historic Area features
the oldest man-made tunnel in the nation.

lieved to have lived here around 800 years ago. Archaeologists say the town was an important political and ceremonial center. If you're interested in visiting Mound Bottom, a park ranger can take you, but be sure to call the park office ahead of time to schedule the trip.

This park doesn't have restroom facilities.

### Long Hunter State Park
**2910 Hobson Pk., off I-40 and I-24 on S.R. 171, Hermitage • (615) 885-2422**

Love water? Have a boat? Want to meet someone with a boat? Like to swim? How about fishing? Then head to Long Hunter State Park, a popular spot for just about any water activity you can think of. If you prefer to stay dry, there are plenty of activities on terra firma too, such as hiking (28 miles of trails), birdwatching, picnicking and backcountry camping. The park also offers boat rentals, playgrounds, a gift shop and more.

The 2,600-acre park is on the east shore of the U.S. Army Corps of Engineers' Percy Priest Reservoir. Spanning more than 14,000 acres, Percy Priest is one of the largest lakes

in the state. The 110-acre, landlocked Couchville Lake is part of Priest Reservoir and is surrounded by a 2-mile paved trail. That barrier-free area also has a fishing pier. Stop by the visitors center for more information on the park or to check in if you plan to camp. If you want to camp, come prepared. You'll hike 6 miles and spend the night at a backcountry (no facilities of any kind) camping area. Long Hunter State Park was named for the hunters and explorers of the 1700s who stayed in the area for months or years at a time. Among them were Uriah Stone, for whom nearby Stones River is named. (See our History chapter for related information.)

The park is open daily 7 AM to sunset.

### Montgomery Bell State Resort Park
**U.S. Hwy. 70, Burns • (615) 797-9052**

This 3,850-acre park is named for the state's first capitalist and industrialist, Montgomery Bell, who operated an iron forge on the Harpeth River. Bell came to Tennessee from Pennsylvania in the early 1800s and for a few years operated the Cumberland Iron Works, which had been established by James

Robertson, a founder of Nashville. Bell soon purchased the business and turned the area into an industrial capital. He built the 290-foot tunnel at Narrows of the Harpeth (see previous related entry) to supply water for the business. The tunnel is now on the National Register of Historic Places and is said to be the oldest remaining man-made tunnel. Other remains of Bell's iron empire include Laurel Furnace, built in 1810, and ore pits.

Another interesting historical note about the park: it was the birthplace of the Cumberland Presbyterian Church, first organized in 1810. Every Sunday during June, July and August, services are held at the park's replica of the Rev. Samuel McAdow's chapel. Everyone is welcome. The church is a popular site for weddings, which are held Monday through Saturday. Montgomery Bell's accommodations and recreational opportunities make it a popular choice for family reunions, church groups and company outings. There are 118 tree-covered campsites, 93 of which have water and electrical hookups. All sites have a picnic table and grill. A 120-person–capacity group camp — open May through September — contains individual cottages, a dining hall, bathhouses and a fishing dock.

The Montgomery Bell Inn & Conference Center offers 120 rooms plus five suites, and includes a restaurant that serves three meals a day. Other accommodations include eight two-bedroom, fully equipped cabins that are available year round. During the summer, the cabins are available on a weekly basis Monday through Saturday; a minimum two-night reservation is required during other seasons. Call the listed number for reservations. (See our Campgrounds chapter for details.)

In addition to its great accommodations, Montgomery Bell Park boasts one of the few sandy beaches in Middle Tennessee. The park's beach is on Acorn Lake. The boat dock next to the beach rents rowboats and paddleboats. Lifeguards and a two-story bathhouse with vending station and recreation pavilion make for a safe and comfortable day at the beach. Hikers will find about 20 miles of trails plus an 11.7-mile overnight trail with three primitive overnight shelters. The park also offers a challenging 18-hole golf course, lighted tennis court, playground, ball field, archery range, basketball courts, croquet courts, volleyball courts, shuffleboard, 125 picnic tables and three picnic pavilions. During the summer, a naturalist and a recreation coordinator conduct tours, arts and crafts programs, canoe floats and other activities.

Hours are 8 AM to 10 PM. The park is north of I-40 on U.S. 70, 7 miles east of Dickson.

## Radnor Lake State Natural Area
### 1160 Otter Creek Rd.
### • (615) 373-3467

In photographer John Netherton's book *Radnor Lake: Nashville's Walden* (Rutledge Hill Press, 1984), Nashville author John Egerton writes, "Words will never suffice to describe it. Radnor must be experienced through the senses. It must be seen, smelled, heard."

It's true. Radnor Lake, an 1,125-acre natural area just 6 miles south of downtown Nashville, must be experienced — in every season. But beware — Radnor Lake can become addictive.

The lake is just a half-mile east of Granny White Pike and 1.5 miles west of Franklin Pike (U.S. Highway 31). Otter Creek Road winds its way around the 85-acre lake, offering wonderful views of the lake and surrounding hills. On weekends, you'll find people of all ages and all walks of life taking in the natural beauty along the route. Walkers, joggers, bird watchers, bicyclists, babies in strollers, photographers and pets (on leashes) share the road, which is closed to motor vehicles from 7 AM to sunset. Hours of operation are 7 AM to sunset.

Radnor is a state natural area and therefore not a recreation-oriented park. Primary activities are hiking, nature observation, photography and research. Some activities, such as jogging on the wooded trails, boating, swimming and picnicking, are not permitted. All plants, animals, rocks, minerals and artifacts are protected by state law — so observe and enjoy, but don't disturb!

Many of the lake's 1 million annual visitors come for the hiking trails. Radnor offers six connecting trails, ranging in length from a quarter-mile to 1.5 miles. The Spillway Trail and Lake Trail are the easiest. Ganier Ridge Trail and South Cove Trail are the most strenuous. The trails are especially nice and fragrant to walk in January, after they have been paved

Photo: Cindy Stooksbury Guier

Radnor Lake is one of Nashville's most scenic parks.

with the mulch of hundreds of recycled Christmas trees. Along the trails, don't be surprised if you come upon one or more deer just feet away from you. This nature preserve is also home to coyotes and bobcats, although we've never seen them here. Before or after your hike or walk, be sure to spend at least a few relaxing moments at the lake near the nature center, just off the Spillway Trail. You can get up-close looks at one or more of the 26 species of ducks and Canada geese as well as frogs and turtles — including large snappers. Radnor is also home to some 240 bird species.

Radnor naturalists conduct a variety of environmental activities such as birds of prey programs, wildflower hikes, canoe floats and nighttime owl prowls. You can make reservations for these programs by phone (call the listed number) or by stopping in at the visitors center in the west parking lot.

Many are surprised to learn that Radnor Lake is man-made. It was created in 1914 by the Louisville and Nashville Railroad Company to provide water for steam engines and livestock at the Radnor Railroad Yards. L&N officials and their guests also used the site as a private hunting and fishing ground. At the re-

quest of the Tennessee Ornithological Society, L&N in 1923 declared Radnor a wildlife sanctuary and banned all hunting. In 1962, when the area was purchased by a construction firm that had plans for a housing development, Nashvillians protested and were able to preserve the area. With the financial support of the federal government and thousands of Nashvillians, the Tennessee Department of Conservation purchased the land in 1973, and it became the state's first natural area.

# Metro Parks and Greenways

### Bellevue Greenway
### Morton Mill Rd. • (615) 862-8400
This greenway is along the Harpeth River on Morton Mill Road near Old Harding Pike. Along the boardwalk following Morton Mill Road, you'll find an overlook with benches.

### Cedar Hill Park
### 860 Old Hickory Blvd.
### • (615) 865-1853
This 225-acre, hilly park is near

Goodlettsville on Dickerson Road at Old Hickory Boulevard. With a four-diamond baseball and softball complex, it's a top pick for the area's teams; the complex is used by leagues five days a week and is the site of tournaments on weekends. The director of the Amateur Softball Association once called the complex the finest softball facility in the nation.

Cedar Hill Park was originally known as Old Center Park, taking its name from a nearby school. Metro purchased the property on 1964 and in 1965 it was renamed Cedar Hill Park because it was covered with cedar trees. It reopened to the public in 1977 and that year hosted the National Men's Fast-Pitch Softball Tournament.

In addition to its baseball and softball diamonds, Cedar Hill Park has seven tennis courts, a playground, walking and jogging track, seven picnic shelters that stay very busy and restrooms. Many visitors come here just to walk the path around Cedar Hill Lake. The lake is also the site for regional fishing rodeos for the disabled.

The park is open from sunrise to 11 PM.

## Centennial Park
### 2500 West End Ave. • (615) 862-8400

Home of Nashville's famous replica of the Greek Parthenon, Centennial Park sits on 132.3 acres at West End Avenue and 25th Avenue N., 2 miles west of downtown. The land was once a farm, purchased in 1783 by John Cockrill, brother-in-law of Nashville founder James Robertson. After the Civil War, the land served as the state fairgrounds, and from 1884 to 1895 it was West Side Park racetrack. In 1897 it was the site of the Tennessee Centennial Exposition, which celebrated (one year late) Tennessee's 100th anniversary of statehood. Construction on the exposition buildings began in October 1895, when the cornerstone for a Parthenon replica was laid. Several elaborate, temporary white stucco buildings were constructed for use during the event, which attracted more than 1.7 million people from around the world.

When the celebration was over, the buildings were removed, but Nashvillians chose to keep the magnificent Parthenon (see our History and Attractions chapters), the only full-size replica of the Athenian structure. The Parthenon and Centennial grounds were preserved as a public park. The city's new park system, which was begun in 1901, built a pool, driveways and walkways, stocked the lake with fish and planted flowers and shrubs. Centennial Park opened to the public in 1903 as Nashville's second city park. The Parthenon was rebuilt of concrete from 1921 to 1931, and the structure received renovations in 1962. A long-term renovation began in the 1980s. A highlight of the Parthenon is the 42-foot *Athena Parthenos*, the largest piece of indoor sculpture in the Western world.

Various other changes and additions have been made to the park over the years. Today, Centennial Park offers playgrounds, paddleboating on Lake Watauga (a large pond), picnic facilities, swings, a band shell, a sand volleyball court and plenty of grassy areas, just perfect for spreading out a blanket. Various monuments around the park are reminders of Nashville's history. Monuments of James Robertson and leaders of the Centennial Exposition were erected in 1903. The steam locomotive was put in place in 1953, and the F-86 jet aircraft landed in Centennial in 1961. Despite the park's many attractions, one of the most popular activities for kids (and grownups) seems to be observing and feeding the ducks and pigeons at the pond.

The park is the site of various arts and crafts exhibits, concerts and other popular events that draw thousands every year. During the weekdays, it's a popular escape from the office for many workers, who walk over or drive and park their cars along the lake to enjoy a quick lunch. The Art Center in the northernmost corner of the park features works by local artists and offers arts classes.

Across 25th Avenue, the Centennial Sportsplex has an indoor ice rink, tennis courts and an Olympic-size pool.

## INSIDERS' TIP

**Centennial Park's Watauga Lake is named for the East Tennessee community from which Nashville's first settlers came.**

## Fannie Mae Dees Park
**2400 Blakemore Ave. • (615) 862-8400**

Fannie Mae Dees Park is known by many as Dragon Park, because of the mosaic sea-serpent centerpiece sculpture that winds its way through the playground area. A grant from the Tennessee Arts Commission brought artist Pedro Silva from New York to Nashville to design the serpent. The work itself was funded by grants from Vanderbilt University and local businesses. Individual artists created the graphics in the mosaic design of the serpent's coils. Nashville children were involved in the work, piecing the tiles together at various community centers and then bringing them to the park. The piece was dedicated April 25, 1981.

If you've never visited this park, it's worth stopping by just to marvel at the sea serpent. Look closely — you'll see many interesting and fanciful designs including sailboats, scuba divers, mermaids and flowers. A portrait of local civic leader Fannie Mae Dees, the park's namesake, can be found on the loop near the serpent's tail. The sculpture is more than art, however; its tail serves as a bench — a great spot to relax while the kids enjoy the playground. (See Kidstuff for related details.)

In addition to playground equipment, the 7.6-acre park features three tennis courts and four picnic shelters. The park is on Blakemore Avenue at 24th Avenue S., a couple blocks from Hillsboro Village.

## Elmington Park
**3531 West End Ave. • (615) 862-8400**

This park, on 13.34 acres at West End and Bowling avenues, was developed by the Works Progress Administration during the 1930s. The property the park encompasses was once part of Edwin Warner's "Elmington Estate." The park board purchased the property in 1927 with assistance from area citizens.

Today, Elmington is a multipurpose park, offering two tennis courts, a baseball diamond,

various playground pieces and picnic tables. A community group helped raise funds for a new playground and trees for the property. The grassy front field is the site of a nearby college's cricket games as well as an annual Swing for Sight hole-in-one golf benefit, dog shows and various community events. It is also used by students of West End High School, which sits at the top of the hill in back of the park. (See Kidstuff for more information.)

## Hadley Park
**1037 28th Ave. N. • (615) 862-8400**

The band shell and picnic shelters are popular attractions at this 34-acre park, at 28th Avenue N. and Centennial (John Merritt) Boulevard. The park also has a community center, softball and baseball diamonds, 12 lighted tennis courts, playground and restrooms.

The park board purchased the property in 1912 at the request of Fisk University's president and leaders of the north Nashville community. That year, Nashville Mayor Hilary Howse proclaimed Hadley Park to be the first public park for black citizens that had been established by any government.

A park board member named the park Hadley Park, but did not specify which Hadley he had in mind. The city's black newspaper assumed it to be John L. Hadley, whose family had a house on the property. Around the time the park was purchased, the family's plantation became the site of Tennessee State University. Some say the park might have been named for Dr. W.A. Hadley, a pioneering black physician who worked with the park board on the 1897 Centennial Exposition.

The entrance gates were built in the late 1930s by the Works Progress Administration. On each side of the main entrance, next to the library, the stone columns contain a listing of the 11 African-American soldiers from Davidson County who were killed during World War I.

---

**INSIDERS' TIP**

If you're looking for a good downtown meeting spot where you can hook up with your friends before a trip to The District, "radio tower" facing Broadway at the Gaylord Entertainment Center (it used to be called the Nashville Arena) is a can't-miss location.

## Hamilton Creek Park
**2901 Bell Rd. • (615) 862-8400**

Biking and boating are popular activities at Hamilton Creek Park, a 790-acre park on Bell Road along the east side of J. Percy Priest Lake. The U.S. Army Corps of Engineers leases the property to Metro Parks. In 1975 the parks board participated in the construction of a sailboat marina at the Hamilton Creek embayment; it opened in 1980, and today it stays busy. Boat slips and boats are available for rent. The park also has a boat-launching ramp, concessions stands, restrooms, and hiking and nature trails.

The BMX track is the site of national races that attract anywhere from 2,000 to 3,000 people. The park boasts 10 miles of mountain biking trails maintained by a local biking organization, which is planning several additional miles of trails. Bike trails range in difficulty from challenging beginner to advanced. The beach area along the lake is used as a remote-control motorboat area. Some visitors come here to swim, but there are no lifeguards.

## Mill Creek/Ezell Park Greenway
**Harding Pl. at Mill Creek**
**• (615) 862-8400**

A 1-mile trail in Ezell Park is the first segment of what will eventually be a 7-mile greenway corridor on Mill Creek.

## Red Caboose Playground (Bellevue Park)
**656 Colice Jean Rd. • (615) 862-8435**

This is one of Metro's most popular parks. It's in the west Nashville community of Bellevue along U.S. Highway 70 S. Formerly the site of Bellevue Junior High School, the land was transferred from the Metro Board of Education to the park system in 1982. A community center and park were completed in 1984. In the mid-1990s, the community raised the funds and volunteered time and labor to renovate the playground; with matching funds from Metro Parks, the nearly 8-acre park now boasts the most expensive structures in the park system.

The natural wood play structure is the fo-

Photo: Nashville CVB

Nashville's Parthenon is the world's only full-scale reproduction of the famous Greek Parthenon.

cus of the park. Its connecting slides, bridges, tunnels and other features entertain children for hours. Tire swings, toddler swings, a sand area and the much-loved old red caboose provide other options for fun. While the youngsters are playing, grownups might enjoy getting some exercise on the quarter-mile paved walking track that surrounds the playground. Three gazebos provide shade and a spot for picnicking, and a new restroom facility has been built on the park grounds.

The on-site Bellevue Community Center is open Monday through Friday; hours of operation vary according to season. The community center features a basketball gym, weight room with free weights and machine weights, two club rooms, a game room with pool tables and Ping Pong tables, and restrooms. These activities are free. In the winter, adult volleyball leagues and church basketball leagues play here. The center also has a pottery and ceramics room, where classes are conducted by the arts department. The community center staff can provide information on class fees and instructions on how to sign up. Bellevue's park is also the traditional location for the Bellevue Community Picnic, an annual spring event featuring arts and crafts, exhibits, music, food and a fireworks display.

## Riverfront Park
**100 First Ave. N. • (615) 862-8400**

Riverfront Park is where you can join thousands of Nashville revelers each Thursday during the summer for Dancin' in the District, a free concert series that features some of the best performers in popular music. It's along the Cumberland River, just a short walk from bustling Second Avenue and Broadway. The 7.5-acre park attracts tens of thousands for annual events such as the big Fourth of July fireworks display and the Italian Street Fair in September. (These events are described in the Annual Events chapter.) Prime viewing spots along the sidewalk and on the tiered, grass-covered hill fill up fast, so come early.

Commercial and private boats dock at Riverfront Park. You can also find a replica of Fort Nashborough here that is open to the public. The replica is near where the original Fort Nashborough of the late 1700s stood.

The park was created to commemorate Nashville's bicentennial and pay tribute to the city's river heritage. The first phase opened July 10, 1983.

## Shelby Bottoms Greenway and Nature Park
**East end of Davidson St., adjacent to Shelby Park • (615) 880-2280**

Under development for several years, by the end of 1999, this greenway project is expected to have about 12 miles of trails, including 5 miles of paved trail along the Cumberland River. The area also includes an observation deck for birders, lots of bluebird boxes, a river overlook and a wetlands waterfowl refuge. Level, paved trails make this a great place for in-line skating. Plans call for a major visitors center/nature center to be located here. It will merge with the existing nature center at Shelby Park (see next entry).

## Shelby Park
**Shelby Ave. and S. 20th St.**
**• (615) 862-8467, (615) 880-2280 (nature center)**

Shelby Park, a historic and scenic park covering 361.5 acres, recently received a boost to its reputation with renovations as well as improvements to the adjacent 810-acre Shelby Bottoms (see previous entry). When the park board opened Shelby as a public park in 1912, it was a showpiece park, but it deteriorated along with the east Nashville neighborhoods in later years. It's enjoying a renewed popularity today.

A true community-use park, Shelby Park is bordered on various sides by a renovated historic neighborhood, middle-class contemporary homes and lower-income homes, bringing a diverse mix of visitors to the park. Some come to fish in the lake, walk the paved winding roads or play golf at the 27-hole golf course or the nine-hole course. With a four-diamond softball complex, Shelby Park is one of the five large ballparks operated by Metro Parks. Four tennis courts, a playground, hiking/nature trails, eight picnic shelters, restrooms and a boat ramp are among the other attractions here. (See Kidstuff for additional information.)

At the turn of the 20th century, a real estate development company named the park after John Shelby, an army surgeon who owned much of the original property and built the Fatherland and Boscobel mansions in east Nashville during the 1800s. The company operated an amusement park on the Shelby Park site. The city's first municipal golf course opened here in 1924, and the park was home to Nashville's first city park baseball league, organized in 1915 by the YMCA.

## Two Rivers Park

**3150 McGavock Pk. • (615) 862-8400**

This park, at Briley and Two Rivers parkways, is a great place to cool off on a hot summer day. This is where you'll find the Wave Country water park (see Kidstuff). Wave Country has a wave pool, three water slides, a children's playground and volleyball pits, and it gets packed on summer days. (See our Attractions chapter for more information.)

Other attractions at the 384.8-acre park include 18 holes of golf, baseball and softball diamonds, six tennis courts and a new playground. The park also has concession stands, five picnic shelters, restrooms, Two Rivers Lake, disc golf and a greenhouse where Metro Parks stores plants bound for area parks. The property is the site of Two Rivers Mansion, a restored 1859 Italianate home available for event rentals. The mansion and an adjacent 1802 house are listed on the National Register of Historic Places.

## Warner Parks

**Edwin Warner Park, 50 Vaughn Rd.**
**• (615) 370-8051**
**Percy Warner Park, 2500 Old Hickory Blvd. • (615) 370-8051**
**Warner Parks Nature Center, 7311 Tenn. Hwy. 100 • (615) 352-6299**

The jewel in Metro Parks' crown, Warner Parks encompass more than 2,681 acres in southwest Nashville, making the collective pair one of the largest city parks in the country. Acres of wooded hills, open fields and miles of scenic paved roads and nature trails provide Nashvillians with excellent recreation and environmental-education opportunities. (See Kidstuff for related information.)

The parks are named for brothers Edwin and Percy Warner and were acquired between 1927 and 1930. Col. Luke Lea donated the first 868 acres of the land to the city in 1927 with the encouragement of his father-in-law, Percy Warner, a prominent local businessman, park board chairman and lifelong outdoorsman and nature lover. Following Percy's death, Edwin Warner joined the park board and became the driving force behind the development of the parks and the acquisition of additional acreage. In 1937 the park board designated all the property west and south of Old Hickory Boulevard as Edwin Warner Park.

The impressive stone structures in the park, including the miles of dry-stacked stone retainer walls, were constructed from 1935 to 1941 by the Works Progress Administration, which provided jobs during the Great Depression. The WPA built seven limestone entrances, two stone bridges, a steeplechase course, picnic shelters, stone pillars, scenic drives, overlooks and trails.

The main entrance to 2,058-acre Percy Warner Park is at the intersection of Belle Meade Boulevard and Page Road. Other entrances are off Chickering Road, Tenn. Highway 100 and Old Hickory Boulevard. Percy Warner offers miles of hiking and equestrian trails as well as paved roads that wind along forest-shaded hillsides and through open fields. Bicyclists will find the roads make for a challenging workout. In addition to its recreation opportunities, Percy Warner Park is a nice place for a Sunday afternoon drive or picnic. Percy Warner Park also has a steeplechase course — the site of the annual Iroquois Steeplechase (see Annual Events) — as well as 27 holes of golf, picnic shelters, restrooms and equestrian facilities.

## INSIDERS' TIP

**President Theodore Roosevelt coined Maxwell House coffee's slogan "Good to the last drop" in reference to the delicious brew served at Nashville's Maxwell House Hotel (see the related Close-up in our History chapter).**

Edwin Warner Park, divided from Percy Warner by Old Hickory Boulevard, offers paved and nature trails, playgrounds, ball fields, a polo field, model-airplane field, restrooms and picnic shelters, including 11 reservable shelters. It's a popular spot for company picnics, family reunions and other group events. The main entrance to Edwin Warner is at Tenn. Highway 100 near the Warner Parks Nature Center, but you can also enter the park at Vaughn Road off Old Hickory Boulevard.

The Warner Parks Nature Center serves both parks and includes the Susanne Warner Bass Learning Center, a natural history museum, office and reference library, organic vegetable and herb garden, pond, bird-feeding area and wildflower gardens. The park offers environmental programs year round for adults and children. Programs include wildflower, insect and tree hikes; bird-watching hikes and bird banding; exotic-plant removal; and sunrise celebrations. The programs are free, but reservations are required.

The parks' new 5,000-square-foot learning center features a gathering area where you can review park maps, an exhibit hall, classroom, collections room, offices and a large porch and patio.

Warner Parks is a strictly protected sanctuary. The parks are open from daybreak until 11 PM.

# Parks Information

For additional information on state parks, natural areas and metro parks and greenways, contact:
• Tennessee State Parks (Tennessee Department of Environment & Conservation), 401 Church Street, L&C Tower, 7th floor, (615) 532-0001 or toll-free (888) TN PARKS;
• Metropolitan Board of Parks and Recreation, 511 Oman Street in Centennial Park (Administrative Office), (615) 862-8400; 2565 Park Plaza in Centennial Park (Sports and Recreation Office, Park Rangers), (615) 862-8424.

The Metropolitan Board of Parks and Recreation, informally known as Metro Parks, not only maintains more than 80 parks throughout Davidson County, but also provides ample opportunities for people of all ages to enjoy themselves.

# Recreation

The typical Nashvillian isn't one to sit around idly and let the world go by. No, there's just way too much to do here for that. Whatever your preferred method of recreation, you'll probably find it in this city.

We've mentioned elsewhere in this book how Nashville has earned the nickname "City of Parks," among many others. That's appropriate to bring up again here because many of the recreational opportunities available in Middle Tennessee are at parks. We're talking about such activities as varied as bicycling, hiking, swimming, tennis and ice skating, to name just a few. And many parks have fields for team sports like baseball, softball and soccer.

But parks don't have a monopoly on the action in Nashville. Tens of thousands of acres of water in area lakes just beg to be swum, fished, boated and skied. You can put on your boots and cowboy hat and, instead of boot-scootin', go for a horseback ride through the country. You can enjoy nature's beauty on an easy-paced walk or a strenuous hike.

Bad weather? That's OK. It doesn't have to ruin your day. As you'll discover in this chapter, we have plenty of indoor recreational opportunities as well, like indoor swimming and tennis, bowling, billiards and pumping iron. So you don't need to climb the walls — although, if you really want to, that's an option as well (see the "Climbing" section in this chapter for details).

You'll also find recreational opportunities in our Campgrounds, Golf, Kidstuff and Parks chapters as well as in Daytrips and Weekend Getaways.

## Public Parks, Playgrounds and Programs

### Metropolitan Board of Parks and Recreation
**Administration Office, 511 Oman St.**
• **(615) 862-8400 (general information)**
**Centennial Sportsplex, 222 25th Ave. N.**
• **(615) 862-8480**
**Sports and Recreation Office, 2565 Park Plaza** • **(615) 862-8424**

The Metropolitan Board of Parks and Recreation, informally known as Metro Parks, not only maintains more than 80 parks throughout Davidson County, but also provides ample opportunities for people of all ages to enjoy themselves. Facilities include more than 60 ball fields; 20 community centers; 13 swimming pools, some of which are open year round; more than 50 picnic shelters; and more than 50 playgrounds.

Metro Parks programs range from sports leagues for youths and adults to arts classes and workshops for all ages. The Community Centers offer activities including arts and crafts, exercise classes, sports, games, tutorial help, nature, anti-drug programs, Boy Scouts and Girl Scouts.

INSIDERS' TIP

**Dozier's Restaurant, (615) 792-9175, at the mouth of the Harpeth River on Cheatham Lake invites anglers to park their boats at the dock while they eat. There is a boat ramp at Dozier's, and there's another about 2 miles upriver at the Harpeth River Bridge, on Tenn. Highway 49, southwest of Ashland City. A mile upriver from Dozier's is Sycamore Creek, a very good fishing spot.**

Centennial Sportsplex, at the edge of Centennial Park (see our Parks chapter), contains an ice rink offering lessons for all ages and skill levels, as well as open skating sessions; an aquatic center offering lessons and open swim times; a tennis center with indoor and outdoor courts, including a stadium court; and a full fitness center.

More information about activities available at Metro Parks is in this chapter under the specific activity, such as swimming or tennis. You can also find more detailed descriptions of some parks in our Parks chapter.

In addition to the playgrounds maintained by Metro Parks, most area elementary schools also have playgrounds, so there's bound to be one near you.

# Bicycling

Nashville's many parks make it an ideal city for bikers of varying experience. If you're a beginner, you can find relatively flat paths that require little exertion; if you're eager for a challenge, there are plenty of hills that will test your stamina.

One excellent guide to biking throughout Nashville and surrounding areas is *Bicycling Middle Tennessee: A Guide to Scenic Bicycle Rides in Nashville's Countryside*, by Ann Richards and Glen Wanner (Pennywell Press, Nashville). You can also request "Cycling Tennessee's Highways," a free collection of bicycling touring maps covering various sections of the state, from the Tennessee Department of Transportation by writing to Bicycle & Pedestrian Coordinator, Department of Transportation Planning, 5050 Deaderick Street, Suite 900, James K. Polk Building, Nashville TN 37243.

Here are some highly recommended areas to bike in the Nashville area.

## Bowie Nature Park
**766 Fairview Blvd. W., Fairview**

This park west of Nashville is a popular spot for mountain biking. The trails are in good shape and can be fairly challenging, especially for beginners, though the park has smoother areas through sections of woods and fields.

## Hamilton Creek Park
**2901 Bell Rd. • (615) 862-8400**

Ten miles of mountain biking trails, with varying degrees of difficulty, are available at this park, and more are in the works. Some of these trails are considered quite challenging. Hamilton Creek Park, near Percy Priest Lake, also has a BMX track used for national races. For more information, see our Parks chapter.

## Radnor Lake State Natural Area
**1160 Otter Creek Rd. • (615) 373-3467**

Otter Creek Road, which encircles the lake, is a great route for biking, and it's closed to motor vehicles from 7 AM to sunset. Just be sure to watch out for walkers and joggers! For more information, see our Parks chapter.

## Shelby Bottoms Greenway and Nature Park
**East end of Davidson St., adjacent to Shelby Park • (615) 880-2280**

Some of the trails at this still-developing 810-acre greenway and nature park are paved and others are mulched. For more information, see our Parks chapter.

## Warner Parks
**Tenn. Hwy. 100 • (615) 370-8051 (headquarters), (615) 352-6299 (nature center)**

An 11-mile loop begins at the main drive near the Belle Meade Boulevard entrance to Percy Warner Park. The one-way road, which winds through fields and wooded areas, is suited for all skill levels, though the hills make it challenging in spots. For more information, see our Parks chapter.

## Natchez Trace Parkway

The Natchez Trace Parkway is very popular with bicyclists, even though there's no shoulder. Begin at the northern terminus at Tenn. Highway 100, just across from Loveless

Cafe, and — if you are so motivated — you can bike the road, which is part of the National Park system, as far as Natchez, Mississippi.

# Boating

## Registration, Rules and Regulations

It is legal to travel on any navigable stream in Tennessee. But before you do, you should know the rules, so you can avoid hurting someone or ending up in trouble with the law.

If you have bought a new boat, your dealer generally will register it for you. If you've bought the boat from an individual, or are new to the area, you'll need to go to the county court clerk's office in your county — in Davidson County, the clerk is at 700 Second Avenue S., (615) 862-6050. Bring a bill of sale and other appropriate information on the boat; you'll pay sales tax on the amount paid plus $2. While there, you should apply for registration in your name; the office will notarize the card and give you a 30-day temporary registration, then you mail the card to the Tennessee Wildlife Resources Agency (TWRA). You can register for a one-, two- or three-year period.

TWRA enforces and administers the provisions of the Tennessee Safe Boating Act. Enforcement officers are on the water to assist boaters, enforce laws and provide control. Every TWRA officer has the authority to stop and board any vessel, issue citations and make arrests. Most TWRA boats are identified by orange and green stripes near the bow and the words WILDLIFE RESOURCES on the sides; some, however, are unmarked. Boaters who are signaled to stop must do so immediately.

It is unlawful to operate any sail or powered vessel while under the influence of alcohol or drugs. A person with a blood-alcohol content of .10 is presumed to be under the influence and can be fined up to $1,000 on the first offense, $2,500 on the second offense and $5,000 on the third offense; jailed for 11 months and 29 days; and be prohibited from operating a vessel for one to 10 years. As with motor vehicles, anyone operating a sail or pow-

ered vessel has given implied consent to a sobriety test. Failure to consent to testing is a separate offense that may result in suspension of operating privileges for six months.

Reckless operation of a vessel, including water skis, is an offense punishable by a $500 fine and six months in jail. The Coast Guard can also impose civil penalties up to $5,000 and one year in prison. Examples of reckless operation include operating a vessel in swimming areas; riding on seat backs, gunwales, transoms or pedestal seats in a boat traveling faster than an idle speed; excessive speed in crowded, dangerous or low-visibility areas; operating an overloaded vessel; towing a skier in a crowded area where he or she is likely to be hit by other vessels or to strike an obstacle; and using a personal watercraft to jump the immediate wake of another vessel.

People younger than 12 are prohibited from operating any vessel of 8.5 horsepower or larger unless they are under the direct supervision of an adult who can take immediate control of the vessel.

A life jacket or other approved personal flotation device must be worn by each person on board a vessel being operated within specifically marked areas below any dam, including the lock discharge area. In fact, it's a good idea to wear one any time you're in a vessel, wherever you are; the law requires that an approved personal flotation device be on board and readily accessible for every person in the vessel.

Boating safety classes are available through TWRA. For more information about these classes or about other rules of the waterways, call TWRA's Boating Safety Office at (615) 781-6522.

## Popular Waterways

Nashville's two big lakes, J. Percy Priest and Old Hickory, are both managed by the U.S. Army Corps of Engineers, which also manages some launching ramps on Cheatham Lake (Cumberland River). You'll see a variety of watercraft on these lakes, from fishing and skiing boats to houseboats, sailboats and Jet Skis. Signs to boat ramps are marked at various locations around the lakes.

The Corps of Engineers operates nearly a

dozen launching ramps on Old Hickory Lake in such areas as Hendersonville, Old Hickory, Hermitage and Gallatin. The Corps has 20 ramps at various sites on Priest Lake.

A number of private marina operators lease land from the Corps, and their offerings vary. Most, but not all, have a launching ramp, for example, and while most sell fishing and marine supplies, only a few sell fishing licenses.

## J. Percy Priest Lake

Launching ramps are available at the following Corps Recreation Areas (most don't have phones; listed numbers are for campsite reservations): Cook, (615) 889-1096; Seven Points, (615) 889-5198; Anderson Road, (615) 361-1980; Poole Knobs, (615) 459-6948; Elm Hill; Vivrett; Smith Springs; Hurricane Creek; Fate Sanders; Lamar Hill; Stewart Creek; Fall Creek; Jefferson Springs; West Fork; East Fork; Mona; Four Corners; Gregory Mill; Nice's Mill; and Damsite.

Commercial marinas on Priest Lake include the following:

### Elm Hill Marina
**3361 Bell Rd., Antioch • (615) 889-5363**

Elm Hill, the largest marina on Priest Lake, has a launching ramp and sells cold sand-wiches, along with gasoline and fishing and marine equipment. The marina also has private docking and restrooms. Wet-N-Wild Waterfun Rentals, an affiliated company on an adjacent dock, rents Jet Skis, pontoons, fishing boats and paddleboats.

### Fate Sanders Marina
**3157 Weakley Ln., Smyrna**
**• (615) 459-6219**

In addition to a launching ramp and fishing supplies, Fate Sanders also offers a restaurant that serves catfish daily. The marina got a face-lift in summer 1999, adding new concrete-and-steel slips.

### Long Hunter State Park
**2910 Hobson Pk., Hermitage**
**• (615) 885-2422**

At Couchville Lake, a 110-acre lake off Percy Priest, you can rent 14-foot johnboats with electric motors as well as canoes and hydrobikes, which essentially are bicycle frames on pontoons.

## Old Hickory Lake

Launching ramps are available at the following Corps Recreation Areas (not all have phones): Rockland; Tailwater Left Bank; Lock

The Natchez Trace Parkway is popular for cyclists, hikers and weekend adventurers.

3; Shutes Branch, (615) 754-4847; Avondale; Cages Bend, (615) 824-4989; Cedar Creek, (615) 754-4947; Lone Branch; Old Hickory Beach, (615) 847-8091; Martha Gallatin; and Laguardo, (615) 449-6544. Please note that listed numbers are NOT for making campsite reservations; for that, call the toll-free National Recreation Reservation Service line at (877) 444-6777. (See our Campgrounds chapter for more info.)

Commercial marinas include:

### Anchor High Marina
**128 River Rd., Hendersonville**
**• (615) 824-2175**

Anchor High has a "ship store" with fishing and marine supplies, sandwiches and drinks, plus the Anchor High Bar and Grill, which opened in May 1999. You'll also find a picnic area with tables, drinking water and restrooms. Private and transit docking are available, though all spaces were filled at this writing.

### Cedar Creek Marina
**9120 Saundersville Rd., Mt. Juliet**
**• (615) 758-5174**

Cedar Creek has a launching ramp and a small store that sells fishing licenses, bait, oil and other supplies as well as sandwiches during the warmer months. There's also a picnic area and shelter with tables and grills, private boat docking and a vessel pump-out station.

### Cherokee Resort
**350 Cherokee Dock Rd., Lebanon**
**• (615) 452-1515, (615) 444-2783**

Cherokee Resort offers a marina with private and transit docking as well as a swimming pool and a 150-seat steakhouse restaurant with an additional 175-seat banquet room.

### Drakes Creek Marina
**441 Sanders Ferry Rd., Hendersonville**
**• (615) 822-3886**

Drakes Creek, which sells Regal luxury performance boats and has a complete service department, offers private and transit docking as well as dry storage. It also offers electrical hookups and marine supplies, and there's a restroom.

### Gallatin Marina
**1198 Lock 4 Rd., Gallatin**
**• (615) 452-9876**

Gallatin Marina has a restaurant, a store that sells limited marine supplies, a private launching ramp (there's a $5 fee for nonmembers), a picnic area for boaters, private and transit docking, a gas dock and, for members, a swimming pool.

### Old Hickory Marina
**2001 Riverside Rd., Old Hickory**
**• (615) 847-4022**

Old Hickory Marina has a launching ramp, private and transit docking, an eating area with concessions, gas, bait and restrooms.

### Shady Cove Resort and Marina
**1115 Shady Cove Rd., Castalian Springs**
**• (615) 452-8010**

Shady Cove has a launching ramp, private and transit docking, a snack bar serving sandwiches and other deli-type foods during warmer months, gas, fishing and marine supplies, bait and licenses, a campground with camper dumping station (propane and a grill are available), electrical hookups, a swimming pool with bath house, boat and motor rentals (fishing boats, pontoons, canoes and paddleboats), a laundry facility, picnic area and playground.

## Cheatham Lake (Cumberland River)

The Corps maintains launching areas (no phones) at Cheatham Dam Right Bank, Lock A, Sycamore Creek, Johnson Creek, Pardue, Harpeth River Bridge, Big Bluff, Bull Run, Brush Creek, Sam's Creek, Cleese's Ferry Right Bank and Cleese's Ferry Left Bank. In addition, Metro Parks maintains a ramp in Shelby Park.

# Bowling

Bowling in Greater Nashville generally will cost you around $3 a game. You may pay as little as $2 or as much as $3.35 at regular rates plus an extra $1 to $2.50 for shoes if you need them. Most facilities, however, have reduced-price hours (generally in the morning or afternoon), and some offer all-you-can-bowl specials at certain times. Be aware that, during league play (hours vary from location to location), some bowling centers will have limited or no lanes open — so, as with many businesses, it's always a good idea to call first.

## Cumberland Lanes
**3930 Apache Tr. • (615) 834-4693**

The recently renovated Cumberland Lanes, a Brunswick facility, offers 32 lanes, automatic scoring, a game room, snack bar and lounge. Friday night it stays open until 2 AM, Saturday until 3 AM.

## Donelson Bowling Center
**117 Donelson Pk., Donelson**
**• (615) 883-3313**

Donelson Bowling Center has 24 lanes with automatic scoring, a game room and a kitchen serving beer and food.

## Donelson Plaza Bowling Center
**2715 Old Lebanon Pk. • (615) 889-4710**
## Gallatin Bowling Center
**683 S. Water Ave., Gallatin**
**• (615) 230-7967**
## Hendersonville Bowling Center
**460 W. Main St., Hendersonville**
**• (615) 824-5685**

These Holder Family Fun Centers, all of which are open 24 hours a day, offer automatic scoring, snack bar, video games, electronic darts, full-service pro shop, jukebox, big-screen TV and more. Donelson Plaza has 24 lanes, Gallatin 32 lanes and Hendersonville 36. The Hendersonville location has two lounges, one with pool tables and the other with karaoke and live music.

## Franklin Lanes
**1200 Lakeview Dr., Franklin**
**• (615) 790-2695**

Franklin Lanes, with 24 lanes and automatic scoring, frequently offers "Cyber Bowl" with all-you-can-bowl prices and music accompaniment; disco, laser and black lights; and a general party atmosphere.

## Hermitage Lanes
**3436 Lebanon Pk. • (615) 883-8900**

Hermitage Lanes has 32 lanes with automatic scoring, 17 pool tables and more than 40 video games.

## Melrose Lanes
**2600 Franklin Pk. • (615) 297-7142**

Melrose Lanes has 30 lanes, a lounge and restaurant and a complete pro shop.

## Pla-Mor Bowling Lanes
**2906 Foster Creighton Dr.**
**• (615) 254-5809**

Pla-Mor, an AMF Bowling Center, has 24 synthetic lanes, automatic scoring and a pro shop.

## Tusculum Lanes
**5315 Nolensville Rd. • (615) 833-2881**

Tusculum Lanes, a Brunswick facility, offers 24 lanes with automatic scoring, snack bar, pro shop and video games. Like its sister Franklin Lanes, Tusculum frequently offers "Cyber Bowl" (see Franklin Lanes entry). It also offers a summer youth club that offers significant savings.

# Canoeing

The Harpeth River is a blessing to canoeists who don't want to drive far. Three businesses on the river in nearby Kingston Springs rent canoes for trips of varying lengths and times on the Harpeth, which is designated a state scenic river and nature sanctuary. Because of the Harpeth's 5-mile "hairpin" loop in this area, you can put in and take out at nearly the same spot. Along the quiet, relaxing route

— there are no major rapids to negotiate —
you'll pass peaceful farmland and green, rolling hills. It's a great way to get away from it all
for a few hours. The following renters of canoes are generally open from March through
October, weather permitting. Each canoe will
carry three adults, or two adults and two small
children.

### Foggy Bottom Canoe Rental
**1270 U.S. Hwy. 70, Kingston Springs**
**• (615) 952-4062**
Foggy Bottom rents canoes and flat-bot-
tom john boats. Rates start at $22 for a 2½- to
3-hour trip; you can keep your canoe all day
for $28. Primitive campsites nearby come free
with canoe trips.

### Pizza Shack Restaurant and Marketplace
**1203 U.S. Hwy. 70, Kingston Springs**
**• (615) 952-4211**
"We feed 'em and we float 'em," says the
operator of the Pizza Shack, which is, yes, a
pizza restaurant that rents canoes. Canoes rent
for $22 for 2 hours, $26 for 4 hours, $30 for all
day and $45 overnight. Gourmet pizza, along
with picnic tables near the river, makes this a
popular site for reunions and parties.

### Tip-A-Canoe Stores Inc.
**Harpeth River Outpost, 1279 U.S. Hwy.
70, Kingston Springs • (615) 254-0836**
Canoes rent for $29.95, including shuttle
service, for anywhere from 2 to 4½ hours. An
eight-hour trip is an additional $10. Three-,
four- and five-day tours are also available.

## Climbing

### Classic Rock Gym
**121 Seaboard Ln., Unit 10, Franklin**
**• (615) 661-9444**
Classic Rock Gym, an indoor climbing gym
near CoolSprings Galleria, offers 7,000 square
feet of climbing walls of various shapes and
sizes. First-time climbers must take lessons
before hitting the walls; the $18.50 fee includes
harness and shoe rental, lesson and climbing
fee. After that, you can climb all day for $8.
Shoe rentals are $5, harness rentals $2. The
gym, which presents clinics four times a year,

also has a guiding service for real mountain
climbing expeditions. Classic Rock Gym is
open 4 to 10 PM Monday through Friday, noon
to 10 PM Saturday and 2 to 8 PM Sunday.

### South Cumberland State Park Visitor Center
**Rt. 1, Box 2196, Monteagle**
**• (931) 924-2980**
This visitor center offers information on
climbing at Stone Door (see next entry) as
well as at Foster Falls, which is 11 miles south
of the center.

### Stone Door Ranger Station
**Stone Door Rd., Beersheba Springs**
**• (615) 692-3887**
The Great Stone Door geographic feature in this area about 100 miles southeast of
Nashville lies in the Savage Gulf Natural Area,
which is part of the South Cumberland State
Recreation Area. Like the rest of the
Cumberland Plateau, this area is distinguished by a plateau top that is flat and easy
to traverse, with a gulf — a canyon or gorge
— that is extremely rocky and challenging.
You'll find disappearing waterfalls, bluff-top
overlooks, caves, sinkholes and other stunning natural formations.
Rappelling is allowed only with a permit,
which you can get free at the ranger station.
But one ranger cautioned that rappelling is
becoming "way too popular" in this area and
is having an adverse effect on the rock formations. He touted the area's hiking, which features "miles and miles of trails with some of
the best scenery in Tennessee."
To get to Beersheba Springs, take Interstate 24 toward Chattanooga for about 80
miles to Exit 127, Tenn. Highway 50. Proceed
to Altamont, then turn left on Tenn. Highway
56. Watch for Stone Door Road on the right.

## Fishing

Middle Tennessee has 10 lakes and more
than a dozen rivers and streams within a two-
hour drive of Nashville, which is good news
for anglers. The three closest lakes to Nashville are Cheatham, Percy Priest and Old
Hickory.
Vernon Summerlin, author of *Two Dozen*

*Fishin' Holes: A Guide to Middle Tennessee* (Rutledge Hill Press,1992) and former co-publisher of the now-defunct *Tennessee Angler* magazine, was gracious enough to answer some of our questions and share his thoughts on Nashville-area fishing with us. You'll find Vern's insights throughout this section of the chapter.

Gamefish species caught in Middle Tennessee include rainbow and brown trout, walleye, sauger, rockfish (also known as stripers), stripe (also known as white bass), bream, black bass (largemouth, smallmouth and spotted), catfish and crappie. Not all species will be found in all waters — their presence is often dependent upon habitat and Tennessee Wildlife Resources Agency (TWRA) stocking programs.

Anyone 13 or older who fishes in Tennessee must have a license. You are exempted if you are: (1) a landowner fishing on your own farmland; (2) on military leave and carrying a copy of your leave orders; or (3) a resident born before March 1, 1926. Disabled resident veterans and blind residents are eligible for free licenses. An annual resident fishing and hunting combination license costs $21. A stamp permitting you to fish for trout costs an additional $12. Nonresident licenses start at $10.50 for a three-day (no trout) fishing license and $20.50 for a three-day all-fish license. In addition, special permits are available for TWRA-managed lakes and Reelfoot Preservation (Reelfoot Lake). Fishing licenses are available at sporting goods stores, marinas and bait-and-tackle shops. For more information, call or visit the TWRA (see subsequent entry).

Tennessee has a Free Fishing Day each June, when everyone can fish without a license, and a Free Fishing Week in June for children ages 13 through 15. Contact TWRA for dates (see the subsequent entry for information).

Here are some resources for additional information on fishing in Middle Tennessee:

## Tennessee Wildlife Resources Agency
**Ellington Agricultural Center, 440 Hogan Rd. • (615) 781-6622, (800) 624-7406**

The latest laws governing fishing in Tennessee are available in the booklet "Tennessee Fishing Regulations." The booklet, as well as other information about fishing, hunting and other outdoor activities, is available from this office, which is responsible for Middle Tennessee, or Region II.

## Tennessee Outdoorsman
This TV show airs on WDCN Channel 8 at 7:30 PM Thursdays and 6:30 PM Saturdays.

## Audio tapes
*Largemouth Bass through the Seasons*
*Smallmouth Bass through the Seasons*
*Crappie through the Seasons*
*Striper and Hybrids through the Seasons*

These one-hour audio cassettes cover where and how to catch particular gamefish species during each of the four seasons. Guides and expert anglers from across the state share their knowledge. For more information, write to Vernon Summerlin, 5550 Boy Scout Road, Franklin TN 37064.

# Lake Fishing

## Cheatham Lake
Cheatham Lake is 67.5 miles long, with 320 miles of shoreline, and looks like a river until you get to the lower section. It is an impoundment of the Cumberland River downstream from Old Hickory Dam to Cheatham Dam, and it runs right through downtown Nashville, which is 42 miles upstream from Cheatham Dam. (Most people simply refer to this lake as the Cumberland River.)

Largemouth bass are taken on ¼-ounce jigs and plastic worms at creek mouths where the current is quiet — next to downed trees or other completely or partially submerged structure. Spinnerbaits and crankbaits also can be effective. Top-water baits work best early and late in the day. Similar tactics work for smallmouth and Kentucky bass.

Crappie take small jigs and minnows. Bream, including bluegill, like worms and crickets. Catfish prefer minnows, chicken livers and nightcrawlers. Walleye and sauger like minnows and jigs fished near the bottom in the cold-weather months (November through March). Fish for rockfish below the dams year round.

The 14 public launch access points are fairly limited, but the easiest access is from Shelby Park in Nashville, Cleese's Ferry west of Nashville off Tenn. Highway 12 and at Cheatham Dam in Ashland City. Six of the ramps are within 6 miles of the dam, which is also where the best fishing is found.

Vern Summerlin thinks the best fishing is at Lock A, Brush Creek and Sycamore Creek. Bank-fishing opportunities are available at the ramps and the recreation areas at Lock A, Harpeth River and Sycamore Creek. Camping is available at Lock A and Harpeth River Bridge.

## J. Percy Priest Lake

J. Percy Priest Lake, an impoundment of the Stones River, is the most popular lake in Middle Tennessee. It is 42 miles long with 213 miles of shoreline. Twenty recreation areas, some with camping and all with boat ramps, make the lake very accessible; parts of it are only a five-minute drive from Nashville.

Many people consider Priest Lake's mid-section — from Fate Sanders Marina to Hobson Pike Bridge — to be the most productive. The many islands in this section are usually home to bass on the deep side in summer and winter and on the shallow side in spring and fall.

Priest Lake offers excellent fishing for crappie, largemouth and smallmouth bass, rockfish, white bass and hybrids, thanks to an abundance of cover and a strong forage base.

Smallmouth tend to dwell near Cook, Elm Hill, Seven Points and Vivrett recreation areas as well as Long Hunter State Park and Hamilton Creek Park. They are generally receptive to jigs dressed with pork, crawfish and tubes. In spring, you're likely to catch smallmouth using artificial deep-diving crankbaits including Deep Wee-R, Hellbender and Rapala, along with spinnerbaits, 4-inch worms and jigs.

Largemouth bass prefer worms, spinnerbaits and crankbaits offered near cover like stumps, trees and humps in the upper section of the lake above Fate Sanders Marina, but they are found throughout the lake in all seasons.

Rockfish congregate during summer nights on Suggs Creek and between Seven Points

and Long Hunter State Park. They are receptive to live shad or shiners drifted, or surface lures like Red Fin or a jointed Thunderstick retrieved through what is known as "the jumps" (rockfish feeding on schools of shad).

Crappie are taken year round but are easiest to find in the spring when they're spawning in the shallows and are receptive to a minnow dropped among the limbs of downed trees and bushes along the bank.

Worms and crickets are reliable for catching bream close to the banks and rocky bluffs. There are lots of good spots for bank fishing around the recreation areas like Elm Hill and Cooks.

## Old Hickory Lake

Old Hickory Lake is another impoundment of the Cumberland River, and its flow is regulated by Old Hickory Dam. There are 97.3 river miles from Old Hickory Dam upstream to Cordell Hull Dam and 440 miles of shoreline. There are 12 Army Corps of Engineers ramps on the lake between Old Hickory Dam and Tenn. Highway 109 south of Gallatin, and you'll also find nine marinas on the lake.

Presence of coontail milfoil, an aquatic plant, from Shutes Branch to Bull Creek makes for a prime largemouth habitat. Spinnerbaits, crankbaits and artificial worms are the favored offerings.

Catfish are plentiful throughout Old Hickory, with heavy concentrations around the Gallatin steam plant and Cedar Creek. You'll also find plenty of bream, stripe and crappie. Sauger are taken below the dam in winter. Occasional rainbow trout are taken from Old Hickory — escapees from the Caney Fork River, which is Middle Tennessee's trout hot spot.

Old Hickory also offers good fishing from its banks.

## Laurel Hill Lake

This pretty 320-acre lake, which lies about 80 miles south of Nashville via the Natchez Trace Parkway, is stocked with all three types of black bass plus crappie, catfish and walleye. Laurel Hill Lake is managed by TWRA, which charges $3 a day (in addition to your license fees) to fish here; pay your fee at the shed near the concession stand. You can rent rowboats here (motorized boats are not allowed).

# River and Stream Fishing

Several Middle Tennessee rivers and streams are popular with creek fishermen seeking smallmouth bass. Preferred waters for stream fishing include the Buffalo, Duck, Elk and Harpeth rivers in addition to the Caney Fork below Center Hill Dam. The information we include for these areas is general rather than specific; experienced stream fishermen realize that streams are fragile ecosystems that are more susceptible than reservoirs to heavy fishing pressures.

Author and angler extraordinaire Vernon Summerlin was a great source of information, with much of the following coming from his book *Two Dozen Fishin' Holes: A Guide to Middle Tennessee* (Rutledge Hill Press, 1992).

While it is legal to travel on any navigable stream in Tennessee, please keep in mind that the banks are often privately owned land. Look to public lands for bank fishing, and get permission before traipsing onto private property.

As a general rule, the area's larger streams contain more species, as you might expect. The smaller streams are good places to find largemouth and smallmouth bass, rock bass, bream and rough fish, such as carp, suckers and baitfish. Summerlin suggests, on smaller streams, fishing deep holes and structure, then moving on. "Go prepared to catch about a 2-pound fish on about 4-pound–test line on an ultra-light rod and reel outfit," he says. "You can retrieve most of your lures, so keep it light with a small tackle box that will fit in your pocket. The heaviest thing you want to carry is your fish."

## Buffalo River

The Buffalo River, a scenic Class I and II waterway, provides good fishing for largemouth and smallmouth bass, rock bass and bream. You'll also find trout in some sections. Good canoe access is available off the Natchez Trace Parkway at Metal Ford.

## Caney Fork

Caney Fork offers fishing on 27 miles from Center Hill Dam to Carthage. Trout fishing is popular below the dam, but be prepared to catch rockfish, walleye, stripe, bream, smallmouth and largemouth bass. Use light to medium equipment unless you're going for the big (up to 40 pounds) rockfish.

You can rent a canoe and arrange shuttle service at Big Rock Market, RR 1, Silver Point, (931) 858-9942. Bank fishing is also available at this spot on Caney Fork.

## Duck River

Rainbow and brown trout are in abundance on the Duck River below Normandy Dam. You'll also find saugeye, muskellunge, bass, bream, crappie and stripe.

## Elk River

The Elk River below Tim's Ford Dam is clear and cold. For the first 12 miles below the dam, trout are plentiful. Anglers like to fish large gravel areas near deep pools here.

## Harpeth River

The four branches of the Harpeth River — Little, Big, South and West — converge near the Paquo-Bellevue area. The Harpeth, a State Scenic River, offers more than 100 miles of largely Class I water that is easily navigable by canoe. Gamefish include bass, bream, catfish, crappie, stripe, rockfish and sauger. There's limited access to the South Harpeth, but you can find bank access and a good place to put your canoe in on the Big Harpeth at Pinkerton Park in Franklin. The section known as the Narrows of the Harpeth has an easy 5-mile loop at Narrows of the Harpeth State Park, off U.S. Highway 70. Canoe rentals are available at various canoe liveries in the area (see the "Canoeing" section of this chapter for more information).

# Fitness Centers

## Baptist Health & Fitness Center
**2011 Church St. • (615) 329-5066**

Baptist Health & Fitness Center, on the campus of Baptist Hospital (see Healthcare), provides fitness testing and individualized programs supervised by exercise professionals. The cardiovascular center features treadmills, exercise bikes and rowing, ski and stair machines. Other features include a complete weight room with free weights and a variety of machines, steam room, saunas, whirlpool, aerobics classes, a cushioned indoor track and a heated lap pool. Membership is not required. A one-time visit "off the street" costs $10. For five to 10 visits, you'll pay $7 a day; 11 to 19 visits, $6 a day; and 20 or more visits, $5 a day.

## Centennial Sportsplex
### 222 25th Ave. N. • (615) 862-8480
Machine weights, a separate free-weight room, stationary bikes, treadmills, step machines, aerobics, steam room and sauna are available at Centennial Sportsplex, the complex run by the Metropolitan Board of Parks and Recreation. Sportsplex also has two pools, one Olympic and one recreational, two ice skating rinks and 17 outdoor tennis courts (new indoor courts were scheduled to open sometime in fall 1999). Annual memberships are available; you can also pay $6 a day ($5 for children) or buy 10-pass packages.

## Cummins Station Fitness Center
### 209 10th Ave. S. • (615) 777-3838
You can pay $10 a day to work out at Cummins Station, which has free weights, circuit training, cardiovascular equipment, personal trainers and tanning beds.

## Downtown Athletic Club
### 520 Commerce St. • (615) 271-2616
## Hermitage Fitness Center
### 3924 Lebanon Rd. • (615) 889-4491
One membership gets you into both of these clubs that also offer daily rates (a $10 guest fee) for visitors. Downtown Athletic Club has an indoor track, aerobics, cardio room, weight room, racquetball, basketball, saunas.a steam room and tanning beds. Hermitage Fitness has Nautilus, free weights, a cardio center, aerobics and bench classes, a swimming pool, whirlpool, sauna, steam and tanning beds.

## Fairlane Fitness
### 4898 Nolensville Rd. • (615) 834-9400
This comfortable fitness center offers Nautilus and Universal machines, free weights, treadmills (with TVs to watch while running),

massage therapy, a steam room, sauna, Jacuzzi, whirlpool, exercise cycles, aerobics classes, nutritional counseling, an indoor pool, indoor track and free nursery. Several memberships are available; you can join for as few as four months or pay $10 a day.

## Westside Athletic Club
### 11 Vaughns Gap Rd. • (615) 352-8500
Tennis is big at Westside, with six indoor hard courts and 10 outdoor clay courts. Westside, which also specializes in physical therapy and sports medicine, has a full fitness center, indoor track, whirlpool, saunas, a steam room, massage therapists, yoga, basketball, volleyball, racquetball and squash courts, a year-round outdoor pool, personal trainers, nutrition and weight-loss counseling, aerobics, child-care services, children's gymnastics, youth development programs, restaurant and hair salon. There's a $10 daily guest fee.

# Hiking
For more information on the following areas, see our Parks chapter.

## Harpeth Scenic River and Narrows of the Harpeth State Historic Area
### off U.S. Hwy. 70 at Cedar Hill Rd., Kingston Springs • (615) 797-9052
The three trails here are short (about 1.5 miles combined) but steep, leading to the top of a bluff over a tunnel cut through solid rock — and a gorgeous view of the Harpeth River Valley. For canoeing information, see the "Canoeing" section earlier in this chapter.

## Long Hunter State Park
### 2910 Hobson Pk., Hermitage • (615) 885-2422
This 2,315-acre park has 28 miles of trails for day hiking and overnight backpacking.

## Montgomery Bell State Resort Park
### U.S. Hwy. 70, Burns • (615) 797-9052
This 3,850-acre park includes 19 miles of trails plus an 11.7-mile overnight trail.

## Radnor Lake State Natural Area
### 1160 Otter Creek Rd. • (615) 373-3467
Radnor Lake State Natural Area is a point

of pride for many Nashvillians, whose protests in the '60s saved it from a housing development. The beautiful and peaceful area is surrounded by both level walking paths and steep climbs — six in all — offering something for everyone. No fishing, boating or hunting is allowed, but there are plenty of opportunities for bird watching and photography.

## Shelby Bottoms Greenway and Nature Park
**East end of Davidson St., adjacent to Shelby Park • (615) 880-2280**

The first phase of Shelby Bottoms' development is complete, with 2 miles of paved trails and 1.5 miles of primitive (foot traffic only) over 165 acres. The park — which is popular with hikers, bikers, skaters and birdwatchers — also features a river-look observation deck and a shore-bird pond. By the end of 1999, Metro officials expect to have completed the development, with 12 miles of trails spread over 810 acres.

## Warner Parks
**Tenn. Hwy. 100 • (615) 370-8051 (headquarters), (615) 352-6299 (nature center)**

Percy Warner Park and Edwin Warner Park, more than 2,680 acres combined, are ideal for hiking, jogging or biking, with miles of nature trails as well as scenic paved roads and much, much more.

# Horseback Riding

## The Ranch at Biota
**Biota Tr., Joelton • (615) 876-6062**

The Ranch at Biota, part of the 750-acre Biota Nature Preserve, offers trail rides through beautiful countryside for $15 an hour, as well as saddlebag lunches, dinner rides and overnight trail rides. Riders must be 8 or older, and reservations are required. Camp Biota has a horse camp for ages 10 through 16.

## Ju-Ro Horseback Riding Stables
**7149 Cairo Bend Rd., Lebanon**
**• (615) 449-6621**

At Ju-Ro Stables, named after the first two letters of owners Judy Martin and Roger West's names, anyone from beginner to seasoned riders can take a trip — paced to suit the rider — through wooded trails along Old Hickory Lake or gallop along the "back 40," an open field. Rates are $20 an hour, and full-moon rides are $30. Ju-Ro, which also has primitive camping and cookout facilities, gives English and Western riding lessons, on the trail or in the ring.

## Percy Priest Stables
**3365 Hobson Pk. • (615) 874-0868**

Owner Judy Grice describes her horses as "big, gentle and well trained." Her stables include a few walking horses, a couple of Tennessee Walkers and the rest quarter horses. All rides are guided and limited to eight people. The pace can be modified — walk, trot or canter, but no galloping — depending on the desires and skills of the party.

Rates are $20 an hour or $25 for two hours, with more than 15 miles of trails available. In summer, Grice offers, for $30, a three-hour package that includes a stop to go swimming in the lake. She also gives lessons.

## Ramblin Breeze Ranch
**3665 Knight Rd., Whites Creek**
**• (615) 876-1029**

Ramblin Breeze Ranch has 120 acres of scenic trails. Rides are $15 an hour, and no reservations are needed. The ranch also offers hiking and hayrides.

# Pool and Billiards

## Bailey's Sports Grille
**786 Two-Mile Pkwy., Goodlettsville**
**• (615) 851-9509**

Bailey's, behind Rivergate Mall, has 17

**INSIDERS' TIP**

The section of the Cumberland River that runs through Nashville is part of Cheatham Lake, a 67.5-mile-long impoundment of the river.

regulation pool tables, Foosball, shuffleboard, darts, table tennis and other games plus wide-screen satellite TVs and a full bar.

### Eight Balls
**3314 Nolensville Pk. • (615) 834-6403**
Eight Balls has 13 tables of varying types and sizes, including a tournament table and a snooker table.

### Hermitage Lanes
**3436 Lebanon Pk. • (615) 883-8900**
Hermitage Lanes has 17 pool tables and more than 60 video games in addition to its 32 bowling lanes.

### J.O.B. Billiards Club
**960 S. Gallatin Rd. • (615) 868-4270**
Thirty tables are available in this clean 18,000-square-foot playing area that stays open until 3 AM daily. The club also has a pro shop and a sports lounge.

### Melrose Billiards
**2600 Franklin Pk. • (615) 383-9201**
Melrose has 11 regulation tables and one snooker table plus table tennis.

## Skating

Many skating rinks, while offering limited hours during the week, are available for private party rentals during the "closed" hours. Call the specific rink for details.

### Centennial Sportsplex
**222 25th Ave. N. • (615) 862-8480**
Public ice-skating sessions are held for two to five hours a day at Sportsplex, which has two rinks open to the public (one doubles as the Nashville Predators hockey practice facility). Visit the Sportsplex for a schedule. Admission is $6 for adults, $5 for seniors and ages 12 and younger. Hours for public skating vary, so call ahead.

### Hendersonville Skating Rink
**750 W. Main St., Hendersonville**
**• (615) 824-0630**
Hendersonville Skating Rink specializes in private parties during the week. In-line skaters and roller skates are allowed on the wooden

floor, though only roller skates are available for rent. Cost is $3.75, or $4.50 with skate rental, Friday and Saturday night. Saturday and Sunday afternoons, prices are $1 lower. Hours are 7 to 11 PM Fridays, 2 to 5 PM and 7 to 11 PM Saturdays and 2 to 5 PM Sundays.

### Skate Center
**402 Wilson Pike Cir., Brentwood**
**• (615) 373-8611, (615) 373-1827**
**(information line)**
**119 Gleaves St., Rivergate**
**• (615) 868-7655, (615) 868-3692**
**(information line)**
These two centers, both with wooden floors, generally charge $3.75 admission (prices can vary for special events). Roller skate rental is $1.50. In-line skates are also allowed. Both Skate Centers have a variety of special events, including after-school fun skates, Christian night and ladies night. On family night, up to five people from the same family can skate for just $8. The rinks are also available for private and semiprivate parties.

Brentwood hours are 4:30 to 6:30 PM Tuesdays and Thursdays, 7 to 11 PM Fridays, 1 PM to 11 PM Saturdays and 1 to 5 PM Sundays. Rivergate hours vary, so call first.

### XXX Sports
**1180 Antioch Pk. • (615) 781-8766**
XXX Sports, owned and operated by skaters, is a full skate park and pro shop for in-line skaters and skateboarders. The "arsenal of ramps," as one owner put it, includes quarter- and half-pipes, bowls, ledges, a pyramid and much more. Cost for all-day skating is, for non-members, $15 for a day and $10 for a half-day; and, for members, $7 a day and $5 for a half-day. Membership is $40 a year, including a free video. XXX Sports is open 10 AM to 8 PM Monday through Saturday and 1 to 6 PM Sunday.

## Sports Leagues

### Metropolitan Board of Parks and Recreation
**Sports and Recreation Office, 2565 Park Plaza • (615) 862-8424**
Metro Parks offers adult sport leagues in

softball (men's, women's and coed), basketball (men's and women's) and volleyball (recreational and "power"). Youth leagues are available in basketball, flag football, soccer, kickball, tennis, volleyball and track and field; other youth competition includes a T-ball "hot shot" contest, Iron Kids Triathlon and Punt, Pass & Kick contest. There is no charge for participation in youth sports leagues.

Information on other youth leagues, such as Little League and Babe Ruth baseball, is generally made available through the schools.

# Swimming

With the abundance of water in and around Nashville, many people enjoy taking dips at J. Percy Priest and Old Hickory lakes as well as at Acorn Lake in Montgomery Bell State Resort Park. Those who prefer pools have plenty of options as well.

## Lakes

### Acorn Lake
**Montgomery Bell State Park, U.S. Hwy. 70, Burns • (615) 797-3101**

Thirty-five–acre Acorn Lake has a swimming area with diving dock and slide, open Friday through Monday. The fee is $2 a person 8 and older, free for kids 7 and younger.

### Old Hickory Lake

Most of Old Hickory Lake is controlled by the U.S. Army Corps of Engineers, which maintains swimming areas at several beaches on the lake. In areas where there is a beach only, there is no fee for swimmers. If the site also includes a launching ramp and picnic facilities, the fee is $1 a person or $3 a carload for adults and teens, with no charge for children 12 and younger.

### J. Percy Priest Lake
**Anderson Road Campground, 4010 Anderson Rd. • (615) 361-1980**
**Cook Campground, 12231 Old Hickory Blvd. • (615) 889-1096**
**Seven Points Campground, 1810 Stewarts Ferry Pk. • (615) 889-5198**

The U.S. Army Corps of Engineers maintains three swimming areas on Priest Lake: at Anderson Road, Cook and Seven Points campgrounds. Anderson Road and Cook charge a day-use fee of $1 a person or $3 a carload for adults; there is no fee at Seven Points, which does not have much of a beach and is relatively less popular.

### Nashville Shores
**4001 Bell Road • (615) 889-7050**

Nashville Shores, a campground and water park, features a private beach on Priest Lake. There's also a lot more for your wet and dry amusement. For one price — $11.95 for adults, $8.95 for 12 and younger and 65 and older — you can spend a day cavorting on two 400-foot tube water slides, getting soaked by the Bucket of Fun Waterfall, swimming in the lake or a pool, cruising the lake in paddleboats or the 100-passenger Nashville Shoreliner, playing miniature golf and more. Hours are 10 AM to 7 PM during the summer.

## Pools

The Metro Parks department operates more than a dozen pools, including two pools at Centennial Sportsplex. The outdoor pools are open seasonally — in general, from early June to mid-August — while the indoor pools are open year round, with the exception of Napier, which is open only during the summer. Hours vary.

Wave Country, which is outdoors, and Centennial Sportsplex, which is indoors, have admission fees, but there is no charge for open swimming at any of the other pools. The only charge is for classes, which are generally $25 for 10 sessions, $50 at Sportsplex.

Although lifeguards are on duty at all pools, children younger than 12 should be accompanied by an adult, especially if they are shorter than 4 feet.

Most Metro pools offer competitive swim teams during the summer, with competitions culminating in a big meet at Centennial Sportsplex at the end of summer. For specific hours and other information, call the individual pool or the aquatics office, (615) 862-8480.

Nashville YMCAs operate a total of 21 pools: 11 outdoor and 10 indoor. See the subsequent "YMCAs" section of this chapter for

Photo: Cathy Summerlin

The two Warner Parks together encompass more than 2,680 acres with miles of nature trails and paved roads.

more information, or call or drop by the organization's corporate office at 900 Church Street, (615) 259-9622.

## Metro Parks' Indoor Pools

### Centennial Sportsplex
**222 25th Ave. N. • (615) 862-8480**

The Sportsplex's Aquatic/Fitness Center features two pools: one for recreational swimming and the other, which is Olympic size, for lap swimming. The daily rate is $6 for adults and teens and $5 for children 12 and younger

(children younger than 12 must be accompanied by an adult guardian). Lessons are available.

### Glencliff Pool
**160 Old Antioch Pk. • (615) 862-8470**
### Napier Pool
**73 Fairfield Ave. • (615) 242-9212**
### Pearl-Cohn Pool
**904 26th Ave. N. • (615) 862-8471**
### Whites Creek Pool
**7277 Old Hickory Blvd. • (615) 876-4300**

These indoor pools are heated and have

large locker rooms. Most have low diving boards. Glencliffe, Pearl-Cohn and Whites Creek offer lessons year round; lifeguard training is also available. Depending on available staff, Napier may or may not be offering lessons. Admission is free.

### Metro Parks' Outdoor Pools

**Cleveland Pool**
N. Sixth and Bayard sts.
• (615) 880-2253
**Coleman Pool**
Thompson Ln. at Nolensville Rd.
• (615) 862-8445
**East Pool**
Woodland St. at S. Sixth St.
• (615) 726-8657
**Hadley Pool**
28th Ave. N. at Albion St.
• (615) 327-9898
**Looby Pool**
2301 Metro Center Blvd.
• (615) 726-8631
**Richland Pool**
46th Ave. N. at Charlotte Pk.
• (615) 385-9164
**Rose Pool**
1000 Edgehill Ave. • (615) 726-8627

The big outdoor pools (Cleveland, Hadley, Looby and Rose) are in parks or by community centers. They are about three times larger, in general, than the smaller playground pools (Coleman, East and Richland). The larger pools feature locker rooms and have five or six lifeguards on duty, and most have diving areas. Although there are no concession stands, and no food is permitted inside the pool gates, most have picnic tables nearby.

The playground pools have shallower water and only one or two lifeguards. Unlike the larger pools, they are closed weekends. Admission is free.

**Wave Country**
2320 Two Rivers Pkwy. • (615) 885-1052

Wave Country features simulated surf, along with two water slides and one kiddie slide. Hours are 10 AM to 8 PM daily from Memorial Day weekend through Labor Day. Admission is $6 for adults and teens, $5 for youth ages 5 through 12 and free for kids 4 and younger.

# Tennis

**Centennial Sportsplex**
222 25th Ave. N. • (615) 862-8490

The Metro Board of Parks and Recreation has more than 160 tennis courts available free at parks around town. Call for information on courts near you. In addition, Metro Parks' Centennial Sportsplex has 17 outdoor courts, with new indoor courts in the works at this writing. Outdoor courts are $4 an hour before 5 PM and $5 an hour after 5 PM during spring and summer; the rate drops to $3 an hour during fall and winter. The outdoor courts are open year round, weather permitting.

**YMCA Indoor Tennis Center**
207 Shady Grove Rd. • (615) 889-8668

Membership in the YMCA makes you a member here, or you can belong to the Tennis Center only. Four indoor courts are available at $12 an hour; three outdoor courts are free to members.

# YMCAs

The YMCA of Middle Tennessee is a not-for-profit health and human services organization committed to helping persons grow in spirit, mind and body. The organization operates 21 YMCA centers in seven counties. The Y offers its members a wide variety of programs and services, including indoor and outdoor pools, aerobics classes, wellness equipment, athletic fields and gymnasiums. In addition, the YMCA has programs like youth sports, year-round child care, summer camp, personal fitness, family nights, volunteer opportunities, outreach and activities for teens and older adults.

YMCA centers are community-based, and each center is designed to meet the needs of its community.

For information on how to become a member of the YMCA, call your local Y or (615) 242-9622. Membership requires a joining fee, which is one-time as long as you keep your membership current, plus a monthly charge. Joining fees range from $25 for youth ages 7 to 12 to $175 per family. Monthly charges range from $14 for youth to $65 for family. Membership entitles you to use the facilities at any of the Y's; those who wish to use only the East or Northwest Y's pay a significantly reduced rate. Financial assistance is available at all centers, in accordance with the Y's philosophy that its programs and services should be available to everyone, regardless of ability to pay.

**YMCA Corporate Office,** 900 Church Street, (615) 259-9622

**Brentwood Family YMCA,** 8207 Concord Road, (615) 373-0215

**Clarksville YMCA (Program facility),** 260 Hillcrest Drive, (931) 647-2376

**Cool Springs YMCA,** 121 Seaboard Lane, (615) 661-4200

**Donelson-Hermitage Family YMCA,** 3001 Lebanon Road, (615) 889-2632

**Downtown District YMCA,** 1000 Church Street, (615) 254-0631

**East Family YMCA,** 2624 Gallatin Road, (615) 228-5525

**Franklin Family YMCA,** 501 S. Royal Oaks Boulevard, Franklin, (615) 591-0322

**Green Hills Family YMCA,** 4041 Hillsboro Circle, (615) 297-6529

**Harding Place Family YMCA,** 411 Metroplex Drive, (615) 834-1300

**Indoor Tennis Center,** 207 Shady Grove Road, (615) 889-8668

**Joe C. Davis YMCA Outdoor Center,** 3088 Smith Springs Road, (615) 360-2267

**Madison YMCA,** 900 Madison Square, Madison, (615) 869-6061

**Margaret Maddox Family YMCA East Center**, 2624 Gallatin Road, (615) 228-5525

**Maryland Farms Family YMCA,** 5101 Maryland Way, (615) 373-2900

**Maury County Family YMCA,** 1446 Oak Springs Drive, Columbia, (931) 540-8320

**Northwest Family YMCA,** 3700 Ashland City Highway, (615) 242-6559

**Robertson County Family YMCA,** 3332 Tom Austin Highway, Springfield, (615) 382-9622

**Rutherford County Family YMCA,** 205 N. Thompson Lane, Murfreesboro, (615) 895-5995

**Sumner County YMCA (Program facility),** 115 Hazel Path Drive, (615) 826-9622

**Uptown YMCA,** 424 Church Street, (615) 251-5454

**Urban Services YMCA (Outreach programs),** 213 McLemore Street, (615) 226-6442

**Country music and golf go together like country ham and made-from-scratch biscuits.**

# Golf

It should come as no surprise that Nashville is full of golf courses. First of all, there's the terrain, which varies from flat to gently rolling to downright hilly. That means whatever your playing style, you can find a course with a layout to your liking. Second, consider that this is, after all, a city of business. What better way to clinch a plum contract than with a putter in your hand?

Add in the fact that a lot of us around here like sports of any kind. And don't forget the music. Country music and golf go together like country ham and made-from-scratch biscuits. Just ask Vince Gill, well-known golf tournament host. Gill is renowned for his vocal and guitar skills, but he's equally passionate about his golf. His annual pro-celebrity tournament, The Vinny, attracts thousands of fans each year to The Golf Club of Tennessee in Kingston Springs to see a world of country stars, PGA pros and other celebrities. Since it began in 1993, The Vinny has raised more than $1 million to benefit the state's high-quality junior golfers program, becoming one of the nation's top pro-celebrity events in the process.

Gill has also lent his considerable drawing power to other local golf events, including the now-defunct LPGA Sara Lee Classic at Hermitage Golf Course (the tournament, with any luck, will resume in 2000 with a new sponsor). Another annual tournament is the BellSouth Senior Classic, played each June at Opryland's Springhouse Golf Club. And Legends Club of Tennessee, in Franklin, was host of the 1997 USGA Girls' Junior Amateur. The popularity of these events serves notice that Nashville is a prime location to watch and play competitive golf. The area's public courses have been ranked among the best in the nation, and most of them are reasonably priced. The seven courses operated by Metro Parks in particular are bargains. Golfers with more discriminating standards can pay more to play on tournament-quality courses like Springhouse, Hermitage and Legends Club.

This chapter covers area courses that are open to the general public. We'll also look at practice ranges and opportunities for instruction. Distances are measured from the white (middle) tees. Greens fees include riding cart unless otherwise indicated; please note that these prices were in effect in 1999 and are subject to change. Walkers are allowed, generally for a lower fee, unless otherwise indicated.

Fore!

## Metro Parks Courses

Metro Parks maintains seven public golf courses throughout the city. All are open year round, weather permitting, with the exception of Riverview, which is open May through October. Please note that each course is closed two days a week during January and February, with scheduling staggered so that at least three courses are open each day in winter. During these months, it's a good idea to call first to ensure your course is open. Each course has a snack bar and pro shop; lessons are available at Harpeth, Percy Warner and Two Rivers.

These courses, which range from nine to 27 holes, charge $9 per nine holes, with the exception of the Percy Warner and Shelby courses, which are only $8. Riding cart rental, for those courses that have riding carts, is an additional $8 unless otherwise indicated. Club rental is available.

Annual memberships entitle members to play at any Metro course; from April 1 through September, members pay a $1 surcharge for each nine holes, but the rest of the year there's no additional greens fee. Memberships are $545, $365 for seniors, $815 for couples and $240 for those 18 and younger. If you play a lot, this may be a good deal for you.

## Harpeth Hills Golf Course
**2424 Old Hickory Blvd. • (615) 862-8493**

Harpeth Hills, one of two Metro courses in Percy Warner Park, is a busy course, and you'll generally need to reserve your tee times a week in advance. This scenic, slightly hilly 18-hole course is 6481 yards and par 72, with bentgrass greens and no water.

## McCabe Golf Course
**46th St. and Murphy Rd.**
**• (615) 862-8491**

McCabe is a fairly level, easy-to-walk course with 27 holes — par 70 and par 36. The par 70 covers 5847 yards. There's no water, but there are some challenges, notably the 162-yard 15th hole, a par 3 with a trap on each side. The course's old clubhouse and attached cart garage were destroyed in a fire in June 1999, but the course has remained open even. Metro Parks and Recreation officials said it might take as long as a year, and as much as $1.5 milllion, to rebuild the facilities.

## Percy Warner Golf Course
**Forrest Park Dr. • (615) 352-9958**

This nine-hole, 2474-yard course at the Belle Meade Boulevard entrance to Percy Warner Park features traditional, tree-lined fairways and is par 34. There's no water. Percy Warner has no riding carts, but pull carts are available for $1.

## Ted Rhodes Golf Course
**1901 Ed Temple Blvd. • (615) 862-8463**

There's water everywhere at Rhodes, coming into play on about 14 of the 18 holes. The scenic par 72 course is 6207 yards.

## Riverview Golf Course
**S. 17th and Sevier St. • (615) 226-9331**

Riverview, which lies on the Cumberland River, is a nine-hole, 1314-yard, par 29 course. It rents pull carts only, but you can pay a $2 trail fee and use your own riding cart.

## Shelby Golf Course
**2021 Fatherland St.**
**• (615) 862-8474**

Shelby is very hilly — fit for a mountain goat, as one golfer put it. The 18-hole, 5789-

yard, par 72 course has a pond on the 11th hole and creeks running throughout.

## Two Rivers Golf Course
**3140 McGavock Pk. • (615) 889-2675**

Two Rivers is marked by rolling hills, with one water hole on both the front and the back nines. It's 18 holes, 6230 yards and par 72.

# Other Public Courses in Metro Nashville

## Country Hills Golf Club
**1501 Saundersville Rd., Hendersonville**
**• (615) 824-1100**

Country Hills is a short course, at 5800 yards, but it's a hilly, wooded and tough par 70. The biggest challenge is the No. 3 hole, a 380-yard par 4 dogleg left with water. Holes 4 and 5 feature water. Greens fees are $27 weekdays and $35 weekends, with varying morning and afternoon specials offered. Country Hills has a pro shop and snack bar, and lessons are available from pro Chris Ferguson.

## Forrest Crossing Golf Course
**750 Riverview Dr., Franklin**
**• (615) 794-9400**

During the Civil War, Confederate Gen. Nathan Bedford Forrest and his men built a stone bridge and crossed the picturesque Harpeth River at a spot between where holes No. 3 and No. 4 are today. While he most likely didn't stop for a round, the bridge is still visible, and the name of the rolling course commemorates the event. Water comes into play on 15 of the 18 holes on this 6300-yard, par 72 course. Forrest Crossing, which offers corporate events and tournament packages, also has a putting facility, driving range and full-service snack bar. Greens fees are $33 weekdays and $43 weekends. Walking is allowed after 2 PM.

## Hermitage Golf Course
**3939 Old Hickory Blvd., Old Hickory**
**• (615) 847-4001**

In May 1997, Hermitage marked its 10th and final year as host of the LPGA Sara Lee Classic; at this writing, tournament official were

Photo: Nashville CVB/Robin Hood

Golf is a popular pastime among Nashville Insiders.
A number of tournaments are held here every year.

scrambling to find a new sponsor. The 18-hole, par 72 course measures 6011 yards. It's largely a flat, open course with some elevated greens. The bentgrass greens are large and undulating. Fairways are bermudagrass in summer and rye the rest of the year. Six lakes come into play on the course, which lies along the Cumberland River.

Hermitage, which is noted for its driving range and putting green, (see Practice Ranges in this chapter), also has a snack bar, pro shop and PGA instructors. It specializes in golf outings. Fees are $40 plus tax weekdays, $45 plus tax on weekends and $50 plus tax on holidays. Call for tee time. You can reserve your time up to five days in advance at regular rates, or pre-book up to a year in advance by paying $5 extra per person and using a credit card to guarantee it.

### Hunter's Point Golf Course
**1500 Hunters Point Pk., Lebanon**
**• (615) 444-7521**

Hunter's Point, a 6017-yard, par 72 course, is flat, with water coming into play on many of the 18 holes. No. 15, a 458-yard par 4, challenges you with water to the left and right of the green and trees to the left of the fairway. Greens fees are $22 on weekdays and $29 on weekends. Hunter's Point has a pro shop.

### The Legacy Golf Course
**100 Ray Floyd Dr., Springfield**
**• (615) 384-4653**

This par 72 course, designed by PGA veteran Raymond Floyd, opened on Memorial Day 1996. But it looks a lot older. That's because Floyd designed the 6133-yard Legacy — which is marked by undulating greens and water on 12 of the 18 holes — around a collection of mature trees. Fees are $26 weekdays, $32 weekends. The Legacy has a snack bar and pro shop, and lessons are available.

### Legends Club of Tennessee
**1500 Legends Club Ln., Franklin**
**• (615) 790-1300**

PGA professional Tom Kite and architect Bob Cupp designed the Legends Club, which opened in 1992. The course, host of the 1997 USGA Girls' Junior Amateur, has 36 holes, but only 18 are open to the public.

The public portion is par 71 and 6001 yards, featuring a links design with rolling, open fairways and lots of sand. There's not a lot of water, though the 434-yard, par 4 No. 10 hole requires a shot over water. Fees vary according to the time, but during peak times they're $65 weekdays and $81 weekends and holidays. Twilight and evening rates, however, can reduce your cost to as little as $30 . Walkers are not allowed. Legends Club has a snack bar and pro shop, and lessons are available.

## Long Hollow Golf Course
**1080 Long Hollow Pk., Gallatin**
**• (615) 451-3120**

Long Hollow, a 5650-yard, par 70 course, is on rolling land, with water a factor on seven of its 18 holes. Watch out for No. 10, a 420-yard par 4 — there's water out of bounds to the right on the second shot, and trees to the left. Greens fees are $27 Monday through Thursday and $30 Friday through Sunday and on holidays. Long Hollow has a snack bar and pro shop and offers lessons.

## Montgomery Bell Golf Course
**800 Hotel Ave., Burns • (615) 797-2578**

This course, part of Montgomery Bell State Park, is 5927 yards and par 71. It's hilly and features water on three holes. Reserve your tee times up to six days in advance. Fees are $29. The course has a pro shop and snack bar.

## Nashboro Golf Club
**1101 Nashboro Blvd. • (615) 367-2311**

Nashboro Golf Club, five minutes south of the airport off Murfreesboro Road, is set on rolling hills and beautifully lined with trees. Half of the 18-hole course runs through the Nashboro Village housing development (resi-

dents get a 10 percent discount), and water comes into play on several holes. The course covers 6500 yards and is par 72.

Nashboro has PGA golf pros on staff and offers a driving range, practice putting green, pro shop and large snack bar with satellite television. Tournament and league packages are available. Fees are $37 weekdays and $45 on weekends. Walkers are permitted Monday through Thursday only.

## Pine Creek Golf Course
**1836 Logue Rd., Mount Juliet**
**• (615) 449-7272**

Smaller, undulating greens that can be hard to reach are characteristic of this 6250-yard, par 72 course, which was built on a farm and has remained largely unaltered. Pine Creek's rolling layout is marked with water and pine trees, both of which come into play on many of the 18 holes. A lake marks the 140-yard, par 3 No. 6 hole. Fees are $31 weekdays and $40 weekends. You can schedule tee times up to five days in advance. The course has a snack bar and pro shop. Lessons are available.

## Riverside Golf Course
**640 Old Hickory Blvd., Old Hickory**
**• (615) 847-5074**

This 18-hole course on the Cumberland River is 3407 yards and par 60. It's flat, and water comes into play on three holes. Fees are $24.50. Riverside has a snack bar and pro shop, and lessons are available.

## Smyrna Municipal Golf Course
**101 Sam Ridley Pkwy., Smyrna**
**• (615) 459-2666**

This 6011-yard, par 72 course is fairly flat with just a few water hazards. Fees are $27,

## INSIDERS' TIP

The Vinny, Vince Gill's annual pro-celebrity tournament at The Golf Club of Tennessee in Kingston Springs, is the second-best place (after Fan Fair) to see a bunch of country music stars together.

Photo: Donnie Beauchamp

Shelby Park has an 18-hole municipal golf course and
boat-launch access to the Cumberland River.

plus a $1 key deposit. Smyrna Municipal has a snack bar and pro shop.

## Springhouse Golf Club at Opryland USA
**18 Springhouse Ln. • (615) 871-7759**

Springhouse, a links-style course designed by Larry Nelson, lines the Cumberland River. Each June since 1994 it has been site of the BellSouth Senior Classic, where champions have included Lee Trevino, Jim Dent, two-time winner Isao Aoki and Gil Morgan. The course, highlighted by large mounds and a bunch of water, has five sets of tees. The "everyday" tees at this course are blue instead of white, with a total distance of 6185 yards. A 19th-century springhouse sits at the back of the green on the signature hole, the 345-yard No. 4. In-season (April through October) fees are $75; the rest of the year they're $50. Walking is permitted only in winter.

The 43,000-square-foot clubhouse is a complete facility with rooms for meetings and banquets, a grill room and complete locker room facilities for men and women. The pro shop offers high-quality rental clubs and golf shoes as well as brand-name balls for the driving range. PGA pros on staff are available for lessons; since 1998, the course has featured the John Jacobs Practical School of Golf every weekend from April through October.

## Sycamore Golf Course
**1 Fairway Ln., Ashland City**
**• (615) 792-7863**

Sycamore Creek circles this beautiful 18-hole course, which is par 72 and 6219 yards. Bermudagrass fairways and bentgrass greens

Photo: Cindy Stooksbury Guier

Metro Parks operates several golf courses, including Harpeth Hills, pictured here.

highlight Sycamore, which is flat and open on the front nine but tighter on the back. Ponds come into play on three holes. The course also features a pro shop and snack bar. Fees are $20 weekdays and $26 weekends. Seniors can play for $12 Mondays before noon.

## Windtree Golf Course
### Nonaville Rd., Mount Juliet
### • (615) 754-4653

The front nine is relatively flat, but the back nine is hilly at Windtree, which features bermudagrass fairways, bentgrass greens and water on several holes along the 6099-yard, par 72 course. The signature hole is the scenic No. 16, a 420-yard, par 4 downhill shot from the highest point on the course; don't let the view distract you. Fees are $38 Monday through Friday and $43 weekends; regular players will find it worthwhile to join the free Partners Club, which reduces fees to $34 and $40. Walkers are allowed during week and after 2 PM on weekends. Windtree has a pro shop, driving range and practice putting green. Three pros are available for lessons.

# Golf Instruction

## Art Quick's Golf Academy
### 501 Metroplex Dr. • (615) 834-8121

Art Quick, a PGA professional who still plays the Senior Tour, has been teaching since 1950. But there's nothing old-fashioned about his approach, which uses computerized TV simulators much like those used in baseball and football training. He says it's "one of the best setups in the nation." Rates are $35 for a half-hour or $180 for six lessons.

## The Nancy Quarcelino School of Golf
### 1500 Legends Club Ln., Franklin
### • (615) 599-1344

Nancy Quarcelino, former head pro at the Hermitage Golf Course, moved her school in 1999 from its former site at Heritage to Legends Club of Tennessee. The school provides private and group instruction to golfers of all ages. Quarcelino, a member of the PGA and LPGA who started the school in 1992, has been involved in the sport for more than 30 years. There's a wide range of programs and rates; a private one-hour lesson with Quarcelino is $60.

## Through the Green
**3000 Columbia Ave., Franklin**
**• (615) 791-6905**

Through the Green, a 50-acre indoor/outdoor golf teaching center that's geared especially for women and children, offers complete video analysis of your golf game. Women can benefit from accelerated programs taught by PGA and LPGA professionals. There's a lighted nine-hole executive course with bentgrass greens and zoysia fairways, a driving range with 20 target greens and five USGA regulation practice greens. A short-game practice area simulates course situations. Prices vary, so call for details.

# Practice Ranges

## Bellevue Valley Golf
**7629 Old Harding Pk. • (615) 646-8858**

Bellevue Valley's large, lighted grass range features grass tees and sand. There's also a chipping green, and the resident teaching pro can give you tips.

## Hermitage Golf Center
**4000 Andrew Jackson Pkwy.**
**• (615) 883-5200**

Hermitage is noted for its driving range and its 10,000-square-foot putting green.

## Riverside Golf Center
**640 Old Hickory Blvd., Old Hickory**
**• (615) 847-5074**

Riverside has a lighted driving range, a 150-yard grass tee, PGA instructors, two miniature golf courses, a baseball-softball range, bumper boats and go-carts.

**After a tumultuous courtship, much of Nashville appears ready to welcome the Tennessee Titans, the city's new NFL team.**

# Spectator Sports

When it comes to spectator sports, Nashville has officially — and convincingly — become a major-league city. In the last couple of years, we have made a double mark on the map of big-time professional athletics with the acquisition of both a National Football League team and a National Hockey League team. Meanwhile, Nashville has been mentioned as a possible site for a franchise in a revived American Basketball Association.

Meanwhile, football continues to be king in this city, and across the state. Tennesseans proudly and joyously welcomed the 1998 national college football championship when the University of Tennessee Volunteers defeated Florida State 23-16 in the Fiesta Bowl on January 4, 1999. (Although the Volunteers' real home is three-plus hours away in Knoxville, they are "the state's team." You can see those orange-and-white flags waving in the wind a mile away as you drive around Nashville.)

In other football news, Nashville made an impressive showing on December 29, 1998, with the inaugural American General Music City Bowl, as a sold-out crowd of 41,600 watched Virginia Tech defeat Alabama at Vanderbilt Stadium.

At this point, it's too early to tell what kind of impact the competition from a professional challenger will have on college football here. But, after a tumultuous courtship, much of Nashville appears ready to welcome the Tennessee Titans, the city's new NFL team. A brief history: in 1997 the Houston Oilers became the Tennessee Oilers after owner Bud Adams decided to relocate the team. The ensuing saga has been a controversial and entertaining one of big bucks, intrastate rivalry, politics, a referendum, divided loyalties, finger-pointing and the power of a name. Nashvillians had disagreed about whether or not they wanted to use tax money to build a stadium to lure a professional team, a majority finally deciding in a referendum that the answer was yes. Resentment built, however, when the team's administration made a number of public-relations gaffes even some supporters wondered if they'd made the right decision.

The replanted Oilers spent their initial season playing home games at Liberty Bowl Stadium in Memphis, a city that, having failed in its efforts to land its own expansion franchise, generally welcomed the "borrowed" team with less than open arms. They then moved to their intended base, Nashville, where they played 1998 home games at another temporary site, Vanderbilt Stadium. At the end of the 1998 season, Nashville supporters of the team finally got their wish of a new team nickname, logo and colors when the team was renamed the Tennessee Titans.

The 1999 season was to kick off in a new, $292 million stadium downtown on the east bank of the Cumberland River. Following the growing trend of corporate sponsorship, the Titans in June 1999 signed a $30 million dollar, 15-year deal to christen the new facility Adelphia Coliseum after a Pennsylvania-based communications company.

While we're still on the subject of football, we'll also mention the Nashville Kats, our entry in the Arena Football League. This is a different breed of the sport altogether — a high-scoring, crowd-pleasing, rock 'n' roll indoor hybrid of the game. The inaugural 1997 season and the 1998 follow-up were largely successful ones for the Kats, who play their home games at the newly renamed Gaylord Entertainment Center, formerly the Nashville Arena.

Maybe your game is ice hockey. That scene also is jumping. The 1998-99 season saw the debut of the Nashville Predators, an NHL expansion franchise.

On the downside, 1999 saw the demise of the Nashville Noise women's professional basketball team; the Nashville Metros profes-sional soccer team (an-other pro soccer team, the Tennessee Rhythm, had been founded and was struggling to drum up support at this writing); and the Nashville Ice Flyers, a minor-league professional hockey team. At least part of the reason for these teams' folding was their inability to compete for attendance and sponsorships with the growing number of local professional teams.

Meanwhile, there's a wide world of sports available for local spectators. In addition to the above opportunities, we also have several kinds of auto racing (including a new super-speedway that is being built at this writing), a AAA baseball team and plenty of collegiate competition, along with the occasional spe-cial event. You'll find them all here in this Spec-tator Sports chapter. Golf has its own chapter, by the way; for participant sports and other recreational activities, see our Recreation chap-ter.

Tickets for many sporting events are avail-able through Ticketmaster, (615) 255-9600.

# Auto Racing

## Nashville Speedway USA
### 625 Smith Ave. • (615) 726-1818

It's only appropriate that Nashville, the country music capital of the world, should have a NASCAR track. Country fans, in general, are huge fans of the sport, and many country stars are participants. But, as far as Nashville Speed-way is concerned, there is good news and bad news. The bad news is the days may well be numbered for this track on the Tennessee State Fairgrounds. The good news is that the

Nashville area is expected to have, by the start of the 2001 racing season, a new super-speed-way in nearby Wilson County. But more on that in a moment; first we'll focus on the exist-ing track.

Nashville Speedway opened in the early 1900s as Fairgrounds Speedway, a site for horse racing, which is now illegal in Tennessee. The track's first auto race was in the 1930s. The speedway consists of a $5/8$-mile, high-banked, oval asphalt track, which encircles a quarter-mile, flat, oval asphalt track. The grandstand seats more than 15,000, about 8,000 in the covered upper area and the rest in the uncovered lower area.

The weekly Winston Racing Series pro-gram consists of five divisions: Late Model Stock Cars (the premier division), SuperTrucks, Street Modifieds, Pure Stocks and Legends Cars. Special events include the NASCAR Busch Grand National Series, the NASCAR Craftsman Truck Series, NASCAR Slim Jim All-Pro Series, Southern All Stars, Mark Collie Celebrity Race and American Speed Associa-tion series.

Now, about that other track. In November 1997, Mayor Phil Bredesen and other officials announced plans for a new superspeedway — with a 1¼-mile track — that they originally hoped would be complete by the end of 1999, and that they hope will eventually bring major NASCAR events to Middle Tennessee. Plans have been delayed by struggles to find ac-quire the needed land, legal issues and a fight by some Wilson County residents who say bringing a racetrack to their neighborhood will disrupt their rural tranquillity.

In the meantime, Dover Downs Entertain-ment Inc., owner of the yet-unnamed super-speedway, has acquired the lease for Nash-ville Speedway USA. When completed, the super-speedway — scheduled to begin con-struction in late August or early September 1999 and projected to cost $125 million — will include facilities for a road course, a drag strip, a "short track" dirt track and a "short track" asphalt speedway. It will initially seat 50,000, though owners hope it could eventually ex-

www.insiders.com
See this and many other Insiders' Guide® destinations online.
Visit us today!

pand to the 100,000-seat capacity needed for the big NASCAR events. The events that are now at the existing speedway would carry over to the new one; the owners also hope to attract Winston Cup events and NHRA drag races.

Attendance for races at Nashville Speedway USA was more than 200,000 in 1999. Admission for the regular Saturday racing is $10, with children 11 and younger admitted free. Prices vary for special events.

### Highland Rim Speedway
**6801 Kelly Willis Rd., Ridgetop**
**• (615) 643-8725**

Highland Rim Speedway, a $\frac{1}{3}$-mile, D-shaped track with high-banked turns, features stock car racing every Saturday night from April through October as well as special events throughout the year. Weekly races are held in six divisions: Late Model Stock Car, Sportsman, Mini Cup Series, Pro Modified, 4-Cylinder Sport Truck/Car Series and Taxi Cab.

Before achieving their current NASCAR stardom, drivers such as Darrell Waltrip, Bobby Hamilton, Donnie and Bobby Allison and Red Farmer raced at Highland Rim, which has benefited from a repaved surface and other improvements since new ownership took over in 1990. Seating is about 5,000, including VIP sky boxes, and the atmosphere is family-friendly, with no alcohol. Admission is $8 for general admission, and children 11 and younger get in free with paid adult admission. Tickets for special events are generally $10 but sometimes $12.

Highland Rim Speedway is 20 miles north of Nashville; just take Interstate 65 north to Exit 104, then take Tenn. Highway 257 west for 2 miles. Parking is free.

### Music City Raceway
**3302 Ivey Point Rd., Goodlettsville**
**• (615) 876-0981**

Music City Raceway offers National Hot Rod Association drag racing on Tuesday, Friday and Saturday nights. Admission varies from $5 Tuesday and Friday nights to $8 for regular Saturday night NHRA races and up to $12 for special events. For directions to the track, call (615) 876-3406.

# Baseball

### Nashville Sounds
**Herschel Greer Stadium,**
**534 Chestnut St. • (615) 242-4371**

The 1999 season marked the 22nd in Nashville for the Sounds, the AAA affiliate of the major-league Pittsburgh Pirates. At this writing, the Sounds had the best record in their Pacific Coast League for the 1999 season.

The team, originally a AA affiliate of the Cincinnati Reds when it came to town in 1978, had a memorable second season, setting a minor-league season attendance record and winning the Southern League championship. Nashville was a AA affiliate of the New York Yankees from 1980 to 1984, then moved to AAA and affiliated with the Detroit Tigers in 1985. From 1987 to 1992, the Sounds were the Cincinnati Reds' AAA farm team, and they joined the White Sox organization in 1993 before affiliating with the Pirates in 1998. The Sounds have won two league championships — in 1979 and 1982 — and were runners-up in 1981, 1993 and 1994. In 1998 they finished with a losing record, 67-76, but finished the season by winning 21 of their last 32 games.

Greer Stadium, a 11,500-seat facility highlighted by a guitar-shaped scoreboard, underwent a major renovation in 1997. New ownership — including longtime investor Jerry Reed and the Oak Ridge Boys' Richard Sterban — put a heightened emphasis on fun, family-oriented promotions and entertainment. Entertainment highlights include team mascot Ozzie, with plenty of promotional events and giveaways as well as regulars visits by Jake

---

**INSIDERS' TIP**

**Grantland Rice, a Murfreesboro native who wrote for Nashville's old *Daily News*, went on to become a legendary sportswriter. He came up with the nickname for Notre Dame football's famed "Four Horsemen of the Apocalypse."**

the Diamond Dog, the Famous Chicken and other crowd-pleasers.

1999 marked the return of Trent Jewett as the Sounds' manager; he had previously coached the Sounds for one season.

The nature of a "farm team" can make being a fan both rewarding and frustrating. It's rewarding because you have the opportunity to watch the stars of tomorrow; frustrating because, when they start becoming stars, they are generally shipped up to the major leagues. Nashville Sounds fans have had the opportunity to enjoy the early careers of such stars as Steve Balboni, Don Mattingly, Willie McGee, Otis Nixon, Buck Showalter, Hal Morris, Chris Sabo and Doug Drabek, who as a Pittsburgh Pirate was the National League's 1990 recipient of the Cy Young Award.

Game times vary; gates open two hours before starting time. Box seats are $8, and general admission is $5. Prices for children 12 and younger are $1 less. You can usually park in the stadium lot or at the nearby Cumberland Science Museum (see Attractions).

# Basketball

## Vanderbilt University
**Memorial Gym, 25th Ave.**
**• (615) 322-GOLD (tickets)**

Vandy's men's team starts the 1999-2000 season under a new coach: Kevin Stallings, previously at Illinois State University. Former coach Jan Van Breda Kolff — a Vandy player from 1971 to 1974, and SEC player of the year in 1974 — resigned under pressure at the end of a 1998-99 season in which the Commodores went 14-15 (7-9 in Southeastern conference games). In six seasons at Vanderbilt, Van Breda Kolff compiled a 104-81 record (42-53 SEC), taking the team to three National Invitation Tournaments and one NCAA Tournament appearance; he was subsequently hired by Pepperdine.

The Commodores are always a formidable opponent at Memorial Gym, where they have never had a losing record.

As for the Vanderbilt women, they were looking to rebound in 1999-2000 from a 1998-99 season in which they finished with their worst record (13-14) in 16 years. It was the

first year that Jim Foster, now in his ninth season, had failed to take the Lady Commodores to the NCAA Tournament.

No single-game tickets were available during the 1997-98 season for men's basketball games at 15,000-seat Memorial Gym. You could buy either a "black pack" or a "gold pack," each consisting of upper-level seating at four men's and one women's game, for $70. Season tickets were $265 and $133 for men's games.

Women's tickets were $9 for SEC games ($12 for Tennessee) and $7 for non-conference games. Season tickets for women's games were $80 for adults and $30 for anyone 17 and younger. The four-game super pack is $35. Call (615) 322-GOLD for single-game tickets.

## University of Tennessee
**Thompson-Boling Arena, 1600 Stadium Dr., Knoxville • (423) 974-2491 (tickets)**

It's only fair to start this write-up with the University of Tennessee women's team, which during the 1990s under Coach Pat Summitt has truly earned the right to be called a dynasty — and, many say, the best women's team in history. The Lady Vols' upset loss to Duke in the NCAA East Regionals in March 1999 thwarted their bid for a fourth straight (and seventh overall) NCAA championship. On the court, the team, which finished the 1998-99 season at 31-3, has been led by the phenomenal Chamique Holdsclaw, the first three-time All-American and first to repeat as Associated Press women's player of the year. Now that Holdsclaw has graduated and been taken as the No. 1 draft pick by the WNBA's Washington Mystics, the Lady Vols have some huge shoes to fill.

The men's team finished the 1998-99 season, the second under Coach Jerry Green, with a 21-9 record that included their first NCAA tournament victory in 16 years. But a devastating 81-51 loss to Southwest Missouri State in the second round of the NCAA East Regionals ended the season prematurely. A year earlier, Green had led the Vols to a 20-9 record and their first trip to the NCAA Tournament in 16 years.

Individual reserved tickets for men's games are $12, and general admission seats are $6. Typically, single tickets for four popular games

— Kentucky and three others — are not sold early in the season, but rather are available only in a package, which cost $48 in 1998-99. Reserved season tickets cost $208 .

For women's games, tickets are $12 for reserved seating and $6 for general admission. Reserved season tickets are $125 for adults and $95 for children.

## Tennessee State University
## Howard Gentry Complex,
**John Merritt Blvd. • (615) 963-5841 (tickets)**

The men's Tigers basketball team, coached by Frankie Allen, were 12-15 in 1998-99 (9-9 in conference games). The women's team, coached by Teresa Lawrence Phillips, finished its injury-plagued 1998-99 season with a 13-15 record (7-11 OVC). Individual game tickets are priced at $6 and $8. Season ticket prices vary.

## Middle Tennessee State
**Hale Arena, Murphy Athletic Center, Tennessee Blvd., Murfreesboro • (615) 898-2103 (tickets)**

The Blue Raiders, men and women, play in the Ohio Valley Conference. The men's team, coached by Randy Wiel, was 12-9 (9-9 in OVC games) in 1998-99. The women's team, coached by Stephany Smith, was 18-10 (11-2), including a first-round loss in the post-season Women's National Invitation Tournament. Men's single-game basketball tickets are $8. Women's tickets are $4 a game general admission when only the women's team is playing; when it plays before the men's game, you get two games for the $8 price of a men's ticket.

# Football

## Tennessee Titans
**Stadium and ticket office, Adelphia Coliseum, 1 Titans Wy. • (615) 565-4300
Practice facility, Baptist Sports Park, 7640 U.S. Hwy. 70 S. • (615) 673-1500**

The Tennesse Titans — formerly the Houston Oilers and then, for two seasons, the Tennessee Oilers — finally got their own home

(and a name, logo and color scheme that locals can call their own) for the 1999-2000 season. With the completion of a new stadium on the east bank of the Cumberland River in downtown Nashville, Middle Tennesseans appear to be embracing the team, and hopes and expectations are high.

When the team relocated from Houston in 1997, it spent its first season in a temporary home at Memphis's Liberty Bowl. For the 1998-99 season, the team, still known as the Oilers, played its home games at Vanderbilt Stadium in Nashville. Now there's a $292 million, 67,000-capacity, open air, natural gas stadium, christened Adelphia Coliseum ("The Delph" for short) thanks to a 15-year, $30 million sponsorship deal with a Pennsylvania-based computer company.

The Oilers finished with an 8-8 record in both 1997-98 and 1998-99. But in 1998-99 there was improvement, as the Oilers went a club-record 7-1 against AFL Central division opponents (compared with 2-6 a year earlier). Also, five of their eight losses were by eight points or less. Their division opponents are the Cincinnati Bengals, Pittsburgh Steelers, Baltimore Ravens and Jacksonville Jaguars. In 1999-2000, as the Titans, the team is seeking its first trip to the playoffs since 1993.

Stars include running back Eddie George, a Heisman Trophy winner at Ohio State and 1996 NFL Offensive Rookie of the Year, and quarterback Steve McNair. Head coach Jeff Fisher, the NFL's youngest head coach, played defensive back and returned punts for the Chicago Bears during their mid-1980s glory days under Mike Ditka.

Individual game ticket prices for 1999, available through TicketMaster, range from $18 to $250 plus convenience and handling charges. Season tickets for eight regular-season home games and two preseason games in 1999 range from $250 to more than $2,500, plus PSL (permanent seat license) charges.

## Nashville Kats
**Offices, 150 Second Ave. N., Ste. 305 • (615) 254-KATS (tickets)
Games at Gaylord Entertainment Ctr. (former Nashville Arena), 501 Broadway**

Nashvillians are eating up the exciting, though unconventional, brand of football

The Nashville Kats' Cory Fleming, No. 12, was 1997
Rookie of the Year in the Arena Football League and made All-Arena in 1998.

played by Arena Football League teams. The 1997 debut of the Nashville Kats, who play their home games in the Gaylord Entertainment Center (also known, for the Kats' purposes as "The Alley"), made them the most successful new franchise in league history.

The Kats, who compiled a 27-16 record in their first three seasons (10-5 in 1997 and 9-4 in 1998 and 8-7 in 1999), are the first-ever expansion team to win an Arena Football League division title and have made playoff appearances in each of their first three seasons, losing in the first game each time.

Final tallies in AFL games are a lot more like basketball than football (the 1997 regular-season home finale, where Nashville beat the Orlando Predators 74-55, is typical). Games are played on indoor padded surfaces that are 85 feet wide and 50 yards long — half the length of a conventional football field (one slogan for the game is "half the field, twice the excitement"). Each team fields eight players, most of whom play both offense and defense. Other differences in this version of football are that there is no punting — on fourth down, you can go for a first down, touchdown or field goal — and that forward passes that bounce off the "rebound nets" in the end zone

remain in play until they hit the ground. Loud music between plays, pyrotechnics and a general "party" atmosphere contribute to the excitement.

The Nashville Kats' new head coach for the 1999 season was Pat Sperduto, who took over coaching responsibilities from Eddie Khayat, who remains as general manager. Star wide receiver and defensive back Cory Fleming, a University of Tennessee alum, earned league Rookie of the Year honors in 1997. Other stars include quarterback Andy Kelly, also a former Vol standout, and offensive specialist Tyronne Jones, who set a league record in 1998 by returning five kicks for touchdowns in a four-game span. The ownership group, led by team president Mark J. Bloom and AFL board member Hollis D. Godfrey, also includes country star Travis Tritt.

Season ticket prices in 1999 for seven regular-season games and one preseason game ranged from $800 for the limited-availability "in your face" seats — the first two rows along the sideline — to $70 for upper north end zone seats. Individual game tickets, which go on sale through Ticketmaster the week before each game, average $17 plus handling and service charges.

The AFL season runs from April through August and therefore does not conflict with the NFL.

## Vanderbilt University
**Vanderbilt Stadium/Dudley Field, Natchez Trace • (615) 322-GOLD (tickets)**

The Vanderbilt Commodores' 1999 season is their third under Coach Woody Widenhofer, who had been the team's top defensive coach for two years before taking the head position. Widenhofer, who made his name as defensive coordinator for the Pittsburgh Steelers' much-feared "Steel Curtain" — Jack Ham, Jack Lambert, "Mean" Joe Green and L.C. Greenwood — that contributed to four Super Bowl wins between 1973 and 1983, helped Vandy finish 28th nationally in total defense in the 1996 season.

Upon becoming the Commodores' head coach, Widenhofer defined his "Woodyball" philosophy: "Have fun. Expect to win." But it is be a major challenge bringing winning ways to Vanderbilt, whose last winning season was in 1982. In 1997, the Commodores finished 3-8, and in 1998 they were 2-9.

Vanderbilt has been to three bowl games in its history: defeating Auburn 25-13 in the 1955 Gator Bowl, losing to Texas Tech in the 1974 Peach Bowl and falling to Air Force in the 1982 Hall of Fame Bowl.

The Commodores play their home games at 41,448-seat Vanderbilt Stadium. Ticket info had not been released at this writing, but in recent years, season tickets have been in the $80-120 range, and individual game tickets in the $20-25 range.

## University of Tennessee
**Neyland Stadium, Volunteer Blvd., Knoxville • (423) 974-2491 (tickets), (800) 332-VOLS**

January 4, 1999, is a day that UT football fans will treasure forever. It was the day that the Volunteers, for years seemingly perennial contenders, finally got another national championship, defeating Florida State 23-16 in the Fiesta Bowl to cap a perfect 13-0 season under coach Phillip Fulmer.

Even without that glorious championship, however, the school's football tradition is a proud one with 39 post-season bowl appearances. From their first bowl appearance, a 17-0 victory over Oklahoma in the 1939 Orange Bowl, to their landmark Fiesta Bowl victory, the Vols have compiled a 22-17 bowl record (including a 42-17 loss to Nebraska, 1998 national co-champion with Michigan, in that year's Orange Bowl). They were national champions in the 1951 Associated Press and United Press International polls (and also earned national championships in 1938, 1940, 1950 and 1967 under such systems as the Dunkel and Williamson power ratings systems and the Litkenhouse difference-by-score system).

More than 200 University of Tennessee players have played professionally; 27 of them have been first-round NFL draft choices, including eight in the 1990s. Since 1987, 66 Volunteers have been taken in the NFL draft. NFL stars who played for Tennessee include Cincinnati Bengals receiver Carl Pickens, Green Bay Packers defensive lineman Reggie White, New Orleans Saints quarterback Heath Shuler, Kansas City Chiefs cornerback Dale Carter, Dallas Cowboys defensive back Bill Bates and St. Louis Rams linebacker Leonard Little.

Season tickets and individual game tickets always sell out before the season begins. Neyland Stadium is the nation's largest collegiate football stadium, with an official capacity of 102,544, and attendance often exceeds capacity. An NCAA record crowd of 107,608 was on hand for the Tennessee-Florida game September 21, 1996.

After star quarterback (and Heisman Trophy candidate) Peyton Manning graduated in 1997, Tee Martin took over the field general's role. Despite the pressures of having to follow in Manning's already-legendary footsteps, Martin — with ample help from such stalwart teammates as the aptly named receiver Peerless Price — managed to give the Vols the NCAA title that had eluded his predecessor.

Good luck getting tickets if you don't already have them. If it's any consolation, the games are frequently televised regionally and nationally, and The Vol Network broadcasts games on 29 Middle Tennessee radio stations, including WLAC AM 1510 in Nashville.

Gaylord Entertainment Center, formerly the Nashville Arena, is home
to the NHL's Nashville Predators and the AFL's Nashville Kats.

## Middle Tennessee State University
**Floyd Stadium/Jones Field, Greenland
Dr., Murfreesboro • (615) 898-2103
(season tickets)**

The 1999 season was destined to be a
landmark one for the Blue Raiders. Not only
did they start the season with a new coach —
Andy McCollum, who replaced the retired legend James "Boots" Donnelly — but they also
moved from the NCAA Division I-AA to the top
Division I-A. The school's other athletic programs have been in Division I-A since 1952,
when Middle Tennessee joined the Ohio Valley Conference in those sports. The football
team, at this writing, was still independent
though it was considering the possibility of
joining a conference. A renovation and expansion of the football stadium resulted in a seat-

ing capacity of more than 30,000 at the start
of the 1998 season.

Middle Tennessee was 5-5 overall, 5-2 in
the OVC, in 1998. Between 1983 and 1996,
the Blue Raiders were ranked in the Division I-
AA top 20 nine times, including first-place finished in 1985 and 1990, a fourth-place finish
in 1992 and a sixth-place finish in 1984.

Season football tickets are $32 for four
home games. Individual game tickets are $10.

## Tennessee State University
**Home games at Adelphia Coliseum, 1
Titans Wy. • (615) 963-5907 (tickets)**

TSU kicked off its 1999 season with a major change on the field — or rather, a change
*of* field. Home games are now played at
Adelphia Coliseum, home of the Titans. The

Tigers, coached by L.C. Cole, had a 1998 season filled with highs and lows. On the positive side, the team finished 9-3, winning the Ohio Valley Conference championship and making its first trip since 1986 to the NCAA Division I-AA playoffs before losing to Appalachian State. On the downside, the team also faced off-the-field troubles in an NCAA investigation into alleged violations by Cole and his brother Johnnie, the team's offensive coordinator.

TSU football has a proud legacy as one of the nation's great historically black football programs, compiling an overall 232-65-11 record in their heyday under Coach "Big" John Merritt. But a few years after Merritt's death in 1983, things got tough for the program and generally stayed so until the Tigers' recent turnaround. About 100 TSU football players have been drafted by the NFL, including Ed "Too Tall" Jones, Richard Dent, Joe Gilliam Jr., Eldridge Dickey, Larry Kinnebrew, Claude Humphrey and Jim Marsalis.

Season tickets are $50 for five home games. Individual game tickets are $12.50 or $18, depending on the game.

# Hockey

Nashville's relationship with professional hockey dates back to the Dixie Flyers, a minor-league team that was here from 1962 to 1971. The Nashville Knights of the East Coast Hockey League were here from 1989 to 1996, and the Nashville Nighthawks of the Central Hockey League lasted just one season, disappearing in 1996. A second Central Hockey League team was also short-lived, but now Nashville is truly in the big leagues with the 1998 arrival of the Predators, who play in the National Hockey League.

## Nashville Predators
**Gaylord Entertainment Ctr., 501 Broadway • (615) 770-PUCK (ticket information)**

The Predators began play in the 1998-99 season after a two-year pursuit of a NHL expansion franchise by Nashville officials and private investors bore fruit in June 1997. A public vote helped name the team; ballot options included "Ice Tigers," "Tigers," "Predators" and "Fury." (A partial skeleton of a saber-tooth tiger was found during excavations in downtown Nashville in the '70s; the team's cool logo features a saber-tooth tiger.)

Nashville, the NHL's 27th franchise, is part of the Central Division of the Western Conference, with the Chicago Black Hawks, Detroit Red Wings, St. Louis Blues and Toronto Maple Leafs. The Predators play their home games at Nashvlle Arena. Barry Trotz, the head coach, and Paul Gardner, assistant coach, came to Nashville after several years with the Portland (Maine) Pirates of the American Hockey League. Under their direction, Portland won the league championship, the Calder Cup, in 1994 and made it to the finals in 1996. Craig Leipold is majority owner of the franchise.

The Predators finished their injury-plagued inaugural season with a 28-47-7 record, including a 4-13-1 count in division games. They were 15-22-4 in home games. Despite the losing record, however, the team was a huge hit with fans, playing before 17 sold-out crowds at the Arena. Stars include right wing and team captain Tom Fitzgerald, right wing Sergei Krivokrasov, center Sebastien Bordeleau, defenseman Drake Berehowsky and top draft pick David Legwand, who made his Predators debut in the 1998-99 season finale.

Single-game ticket prices range from $10 to $95. 1998-99 season tickets for 41 games ranged from $585 to $2,340.

Three interstates travel through Music City, offering easy access to a number of great destinations in any direction.

# Daytrips and Weekend Getaways

There is plenty do in Nashville. If you don't believe that, just take a look through some of the other chapters in this book. We have some spectacular annual events and attractions to visit, interesting shops and neighborhoods to explore, parks and green spaces where you can exercise your body and rejuvenate your spirit, and all sorts of dining establishments that will delight your taste buds and satisfy your tummy.

But every now and then, we get the urge to hit the road, to get away from it all and explore new territory. Lucky for us, Nashville is centrally located. Three interstates travel through Music City, offering easy access to a number of great destinations in any direction. Highways and back roads can provide an altogether different experience, taking us on a slower pace through charming towns, historic locations, beautiful farmland, rolling hills and mountain villages.

In this chapter, we feature some of our favorite daytrips and weekend getaways. Most of these are within an easy three-hour drive from Nashville. Hours of operation, admission rates and hotel rates are always subject to change, so if you have specific attractions or other locations you want to visit, it's a good idea to call ahead for the latest information and rates.

The next time you're feeling a little restless, stressed out or bored, or if you're just in search of a fun way to spend a day or weekend with your family, consider one of these trips, or pick up a map and plot your own getaway. Think of it as a minivacation.

## Huntsville, Alabama

For a quick but fun getaway check out Huntsville, Alabama. Huntsville's location and attractions make it an easy, educational and enjoyable trip for adults and kids alike. It's 121 miles south of Nashville. Head down I-65 south and take either Exit 351, for U.S. Highway 72, or Exit 340B for I-565, if you want to go straight to the U.S. Space & Rocket Center.

If you've chosen Huntsville as your get-

---

away destination, it's most likely because of the U.S. Space & Rocket Center, Alabama's top tourist attraction. We'll tell you more about that in just a minute. But first, a little background info on the Rocket City.

Huntsville is named for the area's first settler, Tennessee pioneer John Hunt, who settled here in a log cabin 10 miles north of the Tennessee River in 1805. When the city was designated as the county seat in 1810, its name was changed to Twickenham, but the name was unpopular and was changed back to Huntsville within a year.

In 1940, Huntsville, then a cotton mill town, was selected as the site of a U.S. Army chemical weapons manufacturing plant. The city suited the Army's requirements: it was inland and out of the enemy's bombing reach. The Army turned nearly 40,000 acres of cotton fields into the Redstone Arsenal, which produced chemical weapons and other ammunition. After the war, the arsenal switched its focus to missiles and rockets. In 1950, the Army brought Dr. Wernher Von Braun and 117 German rocket scientists to this small mill town, where they produced the United States' first rocket. That rocket, the *Redstone*, launched an artificial satellite in 1959, followed a couple of years later by the launch of astronaut Alan B. Shepard Jr. on a 15-minute suborbital tour. When the National Aeronautics & Space Administration (NASA) was established, Von Braun's team led the organization's new Marshall Space Flight Center.

During the 1960s, Huntsville welcomed the world's greatest rocket scientists to work toward the goal of putting a man on the moon. The town's population grew by 50,000 in four years. The Huntsville scientists developed the Saturn rockets for the Apollo moon program. On July 15, 1969, the world's most powerful rocket, the 363-foot *Saturn V*, was launched,

**www.insiders.com**
See this and many other
**Insiders' Guide®**
destinations online.
**Visit us today!**

propelling three astronauts to the moon. Neil Armstrong walked on the moon July 20.

Today, Huntsville's population is nearly 180,000. The city has the highest annual median income in the South — $29,400 — and has been listed by *Kiplinger's Personal Finance Magazine* as among America's best 15 small- to medium-size cities in which to live.

In case you didn't know before, you now know why that enormous rocket sits at the Alabama welcome center off southbound I-65. Huntsville is America's space capital. And now you know why the world's largest space attraction is in Huntsville.

For more information on Huntsville, call 1-800-SPACE4U.

## Attractions

### 1819 Weeden House Museum
**300 Gates Ave., Huntsville, Ala.**
• **(256) 536-7718**

The 1819 Weeden House Museum is the state's oldest building open to the public. It's a block from Alabama Constitution Village (see subsequent entry). Inside the Federal-style brick structure, you can get a glimpse of the life of prominent families of the 1800s. The works of artist and poet Maria Howard Weeden, who lived in the house all her life, are on display here. This attraction is open March through December, from 1 to 4 PM Tuesday through Sunday. Admission is $3 for adults, $1 for children ages 12 and under.

### Burritt Museum & Park
**3101 Burritt Dr., Huntsville, Ala.**
• **(256) 536-2882**

Sitting atop Monte Sano Mountain is the Burritt Museum & Park, a museum of regional history housed in the 14-room mansion of prominent physician Dr. William Henry Burritt.

**INSIDERS' TIP**

During Prohibition, Golden Pond, Kentucky, in Land Between The Lakes, was considered the moonshine capital of the world.

You might find it interesting to know that this 1930s home is built in the shape of an X and is insulated with 2,200 bales of wheat straw.

This attraction includes the mansion, which serves as a museum; Historic Park, which features 19th-century restored farm structures; and award-winning nature trails that wind through the dense forest surrounding the buildings. Living-history demonstrations are presented at Historic Park. Be sure to check out the panoramic view from the front of the mansion. Buildings are open Tuesday through Saturday, 10 AM to 4 PM, and from noon to 4 PM Sunday. The structures are closed from mid-December through February. The grounds are open year round; hours are 7 AM to 7 PM April through September, and 7 AM to 5 PM October through March. Admission to the mansion, grounds, museum store and trails is free. Admission to Historic Park is $5 for adults; $4 for students, seniors 60 and older and military personnel; and $2 for children ages 2 through 18. Admission is free to everyone on Wednesdays.

## EarlyWorks History Museum Complex
**404 Madison St., Huntsville, Ala.**
• **(256) 564-8100, (800) 678-1819**

EarlyWorks, a new history complex located in downtown Huntsville, offers three fun attractions: the EarlyWorks Hands-On History Museum, Alabama Constitution Village and Huntsville Historic Depot (see below for individual descriptions). All three are located within a mile of each other. Tickets for all attractions can be purchased at the Madison Street location. Tickets can be purchased per attraction, but if you want to visit two or three of the attractions, the combination ticket is the best value. Combination tickets for all three attractions are $13 for adults, $12 for senior citizens 55 and older and $10.50 for children ages 4 through 17. Tickets to EarlyWorks Museum and Alabama Constitution Village or to EarlyWorks Museum and The Depot are $12, $11 and $9.50.

## EarlyWorks Hands-On History Museum
**404 Madison St., Huntsville, Ala.**
• **(256) 564-8100, (800) 678-1819**

This museum, the only one of its kind in the Southeast, makes learning about history fun for everyone. There's a 16-foot storytelling tree, a musical bandstand where you can hear tunes made popular by Alabama performers, a "floating" keelboat, a rustic gristmill with a working water wheel, a log cabin, Federal- and Victorian-style houses and more.

Hours are Monday through Saturday, 9 AM to 5 PM. Admission is $10 for adults, $9 for seniors and $7.50 for children ages 4 through 17. For combination ticket prices, see the EarlyWorks History Museum Complex listing above.

## Alabama Constitution Village
**109 Gates Ave., Huntsville, Ala.**
• **(256) 564-8100, (800) 678-1819**

Alabama Constitution Village is a living-history museum that offers a trip through Alabama's nearly 200-year history. This attraction is just off the Courthouse Square, on the same block where, in 1819, delegates wrote the Constitution that made Alabama the 22nd state. Costumed "villagers" will take you on a guided tour through eight reconstructed Federal-style buildings. You'll visit reconstructions of a cabinet maker's shop, print shop, confectionery shop, library and post office. You can purchase fresh-baked cookies and Alabama crafts at the confectionery shop. Plan to spend a minimum of an hour here.

Alabama Constitution Village is open Monday through Saturday, 9 AM to 5 PM. Admission is $6 for adults, $5 for senior citizens 55 and older, and $3.50 for children ages 4 through 17. For combination ticket prices, see the EarlyWorks History Museum Complex listing above.

## Huntsville Historic Depot
**320 Church St., Huntsville, Ala.**
• **(256) 535-6565, (800) 678-1819**

The Huntsville Historic Depot is the site of one of the oldest railroad buildings in America. During your self-guided tour of the two-story brick 1860 depot, look for Civil War graffiti — actual messages left by imprisoned soldiers. There are also a number of Civil War artifacts along the way. A robotic ticket agent at the restored 1912 ticket office tells about what life was like as a Southern Railway worker in the early 1900s. Outside, you can explore historic locomotives and rail cars. Every hour and half-hour, a 1920s trolley departs for a 30-minute tour of historic downtown Huntsville, including the Twickenham district, which features lots of antebellum houses.

The Huntsville Depot Museum is open 9 AM to 5 PM Monday through Saturday. Admission is $6 for adults, $5 for seniors 55 and older, and $3.50 for children ages 6 through 18. The trolley tours are available Monday through Saturday from 9:30 AM to noon and from 1:30 to 4 PM. Admission to the historic downtown trolley tour is $2 for adults, $1 for seniors and $1 for children. For combination ticket prices, see the EarlyWorks History Museum Complex listing.

### Harrison Brothers Hardware
**South Side Sq., Huntsville, Ala.**
• **(256) 536-3631**

If you're looking for free attractions, you might want to visit Harrison Brothers Hardware. This store opened in 1879 on the Courthouse Square. Little has changed here since then. The store sells nostalgic hardware, gifts, locally made crafts, rocking chairs, garden ornaments, old-fashioned toys and other souvenirs. It is owned by the Historic Huntsville Foundation. Hours are 9 AM to 5 PM Monday through Friday, 10 AM to 2 PM Saturday. Admission is free.

### Huntsville Botanical Garden
**4747 Bob Wallace Ave., Huntsville, Ala.**
• **(256) 830-4447**

Just a half-mile from the Space & Rocket Center is the Huntsville Botanical Garden. This 112-acre garden features wooded paths, grassy meadows and a beautiful collection of tended gardens filled with the colorful blooms of annuals and perennials from early spring through late fall. Enjoy the beautiful roses, daylilies and irises, and visit the fern glade and demonstration vegetable garden to learn about the benefits of these plants. An aquatic garden features a large gazebo where you can rest and enjoy the view. The Center for Biospheric Education and Research even features an "astronaut garden" designed for the moon.

If you'd like, bring your lunch and kick back in the shade at the picnic area. The garden shop offers a selection of books and gifts. May through October, the Huntsville Botanical Garden is open Monday through Saturday from 8 AM to 6:30 PM, and Sunday from 1 to 6:30 PM. November through April, hours are 9 AM to 5 PM Monday through Saturday, and 1 to 5 PM Sunday. Admission is $4 for adults, $3 for seniors 55 and older and $2 for students.

### Huntsville Museum of Art
**300 Church St., Huntsville, Ala.**
• **(256) 535-4350**

The museum's permanent collection features largely American art from the 19th and 20th centuries, with an emphasis on Southern art. There is some European art as well. The museum features six to eight major traveling exhibitions each year plus shows organized by the museum's chief curator and shows by emerging regional artists. Hours are 10 AM to 5 PM Tuesday through Saturday and 1 to 5 PM Sunday. Admission is usually free, but a fee may be charged for some major exhibits.

### U.S. Space & Rocket Center
**1 Tranquility Base, Huntsville, Ala.**
• **(256) 837-3400**

The U.S. Space & Rocket Center is near where Bob Wallace Avenue/Sparkman Drive

---

**INSIDERS' TIP**

Each fall, from September 15 to November 15, the Tennessee Department of Tourist Development opens its FallColor Forecast Line, (800) 697-4200, which provides weekly recorded updates about the changing leaf colors across the state and about upcoming outdoor events. The message is updated each Monday morning. For a copy of the department's *Tennessee Vacation Guide*, leave your name and phone number after the message, or call the Tennessee Department of Tourist Development at (615) 741-2159.

crosses I-565. From Nashville, take I-65 south, turn on to I-565 and take Exit 15.

The space center welcomes 400,000 visitors each year. This attraction features dozens of interactive exhibits, displays of NASA artifacts and actual Apollo, Mercury and Space Shuttle spacecraft. You can see the *Apollo 16* command module that returned from the moon and check out the moon buggy that was developed here.

If you ever wanted to fly in the Space Shuttle, here's your chance, sort of. You can command an "orbiting" craft in the Land the Shuttle simulator, or experience a shuttle launch and a few seconds of weightlessness aboard the Space Shot simulator, which speeds you 180 feet to the top of a tower at 45 mph with 4 G's of force. Take a trip into deep space on the Journey to Jupiter and Mission to Mars simulators. The IMAX movies on the Spacedome Theater's 67-foot domed screen are a thrill too.

If space flight isn't for you, take the bus tour to NASA's Marshall Space Flight Center, where you can see the International Space Station under construction. Buses depart several times a day from the museum. The two-hour tour includes a stop at the Neutral Buoyancy Tank, where astronauts prepare for walks in space. Back at the museum, you can check out the U.S. Space Camp, (800) 63 SPACE, where children and adults participate in intensive astronaut training activities. You can watch some of the activities, but if you want to participate, you'll need to make reservations about two weeks in advance. When you're ready for lunch, head to the museum's Lunch Pad.

There are a variety of admission prices to the U.S. Space & Rocket Center. A combination ticket that includes the museum, bus tour, IMAX theater, and rocket and shuttle park is $14.95 for adults and teens, $10.95 for children ages 3 through 12. Group discounts are available. One-week Space Camp registration is $675 for children. Adults can register for a weekend at Space Camp for $500. There is also a parent/child Camp, which allows one parent and one child to attend a weekend program for $600

The U.S. Space & Rocket Center is open 9 AM to 5 PM daily after Labor Day and until Memorial Day; from Memorial Day through Labor Day, hours are 8 AM to 6 PM. The attractions are closed Thanksgiving Day and Christmas Day.

# Fall Creek Falls

### Fall Creek Falls State Resort Park
**Rt. 3, Pikeville, Tenn. • (423) 881-3297, (800) 250-8611**

Spectacular scenery and abundant recreational opportunities await you at Fall Creek Falls State Resort Park. This park is an excellent destination at any time of year, but it's especially beautiful during the fall, when the air is crisp and the forest exhibits a stunning patchwork of fall colors.

The park is about 100 miles east of Nashville. It's in Bledsoe and Van Buren counties, 11 miles east of Spencer and 18 miles west of Pikeville. For the quickest route from Nashville, take I-40 east to Cookeville, then travel south on Tenn. Highway 111. The park is also accessible via Tenn. Highway 30.

Fall Creek Falls, Tennessee's largest state park, was named the top state park in the Southeast in *Southern Living* magazine's 1997 poll. On the western edge of the Cumberland Plateau, it covers more than 19,000 acres and offers some of the most beautiful scenery in the state. Sparkling cascades and streams, deep chasms, virgin timber and wildlife are among the attractions, but the highlight is 256-foot high Fall Creek Falls, the highest waterfall east of the Rocky Mountains. The park's other waterfalls are the Piney, Cane Creek and Cane Creek Cascades — all smaller, but impressive nonetheless. If you're planning to do some photography, visit after a good rainfall, when the waterfalls are roaring; after a dry spell, Fall Creek Falls might resemble more of a trickle than a waterfall.

To make your trip more meaningful, make your first stop the nature center, (423) 881-5708, beside Cane Creek Falls. The nature center features exhibits on the natural and cultural history of the park. Parking, restrooms, snack machines and picnic tables are nearby. If you plan to hike, this is also a good spot to pick up a map of the trails and plan your route.

During the summer, naturalist and recreation programs are presented daily. Planned activities might include a Spring Wildflower Pilgrimage, a tree planting, rappelling workshop and the annual Mountaineer Folk Festival.

## Hiking

Hiking is one of the most popular activities at Fall Creek Falls. There are several well-maintained day-use hiking trails that will take you to some of the park's most scenic areas. They range in length from less than a quarter-mile to 4.6 miles. Novice and experienced hikers alike will find suitable trails. Most of the trail heads begin near the park's north entrance, near the nature center. The trails are marked with a color-code system to help keep you on the right path.

A hike to Fall Creek Falls is a must. The .8-mile Woodland Trail is the shortest trail to Fall Creek Falls. This is an easy, 20-minute trail that begins behind the nature center. It takes you across the swinging bridge above Cane Creek Cascades, then continues straight to the Fall Creek Falls Overlooks. From the overlooks, you can continue to the shaded plunge pool of Fall Creek Falls by taking the Fall Creek Falls Trail to the left of the upper overlook. This trail is .4 mile and is classified as medium-difficult. If you're a novice hiker, don't despair: we've seen everyone from tiny tots to senior citizens along this trail — it really isn't too difficult. The trail takes you down through a portion of Fall Creek Gorge. As you near the bottom, watch your footing (sturdy shoes are recommended) — it's a bit rocky in places, and some of the rocks nearest the falls might be slippery. Once you make it to the bottom, reward yourself by taking a break and enjoying the cool temperatures and the mist floating off the falls. If you're really adventurous — and sure-footed — you can make your way over to the waterfall and walk behind it.

What comes down must go up, so after you've enjoyed an up-close look at the falls, you'll have to turn around and head up the mountain. It's steep — some might say strenuous — but just think of what a good workout you're getting! It's OK to stop and rest along the way. It seems that just about everybody does. You might even want to bring a snack in case you need an energy boost. If you didn't notice it on the way down, take the opportu-

nity to examine the ancient layers of rock in the gorge as you head back to the top. If you prefer to skip some of the hiking on the way to the falls, you can park at the Falls Parking area instead of at the nature center.

Fall Creek Falls has several other trails. The Gorge Overlook Trail extends to the right of the Woodland Trail, forming a loop around the bluff above the Cane Creek Gorge. The 1.1-mile trail takes about 25 minutes to hike and will lead you to three overlooks — the Cane Creek Overlook, Cane Creek Gorge Overlook and Fall Creek Falls Overlook.

The longest of the day-use trails is the 4.6-mile Paw Paw Trail. It's an easy trail that you can hike in less than two hours. The trail starts near the nature center and takes you across Rockhouse Creek and up a hill to incredible views of Cane Creek Falls. You can even see Fall Creek Falls at one point. Immediately after crossing Rockhouse Creek, the quarter-mile Cable Trail veers off to the left from the Paw Paw Trail. The Cable Trail is a difficult, rugged trail that goes to the base of Cane Creek Falls. It takes about 20 minutes to get to the bottom. If you take this trail, be sure to use the cable to help make your way down.

The Piney Falls Trail is a quarter-mile trail that begins at the parking lot in the Piney Falls area. The trail takes about 25 minutes and leads you to the Piney Falls Overlook on the right and to the swinging bridge over Piney Creek on the left.

If you're looking for a little more adventure, you might be interested in the long-distance backpacking trail. On the other hand, if you're not feeling very active, you can take the self-guided motor nature trail along the park's scenic loop. Biking enthusiasts will be pleased to know that there is a 3-mile paved bike path that leads from Fall Creek Falls Inn to the falls. Bike rentals are available.

## Other Recreation

The beautiful 345-acre Fall Creek Lake provides opportunities for water-based recreation. You can rent canoes, paddle boats and fishing boats at the boat dock. Privately owned boats are not permitted on the lake, but you can bring your own electric trolling motor. You can pick up bait, tackle, snacks and a park fishing license at the dock. A fishing permit is

Land Between the Lakes has the largest publicly owned bison herd east of the Mississippi. Some of them can be seen at the 750-acre Elk and Bison Prairie.

required unless you are staying at the inn or cabins. Anglers take note: this lake has yielded some record-size fish.

Fall Creek Falls State Resort Park has an Olympic-size swimming pool and a wading pool for children. The park also has an 18-hole, par 72 championship golf course that was named one of the top 25 public golf courses in the United States by *Golf Digest* magazine. A pro shop, (423) 881-5706, on-duty golf pro, driving range and practice green are available.

## Accommodations

If you plan to spend more than a day at Fall Creek Falls, you can choose from a number of accommodations. Fall Creek Falls Inn and Restaurant overlook the lake. The 144-room inn is in demand among vacationing families. Meeting space makes it a popular choice for conferences too. Each comfortably appointed guest room opens onto a private patio or balcony overlooking the lake. You'll

generally need to make reservations well in advance for the inn. Call (800) 250-8610. The 250-seat restaurant offers reasonably priced menu items. The inn also has a recreation room, exercise room, shuffleboard and games.

Another lodging option is a cabin. Each of the park's 20 two-bedroom cabins sleeps up to eight people. The cabins have central heat and air and are fully furnished. There are 10 fishermen cabins directly on the lake. On the hill overlooking the lake are 10 more cabins, two of which are wheelchair-accessible. All cabins are near the inn and restaurant.

Groups can stay at the group camps or group lodges. There are two group camps featuring rustic bunkhouses and central dining halls and bathhouses. Both camps provide private recreational opportunities. There are two group lodges. A two-story dorm lodge accommodates 104, while the other lodge has two buildings that sleep 40 each.

Fall Creek Falls has 227 campsites at three campgrounds. Some sites can be reserved.

All sites are equipped with tables, grills, water and electric hookups. There are central bathhouses with showers. For camping reservations, call (800) 250-8611.

# Land Between The Lakes

## Land Between The Lakes
**100 Van Morgan Dr., Golden Pond, Ky.**
**• (502) 924-2000, (800) LBL-7077**

If you're looking for fun in the great outdoors, TVA's Land Between The Lakes, about 90 miles northwest of Nashville, is an excellent getaway destination. This 170,000-acre natural recreation area nestled between Kentucky Lake and Lake Barkley in Western Kentucky and Tennessee lures more than 2 million visitors each year. They come for the fishing, hiking, camping, hunting, biking, wildlife viewing opportunities and more. It's a favorite spot of many in the Midwest and Mid-South regions and is the focal point of a $500 million-per-year tourism industry.

At 8 miles wide and 40 miles long, LBL is the largest inland peninsula in the United States and the second-largest contiguous block of forested public land east of the Mississippi. It was created by President John F. Kennedy in the early 1960s as the country's only "national demonstration area," combining environmental education, outdoor recreation and natural resource management to stimulate the area's economic growth.

Kentucky Lake was created in 1944 when TVA dammed the Tennessee River. In 1959, the U.S. Army Corps of Engineers began building Barkley Dam on the Cumberland River. Recognizing the recreation potential of the land between what would be two lakes, TVA acquired additional acreage and moved nearly 800 families in Tennessee and Kentucky — more than 2,500 people — from their homes. LBL officially opened in 1964.

Today, this 270-square-mile unspoiled forested peninsula has more than 200 miles of hiking and biking trails, more than 80 miles of horse and wagon trails, 300 miles of undeveloped shoreline, nearly 1,000 camp sites, the largest publicly owned bison herd east of the Mississippi, more than 1,300 plant species, more than 230 bird species and 53 different mammal species. In the 1980s, LBL began the first bald eagle restoration project in the southeastern United States, and there are now several active bald eagle nests in the recreation area, and more in the region.

If you've never been to LBL, Golden Pond Visitor Center is a good place to begin your first visit. It's in the center of LBL, right off The Trace, the main road that travels through the center of LBL.

If you plan to visit attractions at the central and north end, take I-24 west into Kentucky to Exit 65 (Cadiz/Hopkinsville exit). Then take U.S. Highway 68/80 west (left) past Cadiz and across the Lake Barkley Bridge into LBL. About 4 miles into LBL, you will see several signs. Turn left, go through the LBL Gatehouse to The Trace. Follow the signs to the facilities of your choice.

Visitors to the south area of LBL can take I-24 west to U.S. Highway 79 (Exit 4). Follow U.S. 79 south through Clarksville toward Fort Donelson National Battlefield and Dover. After you pass Dover, watch for the large, brown sign directing you to turn right for LBL. Turn right and follow it for about 4.5 miles; this road turns into The Trace, the main artery through LBL. This will take you to the South Welcome Station.

## Attractions

### Elk & Bison Prairie
**Located north of the Golden Pond**
**Visitor Center, off The Trace**

The 750-acre Elk & Bison Prairie is a restoration project of LBL. Here, you can see how this area looked during the days of Daniel Boone, the longhunters and the Shawnee Indians. Two hundred years ago, this area of Kentucky and Middle Tennessee featured rolling hills of grasses. Today, visitors can drive along a 3.5-mile winding road through the prairie, observing animals in their native habitat as well as the native grasses and flowers, which are being re-established. Dusk and early morning are good times for spotting wildlife. Be sure to stay near your vehicle at all times and stay inside the vehicle if large animals are nearby (bison can run as fast as 35 mph!). The prairie is open year round from dawn 'til dusk. You can purchase a token on site for entry. Rates are $3 for automobiles; they vary for buses, commercial vans and guided van trips.

## The Golden Pond Planetarium

LBL's Golden Pond Planetarium, (502) 924-2000 or (800) 455-5897, near the Golden Pond Visitor Center off Van Morgan Drive, features astronomy programs and seasonal specials. Visual effects are projected onto the 88-seat planetarium's 40-foot dome. Shows are held daily on such topics as black holes and life on Mars. A live program on that evening's sky concludes each show. The planetarium is open March through mid-December. Admission is $2.75 for anyone 13 and older, $1.75 for children ages 5 through 12. Groups with advance reservations get a discount.

## The Homeplace – 1850

Step back in time and experience life on a mid-19th century farm during a visit to LBL's The Homeplace – 1850. This is a living history farm where you can see the work, play and customs of family life in this area as they were in the mid-1800s. The Outdoor Museum area features 16 log structures, including two restored log homes, a woodshed, smokehouse, springhouse and work barn. Knowledgeable interpreters dressed in period clothing engage in housework, farm work and other everyday chores necessary to farm life of the period. Plowing, farming tobacco, spinning, churning butter and cooking meals on a wood stove are some of the activities that take place. Interpreters also talk with visitors and answer questions about what life was like for rural residents here 150 years ago. Special events such as weddings and harvest celebrations are scheduled throughout the year.

The living-history farm also features a variety of livestock typical of animals that would have been kept on a mid-19th century farm. You can get an up-close look at Cotswold sheep and other rare and endangered breeds of farm animals. The Homeplace's fields and gardens feature historic varieties of plants and crops that are no longer commonly grown.

The Homeplace – 1850 is in the south portion of LBL in Tennessee, a little more than 10 miles from the South Welcome Station. It's about the same distance from the Golden Pond Visitor Center. It is open from March to November, but hours vary. It is closed December through February. In March and November, hours are 9 AM to 5 PM Wednesday through Saturday, 10 AM to 5 PM Sunday; April through October, hours are 9 AM to 5 PM Monday through Saturday, 10 AM to 5 PM Sunday. Admission is $3.50 for adults, $2 for children ages 5 through 17. Advance group rates are available.

## The Nature Station

The Nature Station is a good place to get up-close looks at live plant and animal exhibits before you begin exploring Land Between The Lakes. The Nature Station is north of the Golden Pond Visitor Center, in the woods between Honker and Hematite lakes. To reach it, travel north on The Trace for about 8 miles, turn on Mulberry Flat Road and travel another 3 miles. Check out the facility's indoor discovery center and "Backyard" exhibits, then head out to explore the world on an organized or self-guided hike. LBL offers easy to moderate hikes along trails, streams, ponds and lakes plus canoe trips and other programs that teach about the area's plants and wildlife. You may see wild turkey, fallow deer, white-tailed deer, songbirds and many of the 53 mammal species that live at LBL. The organized hikes include van transportation to the site.

If you seek more challenging outdoor experiences, you can rent mountain bikes and canoes at The Nature Station. Biking helmets, child seats for bikes, paddles and life vests are provided. In March and November, The Nature Station is open 9 AM to 5 PM Wednesday through Saturday, 10 AM to 5 PM Sunday. April to October, hours are 9 AM to 5 PM Monday through Saturday, 10 AM to 5 PM Sunday. The Nature Station is closed December through February. Admission is $3.50 for anyone 13 and older, $2 for children ages 5 through 12. Group rates are available with advance notice.

## Turkey Bay Off-Highway Vehicle Area

Off Kentucky Lake, the 2,500-acre Turkey Bay Off-Highway Vehicle Area offers terrain for various skill levels. This is the first federally designated area for off-highway vehicle riding and camping. It is open year round. A vehicle permit is required — $35 annually, $20 for seven consecutive days, or $10 for three consecutive days — and may be purchased on site or at the Golden Pond Visitor Center.

## Camping

There are all sorts of camping options at LBL. There are three family campgrounds: Hillman Ferry in the north end, Piney in the south end and Energy Lake north of the Golden Pond Visitor Center. Each has scenic campsites along the lake shore and in the woods. Water, electric and sewer hookups are available at Hillman and Piney. LBL also has the only horse camp in the region — Wranglers, which opened a $2 million expansion in 1997. The camp offers more than 70 miles of horse and wagon trails, an outpost center, stalls, tack gear and farrier service. Guided horse trail rides and pony rides are available for other LBL visitors.

In addition to the developed campgrounds, there are other campsites with basic amenities. Informal camping areas are at Birmingham Ferry, Fenton, Rushing Creek, Cravens Bay, Gatlin Point and Turkey Bay OHV Area (see previous entry). Backwoods camping permits are available as well and can be purchased in the Welcome Areas. Backpackers on the North/South Trail can spend the night in metal huts along the way. Wooden camping shelters with electricity and bunk beds are available at Piney and Wranglers. Colson Hollow Group Camp can accommodate groups of as many as 200. Camping fees vary depending on time of year and campsite.

## Hiking

LBL has more than 200 miles of trails that will take you through rolling woodlands and along isolated shorelines. Trails range in length from less than a mile to 65 miles. Some of the shorter nature trails have wildlife blinds, where you can blend in with the natural surroundings and get up-close looks and take photographs of wildlife.

The trails are divided into three systems. The Canal Loop, a 14-mile connecting loop system that begins at the North Welcome Station, is a good starting point. The 26-mile loop Fort Henry Trail system is near the South Welcome Station. This trail system features several historically significant points. Serious hikers might consider the 65-mile North/South Trail, which runs almost the entire length of LBL, in between the North Welcome Station and the South Welcome Station. Metal shelters that sleep up to six people each are provided for backpackers along this trail, so there's no need to pack a tent. In addition to the three main trail systems, there are numerous shorter nature trails throughout the area. LBL offers several organized hikes, such as the spring "Volksmarch," which attracts hikers from as far as 10 hours away.

## Hunting and Fishing

With abundant populations of white-tailed deer and wild turkey and more than 230 days of hunting seasons for large and small game and waterfowl, LBL is a prime location for hunting. It's a pretty good fishing spot too: Kentucky Lake and Lake Barkley, which comprise one of the world's largest man-made bodies of water, are home to plenty of crappie, bass, sauger, catfish and bluegill. There are 21 lake-access areas; five are maintained for camping, and the others are boat ramp areas, some with campsites, picnic tables and grills.

## Mountain Biking

For mountain biking enthusiasts, LBL offers miles of trails, backroads and shorelines where you can enjoy the outdoors and venture into more remote areas where wildlife-viewing opportunities are superb. Trails wind along old logging roads and fire-access lanes, covering a variety of terrain. Mountain bikers have three trails to choose from, including the scenic Canal Loop hiking trail, which includes rugged hills and smoother forest paths along the shore of Kentucky Lake. On the Jenny Ridge Mountain Bike Trail, a 12-mile looping segment of the North/South Hiking Trail, you'll travel past old homestead sites and through valleys once inhabited by Golden Pond moonshiners. The Energy Lake Mountain Bike Trail is a 12-mile loop beginning at Energy Lake Campground and traveling along road beds, gravel roads and dirt roads around the lake. Mountain bikes, helmets and child seats are available for rent at The Nature Station and Hillman Ferry Outpost at Piney Campground. Bicycles suitable for traveling LBL's paved roads are available for rent at Piney Campground's Piney Outpost.

# Chattanooga, Tennessee

Chattanooga is a great getaway destination. You can make it a daytrip if you're really determined, but this city is best enjoyed as a weekend getaway. You'll need at least that much time to visit a selection of the city's many attractions.

Chattanooga is an easy 133-mile drive from Nashville via I-24 east. You'll enjoy some nice scenery along the way. Chattanooga is in the Eastern Time Zone, so set your watch ahead an hour to keep up with local time.

The Chattanooga Visitor Center, next to the Tennessee Aquarium downtown, is a good first stop. You can pick up brochures on attractions, accommodations, shops and restaurants as well as tickets to attractions. The visitor center is open 8:30 AM to 5:30 PM daily except Thanksgiving and Christmas days.

Chattanooga has changed enormously in recent years. A few decades ago, this river city was declared the "dirtiest city in America" by the Environmental Protection Agency, but after an $850 million riverfront and revitalization plan, Chattanooga is now often called the "best midsize city in America." The revitalized downtown area includes the $45 million Tennessee Aquarium (see subsequent entry), which opened in 1992 and continues to spur new development in the area, and the Tennessee Riverpark, a greenway that, when complete, will span 22 miles. Numerous other attractions, including museums, restaurants, festivals and excellent retail shopping, have done much for the city's image. Today the city's population exceeds 153,000, while more than 446,000 live in the Metropolitan Statistical Area.

Chattanooga is known worldwide thanks to "King of Swing" Glenn Miller's No. 1 hit single "Chattanooga Choo Choo," released in 1941. The song sold more than 1 million copies. But before that, the city was known as a major center of trade and, later, as one of the key strategic locations during the Civil War.

As far back as 10,000 years ago, Chattanooga was a center of trade and migration among Native Americans. In 1815 Cherokee descendant John Ross established a trading post and ferry across the Tennessee River. His post was at Ross's Landing, where the Tennessee Aquarium is today. A small town of Cherokee and white settlers grew up around the trading post.

Chattanooga became a railroad hub before the Civil War, linking producers in the South with Northern manufacturers. In fall 1863, a series of Civil War battles took place on Lookout Mountain, Missionary Ridge and at Chickamauga, which is considered the bloodiest battle of the Civil War. The city was a key to the Union's control of the South. Many attractions tell the stories of the Civil War battles that took place in the area. Those interested in Civil War history should visit the Chickamauga/Chattanooga National Military Park, Point Park and the Battles for Chattanooga Electric Map & Museum (see subsequent entries). There are several other attractions and locations that would be of interest to Civil War buffs.

We list some of Chattanooga's best-known attractions as well as a few off-the-beaten-path locations. We also provide a few choices for dining and overnight accommodations. Call the Chattanooga Area Convention and Visitors Bureau, (423) 756-8687 or (800) 322-3344, for more information on the city's attractions, accommodations and dining choices.

## Attractions

### Battles for Chattanooga Electric Map & Museum
**Lookout Mountain, 1110 E. Brow Rd., Chattanooga, Tenn. • (423) 821-2812**

This is an electronic battle map of Chattanooga's Civil War history, with more than 5,000 miniature solders and hundreds of

---

lights. The museum (formerly known as Confederama) displays include a weapons collection and other relics. You'll also find a bookstore and gift shop. After learning about the battles, walk to Point Park (see subsequent entry), the site of Chattanooga's famous "Battle Above the Clouds." General hours are 10 AM to 5 PM daily; summer hours are 9:30 AM to 6 PM. Admission is $5 for adults and teens and $3 for kids ages 3 through 12.

### Bluff View Art District
**Corner of High and E. Second sts. (next to the Hunter Museum), Chattanooga, Tenn. • (423) 265-5033**

The Bluff View Art District is in a quiet area of downtown Chattanooga, along the Tennessee Riverwalk and just a quarter-mile walk from the Tennessee Aquarium. The district includes the Hunter Museum of American Art, the Houston Museum of Decorative Arts, the River Gallery, the Bluff View Inn (see separate listings in this section) and a handful of restaurants. From this area, you can climb the steps to the century-old steel-truss Walnut Street Bridge, a .75-mile linear park and pedestrian bridge, the longest pedestrian-walkway bridge in the world.

### Chickamauga/Chattanooga National Military Park
**Fort Oglethorpe, Ga.**
**• (706) 866-9241**

History and Civil War buffs will want to visit this attraction, America's first and largest National Military Park. Just across the state line from Chattanooga, Chickamauga/Chattanooga National Military Park is dedicated to the memory of Union and Confederate soldiers who died in the 1863 battle here. An audiovisual presentation explaining the battle and its significance in the war is offered at the Chickamauga Battlefield Park Headquarters and Visitor Center. A collection of Fuller guns is also on display. Point Park (see subsequent entry), atop Lookout Mountain, is an extension of the park and serves as a memorial to the soldiers. Admission is free.

### Creative Discovery Museum
**321 Chestnut St., Chattanooga, Tenn.**
**• (423) 756-2738**

Creative Discovery Museum is a neat place for kids. It's two blocks from the Tennessee Aquarium at the corner of Fourth and Chestnut streets in downtown Chattanooga. Open since 1995, the 42,000-square-foot museum is loaded with interactive, hands-on attractions that make learning fun. Based on the key education programs of art, music, science and invention, the museum's four main exhibit areas include the Artist's Studio, where kiddies can learn about and participate in printmaking, sculpting and painting; the Inventor's Studio, which allows visitors to manipulate various pulleys, motors, magnets and other devices to create their own inventions; a Musician's Workshop, with instruments from around the world and a recording studio where the little ones can play instruments, compose songs and experiment with studio recording; and a Science Field Lab, where kids can dig for "bones," study paleontology, play with a computer and see what it's like to be a field scientist. You'll also find a three-story observation tower, an optics gallery, the Little Yellow House for preschoolers, a gallery for temporary exhibits and an auditorium where science demonstrations are presented. The Museum Shop has a good selection of educational and fun toys. Admission to the museum is $7.75 for adults and teens, $4.75 for children ages 2 through 12. Memorial Day through Labor Day, hours are 10 AM to 8 PM daily. September through May, hours are 10 AM to 5 PM Tuesday through Saturday and noon to 5 PM Sunday.

### The Heritage Center
**200 Martin Luther King Blvd., Chattanooga, Tenn. • (423) 266-8658**

The Heritage Center, in a renovated warehouse at the corner of Martin Luther King Boulevard and Lindsay Street, houses the Bessie Smith Performance Hall and the Chattanooga African-American Museum. Bessie Smith Performance Hall, named for the legendary "Empress of the Blues," a Chattanooga native, is a performance hall/cabaret/restaurant that also contains practice rooms for students. The 264-seat performance hall presents prominent blues acts as well as other music and arts programs.

The Chattanooga African-American Museum is dedicated to preserving the history of African Americans in the Chattanooga area.

Exhibits include a wall dedicated to African Americans who have achieved "firsts" in their professions, an authentic African dwelling and exhibits on the lives of blacks in Chattanooga, including Civil War displays and displays highlighting achievements in performing arts and sports. Museum admission is $5 for adults, $3 for teens and seniors and $2 for children ages 6 through 12. Hours are 10:00 AM to 5 PM Monday through Friday, noon to 4 PM Saturday.

## Houston Museum of Decorative Arts
**201 High St., Chattanooga, Tenn.**
• **(423) 267-7176**

This museum houses a collection of 10,000 pieces of antique glass, china and furniture owned by the late Anna "Antique Annie" Safley Houston, an interesting, eccentric woman who once operated an antique shop. Approximately 30 percent of the collection is on display at a time. The museum is across the street from the Hunter Museum of American Art (see next entry). Guided tours begin at 9:30 AM Monday

through Saturday; the last tour begins at 4 PM. On Sundays during the summer, tours begin at noon. The museum may be closed Sundays during the winter; call ahead if you're planning to visit during that season. Admission is $5.

## Hunter Museum of American Art
**10 Bluff View, Chattanooga, Tenn.**
• **(423) 267-0968**

Called the most important and complete collection of American art in the Southeast, the Hunter Museum of American Art has more than 1,500 works in its permanent collection. Among them are works by Mary Cassatt, Childe Hassam, Thomas Hart Benton, Ansel Adams, Albert Bierstadt, George Inness, Helen Franhenthaler, Louise Nevelson, George Segal, Hans Hoffman, William de Kooning, Albert Paley and Alexander Calder. Its collection of contemporary glass sculpture includes works by Harvey K. Littleton, William Morris, Dale Chihuly and Toots Zinsky. Because space is limited, only about 20 percent of the

Photo: US Space and Rocket Center/Bob Gathany

The U.S. Space and Rocket Center is Alabama's number one tourist attraction.

museum's collection is on view. Pieces are rotated every two to four years.

The recently renovated museum sits on a 90-foot limestone bluff overlooking the Tennessee River on one side and downtown Chattanooga on the other. The museum is actually two different buildings, one a 1904 Greek Revival mansion and the other a contemporary structure built in 1975. The two buildings are connected by an elliptical stairwell and outdoor sculpture garden. To get there, take 4th Street to High Street, turn left and go two blocks. Museum hours are 10 AM to 4:30 PM Tuesday through Saturday and 1 to 4:30 PM Sunday. Admission is $5 for adults, $4 for seniors, $3 for students 12 and older with ID and $2.50 for children ages 3 through 11.

## International Towing & Recovery Hall of Fame & Museum
**401 Broad St., Chattanooga, Tenn.**
• **(423) 267-3132**

Two blocks from the Tennessee Aquarium is one of Chattanooga's more offbeat attractions. The International Towing & Recovery Hall of Fame & Museum is all about the history of wreckers and tow trucks. Exhibits include wreckers and towing equipment dating back to 1916. Hours are 10 AM to 4:30 PM Monday through Friday, 11 AM to 5 PM Saturday and Sunday. Admission is $3.50 for adults, $2.50 for children ages 5 through 18 and senior citizens.

## Lookout Mountain Hang Gliding
**7201 Scenic Hwy. (Tenn. Hwy. 189 S.), Rising Fawn, Ga.**
• **(706) 398-3541, (800) 688-5637**

You can watch hang gliders fly off 1,340-foot Lookout Mountain, or take a tandem flight with a certified tandem pilot. No experience is necessary. Spectators can watch free, but there are fees for lessons, tandem flights and aero towing. To get there, follow the Rock City signs past Rock City, stay on Tenn. Highway 157, turn left onto Tenn. 189 and go about 8 miles.

## Lookout Mountain Incline Railway
**At St. Elmo Ave., at the foot of Lookout Mountain, Chattanooga, Tenn.**
• **(423) 629-1411**

Put the Incline Railway on your must-do list. A ride on the Incline Railway, the world's steepest passenger railway, is a memorable and breathtaking experience. The Incline's trolley-style rail cars take you to the top of scenic Lookout Mountain and back; near the top of the track, the grade reaches 72.7 percent. As you ride toward the clouds, you'll get a panoramic view of Chattanooga. The observation deck at the top is the highest overlook on Lookout Mountain. On a clear day, you can see as far as 100 miles. At the upper station, you can visit the Incline's machine room and see how the giant gears and cables make the whole thing work. After checking out the views at the top, visit Point Park (see next entry), just a short, three-block walk from the upper station, for other spectacular views.

The Incline is both a National Historic Site and a National Historic Mechanical Engineering Landmark. It was built in 1895 as a fast and inexpensive way to transport residents and visitors to and from the St. Elmo neighborhood and the top of Lookout Mountain. The mountain soon developed as a popular summer vacation resort of the late 1800s and early 1900s.

To get to the Incline from I-24, take any Lookout Mountain exit and follow the signs. Free parking is available at the lower station. Incline Railway is open 8:30 AM to 9:30 PM daily in the summer, 9 AM to 6 PM in the spring and fall, 10 AM to 6PM in the winter. Round-trip tickets are $8, and one-way tickets $7 for adults and teens; tickets for children ages 3 through 12 are $4 round trip and $3 one way.

## INSIDERS' TIP

A 65-foot reproduction of the Eiffel Tower, the world's second-tallest Eiffel Tower in a city called Paris, can be found in Memorial Park in Paris, Tennessee. Paris is in the northwest section of the state, in Henry County. For more information, call the Paris/Henry County Chamber of Commerce, (800) 345-1103.

## Point Park

**Atop Lookout Mtn., Lookout Mountain, Tenn. • (423) 821-7786**

A unit of the Chickamauga/Chattanooga National Military Park, Point Park is the site of one of the most dramatic battles of the Civil War. Panoramic views of Chattanooga and the Tennessee River and a history of the Battle of Lookout Mountain await visitors. Monuments, markers and a museum pay tribute to the soldiers who died in the Battle of Chattanooga. The park is on the northern crest of Lookout Mountain.

Point Park is open 9 AM to sunset. Admission costs $2 for visitors 16 and older, while anyone younger than 16 gets in free; call for senior and group rates.

## River Gallery

**400 E. Second St., Chattanooga, Tenn. • (423) 267-7353**

In the Bluff View Art District (see previous entry), River Gallery has an eclectic collection of regional and national fine art and crafts. The gallery rotates exhibits monthly. Hours are 10 AM to 5 PM Monday through Saturday, 1 to 5 PM Sunday. Admission is free.

## River Gallery Sculpture Garden

**214 Spring St., Chattanooga, Tenn. • (423) 267-7353**

Just around the corner from River Gallery and Bluff View Inn, overlooking the Tennessee River, the 2-acre River Gallery Sculpture Garden features dozens of pieces of original sculpture, some of which are available for purchase. It is open daily during regular gallery hours (see previous entry for details). Admission is free.

## Rock City Gardens

**1400 Patten Rd., Lookout Mountain, Ga. • (706) 820-2531**

"See Rock City." You've seen the barns and birdhouses painted with that slogan, and if you've ever been to Chattanooga, chances are that you have seen Rock City. If you haven't visited Rock City, one of Chattanooga's best-known attractions, be sure to stop by on your next visit. Rock City Gardens began more than 60 years ago, when Frieda Carter and her husband, Garnet, developed a 10-acre garden

among huge boulders and natural rock formations on this mountaintop. It opened to the public in 1932. The ingenious advertising campaign followed not long after, when Garnet Carter hired a young man named Clark Byers to paint barn roofs with messages. Over the next 32 years, Byers painted the "See Rock City" slogan on more than 900 barns in nearly 20 states. In the '50s, Rock City added birdhouses to its campaign. The campaign was brought to an end after the Beautification Act of 1965. Barns and birdhouses were painted over. Today, fewer than 100 of the painted barns remain, but the legend lives on. The "See Rock City" slogan can be seen on subways, gardens, birdhouses and other spots around the world. During Desert Storm, soldiers erected a Rock City birdhouse in the Kuwaiti desert.

Now that you know the history, what can you expect at Rock City Gardens? Lovely gardens and great scenery mostly. Take a self-guided tour along the Enchanted Trail, where you'll observe unique rock formations and various gardens with more than 400 species of wildflowers, shrubs and other plants. The trail takes you through a couple of tight squeezes — the Needle's Eye and Fat Man's Squeeze — between massive boulders. At the top, at famous Lover's Leap, you can supposedly see seven states — Tennessee, Kentucky, Virginia, North Carolina, South Carolina, Georgia and Alabama. The walk through the charming Fairyland Caverns and Mother Goose Village is especially fun for the kids. The whole trip takes about 60 to 90 minutes.

Rock City Gardens is open daily except Christmas. Hours are 9 AM to 5 PM from the day after Labor Day through Memorial Day, and 9 AM to 8 PM June 1 through Labor Day. Admission is $9.95 for adults, $5.50 for children ages 3 through 12.

## Ruby Falls

**Lookout Mountain, 1720 S. Scenic Hwy., Chattanooga, Tenn. • (423) 821-2544**

Ruby Falls, America's highest and most visited underground waterfall, is one of Chattanooga's oldest and most popular attractions. This 145-foot natural waterfall is more than 1,100 feet inside Lookout Mountain. Your guided tour begins with a 260-foot elevator ride into the caverns. Then you make the trek to the falls. Along the way, your guide will tell you all about the history of the falls and point out interesting calcite formations.

Lookout Mountain Caverns is a National Landmark and is on the National Register of Historic Places. Lookout Mountain Tower provides a spectacular panoramic view of Chattanooga. Ruby Falls also has a Fun Forest play area for kids. A gift shop and concession stand are nearby. Ruby Falls is open 8 AM to 9 PM Memorial Day through Labor Day; 8 AM to 8 PM September, October, April and May; and 8 AM to 6 PM November through March. Admission is $9 for adults and teens, $8 for senior citizens and $4.50 for children ages 3 through 12.

## Tennessee Aquarium
**1 Broad St., Chattanooga, Tenn.**
**• (423) 265-0695, (800) 262-0695**

The Tennessee Aquarium, the world's first and largest freshwater aquarium, is an attraction you don't want to miss. In fact, it's the reason many people visit Chattanooga. The aquarium opened in 1992 as the centerpiece of Chattanooga's downtown revitalization effort and has been drawing tens of thousands of visitors each year. It can be quite crowded during peak times. It's busiest Memorial Day through Labor Day. You might consider visiting during the week — especially in spring, fall or winter — if you want to avoid the crowds.

The aquarium is in the center of Ross's Landing Park and Plaza, next to the Chattanooga Visitors Center. A self-guided tour through the aquarium takes as long as two hours. During your visit, you'll travel through a number of natural freshwater habitats, including a 60-foot canyon and two living forests. The aquarium provides habitat for more than 7,000 animals, among them a 60-pound catfish, river otters, alligators, piranhas, a boa constrictor, stingrays, sharks and colorful fish that can be found in the Gulf of Mexico.

Tickets are sold daily from 10 AM to 6 PM, except Thanksgiving and Christmas. Admission is $10.95 for adults and teens, $5.95 for children ages 3 through 12. Various discounted combination tickets good for admission to the aquarium, IMAX 3-D Theater and Creative Discovery Museum are available as well.

To get there from Nashville, take I-24 east to downtown Chattanooga, get off at U.S. Highway 27 N., then take the Fourth Street exit (Exit 1C), turn right onto Fourth Street, then take a left at the second traffic light onto Broad Street. The aquarium and IMAX theater are two blocks ahead.

## Tennessee Aquarium IMAX 3-D Theater
**201 Chestnut St., Chattanooga, Tenn.**
**• (800) 262-0695**

This theater, next to the Tennessee Aquarium, is one of only a handful of IMAX 3-D theaters in the country. It has a six-story screen and offers a choice of films, which are scheduled several times daily, beginning at 11 AM. You can order tickets by phone or purchase them on site. If you want to see one film, tickets are $6.95 for adults and teens, $4.95 for children ages 3 through 12. For two movies, prices are $10.95 for adults and teens and $7.95 for children. Tickets to all three movies are $14.95 and $10.95. Various discounted combination tickets good for admission to the theater, the Tennessee Aquarium and Creative Discovery Museum are available as well.

## Tennessee Valley Railroad Museum
**4119 Cromwell Rd., Chattanooga, Tenn.**
**• (423) 894-8028**

This is the largest operating historic railroad in the South. The museum was founded in 1961 by a group of Chattanoogans who wanted to preserve operating steam passenger trains. The museum features a number of classic pieces from railroad's golden age, among them a 1911 steam locomotive, 1926 dining car and 1929 wooden caboose. Passenger trains depart regularly for various Chattanooga destinations. The schedule varies according to season. Admission is $9 for adults, $4.50 for children ages 3 through 12.

## Accommodations

Chattanooga has all types of hotel, motel and bed and breakfast accommodations. We list just a few. For other options, check out the many brochures available at the Chattanooga Visitor Center downtown, or contact the Chattanooga Area Convention and Visitors Bureau, (423) 756-8687 or (800) 322-3344.

## Bluff View Inn
**412 E. Second St., Chattanooga, Tenn.**
**• (423) 265-5033**

A bed and breakfast overlooking the Tennessee River, Bluff View Inn offers accommodations in three early 1900s restored homes. Your room comes complete with a complimentary gourmet breakfast. Expect a room here to run approximately $100 to $250 a night.

## Chattanooga Choo Choo Holiday Inn
**1400 Market St., Chattanooga, Tenn.**
**• (423) 266-5000, (800) TRACK 29**

A fun place for the whole family, the Chattanooga Choo Choo Holiday Inn downtown is the city's most famous place to spend the night. For some 60 years, this was the site of Chattanooga's Terminal Station, which saw dozens of arriving and departing trains each day during the height of the railroad era. Today, visitors here can sleep and eat in authentic railcars. The Chattanooga Choo Choo Holiday Inn is a 30-acre complex with 315 guest rooms, 48 sleeping parlors aboard railcars, meeting space, restaurants, indoor and outdoor pools, a Model Railroad Museum, formal rose gardens and more. The lobby has the largest freestanding brick dome in the world. Rates range from approximately $79 to $115 a night.

## Chattanooga Marriott
**2 Carter Plaza, Chattanooga, Tenn.**
**• (423) 756-0002, (800) 841-1674**

Adjacent to the convention center in downtown Chattanooga, this hotel features recently renovated guest rooms and public areas. Restaurants and numerous recreation facilities, including indoor and outdoor pools and an exercise room, are among the extras. Rates run from about $70 to $115 nightly.

## Chanticleer Inn
**1300 Mockingbird Ln., Lookout**
**Mountain, Ga. • (706) 820-2015**

On the Georgia portion of Lookout Mountain, one block from Rock City and about 6 miles from downtown, Chanticleer Inn is a bed and breakfast inn offering accommodations in mountain stone buildings. Each has two to four units with a private entrance and bath,

plus cable TV. Some units have gas fireplaces. A swimming pool with picnic and play areas also is on the property. Rates run about $40 to $86 a night.

## Comfort Suites Downtown
**2431 Williams St., Chattanooga, Tenn.**
**• (423) 265-0008**

This downtown all-suites hotel has in-room hot tubs, an indoor heated pool and in-room microwaves, refrigerators and hair dryers. Rooms run from about $60 to $90 a night.

# Restaurants

## Back Inn Cafe
**412 E. Second St., Chattanooga, Tenn.**
**• (423) 757-0108**

Pasta is the specialty at this Italian bistro in the Bluff View Art District. The cafe is in a turn-of-the-century mansion, which offers a spectacular river view. Dine indoors or out. Wine and a selection of imported and domestic beers are available. The cafe is open daily for lunch and dinner.

## Big River Grille and Brewing Works
**222 Broad St., Chattanooga, Tenn.**
**• (423) 267-BREW**

Just a few steps from the Tennessee Aquarium, this eatery is a fun and casual spot to grab a bite or sample a handcrafted ale. The brewing apparatus overlooks the bar area. In addition to fresh-brewed beers and homemade sodas, the menu features such tempting entrees as smoked chicken enchiladas, fresh-grilled seafood and fresh salads. Next door is Big River Billiards, where you can order a wood-fired pizza to munch on while you enjoy a game of billiards.

## Chattanooga Choo Choo
**1400 Market St., Chattanooga, Tenn.**
**• (423) 266-5000**

The Chattanooga Choo Choo's Dinner in the Diner offers gourmet meals aboard an authentic dining car. At the Choo Choo's The Station House, singing waiters and waitresses will deliver your meals. Southern favorites are served for breakfast, lunch and dinner at The Gardens, while Café Espresso offers gourmet coffee and desserts.

### The Loft
**328 Cherokee Blvd., Chattanooga, Tenn.**
**• (423) 266-3061**

A local favorite for more than 20 years, The Loft is across the river from the Tennessee Aquarium. Aged prime rib, steaks, fresh seafood, lobster, king crab, Cajun specialties, poultry, pasta and delicious desserts are served daily in a casual atmosphere. The Loft serves lunch Monday through Friday, dinner nightly and brunch on Sunday .

### Rembrandt's Coffee House
**205 High St., Chattanooga, Tenn.**
**• (423) 265-5033**

Rembrandt's is a good spot to stop for a cup of gourmet java and indulge in handmade chocolates and fresh-baked pastries. Seating is available indoors or on the garden terrace outdoors. Rembrandt's is open daily for breakfast, lunch and dinner.

# Franklin/Bowling Green/ Mammoth Cave, Kentucky

Feeling lucky? . . . Adventurous? . . . Dashing? Head north on Interstate 65 to south-central Kentucky, where you'll find experiences you can only dream about in Tennessee — vices like lotteries, horse racing and bingo, for example. You can also wander through the world's largest cave system, speed through time with America's favorite sports car and more.

While the quickest route to our destinations is I-65, if you're not in a hurry and you want to enjoy some two-lane country scenery along the way, consider taking U.S. Highway 31W (Dickerson Pike) out of Nashville. You'll wind around a bit more, but you'll get to the same places: Franklin, Bowling Green and the Mammoth Cave area.

As you approach the Tennessee-Kentucky state line on I-65, be especially aware of truckers. Weigh stations are in operation on both sides of the line, within just miles of each other, so there will often be a lot of truck traffic exiting and entering the interstate.

For more information about Bowling Green/Franklin/Mammoth Cave area, contact the following agencies:

•Bowling Green–Warren County Tourist and Convention Commission, 352 Three Springs Road, Bowling Green, Kentucky, (502) 782-0800

•Cave City Convention Center and Tourism, 502 Mammoth Cave Road, Cave City, Kentucky, (800) 346-8908

•Simpson County Tourism Commission, 201 S. Main Street, Franklin, Kentucky, (502) 586-3040

# Franklin

The first Kentucky exit you'll come to is Exit 2, Franklin (U.S. Highway 31W), where you'll find:

### Dueling Grounds
**5629 Nashville Rd., Franklin, Ky.**
**• (502) 586-7778**

After a three-year absence, live racing returned in September 1998 to Dueling Grounds, the only all-turf thoroughbred course in North America. The season is short — September 10-20 in 1999, for example — but when the horses aren't actually running at Dueling Grounds, you can bet on simulcast races from other tracks around the country, including Belmont, Churchill Downs, Keeneland, the Meadowlands and Santa Anita.

The all-turf track is a 1 5/16-mile, European-style oval with an incline at the start and a long stretch. Since reintroducing live racing in 1998, the track has already played host to the $300,000 Kentucky Cup Turf and the $200,000 Kentucky Cup Mile, both designated prep races for the Breeder's Cup.

The track's name, incidentally, comes from the fact that Franklin, Kentucky, once had a reputation as a dueling ground — a place where "civilized" men fought one-on-one battles of honor with pistols. One enterprising local, Sanford Duncan, even built an inn where Sam Houston and others gathered before dueling on the Duncan farm.

Dueling Grounds is open year round for simulcasts. It's closed some days, however, so call to be sure there's racing on a particular day. There's a restaurant and bar with TVs and betting windows. Admission is $2, and

Photo: Russ Guier

Many scenic spots await hikers in the Great Smoky Mountains, like this stream that runs along the trail to Rainbow Falls.

parking is free. Gates open one hour before the first post time, which generally ranges from 11 AM to 12:15 PM.

## Kentucky State Line Bingo
**5950 Nashville Rd., Franklin, Ky.**
**• (502) 598-0735**

This building, just across the road from Dueling Grounds, is one of about four bingo joints in Franklin. Its convenient location near the state line helps it lure an estimated 100,000 Tennessee players a year.

Doors open at 4 PM. Games start at 6:45 PM Monday and Thursday through Saturday and at 4:45 PM Sunday and continue for about three hours. Kentucky State Line Bingo is closed Tuesday and Wednesday. Packages are $15, $20 and $30, with a different nonprofit group running the show and benefiting each night.

## Lotto Land
**3765 Nashville Rd., Franklin, Ky.**
**• (502) 586-7281**

About 10 percent of the people who buy Kentucky Lottery tickets are from Tennessee, it's been estimated, and six of the state's biggest lottery ticket sellers are on the Tennessee border. At Lotto Land, "we get swamped" with lottery customers from Nashville and other parts of Middle Tennessee, says one employee. You can also get cigarettes, candy and soft drinks, but it's the lottery tickets — including a number of pull-tab game machines — that provide the bulk of the business.

If you're back in Tennessee and want to find out the winning lottery numbers, you can call (615) 737-5686.

By the way, we don't mean to imply that Franklin, the Simpson County seat, is simply for gamblers. It's a nice, small (population about 7,600), homey town filled with friendly people (and no more duels). Before leaving Franklin, drive around the town square and maybe check out an antique store or two. And, if you like, instead of getting back on I-65, you can continue toward Bowling Green on U.S. 31W.

## Bowling Green

Bowling Green, population about 41,000, may have been named for a bowling-type game that early residents, in the late 1790s, played on the grass at one host's home. It may also have been named after Bowling Green, Virginia. At any rate, while there's also a Bowling Green in Ohio, this is definitely the one that Kentucky boys The Everly Brothers sang so wistfully about.

Take Exit 20, the first of three Bowling Green exits off I-65, for a visit to the Kentucky Museum and Library, on the campus of Western Kentucky University.

### Attractions

**Kentucky Museum and Library**
Western Kentucky Univ. campus, 1 Big
Red Wy., Bowling Green, Ky.
• (502) 745-2592
Exhibits include one celebrating the recent

bicentennial of Bowling Green and Warren County (the city was founded in 1798); a 200-year-old log house from nearby Logan County, complete with period furnishings; and many more examples of Kentucky heritage. You'll also find an extensive collection of manuscripts and books detailing the state's and the area's history. The museum galleries are open for self-guided tours from 9:30 AM to 4 PM Tuesday through Saturday and 1 to 4 PM on Sunday. Admission Tuesday through Saturday is $2 for adults, $1 for children 6 and older and free for students with ID. On Sunday afternoon, everybody gets in free.

After leaving the Western campus, you can drive through town or get back on I-65 and drive to Exit 28, the third Bowling Green exit. At this exit, you'll see a strange sight: a futuristic yellow conical structure with a red spike protruding from the top. Inside this unusual building is a Corvette-lover's fantasy.

**National Corvette Museum**
350 Corvette Dr., Bowling Green, Ky.
• (502) 781-7973, (800) 53VETTE
More than 50 Corvettes, those fabulous fiberglass fliers, are on display in this 68,000-square-foot museum. Displays include race cars, experimental prototypes and one-of-a-kind models as well as all the classics you remember. You'll also see performance exhibits, and the 165-seat Chevrolet Theater shows an entertaining and educational film about the history of the Corvette.

Hours are 8 AM to 6 PM April through September and 8 AM to 5 PM October through March. Admission is $8 for adults, $4.50 for ages 6 to 16 and free for ages 5 and younger.

**General Motors Corvette Assembly Plant**
600 Corvette Dr., Bowling Green, Ky.
• (502) 745-8419 (tour information)
This plant produces every single Corvette

**INSIDERS' TIP**

Have you ever wondered where East Tennessee's Frozen Head State Natural Area got its name? The 11,869-acre wilderness area, in Wartburg, is named for a 3,324-foot peak that often is capped in ice or snow. For more information, call the park at (423) 346-3318.

made in the United States today, and a free tour shows you how they do it. The plant was shut down during the development of the new model (representing the Corvette's fifth generation), but now that the car is out, the tour has resumed. No cameras are allowed; call (502) 745-8287 to make reservations for parties of 10 or more. Free tours, which last about an hour, start promptly at 9 AM and 1 PM Monday through Friday, so arrive 15 minutes early to allow time for parking and registration.

## Restaurants

### The Parakeet Café
**951 Chestnut St., Bowling Green, Ky. • (502) 781-1538**

Al Baker, who bought the storied Parakeet from Elizabeth Durbin in early 1999, plans to return the cozy, bistro-style cafe to its "heyday of 1975 to 1979," even reintroducing the old menu. In those days, the Parakeet was known for "upscale casual" dining, with menu choices including baked trout, prime rib, grilled filet mignon with artichoke hearts and Bèarnaise sauce, Delmonico steak, shrimp provencale, sautéed scallops and boneless chicken breast in brandy cream sauce.

While much of the atmosphere remains, changes are noticeable. Baker is refurbishing the building, which during the mid-1800s was a blacksmith shop. He's also eliminating the white tablecloths, but leaving the brick walls and wood trim.

### West Kentucky Barbecue
**430 U.S. Hwy. 31W Bypass, Bowling Green, Ky. • (502) 781-5719**

This friendly restaurant, which relocated from Lexington, Kentucky, in 1996, specializes in Western Kentucky-style barbecue. Beef, pork, chicken, mutton, turkey and ribs are basted in a thin, vinegar-based sauce, or "dip," then slow-cooked in a hickory smoker. The mutton and the pork shoulder are our favorites, but you can't go wrong with anything on the menu. The side items, especially the mashed potato salad, are also excellent.

# Mammoth Cave

Continue north on I-65 to Exit 53, Cave City, and follow the signs for about 10 miles to the park entrance. If you prefer, you can take the earlier Exit 48, Park City, which also will lead you to the park; or, as before, you can continue to follow U.S. 31W.

This area of the state is known for its karst topography — consisting of limestone formations, sinkholes and caves. There are hundreds of caves in this area, some privately owned, and many of them are open to the public. The best place to start is with the granddaddy of all caves, Mammoth Cave.

## Mammoth Cave National Park
**Cave City, Ky. • (502) 758-2328 (information)**

The surface area of this highly popular tourist site covers 80 square miles, but that is literally just scratching the surface. Mammoth Cave, the centerpiece of Kentucky's only national park, is part of the world's longest cave system — more than 330 miles of underground passages. As many as a dozen guided tours are offered, ranging from easy to strenuous, most of them around $6. For the more adventurous, a guided "wild cave" tour through unlighted portions of Mammoth Cave provides more of a true caving experience, while another tour is accessible to disabled visitors. Structure your visit to fit your own interests, physical abilities and sense of adventure.

Also available is a demanding, self-guided tour through Ganter Cave. This tour is restricted to groups of four to nine who meet age, fitness, experience and equipment guidelines; reservations for the Ganter Cave tour must be made through the chief ranger's office.

Often called one of the wonders of the Western Hemisphere, Mammoth Cave was named a World Heritage Site by the United Nations in 1981. In recent years, it has drawn nearly 2 million annual visitors, who come to see such awe-inspiring sights as Floyd Collins Crystal Cave, Crystal Lake, Frozen Niagara and, of course, the multilevel main cave. You'll find stalactites, stalagmites and numerous other types of rock formations. Echo River, which runs through Mammoth Cave and is still making changes to it, is home to rare, eyeless fish.

Mammoth Cave's history is nearly as intriguing as its features. Evidence shows that prehistoric Indians visited the cave. According to some accounts, a hunter in pursuit of a wounded bear in the late 1700s was the first white person to discover the cave. During the War of 1812, a commercial saltpeter-mining operation provided gunpowder for the American troops; in 1842, the cave became a tuberculosis hospital during a brief and unsuccessful experiment. Before long, the public was flocking to take in the cave's natural splendor. It became a national park, the nation's 26th, in July 1941.

Crystal Cave was discovered in 1917 by Floyd Collins, a good spelunker with a fatally bad run of luck. Collins received worldwide attention in February 1925 when he became trapped in Sand Cave while trying to find a passage linking it with Crystal Cave. Pinned in a narrow passageway by a rock that would-be rescuers could not reach, he eventually died.

If that kind of story keeps you out of caves, we're sorry for telling you; stick with a guided tour and you'll be fine — and you'll be glad you took it. But even if you steadfastly refuse to set foot in a cave, you'll still enjoy the park. You can hike more than 70 miles of forest trails, camp and take a canoe or cruise boat down the Green River. And there are plenty of picnic shelters.

# Natchez Trace

The Natchez Trace has always been a fascinating road, since its early days. Back then it was known for Mississippi River pioneer merchants, bloodthirsty bandits who attacked overland travelers, Native American innkeepers, "postriders" delivering news and mail, and soldiers bound for the Battle of New Orleans. Today, it remains fascinating, though for different reasons, such as bikers, bed and breakfast inns, speeding tickets, and plentiful reminders of its rich history.

If you travel all 450 miles of the Trace, heading southwest from Nashville, you'll arrive in Natchez, Mississippi, the oldest city on the Mississippi River. Because this is a daytrip, we won't go that far. But we will give you some options, along with suggested side trips, that will allow you to make your excursion as short or as long as you want it to be (if you like, you also can choose to stay in a bed and break-

fast inn and make your trip a weekend getaway).

But, first, a little history. The Old Natchez Trace, which developed from game and Indian trails, was especially important during the late 1700s and early 1800s, when early pioneers from Tennessee, Kentucky and Ohio floated their wares on flatboats down the Mississippi River to Natchez, then walked back overland to Nashville with their earnings.

This situation attracted bands of robbers from all over the Southeast. Among them were the murderous Harpe brothers, Big and Little, who not only robbed travelers, but also exhibited senseless brutality. They supposedly tied one man to his horse, then drove horse and rider over a cliff. One brother, annoyed by a crying infant, killed it by dashing its head against a tavern wall. (Some accounts have suggested a connection between the Harpes and the Harpeth River's name, though the brothers hardly seem worthy namesakes.)

Bandits weren't the only threats. The long route also passed through rugged wilderness that included Chickasaw and Choctaw lands. Travelers, who formed groups for protection whenever possible, found food and usually humble shelter at a series of stands, or inns, placed at one-day intervals and operated by the Choctaw and Chickasaw, or their agents, at the request of the U.S. government.

In the 1790s a steady stream of Americans, including Andrew Jackson and his fiancée, Rachel Robards, visited Natchez, although Spain had seized it from the British in 1779. Jackson and Robards were married in Natchez in August 1791. By 1798 the United States was in undisputed possession of Natchez and wanted to keep in as close contact as possible with the city, a strategic link to the Mississippi Territory, which had been established that year.

By 1801 the government began a project to improve the Natchez Trace, also known as Post Road, because postriders regularly traveled the route carrying mail and news between Nashville and the Natchez District. They were expected to make the one-way journey in 10 days and four hours.

Andrew Jackson again traveled the road to Natchez with 5,500 soldiers to defeat 10,000 British in the Battle of New Orleans on Janu-

The view from Lover's Leap at Rock City in Chattanooga is at once breathtaking and serene.

ary 8, 1815, and was the toast of New Orleans before returning to Nashville a hero. (A peace treaty had been signed with Britain two weeks before the battle, but the combatants didn't know this.)

The steamboat's arrival eliminated the need for an overland route, and the road "settled peacefully into its well-worn ruts," as Cathy and Vernon Summerlin relate in *Traveling the Trace: A Complete Tour Guide to the Historic Natchez Trace from Nashville to Natchez* (Rutledge Hill Press, 1995). In 1934, Mississippi congressman Thomas Jefferson "Jeff" Busby introduced a bill authorizing a survey of the Old Natchez Trace. Four years later, the historic road was designated a unit of the National Park system. Today all but a section around Jackson, Mississippi, and the southern terminus at Natchez is completed.

To arrive at our starting point, travel west from Nashville to the northern terminus of the Trace at Tenn. Highway 100, just across from Loveless Cafe. Keep in mind that the park is long, narrow and highly scenic — you should expect to find visitors enjoying themselves and motorists strictly observing the speed limit. The rangers who patrol the 450-mile parkway are diligent in their enforcement of the posted speed limit, which is a maximum of 50 mph for most of the route. In the area closest to Nashville, the posted limit is even slower.

The Trace is a popular biking route, even though there's no shoulder. Please watch out for bicyclists if you're driving; if you're biking, watch out for motorists. Also keep in mind that there are no gas stations on the Trace.

The first exit is at the Tenn. Highway 96 bridge in Williamson County. The $12 million bridge, which is 1,610 feet long and rises 160 feet above the valley, is one of only two "post-tensioned, segmental concrete arch" bridges in the world and is considered an engineering marvel. If you exit, head east to drive into Franklin on Tenn. Highway 96.

For more information about the Trace, contact the Natchez Trace Parkway Headquarters, (800) 305-7417, or Meriwether Lewis Park, (615) 796-2675. We also suggest you pick up a copy of the Summerlins' aforementioned book.

## Williamson County

Traveling the Trace through rural Williamson County, the second exit is at the small community of Leiper's Fork. It's a good place to grab a snack or a picnic for later on the Trace. If you want to spend a little more time here, you can shop for heirlooms at Leiper's Fork Antiques, 4149 Old Hillsboro Road, (615) 790-9963; enjoy a home-cooked meal at Country Boy Restaurant, 4141 Old Hillsboro Road, (615) 794-7680; get a great burger at Puckett's Grocery, 4146 Old Hillsboro Road, (615) 794-1308; or pick up some cold-cut sandwiches at Leiper's Fork Market, 4348 Old Hillsboro Road, (615) 794-0958 (gas, soft drinks and other needs of the road are available at both the grocery and the market).

As you continue on the parkway, take time to notice the historic markers along the way.

### Attractions

#### Along the Trace . . .

Mile marker 407.7 highlights the Gordon House/Ferry Site. This house, one of the few remaining buildings associated with the Old Natchez Trace, was the home of John Gordon, an Indian scout who struck a deal with the Chickasaw to operate a trading post and ferry on the Duck River. It's a 10-minute walk from the house to the ferry site and a section of the original Natchez Trace.

Mile marker 404.7 indicates Jackson Falls. A steep, 900-foot concrete trail leads to a clear pool at the base of the falls. It's a great place to while away a few hours, especially in the summertime.

Mile marker 401.4 is at the site of an early 1900s tobacco farm, where tobacco still dries in a barn a 10-minute loop walk away.

### Carnton Plantation
**1345 Carnton Ln., Franklin, Tenn.**
• **(615) 794-0903**

The Carnton Plantation house, built by former Nashville mayor Randal McGavock in 1826 and home to his family, was caught in the middle of the Civil War's bloody Battle of Franklin, which claimed the lives of 8,578 soldiers in just five hours November 30, 1864. President Andrew Jackson and his wife, Rachel, were frequent visitors to the neoclassical house, which has been designated a National Landmark museum house. For more information, see our Attractions chapter.

The McGavock Confederate Cemetery, which adjoins Carnton Plantation, is the final resting place for 1,481 Confederate soldiers who died in the battle. John McGavock provided the 2 acres for this purpose after the war. It is the largest privately owned Confederate cemetery in the country and is maintained by the United Daughters of the Confederacy. It is always open, and there is no admission charge.

### Carter House
**1140 Columbia Ave., Franklin, Tenn.**
• **(615) 791-1861**

Like Carnton Plantation, Carter House has a history closely tied to the Battle of Franklin. For more information, see our Attractions chapter.

### Accommodations

#### Namaste Acres
**5436 Leipers Creek Rd., Franklin, Tenn.**
• **(615) 791-0333**

This bed and breakfast inn, run by some really nice people, Bill and Lisa Winters, makes for a fun overnight stay. It has bedrooms with private baths, an outdoor swimming pool and a hot tub, and facilities for those traveling with horses to ride on the 26-mile-long Garrison Creek horseback-riding and hiking trail. A variety of "themed" lodging is available, from the Confederate decor of The Franklin Quarters to The Frontier Cabin, The Indian Lodge and The Cowboy Bunkhouse, which has a bedroom done up in Western-style decor complete with a modern "indoor outhouse" that's a real hoot. (See our Bed and Breakfasts chapter for more.)

# Columbia, Tenn.

An eastern exit on Tenn. Highway 7 takes you for a nice "loop tour" through Columbia, where you'll find several historic homes including the boyhood home of the 11th U.S. president as well as antique shops and more. If you continue northward on U.S. Highway 31 you'll reach Nashville by way of Spring Hill, Franklin and Brentwood.

## Attractions

### Along the Trace . . .

Mile marker 385.9 is a monument to Meriwether Lewis (1774–1809). "Beneath this monument . . . reposes the dust of Meriwether Lewis, captain in the U.S. Army, private secretary to President Jefferson, senior commander of the Lewis and Clark Expedition and governor of the Territory of Louisiana." Lewis died here at the Grinder House under mysterious circumstances that continue to generate controversy. Suicide? Murder? An exhibit tells the story of his death at this site, which also contains a campground and a good picnic spot. The campground offers RV pads, primitive campsites, bath houses, restrooms, picnic tables and grills.

Mile marker 382.8 indicates Metal Ford Steele's Ironworks. Not much remains of the ironworks, but this is a great canoe access for the Buffalo River.

Just north of U.S. Highway 64 is a sign to Laurel Hill Lake (see "Fishing" in our Recreation chapter). This 320-acre lake has a concession stand (open daily except Mondays) and rents boats for fishing. Or you can fish from the bank. A daily permit costs $3. The lake has largemouth bass, bream, crappie and catfish, is open year round and is managed by the Tennessee Wildlife Resources Agency.

Mile markers 365.1 and 364.5 indicate Glenrock Picnic Area. Trails at both markers lead to streamside picnic sites that are ideal for families, and continue along the stream to Glenrock Branch Area, .67-mile south on the parkway. The creek is perfect for wading, and

the round-trip hike is less than 1.5 miles, so anyone can enjoy it.

The Alabama state line is at mile marker 341.8 — or about 108 miles from our starting point. It's also where we'll end this daytrip. Before heading back to Nashville, however, you might want to turn east on State Route 20 to visit the "Quad Cities" of Florence, Tuscumbia, Sheffield and Muscle Shoals.

### James K. Polk Home
**301 W. Seventh St., Columbia, Tenn.**
• **(931) 388-2354**

James K. Polk, 11th president of the United States, began his legal and political career here at the home of his parents. Before becoming president, an office he held from 1845 to 1849, Polk served in Congress for 14 years, including four years as House Speaker, and was governor of Tennessee. This house, his only surviving residence other than the White House, is furnished today with many of his personal belongings.

The Polk Home is open Monday through Saturday from 9 AM to 5 PM (it closes at 4 PM November through March) and Sunday from 1 to 5 PM. Admission is $5 for adults, $4 for seniors 60 and older, $2 for anyone 6 years through college-age and free for kids 5 and younger.

# Florence and Tuscumbia, Ala.

## Attractions

### W.C. Handy Home and Museum
**620 W. College St., Florence, Ala.**
• **(256) 760-6434**

W.C. Handy, remembered today as the Father of the Blues, was born in a log cabin here in 1873. Today the home is a museum to Handy, with historical artifacts including the piano on which he composed such landmark songs as "Beale Street Blues" and "St. Louis Blues." Every August, this is also the site of the W.C. Handy Music Festival. Hours are 10 AM to 4 PM Tuesday through Saturday. Admission is $2 for adults and 50¢ for students in kindergarten through college.

### Ivy Green, the Helen Keller Birthplace
**300 W. Commons, Tuscumbia, Ala.**
**• (256) 383-4066**

Ivy Green, the family home of Helen Keller's parents, was the second house built in Tuscumbia. Helen was born here June 27, 1880. In 1887, 20-year-old Anne Mansfield Sullivan arrived to become the personal teacher to the deaf and blind child. She stayed for 49 years, even after her marriage in 1904. The pump with which Sullivan taught Keller the word "water" — a dramatic moment in the movie *The Helen Keller Story* — is behind the house.

Hours are 8:30 AM to 4 PM Monday through Saturday and 1 to 4 PM Sunday. Admission is $3 for anyone 12 and older, $1 for children ages 6 to 11 and free for kids ages 1 to 5.

# Memphis, Tennessee

Just about three hours away from Nashville by way of Interstate 40 is Memphis, Tennessee's largest city, the adopted home of The King — and much more.

Memphis, named after the ancient Egyptian capital (you were wondering about that pyramid?), has a rich history filled with proud events as well as shameful ones. It's a jumpin', swingin' Mississippi River town that, essentially, is to blues, rhythm-and-blues and rockabilly what Nashville is to country music. It's a city with a past inextricably linked to the civil rights movement. It's one of less than a handful of cities that legitimately can claim the title Barbecue Capital of the World. And it's a city that, perhaps not surprisingly, shares a sometimes intense sibling rivalry with Music City.

The city of Memphis is in the southwest corner of Tennessee, with Arkansas to the west and Mississippi to the south. It's a city built on cotton and river trade that has grown into a major commercial hub. The river remains a major transportation route, and the sky is another. Northwest Airlines has its headquarters

here, at Memphis International Airport, as does Federal Express.

Memphis's past includes a role as one of the South's largest slave markets in the early and mid-1800s. Because of its location, it was a strategic city during the Civil War. At the start of the war, it was a Confederate center, but Union forces captured it in 1862. The racial problems that plagued the city came to a climax in 1968, when escaped convict James Earl Ray assassinated Rev. Martin Luther King Jr. at the city's Lorraine Motel. (One positive outcome in the aftermath of King's assassination was an effort by local, state and federal officials to improve relationships with, and conditions within, the black community.)

Today there are many reasons to visit Memphis. Many people immediately think of Elvis Presley when they think of Memphis, but he isn't the only King enshrined here. You also can celebrate the legacies of Martin Luther King Jr. and the still-vibrant bluesman B.B. King, while contemplating the mysterious power of the mighty Mississippi, that natural force often referred to as Old Man River.

## Attractions

### Beale Street

This short downtown street packs a lot of action, most of it music-related, into four blocks. W.C. Handy, the musician and composer who became known as "Father of the Blues" for his efforts to popularize the genre, made the street famous with his song "Beale Street Blues." A statue of Handy stands on Beale Street today. Other attractions on this street include B.B. King's Blues Club, Elvis Presley's Memphis, Rum Boogie Cafe, A. Schwab and the W.C. Handy House Museum, all of which are described subsequently.

### Graceland
**3765 Elvis Presley Blvd., Memphis, Tenn. • (901) 332-3322, (800) 238-2000 (outside Tennessee)**

We've heard many people use the word "tacky" to describe the 15,000-square-foot Memphis mansion of Elvis Presley — and it is true that the home does have its garish highlights. But it was, honestly, nowhere near as bad as we'd expected (maybe that just means we're tacky too). Remember, much of the decor was from the '70s, a period not generally associated with subtlety and good taste. Keep in mind, too, that Elvis was a rock 'n' roll star. Beyond that, he was just a poor country boy who got way too rich and way too famous way too soon.

Visiting Graceland, for us at least, actually served to make The King seem more human. By the time we reached the backyard memorial gardens, where Elvis and family members are buried, we felt a genuine sadness.

The Graceland mansion tour, which takes about 1½ hours to complete, takes visitors through selected portions of the mansion. You won't see The King's bedroom, or the infamous bathroom where the music died August 16, 1977, but you will see the pool room where he hung out with his friends in the Memphis Mafia, and the kitchen where so many of those famed peanut butter and banana sandwiches were made. You'll see the TV room, the music room, the all-white formal living room, his baby grand piano, his dining rooms and den. You'll visit his racquetball building and his trophy room, which features gold records, stage costumes and other mementos. Finally, you can spend a quiet moment in the Meditation Garden, where Elvis and members of his family are buried. Tours of the mansion plus a viewing of the 20-minute film *Walk a Mile in My Shoes*, are $10 for adults and teens, $9 for seniors and $5 for children ages 7 through 12. Or you can take the "platinum tour," which includes The King's private airplanes and car collection, for $19.50 adults and teens, $17.55 seniors (62 and older) and $11 children.

Tours start every three to five minutes. Hours are 8 AM to 6 PM daily from Memorial Day through Labor Day and 9 AM to 5 PM the rest of the year. Graceland is closed Tuesdays from November through February, and on Thanksgiving, Christmas and New Year's Day. Parking is available across the street from the mansion.

## Memphis Music Hall of Fame
### 97 S. Second St., Memphis, Tenn.
• (901) 525-4007

With all the other musical attractions in Memphis, you might think this nondescript (from the outside) building couldn't have much

to offer. You'd be wrong. The original recording equipment from Sun Record Company, W.C. Handy memorabilia and a lot of Elvis stuff are among the highlights. You'll also find a complete collection of Charlie Rich memorabilia, tons of photos, rare recordings, original instruments from Memphis legends, biographies and more. The Memphis Music Hall of Fame opens at 10 AM seven days a week; closing times vary, so call for information. Admission is $7.50 for anyone 15 and older, $2.50 for ages 7 through 14 and free for kids 6 and younger.

## Memphis Pink Palace Museum and Planetarium
### 3050 Central Ave., Memphis, Tenn.
• (901) 320-6320

The Pink Palace is a 1920s house that has been converted into a museum of natural and cultural history, with special emphasis on the region around Memphis. In addition to regular exhibits on birds, insects, fossils, geology and the Civil War, the Pink Palace features traveling exhibits. It's home to the hand-carved Clyde Park Miniature Circus and a replica of the first Piggly Wiggly store (the house is the former home of the grocery chain's founder, Clarence Saunders). An IMAX theater presents special movies on a huge screen, and the Planetarium features astronomy and laser shows.

Hours from Labor Day to Memorial Day are 9 AM to 4 PM Monday through Wednesday, 9 AM to 8 PM Thursday, 9 AM to 9 PM Friday and Saturday, and noon to 5 PM Sunday. The rest of the year, the Pink Palace stays open an hour later every day except Sunday. Last admission is an hour before closing.

Several admission packages are available. Admission to the museum exhibits only costs $6 for adults and teens, $5.50 for seniors and $4.50 for children ages 3 through 12. IMAX theater showings cost the same as admission prices. Planetarium admission is $3.50 for adults and $3 for seniors and children. A combination ticket for either IMAX plus exhibits or IMAX plus planetarium is $9 for adults, $7.50 for seniors and $6 for children. For the exhibits plus planetarium, it's $7.50 for adults, $7 for seniors and $6 for children. Finally, your best buy, a ticket that lets you enjoy it all, is $11, $10 for seniors and $8 for children.

## The Memphis Zoo
**2000 Galloway St., Memphis, Tenn.**
**• (901) 725-3400, (800) 288-8763 (group reservations)**

The Memphis Zoo, considered by many to be one of the best in the country, is in Overton Park. Favorite exhibits include Cat Country, Primate Canyon, an aquarium and tropical birdhouse. The zoo is open every day except Thanksgiving, Christmas Eve and Christmas Day. Hours are 9 AM to 5 PM March through October and 9 AM to 4:30 PM the rest of the year. During July and August, closing time on Saturdays and Sundays is extended to 9 PM. Admission is $8 for folks 12 and older, $7 for seniors, $5 for kids ages 2 through 11 and free for tots younger than 2.

## Mud Island
**125 N. Front St., Memphis, Tenn.**
**• (901) 576-7241**

How'd you like to walk along — or *in*, if you prefer — the Mississippi River from Cairo, Illinois, to the Gulf of Mexico? You can do just that — and all in a matter of minutes — at Mud Island. The River Walk, a five-block-long scale model of the lower Mississippi River, is just one highlight of this fascinating attraction devoted to the river, its history and its culture.

Mud Island, a 52-acre island just off shore, is connected to downtown Memphis by an automobile bridge, a pedestrian bridge and a monorail. Other highlights here include the Mississippi River Museum, with exhibits that include a reproduction of an 1870s steamboat, a Union gunboat and other river vessels; American Indian artifacts; and a Hall of River Music, which offers insights into the development of jazz, blues and rock 'n' roll. Back outside on the pavilion, you'll find the *Memphis Belle*, a B-17 bomber from World War II, as well as a swimming pool and beach. (The pool, incidentally, represents the Gulf of Mexico, at the end of the River Walk.)

During the spring season, from early April to late May, Mud Island is open from 10 AM to 5 PM Tuesday through Sunday. During the summer season, from late May to early September, it is open from 10 AM to 8 PM seven days a week. During the fall season, from early September to late October, it is again open from 10 AM to 5 PM Tuesday through Sunday. The last admission is one hour before closing time. The beach and pool are open only during summer. Admission to the pavilion, which includes the River Walk, is $4 for anyone 12 and older, with seniors and children ages 4 through 11 getting in for $3. Museum admission is $4 extra, or $2 for seniors and children.

## National Civil Rights Museum
**Lorraine Motel, 450 Mulberry St.,**
**Memphis, Tenn. • (901) 521-9699**

The Lorraine Motel is where, on April 4, 1968, Rev. Martin Luther King Jr. was assassinated. So it is fitting that the building today be devoted to the ideals of King and other leaders of the civil rights movement. An introductory film provides an overview, and interactive audiovisual exhibits evoke the emotions and tensions of the times.

The "Brown v. Board of Education of Topeka" exhibit explores the 1954 Supreme Court decision that ruled segregation in public schools unconstitutional. In another dramatic exhibit, visitors can sit on a bus and put themselves in the place of Rosa Parks, whose refusal to surrender her bus seat in Montgomery, Alabama, in 1955 was a catalytic event in the struggle for civil rights.

The National Civil Rights Museum is open 9 AM to 5 PM Monday through Saturday — except Tuesday, when it is closed — and 1 to 5 PM Sunday. Thursday hours are extended to 8 PM, and from June through August the regular closing time is extended to 6 PM. Admission is $6 for adults, $5 for seniors and college students with ID, and $4 for ages 4 through 17. Audiotape guided tours are $2.50 a person. Group rates are available for 20 or more people with reservations.

## The Peabody Hotel
**149 Union Ave., Memphis, Tenn.**
**• (901) 529-4000, (800) PEABODY**

The Peabody, a luxury hotel, is famous for its ducks, a pampered quintet who twice a day march through the lobby amid great ceremony. At 11 AM, the ducks leave their hotel room, take an elevator ride to the main floor, then march across the red carpet, rolled out just for them, to the lobby fountain. There they frolic until 5 PM, when they reverse the process. It's a great photo opportunity, especially for the little ones, and it's free. (Just for kicks, we asked the maitre d' of Mallards, one of the hotel restaurants, whether duck was on the menu. "No, it is not," he said. He was not amused.)

## The Pyramid
**1 Auction Ave., Memphis, Tenn.**
• **(901) 521-9675**
The original Memphis was the capital of ancient Egypt. This glistening 32-story structure, with a 20-foot statue of the Pharaoh Ramses II guarding the entrance, makes that connection explicit. The stainless-steel covered Pyramid, on the downtown riverfront, is an arena that seats up to 22,500 people for sports events and concerts; it also plays host to special events such as the 1997 world premiere of the "*Titanic*" exhibit and exhibits highlighting Peru and World War II.

Tours of The Pyramid include locker and dressing rooms, a luxury suite and a short video of the building's history. Tours are offered hourly 9 AM to 5 PM May through September, and at noon, 1 and 2 PM the rest of the year. Cost is $4 for adults and $3 for seniors and kids ages 4 through 11.

## A. Schwab
**163 Beale St., Memphis, Tenn.**
• **(901) 523-9782**
Students of Delta blues lore can pick up a mojo hand or other voodoo talismans at this funky little general store, open since 1876. You can also find clothing, blues albums and other merchandise; the store's longtime motto is "If you can't find it at Schwab's, you're better off without it!"

A. Schwab is open 9 AM to 5 PM Monday through Saturday year round.

## Sun Studio
**706 Union Ave., Memphis, Tenn.**
• **(901) 521-0664**
Graceland may attract most of the attention, but Sun Studio has the ghosts. Here, at Memphis Recording Service, part of the Sun Records company, is where 18-year-old Elvis Presley cut his first tracks in 1953. By the next year, Sun owner Sam Phillips had signed Presley to his label and released his first single, "That's All Right, Mama," with "Blue Moon of Kentucky" on the flip side.

Despite two top-5 hits, including a No. 1, in the next year, Phillips soon sold Elvis's contract to the larger RCA Victor label for $35,000 — a huge sum then, but nothing when you consider what was to come. Yet Phillips says he never regretted his decision. Sun also recorded such legends as Johnny Cash, Roy Orbison, B.B. King, Muddy Waters, Carl Perkins, Jerry Lee Lewis and Charlie Rich — pioneers whose music has shaped the face of popular music with an influence that continues to be felt today.

Sun, which reopened in the 1980s after being closed for years, has recently been the studio for recordings by acts including U2, Bonnie Raitt and Def Leppard. There's still magic between these walls, as you'll discover when you take the 45-minute tour. Actually, "tour" can be something of a misnomer because most of the presentation takes place in a single room. But what a room it is! The outtakes you'll hear from those early recording sessions serve as a brief audio history of rock 'n' roll's formative years. And you can hold the microphone once used by the poor teenager from Tupelo, Mississippi, who became The King of Rock 'n' Roll.

Sun Studio is open from 9 AM to 7 PM daily from Memorial Day to Labor Day and from 10 AM to 6 PM daily the rest of the year. Daily year-round tours start at 10:30 AM, continuing every hour on the half-hour until 5:30 PM. Admission is $8.50 for anyone 12 and older; children younger than 12 get in free. Get your tickets next door to the actual studio at Sun Studio Cafe and Gallery, which contains a collection of rare recordings, photos and memorabilia.

## W.C. Handy House Museum
**352 Beale St., Memphis, Tenn.**
• **(901) 522-1556**
This small, wood-frame house is where W.C. Handy lived after moving from Florence, Alabama. He went on to write such classic blues songs as "Beale Street Blues" and "St. Louis Blues." Here you can see artifacts relating to Handy's life. Hours are 10 AM to 5 PM Tuesday through Sunday during summer and 11 AM to 4 PM Tuesday through Saturday the rest of the year. Admission is $2 for adults and $1 for children and students.

## Restaurants and Nightclubs

### B.B. King's Blues Club
143 Beale St., Memphis, Tenn.
• (901) 524-5464

Listen to live blues while savoring some down-home Southern cooking, like barbecue and catfish. We highly recommend the catfish, fried in cornmeal batter. (Here's a tip: skip the tartar sauce and eat your catfish with hot sauce, the way they do in Mississippi, where B.B. King grew up.) B.B. King's is open seven days a week, with live entertainment nightly.

### Elvis Presley's Memphis
126 Beale St., Memphis, Tenn.
• (901) 527-6900

This theme restaurant, which opened in July 1997, is decorated with Elvis gold records and loads of other memorabilia. Menu favorites include meat loaf, burgers and, yes, those fried peanut butter and banana sandwiches you've heard about. The sound system plays mostly Elvis, and live bands — primarily rockabilly — play at least four nights a week. Elvis Presley's Memphis is open daily.

### The Rendezvous
52 S. Second St., Memphis, Tenn.
• (901) 523-2746

The entrance to this barbecue restaurant is actually in the alley across from the Peabody Hotel's main entrance. The Rendezvous is noted for its ribs and pork.

### Rum Boogie Cafe
182 Beale St., Memphis, Tenn.
• (901) 528-0150

Rum Boogie has great barbecue and sandwiches as well as a great collection of autographed photos and musical instruments. It's open seven days a week, with live entertainment nightly.

# The Great Smoky Mountains

An acquaintance of one of our friends recently made a weekend getaway with his wife to Pigeon Forge, Tennessee. Upon returning to his home in Kentucky, he was excitedly relaying the experience to our friend. The couple had caught two musical shows, shopped at outlet malls and flown in a helicopter. "What did you think about the national park?" our friend asked. To which his acquaintance replied, "Oh, we never made it to the park."

Our friend, like us a frequent visitor to the Smokies, related this story to us with great amusement. He found it hard to believe that someone would visit the area without venturing into the Great Smoky Mountains National Park. Sure, it's possible to do, what with all the other attractions in the vicinity — but why would you want to?

The Great Smoky Mountains are a range of the Blue Ridge Mountains, which are part of the Appalachian Mountains. The Great Smokies, which earned their name from the bluish, smoke-like haze that rises from the dense tree growth and other vegetation, are truly a natural wonder, filled with scenic beauty. In the 520,000-acre park itself — roughly half of which is in Tennessee and half in North Carolina — you can see more than 100 native species of trees; more than 1,000 types of flowering shrubs and plants; several hundred miles of clear, sparkling streams fed by mountain springs; and all kinds of mammals, birds, fish, reptiles and other animals. As a result, the park has been designated an International Biosphere Reserve.

The Smokies' most famous animal resident is *Ursus (Euarctos) americanus*, more commonly known as the black bear. Park officials say the bear population, which has risen in recent years thanks to plentiful food supplies, is about 700. If you spend much time in these mountains, chances are very good that you will see one or more black bears.

You will also find plenty of activities. Nature lovers will relish the opportunities for hiking, swimming, fishing, camping, whitewater rafting, horseback riding and nature watching. In the towns of Gatlinburg and Pigeon Forge, you can get married in one of many wedding chapels, play golf, shop, browse for arts and crafts, be entertained by top-notch singers and musicians, bungee jump and ride go-carts. You can visit Cherokee, North Carolina, an Indian reservation, and gamble in a casino.

There's something for almost everybody, which may be why this is such a popular place. The Great Smoky Mountains National Park attracts an average of 9 million visitors a year — more than any other national park. (And that's not counting the people who don't actually make it into the park.)

To get to the Great Smoky Mountains National Park, take Interstate 40 east from Nashville to Knoxville — about a three-hour drive. Then continue east on the I-640 bypass toward Asheville, North Carolina (you can bypass downtown Knoxville via I-640 if you wish). Exit onto U.S. Highway 441 S. and follow the signs. You'll pass through Sevierville and the resort towns of Pigeon Forge and Gatlinburg before arriving at the entrance to the park. (The part of U.S. 441 that passes through Sevierville, Pigeon Forge and Gatlinburg is known as Parkway; as it enters the park and leads on to North Carolina, it becomes known as Newfound Gap Road.) Incidentally, the Smokies are in the Eastern Time Zone, so set your watch ahead one hour.

In addition to the towns we just mentioned, this section covers attractions in Townsend, Tennessee, as well as Cherokee, North Carolina. In this area, literally thousands of possibilities await you. To describe them all would require a thick book. We've chosen to cover some of our favorite activities, which, with a few exceptions, lean toward the "natural." If you prefer to bungee jump or ride go-karts or helicopters, don't worry if you don't find those activities described in this section. We guarantee that, once you get here, you won't have any trouble finding them. They are everywhere, especially in "action-packed Pigeon Forge," to quote the advertisements.

For more information on opportunities in the Smoky Mountains, these numbers may be of help:

• Cherokee Visitor Center, (800) 438-1601
• Gatlinburg Visitors and Convention Bureau, (423) 430-4148 or (800) 568-4748
• Great Smoky Mountains National Park, (423) 436-1200
• Pigeon Forge Department of Tourism, (423) 453-8574 or (800) 251-9100
• Sevierville Chamber of Commerce, (423) 453-6411 or (800) 255-6411
• Sugarlands Visitor Center, (423) 436-5615
• Townsend Visitor Center, (423) 448-6134 or (800) 525-6834

## Natural Attractions

### Cades Cove

Take scenic, winding Little River Road (U.S. Highway 73), off U.S. 441 near the Sugarlands Visitor Center, to reach Cades Cove, about 25 miles away. This 4,000-acre valley was once home to a thriving frontier community that lasted from the mid-1700s to the mid-1800s. As you pass through the valley on a one-way, 11-mile loop road, you'll see old log homesteads and barns, smokehouses, a working corn mill and three historic churches with cemeteries. Cades Cove offers several hiking trails, ranging from 2 to 11 miles round trip.

On the way to Cades Cove, stop at the Townsend "Y," where the middle and west prongs of the Little Pigeon River come together. This peaceful and popular spot is ideal for picnicking, swimming or floating on inner tubes. A large, grassy bank looks down on the curve of the river. Some young people like to jump or dive from a cliff above a deeper section of the river here, but we don't recommend doing this.

### Newfound Gap Road

Newfound Gap Road, or U.S. Highway 441, leads through the center of the Great Smoky Mountains National Park, winding southeast on its way over the mountains and into North Carolina. This route will take you to or near a number of scenic overlooks, hiking trails and other points of interest including Chimney Tops, Mount LeConte, Clingmans Dome, Newfound Gap and Cherokee (descriptions follow).

### Chimney Tops

The gap between these dual peaks, about 2,000 feet high, has the appearance, to some, of a flue; hence the name. You can see the peaks from the Chimney Tops overlook on Newfound Gap Road. Just 5 miles up the road from the Sugarlands Visitor Center is The

Chimneys picnic area. This highly popular spot, in a ravine, contains plenty of picnic tables and a mountain stream filled with big boulders that are perfect for resting, sunning or walking across the stream.

## Mount LeConte

Mount LeConte, which at 6,593 feet is the Smokies' third-highest peak, is visible throughout the park. But you must hike or ride on horseback to reach it, as it is accessible only by five trails ranging from 11 to 16 miles round trip. Two overlooks provide magnificent views from the top of Mount LeConte, and you can make reservations for rustic mountaintop lodging by calling Wilderness Lodging at (423) 429-5704.

## Newfound Gap

At this site, 15 miles up Newfound Gap Road from Sugarlands Visitor Center, President Franklin Delano Roosevelt officially dedicated the Great Smoky Mountains National Park in 1940. A parking area includes restrooms and provides some great photo opportunities of Smoky Mountain ranges. Here you can also get on the Appalachian Trail, a 2,000-mile trail that stretches south to Georgia and north to Maine. Charlie's Bunion, a 1,000-foot sheer drop-off, is a 4-mile eastward hike from here.

## Clingmans Dome

Clingmans Dome, at 6,643 feet, is the highest point in all of Tennessee. A 7-mile road from Newfound Gap Road takes you to a parking area from which you can you can take a steep half-mile hike to the peak's observation tower. Here you'll discover a spectacular 360-degree panorama of the Smokies — one of the most incredible vistas you'll encounter. Sometimes Clingmans Dome is above the level of the clouds; while this can limit visibility, it also offers an eerily dreamlike view.

## Roaring Fork Motor Nature Trail

The Roaring Fork Motor Nature Trail, off U.S. Highway 321 E., is a one-way, 6-mile loop that contains a number of homesteads from the early 19th century as well as an abundance of natural beauty. Several hiking trails are accessible from the Roaring Fork road, and these range from the easy, 3-mile Grotto Falls round trip to the strenuous, 9-mile Trillium Gap round trip. This area contains three waterfalls, one of which is visible from the road.

## Greenbrier

The entrance to this wooded area, which lies along the middle prong of the Little Pigeon River, is a few miles outside downtown Gatlinburg off U.S. Highway 321 E. It's a popular place to float in inner tubes — various stores and gas stations on U.S. 321 rent them — over the river's rapids, which range from mild to moderate in this area. Other people prefer simply to relax on rocks, enjoy a picnic lunch or hike on one of several trails, which range from about 3 to 8 miles round trip. The narrow 4-mile road that winds through the Greenbrier area is secluded and filled with beautiful scenery, including plants and wildlife; a deer ran across our path on a recent visit.

# Other Attractions

## Cherokee, N.C.

Cherokee, an Indian reservation 35 miles from Sugarlands Visitor Center, contains the Cherokee Museum and Gallery as well as numerous shops that sell Native American arts and crafts. The reservation is also home to Harrah's Cherokee Casino, featuring video poker, craps, blackjack and pull tabs, along with live entertainment and dining; call (800) HARRAHS for details.

## Dollywood
**1020 Dollywood Ln., Pigeon Forge, Tenn. • (423) 428-9488**

Dollywood, owned by Dolly Parton, is a theme park devoted to music, arts and crafts, and rides for the entire family. Many of the park's attractions reflect Dolly's down-home mountain heritage. Rides include Thunder Road, a "turbo action" ride based on the classic Robert Mitchum movie about a moonshiner; the Slidewinder coaster ride; The Dollywood Express, a steam train; and a Country Fair area of old-fashioned rides and games. New for the 1999 season are the Tennessee Tornado, a roller coaster with a spiral loop; and the Southern Gospel Music Hall of Fame and Museum. Popular entertainer James Rogers also has returned.

The Dolly Parton Museum tells the singer's life story through mementos and video presentations. Imagination Station features a LEGO Construction Zone, where kids can play with the popular building bricks, as well as other hands-on activities. Dozens of daily shows range from contemporary country and '50s rock 'n' roll to Southern gospel and the music of Dolly and other songwriters of the Smokies. In addition, weekends September through early November feature, for an additional charge, concerts by many of today's country superstars.

Dollywood, 1 mile off the Parkway in Pigeon Forge, is open most days from May through August, on weekends in April, every day except Thursday in October. The schedule for September, November and December varies, so call first. The park is closed January through March. Ticket prices in 1999 were $29.99 for folks 12 and older, $24.99 for seniors 60 and older and $20.99 for kids ages 4 through 11.

### Great Smoky Arts and Crafts Community
**U.S. Hwy. 321 N., Glades and Buckhorn rds., Gatlinburg, Tenn.**

Glass blowers, candle makers, potters, basket weavers, visual artists, doll makers, woodcarvers and many other types of artists and crafts people have their wares on display and for sale on this 8-mile loop of shops, studios and galleries. Many offer free demonstrations of their work. The loop begins 3 miles from traffic light No. 3 in downtown Gatlinburg.

The Arts and Crafts Community holds spe-cial shows during Thanksgiving week, early December (Christmas) and early April (Easter).

### Ober Gatlinburg
**Ski Mountain Rd., Gatlinburg, Tenn.**
**• (423) 436-5423, (800) 251-9202**

Ober Gatlinburg is a ski resort and amusement park atop 3,500-foot Mount Harrison. You can drive to it by way of the winding and often steep Ski Mountain Road, or ride the aerial tramway at 1001 Parkway (traffic light No. 9) in downtown Gatlinburg. Skiing is seasonal, with primarily man-made snow, but the rest of the park is open year round. Amusements include an alpine slide, bungee jumping, an ice skating rink, arcade games and a black bear habitat. Admission is free, with prices varying per attraction.

### Smoky Mountain Winery
**Winery Sq., U.S. Hwy. 321 E.,**
**Gatlinburg, Tenn. • (423) 436-7551**

This small winery produces a range of wines, from dry to sweet. You can take a free tour of the facility and view the oak barrels, casks, tanks, aging cellar and other equipment. You can also sample the product. The winery's regular hours are 10 AM to 6 PM daily, with occasional seasonal adjustments.

## Recreation

### Deer Farm Riding Stables
**Happy Hollow Ln., Sevierville, Tenn.**
**• (423) 429-BARN**

Half-hour ($10 per person) and hour-long ($15) rides in the foothills of the Smokies are available year round, weather permitting, at Deer Farm, which is also the site of an exotic petting zoo.

### INSIDERS' TIP

If you're visiting East Tennessee's Great Smoky Mountains National Park, consider spending some time in the peaceful mountain town of Townsend, Tennessee, just 30 minutes from Pigeon Forge and Gatlinburg. Townsend has beautiful scenery, recreation, attractions, entertainment, shopping, dining and accommodations. For more information, call the Townsend Visitors Center, (423) 448-6134. For a free vacation guide, call the Smoky Mountain Visitors Bureau, (800) 525-6834.

## Smoky Mountain Outdoors Unlimited
### 3229 Hartford Rd., Hartford, Tenn.
- **(800) 771-7238**

Smoky Mountain Outdoors Unlimited takes rafters onto the Big Pigeon and French Broad rivers. For the Big Pigeon trip ($30 per person), you and your rafting colleagues, with guide, will take a bus to your entry point near the North Carolina state line. (First you'll receive a thorough briefing on proper use of oars and general rafting safety.) Then you'll put your canoe into the water for a 6.5-mile trip back to headquarters. Along the way, you'll pass through more than 40 Class I and II rapids, more than a dozen Class IIIs and four Class IVs (the roughest of the trip). No experience is necessary, but whitewater rafting can be a risky activity, and you'll have to sign a waiver releasing the company from liability. We came through our trip unscathed, exhilarated and determined to try it again someday.

## Accommodations

We'd like to caution you from the start that, while you certainly can take a daytrip to the Smokies, you'll more than likely want to make the trip last more than one day. There are many hotels and motels in the area, but our preferred lodging would be a mountain cabin, cottage or chalet. You can rent anything from a cozy one-room cabin to a luxury chalet with five or more bedrooms accommodating 15 or more people. Features, which vary according to property, include fireplaces, gorgeous mountain or forest views, mountain streams, decks, barbecue grills, outdoor hot tubs, indoor whirlpools, pool tables, TVs and VCRs and much more, including all the amenities of home. Prices also vary significantly, with such a wide range of properties available. You can pay less than $100 a night or as much as $500 or more. The average price for a fully equipped two-bedroom chalet is generally around $125 a night.

Some rental companies whose Smoky Mountain properties we have enjoyed in recent years include:

- Alpine Chalet Rentals, 205 Parkway, Gatlinburg, Tennessee, (423) 439-4336 or (800) 235-2661

- Chalet Village Chalets, 631 Ski Mountain Road, Gatlinburg, Tennessee, (423) 436-0254 or (800) 545-4199
- Jackson Mountain Homes, Winery Square, U.S. Highway 321 E., Gatlinburg, Tennessee, (423) 436-8876 or (800) 473-3163
- Smoky Mountain Rentals, 204 Parkway, Suite 3, Sevierville, Tennessee, (423) 908-7055 or (800) 360-5978

Just be sure to make your reservations in advance, especially during peak times like the start of autumn, when the changing leaves turn the mountains into a beautiful canvas of golds, oranges, reds and browns.

## Shopping

Many people travel to the area simply to shop. Pigeon Forge has several major outlet malls offering discounted prices on brand-name merchandise.

### Belz Factory Outlet World
**2655 Teaster Ln., Pigeon Forge, Tenn.**
- **(423) 453-3503**

Belz stores include American Eagle Outfitters, American Tourister, Burlington Brands, Converse, Fuller Brush, Geoffrey Beene, Hush Puppies, Izod, Jockey, Maidenform, Naturalizer, Petite Sophisticate and Van Heusen.

### Governor's Crossing Outlet Center
**212 Collier Drive, Sevierville, Tenn.**
- **(423) 429-2320**

Governor's Crossing, the Smokies' newest collection of factory outlets, is home to Books a Million, GNC, Golf Depot, Oneida, Shoe Carnival and other stores; the list is sure to grow.

### Pigeon Forge Factory Outlet Mall
**2850 Parkway, Pigeon Forge, Tenn.**
- **(423) 428-2828**

This orange-roofed mall, the Smokies' first, has about 40 "factory direct" stores featuring name-brand merchandise from such companies as Bass, Black & Decker, Book Warehouse, Bugle Boy, Chicago Cutlery, Corning/Revere, Dexter Shoe, London Fog, Oshkosh B'Gosh, Pfaltzgraff, Samsonite and Van Heusen.

## Riverview Factory Stores
2668 Teaster Ln., Pigeon Forge, Tenn.
• (423) 429-2781
## Rivervista Factory Stores
2732 Teaster Ln., Pigeon Forge, Tenn.
• (423) 429-2781

These malls, which share management, are near the huge Belz Factory Outlet World and Tanger Outlet Center. Stores include Corning/Revere, Home & Garden, Hoover, Tool Factory Outlet, Brass Crafters and Dalton Rug.

## Tanger Five Oaks Factory Stores
145 Parkway, Sevierville, Tenn.
• (423) 453-1053

The growing Tanger Five Oaks has close to 50 outlet stores, including Anne Klein, Brooks Brothers, Gap, Guess?, Haggar, Lenox China, Liz Claiborne, Magnavox, Nautica, Nine West, Reebok/Rockport, Tommy Hilfiger and Woolrich.

## Tanger Outlet Center
175 Davis Rd., Pigeon Forge, Tenn.
• (423) 428-7002

Tanger Outlet Center features two dozen stores, including Eddie Bauer, Gant, J. Crew, L'eggs/Hanes/Bali, Liz Claiborne, London Fog, Oshkosh, Polo Jeans, S&K Famous Brand Menswear and Smith & Wesson.

## Restaurants

Please note that no alcohol is available in Pigeon Forge or Sevierville restaurants.

## Applewood Farmhouse Restaurant
Apple Valley Rd., Sevierville, Tenn.
• (423) 428-1222

People don't seem to mind waiting to eat at this quaint restaurant in a farmhouse in the midst of an apple orchard. The Southern fried chicken is outstanding, as is the country ham, and all meals start with tasty homemade apple fritters.

## Country Kitchen
2794 Parkway, Pigeon Forge, Tenn.
• (423) 453-1750

Country Kitchen offers a varied, family-oriented menu with prices and friendly, efficient service to match. It fills up quickly at dinnertime.

## Hofbrauhaus Restaurant
The Village, 634 Parkway, Ste. 15,
Gatlinburg, Tenn. • (423) 436-9511

Reubens made with steamed, lean corned beef on pumpernickel rolls are the specialty at this cozy little restaurant, upstairs from The Cheese Cupboard in The Village collection of shops. The restaurant also serves roast beef, turkey, pastrami and other deli sandwiches, bratwurst and beer.

## Mountain Smoke Barbecue
Winery Sq., U.S. Hwy. 321 E.,
Gatlinburg, Tenn. • (423) 436-9643

The aroma of Mountain Smoke tempts you from a block away. It's not fancy, but barbecue fans won't mind. Specialties include slow-cooked pork, beef brisket, chicken and ribs.

## The Old Mill & Restaurant
2934 Middle Creek Rd., Pigeon Forge,
Tenn. • (423) 429-3463

This restaurant serves Southern specialties like catfish and fried chicken in a scenic location next to a working mill on the Little Pigeon River. Before or after your meal, you can visit the mill and even buy some cornmeal.

## The Park Grill
1110 Parkway, Gatlinburg, Tenn.
• (423) 436-2300
## The Peddler Restaurant
820 River Rd., Gatlinburg, Tenn.
• (423) 436-5794

Both of these restaurants, which share ownership, are in big log buildings. The Peddler is noted for its steaks, marinated chicken, grilled seafood and salad bar. The newer Park Grill is a little more family-oriented, with a wide children's menu.

# Nashville Area Neighborhoods

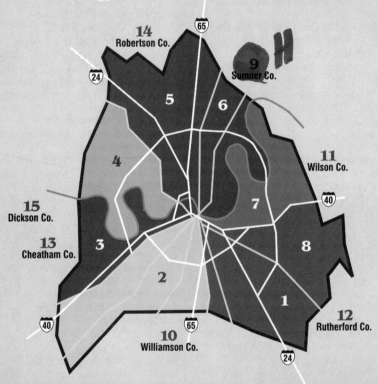

14 Robertson Co.

9 Sumner Co.

5

6

11 Wilson Co.

4

15 Dickson Co.

13 Cheatham Co.

3

7

8

2

1

10 Williamson Co.

12 Rutherford Co.

## Where the Neighborhoods Are

| | | | | | |
|---|---|---|---|---|---|
| Antioch | Area 1 | Forest Hills | Area 2 | Inglewood | Area 6 |
| Ashland City | Area 13 | Franklin | Area 10 | Kingston Springs | Area 13 |
| Belle Meade | Area 2 | Gallatin | Area 9 | Madison | Area 6 |
| Bellevue | Area 2 | Germantown | Area 3 | Oak Hill | Areas 1 & 2 |
| Belmont | Area 2 | Goodlettsville | Area 5 | Sylvan Park | Area 2 |
| Brentwood | Area 10 | Green Hills | Area 2 | Vanderbilt | Area 2 |
| Crieve Hall | Area 1 | Hendersonville | Area 9 | West End | Area 2 |
| Donelson | Areas 7 & 8 | Hermitage | Area 7 | West Meade/Hillwood | Area 2 |
| Fairview | Area 10 | Hillsboro Village | Area 2 | Whitland | Area 2 |

# Neighborhoods and Real Estate

Nashville has come a long way since the pioneering folks of 1779 established a settlement on the banks of the Cumberland River. The city has continued to grow and expand its boundaries in every direction, and the population has boomed. Today, more than 1.1 million people live in the eight-county Nashville Metropolitan Statistical Area (MSA). The population grew nearly 19 percent between 1990 and 1999, and is expected to increase nearly 32 percent — to 1.57 million — by 2020.

Nashville is one of the most affordable cities of its size. Its overall cost of living consistently ranks below the national average. According to the American Chamber of Commerce Researchers Association, Nashville's cost of living in 1998 was rated 95.9, compared with a national average of 100.

Housing costs in Nashville are among the most affordable in the country. According to one 1999 report that compared housing costs of 300 U.S. and Canadian cities, a typical 2,000-square-foot suburban home in Nashville would cost $152,600, well below the median of $173,000.

Nashvillians live in the city, in the suburbs and out in the country. We make our homes in modern houses, high-rise condos, renovated historic houses, downtown lofts, apartments, farmhouses, mansions, cottages and townhouses in communities and neighborhoods that are as diverse as the people who live in them. We are sometimes surprised and amused at the view non-Insiders have of Nashville and Nashvillians. Their images include barns and hay bales, but that's not Nashville; Music City is much more cosmopolitan than

that. Of course we do have some spectacularly beautiful scenery and some charming and peaceful rural communities nearby, but you'll have to drive a few miles to find them.

If you're a newcomer, you will soon find out that the Nashville area is made up of many suburbs, urban and rural areas and historic districts, each with its own personality and appeal. Belle Meade is as different from Madison as Hillsboro Village is from Bellevue. Because Nashville is so spread out and has so many well-developed areas, many of us who have lived here for years still aren't familiar with some neighborhoods. A lot of Nashvillians tend to keep to their own part of town most of the time. Why drive 15 to 30 miles across town to shop, dine or enjoy a day of recreation when everything you need is practically in your own back yard? Of course, when we do make an excursion into a far-away neighborhood, we usually come across some great homes, shops, restaurants and other new discoveries.

With few exceptions, the top restaurants, clubs and shops are on the west side of the Cumberland River, starting in The District and spreading westward. But if you never cross the river and explore the east side, you're missing a treat — lots of good neighborhoods, interesting homes, plenty of shopping, good food and numerous recreation opportunities.

Within Metro Nashville are several satellite cities that were incorporated before Nashville and Davidson County merged in 1963 to form Metro. These cities — Belle Meade, Berry Hill, Forest Hills, half of Goodlettsville, Lakewood and Oak Hill — have their own planning and zoning boards, city officials and various city

services. They are somewhat indistinguishable from surrounding Nashville areas and generally have a suburban feel.

While people relocating to the Nashville area often head straight to Davidson County, existing residents are moving to surrounding counties in the Nashville MSA: Cheatham, Dickson, Robertson, Rutherford, Sumner, Williamson and Wilson. The Nashville Economic Market includes these eight counties as well as Maury County to the southwest and Montgomery County to the north, adding an additional 214,000 or so to the population.

Populations in the MSA are increasing steadily. Large numbers of Nashvillians began exiting the city for life in the suburbs in the 1950s, and now that those suburbs are well established, many residents are looking for a little more space and moving even farther from the city. Many cite taxes, schools, housing prices and quality of life as their reasons for moving to outlying areas. According to a study by the UT Center for Business and Economic Research, between the years 2000 and 2020, Davidson County's population is expected to increase 11 percent — from 543,102 to 605,030 — while surrounding counties will experience growth rates ranging from 34 percent to 81 percent.

Not surprisingly, major development is occurring along the interstate system and major secondary arteries into Davidson County. Easy access to I-40, I-24 and I-65 makes living in a surrounding county an appealing option for many Nashville workers. According to the Rutherford County Chamber of Commerce, for example, at least 18,000 residents make the 30- to 50-minute commute from Rutherford County to Nashville every Monday through Friday. The Federal Highway Administration reports that Nashvillians travel an average of about 32 miles per person per day. A good portion of that is the commute to and from work. The construction of I-840, a loop connecting all three interstates on both the north and south sides of Nashville, is expected to make it even easier to zip around the area.

Regardless of the area in which you choose to live, it's a good idea to learn about the school districts, tax rates, level of services, restrictions and zoning laws. For example, if you want to live on a lake, you should know that most lake areas allow for very limited shoreline access, but there are some areas designated for shoreline development that might allow for a dock (a permit is necessary). If you plan to build on acreage that requires a well and septic tank, consult local officials to make sure the land will percolate — a necessary component in obtaining a permit to install a septic system. Some areas in Middle Tennessee are rocky, making it difficult to support septic systems.

Of course, you also have price to consider.

Fortunately, Nashville has something for every budget. With a little patience, you will find what you're looking for, whether it's an efficiency apartment or a custom-designed new home.

# NashvilleArea County Property Tax Rates

The following are the 1999 property tax rates per $100 assessed value listed by county. Check cities for additional rates.

**Cheatham** — $2.95
**Davidson**
　(General Services District) — $3.39
　(Urban Services District) — $4.24
**Dickson** — $2.45
**Rutherford** — $2.78
**Sumner** — $2.42
**Williamson** — $ 2.96
**Wilson** — $2.82

# Neighborhoods

With so many great neighborhoods, choosing one in which to live can be tough. You can use the neighborhood descriptions in this section to aid you in your search or just to learn more about the different communities in and around Nashville. We use the term "neighborhood" pretty loosely. While Green Hills could be considered a neighborhood, the area also has several smaller neighborhoods that have their own character and style. The same is true for most other areas we call "neighborhoods." If you are relocating or are considering moving to another part of town, we highly recommend making several exploratory visits to different neighborhoods so you can get a good feel for what these areas are like.

In what follows, we describe some of the major neighborhoods, starting with those in Metro; these are grouped by area. A listing of counties follows. In local real estate and apartment guides, most listings are categorized into numbered areas that correspond to areas on the real estate map. Area 2, for example, includes Green Hills, Bellevue, Belle Meade and some surrounding neighborhoods; Area 13 is Cheatham County; Area 8 lies between Murfreesboro Road and Donelson Pike and is bordered by Percy Priest Lake; and so on. To benefit those of you who might be using a real estate map for reference, we'll refer to these well-known numbered areas to help orient you to a particular neighborhood or county.

Information on average sale prices was provided by several sources, including the Middle Tennessee Regional Multiple Listing Service, real estate agents and chambers of commerce. Keep in mind that prices have been climbing, so by the time you read this, prices could have increased a bit.

Following this "Neighborhoods" section is a listing of real estate agencies, services and publications that can assist you in relocating or finding a new home.

# Metropolitan Nashville– Davidson County

When you drive across the county line into Davidson County, you'll be greeted by a sign informing you that you are entering "Metropolitan Nashville Davidson County, Home of the *Grand Ole Opry*." This is Music City U.S.A. This very urbanized county includes those six satellite cities mentioned previously as well as other extensive residential areas.

The Nashville Area Chamber of Commerce estimated the 1999 population at 541,490, a 6 percent increase from 1990. In 1998, the average selling price for a home in Davidson County was approximately $126,200.

## Downtown Area

### Second Avenue

Among downtown Nashville's historic neighborhoods, the oldest — Second Avenue, or "The District" as we call it — offers city living in the truest sense. Serious urbanites who want to feel the pulse of the city — day and night — can live here in the heart of downtown Nashville, among the neon lights and hustle and bustle of Music City.

Second Avenue Historic District is listed on the National Register of Historic Places.

Until 1903, Second Avenue was called Market Street. The center of commercial activity in the last half of the 1800s, the street was lined with two- to five-story brick Victorian warehouses that were one block deep. Their back entrances on Front Street (First Avenue) received goods unloaded from vessels that had traveled down the Cumberland River. Groceries, hardware, dry goods and other items were sold out of the buildings' Market Street entrances. Most of the buildings were built between 1870 and 1890. Later, as the railroads became the preferred method of transporting goods and as shipping on the Cumberland declined, many of the buildings closed their doors; others served as warehouses. In the 1960s, when Nashvillians were moving to the suburbs in droves, these historically significant buildings were largely unoccupied.

Burgeoning interest in historic preservation during the 1970s was a boon to this district. Businesses such as restaurants and retail shops opened in the old warehouses, and development boomed during the late 1980s. Today, Second Avenue's restored 100-year-old warehouses contain unique shops, galleries, restaurants, nightclubs and offices. The upper levels of some of these buildings have been turned into upscale lofts, apartments and condos. Second Avenue lies in both Area 1 and Area 7. According to information from the Middle Tennessee Regional Multiple Listing Service, in 1998 the average sale price of a single-family home in Area 1 was approximately $143,500; in Area 7, it was $121,400.

There are some condo and apartment complexes nearby. At the 12-story Bennie Dillon by Post apartment building on Church Street, for example, the rent ranges from about $810 for a 600-square-foot studio apartment to $1,800 for a 1,200-square-foot two bedroom.

## Germantown

Bordered by Eighth and Third avenues N. between Jefferson and Hume streets, 18-block historic Germantown is Nashville's oldest residential neighborhood. German immigrants established the community in the late 1850s, and it grew into a truly diverse neighborhood, home to both wealthy and working-class families. The diversity is reflected in many of the area's homes. Architectural styles range from impressive Italianate, Eastlake and Queen Anne Victorian homes to modest worker cottages. After World War II, many German residents moved away from this neighborhood. That exodus, the rezoning of the area to industrial in the 1950s and the city's urban renewal projects in the 1960s led to the demolition of many of Germantown's historic homes. Preservationists arrived in following decades, however, and have renovated many of the buildings.

Today, Germantown boasts an interesting mixture of residential, commercial, office and retail. The area attracts lots of single professionals and older professionals who work from their homes. In 1998, the average sales price for a single-family home in Area 3 was $84,600, but properties in Germantown are generally more expensive than that. You won't find many properties available here, but there are some new developments, such as the row of frame townhouses along Fifth Avenue N. that are modeled after the area's older buildings; in 1999 the townhouses were priced from $150,000 to $200,000.

A couple of mid-1999 listings included a 1,670-square foot late 1800s Victorian wooden cottage with only a half bath, which sold for about $165,000, or about $98.80 per square foot, and a fixer-upper available for about $150,000. Properties in mint condition would sell perhaps $105 per square foot.

## INSIDERS' TIP

**Is it a pike or a road? Newcomers and visitors could be easily befuddled by Nashvillians' seemingly arbitrary usage of the two words. While many official street names contain the word "pike," we locals often substitute "road." Street signs and maps might say "Hillsboro Pike" or "Nolensville Pike," but if you ask us for directions, we're likely to send you to "Hillsboro Road" (or simply "Hillsboro") and "Nolensville Road" (or "Nolensville").**

Brentwood is a Nashville suburb located in Williamson County.

Germantown, like Edgefield and some other communities on the perimeter of downtown, is surrounded by areas with a relatively greater incidence of crime, and many consider this more of an industrial area than a residential neighborhood.

Germantown is within walking distance of the Farmer's Market on Eighth Avenue N. and the Bicentennial Capitol Mall. Other neighborhood hot spots include the Mad Platter and Monell's restaurants on Sixth Avenue N. On the second Saturday in October, Germantown invites all of Nashville to Oktoberfest, its celebration of German and American food, music, arts and crafts. Germantown's annual Maifest Tour of Homes and Progressive Dinner takes place in May, hosted by Historic Germantown Nashville, 1215-D Fifth Avenue N. The 1999 tour featured 12 homes, businesses or gardens and food from the Mad Platter and Monell's plus wine tastings and entertainment along the way. Read more about Germantown restaurants, shopping and events in our Restaurants, Shopping and Annual Events chapters.

## Buena Vista

Just west of Eighth Avenue N., on a 10-block area adjacent to Germantown, is Buena Vista. This late 19th- and early 20th-century neighborhood lies in between Jefferson Street and I-265. Affordable renovation opportunities, including some spacious historic homes, await investors here. It's only a matter of time before renovators expand their focus from nearby north Nashville communities to Buena Vista. The wide, tree-lined Monroe Street and Arthur Street are particularly attractive. Before the 1890s, Buena Vista, named for its nice view of downtown Nashville, was originally the town of McGavock, named after property owner David McGavock.

## Fisk-Meharry

Between Charlotte Avenue and Jefferson Street and 12th Avenue N. and 28th Avenue S., Fisk-Meharry is a large historic neighborhood full of renovation potential. It is named for nearby Fisk University and Meharry Medical College. Fisk opened in 1866 as a free school for newly freed slaves and is the home of the world-famous Jubilee Singers. Meharry, founded in 1876, was the first medical college for African Americans and today educates six out of every 10 of the country's black physicians and surgeons.

Architectural styles here include late 1890 and early 1900 two-story post-Victorian brick homes and American foursquares, and stone and brick Tudors and clapboard cottages built from 1910 to 1940. In mid-1997, the average price for two sales during the previous 13-month period was $34,000.

## Rutledge Hill

This tiny Area 1 neighborhood, bordered by Lindsley and Franklin streets from Fourth Avenue S. to Hermitage Avenue, is home to businesses, residences, government agencies and offices. It has been dubbed "attorney hill," due to the concentration of law firms and attorney homes. Rutledge Hill is within walking distance of the downtown business district and easily accessible from I-40. It's popular with downtown professionals who don't want to drive.

Many of the homes and buildings here were built from the mid-1800s to the 1890s, and the majority have been nicely renovated. Two- and three-story brick townhouses and buildings of varied architectural styles, including Second Empire, Gothic Revival and Italianate, can be found. In addition to the historic properties, new apartments and condos have been built nearby. The area is primarily historical/commercial, and properties here are rarely available. Those that have been on the market recently are selling in the $300,000-plus range.

This was Nashville's first university neighborhood. Davidson Academy, Nashville's first school (later known as Cumberland College and the University of Nashville), was founded here in 1785.

## Cameron-Trimble

Just south of Rutledge Hill is Cameron-Trimble, a historic Area 1 neighborhood and one of the early "streetcar suburbs" that developed along Nashville's electric streetcar lines around 1900. It surrounds Second Avenue between Fourth and Lafayette and encompasses Fort Negley, Greer Stadium, Old City Cemetery, St. Patrick's Cathedral and the Tennessee State Fairgrounds. This largely blue-collar neighborhood features homes in a wide variety of styles and sizes. You'll find everything from spacious Italianate Victorian homes to tiny brick and frame bungalows that date to the early 1900s. If you're into renovating, you'll find a good assortment of moderately priced homes here. In 1998, the average

sale price in Area 1 was $143,500; prices in Cameron-Trimble tend to be lower than that.

## Edgefield

There are several historic districts on the east side of the Cumberland River. The closest to the downtown business district is historic Edgefield. This neighborhood, which extends from Fifth Street to 10th Street between Woodland and Shelby streets, is one of Nashville's oldest suburbs and was the city's first historic-preservation district. The first major residential development east of the Cumberland, this community dates from the mid-1800s, when landowner Dr. John Shelby subdivided much of his property into residential lots. At that time, a suspension bridge over the Cumberland River connected downtown Nashville with this east-bank area. A railroad bridge connected the areas by 1857.

This area was dubbed Edgefield by another resident, Neil S. Brown (Tennessee's governor from 1846 to 1850), who was inspired by his view of the distant fields enclosed by forests. By 1869, Edgefield, which had incorporated as a city, had more than 3,400 residents, 675 homes and seven churches. Italianate and Eastlake homes, including middle-class frame cottages and large brick mansions, could be found throughout the area. In 1880, Edgefield was incorporated into Nashville's city limits.

The devastating east Nashville fire of 1916 destroyed nearly 650 homes in the area and claimed one life. The Queen Anne and Italianate homes that burned were replaced by modern bungalows. In the 1950s and 1960s, as Nashvillians moved to more distant suburbs, Edgefield lost some of its prestige, becoming a largely working-class neighborhood. Many homes were turned into apartments, while urban renewal projects further chipped away at the neighborhood's character.

Thanks to the arrival of preservationists in the 1970s, Edgefield today boasts a wonderful assortment of lovingly restored old homes, including two- and three-story Victorians, post-Victorian Princess Anne cottages, American foursquares and bungalows. In addition to restoration of historic properties, Edgefield has seen the construction of new single-family homes, apartments and condominiums. Residents formed the nonprofit neighborhood association Historic Edgefield Inc. (P.O. Box 60586, Nashville TN 37206) in 1976. The organization sponsors a tour of homes each spring, proudly showcasing some of the neighborhood's best restoration projects as well as homes in the process of being restored. Historic churches and a museum of neighborhood history have been featured also

Though it has changed over the years, Edgefield retains much of the charm of an early Nashville suburb. Tree-lined streets, "Historic Edgefield" signs marking neighborhood boundaries, an active neighborhood association and a mix of professionals, young families and longtime residents combine to create a definite neighborhood feel.

With the construction of the Tennessee Titans' stadium nearby, interest in east Nashville is increasing. Members of Historic Edgefield Inc. say property values are going up, but this is still an affordable neighborhood for first-time home buyers. From January through May of 1999, the average sale price of 10 homes sold in Edgefield was $79,300.

## East End

This small, middle-class, urban neighborhood east of downtown Nashville is home to professionals, blue-collar workers and artists, many of whom were drawn to its historic appeal, quietness and convenience to downtown. East End is between the neighborhoods of Edgefield and Lockeland Springs, extending from Woodland Street to Shelby Avenue between 10th and 14th streets. The 360-plus-acre Shelby Park is nearby, as is the revamped Five Points commercial district.

The neighborhood was named East End because at one time it was at the eastern city limits of Edgefield, which was incorporated in 1868. Electric streetcar lines linking east Nashville to the downtown business district were installed by 1890 and contributed to the influx of residents. Development took place here from about 1875 to the early part of this century, when East End was considered a working-class neighborhood. East End boasts nice examples of a variety of architectural styles, including Eastlake, Queen Anne and neo-Classical.

East End is in Area 6, where the average sales price in 1998 was $115,300. In March 1999, one East End property sold for $121,500. Two sample listings from mid-1999 included a 1,636-square-foot property on South 11th Street available for $49,900 and a 1,307-square-foot property on Woodland for $118,900.

## Lockeland Springs

The third historic neighborhood in the urban area of east Nashville is Lockeland Springs, just past East End, between Gallatin Road and Shelby Avenue. It's bordered by 14th Street, Eastland Avenue and Shelby Park. The area was named for Lockeland Mansion, built in the early 19th century by Col. Robert Weakley, whose wife, Jane Locke, was the daughter of Gen. Matthew Locke of North Carolina. Water from the property's Lockeland spring, which some believed to have curative powers, won a grand prize for its mineral composition and "salubrious quality" at the St. Louis Exposition in 1904. The city of Nashville purchased the mansion in 1939, demolished it and built Lockeland School on the site.

Like East End, Lockeland Springs benefited from the electric streetcar lines installed in the late 1800s. Streetcars allowed residents to travel easily to Nashville's business district across the Cumberland River and made it practical for the middle class to move away from the crowded city.

The well-preserved and architecturally diverse homes in this neighborhood were built from about 1880 to 1940. More recently, in the past two decades, the neighborhood has seen quite a bit of renovation. This large area is popular with professional renovators as well as first-timers eager to try their hand at restoring a home. Middle-class workers, professionals and artists enjoy the community feel of this neighborhood.

Lockeland Springs has been called the next Hillsboro Village. In fact, in 1999, some investors from trendy Hillsboro Village businesses were looking to buy and lease in this area. This is a good area for buyers looking for value. From January through May of 1999, the average sale price in Lockeland Springs was approximately $113,100, but many properties sell in the $130,000 to $140,000 range (about $83 per square foot, versus $110 per square foot in Hillsboro Village). Listings from mid-1999 ranged from a 766-square-foot home on Boscobel for $49,900 to a 1,995-square-foot home on Stratton Avenue for $229,900.

# North and Northeast Nashville

## Inglewood

Inglewood is a friendly and pleasant community that, according to some local Realtors, is one of the best investment values in Nashville, appealing to first-time buyers as well as investors looking for good rental properties. The neighborhood is just east of Lockeland Springs, off Gallatin Pike. It is bordered roughly by the railroad track at Gallatin Pike, north of Trinity Lane, and extends to Briley Parkway.

Lovers of historic houses will feel right at home here. Inglewood boasts lots of 1920s and 1930s homes with brick and stone exteriors, marble fireplaces, ceramic tile and excellent structural quality. There are some newer ranch-style homes too. You'll find small lots as well as large, well-shaded lots with houses set back off the road. Tidy, well-maintained yards, colorful window boxes, perennial gardens and lots of green areas add to Inglewood's cheerful personality. Many 30- to 45-year-old residents, as well as younger professionals, make their home in this settled community. Parents often send their children to B.C. Goodpasture, Davidson Academy or the Metro Magnet Schools.

From January through May 1999, the average sale price in Inglewood was $91,700.

## Madison

Until recently, it was sort of hard to pinpoint the location of the Madison community. If you weren't familiar with the north and east Nashville areas, you could drive right through Madison without even knowing it. Even some longtime Nashvillians are not quite sure where Madison begins and ends. To help identify itself, the community in 1999 installed signs at five entry points to the area. Madison doesn't have an identifiable town square or center, just lots of retail areas lining Gallatin Road and established neighborhoods tucked along the side streets.

This neighborhood sits on the northeast edge of Metro Nashville–Davidson County, 8 miles from downtown Nashville. It's south of Goodlettsville and southwest of Old Hickory. The busy part of town extends along Gallatin Road between Neeley's Bend Road and Old Hickory Boulevard. The community was established in 1840, although a church known as the Spring Hill Meeting House existed in what is now south Madison in the late 1700s.

Between 1859 and 1865, Madison Stratton was hired as a contractor for the L&N Railroad, which passed through the area. The depot he constructed was named for him, putting Madison on the map. The Nashville-Gallatin interurban streetcar track also ran through this community. The old depot was in an area known as Amqui. As the story goes, trains came to such a quick stop in Madison that if you wanted to load something on the train, you'd better do it "damn quick." Madison residents dropped the "d," "n" and the "ck" and came up with the more respectable "Amqui" to name their section of town.

Today, Madison is home to some 60,000 residents and has one of the oldest commercial districts in the state. Here you'll find the more than 200-year-old Spring Hill Cemetery (not to be confused with the community of Spring Hill between Franklin and Columbia). Madison Park and Cedar Hill Park offer lots of recreation opportunities. There are also facilities for bowling, golfing, horseback riding and skating.

This area is especially appealing for first-time buyers. In some sections, you'll find tree-lined streets and large lots with ranch-style houses; others feature older cottages on small lots. From January through May 1999, the average sale price in Madison was $99,000.

## Goodlettsville

Goodlettsville is one of those cities that offers the best of both worlds: a quiet, small-town feel with all the conveniences of city life close by. An incorporated city within Metropolitan Nashville–Davidson County, Goodlettsville is north of Nashville and Madison and east of Hendersonville. It encompasses areas around Dickerson Pike, Long Hollow Pike and I-65. Goodlettsville incorporated in 1857 and again in 1958, but like Nashville's other satellite cities, it remains part of Metro government. Goodlettsville straddles the Davidson and Sumner county lines, so the property taxes vary depending on the county.

Goodlettsville residents receive Goodlettsville city services, not Metro services. The city has a separate police department, including 30 uniformed officers (the highest officer-to-citizen ratio in the state); a separate fire department with 15 full-time firefighters plus volunteers; and a separate public works departments, a planning commission and city manager/city commission government structure. Goodlettsville's easy access to I-65 and the excellent security provided by its police and fire departments make the area appealing to industries. Many businesses have relocated or moved their distribution operations here.

Goodlettsville was originally known as Manskers Station, established by pioneer Kasper Mansker around 1780. The road connecting the area to "Nashborough" was built in 1781. Today Goodlettsville is home to some 20,000 people, including several country music stars. The area has a real mix of residential properties — everything from large homes surrounded by acres of lawns to historic houses to mobile-home parks. Lots of fields and green spaces give this area a rural feel, but the bustling Rivergate Mall area is just minutes away.

According to the Goodlettsville Chamber of Commerce, (615) 859-7979, homes here typically sell for anywhere between $90,000 and $300,000. From January through May 1999, the average sale price in Goodlettsville was $162,000.

## East Nashville

### Donelson

Affordable homes draw lots of young families to this east Nashville community, which was developed in the 1950s and '60s. From January through May 1999, the average sale price in Donelson was $115,100, but homes have sold for as little as $60,000 and for as much as $270,000 in the past couple of years. The dominant architectural style here is the one-story ranch. In addition to affordability, good location is another plus here. Situated between the Stones and Cumberland rivers, Donelson offers easy access to the airport and downtown (via I-40) as well as J. Percy Priest Reservoir and Opryland. The Tennessee School for the Blind and the Cloverbottom hospital and school also are here.

Donelson, named for John Donelson, one of Nashville's founders, is a conservative com-

---

**INSIDERS' TIP**

A 1997 study conducted by the Nashville Area Chamber of Commerce showed that 93 percent of Middle Tennessee residents are satisfied with the overall quality of life in their county and region. Fifty-one percent of residents felt the overall quality of life is improving, 38 percent feel it is static, and 10 percent feel it is worsening. The top five quality-of-life issues in need of attention: improving public schools, reducing crime, attracting more jobs, cleaning up the environment and reducing traffic congestion. According to the study, at least 80 percent of residents are satisfied with current economic conditions, police protection, access provided by roads and highways, level of air pollution, fire protection and quality of airline service.

munity with many longtime residents. It boasts a strong chamber of commerce and lots of civic-minded residents. As in the Bellevue community, residents here joined to raise money for improvements to the neighborhood playground at Two Rivers Park. The hot spot is Lebanon Road, which is lined with lots of shops, churches and fast-food restaurants. Upscale stores and restaurants, however, are scarce here, so folks in search of other shopping and dining choices need to go into town, or perhaps head to the Rivergate Mall area.

## Hermitage

This northeast Davidson County community lies between the Stones and Cumberland rivers. Hermitage Station, a stop along the Tennessee and Pacific railroad line, once was here. The Hermitage, home of President Andrew Jackson, is nearby (see our Attractions and History chapters).

Affordable land and fairly easy interstate-highway access encouraged a lot of speculative building in the Hermitage–Priest Lake area in the 1980s, and the community experienced one of the largest population gains in the area. Today, lots of affordable single- and multifamily residences lure home buyers to this neighborhood. From January through May 1999, the average sale price in Hermitage was $134,300.

## Old Hickory

On the banks of the Cumberland River to the west and with Old Hickory Lake to the east, this well-established neighborhood offers lots of affordable housing. Old Hickory is north of Madison and Hermitage and south of Hendersonville.

From January through May 1999, the average sale price in Old Hickory was $141,300.

# West End/Vanderbilt/ Hillsboro Village

## Belmont-Hillsboro

Popular with the academic crowd, arts community and young professionals, and home to many longtime residents, this middle-class neighborhood is situated between 21st Avenue S./Hillsboro Road and Belmont Boulevard and extends north toward Wedgewood

and south toward I-440. It's convenient to downtown, Music Row, Vanderbilt University, Belmont College, Green Hills, West End, hospitals and bus lines.

In the 19th century, the area was part of the estate of Adelicia Acklen (see the Belmont Mansion entry in our Attractions chapter). In the early 1900s, an electric streetcar line along Belmont Boulevard accelerated the neighborhood's transition to a streetcar suburb. Most homes here were built between 1910 and 1940 and range from 1,200-square-foot cottages to 3,500-square-foot bungalows and foursquares. Renovators will find some good opportunities here. The streets feature wide, tree-lined sidewalks and small shaded lots. Expect to spend anywhere from $145,000 to $450,000 for a home in this neighborhood. In 1999, most properties were selling for between $180,000 and $295,000. Belmont-Hillsboro Neighbors (P.O. Box 120712, Nashville TN 37212), a neighborhood association that formed in 1970, sends out a newsletter every other month.

The nearby hot spot is Hillsboro Village, a neighborhood shopping district of eclectic shops, restaurants and pubs that scores high on the "hip" meter. This is where you'll find Sunset Grill, the Fido/Bongo Java Roasting Company coffeehouse, Pancake Pantry (a Nashville landmark), Provence bakery and restaurant, and Watkins Belcourt Theatre, the best venue in town to catch critically acclaimed, foreign and independent films. On Belmont Boulevard, you'll find Sunshine Grocery natural foods store, Bongo Java coffeehouse, the International House Restaurant, the International Market and Tabouli's restaurant, all popular with the Belmont College crowd.

## Hillsboro–West End

One of Nashville's oldest neighborhoods, Hillsboro–West End is a large middle- and upper-middle–class neighborhood extending from around Blakemore Avenue to just past I-440, and from Hillsboro Road to West End.

Many Nashvillians refer to this neighborhood as the "Vanderbilt area." The location is great: it's close to Vanderbilt University, Hillsboro Village, Belmont College, Green Hills and West End, which means there are plenty of places to shop and dine. In fact, many of

# Going Postal with Larry Wall

"There's only so many ways you can sell a stamp," says Larry Wall, who might best be described as a gruntled (it's a word, look it up!) postal clerk. "You've got to like people. If you can get a little twinkle in their eye, it makes the day go along."

Close-up

Wall's Acklen Station customers typically have twinkling eyes. Often he'll do more than make you smile — he'll give you a chuckle or even a belly laugh with your stamps, no extra charge. When a woman mutters "Shoot" after realizing she has the wrong postage, Wall gently chides, "Now, lady, that's the wrong thing to say in the post office. We might take you seriously." Everybody laughs.

OK, Larry, since you mention that . . . "Pressure's going to get to everybody," he explains later over a cup of coffee. "The stresses are there. They may not look like they're there, but they're there. How you react to that stress is an individual thing. . . . You've got to make jokes about it, laugh about it. Because if you take it seriously, it will wear on you."

Larry Wall has been at this business for going on three decades, the last half of that at Acklen Station, which happens to be the closest station to Music Row. Perhaps 50 percent of the customer traffic is tied to the music industry. As a result, this post office is distinguished by a wall of autographed and framed 8-by-10 publicity photos, about 200 of them. A number are easily recognizable, but others are far from household names.

The post office started that around 1993, Wall says. "We had a supervisor who thought the wall looked bare. Which it did; it just had some posters on it. So he framed those Elvis Presley stamps you see there. And since so many country stars and producers get their mail here, we started asking a few of them if they'd mind autographing a picture that we could frame and hang. And it mushroomed."

Now there are dancers. Actors. Hand models. Some guy who's worked at Vandy for 50 years or so. "Greats, near-greats and wanna-be-greats," Wall says with a laugh. "They'll ask us to put their picture up, or we'll ask them, whatever. As long as they're regular customers, it makes no difference. If you've got an 8-by-10, bring it in! Actually I've got two waiting to hang now, but the boss has closed the wall. I've got one slot left, that's about it."

Wall likes music, listens to everything from rock 'n' roll to country to Big Band, but he's not one to buy CDs or tapes. His favorite performers are the ones who have been his regular customers and gone on to make it. "Faith Hill used to

Photo: Cathy Summerlin

Larry Wall with the "Wall of Fame."

— continued on next page

come in every day for two or three years to pick up her mail. She's one of the sweetest people who ever stood in our line. She never had a cross word for anybody, no matter how long she had to wait."

Not all stars go to the post office themselves. But it's not uncommon for someone like Chet Atkins or Randy Travis or Tanya Tucker to drop by to pick up mail or buy stamps or get passports made — the latter being something one must do in person, the clerk wryly points out. Aaron Tippin shot (with a camera, of course!) one of the window clerks for a video.

Someone Wall would like to have for a customer is President Bill Clinton. With a mischievous grin, he tells why: "We had the Western stamps, and we had displays in the lobby of the Old West — cactus, tombstones and stuff. And one of the displays was a tombstone that had 'Rest in Peace. Snake Oil Willie.' So I packaged it up, along with a little letter, and told him to come to the post office next time he's in Nashville. I keep waiting; he hasn't made it yet. I'm not sure he had a real big sense of humor about 'Snake Oil Willie.'"

Nashville's best restaurants are just minutes away. On West End, Cakewalk/Zola, Rio Bravo and Houston's restaurants are longtime favorites. The area is also home to Eakin Elementary School, which is regarded as one of the city's best.

Residents of Hillsboro–West End include young professionals, some music-business types, physicians and university professors, many of whom can be found daily walking their dogs or jogging on tree-lined sidewalks. Homes are situated on small lots, and there are lots of winding, shaded streets leading to little pocket neighborhoods that have their own unique personalities. As for architectural styles here, you'll find mostly classic Tudors, Cape Cods and bungalows built between 1920 and 1940. There also are some newer properties, including condos. Prices start at about $150,000 and can go as high as $500,000, though most are priced in the $200,000 to $325,000 range. Homes here often offer a substantial value for their price and are generally considered good investments. Renters will find some good older homes and some apartments too.

## Waverly-Belmont to Melrose

### Waverly-Belmont/Sunnyside

In the late 1990s, this urban neighborhood was becoming one of the hottest areas for renovation. In the past few years, the "12th South Neighborhood Commercial District," which borders Waverly-Belmont and Belmont-Hillsboro, received several hundred thousand dollars in improvements from the Metropolitan Development & Housing Agency and Public Works, including new lights, sidewalks and banners designed to encourage pedestrian-friendly retail and office spaces and to create a more friendly neighborhood feel.

Renovators are also doing their part, restoring many of the area's old homes, most of which were built from the 1890s to 1930s. These homes provide the first impression of the area's personality, but the neighborhood also gets some of its character from its racially and socioeconomically diverse residents.

Waverly-Belmont is a large neighborhood extending from Belmont Boulevard to Ninth Avenue S. and from Gale Lane north to Bradford Avenue, near Wedgewood. The area includes Waverly Place, adjacent to Woodland-In-Waverly, which is also sometimes considered part of the Waverly-Belmont district. It is convenient to I-440, Music Row, Green Hills, colleges, downtown and the Melrose shopping district. In the center of the neighborhood is Sevier Park and its antebellum Sunnyside Mansion.

Part of this district is viewed by many as a high-crime area, but its great assortment of historic homes makes it appealing to those with an eye to the future. The neighborhood is filled with large Queen Anne, American four-square and 1900-1915 Princess Anne homes as well as smaller 1900s shotgun homes and 1920s and 1930s Tudors and bungalows awaiting a renovator's touch. Homes in Waverly-Belmont start at about $90,000 and go as high as about $225,000, with most in the $120,000 to $175,000 range. You can occasionally find a good fixer upper for less than $90,000.

## Waverly Place

When you turn off Eighth Avenue S. onto Douglas Avenue (at Zanies), you'll be greeted by a "Welcome to Waverly Place" sign. Waverly Place is a small historic district tucked between Woodland-In-Waverly and Waverly-Belmont, from Eighth to 10th avenues S. and Wedgewood to Bradford avenues. Is it often considered part of the larger Waverly-Belmont, also referred to as Sunnyside (see separate listings in this section), a larger district that is ripe for renovation.

Sidewalks line both sides of the street, and the small lots are accented with numerous tall trees, ivy and colorful flowers. Waverly Place features a wide mix of architectural styles, including frame and brick cottages, American foursquares, Tudors and one- and 1½-story bungalows from the 1890s and 1930s. The area's population is as diverse as its properties, and people of various races and income levels find this pleasant little neighborhood to their liking. First-time home buyers and renovators have shown increasing interest in this area in the past decade.

Neighborhood hot spots include Zanies comedy club, Douglas Corner songwriters club and the Eighth Avenue antique district.

## Woodland-In-Waverly

One of Nashville's first streetcar suburbs, Woodland-In-Waverly is south of Wedgewood Avenue, between I-65 and Eighth Avenue, convenient to downtown, Music Row, colleges, the Melrose area and Eighth Avenue antique shops. This is the second of Nashville's two locally zoned "historic preservation districts," the first being Edgefield. This zoning means that all exterior additions, alterations, demolitions, new construction and fences must meet the approval of the Metro Historical Commission.

According to the Historical Commission,

Woodland-In-Waverly could serve as a model for neighborhood design now being emulated by progressive new subdivision developments. Part of Woodland-In-Waverly was listed in the National Register of Historic Places in 1980. The neighborhood features many well-preserved homes built mainly from the 1890s through the 1930s. Queen Anne, English Tudor and American foursquares and bungalows are among the architectural styles found in this small neighborhood, which offers plenty of choices for renovators.

In the 1830s, the area was farmland owned by historian and author A.W. Putnam, who named his house Waverly and his farm Waverly Place after the novel by Sir Walter Scott. The name stuck after the farm was sold in 1858. Development increased in the late 1880s following the installation of an electric streetcar line on Eighth Avenue S. that provided easy access to downtown Nashville. This streetcar suburb was a fashionable address and remained so until around 1940, when automobiles became the preferred method of transportation. The neighborhood eventually evolved into an urban middle-class neighborhood. A few houses built during this period still remain.

In the mid-1960s, many of the historic homes were demolished to make room for I-65, which divided and reduced the size of the neighborhood. At the same time, many buildings had fallen into disrepair, and Nashvillians were moving to outlying suburbs in droves. Today, a few duplexes and ranch-style homes dot the areas around I-65.

This is a good area for first-time buyers who want to live in an urban neighborhood. Most homes in this area sell for between $90,000 and $225,000.

## Melrose

This neighborhood was named for the Melrose Estate, which was granted to its first owner, John Topp, in 1788. Named for the Scottish ancestry of the then-reigning mistress, the mansion was the site of many notable events in Nashville society. The original two-story brick building, which had a large portico, burned in 1950 and was rebuilt as a one-story structure. The rebuilt home was gutted by fire in 1975.

Melrose is bounded by Wedgewood Avenue and I-440 between Franklin Pike and Granny White Pike. It's convenient to downtown, I-440 and Nolensville Road. You'll find a variety of home styles here, ranging from late Victorian to contemporary.

The Eighth Avenue S. antique stores are nearby. The Sutler, next to the Melrose Lanes bowling alley on Franklin Pike, has become a popular showcase club and has a "neighborhood pub" feel.

From January through May 1999, the average sale price in Melrose was $243,400.

## West and Southwest Nashville

### Richland–West End

Historic Richland–West End encompasses a triangular area between Murphy Road, I-440 and West End. Developed in the early 1900s on the outskirts of the city, this was an upscale suburb popular with professionals who wanted to escape the noise, smoke and crime of the city. After World War II, some homes were converted to apartments, but young professionals and upper- and middle-income families have been restoring them since the 1970s.

The neighborhood also has lots of longtime residents, and many take an active part in the community. The Richland–West End Neighborhood Association (3714 Richland Avenue, Nashville TN 37205), formed in 1974, keeps watch over the area's residential quality and sponsors an annual tour of homes. Richland–West End features lots of well-preserved early 1900s homes, including spacious bungalows, built from 1910 to 1930, and American foursquares. Prices in this neighborhood range from about $220,000 to $750,000-plus.

Sidewalks, lots of trees and a definite community feel are strong selling points for this neighborhood. Location is another plus: it's a straight shot down West End/Broadway to downtown, I-440 access is right off West End, and it's close to Music Row, Green Hills, Belle Meade and Hillsboro Village.

### Sylvan Park

This historic west Nashville neighborhood has enjoyed a wave of popularity in the past decade. Young professionals, families, creative types and retirees in search of affordable homes have been moving to this former blue-collar area and carefully restoring homes.

Lots of trees, sidewalks, nice landscaping, cheerful window boxes and a business district contribute to the personality and close-knit feel of this charming neighborhood. There are a lot of 800- to 1,000-square foot houses here, but they can be pricey, typically starting at about $110 per square foot. You'll find mostly 1910 to 1940s frame and brick bungalows, and these can range from 800 to 2,500 square feet. A tour of the neighborhood also will reveal some 1900 to 1915 Princess Annes, 1930s brick cottages and spacious Queen Anne homes. This neighborhood definitely represents a good investment: houses recently have appreciated as much as 20 percent a year. As of mid-1999, most homes were selling for between $100,000 and $200,000.

Sylvan Park is between West End Avenue and Charlotte Pike, and is convenient to West End, I-40, I-440 and downtown. A neighborhood hot spot is McCabe Park and Community Center, offering golf and other recreational opportunities. There are also some good restaurants and markets nearby, including Sylvan Park, McCabe Pub and Produce Place.

### Green Hills

Green Hills is considered one of Nashville's most desirable addresses. This Area 2 community is bounded by I-440, Belle Meade, Oak Hill at Harding Road and Forest Hills. It's minutes from Vanderbilt, West End, Music Row, Hillsboro Village and downtown. If you're looking for an upscale neighborhood, large, well-landscaped lots and tree-lined streets, you can't miss with Green Hills. Families will find the good schools a bonus.

The area was developed in the 1930s and '40s, and building continues today, so you'll find everything here from modern and spacious homes loaded with amenities to pockets of cluster housing and smaller, older properties. There are also some nice condominiums/townhouses. Expect to pay a premium for even the tiniest cottage here. From January through May 1999, the average sale price in Green Hills was $340,400, but prices could range from about $120,000 to more than $600,000; the minimum price during that five-month period was $83,000 and the maximum topped $2 million. Those who want the privacy and square footage of a house but aren't in a buying mode might find a suitable private rental here. There is a smattering of apartments too — old and new. The beautifully landscaped Post Green Hills apartment complex, at Woodmont Boulevard and Hillsboro Road, is a popular choice for renters.

The upscale Green Hills Mall (see Shopping) is the centerpiece of the large retail sector that extends for several blocks along Hillsboro Road. Davis-Kidd Booksellers in Grace's Plaza is a Nashville favorite, offering not only one of the best selections of books in town, but also good food in the tiny Second Story Cafe. Another hot spot is the world-famous Bluebird Cafe, a songwriters club that has helped launch the careers of many country singers and songwriters. There are several good restaurants in the neighborhood, including F. Scott's and Green Hills Grille.

One drawback here is traffic, which can get pretty congested along Hillsboro Road. But if you maneuver around Hillsboro on the side streets, you can avoid most traffic jams.

## Forest Hills

This desirable west Nashville neighborhood extends from Harding Road to Old Hickory Boulevard and from Belle Meade toward Oak Hill and Franklin Road. It's popular among professionals, including local physicians and executives.

First developed in the 1950s and '60s, Forest Hills boasts spacious ranch-style homes as well as some architect-designed custom homes. Newer housing developments can be found along Old Hickory Boulevard and Granny White Pike. Houses sit on large, well-tended lots that offer a good amount of privacy. Some have great views. From January through May 1999, the average price of 33 sales was $388,700, with a low price of $164,000 and a high of $2,025,000. Renters

Photo: Cathy Summerlin

American foursquares and spacious bungalows along tree-lined streets make Richland–West End popular with young professionals and upper-middle-income families.

will find an occasional upscale rental. Good schools and a convenient Area 2 location add to the appeal of this neighborhood.

Nearby Radnor Lake offers a wonderful, if sometimes crowded, nature retreat (read all about it in our Parks chapter). Also worth a look: the buffalo park at Hillsboro Road and Tyne Boulevard, featuring "evergreen buffaloes" by artist Alan LeQuire.

## Oak Hill

A popular choice for music-business executives and "move-up" families, Oak Hill is where you'll find the Governor's Mansion and other stately homes, including former homes of the late Tammy Wynette and Minnie Pearl. Oak Hill extends from Forest Hills to I-65 and from Woodmont Boulevard to Old Hickory Boulevard. You'll find Oak Hill divided between Area 1 and Area 2 on the Nashville real estate maps.

As its name suggests, this community boasts lots of rolling, tree-covered hills. Most homes are on at least 1-acre lots. Many of the ranch-style and two-story colonial homes here were built during the past 30 to 35 years. There are also some beautiful contemporary homes. This is a well-established, stable neighborhood, and residents often prefer to renovate rather than move out. You'll occasionally come across a new structure. From January through May 1999, the average price of 20 sales in Oak Hill was $350,600; sales included a low of $167,500 and a high of $1.8 million.

Oak Hill is close to the Melrose shopping area, Harding Mall, 100 Oaks Mall (see Shopping) and Nipper's Corner. Radnor Lake is nearby too.

## Belle Meade

If living in one of the area's most prestigious neighborhoods is a must, look no further than Belle Meade. This old-money west Nashville community is the address of choice for many of the city's most prominent citizens. It is one of Nashville's oldest communities — it's actually a city itself, having incorporated in 1938. Today it has its own police force, street signs and building codes, and the powers that be keep a pretty tight rein on the neighborhood. It was originally part of the Belle Meade Plantation, a world-renowned thoroughbred

farm. The plantation's Belle Meade Mansion is now a tourist attraction (see our Attractions chapter).

Belle Meade's unique and architecturally interesting homes are surrounded by large, beautiful, professionally landscaped lawns. Many homes here were built during the 1920s, but Nashville's elite find this address so *de rigueur* that many are willing to pay top dollar for an older home, demolish it and build an enormous, new traditional home in its place. Homes range from about $250,000 to the millions. From January through May 1999, the average sales price in Belle Meade was $354,400; during that time the minimum price was $80,000 and the maximum $1.75 million.

Belle Meade is bounded roughly by U.S. Highway 70, Woodmont Boulevard, Estes Road and Percy Warner Park at Chickering. Hot spots include Belle Meade Boulevard, popular with residents and nonresidents who come to jog, play Frisbee and hang out at the entrance to Percy Warner Park, the members-only Belle Meade Country Club and Cheekwood.

## West Meade/Hillwood

Another Area 2 community, West Meade/Hillwood is just west of Belle Meade, across the railroad tracks that parallel Harding Road/U.S. Highway 70. The area is bounded by White Bridge Road, Davidson Drive and I-40 and encompasses the Vaughns Gap Road area to the south.

This well-established neighborhood is one of Nashville's oldest planned communities. Most homes were built in the 1950s and '60s, so there are lots of ranch-style dwellings. Houses sit on very large and shady lots, and the neighborhood's winding streets take you over hills and along little forest-like areas. The Hillwood area, which developed around the Hillwood Country Club, has some of the largest and most expensive homes, with prices ranging from $160,000 to more than $500,000. From January through May 1999, the average sale price in West Meade was $227,500, while the average in Hillwood was $279,575.

There is a definite neighborhood feel here, and residents are active in the community. This is a convenient location with lots of good shopping and restaurants nearby on White Bridge

Road and in the Belle Meade/Harding Road area. The Green Hills and Bellevue Center malls are just minutes away. Hot spots include Percy Warner and Edwin Warner parks, Cheekwood and Bookstar bookstore.

## Bellevue

For those who want a fashionable Area 2 address but find such areas as Belle Meade, Hillwood/West Meade and Green Hills a little pricey, Bellevue is a good choice, offering lots of newer, upscale homes that are affordable for many first-time buyers. This west Nashville community is about 2.5 miles west of the U.S. Highway 70–Tenn. Highway 100 split, about 7 miles from Green Hills and about 13 miles from downtown. Most areas are easily accessible to I-40. Bellevue is bordered on one side by the Warner Parks along Tenn. Highway 100 and on the other by Charlotte Pike.

As the "Welcome to Bellevue" sign on U.S. Highway 70 S. informs you, this community was established in 1795. The rolling green hills and wooded valleys inspired the name, which is French for "beautiful view." Bellevue remained a largely rural area until the mid-1900s. Development moved in this direction in the 1940s, but it hasn't taken over yet. Despite rapid growth since the 1970s, the area still offers a pleasing mix of urban and rural life and Bellevue has maintained a sort of small-community feel that some Nashville suburbs lack. A few farms areas remain around the perimeter, but the conveniences of "city life" are close by for those in the more rural areas.

The local chamber of commerce and civic-minded residents keep watch on the area's growth. Though there has been a lot of development on U.S. Highway 70, Bellevue's proximity to the Warner Parks on Tenn. Highway 100 (see our Parks chapter) keeps residents from feeling crowded.

Lots of young professionals and families have joined the longtime residents here. Those looking for a house will find many single-family homes, some in pocket neighborhoods and new subdivisions. There are also condominiums to fit every budget as well as an assortment of apartment complexes, some brand-new or just a few years old. Prices have been increasing steadily since the early 1990s.

Bellevue's average sale price from January through May 1999 was $213,000. Renters will discover that the newer apartments here carry some of the highest rents in Nashville, although some of the older complexes offer significantly lower rates.

Recreational opportunities abound here. In addition to Warner Parks, the northern terminus of the Natchez Trace Parkway is just a few miles down Tenn. Highway 100, offering a scenic retreat for Sunday drivers or biking enthusiasts, and the nearby Harpeth River, with several access points, is a great spot for canoeing. Other retreats include the Bellevue Center mall on U.S. Highway 70 S., Regal Cinemas' Bellevue 12 movie theater near the mall and Loveless Cafe on Tenn. Highway 100.

# South and Southeast Nashville

## Crieve Hall

Development of this Area 1 neighborhood centered around Trousdale Drive and Blackmon Road in the 1950s, so you'll find lots of ranch-style homes here. Unlike many of Nashville's new developments, Crieve Hall boasts large lots accented with big shade trees. Homes are well-maintained and nicely landscaped. It's a nice, quiet area convenient to downtown, Harding Mall, 100 Oaks Mall and the Nashville Wildlife Park at Grassmere.

Crieve Hall is a stable neighborhood, with many longtime residents. Good schools are nearby. In 1998, the average price for a single-family home in Area 1 was $143,500. Selling prices have ranged from about $80,000 to $175,000 in the past few years.

## Antioch

Affordable housing and location lure many Nashvillians to this diverse southeast Nashville community, which has experienced much new construction in the last couple of years. Antioch is convenient to I-24, the airport and the First American Music Center (formerly Starwood Amphitheatre), and is a short drive from downtown via I-24. The area is bordered to the north by Harding Place and extends west from Percy Priest Lake to just past the Interstate 24-Bell Road intersection.

Development boomed here with the opening of the Hickory Hollow Mall and Smyrna's

Nissan plant with an influx of newcomers seeking affordable housing. In the past two decades, Antioch has undergone tremendous growth, including lots of commercial development along Bell Road, Nolensville Pike and Harding Place. Large numbers of new housing developments and apartment complexes have joined the ranch-style homes built here in the 1960s. The arrival of new residents and increase in commercial development have resulted in major traffic snarls in the Hickory Hollow area and along Nolensville Pike. Road construction here seems to be never-ending. Overall, Antioch is a community lots of Nashvillians are proud to call home. Antioch has been praised for its ethnic diversity and integration of its schools.

From January through May 1999, the average sale price in Antioch was $122,400. Renters can choose from many affordable apartment complexes.

Nearby recreational areas include William Pitts Park on Wessex Drive, Long Hunter State Park and J. Percy Priest Reservoir.

# Neighboring Counties

## Cheatham County

The area's best-kept neighborhood secret may be just west of Davidson County: Cheatham County (Area 13). Some real estate agents expect this 305-square-mile county to be the next boom area, but houses are still affordable here, and most of the new developments feature 1-acre lots, large by Middle Tennessee standards. Cheatham County's slogan is "A Great Place to Raise a Family," and apparently many agree: in 1997, this was the state's sixth-fastest-growing county. According to the Cheatham County Chamber of Commerce, (615) 792-6722, a 1997 census showed the county had a population of 33,103. In an effort to keep the growth at a manageable level, the county has a development tax of $7,500 per each new house, which will deter some development. There's also a county adequate facilities tax of $1.00 per square foot of heated living space.

Cheatham County is convenient to Bellevue in west Nashville, easily accessible to I-24 and I-40 and is a 25- to 40-minute drive

to downtown Nashville, depending on which side of the county you're on. In addition to location, strong drawing points of this rural area include quality of life, low property taxes, good schools and lots of outdoor-recreation opportunities. The 20,000-acre Cheatham Wildlife Management Area is popular for hunting, horseback riding and hiking, and the Narrows of the Harpeth State Historic Area is a good spot for canoeing, fishing and hiking. Cheatham Lake is popular with boaters.

Folks interested in lake property should determine eligibility for private-use privileges before beginning any construction. A shoreline-management plan classifies the lake into limited development areas, which are the only areas where private-use privileges such as mowing, moorage, electric lines and construction of steps are permitted. Contact the Resource Manager's Office, 1798 Cheatham Dam Road, (615) 792-5696, for information.

The four largest cities in Cheatham County are Ashland City, Kingston Springs, Pleasant View and Pegram. In 1998, the average sale price in Area 13 was $115,000.

## Ashland City

In central Cheatham County, Ashland City developed around a shallow area along the Cumberland River where riverboats ran aground and had to unload their cargo. Locks have since solved that problem, and today Ashland City is a rapidly growing area.

The county's 1997 census showed that Ashland City, the county seat, had a population of 3,328. Ashland City is home to one of the area's largest employers, State Industries, with a work force of some 2,500, as well as other growing industries. With the widening of Tenn. Highway 12 to Nashville to four lanes, the city has paved the way for more growth. Ashland City is about a 40-minute drive from downtown Nashville; from courthouse to courthouse, it's about 20 miles. Ashland City's courthouse, with its croquet lawn, is still the focus of downtown. The city is also known for its antique shops and catfish restaurants. The 3.7-mile Cumberland River Bicentennial Trail, a former railroad right of way, is popular for walking, horseback riding and bicycling along river bluffs, past waterfalls and wetlands.

Ashland City has some of Cheatham

County's most affordable homes. From January through May 1999, the average sale price was $111,400. Finding a rental property here isn't easy. Those that are available often are snapped up by newcomers awaiting construction of new homes.

## Kingston Springs

Kingston Springs, on the south side of Cheatham County, appears to be one of the next neighborhood hot spots. A 1997 census showed its population at 2,426. According to a 1999 report by the UT Center for Business and Economic Research, during the next 20 years, Kingston Springs is expected to experience an 81 percent growth in population — the highest rate in the eight-county MSA.

Affordable homes, easy access to Nashville via I-40 and a quiet rural setting are part of the appeal here. Those who prefer to live in a country-style home with a big wrap-around porch or in a log cabin or hillside chalet will feel right at home in Kingston Springs. Some of the rolling wooded hills and farmland are being developed into subdivisions, but in an effort to control the growth, Kingston Springs has implemented a 75¢-per-square-foot adequate facilities tax (impact fee) — in addition to the county's $1-per-square-foot tax — on new residential development; there's also a 25¢-per-square-foot building permit fee inside the city limits.

Kingston Springs has some of the county's most expensive homes and lots. A 1-acre or smaller lot might cost $35,000, compared with $10,000 to $20,000 for a lot in Ashland City or Pleasant View. But you can get more for your money here than in nearby west Nashville. From January through May 1999, the average sale price in Kingston Springs was $165,800. Some of the newer homes list for about $175,000 to more than $200,000. There are still some bargains here, especially older homes.

## Pegram

At 3,440 acres, this is the smallest of Cheatham County's four cities. This quaint little rural town is on the south side of the county, next to Bellevue and about a 25-minute drive from downtown Nashville. According to a 1997 census, the population here is 1,928. Like Kingston Springs, Pegram's population is expected to grow by 81 percent by the year 2020, the highest rate in the eight-county MSA. From January through May 1999, the average sale price in Pegram was $141,500.

If you'd like to get a feel for what Pegram is like, visit on July 4th, when the town puts on the big Pegram Fish Fry; you can get all the catfish you can eat.

# Dickson County

Dickson County (Area 15), just west of Nashville past Cheatham County, is a largely rural area with the lowest population density of any county surrounding Metro Nashville. Officials with the Dickson County Chamber of Commerce, (615) 446-2349, say that is changing fast. Like most counties surrounding Metro, Dickson County is growing. A 1997 census showed a population of 42,500.

The 600-acre Dickson County Industrial Park, established in 1976, is attracting a steady stream of industry. The county's chamber of commerce actively recruits new businesses. At the same time, many city dwellers and suburbanites are deciding they want to live in the country and are heading to Dickson County areas such as Dickson, White Bluff, Burns and Charlotte. Lower home and land prices are a big draw.

## Dickson

The "for sale" signs don't stay up long in small-town Dickson these days. Homes get snapped up right after they go on the market. Land sales are strong too, especially small farm properties of 20 acres or less. New subdivisions are being developed, and new construction is turning other neighborhoods into subdivisions. Driving through Dickson, you'll see new houses popping up everywhere. According to the Dickson County Chamber of Commerce, the average home sale price in early 1999 was $90,000. Prices range from about $80,000 to about $250,000. Dickson is about 40 minutes from downtown Nashville and easily accessible to I-40, so it's a feasible choice for Nashville workers who don't mind the commute; it's a shorter drive for those who work in west Nashville.

Dickson County was established in 1803, and the city of Dickson dates back to 1899.

There are a few historic homes here, but most of the area is still rural. Most of the longtime, family-owned businesses in the Main Street downtown district have been replaced with antique stores and specialty shops. Dickson voters approved liquor-by-the-drink a few years ago, so there are a few modern restaurants, grills and pubs sprinkled around the city. Shopping is sparse, but new retail is coming in. Among the offerings are a Wal-Mart Supercenter and a Goody's clothing store. The new Hillcrest Shopping Center strip mall has some new stores, including a Blockbuster Video. For recreation, there are nearby Montgomery Bell State Resort Park, The Great Caves Park and two existing golf courses with a third under development.

Dickson's annual Old Timers festival, honoring senior citizens, is held the first weekend in May and attracts as many as 20,000 to the downtown area for a parade, entertainment and arts and crafts. Special activities are planned for the 1998 event, the festival's 40th anniversary.

A sign of Dickson's progressive growth is the new Renaissance Center, an educational technology center on Tenn. Highway 46. This unique public facility, scheduled to open in August 1999, will offer traditional art, music and drama education, instruction in high-performance computing, a 450-seat performing arts theater, two computer classrooms, a 136-seat domed interactive theater with graphic- and laser-projection systems, a science theater and more.

For more information, call the Dickson County Chamber of Commerce at (615) 446-2349.

## Charlotte

The smallest Dickson County town, Charlotte (population 1,400) has been the county seat since 1804. The 1834 courthouse, the oldest in the state, is still in use. The public square has more than 20 buildings dating from 1804 to 1920 and is listed on the National Register of Historic Places. Availability in this small community is limited. Average home prices range from the high $90,000s to the low $100,000s.

## Robertson County

With a strong agricultural base and diverse manufacturing industries, Robertson County (Area 14), about a 35-minute drive north of Nashville, is growing fast. By 1997, the county's population had already exceeded projections for the year 2000. In 1999 there were 50,000 residents. County officials attribute the growth to improved quality of life. Recent developments in the county include an 18-hole public golf course, a $4 million-plus YMCA, a new hospital and improvements to schools. A portion of U.S. Highway 41 was widened to four lanes, improving access to Springfield, the county seat and largest community.

Nearly 90 percent of this 476-square-mile county is farmland. The county ranks fifth in the state in the production of corn, wheat, cattle and other agricultural products. Acres of farmland, historic family farms and beautiful country scenery surround Robertson County's incorporated cities and towns, which include Adams, Cedar Hill, Coopertown, Cross Plains, Greenbrier, Orlinda, Ridgetop and White House.

Robertson County has 17 public schools and two private schools. The county's per capita income ($19,341) ranks 25th in the state. To contact the Robertson County Chamber of Commerce, call (615) 384-3800.

### Springfield

Renovations and new construction are increasing in busy Springfield, population 14,000. Buyers have snapped up and begun renovating several historic homes. The highest concentration of older residences, including Victorian homes, is in the district north and west of the historic town square. New-home prices are keeping pace with the increase in new construction. As of late 1998, the average sale price was about $105,000. Springfield has three golf courses, a bowling alley and a movie theater. The largest city park, J. Travis Price Park, has soccer fields, a baseball complex, trails, a playground, picnic shelters and a lake. Retail and dining choices are limited but increasing. Residents who want a night on the town can drive to Nashville in about 45 minutes.

## Rutherford County

In the geographic center of Tennessee, Rutherford County (Area 21-34), southeast of Nashville, is one of the fastest-growing areas in the nation. Most statistics put it neck-and-neck with adjacent Williamson County in population growth. From 1990 to 1999, Rutherford County's population grew 43.3 percent, reaching an estimated 169,862. With Murfreesboro's Middle Tennessee State University, Smyrna's Nissan Motor Manufacturing Corporation USA plant (the county's largest employer), three hospitals and other industries, the county has a diverse economic base and is enjoying a booming economy.

Despite the growth, Rutherford County maintains a small-town charm. Its 615 square miles still have nearly 234,000 acres of farmland. The area is also rich in history. The Battle of Stones River, one of the major battles of the Civil War, was fought near Murfreesboro. You can take a self-guided tour of the battlefield today (see our Attractions chapter). In 1996, Murfreesboro, the county seat, was a national finalist in the Great American Main Street Award Program honoring downtown preservation and revitalization.

Affordable homes and easy access to Nashville via I-24 are among the county's other pluses. When it comes to buying a home or property, you'll get more for your money here than in Williamson County. In 1998, the average home sale price in Rutherford County was $122,000. Rutherford County encompasses Murfreesboro, LaVergne, Smyrna and tiny Eagleville (population 501).

For more information, you can contact Rutherford County Chamber of Commerce at (615) 893-6565.

## Murfreesboro

Rutherford County's largest city, Murfreesboro was home to 59,506 plus some 18,000 students at MTSU, as of 1997. And the population is growing every day. This city, established in 1812, still has the feel of a small town. Its charming and historic downtown area received a boost in 1985 with the initiation of the Main Street program, which included new sidewalks, underground wiring, landscaping and more than $6 million in interior and exterior renovations. The first-floor occupancy rate in downtown buildings is now 98 percent. The beautiful courthouse, built in 1859, is the focal point of the historic and still lively town square. (The first courthouse, built in 1813, burned before the Civil War. It served as the State Capitol from 1819 until 1826, when Nashville became the capitol.) A variety of shops and businesses line the square. The landmark City Cafe continues to be the hot spot with Murfreesboro seniors and the downtown business crowd.

On the tree-lined streets surrounding the square, you'll find some wonderfully restored old homes, the grandest of which are on W. Main, between the courthouse and MTSU's campus. East Main Street has some especially lovely Victorian architecture. There are several neighborhoods of 1950s and 1960s ranch-style brick homes as well as newer developments around the city's perimeter.

In mid-1999, the average home sale price in Murfreesboro was about $140,000. In a new upscale development, you can expect to pay at least $78 per square foot for new construction; that figure drops to about $68 per square foot for an existing home in a more modestly priced neighborhood.

Recreation opportunities in Murfreesboro abound. Hot spots and activities include Stones River; Old Fort Park, a 20,000-square-foot playground; Children's Discovery House, a hands-on museum designed for children 12 and younger; historic Cannonsburgh, a reconstructed pioneer village; Uncle Dave Macon Days, an old-time festival held in July; Old Fort Golf Course; Stones River Greenway, a 3-mile walking and biking trail; and outlet mall shopping. Concerts and sporting events on the MTSU campus are other options.

## Smyrna

This former farming community between LaVergne and Murfreesboro enjoyed a boost when the Nissan plant came to town, bringing

6,000 jobs and hastening the development of farmland into subdivisions. In 1997, Smyrna's population was 24,077, the second highest in the county. While you won't find many tree-lined streets here, you will find plenty of new construction and affordable housing. The average selling price as of mid-1999 was between $120,000 and $125,000. Nearby I-24 provides easy access for Nashville commuters.

Aviators will want to take note of this city. The Smyrna Air Base airfield is still active, and the Tennessee Aviation Days air show at the Smyrna Airport is a big draw each September (see our Annual Events chapter). East of downtown are the remnants of the Smyrna Air Base housing. Area hot spots include Stones River, Smyrna Town Center (fitness center), Smyrna National Golf Course and Smyrna Recreation Park.

## LaVergne

Just across the Davidson County line in northeast Rutherford County, LaVergne has experienced dramatic growth in this decade. According to some statistics, the city's population grew 90 percent from 1990 to 1995. The 1997 census showed LaVergne had 16,001 residents. The city is a top pick for incoming industries. The largest employer is book distributor Ingram Book. It's about a 30-minute drive from downtown Nashville and is close to the Nashville International Airport. Relatively inexpensive homes make this area a viable choice for first-time home buyers. As in Smyrna, the average selling price here falls between $120,000 and $125,000.

Neighborhood hot spots include Percy Priest Lake and LaVergne Park.

## Sumner County

Sumner County (Area 9), Nashville's northeastern neighbor, has several diverse communities and recreational opportunities that make it a popular choice for everyone from young families to country music stars. This county's communities have distinct personalities. Some remain largely rural, while others have a definite urban feel. Country general stores, pastures, rolling creeks and antebellum homes are common sights in the more rural areas, while Old Hickory Lake, with its hundreds of miles of shoreline on the county's southern border, boasts some luxurious, upscale properties. Sumner County is also a historic area, the site of two settlements established by long hunters in the late 1700s (see our History and Attractions chapters for details).

Like many other Middle Tennessee counties, Sumner County is growing. It is the third-most-populous county in the MSA, behind Davidson and Rutherford. In 1999, the estimated population was 126,227. Lots of major business developments in Gallatin, numerous recreational and upscale residential areas in Hendersonville, abundant retail stores in Goodlettsville and an extensive industrial base in Portland have contributed to the growth.

In 1998, Sumner County's average home sale price was $144,100. You'll pay a premium for anything along Old Hickory Lake, however, where Nashville-area residents flock for boating, fishing and recreation. If you're interested in lake property, be sure you understand the regulations that govern the property and where the property lines lie. Docks are allowed along certain areas.

## Hendersonville

Hendersonville, Tennessee's 10th-largest city, offers small-town appeal, resident country music stars, Old Hickory Lake, good schools and plenty of shopping in nearby Rivergate. It's about a 30-minute drive from downtown Nashville, with easy access from I-65 and Gallatin Pike/U.S. Highway 31E. Some of the biggest country music stars, including Garth Brooks and Johnny Cash, live here, along with lots of retirees, families and professionals. In 1999, the city's population was approaching 40,000.

Hendersonville's 534 square miles offer plenty of residential choices. There is a rural side, a lake side and lots of apartments, condominiums and high-density developments. Houses on Old Hickory Lake are in big demand, and generally range from $250,000 to nearly $2 million. You can find homes in older neighborhoods for less than $100,000; new homes will start a little higher. From January through May 1999, the average sale price was $174,000. In addition to recreation on Old Hickory Lake, residents can go out and play at the 135-acre Drakes Creek Park, which has a lighted jogging and fitness trail, 15 soccer fields, 11 softball and baseball fields, a youth football field, picnic areas and playgrounds.

For more information, call the Hendersonville Chamber of Commerce at (615) 824-2818.

## Gallatin

About 45 minutes from downtown Nashville, 10 to 15 miles northeast of Hendersonville on U.S. Highway 31E, is Gallatin, the Sumner County seat. Gallatin is one of Tennessee's original five "Main Street Communities." Its quaint downtown district features more than 25 historic buildings, some of which were built before the Civil War. There are also several historic attractions nearby, including Cragfont and Wynnewood.

In 1999, Gallatin's population was 20,551. The economic base here is 50 percent industrial and 50 percent agricultural.

Old Hickory Lake, Bledsoe Creek State Park and numerous city parks offer lots of recreation opportunities. The Gallatin Civic Center, opened in 1994, has an indoor swimming pool, volleyball and racquetball courts, two basketball courts, a track for walking and running, fitness room, aerobic room, weight room, meeting rooms and a video arcade.

Contact the Gallatin Chamber of Commerce, (615) 452-4000, for additional information.

## Goodlettsville

Half of this historic area, 20 minutes from downtown Nashville, is in Davidson County, and half is in Sumner County. See the listing under Metro Nashville–Davidson County Neighborhoods for more information.

## Wilson County

As the Nashville area continues to expand on all sides, Wilson County (Area 11), about 20 minutes east, is experiencing a boom in residential, commercial and industrial development. From 1980 to the mid-1990s, the population increased nearly 44 percent. As of mid-1999, the estimated population was 80,000.

An abundance of affordable land is luring families in search of a more peaceful lifestyle. The median home sale price here in 1998 was nearly $142,000.There are some big budgets here too: Wilson County has the second-highest median household income in Tennessee: $43,932. With its wide-open spaces, small historic towns and easy access to Nashville via I-40, Wilson County offers what many are finding to be the right mix of country and city life. Businesses also have chosen to make Wilson County home, and Cracker Barrel Old Country Stores, Bay's Bread and Texas Boots are among those with corporate headquarters or offices here. Dell Computer has plans to open a manufacturing facility here in August 1999. For more information, contact the Wilson County Chamber of Commerce at (615) 444-5503.

## Mt. Juliet

How this small town got its name is something of a mystery. Some say it was named for Aunt Julie Gleaves, a sort of guardian angel of the area, someone who was always helping others. The problem with that story is that she was only 18 years old in 1835, the year Mt. Juliet was formed. Most believe the city was named after a castle in Kilkenny County, Ireland. Whatever its beginnings, Mt. Juliet, incorporated in 1972, is reputed to be the only town in the world with that name.

If you like rolling green hills, spacious lots and a relaxed lifestyle, Mt. Juliet, home of music star Charlie Daniels, may be for you. Just about 25 minutes from downtown Nashville and a short drive from the Nashville International Airport, Mt. Juliet is an increasingly popular choice for families. In 1999, 10,953 people called Mt. Juliet home. Affordable housing is a big draw, although Mt. Juliet's prices are generally the highest in Wilson County. The average sale price for a home in Mt. Juliet was

## INSIDERS' TIP

**Nissan's pickup truck, Sentra and Altima are produced at its 5.3 million-square-foot plant in Smyrna. Free tours of the plant are offered Tuesdays with advance reservations; call (615) 459-1444.**

Photo: Cathy Summerlin

Considered by many to be Nashville's premier address, Belle Meade features homes surrounded by large, lovely lawns with lush landscaping.

$190,500 according to sales closed from January through May 1999. Old Hickory and Percy Priest lakes are nearby.

## Lebanon

Lebanon, named for the biblical land of cedars, may be the largest city in Wilson County, but it's also big on small-town appeal. About a 30-minute drive from Nashville, Lebanon (population 19,553 in 1999) offers a slower pace.

The city was laid out in 1802 and chartered in 1819. A Civil War battle was fought on the town square in 1862, and after the Confederates' defeat, many homes and businesses were burned. The town rebuilt, and today the Public Square boasts lots of historic buildings. This area, once the site of mule sales, is known mainly for is great collection of antique shops. In fact, Lebanon has earned the nickname "Antique City of the South" — for antique lovers, a visit to this town is a must — and has been featured in *Southern Living* magazine.

Homes in Lebanon range from around $65,000 to $350,000 — less than Mt. Juliet but higher than some other areas in the county. From January through May 1999, the average sale price here was $131,700. Some historic properties can be found near Cumberland University as well as on W. Main and W. Spring streets.

Nearby hot spots include Cedars of Lebanon State Park, south of Lebanon on U.S. Highway 321; Fiddlers Grove at James E. Ward Agricultural Center; Lebanon Golf and Country Club; Cumberland River, north of town; Don Fox Park; and Lebanon Community Playground.

## Watertown

This historic town hasn't changed much since it was founded in the mid-1800s, and that's OK with its 1,354 residents. Historic Watertown has gotten spruced up just a bit recently, however, with new period streetlights, improved sidewalks and nice landscaping. The old train depot is being refurbished too. Excursion trains from Nashville visit about eight times a year. Travelers can unload for a couple of hours and visit the numerous antique shops.

The historic railroad hotel, just off the square, is now the site of the Watertown Bed and Breakfast.

Historic homes and commercial buildings are available in this family-oriented community. Prices range from about $55,000 to $100,000, with the average price from January through May 1999 at $90,800. For more information on Historic Watertown, contact the town's director of tourism at (615) 237-3318.

## Williamson County

Williamson County (Area 10), south and southwest of Nashville, boasts the highest per capita income in the state and the 11th-highest income per capita in the nation. According to the county chamber, per capita income in 1998 was $32,775. Williamson County is a definite relocation hot spot in Middle Tennessee, luring more and more Nashvillians and newcomers with its high quality of life, excellent schools, beautiful rural settings and upscale shopping. It's about a 20- to 25-minute commute to Nashville via I-65 (if there are no traffic snarls, that is), so neighborhoods here are popular with Music City workers who prefer the Williamson County lifestyle. Lots of music-business executives, country stars, professionals and families live in Brentwood, Franklin, Leipers Fork and areas in between.

In 1999 Williamson County's estimated population was 106,000 and growing. Given the high per capita income, it's no surprise that you'll find some spectacular homes here. Of course, if you're shopping for real estate in this area, be prepared to spend big. Property and homes here can be pricey. In 1998, the average sale price in Williamson County was $251,200.

Williamson County has two public school districts, four private schools and one hospital. Recreation-wise, there are plenty of options, including several public and private golf courses, more than 20 parks, Natchez Trace Parkway and several historic attractions. And there are plenty of good country roads — just perfect for a Sunday afternoon drive.

For more information about the county, call the Williamson County Chamber of Commerce, (615) 794-1225.

## Brentwood

Nestled among green rolling hills, about 8 miles south of downtown Nashville, is the popular middle-class suburb of Brentwood. A mix of suburban and rural areas covering 35.4 square miles, Brentwood has seen its population grow dramatically since the city incorporated in 1969. Since 1980, the population has doubled to about 20,000, some of whom work in nearby Maryland Farms office park. Brentwood's location along I-65 and Franklin Road just across Old Hickory Boulevard offers easy commuter access to Nashville.

The city's well-planned new residential and commercial developments lend a brand-new, fresh look. Planned growth includes green spaces around office buildings and commercial complexes and 1-acre lots in subdivisions. The attention to detail is impressive. If you've ever driven through the Maryland Farms area along Old Hickory Boulevard in the spring, you likely have seen the rows of carefully spaced, brilliant white Bradford pear trees in bloom.

Home buyers can choose from established neighborhoods of two-story or ranch-style homes and newer developments in upscale subdivisions offering super-spacious floor plans, modern amenities and security. From January through May 1999, the average sale price was $383,300, but prices range from about $150,000 to more than $600,000. Current development is pushing toward the CoolSprings Galleria mall area, and you'll find some condominiums and apartments here. Several city parks offer tennis courts, ball fields, playgrounds, trails and picnic pavilions.

## Franklin

Although it's only about a 30-minute drive from downtown Nashville, Franklin seems worlds away. Its old-fashioned but revitalized town square remains the hub of this town of

## INSIDERS' TIP

The world-record walleye — a 25-pound whopper — was caught in Old Hickory Lake in 1960.

about 25,000 to 30,000 residents. The 15-block original downtown area is listed in the National Register of Historic Places. The restored 19th-century buildings downtown house trendy boutiques, antique stores, restaurants, art galleries and other unique shops. Franklin's participation in the National Main Street Program brought brick sidewalks, period lighting, underground wiring and trees to the downtown area.

Many fine old homes on the streets near the square have been restored. The two-block Lewisburg Avenue Historic District features numerous late 19th- and early 20th-century homes. If you're shopping for a historic home, take note: these properties get snapped up quickly, and they've been selling for higher than market value. Homes in Franklin generally are on smaller lots and have less square footage than Brentwood properties, but they're also less expensive. From January through May 1999, the average sale price in Franklin was $255,400. Folks looking more for a lifestyle than a house feel that's a fair trade.

Franklin's farmland also is in great demand for development.

### Fairview

This quiet, rural community about 25 miles southwest of downtown Nashville has little in common with its Williamson County neighbors Brentwood and Franklin. Fairview is about 10 miles from Bellevue on Tenn. Highway 100; it's also accessible via I-40. As of 1999, Fairview's population was 5,531. Many of its residents work in nearby Franklin, Brentwood and Dickson. Fairview's industrial park, developed in the early 1990s, continues to attract new industries.

Fairview incorporated in 1959, so many of the homes here are brick ranches. Properties are much more affordable than in other parts of Williamson County, with prices starting well below $100,000. The average sale price from January through May 1999 was $144,800. Lots in some subdivisions are 2 acres or more, while others feature the tiny parcels commonly found in Middle Tennessee's new developments. There are also some small-acreage listings for "gentleman farmers" whose budgets make trendy Franklin and Leipers Fork areas off-limits.

The hot spot in Fairview is the Bowie Nature Park, which encompasses approximately 800 acres. Bicycling and horseback-riding trails, picnicking and a small lake are among the attractions at this lovely and rarely crowded park.

# Real Estate

There's plenty of buying, selling and building going on in and around Nashville. In some areas, new subdivisions and apartment complexes seem to pop up almost overnight.

Local Realtors report a robust real estate market — in-town and suburban homes as well as condos — in Nashville, continuing a trend that's lasted several years.

New jobs, a diversified economy and incoming business have contributed to the housing boom. Relatively low interest rates also are fueling the market, making it easier for first-time buyers to purchase a home and for families moving up to buy a more upscale property. From the mid- to late 1990s, for example, area lenders were offering 30-year, fixed-rate mortgages for as low as 6.88 percent interest and one-year adjustable mortgages for as low as 4.50 percent.

As a result of recent accelerated construction, there are tons of new homes on the market. Counties surrounding Metro Nashville are growing rapidly. Williamson and Rutherford counties have been growing fastest, but some local Realtors expect to see more buyers looking to other counties — Cheatham and Dickson, in particular — in search of more value for their dollar.

## Real Estate Agencies

If you are considering buying or selling a home, you may want to consider working with a real estate agent. An agent can help ensure your home search, purchase or sale goes more smoothly. An agent's knowledge of the market and the ins and outs of real estate transactions can save buyers and sellers time, headaches and hassles.

We've compiled a sample of several of the area's best-known real estate firms as a place to start. Certainly, there are many other good firms in and around Nashville, so don't limit your options. For information on other companies, call the Greater Nashville Association of Realtors, (615) 254-7516, and the Tennessee Association of Realtors, (615) 321-0515. In addition, the Tennessee Real Estate Commission, (615) 741-2273, which issues real estate licenses to brokers, affiliate brokers and firms as well as timeshare licenses, also offers information to the public on how to proceed with complaints against firms.

The Sunday edition of *The Tennessean* is a great source for information on properties for sale or rent. Each week, you'll find hundreds of properties, a list of interest rates from some 25 area lenders, information on Realtors plus news on the housing market. Also check out our list of several free real estate and apartment guides at the end of this chapter.

# Metro Nashville– Davidson County

## Century 21 Dawson & Associates Inc.
**6950 Moore's Ln., Brentwood**
**• (615) 371-0021, (800) 843-7962**

In business since 1986, this company specializes in Williamson County properties. There are 15 brokers and agents. The office is open daily and offers 24-hour paging. If you call after hours, you can enter your agent's extension, and he or she will be paged until the message is retrieved. The office directory is extension 800; the relocation department, extension 117.

## Century 21 Jerry Drake Realtors
**103 White Bridge Rd.**
**• (615) 356-2030, (800) 344-7963**

This agency has 18 agents and brokers and has been in business 11 years. Century 21 Jerry Drake Realtors has built a good reputation for customer service. The company handles residential properties, including rural properties and small farms.

## Crye-Leike Realtors Inc.
**5111 Maryland Wy., Brentwood**
**• (615) 373-2044, (800) 373-8893**

In the Nashville area since 1992, Crye-Leike is the largest real estate company in the state. After purchasing longtime Nashville real estate firm Folk Jordan in 1999, Crye-Leike has 1,200 employees and 22 offices in Middle Tennessee.

Crye-Leike handles residential, commercial and rural properties throughout Middle Tennessee. The company publishes the *Crye-Leike Homebuyer's Guide*, available free at area grocery stores, convenience stores and other locations. Call the central office number (listed above) to get connected with the office nearest you. The Crye-Leike Smartline, (615) 661-5800 or (800) 404-9874, is a 24-hour hotline that provides recorded information on listings. You can find out information on a specific property by entering the four-digit code from an advertisement, or search by category, such as lots and land, single-family homes, commercial, new construction, etc.

## Haury and Smith
**2033 Richard Jones Rd.**
**• (615) 383-3838**
**8327 Sawyer Brown Rd.**
**• (615) 646-3838**

This locally owned and operated company has been in business since 1960. Twenty agents and brokers handle residential, commercial, farm land and resort properties. The company also offers relocation services.

## Realty Executives Fine Homes
**3902 Hillsboro Rd. • (615) 463-7900**
**111 Westwood Pl., Ste. 104, Brentwood**
**• (615) 376-4500, (800) 291-1966 (relocation)**
**114 E. Main St. • (615) 595-5999**

Realty Executives' international network has more than 300 franchised offices. The company has been in business nationally since 1965, making it the second-oldest real estate company in the United States. The local Realty Executives offices opened in 1997. The Nashville-area offices boast 90 employees. This company puts a strong emphasis on service and attitude. The company serves all needs, including residential, land, new homes and commercial properties. Offices are open daily and offer both buyer and seller representation.

## RE/MAX BCA Partners
**109 Kenner Ave. • (615) 383-0000**

RE/MAX BCA Partners has been in business here for 27 years. The two offices combined have about 46 agents who cover all areas of Nashville and surrounding counties. The company handles residential and commercial properties, farms and vacant land.

## Sharon Langford and Associates
**2319 Crestmoor • (615) 383-6600**

This Green Hills–area office has 45 brokers and agents who handle residential and historic properties, farms and new and existing properties. Owned by Bob Parks Realty since mid-1999, the agency handles listings in Nashville and adjoining counties in every price range, so agents most likely will find something to suit your budget. Sharon Langford and Associates has been in business since 1992.

## Shirley Zeitlin and Co.
**4301 Hillsboro Pk. • (615) 383-0183**
**278 Franklin Rd. • (615) 371-0185**

Founded in 1979, Shirley Zeitlin and Company is one of the most recognizable names in Nashville real estate. The full-service company has two offices and 70 full-time agents. It landed the exclusive agreement to relocate the Houston Oilers (now Tennessee Titans) football team to Nashville — a real coup for Zeitlin, who has served as president of the Greater Nashville Association of Realtors and the State of Tennessee Association of Realtors during her 30-plus years in the business. The company was a finalist in a competition conducted by the United States Chamber of Commerce and Dun and Bradstreet to determine the best businesses in the Southeast.

This company's HomeSource hotline, (615) 385-HOME, offers information on homes and mortgages. Several of the company's advertised properties have code numbers. Call the hotline and enter the code from the advertisement to receive more info on the property.

## Village Real Estate Services
**1912 21st Ave. S., Ste. 100**
**• (615) 383-6964**
**615 Woodland St. • (615) 369-3278**

This agency specializes in unique, eclectic and historic urban homes in areas such as Belmont/Hillsboro, Hillsboro/West End, Richland, Sylvan Park, Historic Edgefield, Inglewood, Forest Hills, Oak Hills, Green Hills and Belle Meade.

In business since October 1996, this company made a big splash in its first year. Principal broker Mark Deutschmann has been voted Realtor of the Year in the *Nashville Scene* readers poll for several years. The full-service agency has 35 agents and staff members between its two offices.

# Surrounding Area

## Agee and Johnson Realty and Auction
**728 W. Main St., Lebanon**
**• (615) 444-0909**

This company has been in business since 1977. It has 22 agents and brokers, many of whom are members of the "Multimillion-dollar Club," recognizing sales of $1.25 million or $2.5 million a year, depending on the county. The company handles residential properties, farm auctions and commercial properties and offers relocation services.

## American Realtors
**102 S. Main St., Ashland City**
**• (615) 792-6400**

This office has five brokers and agents and handles residential, land and commercial properties in Cheatham, Dickson and Robertson counties.

---

**INSIDERS' TIP**

**The U.S. Army Corps of Engineers Visitor Center at Hendersonville's Rockland Recreation Center offers an interactive history of Old Hickory Lake and the navigational lock-and-dam system.**

Photo: Courtesy of Norma Mason

Homes of all sizes and styles are available in and around Nashville.

### B.J. Mitcham Real Estate
**121-A Luyben Hills Rd., Kingston Springs • (615) 952-4444**

In business since 1989, this agency in the small community of Kingston Springs has five agents and specializes in residential properties and land in Cheatham, Dickson, Williamson and Davidson counties.

### Century 21 – Roy Barker Company
**1117 Columbia Ave., Franklin**
**• (615) 791-0173, (800) 221-0949**

The only Century 21 office in Franklin, this office has about 20 agents and is part of an independently and locally owned franchise. The company has been in business since 1978 and handles residential and commercial properties, farmland, lots and auctions.

### Clark Maples Realty and Auction
**123 E. College St., Murfreesboro**
**• (615) 896-4740**

Lots of referrals and repeat customers have helped keep this locally owned company in business for 30 years. The company offers a full range of properties, including residential,

commercial and acreage, and handles as many as 40 auctions in Tennessee each year. There are approximately 25 brokers and agents.

### Coldwell Banker Lakeside Realtors
**530 W. Main St., Hendersonville**
**• (615) 824-5920, (800) 933-5920**
**3735 N. Mt. Juliet Rd., Mt. Juliet**
**• (615) 758-0401, (800) 884-8710**

Established in the early 1970s, this is one of the oldest real estate companies in Hendersonville. The offices specialize in residential properties, including lakefront. Each office has about 45 agents.

### Crye-Leike Realtors
**917 Conference Dr., Goodlettsville**
**• (615) 851-0888**

One of Crye-Leike's numerous Middle Tennessee offices, this branch in the north Nashville area has about 80 brokers and agents and has been open since 1993. Crye-Leike has a central relocation department, a property management department that handles rentals and leases and an in-house mortgage company.

Nashville has a variety of condominiums and apartments.

## Goldstar Realty
**303 S. Main St., Ashland City**
• **(615) 792-1910**
   This company specializes in new construction and residential properties in Cheatham, Robertson and Davidson counties. It has been in business since 1989 and has 10 brokers and agents.

## RE/MAX Elite Carriage House
**2500 N. Mount Juliet Rd., Mt. Juliet**
• **(615) 754-4766, (800) 548-0131**
**4680 Lebanon Pk., Hermitage**
• **(615) 872-0766, (80) 807-9099**
   This locally owned company has been in business since the late 1980s. It handles residential, commercial and farm properties. With about 25 agents, the company prides itself on its emphasis on personal service. The office is open daily, and agents are available by pager 24 hours a day.

## Snow and Wall Realtors
**1980 Old Fort Pkwy., Murfreesboro**
• **(615) 893-1130**
   Owners Howard and Sally Wall have 50 years' combined experience in the real estate business and represent five builders in the area who build in various price ranges. The com-

pany has 50 residential agents and brokers and an additional 10 who handle commercial properties.

# Real Estate Resources

## Services

## Apartment Selector Relocation Service
**409 Harding Industrial Dr.**
• **(615) 833-3151, (800) 394-2736**
   Call either of the listed numbers for free assistance in locating an apartment in Nashville or surrounding cities. Fees are paid by the landlords. This service is provided in cooperation with the majority of Nashville-area apartment complexes. Listings also include condominiums, houses and duplexes. The database contains information on current availabilities, size, amenities and policies.
   In business since 1959, the company providing this service has 23 offices nationwide. You can move into an apartment in as little as one to three days from your rental application or look two to three weeks in advance of your move and have your new apartment reserved.

## Morris Property Management Inc.
**413 Welshwood Dr. • (615) 833-5117**

Founded in 1969 by Harold F. Morris, this company actually manages and maintains hundreds of units, serving the needs of both the property owner and the resident renter. Morris Property Management also has a Realtor division to assist buyers and sellers with real estate transactions. The company also handles commercial leasing.

# Publications

The following publications are distributed free at participating grocery stores, convenience stores, area chambers of commerce, hospitals, colleges and other locations.

## Apartment Blue Book
**• (800) 222-3651**

This handy guide has loads of color photos and information, including rental rates. Complexes are arranged geographically.

## Apartment Guide Monthly
**2416 Hillsboro Rd. • (615) 292-7045**

This comprehensive publication has a facts and features checklist for an easy comparison of rates and amenities. Page after page of color photos, floor plans and other information will help you choose the apartment community that's right for you.

## Crye-Leike Homebuyers Guide
**(615) 373-2044, (800) 373-8893**

This guide features color photos and a brief description of Crye-Leike properties, arranged by area.

## Greater Nashville Real Estate Listing Magazine
**201 Thompson Ln., Ste. 1**
**• (615) 331-2594, (800) 874-1490**

Published every four weeks, this guide has color photos, descriptions and prices of homes listed by various agencies.

## Homes
**201 Thompson Ln., Ste. 1**
**• (615) 331-2594, (800) 874-1490**

This is the big, thick book filled with more than 200 pages of properties for sale. It's published every two weeks. Listings are arranged by area.

## Nashville and Middle Tennessee Apartment Magazine
**201 Thompson Ln., Ste. 1**
**• (615) 331-2594, (800) 874-1490**

This publication comes out every four weeks. It has color photos and information on several area apartment complexes. Some advertisers list rental rates.

## New Homes & Communities
**9311 Monroe Rd., Ste. K, Charlotte, N.C.**
**• (704) 846-HOME, (800) 773-0377**

This attractive and handy magazine is filled with all sorts of useful information on home builders and new communities. The "Community Profile" section lists homes by area and price range. The publication also features lots of color photos, great maps, mortgage information, information on schools, utilities and more. You can pick up a copy at grocery stores or real estate agency offices, or call the toll-free number for a free subscription.

## Real Estate This Week
**306 Gay St., Ste. 204 • (615) 259-4414**

This biweekly guide features Nashville and Middle Tennessee homes and property for sale, listed by area and price.

**According to the
Nashville Area Chamber
of Commerce,
healthcare costs here
are typically about 15
percent below the
national average.**

# Healthcare and Wellness

Healthcare is a major component of Nashville's economy, and — perhaps because of the abundance of available options — it is fairly economical. According to the Nashville Area Chamber of Commerce, healthcare costs here are typically about 15 percent below the national average.

Of course, it's the quality of healthcare that is most important, and Nashville has established itself as a national leader in that regard. The area has an extensive system of hospitals providing the finest in general and specialized care. Vanderbilt University's school of medicine, which includes two Nobel Prize winners among its staff, has been ranked among the nation's best. The school's Medical Center and The Vanderbilt Clinic are among the nation's top healthcare facilities.

Saint Thomas Hospital ranks in the top five in the United States for number of open-heart surgeries. Baptist Hospital, the largest nonprofit healthcare center in the area, developed the country's first laser surgery center.

Vanderbilt University and Meharry Medical College, both fully accredited medical schools, continue to supply the region with excellent physicians, while many schools in and around Nashville provide training in nursing, medicine and other health-related areas. In town, Belmont University offers undergraduate and master's degrees in nursing and a master's degree in occupational therapy. Tennessee State University offers a degree in allied health and bachelor's and master's degree programs in nursing.

Aquinas Junior College offers a Bachelor of Science degree in nursing. Free Will Baptist College offers degrees in sports medicine.

Trevecca Nazarene University offers Bachelor of Arts degrees in sport and exercise science; pre-professional programs in dental, medicine, pharmacy and physical therapy; and a master's degree in science (physician assistant). Draughons Junior College offers 60-hour Associate of Science degree programs in health information management and medical assisting as well as a diploma programs of 30 to 36 hours in health information management.

In the region, Austin Peay State University, in Clarksville, offers a professional program through its School of Nursing. Cumberland University, in Lebanon, offers an undergraduate nursing degree, as does Tennessee Technological University.

The public school system is also doing its part to prepare young people for health-related careers. The Martin Luther King Academic Magnet for Health Sciences/Engineering, a magnet school for grades 7 through 12, prepares students for post-secondary study leading to careers in health sciences and engineering.

Nashville also has a higher concentration of healthcare management firms than any other area in the nation. More than 250 healthcare management companies and about 70 other health-related firms call Nashville home.

Nashville's healthcare scene, like many other parts of this dynamic city, is in flux. One area to keep an eye on is the continuing development of TennCare, a statewide, experimental replacement for Medicaid. This $3.4 billion, publicly funded program is designed to provide adequate healthcare for those who are not otherwise insured. Under the program, which is about 4 years old, the state has contracts with a number of for-profit, managed-care organizations to serve about 1.2 million Tennesseans. At this writing, the state was working to address complaints about various inadequacies within the TennCare system.

The big healthcare news of 1997 — a still-developing story — revolved around Columbia/HCA Healthcare Corporation, One Park Plaza, (615) 342-1919 (local information). HCA, founded in Nashville in 1968, became, as Columbia/HCA Healthcare Corporation, the nation's largest for-profit healthcare company. As of 1997, it remained the largest, with 8,000 employees and headquarters in Nashville. However, with the major reorganization that was occurring as of this writing, this is all subject to change. Hospital names, ownership and much more are likely to be affected by the changes that are under way, so the picture may be entirely different by the time you read this. Nonetheless, we include Columbia-affiliated medical facilities in the Nashville area in this chapter's "Hospitals" section (see also our History chapter).

While many changes are taking place, one constant is an overall commitment to excellence and public service that will keep Nashville in the forefront among the nation's healthcare providers.

# Health Department

## Metropolitan Health Department for Nashville and Davidson County
### 311 23rd Ave. N. • (615) 862-5900
### (recorded general information)

Since the introduction of TennCare, the state's experimental replacement for Medicaid, the Metro Health Department largely has moved out of primary service and assumed more of a preventive function. Still, the department takes an active role in such areas as HIV testing and the treatment of sexually transmitted and other communicable diseases as well as food inspection, air-pollution control and other environmental issues.

In addition to the Health Department's main clinic, the Lentz Public Health Center at 311 23rd Avenue N., (615) 340-5658, the Health Department also operates clinics at the following locations: downtown, 526 Eighth Avenue S., (615) 862-7900; East, 1015 E. Trinity Lane, (615) 862-7916; and Woodbine, 224 Oriel Avenue, (615) 862-7940

The Sexually Transmitted Disease Clinic, (615) 340-5647, and Communicable Disease Referrals, (615) 340-5632, are housed at the 23rd Avenue center, which also runs special programs such as the Breast-feeding Promotion Program, (615) 340-7778, and Car Seat Loaner Program, (615) 340-5619.

Clinic hours are 8 AM to 4:30 PM Monday through Friday except holidays. For direct-dial numbers of the department's programs, check the blue pages of your telephone directory under Nashville government. Or you can access the audio directory by dialing (615) 862-5900.

# Hospitals

## Baptist Hospital
### 2000 Church St. • (615) 329-5555

Baptist Hospital, Middle Tennessee's largest nonprofit medical center, has 2,900 employees and 1,000 physicians serving 50 locations in Davidson and surrounding counties. Baptist, which is licensed for 759 beds and 64 bassinets, offers a wide variety of services from laser surgery to maternity care to a health and fitness center.

The hospital's mission statement is: "to ensure that our services meet the highest standard of quality and efficiency, are accessible and responsible to the community we serve, and are delivered in a caring manner." Baptist has been an industry leader in many areas, including the creation of Health Net, the area's first and largest independent preferred-provider organization, or PPO. (Saint Thomas Hospital — see its subsequent entry — is a partner in that venture.) Baptist also built the region's first outpatient surgery center and the nation's first facility dedicated solely to laser and laparoscopic surgery. It has instituted fit-

Photo: Cathy Summerlin

Vanderbilt University Medical Center and the Vanderbilt Clinic
are among the top healthcare facilities in the nation.

ness and preventive medicine programs and developed the region's largest community education and corporate wellness programs.

After an annual survey of 170,000 households in the United States, the National Research Corporation in December 1996 named Baptist Hospital a 1996 Quality Leader and the most preferred healthcare provider in the greater Nashville area.

Baptist's emergency room is the busiest in the region, with 54,326 visits in 1995, the last year for which figures are available. That year the hospital also treated 30,499 inpatients; performed 12,248 inpatient surgeries and 16,610 outpatient surgeries; and had the largest obstetrical service in Nashville, with nearly 5,000 births.

Commitment to the community includes Livesmart education programs and more than $26 million in free services, including charity and uncompensated care and community benefit programs. The hospital offered nearly 1,200 community education programs in 1996, most at no charge to participants.

The hospital operates more than a dozen Baptist-Centracare Centers and four Occupational Medical Centers in Middle Tennessee. (This group is one of only 15 multi-site ambulatory-care centers in the country to receive accreditation from the Joint Commission on

Accreditation of Hospitals.) Baptist also co-owns Middle Tennessee Medical Center in Murfreesboro with Saint Thomas Hospital and has joint ventures with Tennessee Christian Medical Center (manages surgery and OB) and Williamson Medical Center (OB, Family Care Center).

Specialty Centers include Arthritis and Osteoporosis, Occupational Medicine, Cancer, Health and Wellness, Chest Pain, Diabetes, 55 Plus (for adults 55 and older), Heart Center, Home Health Services, Institute for Aesthetic and Reconstructive Surgery, Mind/Body Medical Institute (which uses relaxation and other techniques to treat stress-related disorders), Neuroscience, Orthopaedic, Foot and Ankle, Rehabilitation, Sleep, Sports Medicine, Women's Pavilion (which includes screening centers for mammography at Proffitt's in Green Hills and Bellevue malls) and Wound Care (which provides treatment for chronic non-healing wounds).

The Center for Health and Wellness offers assessments and screenings that include hearing testing, treadmill stress tests and stop-smoking programs. The Health and Fitness Center includes an indoor track, pool, fully equipped weight room, multipurpose gym, steam and sauna rooms and a variety of aerobic exercise programs.

According to hospital surveys, 98.7 percent of Baptist patients say they would return. Baptist has also been selected by the Tennessee Titans football team as its sports-medicine provider.

## Centennial Medical Center
2300 Patterson St. • (615) 342-1000

This medical center is the largest of the Nashville Columbia/HCA facilities, with 685 beds and a medical staff of 700. It offers a full array of primary care as well as emergency, cardiac, neurologic, orthopedic, obstetric, psychiatric and other specialty services. Colum-bia Centennial Medical Center is composed of four main facilities: The Sarah Cannon Cancer Center; The Women's Hospital; Parthenon Pavilion, a 164-bed psychiatric facility; and Centennial Tower, a tertiary-care facility.

## Cheatham Medical Center
313 N. Main St., Ashland City
• (615) 792-3030

Cheatham Medical Center, part of the Columbia/HCA system, has served Cheatham County since 1987, has 29 beds. It provides a number of on-site services — including surgery, radiology, respiratory therapy, ultrasound, CAT scans and mammograms — for pediatric through geriatrics as well as transfers to other Columbia/HCA hospitals.

## Hendersonville Hospital
355 New Shackle Island Rd.,
Hendersonville • (615) 264-4000

This Hendersonville facility has been ranked as one of the top 100 hospitals in the. It has 120 beds offering medical and surgical care, obstetrics, gynecology, critical care, 24-hour emergency services, MRI (magnetic resonance imaging), a cardiac catheterization lab and outpatient services.

## Metropolitan General Hospital
1818 Albion St. • (615) 341-4000

The hospital now known as Metro General opened as City Hospital on April 23, 1890, with one physician and seven nurses. Today it is not only the teaching hospital for Meharry Medical College, but it also serves the medically underserved and residents of Davidson County with sliding-scale fees according to income. The hospital is licensed for 150 beds, all private and semiprivate.

In January 1998, General Hospital moved to the renovated former George W. Hubbard Hospital site, which covers more than 350,000 square feet on the Meharry Medical College campus. It houses inpatient medical, surgical, obstetrical, emergency, ancillary and ambulatory services.

Under the alliance announced in January 1999 with Vanderbilt Medical Center, Vanderbilt takes over management of Metro General, while Meharry continues to staff the hospital.

Among the hospital's other special programs and features are a large gymnasium and hydrotherapy areas for patients who require occupational and physical therapy, and an *Activities of Daily Living* component that provides patients with home- and work-related activities, allowing them to return to a normal routine after hospitalization or medical care.

The OUR KIDS Center, supported by General Hospital, Vanderbilt Medical Center and the Junior League of Nashville, provides medical and psychological services for children who are suspected victims of sexual abuse. The center is at 1900 Hayes Street.

## Middle Tennessee Medical Center
### 400 N. Highland Ave., Murfreesboro
### • (615) 849-4100

Middle Tennessee Medical Center is a private, not-for-profit hospital, affiliated with Baptist and Saint Thomas hospitals (see this chapter's separate entries). It is licensed for 288 beds and provides both inpatient and outpatient services. MTMC, which performs an average of 9,000 surgical procedures a year, recently opened a new ambulatory-surgery center for outpatients as well as a cancer center.

The medical center offers CT (computer tomography) scanning, MRI, angiography, cardiac catheterization, X-ray and ultrasound. It has general medical and surgical units, intensive care, coronary care and pediatrics. The Baptist Women's Pavilion offers labor/delivery/recovery facilities and a Level II nursery that offers neonatology services. About 2,000 babies are born here each year.

Additional services include MTMC at Home (home health), Hospice of Murfreesboro, the PACE (Personalized Aerobics and Cardiac Exercise) Center, outpatient radiation oncology and a Level II Emergency Department that treats about 40,000 cases each year. A new service is Senior Life Outlooks, an outpatient program for seniors battling depression.

More than 180 physicians are on staff, representing 26 different specialties including family medicine, internal medicine, pulmonary medicine, OB/GYN, pediatrics, plastic and reconstructive surgery, neurology, neurosurgery, orthopedics and general surgery.

## Nashville Memorial
### 612 Due West Ave., Madison
### • (615) 865-3511

Nashville Memorial, part of the Columbia/HCA system, has 316 beds and is particularly well known for its oncology, neurology and emergency services, in addition to a skilled-care unit, home health services and a community child-care facility. A fitness center, open to the general public, has the largest membership of any hospital-based fitness center in Middle Tennessee.

## Saint Thomas Hospital
### 4220 Harding Rd. • (615) 222-2111

Saint Thomas Hospital, founded in 1898, is recognized as one of the finest cardiac and vascular care centers in the nation. It is consistently listed among the nation's top five cardiac programs and is currently fourth in the number of annual vascular procedures. The hospital, also renowned as a tertiary-care center, was named a "Top 100 Hospital" for three consecutive years in an independent industry survey rating high-quality, cost-effective care.

With 537 beds for acute and primary care, Saint Thomas serves more than 2 million residents of northern Alabama, southwestern Kentucky and Middle Tennessee. It offers a full spectrum of primary care and specialty services including diabetes care, emergency services (including a state-designated Level II trauma center), gynecology and obstetrics, hospital lodging services, medical imaging, neurosciences, oncology treatment, ophthalmology, orthopedics, osteoporosis services, pulmonary services, psychiatric services, rehabilitation, a nationally accredited Sleep Disorders Center, subacute care and surgical services.

Saint Thomas, guided by the Daughter of Charities mission to make a positive difference in the lives and health status of individuals and communities, is dedicated to providing health services that are spiritually centered, accessible and affordable. It provided $44.3 million in charity care and outreach programs during 1996.

The hospital has community-based health centers in Brentwood, on Charlotte Avenue and in Green Hills. It is a partner with Baptist Hospital of Nashville in Health Net, the region's largest independent preferred-provider organization, or PPO. It is one of three Nashville hospitals used to train Vanderbilt residents.

### Southern Hills Medical Center
**391 Wallace Rd. • (615) 781-4000**

Southern Hills, part of the Columbia/HCA system, is recognized for primary care, neurology, orthopedics, a transitional-care center, cardiology, obstetrics, gynecology and oncology. The center has 160 acute-care beds and 20 skilled-nursing beds. It recently received the prestigious Accreditation with Commendation from the Joint Commission on Accreditation of Healthcare Organizations.

### Smyrna Medical Center
**400 Enon Springs Rd., Smyrna**
**• (615) 459-8771**

This small but growing emergency and diagnostic center treats outpatients only. In addition to emergency medical care, Smyrna Medical Center offers ultrasound and mammography capabilities, family practice, internal medicine, obstetrics and gynecology, orthopedics, pulmonary medicine, cardiology, CT scanning and occupational medicine.

### Summit Medical Center
**5655 Frist Blvd., Hermitage**
**• (615) 316-3000**

This medical center, in operation since 1970, moved in 1994 to its current 204-bed medical and surgical facility. It is recognized for emergency care, diabetes management and obstetric services. Summit, a part of the Columbia/HCA system, also has a women's

health center, psychiatric care, neurosurgery, orthopedic and pediatric care.

### Tennessee Christian Medical Center
**500 Hospital Dr., Madison**
**• (615) 865-0300**
### Portland Highland Hospital
**105 Redbud Dr., Portland**
**• (615) 325-7301**

Tennessee Christian Medical Center, a member of the Adventist Health System/Sunbelt, is one of nearly 350 healthcare facilities worldwide operated by the Seventh-Day Adventist Church. Since the opening of the church's first healthcare center in Battle Creek, Michigan, in 1866, these facilities — which include 160 hospitals in addition to nursing homes, dispensaries and clinics — have been "dedicated to helping people achieve physical, mental and spiritual wholeness."

Tennessee Christian Medical Center, which admitted its first patient in 1908, now has 311 acute-care beds at its Madison facility and 48 at its Portland Highland Hospital facilities; 38 of the beds in Madison, and 12 in Portland, are categorized as subacute or skilled-nursing beds.

Portland Highland Hospital has more than a dozen physicians and 165 employees providing intensive and coronary care, medical and surgical care and comprehensive OB/GYN care, including a newborn nursery.

TCMC in Madison has a 350-member medical staff serving 35,000 patients a year and providing outpatient and inpatient acute care as well as behavioral and rehabilitation programs. In addition to the services provided at the Portland facility, the Madison hospital offers cardiac catheterization, cardiopulmonary services, day surgery, 24-hour emergency services staffed by MDs and nurses specially trained in emergency medicine, endoscopy lab, home health services (with offices in Madison, Hendersonville, Portland and Westmoreland), occupational medicine, radiology, inpatient rehabilitation and behavioral services

### INSIDERS' TIP
**Nashville has the nation's highest concentration of healthcare management firms.**

including adolescent treatment with partial hospitalization, aftercare and outpatient services as treatment options, adult acute treatment, an adult stress-disorders unit and center for addictions (based on 12-step programs pioneered by Alcoholics Anonymous).

The Madison hospital also has a Seniorlife Center for people older than 60, an outpatient counseling center for families, adults and children, and a women's program for those suffering from emotional and psychiatric problems such as sexual or physical abuse, depression, anxiety and addictive relationships. For information on behavioral programs, call (800) 467-TCMC.

The TCMC Fitness Center offers a gym, indoor swimming pool, all types of exercise equipment and a number of exercise classes as well as classes in weight control, fitness, nutrition and smoking cessation.

The hospitals also are affiliated with Baptist Hospital for their Women's Pavilion, the Baptist Medical Plaza at TCMC and the free 55 Plus program for seniors, which offers discounted and complimentary services including free transportation for members who live within 25 miles and are scheduled for an inpatient stay. Call the 55 Plus office at (615) 868-5500 for more information.

## University Medical Center
### 1411 Baddour Pkwy., Lebanon • (615) 444-8262

The 261-bed University Medical Center's facilities include an Outpatient Center with a full range of diagnostic and treatment procedures from CAT scans to MRI and cataract surgery to tonsillectomies. The Heart Center is a full-service diagnostic facility with capabilities ranging from nuclear cardiology to cardiac catheterization. The Orthopaedic Center of Excellence performs procedures including total joint replacement as well as back, knee and hip surgeries. The Emergency and Chest Pain Center features the latest in emergency-treatment technology and chest pain testing.

McFarland Specialty Hospital offers rehabilitation (including physical, occupational, speech and recreational therapies), psychiatric care for adult and geriatric patients and skilled nursing for total care of those with physi-cal or cognitive disabilities. The Women's Pavilion offers all-in-one labor/delivery/recovery rooms and dedication to meeting the additional needs of women in all stages of life. The hospital also has a Health Works Program to help business and industry obtain high-quality healthcare in a cost-effective manner.

## Vanderbilt University Medical Center
### 1211 22nd Ave. S. • (615) 322-5000

Vanderbilt University Medical Center and The Vanderbilt Clinic have a world-class reputation for excellence that is unsurpassed in the region. Physicians refer patients to Vanderbilt from throughout not only Middle Tennessee, but also East and West Tennessee, Kentucky and Alabama.

Major facilities at Vanderbilt include The School of Medicine, The School of Nursing, Vanderbilt University Hospital, Vanderbilt Clinic, Vanderbilt Children's Hospital, Vanderbilt Stallworth Rehabilitation Hospital, The Psychiatric Hospital at Vanderbilt and the Kim Dayani Human Performance Center.

Both the medical center and the clinic consistently rank among the premier healthcare facilities in the nation. *U.S. News and World Report* recently listed six of Vandy's specialties — endocrinology, otolaryngology, orthopedics, cancer, gynecology and rheumatology — among the top 40 in the nation.

The hospital is licensed for 658 beds, including the Children's Hospital, which is within the Vanderbilt hospital building. The Vanderbilt Clinic, which contains of 92 specialty clinics, had 535,934 outpatient visits during the 1998 fiscal year.

The School of Medicine, which the 1998 *U.S. News and World Report* survey ranked 15th among 125 medical schools in the country, claims two Nobel Laureates. Earl Sutherland Jr. was awarded the prize in 1971 for his discovery of cyclic AMP, a hormonal mediator on the cellular level; and Stanley Cohen won in 1986 for his discovery with a colleague of epidermal growth factor.

The Vanderbilt Cancer Center, a National Cancer Institute Clinical Cancer Center, provides comprehensive care and state-of-the-art research. The Vanderbilt program provides leading-edge treatments, some of which may not be available anywhere else in the world.

Vandy has several programs that are the only ones of their kind in Middle Tennessee. These include a Level I Trauma Center and a Level I Burn Center, both of which provide the highest level of immediate, 24-hour service available; a Lifeflight air emergency transport system; and a Level IV Neonatal Intensive Care Unit, which provides the highest level of that type of care available.

The Children's Hospital, the only one in Middle Tennessee closer than Jackson or Chattanooga, has 17 specialty units, including neonatal intensive care, pediatric intensive care, pediatric surgery, kidney center, lung center and long-term care unit. In addition, Vandy does high-risk obstetrics.

Vandy also has the only Middle Tennessee transplant program that provides major organ transplants: heart, kidneys, lungs, liver and pancreas. The Vanderbilt Stallworth Rehabilitation Hospital, which has 80 beds, provides complete inpatient and outpatient services for pediatric and adult patients with orthopedic and neurologic injuries or disabilities. It includes the Vanderbilt Center for Multiple Sclerosis.

The Psychiatric Hospital at Vanderbilt, with 88 beds, provides inpatient, partial hospitalization and intensive outpatient services to children, adolescents and adults with psychiatric and substance-abuse problems.

Other special centers include the Adult Primary Care Center, the Arthritis Center, the Breast Center, the Child Development Center, the Geriatric Evaluation Program and the Voice Center. At the Breast Center, women can obtain comprehensive breast healthcare including mammography, breast ultrasound, examination, biopsy and surgical evaluation; the center also offers a breast cancer support group. The Child Development Center evaluates children who have, or are suspected of having, developmental problems. The Voice Center is a one-of-a-kind facility for treating vocal disorders.

The Kim Dayani Human Performance Center offers a wide range of health assessments and screenings, aerobics and exercise programs, rehab programs, nutrition consultation, therapeutic massage and classes in smoking cessation and weight management. Its facilities include an indoor track, indoor pool and fully equipped weight room.

## Williamson Medical Center
**Curd Ln., Franklin • (615) 791-0500**

Williamson Medical Center is a not-for-profit, county-owned community hospital dedicated to "making health care services cost effective, convenient and accessible to area residents and employers." The center offers 26 medical specialties including allergy, cardiology, dermatology, emergency medicine, endocrinology, gastroenterology, neurology, obstetrics and gynecology (the obstetrics unit is The Baptist Women's Pavilion South), oncology, orthopedics and sports medicine, pediatrics, pulmonary medicine and urology, to name a sampling. Facilities include MRI, CT, cardiac catheterization, mammography and ultrasound. More than 80 percent of its 140 beds are in private rooms.

Through Harpeth Health Group, an affiliation of Williamson Medical Center and Baptist Hospital, four clinics serve the community: Grassland Family Center, on Hillsboro Road; Cool Springs Center, on Mallory Lane in the new Baptist Williamson Medical Plaza; Nolensville Family Care Center, near the post office on Oldham Drive; and Franklin Family Walk-in Clinic, beside the Medical Center in Franklin in the Physicians Plaza Building.

# Walk-in Clinics

## Hospital Affiliates

All of the following walk-in clinics (no appointment needed) are affiliated with an area hospital and see patients of all ages.

### Baptist Care Centers

Most Baptist Care Centers are open seven days a week. Hours vary by location. Call the center nearest you during operating hours for specific information. In addition to physician-ordered lab tests, several tests — cholesterol, blood type, colorectal, hemoglobin and pregnancy — are available at all locations without physician referral.

**Bellevue**, 7643 U.S. Highway 70 S., Bellevue, (615) 662-9322

**Donelson**, 2531 Elm Hill Pike, (615) 391-5582

**Downtown** (occupational medicine), 342 21st Avenue N., (615) 321-4800

**Hickory Hollow**, 2553 Murfreesboro Road, (615) 399-7081

**Murfreesboro**, 1203-A Memorial Boulevard, Murfreesboro, (615) 895-0511

**Rivergate**, 1721 Gallatin Road, (615) 265-5961

**South Nashville**, 394 Harding Place, (615) 331-2081

## Company Care White Bridge
**280 White Bridge Rd. • (615) 352-8440**

Company Care White Bridge is open 8 AM to 5:30 PM Monday through Friday.

## Company Care Donelson
**522 Donelson Pk. • (615) 391-3799**

Company Care Donelson is open 8 AM to 10 PM Monday through Friday and 9 AM to 6 PM Saturday and Sunday.

## Company Care Smyrna
**400 Enon Springs Rd., Smyrna**
**• (615) 220-0229**

Company Care Smyrna is open 8 AM to 5:30 PM Monday through Friday.

## Vanderbilt Health Services
**919 Murfreesboro Rd., Franklin**
**• (615) 791-7373**

The Vanderbilt Health Services walk-in clinic is open 8 AM to 8 PM Monday through Friday, until 6 PM Saturday and Sunday.

## Independents

The following clinics, which do not require

appointments and which see patients of all ages, prefer that patients come in no later than an hour or so before closing so there is still time to be seen.

## Brentwood Family Care Center
**5046 Thoroughbred Ln., Brentwood**
**• (615) 370-8080**

Brentwood Family Care Center is open 8 AM to 7 PM Monday through Friday, 9 AM to 4 PM Saturday and noon to 4 PM Sunday.

## Harding Medical Center
**4126 Nolensville Rd. • (615) 834-2170**

Harding Medical Center is open 8 AM to 7 PM Monday, 8 AM to 6 PM Tuesday through Thursday, 8 AM to 4:30 PM Friday, 8 AM to 5 PM Saturday and 9:30 AM to 4 PM Sunday.

## Madison Minor Medical Center
**1114 N. Gallatin Rd., Madison**
**• (615) 868-9959**

Madison Minor Medical Center is open 9 AM to 7 PM Monday through Friday, until 6 PM Saturday.

# Special Services

## Agape
**4555 Trousdale Dr. • (615) 781-3000**

Agape (pronounced "uh-gah-PAY"), meaning "Christian love," is a licensed child-placement agency offering temporary foster-home care and adoptive services in Middle Tennessee since 1966. Maternity services include counseling and foster care for unwed mothers. Professional counseling, available on a sliding scale, includes marriage and family counseling as well as individual counseling. A major objective of the agency is strengthening family life through workshops and seminars.

Hours are 8 AM to 4:30 PM Monday through Friday.

## Crisis Pregnancy Support Center
1810 Hayes St. • (615) 321-0005
1107-A Lakeview Dr., Franklin
• (615) 591-4442

Crisis Pregnancy Support Center offers free pregnancy tests, crisis intervention counseling, post-abortion counseling (individual and support groups), abortion education, maternity clothes and baby items. The center also provides referrals for medical care, social services, adoption and housing. All services are confidential. Hours for the main Hayes Street location are 9 AM to 5 PM Monday, Wednesday and Friday; 9 AM to 8 PM Tuesday and Thursday; and 9 AM to noon Saturday. The smaller Franklin center is open only from 10 AM to 5 PM Tuesday and from 1 to 7 PM Thursday.

## HotelDocs
(800) HOTEL DR

When you're on vacation, you generally travel without many of the conveniences of home — such as your family physician. With HotelDocs, however, if you find yourself in need of medical assistance, you simply can call the listed toll-free number, and a board-certified local physician will be dispatched to your hotel room within about 35 minutes. The charge for being treated in the comfort and security of your hotel room is $150 — or $195 between 10 PM and 8 AM. Medication, which most doctors bring with them, costs extra.

Various types of doctors and specialists are available, including physicians, dentists, chiropractors, optometrists, podiatrists, audiologists, acupuncturists, nurses, pediatricians, ophthalmologists, obstetricians, gynecologists, allergists, dermatologists, nutritionists and internal specialists.

HotelDocs, created and based in San Diego since 1989, now serves more than 150 markets in most U.S. states, with more cities being added weekly. The service, which guarantees satisfaction or your money back, is covered by most insurance plans and is available 24 hours a day, 365 days a year.

## Planned Parenthood of Middle Tennessee
Midtown Clinic, 412 D.B. Todd Blvd.
• (615) 321-7216
Southeast Clinic, 313 Harding Pl.
• (615) 834-4840

Planned Parenthood provides family planning and crisis pregnancy services. Regular hours at the Midtown Clinic are 8:30 AM to 5 PM Monday through Friday. Appointments are available for gynecological exams and Pap smears, all birth-control methods, counseling, abortions from seven to 14 weeks, testing for sexually transmitted diseases including HIV, and hormone replacement and gynecological care for menopausal women.

The clinic accepts walk-ins for pregnancy testing without an appointment during Family Planning Clinic hours. First-time patients may be seen as walk-ins only on Wednesdays between 8:30 AM and 5 PM for an initial exam and birth-control supplies. Emergency contraceptive pills, for use within 72 hours of unprotected sex, are available, but appointments are requested.

At the Southeast clinic hours are Wednesday from 9 AM to 4:30 PM, Thursday from 11 AM to 6:30 PM, Friday from 9 AM to 4:30 PM and the second and fourth Saturdays of each month from 9 to 11:30 AM.

# Hospice Care

## Alive Hospice Inc.
1718 Patterson St. • (615) 327-1085

The goal of Alive Hospice is to "provide support and comfort to meet the special needs arising from the physical, emotional, spiritual and social stresses experienced during the final stages of a terminal illness." Hospice volunteers service those who have a limited life expectancy; have a physician primarily responsible for medical care who will work with the hospice program; and have someone available to assist with continuing care. Patients must live within the Alive Hospice service area, which covers Davidson, Cheatham, Dickson, Robertson, Rutherford, Sumner, Williamson and Wilson counties.

Referrals are accepted from physicians, hospital and other healthcare personnel and families and friends. Nursing services include the complete spectrum of skilled-nursing care and pain management with 24-hour on-call availability. Arrangements can be made for physical, speech and occupational therapies related to symptom control. Social workers offer emotional support and counseling, assistance with financial and practical concerns, and bereavement and follow-up contact with families. Individual counseling is also available for patients and families.

Chaplain services for spiritual support are available, as is assistance with memorials and funeral arrangements. Specially trained hospice volunteers provide companionship, help in the home, respite care and emotional support, and they may run errands as well.

## Friendship Hospice of Nashville
**1326 Eighth Ave. N. • (615) 726-0630**

Friendship Hospice, established in 1991, was the first minority-owned agency of its kind in the country. It began as a volunteer organization but quickly realized the need for its services in Davidson and surrounding counties (Cheatham, Robertson, Sumner, Wilson, Rutherford and Williamson) was too big for volunteers alone. Today, Friendship Hospice uses a combination of hospice staff and volunteers.

The agency provides palliative care to terminally ill patients with a life expectancy of six months or less. Its philosophy stresses that death is a natural part of the life cycle — when death is inevitable, the hospice neither hastens nor postpones death — and focuses on relief of physical, psychological and spiritual pain for patients, their families and loved ones.

Friendship Hospice's team approach includes physicians, nurses, counselors, therapists, aides and volunteers. While patients are usually referred by the primary physician, re-

ferrals can also be made by family, friends, clergy or healthcare professionals.

## Hospice of Murfreesboro
**417 N. Highland Ave., Murfreesboro**
**• (615) 896-4663**

Hospice of Murfreesboro, which serves Rutherford County, is a department of Middle Tennessee Medical Center. Its services, however, are not limited to patients at that hospital. The hospice emphasizes a team approach with nurses, social workers, volunteers and chaplains serving not only the patient, but also the family unit or caregiver. It follows families for at least 13 months after the patient's death.

Most services are provided in patients' homes. The hospice has an active volunteer component that helps out in such ways as occasionally delivering dinner and staying with a patient so family members can run errands or tend to other needs.

Other benefits include grief support groups, which are free and open to the community, and a children's grief day camp in the summer. Hospice of Murfreesboro, which is partly funded by The United Way, accepts what the patient's insurance pays and does not bill the family for any difference.

## Hospice of Tennessee
**115 Castle Heights Ave. N., Lebanon**
**• (615) 453-8723, (800) 889-HOPE**

Hospice of Tennessee, an affiliate of Home Technology Healthcare Inc., serves terminally ill patients residing in Middle Tennessee as well as portions of East and West Tennessee. Services include nursing care; social work; counseling and education; dietary consultation; home medical equipment and supplies; medications; home health aides; spiritual support; speech, occupational, physical and other supportive therapies; volunteer assistance; short-term inpatient support at approved medical facilities; 24-hour on-call availability; and bereavement follow-up for family members and caregivers for a year and one month after the patient's death.

Any patient with limited life expectancy who is no longer receiving treatment toward a cure may be referred for hospice care. The patient should desire and be seeking treatment toward comfort, have a willing and able caregiver, and must be under the care of a physician. The request for hospice services can be made by the patient, family, physician or a hospice team member. After the referral is approved by the patient's primary physician, a hospice nurse visits the patient and caregiver to discuss specific concerns and address any questions. A plan of care is then determined based on the medical, emotional, physical, social and spiritual needs of the patient and family.

Hospice of Tennessee, a member of the National Hospice Organization, is accredited by the Joint Commission on Accreditation of Healthcare Organizations and is Medicare certified. All or part of the hospice care may be covered by Medicare, Medicaid or private insurance companies. Hospice of Tennessee's policy is to provide care when needed, regardless of the patient's ability to pay.

### Willowbrook Hospice
**145 Southeast Pkwy., Franklin**
**• (615) 791-8499**

Willowbrook works with patients who have been diagnosed as having six months or less to live if their disease runs its normal course.

The hospice's main focus is on comfort and pain management, working to help patients spend their final days at home rather than in an institution and teaching family members how to care for their dying loved one. A staff chaplain works with clergy from the church of the family's choice.

Most referrals come from physicians, but also can come from discharge planners and hospitals. Hospice nurses are specialists in pain management, and social workers help the family come to terms with their impending loss. Willowbrook staffers are available 24 hours a day.

## Alternative Healthcare

We've already established that Nashville is a national leader in the field of healthcare. When it comes to "alternative" healthcare, however, this area is not exactly a hotbed. That's not to say you won't find practitioners of holistic medicine, acupuncture and other less conventional methods, it's just that, well, this isn't California. This is the Bible Belt, where people tend to be a little more conservative on the average, and apparently that philosophy

Photo: Tennessee Valley Authority

Taking advantage of nearby recreational opportunities
is one way Nashvillians maintain physical wellness.

largely extends to folks' attitudes toward medicine.

Then again, it may depend on what you mean by "alternative." Chiropractors, for example, once were viewed as being on the fringes of the medical profession. Today, BellSouth's local Yellow Pages directory lists more than 120 chiropractic practices in the Nashville area. Also in the Yellow Pages, you'll find a handful of "holistic practitioners," some of whom apparently practice from their homes.

If you're seeking treatment through such methods as acupuncture (with or without needles), acupressure, iridology, reflexology, meditation, tai chi, yoga or applied kinesiology, you can find someone to help you here. Acupuncturists and reflexologists have their own listings; the "Health & Diet Food Products" section of the Yellow Pages is a good place to find related information.

Keep in mind that not all of these practitioners are licensed medical doctors; some, for example, are merely registered nurses. Be sure to ask plenty of questions if you have doubts about anyone's credentials.

# Emergency, Information and Referral Numbers

**Emergencies** requiring ambulance, police or fire departments — 911
**Baptist Care Finders** (physician referrals) — (615) 329-MD4U, (800) 625-4298
**Crisis Intervention Center** (crises ranging from suicide attempts to people who can't pay their heating bill in winter) — (615) 244-7444.
**Just Ask Saint Thomas** (health information and physician referrals) — (615) 298-3200
**Vanderbilt Physician Referral** — (615) 322-3000
**Vanderbilt Poison Center** — 911 or (615) 936-2034
**Vanderbilt Respond for Psychiatric Referral and Assessment** — (615) 327-7000, (800) 365-2270

The 1855 founding of Hume School made Nashville the first city in the South to establish a public school system.

# Education and Child Care

Education has come a long way since the 1855 founding of Hume School, a notable institution because it made Nashville the first city in the South to establish a public school system. On that site today stands Hume-Fogg High, a "magnet" for academically talented students in grades 9 through 12. The newer school, one of a growing number of public magnet programs in Nashville/Davidson County, represents an ever-expanding number of educational opportunities in the area for young and old alike.

Perhaps it's no surprise to find a large quantity of high-quality learning institutions in a city that has been called the "Athens of the South." But it's reassuring to discover that Nashville schools — technical as well as academic, from pre-kindergarten through doctoral programs — are continuing to explore, innovate and improve, helping to create new generations of leaders in a stunning range of fields. Today's students, even in the early grades, are as likely to be utilizing high-tech tools like CD-ROMs and the Internet as they are books or calculators. One indication of the rapid growth of technology in our area's schools is the number of "21st Century Classrooms," which include student computer workstations and multimedia equipment as part of a na-

tional program to improve the teaching of all academic skills.

*U.S. News & World Report* in 1996 recognized the Nashville region's diverse and outstanding educational institutions. This diversity includes not only the area's public schools, but also literally scores of private elementary and secondary schools, both secular and with church or religious affiliations. Nashville also has two highly respected single-sex institutions, the all-girls Harpeth Academy and the all-boys Montgomery Bell Academy. The national Leonard Bernstein Center for Education through the Arts, based in Nashville, uses art and technology to create new learning approaches.

Higher education, of course, has long been one of Nashville's bragging points. The most prominent institutions are Vanderbilt University, with its highly ranked schools of education, medicine, business and law; Meharry Medical College, a leading educator of black doctors and dentists, that is in the process of building an alliance with Vanderbilt; and Fisk University, which is highly acclaimed not only among historically black colleges and universities but also among all post-secondary schools. And these are far from the only options you'll find in this area. In fact, the region

## INSIDERS' TIP

**Many area churches offer day-care programs. Among the most popular are St. George's Episcopal Day Kindergarten, 4715 Harding Road, (615) 269-9712; Westminster Kindergarten, 3900 West End Avenue, (615) 297-0235; and Woodmont Christian Day Care, 3601 Hillsboro Pike, (615) 297-9962.**

has no fewer than 18 colleges and universities offering baccalaureate, graduate or professional degrees to more than 85,000 students annually.

This chapter looks at the Nashville metropolitan area's public school systems, the "best and brightest" private schools, colleges and universities, and technical and trade schools. We also address the child-care issue — which, in some areas, is becoming more and more inseparable from the school issue, as some schools allow children to enter pre-kindergarten as early as age 3.

www.insiders.com

See this and many other **Insiders' Guide®** destinations online.

**Visit us today!**

# Education

## Public Schools

### Nashville/Davidson County

**Metropolitan Nashville Public School System**
**Central Office, 2601 Bransford Ave.**
• **(615) 259-8400**

All 127 public schools in Nashville/Davidson County are under the direction of the consolidated city-county government. About 58.2 percent of the school budget comes from local property taxes and a 1.75 percent local option sales tax. The school board consists of nine elected members and a director, who is appointed. Sixty-seven elementary schools, 32 middle schools, 11 high schools, four special education schools, three alternative schools and one adult center plus nine magnet schools covering various grade ranges make up the district. Approximately 96 percent of the secondary schools are accredited by the Southern Association of Colleges and Schools, as are 36 percent of the elementaries. (The state average is 60.3 percent for elementaries and 64.1 percent for secondary schools.)

For the 1997-98 school year, 69,337 children were enrolled in the system. The ethnic makeup of the student population reflects the area's diversity: 50.4 percent Caucasian, 43.6 percent African American, 3.3 percent Asian, 2.4 percent Hispanic and 0.2 percent American Indian. (Numbers of Spanish and Kurdish students have been growing, and some schools, including Whitsitt, Gower and Haywood elementary schools, offer English as a Second Language programs.)

The per-pupil expenditure, based on the 1997-98 budget, is $5,568. The average teacher salary in the Metro system is $39,333. About two-thirds of the teachers have a master's degree or higher. The system's Randall's Learning Center provides ongoing teacher education.

About 63 percent of spring 1997 graduates from Nashville public schools went on to higher education.

The 1997-98 composite SAT scores of seniors averaged 1,100, compared with a state average of 1,121. The average ACT composite was 19.1, compared with a state average of 19.8. The district requires 22 credits for graduation, two more than the statewide requirement.

Eleven Metro schools have been recognized with the United States Schools of Excellence designation, the highest award given to any public or independent K–12 school. Those schools are Wright Middle, Brookmeade Elementary, Glendale Middle, Andrew Jackson Elementary, Head Middle, Meigs Magnet, Glencliffe Comprehensive High School, Lakeview Elementary, Dodson Elementary, Eakin Elementary and Hillsboro Comprehensive High. The system also has more than 500 21st Century Classrooms.

In late 1998, a U.S. district judge's ruling effectively ended a voluntary-desegregation lawsuit that had been pending for more than 40 years in Davidson County. That case began when a black father sued to allow his son to attend a school in their neighborhood rather than be bused. Judge Thomas Wiseman's decision pronounced that the Metro school district's $206 million desegregation plan was "in the best interest of all the children and all the citizens of Davidson County." It freed the district from court supervision and apparently will help bring an end to nearly three decades of court-ordered busing. Meanwhile, Commitment for the Future, a plan adopted by the Metro schools in 1996, gives more students the ability to attend schools closer to home and helps provide for some voluntary desegregation through an increase in the number of magnet schools (see subsequent section). Commitment for the Future reorganizes the school system so that students will attend no more than three schools from kindergarten through grade 12. This plan also includes early-childhood centers for pre-kindergarten at various locations including the Hull-Jackson Montessori Magnet; Caldwell Early Childhood Center; Berry, Napier and Warner elementaries; and Carter-Lawrence, Head and McKissack middle schools.

## Kindergarten

One year of state-approved kindergarten is required for enrollment in first grade in the Metropolitan Nashville Public School System. Kindergarten programs are available at 80 elementary and middle schools. Kindergarten enrollment for children who will be 5 years old on or before September 30 requires the child's birth certificate, a record of a recent physical examination, a Tennessee state immunization form, proof of residence (a rent receipt or utility bill will work) and the child's Social Security number.

## Partnership Programs

The Adopt-a-School Program, established in the early '80s, creates partnerships between Nashville schools and area businesses. About 250 organizations, ranging from small local businesses to large international conglomerates, provide millions of dollars' worth of in-kind gifts while working with the schools to enhance the education of all students. Enhancements through this and similar partnership programs can include tutors, mentors, classroom assistance, help with special events or even trading places with a principal or administrator for a day. A partnership with Vanderbilt University called Schools for Thought started with two classrooms in 1993-94. By 1996 it had grown to 25 classrooms, grades 5 through 8, in four schools. Students

in this program use a variety of electronic media to research topics, write and edit reports and prepare graphics.

## Enrichment Programs and Options

Enrichment options offered throughout the Metro school system include weekly "encore" classes for gifted children in kindergarten through grade 6; testing for credit for middle school students (grades 7 and 8), who may take tests to gain high school credit in Algebra I, physical science and first-year French, German, Latin and Spanish; and the High Achievers summer program, which involves some of the top 10th graders.

## Special Education

Special Education programs consist of Individual Education Plans created by committees of parents, teachers, principals and school psychologists. One committee meets to assess the student's needs; another creates the plan for meeting those needs, which is devised according to the student's disabilities. Students in special-education programs may continue in the Metro system until they are 22 years old if they desire. Whenever possible, they are mainstreamed.

## Metro Magnet Schools

Magnets offer alternatives to assigned or zoned schools and help to offer voluntary desegregation for some students. They also allow students to study a theme related to their areas of interest or expertise. No transportation to magnet schools is provided by Metro schools, but bus routes from Metro Transit Authority are available. For information call the transit authority at (615) 862-5950.

All Metro academic magnet schools are accredited by the Southern Association of Colleges and Schools. Magnets have a six-week open application period each year during January and February (dates vary). A selection drawing is held for positions in the entering grades; an application process is used to fill any vacancies that remain. Some grade levels at some magnets have openings as the school year begins, and interested people can apply for these until classes begin.

Students apply by audition or portfolio for high school arts magnets. Students from

Wharton Arts Magnet Middle School have automatic entry into the high school arts program, but with this exception there is no automatic entry from any of the other middle school programs. "Walk-through" days are available year round for families interested in the magnet programs. During the January-February selection period, families can attend Sunday afternoon open houses as well as Magnet School Fairs, which are held in various malls with parent and teacher representatives present.

Applications are accepted for waiting lists for "subsequent grades" (grades other than a particular school's entry level) at any time, but students may enter magnet programs only within the first 10 days of the school year. The advantage to applying for a waiting list as soon as possible is that students who qualify to enter in subsequent years do so on a first-come, first-served basis. Following is a listing of area magnet schools.

### Buena Vista/Jones Paideia Magnet
**1531 Ninth Ave. N. • (615) 291-6360**

Buena Vista/Jones Paideia, for grades K through 8, develops students' abilities for creative thinking and problem solving.

### East Literature Magnet
**110 Gallatin Rd. • (615) 262-6650**

As its name indicates, this school for grades 5 through 12 offers a literature core curriculum. A computer lab provides students with tools for researching and producing their own works.

### Hull-Jackson Montessori Magnet
**1015 Kellow St. • (615) 353-2060**

At Hull-Jackson, in Metro Center behind Luby Library, children ages 3 through 5 attend classes together, as do those ages 6 to 9. This program promotes academic achievement in a noncompetitive environment under the guidance of Montessori-certified teachers.

### Hume-Fogg Academic Magnet
**700 Broadway • (615) 291-6300**

Hume-Fogg, on the site of Nashville's first public school, serves academically talented students in grades 9 through 12 with a rigorous college-preparatory curriculum. More than 95 percent of these students go on to post-

secondary education. High achievement test scores are required for application.

### Martin Luther King Academic Magnet for Health Sciences/Engineering
**613 17th Avenue N. • (615) 329-8400**

This magnet school for grades 7 through 12 prepares students for post-secondary study leading to careers in health sciences and engineering. More than 95 percent of Martin Luther King graduates enroll in higher education.

### Meigs Academic Magnet Middle School
**713 Ramsey St. • (615) 291-6390**

Meigs's academic course of study is open to students with high achievement test scores in grades 5 through 8. The school has computers in every classroom, and a four-year foreign language program is available in Latin, French, German and Spanish.

### Nashville School of the Arts
**3500 Hydes Ferry Rd. • (615) 291-6600**

Nashville School of the Arts provides liberal arts instruction plus visual arts, dance, music and theater to students in grades 9 through 12.

### Pearl-Cohn Business/ Communications High School
**904 26th Ave. N. • (615) 329-8412**

Pearl-Cohn, which opened successfully in fall 1997 as a business/communications magnet for grades 9 through 12, is a 21st Century High School with computers in every classroom. It offers students a unique opportunity to combine media arts and business studies through its television studio and partnership with local cable-access channels. Pearl-Cohn, a member of the National Academy Foundation, is the only Metro high school that offers the Academy of Finance. Magnet students also can participate in college classes and gain real-world work experience.

### Wharton Arts Magnet Middle School
**1625 D.B. Todd Jr. Blvd.**
**• (615) 329-8180**

Wharton, for grades 5 through 8, has an

academic program plus interdisciplinary programs in visual and performing arts including dance, drama and instrumental and vocal music.

# Goodlettsville

Goodlettsville schools are in both Davidson and Sumner counties, as about half the city's area lies in each. There is no central phone number because there is no central school district; schools are in either the Davidson County or Sumner County public systems (see those listings for addresses and phone numbers). Goodlettsville is about 12 miles north of Nashville and has a population of about 12,500. It has a total of six elementaries, three middle schools and two high schools, with a total enrollment of about 7,750.

One school in the system, Hunters Lane High School, uses innovative programs to combine vocational-technical and college preparation. For example, the music program, which works in conjunction with Hillsboro High School in Nashville, teaches music writing and performance on all instruments, with special emphasis on those used in country music. The school also has an "internationally acclaimed string band."

# Ashland City/ Cheatham County

## Cheatham County Schools
### 102 Elizabeth St., Ashland City
• (615) 792-5664

The Cheatham County Schools system consists of eight elementaries, three middle schools and three high schools, with a total 1997-98 enrollment of 6,584. Almost 98 percent of the student population is Caucasian, with African Americans accounting for about 1.6 percent. All secondary schools are accredited by the Southern Association of Colleges and schools, and 44.4 percent of elementary schools have been accredited. The per-student expenditure for 1997-98 was $3,607, average teacher salary was $29,322, average composite ACT score was 18.5, and average SAT was 1,092.

# Murfreesboro/ Rutherford County

## Rutherford County Schools
### 502 Memorial Blvd., Murfreesboro
• (615) 893-5812

The county school system in Rutherford, Tennessee's fastest-growing county, had a 1997-98 enrollment of 23,708. Seventy percent of the district's secondary schools are accredited by the Southern Association of Colleges and Schools, as are 76.5 percent of primary schools. The 1997-98 student population was 87.4 percent Caucasian, 9.2 percent African American, 1.9 percent Asian, 1.3 percent Hispanic and 0.2 percent American Indian.

The average composite ACT score in 1997-98 was 20.0, and average SAT score was 1,180. Average teacher salary was $34,862, and average expenditure per student $4,033.

## Murfreesboro City Schools
### 400 N. Maple St., Murfreesboro
• (615) 893-2313

The Murfreesboro City Schools system, with a 1997-98 enrollment of 5,553, has been designated an A+ system by the Tennessee Department of Education, and all 10 of its schools are accredited by the Southern Association of Colleges and Schools. The state's first Extended School Program was piloted here in 1986; now such programs are under way at all schools in the district. They operate year round, including snow days, teacher in-service days and summer vacation and are closed for only six major holidays.

Students can participate in various enrichment programs including music, art, foreign languages, computers, ballet, typing and Scouting or 4-H. All classrooms have a Macintosh computer and Internet access; the system has a ratio of one computer to every six students. There are 33 21st Century Classrooms, each of which contains a minimum of six computers, a camera, a laser-disc player, a CD-ROM player, a modem and the latest software. The per-pupil expenditure for 1997-98 was $4,551. The average teacher salary was $35,647.

Photo: Cathy Summerlin

Hume-Fogg Magnet School has one of Nashville's finest academic programs.

# Franklin/
# Williamson County

## Williamson County Schools
**1320 W. Main St., Franklin**
**• (615) 595-4700**

All 25 schools — 15 elementary, five middle and five high schools — in the Williamson County system are accredited by the Southern Association of Colleges and Schools. In 1992-93 the system, which enrolls 16,496, met performance standards required by the state for all school districts by the year 2000, and continues to meet them. Based on scores on college entrance exams, the system is among the top 20 percent of the nation's 16,665 school systems. The January 1996 issue of *Money* magazine ranked Williamson County Schools among the nation's top 100 systems. About 80 percent of the district's high school gradu-

ates pursue higher education. There are more than 40 21st Century Classrooms.

The average teacher salary in 1997-98 was $35,802. Per-pupil expenditure was $4,351. Average composite ACT score in 1997-98 was 21.8, and average SAT score was 1,137. Several schools offer before- and after-school child-care programs.

## Franklin Special School District
**507 New Hwy. 96, Franklin**
**• (615) 794-6624**

Franklin Special School District, with a 1997-98 enrollment of 3,780, consistently ranks in the top 10 percent in Tennessee based on academic achievement. It has received the Governor's A+ Award for Excellence each year since 1992. All six of its schools — four elementary (grades K through 4), one intermediate (grades 5 and 6) and one middle (grades 7 and 8) — are accredited by the Southern Association of Colleges and Schools. Two elementary schools (Liberty and Moore) are Tennessee Model schools for art instruction. Students at these schools move on to Williamson County high schools.

The district, started in 1906 as Franklin City Schools and run jointly by the Franklin Board of Mayor and Aldermen, was changed to "special" school district status in 1949 by a resolution of the Tennessee State Legislature. It is now governed by an elected six-member Board of Education and an appointed director of education. The average teacher salary in 1997-98 was $37,092; per-pupil expenditure was $5,522. The district's Teacher Center is home to a distance learning program that allows teachers to participate in live workshops by satellite.

All schools in the district offer special programs in music, art and physical education, and there are 36 21st Century Classrooms. The district was the first school system in Tennessee to implement the DARE (Drug Abuse Resistance Education) program. Franklin Special School District has its own morning and afternoon care program five days a week and in the summer for children enrolled in the system. This program, which runs from 6 AM to 6 PM from early June to mid-August, provides enrichment, tutoring and extracurricular activities such as swimming, bowling, movies, art, karate, dance classes, trips to area museums, fishing trips, movies and baseball games. There is a special-education preschool program for 3- and 4-year-olds at Franklin Elementary School.

# Gallatin/Sumner County

## Sumner County Schools
**225 E. Main St., Gallatin**
• **(615) 451-5200**

Sumner County is one of nine Tennessee communities receiving the governor's A+ Award for "Community Commitment to Excellence in Education." This award requires recognition of outstanding students and teachers, meeting needs of at-risk children, evidence of student academic achievement and community support for all aspects of the educational program. The 1997-98 enrollment was 21,926 in the system, which is made up of 18

elementary schools, nine middle schools, six high schools and one night school. Nearly 86 percent of the secondary schools and 48.1 percent of primaries are accredited by the Southern Association of Colleges and Schools.

The average teacher salary in 1997-98 was $33,018. Average per-pupil expenditure for 1997-98 was $4,159. The average composite ACT score in 1997-98 was 20.6, and the average SAT score was 1,148.

Volunteers are involved with reading programs, computer instruction, tutoring students and building playgrounds. The Sumner County system has nearly 100 21st Century Classrooms. The Adopt-a-School program involves the business and industrial community in educational programs. A magnet school program allows outstanding students to study selected subjects before and after school for special credit. A comprehensive drug education program uses DARE and Just Say No training and provides drug and alcohol counseling.

Adult education at 30 sites, open to those 18 and older who have been out of school at least six months, provides instruction in basic adult education, English as a Second Language and sign language. The district's night school program, started in 1991, was the first of its kind in Tennessee. It's used by currently enrolled students falling behind as well as by some adults returning for diplomas. Special-education programs are available for students with disabilities from ages 3 to 22. Four elementaries, two middle schools and one high school make up Gallatin City Schools, which are part of the county system.

# Lebanon/Wilson County

## Wilson County Schools
**501-B Park Ave., Lebanon**
• **(615) 444-3282**

The Wilson County Schools system prides itself for its ability to provide "a relatively low investment" ($3,900 per pupil in 1997-98) for quality education. (Some taxpayers prefer to spend less money on educational resources.) The system, which encompasses 10 elementary schools, on junior high, three high schools, one vocational school and one adult high school, had a 1997-98 enrollment of 11,545.

The schools are also proud of their technology program, which includes 21st Century Classrooms.

All elementaries provide extended care with an enrichment program for ages 4 through 13. There are also free adult education programs to improve basic skills. Average composite ACT score in 1997-98 was 19.1, and average SAT score was 1,136. The average teacher salary was $31,165.

## Lebanon City Schools
**701 Coles Ferry Pk., Lebanon**
**• (615) 449-6060**

Support teachers and staff at each of the system's five schools — three for grades 1 through 3, one for grades 4 through 6 and one for grades 7 and 8 — in the Lebanon city district include guidance counselors and physical education, computer and music teachers. There are 21st Century Classrooms and computer labs at each school, as well as after-school care and summer programs. Enrollment in 1997-98 was 2,856, and average per-pupil expenditure was $4,063. The average teacher salary was $32,585.

# Private Schools

## Nashville

### Akiva School
**3600 West End Ave. • (615) 383-3223**

Akiva, a coed Jewish day school serving 75 to 100 students in kindergarten through 6th grade, was set to move in fall 1999 to 801 Percy Warner Boulevard. The school, founded in 1954 by Rabbi Zalman Posner, is open to all children who have at least one Jewish parent, without regard to synagogue affiliation. It combines "excellent secular education with intense Jewish education." The student-teacher ratio is 11 to 1. Jewish studies include classical and conversational Hebrew, the Hebrew Bible in its original text, Jewish prayer, laws, traditions, holidays and history, along with Mishnah, Talmus and Jewish thought. "Akiva's history indicates that children of conservative and reform families do not become 'orthodox' as a result of attending Akiva; rather they become active, knowledgeable members of their family's temple or synagogue," reads a school brochure. "Akiva provides a strong atmosphere of Jewish values: love of learning, strong moral principles and pride in our heritage." School officials express pride that Akiva graduates have been accepted at Nashville's "finest, most demanding private and public secondary schools, such as Harpeth Hall, University School of Nashville and Montgomery Bell Academy in the private sector and Martin Luther King and Hume-Fogg Magnet high schools in the public sector."

### David Lipscomb Campus
**4517 Granny White Pk. • (615) 269-1783**

David Lipscomb Campus, part of Church of Christ-affiliated David Lipscomb University, serves children in pre-kindergarten through high school. Enrollment as of September 1998 was 1,556. The private school's mission is "to serve students so that [they] may master knowledge and skills appropriate to them and become Christ-like in attitude and behavior."

The school began in 1891 when Lipscomb and James A. Harding founded the Nashville Bible School, which later became David Lipscomb College and is now Lipscomb University. The original objective of the Nashville Bible School was to provide a well-rounded general education, offering instruction in a full range of academic subjects as well as the Bible. Students of all ages — many of the younger ones children of the college's professors — attended, helping establish a close relationship between the college and campus school. The school, which moved in 1903 to its present location, was renamed in 1918. Four years later, the Campus School was separated in identity from David Lipscomb College, but the Campus School and Lipscomb University continue to share a common organization and commitment to education founded on Biblical principles.

David Lipscomb Campus School offers a comprehensive and challenging academic curriculum designed to prepare students for college. Primary emphasis in all grades is on language skills, math, science, social studies and Bible, with supplemental instruction in art, music, foreign languages, computer skills and physical education. A full range of athletic and extracurricular activities begins with elementary class plays and continues in the middle school and high school with interscholastic and intramural athletics, drama, music, forensics, student publications, academic competitions and various civic and social clubs.

All members of the faculty and administration are Christians, and the curriculum for all grades includes daily Bible instruction and participation in regular chapel services. About 98 percent of all graduates from the Campus School enter colleges and universities. Each year's senior class has included at least one, and as many as five, National Merit Semi-Finalists. David Lipscomb Campus School is accredited by the Southern Association of Colleges and Schools.

## Davidson Academy
**1414 Old Hickory Blvd. • (615) 860-5300**

Davidson Academy, an interdenominational school for 3-year-olds through high school seniors, took its name from the first school west of the Cumberland Mountains. The original Davidson Academy was founded in 1785 in Madison; its namesake, which opened in the fall of 1980, had 1,070 students during the 1998-99 school year. The student-teacher ratio is 20 to 1. The school's mission statement reads: "Davidson Academy is dedicated to providing boys and girls opportunities for intellectual, spiritual, social and physical growth; to instilling and strengthening Christian values in an interdenominational setting; to preparing students for higher education, leadership and service; and to offering programs and services to meet the ever-changing needs of students and their families." Ninety-nine percent of Davidson Academy graduates go on to college.

## Ensworth School
**211 Ensworth Ave. • (615) 383-0661**

Ensworth, founded in 1958, serves boys and girls in grades K through 8. (School administrators prefer the term "pre-first" to "kindergarten" because, they say, the school's program exceeds what is commonly thought of as kindergarten.) The school's 1998-99 enrollment was 558. The average class size is 21, with a student-faculty ratio of 10 to 1. Ninety-eight percent of Ensworth students continue on to college. The curriculum includes English (personal journals are kept at many grade levels), social studies (a thematic, not chronological, approach), foreign language (French studies begin in pre-first grade), computers (two fully equipped computer labs), science (three lab facilities), music (regular instrumental and choral instruction), math (emphasis on problem-solving and logical thinking), art (biweekly art studio offerings), physi-

Photo: Cathy Summerlin

The George Peabody College of Vanderbilt University offers undergraduate and graduate studies.

cal education, outdoor education and life skills (personal responsibility, decision making, health and communication skills); students also have scheduled classes in and free time to use the 15,000-volume library. The school offers competitive sports for boys and girls and is a member of the Harpeth Valley Athletic Conference. Applicants should demonstrate average or above-average abilities on developmental and achievement tests. Priority is given to youngsters who are children or siblings of graduates or children of faculty members.

### Father Ryan High School
**700 Norwood Dr. • (615) 383-4200**

Father Ryan, the only co-educational Catholic secondary school in the Nashville area, is operated by the Catholic Diocese of Nashville and accredited by the Southern Association of Colleges and Schools. For more than 60 years, its mission has been "to develop within each student a sense of purpose, a love of God and one's fellow man, and a strong respect for life."

Faculty consists of two religious and 80 lay faculty; 59 percent of the teaching faculty hold a master's degree or higher. Enrollment for 1998-99 was 1,000 students from seven Middle Tennessee counties. Ninth-grade students are admitted from the parochial schools and other area schools. Placement is based on the results of placement tests, in December, plus academic record and 8th-grade teacher recommendations. The school requires 22¼ credits for graduation, including

one credit in religion for each year attended. Honors and advanced courses are offered at all grade levels in every major subject.

Extracurricular activities include drama, newspaper and yearbook journalism, band and student government. The National Honor Society and Mu Alpha Theta encourage academic achievement. Boys' varsity and freshman teams are offered in football, basketball and wrestling; other boys' teams include soccer, baseball, tennis, golf, swimming, track and cross-country. Girls' teams include volleyball, softball, basketball, tennis, soccer, golf, swimming, track and cross-country.

### Franklin Road Academy
**4700 Franklin Rd. • (615) 832-8845**

"A well-rounded education in a caring Christian environment" is the objective at Franklin Road Academy, founded in 1971. The school, which serves about 850 co-ed students in pre-kindergarten through 12th grade, says its "mission is to prepare students intellectually for higher levels of education while also providing programs and facilities for the physical, social, spiritual, cultural and emotional development of the 'whole child.'"

Pre-kindergarten, for 4- and 5-year-olds, stresses social and academic growth with programs "geared to the cultivation of thinking abilities, language development, reading and math readiness, and refinement of gross and fine motor skills." These youngsters receive an early introduction to computers, and computer science instruction starts in 1st grade. Enrichment classes at Franklin Road Acad-

## INSIDERS' TIP

In 1998, *Nashville Life* magazine retained an academic evaluation company called SchoolMatch to rank area schools based on a formula that rates pupil performance based on scholarship examinations. Among private schools, Montgomery Bell Academy and University School ranked highest with scores of 99 percent. BGA and Harpeth Hall were close behind at 98 percent; St. Cecilia was 97 percent; Franklin Road Academy, 95 percent; and Brentwood Academy and Father Ryan, 94 percent. Among public schools, Hume-Fogg topped the list at 99 percent, with Martin Luther King in second place at 97 percent. Brentwood High School was at 96 percent, followed by Hillsboro Comprehensive High School at 90 percent.

emy include computer science, library skills, physical education, music/band and art. To graduate, students must accumulate 24 units including Old and New Testament Survey, foreign language, fine or performing arts and physical education in addition to math, English, science and social studies. Many teachers hold master's degrees, and some have doctorates. There is a 14 to 1 student-teacher ratio. The school is accredited by the Southern Association of Colleges and Schools, and the preschool program is licensed by the state of Tennessee and accredited by Nashville Area Association for the Education of Young Children.

FRA fields teams in basketball, softball, football, baseball, soccer, tennis, cross-country, indoor track, track and field, riflery, cheerleading, golf, volleyball and wrestling. There's also an extended-hours program and a summer program.

## Harding Academy

**170 Windsor Dr. • (615) 356-5510**

Harding Academy, organized in 1971 as a nonprofit, independent, non-sectarian, coeducational elementary day school, is for children in grades K through 8. It stresses "emotional as well as academic support," with a child-centered curriculum adaptable to the child's level of readiness. The school places strong emphasis on language arts (beginning with kindergarten creative writing programs) and a strong foundation of mastery of skills at each level. The academy also has a challenging middle school program that helps students prepare for high school.

Classes in art, music and computer skills are taught in all grades, and students have physical education in grades 1 through 8. Reading enrichment programs, with small groups of six to eight students, are offered from kindergarten through 4th grade. Sometimes 5th-grade "buddies" read aloud to their kindergarten "pals." Special events such as "favorite book character day" raise the awareness of the importance of books and reading in a fun-filled way. Enrollment was 410 in 1998-98; average class size is 20.

## Harpeth Hall School

**3801 Hobbs Rd. • (615) 297-9543**

Harpeth Hall, Nashville's only independent, college preparatory school for girls, claims a 100 percent rate of graduates matriculating to four-year colleges and universities since its founding in 1951. Singer Amy Grant is a graduate of the prestigious day school, which serves grades 5 through 12, and she returned to her alma mater to be honored as 1996 Distinguished Alumna. Average SAT scores are 200 points higher than the national average, and nine of every 10 girls who take Advanced Placement exams earn college credit, many at the nation's most prestigious institutions.

The school, which has seven academic buildings on a 35-acre campus, had a 1998-99 enrollment of about 535 and a student-teacher ratio of 9 to 1. The school's library contains 21,000 volumes and 366 periodicals. Harpeth Hall, a leader in the integration of technology into a traditional curriculum, also has excellent athletic and arts programs and provides a number of opportunities for service learning. Admission is competitive, based on previous school records, personal qualifications and entrance examinations.

## Montgomery Bell Academy

**4001 Harding Rd. • (615) 298-5514**

Montgomery Bell Academy, a boys-only day school, was founded in 1867 as a separate department within the University of Nashville by a bequest from Montgomery Bell, an iron foundry magnate in Middle Tennessee. The school, originally created to provide for "deserving and needy" students, claims an illustrious legacy and enrolls many of Nashville's finest sons. Its traditionally stated goal is "challenging each young man" to attain his highest level of accomplishment as "gentleman, scholar and athlete."

**INSIDERS' TIP**

**Oprah Winfrey went to high school and college in Nashville, and her dad operates a barber shop here.**

The school, which serves grades 7 through 12, has been at its present 35-acre campus since 1915. Enrollment for the 1998-99 school year was 610, with an average class size of 13 and a student-teacher ratio of 8-to-1. Six percent of students represent minorities, and 15 percent of students receive financial aid. Eighty-three percent of the teaching faculty have master's degrees or higher. Montgomery Bell requires 19 academic credits for graduation. Honors sections are available in most courses, and 16 Advanced Placement courses are offered. Standardized-test results for the middle 50 percent of the class of 1996 were: SAT verbal, 570 to 690; SAT math, 560 to 650. From 1992 to 1996, 26 percent of Montgomery Bell graduates received National Merit Scholarship recognition.

Eighty computers are available for student use. The school's debate program is ranked as one of the top 10 in the country. Athletically, the school fields 32 competitive teams in 11 sports; since 1991, these teams have won six state championships and 38 regional championships. Community service projects include Soup Kitchen, Boys and Girls Club tutoring, YMCA coaching and tutoring and Habitat for Humanity. An Independent School Entrance Exam and application are required for admission. While applications are accepted at any time, students are encouraged to apply one year in advance of anticipated entry.

## Oak Hill School
**4815 Franklin Rd. • (615) 297-6544**

Oak Hill School is an independent elementary school serving kindergarten through grade 6. The "lower school" consists of kindergarten through 3rd grade and the "upper school" of grades 4 through 6. Founded in 1961 as an outreach of First Presbyterian Church, Oak Hill provides "a rich and comprehensive curriculum for qualified students within a nurturing Christian environment." The curriculum emphasizes critical thinking and active problem solving in collaboration with others.

In partnership with students' families, the school also seeks "to recognize, celebrate and develop each student's unique talents and gifts, to foster a love of learning with emphasis on academic excellence; and to prepare students to be persons of integrity with the skills necessary to meet future challenges."

Facilities at the school, which sits on a 55-acre wooded campus, include a 12,000-volume online library/media center, fully equipped playgrounds, sports playing fields, a gymnasium, cafeteria, music center, art room, fully equipped science lab, stage, staffed clinic, monitored Internet access, fully equipped computer lab and computers in every classroom. Enrollment in 1998-99 was 405, with an average class size of 19.

## Overbrook School
**4210 Harding Rd. • (615) 292-5134**

Overbrook, a private, Catholic coeducational school for 3-year-olds through 8th graders, was founded in 1936 and is owned and administered by the Dominican Sisters of the Congregation of St. Cecilia. The school shares its 92-acre Dominican campus in West Nashville with St. Cecilia Academy and Aquinas Junior College. A faculty of religious and lay teachers is dedicated to "high academic standards, belief in the dignity of each child and a Christ-centered approach to education." The curriculum includes daily religious instruction. 1998-99 enrollment was 360, with an average class size of 16.

## St. Cecilia Academy
**4210 Harding Rd. • (615) 298-4525**

St. Cecilia Academy is a private Catholic college preparatory school for girls in grades 9 through 12. It shares a campus with Overbrook School and Aquinas Junior College and, like those institutions, is owned and administered by the Dominican Sisters. The school seeks to enable each student to grow "in her life of faith" and encourages academic excellence (the 1994-95 senior class of 45 students included three National Merit Scholarship Finalists), creativity and the development of leadership qualities within each student. An extensive physical education program and various coeducational activities promote physical and social well being. The interim program suspends regular classes for two weeks each year and offers travel opportunities to study fine arts in New York, marine biology in Florida, democracy in Washington, Mayan ruins in

Mexico or world history in Europe. Enrollment in 1998-99 was 200, with an average class size of 12.

## University School of Nashville
### 2000 Edgehill Ave. • (615) 327-8158

University School of Nashville, which serves grades K through 12, traces its heritage back to the Winthrop Model School established in 1892 by the Peabody Board of Trustees (Peabody College for Teachers is now part of Vanderbilt University). Winthrop, the first model school in the South specifically designed to demonstrate proper teaching methods and traditions, also was the first private school in the South to integrate its student body. In 1915 the school moved to the campus of George Peabody College for Teachers and became the Peabody Demonstration School. In 1974 it became a nonprofit independent institution dedicated to the school's historic legacy. That legacy continues in the school's philosophy, which holds academic excellence as its central value but also encourages pursuit of artistic values (including the appreciation of others' artistic expressions and the development of one's own creativity).

University School consciously draws students from diverse racial, religious and cultural backgrounds and encourages them to appreciate differences while learning about aspirations and values they hold in common. The lower school (grades K through 4) features grade-level teams. Specialists in art, music, Spanish, library and physical education enrich the curriculum, and noncompetitive athletics are also offered. At the middle school level (grades 5 through 8), learning begins to separate into subjects, with continued enrichment courses and physical education. These children also benefit from extracurricular mini-courses, outdoor experiential activities and excursions to historic sites and cultural events, as well as both intramural and competitive team sports.

College preparation is essential at the high school level, where a minimum of 23 credits is required for graduation. At the same time, "a vital part of the school's mission is to produce people of personal integrity who recognize they are part of a global community." Ongoing service projects include sponsorship of a local soup kitchen. Students also take a range of studio and art history classes and enjoy performing arts such as band, chorus, drama, select choir and jazz band. Competitive sports include junior varsity and varsity teams.

The school had a 1998-99 enrollment of 990, with an average class size of 15. New students are admitted at all grade levels with preference to qualified siblings of enrolled students and children of faculty members. In an after-school program for grades K through 8, "students set their own pace and choose their own fun . . . under supervision of an attentive staff." University School also is host to evening classes for the Nashville adult community, an annual program that one resident described as "wonderful." Benefits from this program's tuition, which ranges from $15 to $40, go toward the University School Scholarship Fund. Topics range from archaeology to dog training, computers to travel and massage to financial planning. Phone (615) 321-8019 for information about the school's evening classes.

# Franklin

## Battle Ground Academy
### • (615) 794-3501

Battle Ground Academy, a college preparatory day school serving pre-kindergarten through 12th grade, has a student body of about 900. The school, chartered in 1889, has a long and rich heritage steeped in tradition. It operates three divisions: Lower School (pre-kindergarten through grade 4) on the Harpeth Campus, 150 Franklin Road; Middle School (grades 5-8) on the South Campus, 1314 Columbia Avenue; and Upper School (grades 9-12) on the North Campus, 336 Ernest Rice

Lane. All three campuses are in close proximity to one another in Franklin.

Throughout its long history, BGA, which merged with Harpeth Academy at the start of the 1998-99 school year, has fostered the moral growth of students by ethical example and through the expectation of responsibility, integrity and respect for the worth of each individual. The school's mailing address is P.O. Box 1889, Franklin TN 37065.

# Brentwood

## Brentwood Academy
**219 Granny White Pk., Brentwood**
**• (615) 373-0611**

Brentwood Academy, founded in 1969, is a co-educational, independent, college preparatory day school "dedicated to nurturing and challenging the whole person — body, mind and spirit — to the glory of God." Students of average and above-average ability are admitted to the school on the basis of previous school record, standardized test scores, recommendations and an interview. About 575 students were enrolled in grades 6 through 12 for the 1998-99 school year. Minorities represent 4 percent of the student population, and the school seeks to enroll students from all socio-economic and ethnic backgrounds.

Typically, all members of each graduating class enroll in college. All but three members of the class of 1997 chose to enroll at a four-year college or university. BA has 65 staff and faculty members, three-quarters of whom have master's degrees. The student-teacher ratio is 15 to 1. Students must amass 22 high school credits — including English, math, science, history, foreign language, fine arts, religion, speech, keyboarding, physical education and one year of Bible study — to graduate. Honors and advanced placement classes are available, as are enrichment courses in both vocal and instrumental music.

Although Brentwood Academy offers students a number of opportunities for spiritual growth and renewal, it does not attempt to force any specific religious beliefs upon a student. Each day begins with a five-minute devotional, usually led by a student. Many students also meet during the week on a class-by-class basis for informal Bible study and sharing. A typical course load is made up of five classes and two study halls. Comprehensive exams administered at the end of each semester count for 20 percent to 33 percent of the semester average, depending upon the discipline.

All students are required to participate in some form of after-school athletics at the varsity or intramural level. The school fields 34 teams in 11 different sports including football, boys' and girls' basketball, volleyball, boys' and girls' cross country, boys' and girls' track, boys' and girls' golf, wrestling, baseball, softball, boys' and girls' tennis and junior high soccer. For those students who elect not to participate in interscholastic athletics, BA offers classes in aerobics, racquetball, weight training and other seasonal recreational activities. The football team has won seven state championships and finished as state runner-up six times. The boys' track team has won 10 state championships, and the girls' track team has been state team champion, state runner-up and region champion. The softball team has won back-to-back state championships, the boys' cross-country team holds three state championships, and the girls' team has won twice. The girls' tennis team has won a state championship, and individual state championships have been won in boys' tennis, girls' tennis, boys' cross country, wrestling and boys' golf.

Because the school has no janitors, the academic day ends at 2:45 PM so that all students may assist in a campus-wide cleanup.

All students are required to take the ACT and SAT. The class of 1997 had one National Merit Finalist, six National Merit Commended Students, one Advanced Placement Scholar with Distinction, three AP Scholars with Honor and one AP Scholar. Brentwood Academy is accredited by the Southern Association of Colleges and Schools.

## Montessori Academy
**6021 Cloverland Dr., Brentwood**
**• (615) 833-3610**

Montessori Academy, which serves students in pre-kindergarten through 8th grade, is situated on 24 acres of wooded, rolling ter-

Vanderbilt University was ranked among the top 20 universities in the nation in a 1996-1997 survey by *U.S. News and World Report*.

rain. The stated philosophy for teachers is to "seek to empower every continuing student to become independent, self-directed, self-disciplined" children who are "self-accepting, joyful in learning and responsible as a group member." The school, established in 1983, had a 1998-99 enrollment of 310. Extracurricular activities include Suzuki violin and piano, tumbling, rhythm class, Montessori Singers and a nationally recognized chess club. Montessori Academy also offers before- and after-school care.

## Madison

### B.C. Goodpasture Christian School
**619 Due West Ave., Madison**
**• (615) 868-6171**
B.C. Goodpasture, a college preparatory

school founded in 1966, offers instruction for 3-year-olds through 12th grade. More than 99 percent of Goodpasture graduates enter college, and the 1996-97 senior class received more than $1 million in scholarships. The school, which has a Church of Christ affiliation, has an academic curriculum that includes daily Bible classes. Enrollment in 1998-99 was 1,200, with an average class size of 17.

## Murfreesboro

### Middle Tennessee Christian School
**100 E. MTCS Dr., Murfreesboro**
**• (615) 893-0601**
Middle Tennessee Christian School serves pre-kindergarten through 12th grade on its 25-acre campus. The school, founded in 1960 and affiliated with the Church of Christ, had a

1998-99 enrollment of 600, with an average class size of 20. Enrichment classes are offered in music, art, computer and band along with daily Bible classes. Extended care is available from 3:30 to 5:30 PM daily, and there are non-structured summer programs. The school also has boys' and girls' basketball, soccer, tennis and cross country; boys' baseball and golf; and girls' softball and volleyball.

# Gallatin

## College Heights Christian Academy
**2100 Nashville Pk., Gallatin**
**• (615) 452-4988**

College Heights Christian Academy, established in 1986 as a ministry of College Heights Baptist Church, serves 4-year-olds through 12th graders. It stresses "academic excellence with a Christian distinction," and its mission is "to lead each student to a voluntary commitment of his life to the Lordship of Christ . . . to provide academic excellence . . . to equip each student spiritually, mentally, socially and physically . . . to mature morally bound leaders who will boldly impact their world . . . and to support the Christian family and the local Bible-believing churches."

The school is accredited by the Association of Christian Schools International and the Southern Baptist Association of Christian Schools, and is approved the by state of Tennessee. Graduation requires 24 high school credits in classes including English, math, science, history, wellness, computer, Bible, speech and fine arts. Bible instruction is part of the regular curriculum, and chapel services are held weekly. Academic courses are taught "from a Christian perspective."

Athletic programs include volleyball, basketball, baseball, softball and cheerleading and soccer. Extended care is available.

# Hendersonville

## Hendersonville Christian Academy
**355 Old Shackle Island Rd.,**
**Hendersonville • (615) 824-1550**

Hendersonville Christian Academy serves 3-year-olds through 11th graders (it's adding 10th and 11th grades in fall 1999). The 1998-

99 enrollment was 185 students. The school, a ministry of Bible Baptist Church, has 24 full-time faculty and staff members. Its mission statement reads: "Our goal is to assist the home and church in teaching children the Word of God and the skills necessary to live a productive Christian life."

Students participate in an annual Association of Christian Schools competition in areas of vocal ensemble, charcoal drawing, watercolor, woodworking, science, math, photography, sculpture, poster and crafts. The school also has a basketball team. Before- and after-school care is available.

# Lebanon

## Friendship Christian School
**5400 Coles Ferry Pk., Lebanon**
**• (615) 449-1573**

Friendship Christian School, founded in 1973, puts a strong emphasis on academics and college preparation, with one in every three graduating seniors receiving scholarships to colleges and universities. The school, which runs from pre-kindergarten through high school, had a 1998-99 enrollment of 535 and a student-teacher ratio of 15 to 1. Boys and girls athletics are available, as is an extended after-school child-care program until 5:30 PM each day for kids in pre-kindergarten through grade 6.

# Special-needs Schools

## Tennessee School for the Blind
**115 Stewarts Ferry Pk. • (615) 231-7300**

Tennessee School for the Blind, founded in 1844, serves students ages 3 to 21 with multiple disabilities through three different curricula. In addition to the academic curriculum, in which students pursue a regular high school diploma, there are semi-academic and non-academic programs. The school's 1998-99 enrollment was 169, with a student-teacher ratio of 4 to 1. Students from across the state attend Tennessee School for the Blind, which is a resident school from Sunday through Friday. Buses take everyone home Friday, then bring them back Sunday evening. Students are home for the summer, two weeks at Christmas and a week during Easter break. The school is fully state-funded, so there is no cost to students or their families. A student must be legally blind and a resident of Tennessee to attend.

## Westminster School
**111 N. Wilson Blvd. • (615) 269-0020**

Founded in 1968 by concerned parents and Westminster Presbyterian Church, Westminster was Nashville's first independent day-school program for students with learning disabilities and is now the state's largest such school serving grades K through 8. The school, which started with six students and one teacher, had a 1998-99 enrollment of about 165 students from eight counties.

Westminster touts "a personalized approach to education which is sensitive to the varying learning styles of the children it serves," with an educational philosophy centered on the concept of diversity. It acts on the basic premises that individuals learn differently and that the school's role is to help students, by understanding their differences, reach their full potential. While the school continues to be a ministry of Westminster Presbyterian Church, the curriculum does not include any religious or denominational training.

In 1991, Westminster was named one of the nation's Blue Ribbon Schools by President George Bush. In 1990, the school was recognized as a School of Excellence by the U.S. Department of Education. In 1994, Cherrie Farnette, a 4th-grade teacher, was named Tennessee Teacher of the Year by the state's Council for Learning Disabilities and was honored at an international learning disabilities conference. Westminster was recently accepted into the National Association of Independent Schools and is accredited by the Southern Association of Colleges and Schools.

## Bill Wilkerson Center
**1114 19th Ave. S. • (615) 936-5000**

Bill Wilkerson Center is a regional facility for diagnosis and treatment of communication and related disorders for people of all ages. It's also one of the largest dispensaries of hearing aids in the Southeast. Educational offerings include an Early Intervention Program for children from birth to age 4 with hearing loss or speech and language problems. Other services include individual therapy and preschool classes for children, parent support groups, sign language instruction and afternoon child care. The center also offers a summer program for teens with hearing impairment.

## Benton Hall
**2420 Bethlehem Loop Rd., Franklin**
**• (615) 791-6467**

John McLaughlin saw a need for a "private high school which focused upon intelligent students, who for a variety of reasons, have not performed to the best of their abilities in public or private schools." So in 1977 he established Benton Hall. In 1991 the program expanded to include grades K through 8. Benton Hall's philosophy is "to prepare each student academically, socially, behaviorally and emotionally, through individualized instruction, to work to his or her potential and to make a successful transition into the workplace or into a higher learning experience."

Students may have learning disabilities, experience difficulties in a regular school setting or be high-ability learners. At present the high-ability program is for students in kindergarten through 12th grade. Enrollment in 1998-99 was about 200. Benton Hall offers testing services — including perceptual and motor, psycho-educational, speech and language and Attention Deficit Disorder — to its students as well as students from other schools. Intellectual and academic testing results and school records are required for admission. The school provides a wide range of athletic activities including team sports for grades 6 through 12. Before-school care is available from 7 to 8 AM ; after-school care is offered until 5:45 PM .

# Colleges and Universities

## Nashville/Davidson County

### Aquinas Junior College
**4210 Harding Rd. • (615) 297-7545**

Aquinas Junior College is part of the Dominican Campus that includes Overbrook and St. Cecilia schools (see previous listings under "Private Schools"). As a Catholic institution of higher learning, it strives to "provide an atmosphere of learning permeated with faith, directed to the intellectual, moral and professional formation of the student." Degree programs include a liberal arts program for an associate degree, a weekend associate program, a bachelor's degree in teacher elementary education and a B.S.N. in nursing that is a completion program for graduates of a diploma or associate degree nursing program.

## Belmont University
**1900 Belmont Blvd. • (615) 383-7001**

Belmont University is on grounds known as Adelicia Acklen's Belle Monte Estate, hence the name. The first Belmont College was established here in 1890. It joined the Ward School and became Ward-Belmont College for Women in 1931. In 1951 the Tennessee Baptist Convention founded the second Belmont College, which became a university in 1991. The college does not receive direct assistance from the state or federal government and remains affiliated with the Tennessee Baptist Convention. It is accredited by the Southern Association of Colleges and Schools.

Six schools — Business, Humanities/Education, Music, Nursing, Religion and Sciences — offer undergraduate degrees in 53 major areas of study with 34 minors, and there are master's degrees in business administration, accounting, education, music education, nursing and occupational therapy. The school of business has a unique NAFTA trade internship coordinated with U.S. Commercial Services offices in Nashville and Guadalajara, Mexico.

The nationally recognized Mike Curb Music Business Program enrolls the largest number of majors, with about 600 students. The School of Nursing offers a bachelor's degree. Belmont's annual enrollment is about 2,300. The student-faculty ratio is 11 to 1. Belmont now offers 15 men's and women's sports, and the athletic program had its first-year provisional membership in the NCAA in 1996-97.

## Draughons Junior College
**340 Plus Park Pavilion Blvd.**
**• (615) 361-7555**

Draughons has a total enrollment of about 500 students at its Nashville campus and branches in Bowling Green, Kentucky, and Clarksville, Tennessee. It is accredited by the Association of Independent Colleges and Schools as a junior college of business. The college offers 60-hour associate degree of science programs in accounting, business management, health information management, legal assisting, medical assisting, office administration, radio broadcasting and retail management. It also offers diploma programs of 30 to 36 hours in bookkeeping, computer information processing, health information management, office administration and radio broadcasting.

## Fisk University
**1000 17th Ave. N. • (615) 329-8500**

If your alumni included writer and activist W.E.B. DuBois, historian and author John Hope Franklin and U.S. Energy Secretary Hazel O'Leary, you'd probably feel like singing. Fisk can claim not only those three luminaries but also many more, as well as one out of every six of the nation's black doctors, dentists and lawyers.

And sing it does. Chances are you've heard, or at least heard of, the Fisk Jubilee Singers, who for more than 125 years have been keeping alive the beauty of the traditional spiritual. They're still going strong, and so is this school founded in 1866. Then known as Fisk School, it was named in honor of Gen. Clinton B. Fisk of the Tennessee Freedman's Bureau. In 1867 it was incorporated as Fisk University, with the goal of "providing students with an education that meets the highest standards, not of Negro education, but of American education at its best." Need proof that those standards are still being met? In 1995 *Money Guide* ranked Fisk second overall among all historically black colleges and universities in the United States, fourth among all small liberal arts schools in the country, sixth among colleges and universities in the Southeast and 18th among all colleges and universities nationally.

The now–world-famous singers, who came along in 1871, were originally a group of traveling students who set out from Nashville to raise money for their school. They took the name Jubilee Singers after the "Old Testament's Year of Jubilee marking the deliverance of the Jews who, like all but two of themselves, had been in bondage." (Remember, this was just years after the end of the Civil War.) After a troubled beginning, the singers were endorsed by Henry Ward Beecher and would eventually give command performances for President Grant and the crowned heads of Europe before returning to Nashville with enough money to build Jubilee Hall.

Music isn't the only art that's alive at Fisk. The Carl Van Vechten Art Gallery includes the Alfred Stieglitz Collection of Modern Art and one of the nation's premier collections of African-American art. Current enrollment at the private, coeducational university is about 1,000 undergraduate students, with a student-faculty ratio of 14 to 1. Athletically, the school competes in the NCAA's Division III and the College Athletic Conference.

### Free Will Baptist Bible College
**3606 West End Ave. • (615) 383-1340**

This school, owned and operated by the National Association of Free Will Baptists, was founded in 1942. Its enrollment is about 350. Its mission is to train "Christians for service to Christ and the Church." Free Will Baptist Bible College offers B.A. and B.S. degrees in pastoral training, youth ministry, music, missions, education, business, psychology and sports medicine. It is accredited by the Southern Association of Colleges and Schools and by the Accrediting Association of Bible Colleges.

### John A. Gupton Junior College
**1616 Church St. • (615) 327-3927**

John A. Gupton Junior College, founded in 1948, offers an associate of arts degree in funeral service with a general education component and a professional component in funeral service arts and sciences. It is accredited by the Southern Association of Colleges and Schools.

### David Lipscomb University
**3901 Granny White Pk. • (615) 269-1000**

"The Bible is still at the heart of what is now a greatly expanded liberal arts and professional curriculum." So say the folks at David Lipscomb University, which has grown in size and scope since its 1891 founding as Nashville Bible School. The coeducational university, which now has a 65-acre campus, six residence halls and more than 2,500 graduate and undergraduate students, was renamed in 1917 to honor David Lipscomb, an influential leader in the American Restoration Movement among the Churches of Christ. The school requires regular Bible classes of all students and assists students "in enhancement or selection of a vocation and by equipping students for honorable professions." It employs teachers "who are firmly committed to the worldview and lifestyle of Biblical Christianity."

### Meharry Medical College
**1005 D.B. Todd Blvd. • (615) 327-6111**

When the Freedman's Aid Society of the Methodist Episcopal Church founded the Meharry Medical Department of Central Tennessee College in October 1876, its dream was to educate freed slaves and provide healthcare services to the poor and underserved. Today, their dream is known as Meharry Medical College, the largest private, historically black institution solely dedicated to educating healthcare professionals and scientists in the United States. About 900 students and residents are enrolled in the college's four schools: Medicine, Dentistry, School of Graduate Studies, and Research and Allied Health Professions (a joint program with Tennessee State University). It has graduated nearly 15 percent of all African-American physicians and dentists practicing in the United States.

At this writing, Meharry and Vanderbilt were working on an alliance that would benefit both institutions. Still, Meharry's goal hasn't changed much, as it focuses on "providing promising African-American and other underrepresented ethnic minority students" an "ex-

---

**INSIDERS' TIP**

**Alex Haley Jr., author of *Roots*, was from Henning, in West Tennessee.**

cellent education in the health sciences." The school's mission statement includes a special emphasis on clinical and applied research on diseases that disproportionately affect ethnic minority populations.

## Nashville Auto Diesel College
**1524 Gallatin Rd. • (615) 226-3990**

Established in 1919, Nashville Auto Diesel College is one of the oldest schools of its type in the country. Its more than 1,000 students attend 11-month courses of study leading to associate degrees in applied science, auto diesel technology and auto body technology.

## Nashville School of Law
**2934 Sidco Dr. • (615) 256-3684**

Nashville School of Law was born in 1911 as night law classes at the YMCA for those unable to attend law classes during the day; it has been in operation ever since. It was incorporated in 1927 and authorized by the state to confer the degree of Doctor of Jurisprudence. The school leased space from the downtown YMCA until 1986. Admission is competitive and requires an official transcript showing a bachelor's degree from an accredited college or university, three recommending letters with at least one from a member of the legal community and the LSAT (Law School Admission Test). Unlike most law schools, it welcomes students who are employed full-time.

## Nashville State Technical Institute
**120 White Bridge Rd. • (615) 353-3333**

Nashville State Technical Institute offers two-year associate's degree programs in architectural engineering technology; automation robotics technology; automotive services technology; business management; civil and construction engineering technology; communications technology; computer accounting technology; computer information systems; electrical, industrial and mechanical engineering technologies; occupational therapy assistant technology; office administration; police science technology; and visual communications. One-year technical certificate programs are available in electrical maintenance, photography and surgical technology. Total annual enrollment is around 7,000.

## Tennessee State University
**3500 John Merritt Blvd. • (615) 963-5000**

Tennessee State was founded in 1912 as the Tennessee Agricultural and Industrial State Normal School. In 1922 it became a teachers college capable of granting the bachelor's degree. In 1951 it was granted university status. Today the school, with an enrollment of more than 8,000, offers 43 bachelor's degrees, 24 master's degrees and five doctorates. Programs are offered in agriculture, allied health, arts and sciences, business (TSU is one of fewer than 25 percent of colleges and universities to receive accreditation from the American Assembly of Collegiate Schools of Business), education, engineering and technology, home economics, human services, nursing (bachelor's and master's programs) and public administration. More than three-quarters of TSU faculty hold doctorates or terminal degrees in their fields.

A $6.5 million grant from NASA helped establish a Center for Automated Space Science, which now operates more automated telescopes at one site than any other institution in the world. TSU has two centers of excellence: the Center of Excellence for Research and Policy Basic Skills and the Center of Excellence for Information Systems Engineering and Management. It is also one of a few historically black colleges and universities to offer a bachelor's degree in African studies. TSU operates the Nashville Business Incubation Center, dedicated to the successful start-up of

---

**INSIDERS' TIP**

**Three U.S. presidents have come from Tennessee: Andrew Jackson, James Polk and Andrew Johnson. At press time for this book, Vice President Al Gore was campaigning to be the fourth, and Tennessean Lamar Alexander had just ended his race for the Republican nomination.**

small businesses. Fledgling businesses supported by the center have achieved a 90 percent success rate.

The university competes athletically in the Ohio Valley Conference. The men's basketball team won the OVC title in 1993 and 1994, and the women's basketball team won the conference in 1994 and 1995. More than 100 TSU football players have been drafted into the National Football League. Since 1952, track athletes from TSU have won 29 Olympic medals. Of the 40 famed Tigerbelles (members of TSU's women's track team) who have competed in the Olympics, 39 graduated from college with one or more degrees. The most famous Tigerbelle was the beloved Wilma Rudolph, who won three gold medals at the 1960 summer Olympics in Rome.

## Trevecca Nazarene University
### 333 Murfreesboro Rd. • (615) 248-1200

Trevecca Nazarene was founded in 1901 by the Rev. J.O. McClurkan, a Cumberland Presbyterian minister, to train Christian teachers and ministers to serve in America and foreign countries. It became a four-year college in 1910 and was officially adopted by the Church of the Nazarene in 1917. The school became a junior college in 1932 and was rechartered as Trevecca Nazarene College in 1935 after moving to its present location. In 1969 it earned accreditation from the Southern Association of Colleges and Schools and has kept it ever since. Other milestones include the creation of Tennessee's first physician assistant program in 1978, the addition of graduate degrees in 1984 with a Master of Education program, and achievement of university status in 1995.

Today, Trevecca graduates pursue careers in education, business administration, religion and as physician assistants. Degrees include Bachelor of Arts (communication studies, Christian education), Bachelor of Business Administration (computer information systems, music business), Bachelor of Science (education, sport and exercise science, physics, broadcast technology) and Bachelor of Social Work. In addition, pre-professional programs are offered in dentistry, engineering, law, medicine, pharmacy, physical therapy and veterinary science. Master's degrees are available

in arts, education, marriage and family therapy and science (physician assistant). More than 1,500 students are enrolled at Trevecca, which has a 75-acre campus with 20 major buildings. There are 55 full-time faculty members, 40 of whom have doctorates. The student-faculty ratio is 14 to 1.

## Vanderbilt University
### West End Ave. • (615) 322-7311

Commodore Cornelius Vanderbilt (yes, *that* Vanderbilt) founded this school in 1873 with a $1 million endowment. We'd have to call it money well spent. Today Vanderbilt University is consistently ranked among the nation's best institutions of higher learning. A 1996-97 survey by *U.S. News & World Report* ranked Vanderbilt 20th overall among national universities, 10th among education schools, 14th among medical schools, 27th among business schools and 16th among law schools. The school is the largest private employer in Middle Tennessee and the second largest private employer in the state.

Vandy, as the school is informally known, consists of 10 schools in 223 buildings situated on a beautiful, tree-filled, 308-acre campus that was designated a national arboretum in 1988. Highlights of the school include the W.M. Keck Free-Electron Laser Center, which conducts experiments using the most powerful free-electron laser in the world; a public policy institute, or interdisciplinary think tank, that focuses on such issues as healthcare, education, social services, environment, mental health and economic development; and the Freedom Forum First Amendment Center, a forum for discussion and debate of free expression and freedom-of-information issues.

The university's annual enrollment is nearly 6,000 undergraduates and nearly 4,500 graduate and professional students. The ratio of undergraduate students to faculty is 8 to 1, and 97 percent of faculty have terminal degrees. Vanderbilt's 10 schools are the College of Arts and Science, Blair School of Music, Divinity School, School of Engineering, Graduate School (offering degrees in Master of Arts, Master of Science, Arts in Teaching and Liberal Arts, Doctor of Philosophy and Nursing Science), School of Law, School of Medicine, School of Nursing, Owen Graduate School of

Management and Peabody College. (Incidentally, Peabody College is where Susan Gray, an educational researcher, in 1963 introduced a program for disadvantaged preschoolers that became the prototype for Head Start. Although Peabody College was independent at that time, it joined Vanderbilt in 1979 and remains a top teacher-training center.) The Owen Graduate School of Management offers an executive MBA program on weekends. Students can also earn a master's of liberal sciences with one or more courses a semester in the evening or with weekend classes.

Athletically, Vandy is a member of the highly competitive Southeastern Conference for most men's and women's varsity sports. Men's sports include football, basketball, baseball, soccer, tennis, golf and cross country. Women's sports include a nationally ranked basketball team, soccer, tennis, golf, cross country, indoor track, outdoor track and lacrosse. The appropriately named Commodores ("Corneliuses" just didn't have the same ring) play their basketball games in 15,000-seat Memorial Gym and their football games in 41,000-seat Vanderbilt Stadium.

# Other Metro Area Colleges and Universities

## Austin Peay State University
**601 College St., Clarksville**
• **(615) 648-7011**

This university was founded in 1927 as Austin Peay Normal School, in honor of Tennessee Gov. Austin Peay of Clarksville. The school offers more than 50 majors at associate, bachelor's, master's and education specialist levels in four colleges — Arts and Sciences, Business, Education and Graduate — and professional programs including the School of Nursing. Austin Peay, with a main campus of 51 buildings on 200 acres, has two Centers of Excellence (in field biology and creative arts) and a library that houses 304,014 print volumes.

The school's athletic teams compete in the Ohio Valley Conference. Its men's and women's basketball and men's baseball teams

all captured OVC titles in 1996. Enrollment is about 8,000. Ninety percent of faculty have a doctorate or other appropriate terminal degree for their field.

## Cumberland University
**S. Greenwood St., Lebanon**
• **(615) 444-2562, (800) 467-0562**

Cumberland University was founded in 1842 under "Presbyterian auspices." In 1847 the university added the first law school in Tennessee, and by 1857 it was the largest in the South. Cumberland's evolution included a stint as a law school only (under the control of the Tennessee Baptist Convention from 1951 to 1956), after which the assets of the law school were transferred to Samford University in Birmingham, Alabama. Cumberland offered a two-year junior college program from 1956 to 1982 and returned to its status as a four-year, degree-granting institution in 1982.

The university is a private coed liberal arts institution with undergraduate divisions in sciences and social sciences, business administration and economics, education, nursing, physical education and special education. Graduate degrees are offered in business administration, education, human relations management and public service management. Graduates have included 13 governors, 10 U.S. senators, more than 80 members of the House of Representatives, two Justices of the U.S. Supreme Court and more than 50 college and university presidents. Cordell Hull, former U.S. Secretary of State and Nobel Peace Prize winner, also is a graduate.

Cumberland University offers an off-campus degree program for working adults and an on-campus accelerated evening program. Enrollment is about 1,000. Student-faculty ratio is 12 to 1. Athletic teams include men's baseball, basketball, cross country, football, golf, soccer and tennis, and women's basketball, cross country, golf, soccer, tennis and volleyball.

## Middle Tennessee State University
**1301 E. Main St., Murfreesboro**
• **(615) 898-2300**

Middle Tennessee, the state's third-largest public university, has an enrollment of

18,000. It was founded in 1911 and now offers more than 140 undergraduate degrees in its five colleges: Basic and Applied Sciences, Business, Education, Liberal Arts and Mass Communication. There are more than 55 graduate programs including doctoral degrees in physical education, English, chemistry and economics. The Center for Historic Preservation and the Center for Popular Music are Centers of Excellence established by the Tennessee General Assembly.

The university ranks No. 1 among all Tennessee colleges and universities chosen by valedictorians and salutatorians from the region. Minimum entrance requirements are a 2.8 grade-point average in high school and an ACT score of 20. Of 60,000 total alumni, about 90 percent were born in Tennessee, but the aerospace and recording industry programs attract students from all over the world. The student body is 53 percent female and 14 percent minority, with students from more than 70 countries.

MTSU's Department of Recording Industry is housed in a $15 million facility that includes two world-class recording studios, a digital audio/edit dubbing suite, a complete television studio and two post-production rooms. It is the only school in the world authorized to teach Dolby Surround-Sound. Many graduates are employed in audio production as well as studio engineering. One program focuses on music business management.

## O'More College of Design
### 423 S. Margin St., Franklin
### • (615) 794-4254

O'More College of Design grants bachelor's degrees in fashion design and merchandising, interior design, and graphic design and advertising, as well as an associate degree in fashion design and merchandising. The college is accredited by the Accrediting Commission of Career Schools and Colleges of Technology.

O'More, chartered in 1970, originally opened in the Victorian home of founder Eloise Pitts O'More, who hoped to re-create the ambiance of the French design school she attended in Paris in 1935. In 1979, the college moved to its present 6-acre campus on the

edge of downtown Franklin. The campus contains the historic Abbey Leix Mansion and Fleming-Farrar Hall. Applicants may apply to audit courses.

## Volunteer State Community College
### 1480 Nashville Pk., Gallatin
### • (615) 452-8600

This two-year institution, the fastest-growing state-supported college in Tennessee, awards associate degrees and technical certificates in a wide variety of subjects ranging from art to fire science technology. Volunteer State's enrollment is about 6,500. The college has a modern, computerized $5.5 million library and Learning Resource Center. Besides the traditional classroom, courses are offered by video, through weekend college and on the college cable TV station.

## Tennessee Technological University
### N. Dixie Ave., Cookeville
### • (615) 372-3101

Tennessee Tech University, on the Cumberland Plateau in Cookeville (population 28,000) about 80 miles east of Nashville, is actually outside the metropolitan Nashville area. But we have included it because of the prominence of its wildlife and fisheries science program and its ties to the Columbia Space Shuttle Program.

The university is one of six four-year, state-supported coeducational institutions within the Tennessee State Board of Regents System. It was established in 1915 as Tennessee Polytechnic Institute by an act of the Tennessee General Assembly. It gained university status in 1965, at which time it became known by its current name.

Tennessee Tech's mission is to offer a strong academic program to its students and to preserve and enhance knowledge. Originally known as an engineering school, the university now offers a broader liberal arts component with nearly 70 bachelor's degrees. Academic divisions are agriculture and home economics, arts and sciences, business administration, education, engineering, nursing and military science. Master's degrees are offered in arts, business administration and science, and there is a doctoral program in engineering.

Tennessee Tech has three Centers of Excellence: Electric Power, Manufacturing and Water Resources. The school's wildlife and fisheries science program features course offerings like animal behavior, wild bird ecology and ichthyology. Tennessee Tech graduates are also active in the Columbia Space Shuttle Program. Astronaut Roger Crouch, a Tech alumnus, served as payload specialist aboard the *Columbia* in July 1997 and actually carried the Tech pennant aloft with him. Two other Tech grads participated on the ground: Teresa Vanhooser, an industrial engineer, was mission manager, and a physics grad, Mike Robinson, served as mission scientist.

# Other Educational Opportunities

## University School of Nashville
**2000 Edgehill Ave. • (615) 321-8019**

Classes for adults are offered in various subject areas. See the school's previous listing under "Private Schools" for more information.

## Warner Parks Nature Center
**7311 Tenn. Hwy. 100 • (615) 352-6299**

The nature center offers a variety of classes throughout the year ranging from wildflower walks to tree identification.

## Watkins Institute
**601 Church St. • (615) 242-1851**

Watkins Institute was founded in 1885 after the state received a gift of $100,000 and land from Samuel Watkins on which to build a school "that would strengthen our city." The institute has assumed various roles through the years, including the "Americanization" of Russian and Italian immigrants in the early 1900s, preparation of women for the workplace in the 1930s and 1940s and educational opportunities for returning servicemen after World War II.

Watkins, accredited by the National Association of Schools of Art and Design, has evolved into a community-oriented art and design education facility offering professional certificate programs and associate degrees. Programs include fine art (printmaking, figure drawing, sculpture, painting and water media), photography, graphic design, interior design, young artists (kindergarten to 12th grade), young actors and filmmakers (ages 10 through 18) and film school (programs in animation, cinematography, theatrical design and editing).

# Child Care

For newcomers, finding child care in Nashville can be tough, especially if you're looking to get into one of the more popular centers. Some programs, however, set a few positions aside for people relocating to Nashville. They generally don't advertise that information, so be sure to ask.

According to the Nashville Area Association for the Education of Young Children, parents should find an out-of-home child-care situation that they are secure with and their child is happy in. Talk to your friends, neighbors and co-workers and compare their likes and dislikes. Phone several schools and ask to arrange a visit for both you and your child. Observe the caregivers interacting with children. Do they, for example, speak to children on their level? Attend a school function and observe. Arrange an appointment with the school's director and have a list of questions ready regarding such issues as staff stability and training, teacher education, programs available, fees and policies for holidays and lateness. All nurseries and day-care centers must meet licensing requirements. For more information on these regulations and child-care providers, contact the Tennessee Department of Human Services Child Care Licensing, 1000 Second Avenue N., (615) 532-4410.

# Child-care Information

## Nashville Area Association for the Education of Young Children
**1701 21st Ave. S., Ste. 406**
**• (615) 383-6292**

NAAEYC was established in 1848 with two

primary objectives: to promote standards of excellence in child-care practices and to raise public understanding and support for high-quality educational programs for young children. It does not certify early childhood programs but provides information on how to identify and select high-quality child care. For educators and child-care providers, the association is a resource for information, training and support.

Nashville is one of 28 communities taking part in a national child-care quality improvement campaign (funded by Target stores) known as the Family to Family Project. This program offers a 30-hour curriculum to educate experienced and novice child-care providers about the family child-care profession. Topics addressed include child growth and development, licensing issues, activities and interaction with children.

### Nashville Parent Magazine
**2228 MetroCenter Blvd.**
**• (615) 256-2158**

This monthly publication is a ready source of information on parenthood, as well as edu-cational and recreational opportunities for area children. (See our Media chapter for more details.)

# Child-care Providers

The Nashville metropolitan area does have a number of chain child-care providers, including several KinderCares and couple of La Petites. Check your telephone directory for these listings. There are four preschool programs frequently used by parents who usually enter their children in the more prestigious private schools in Nashville. As you might expect, they are convenient to the Vandy, Green Hills and Belle Meade areas. Three of the four — St. George's Episcopal Day Kindergarten, Westminster Kindergarten and Woodmont Christian Day Care — are church-affiliated (see this chapter's related Insiders' Tip for addresses and phone numbers).

### The Children's House
**3404 Belmont Blvd. • (615) 298-5647**

The name is the English translation of that of Dr. Montessori's first school, Casa dei

Belmont University has a nationally recognized Music Business program.

Mabini. Montessori schools are not structured in a traditional, classroom-based manner. Dr. Montessori recommended that teachers "follow the child" and create a school that is more of a children's community — it allows them to move about freely and select work that captures their interest. Children, for instance, learn responsibility by preparing their own snacks and drinks, going to the bathroom alone and helping one another clean up spills. The Children's House, for 3-, 4- and 5-year-olds, is nonprofit and non-sectarian. All teachers have college degrees and Montessori teaching certificates.

## Other Child-care Options

### EF Au Pair
### (615) 361-6940, (800) 333-6056

EF Au Pair, a nonprofit international organization based in Stockholm, Sweden, matches English-speaking European live-in au pairs with Nashville-area families needing child care for a yearlong cultural exchange program. This agency is designated an official exchange visitor program sponsored by the U.S. Information Agency.

Au pairs, all of whom have prior child-care experience, work a maximum of 45 flexible hours per week. They must receive a private room from the host family and be allowed two weeks' vacation. Host families are asked to fill out applications that ask about the family (its lifestyle and needs), pets, neighborhood and so forth. Both personal and professional references are sought. Personal references, for example, are asked, "Would you feel comfortable having your son or daughter live in this home as an au pair?"

Au pair officials say the costs average out to about $220 a week regardless of the number of children. A $2,000 deposit is due when the au pair is selected, and a second payment of $2,250 is due 10 days before the au pair's arrival. (This payment can be divided into three $750 installments, with the third paid six months after arrival.)

### Brentwood United Methodist Church
**309 Franklin Rd., Brentwood**
• **(615) 373-2523**

Brentwood United Methodist Church cares for children from 6 weeks of age through pre-kindergarten.

### Family YMCAs
**Various Metro locations**
• **(615) 259-9622**

Area YMCAs provide day care for children ages 6 weeks to 6 years. Most schools also have YMCA before- and after-school care for kindergartners through 8th graders.

### Family Care Connection
**5123 Virginia Wy., Ste. C13, Brentwood**
• **(615) 371-0600**

This referral service provides information on in-home child care and companion care in the Nashville area. It also provides these services for major Nashville hotels under the company name Sitter Solutions. Family Care Connection offers an after-hours caregiver request line and will call back as soon as possible for immediate needs or next-day requests.

# Well-child and Drop-in Child Care

### Kiddie Korral
**330 Franklin Rd., Brentwood**
• **(615) 371-5279**

Kiddie Korral offers drop-in child care for children from 6 weeks to 12 years old (reservations are required for children younger than 19 months). It's open 8:30 AM to 11 PM Monday through Thursday, 8:30 AM to 1 AM Friday, 9 AM to 1 AM Saturday and 1 to 6 PM Sunday.

### Kids and Company
**2154 Bandywood Dr.**
• **(615) 269-6114**

Kids and Company is open late — until 11 PM Monday through Thursday and until midnight Friday and Saturday. It accepts children from 6 weeks to 12 years; reservations are required for children younger than 16 months.

A medium-size broadcast market, Nashville ranks as the 44th-largest radio market, the 30th-largest television market and the 126th-largest cable market in the nation.

# Media

TV, cable programming, radio, newspapers, magazines, hit songs, Bibles, books, music videos — when it comes to media, Nashville has it all. Nashville is a major publishing center, and printing/publishing is among the city's top five industries. Numerous cable television programs originate here and are seen by millions of viewers. TNN (The Nashville Network) and CMT: Country Music Television helped take country music to a higher level of exposure and popularity by bringing country artists into the living rooms of viewers worldwide. Many of the videos you see on CMT are shot right here in Music City.

A medium-size broadcast market, Nashville ranks as the 44th-largest radio market, the 30th-largest television market and the 126th-largest cable television market in the nation, according to Standard Rate and Data Service's April 1999 report. Nashville owes much of its heritage to radio. In our "Radio" section later in this chapter, we explain how radio played a role in the city's becoming known as Music City U.S.A.

Here's an overview of the major publications, broadcast stations and cable TV programming providers.

## Publications

Nashville's history as a publishing center dates to the late 18th century. The city's first newspaper, *Henkle's Tennessee Gazette & Mero Advertiser*, was printed in 1799, 20 years after the first settlers arrived and seven years before the city was incorporated. In 1800, the *Tennessee Gazette* began publishing. The first book was published in 1810, and 14 years later, the hymn book *Western Harmony* was published, marking the beginnings of music publishing in Nashville.

Nashville became a center for religious publishing in the 1800s, when there was a huge surge in religion in Tennessee. As Tennesseans flocked to religious revivals, Protestant denominations began publishing their books, Bibles, periodicals and other church materials in Nashville. In 1954, the Methodist Publishing House moved here from Philadelphia, where it had been based since 1789. Baptists and the Church of Christ began publishing here too. The National Baptist Publishing Board was founded in 1896.

By the early 1900s, religious publishing was an important part of Nashville's economy. It remains so today, accounting for about a third of the city's total printed output. Thirty percent of all Bibles printed in the United States are produced in this area, and Thomas Nelson, the world's largest Bible publisher, is based here. (See our Worship chapter for a more detailed look at religious publishing.)

Nashville's publishing industry isn't limited to religious materials, however. Today, there are nearly 500 firms here involved in publishing and printing. These companies employ more than 14,000 and have annual revenues of more than $250 million. Nashville companies publish or print such diverse materials as *USA Today*, the regional editions of *Parade* magazine, and national trade and consumer entertainment publications.

One of the city's interesting publishing success stories is Rutledge Hill Press, which was founded in 1982 and achieved national recognition with the 1990 publication of H. Jackson Brown Jr.'s *Life's Little Instruction Book*. The book — written, designed, typeset, printed and published in Nashville — has sold more than million copies and has been translated into nearly 20 languages. Rutledge Hill Press is also known for its books on the Civil War and local history, regional humor and the history of quilts. Among the company's titles are cookbooks *Aunt Bee's Mayberry Cookbook* and *Cooking With Friends*, *America's Dumbest Criminals*, and travel guides *Traveling the Trace* and *Traveling the Southern Highlands*.

Among the many other major publishing companies in the area are Abingdon Press, Gideons International and Vanderbilt University Press.

Ingram Entertainment, based in nearby LaVergne, is the nation's largest distributor of videos and video games, and a leading distributor of books, music, microcomputer hardware, software and accessories. The company's annual sales topped $1 billion in 1998.

Nashville is also a center of music publishing, the backbone of the country music industry. Among the major music publishers here are Almo/Irving Music Publishing, BMG Music Publishing, EMI Music Publishing, MCA Music Publishing, Acuff-Rose Music Publishing Inc., Sony Tree Publishing, Warner Chappell Music Publishing and Idea Publishing.

Following is a look at some of the newspapers and magazines that serve the Nashville market as well as some published here that have national and international circulations. We include a listing of some of the major country music and music business publications that are either published here or have offices here.

In addition to the following publications, there are several real estate guides and apartment guides that serve the market; we list those in our Neighborhoods and Real Estate chapter.

## Daily Newspapers

When the *Nashville Banner* folded in mid-February 1998, Nashville was left with only one daily newspaper, *The Tennessean*. The two publications had been duking it out since the early 1900s. The *Banner*, the city's conservative voice, was founded in 1876 and had the distinction of being Nashville's oldest continually published newspaper. After its circulation dipped below 40,000 in early 1998, it followed in the footsteps of many afternoon newspapers that had seen their circulations dwindle. *The Tennessean* and the *Banner* had been published under one roof since 1937, sharing advertising, printing, circulation and other costs.

In addition to *The Tennessean* and the other daily newspapers in the cities surrounding Nashville, there are a number of alternative publications, community newspapers and special-interest publications that keep Nashvillians informed.

## Nashville

### The Tennessean
1100 Broadway
• (615) 259-8000

*The Tennessean* is Nashville's daily newspaper, with a weekday circulation of more than 193,00 a Saturday circulation of around 234,000 and a Sunday circulation of 284,000. It dates back to 1907, but the paper evolved from *The Nashville Whig*, which began publication in 1812.

A newspaper with a liberal slant, *The Tennessean* is owned by Gannett Co. Inc., the country's largest newspaper publisher. Gannett bought the paper in 1979 from the family of Silliman Evans, who purchased it in the late 1930s at auction and turned the financially ailing operation into a success. (Gannett had owned the *Nashville Banner*, but opted to sell it in order to be able to purchase *The Tennessean*.)

Popular sections and features include the family/parenting section, working women's section and Brad Schmitt's "Brad About You" entertainment news and gossip column.

*The Tennessean* publishes more than 30 niche publications each year, including *Tennessee Homes*, a glossy color magazine on new homes in the area; and the handy *FYI*, an annual glossy reference guidebook featuring information on everything from schools to shopping.

### Surrounding Counties

### The Daily News Journal
224 N. Walnut St., Murfreesboro
• (615) 893-5860

This afternoon newspaper is published seven days a week. Founded in 1849, it has a circulation of 17,500 Monday through Saturday, and 22,000 Sunday. The Sunday edition is $1.25 at a newsstand; the other editions are 50¢.

## Lebanon Democrat

402 N. Cumberland, Lebanon
• (615) 444-3952

Published since the late 1800s, the *Lebanon Democrat* reaches 9,500 to 10,000 in Lebanon and other Wilson County towns. It is published Monday through Friday. A single copy at the newsstand is 50¢.

# Non-daily Newspapers

## The Advocate

1500 Fallen Tree Rd., Kingston Springs
• (615) 952-5554

Covering the south Cheatham County areas of Pegram and Kingston Springs, *The Advocate* is a free weekly newspaper with a circulation of 4,000. It is published Friday and mailed to all homes in the area.

## The Ashland City Times

202 N. Main St., Ashland City
• (615) 792-4230

*The Ashland City Times* was founded in 1896 and today covers Cheatham County news and happenings on a weekly basis. It comes out each Wednesday and costs 50¢ a copy. Its circulation is 6,000.

## Belle Meade News
## Green Hills News
## West Meade News
## Westside News

GCA Publishing, 2323 Crestmoor Rd.,
Ste. 219-B • (615) 298-1500

These free weekly community newspapers are published each Wednesday by GCA Publishing and cover news in their respective areas. Their combined circulation is more than 20,000. You can pick up a copy at grocery stores, libraries and other locations in each area. Subscriptions are available for $8 a year.

## Brentwood Journal

121 Second Ave. North, Franklin
• (615) 794-2555

The *Brentwood Journal* is a weekly community newspaper that's published on Thursday. Its circulation is 11,000. Copies cost 50¢ each. A one-year subscription is $51.

## The Dickson Herald

104 Church St., Dickson
• (615) 446-2811

*The Dickson Herald*, founded in 1907, is published Wednesday and Friday. It has a circulation of 21,000 and costs 50¢ a copy at a newsstand; subscriptions are $20 if you live inside Dickson County.

## The Gazette

110 Space Park N., Goodlettsville
• (615) 851-2888

This community newspaper began in mid-1999. About half the paper's circulation of 8,000 is distributed free to area homes; the remainder is distributed to local businesses.

## The Hendersonville Star News

110 Sanders Ferry Rd., Hendersonville
• (615) 824-8480

Published since 1951, this free paper comes out every Wednesday and Friday. It features local county news and has a circulation of 13,400. If the paper is distributed via mail in your neighborhood, you can pick up a free copy at the newspaper office or purchase a single copy at a newsstand for 50¢.

## The Messenger

322 E. Old Hickory Blvd., Madison
• (615) 868-0475

This free weekly newspaper has been covering community news in Madison, Goodlettsville and Old Hickory since 1982. It has a circulation of 8,000. You can pick up a copy at retail stores and libraries in those areas and at city hall.

## Mt. Juliet Chronicle
**11509 Lebanon Rd., Mt. Juliet**
• **(615) 754-6111**
Founded in 1980, the *Mt. Juliet Chronicle* is a free weekly community newspaper with a circulation of 12,000. It is published on Wednesday. An annual subscription is $15.95.

## Nashville Today
**2323 Crestmoor Rd., Ste. 219-B**
• **(615) 298-1500**
Published by GCA Publishing, *Nashville Today* is a free weekly community paper focusing on a broader coverage area than GCA's other community papers, with more city-oriented news. An annual subscription is $8.

## The News Beacon
**2740 Old Elm Hill Pk.** • **(615) 391-3535**
With a circulation of 20,000, *The News Beacon* covers news in Southeast Nashville, including the areas around Harding Mall, Hickory Hollow and Murfreesboro Road. It is distributed free to homes and select businesses. An annual subscription is $20.

## The News Examiner
**1 Examiner Ct., Sumner Hall Dr., Gallatin**
• **(615) 452-2561**
Covering news throughout Sumner County, *The News Examiner* began publishing in the mid-1800s. It is published on Monday, Wednesday and Friday and has a circulation of 11,000. A newsstand copy is 50¢; an annual subscription is $39.

## The News Herald
**2740 Old Elm Hill Pk.** • **(615) 391-3535**
Published since the mid-1980s, *The News Herald* is the free community newspaper for Donelson, Hermitage and Old Hickory. An annual subscription is $20.

## Review Appeal
**121 Second Ave. N., Franklin**
• **(615) 794-2555**
This community newspaper, founded in 1813, is published four days per week. The daily circulation rages from 10,000 to 20,000. A single copy costs 50¢, and a subscription is $51 per year.

## Westview
**8120 Sawyer Brown Rd.**
• **(615) 646-6131**
*Westview* is the weekly community newspaper covering Bellevue, Kingston Springs, Pegram, Charlotte Park and West Meade. Published since 1977, its circulation is about 5,000. It's published every Thursday. An annual subscription is $15.

## Wilson World
**113 E. Main St., Lebanon**
• **(615) 444-6008**
This community newspaper began publishing in 1980. It focuses on Wilson County news and has a weekly circulation of 5,400. A single copy costs 50¢; a subscription is $5 per year for those inside the county.

# General Interest

## Nashville In Review
**2021 21st Ave. S., Suite 120**
• **(615) 255-9792, (800) 354-6899**
*Nashville In Review* is sort of the "alternative" alternative newspaper. It started in 1995 as a business publication but later broadened its scope to include politics, lifestyle, arts and leisure. It's published weekly and has a circulation of 30,000. *In Review* takes an in-depth look at Nashville's big issues. The paper prides itself on "responsible criticism" and isn't afraid to challenge local authorities. *In Review* has a music column, restaurant reviews, an "in-out" column of what's "in" and what's "out," and

other fun features. Pick up a free copy at grocery stores, bookstores, other retail stores and restaurants.

## Nashville Scene
### 2120 Eighth Ave. S. • (615) 244-7989

*Nashville Scene* is Music City's leading alternative newspaper. This free weekly publication is so popular that a lot of Nashvillians will go out of their way, if necessary, to pick up a brand-new copy every Wednesday. It's pretty easy to find a copy, however. About 55,000 of them are distributed at grocery stores, convenience stores, book stores, restaurants, record stores and lots of other places all over town.

Founded in 1983, the *Scene* covers politics, business, music and arts in an in-depth fashion. The paper does lots of investigative stories and every now and then causes a stir over some issue or another. The *Scene* has the most comprehensive listings of local entertainment events, with a schedule that runs from Thursday to the following Thursday. Other favorite features include Kay West's restaurant reviews, Jim Ridley's film reviews and Michael McCall's music articles.

Special issues, such as the annual "You're So Nashville If . . . " and the "Best of Nashville" winners issues, get snapped up quickly. The *Annual Manual*, published at the beginning of the year, is a city guide full of information about living in Nashville. The *Scene* also publishes *Nashville Scene Eats*, a restaurant guide, twice a year.

The paper has won numerous awards from the National Newspaper Association and the Association of Alternative Newspapers.

## Around Town
### 2120 Eighth Ave. S. • (615) 244-7989

Each Friday from April through October, the *Nashville Scene* publishes the free *Around Town* publication, geared toward Music City visitors. It's available at hotels, tourist information centers and popular attractions.

## Nashville Sports Weekly
### 4721 Trousdale Dr., Ste. 215
### • (615) 777-5050

This free paper covers the local sports scene, with an emphasis on high school and college sports. There's usually an article on one of Nashville's pro teams too, plus plenty of golf news and info. It is distributed each Tuesday at more than 500 locations around town and has a circulation of 22,000. The paper began publishing in the spring of 1998.

## Nashville Woman
### 1710 Barlin Ct. • (615) 646-8655

*Nashville Woman* is a free resource and networking guide geared especially to career women. Published monthly, it has lots of features on everything from business issues to health and lifestyle. You can find a copy at local grocery stores, retail stores and other outlets.

## The Tennessee Magazine
### 710 Spence Ln. • (615) 367-9284

This monthly magazine is published for members of the Rural Electric Cooperative. It has a circulation of about 443,000 statewide per month, mostly rural readers. A glossy, four-color magazine, *The Tennessee Magazine* does human interest stories and has regular features on food, events and people, places and businesses in the co-op. Nonmembers of the co-op pay $8 for a one-year subscription, $21 for a three-year subscription

# Business

## Business Nashville
### 2817 West End Ave., Ste. 216
### • (615) 843-8000

Nashville's top corporate executives as well as others who want to keep up on the latest local business news turn to *Business Nashville* for reliable information on everything from real estate to healthcare to the environment. This slick-stock color magazine is published 11 times a year by Eagle Communications. *Business Nashville* has a circulation of 15,500 and a readership of about 75,000. A single copy is $3.95; a yearly subscription is $36.

## Music Row
### 1231 17th Ave. S. • (615) 321-3617

A good source of the latest news on Nashville's music business, *Music Row* comes

The BellSouth tower figures prominently in the Nashville skyline.

out on the 8th and 23rd of each month. Read more about it in our section on music publications.

## Nashville Business Journal
**222 Second Ave. N., Ste. 610**
**• (615) 248-2222**

*Nashville Business Journal,* published since 1985, is a weekly business newspaper with a circulation of 8,500. A single copy is $1.50 at newsstands; a one-year subscription is $58. Each edition has a special-emphasis section covering such issues as employee benefits, education, commercial real estate, travel and home business. The *Nashville Business Journal* also publishes about a dozen special publications each year on such topics as small business, real estate, health care, economic development, sports business and the arts.

## Nashville Record
**1100 Broadway • (615) 664-2300**

This weekly legal and business newspaper, published by Gannett, has been around since 1936. It's the source for information on foreclosures, tax sales, marriage licenses, business licenses and the like. A single copy costs 75¢ at newsstands and bookstores; a one-year subscription is $35. *Nashville Record's* circulation is 1,500.

# Special Interest

## Blast!
**2228 MetroCenter Blvd.**
**• (615) 256-2158**

*Blast!* is a free monthly magazine geared mainly to high school students. Most of the articles are written by students. You can find a copy at record stores, high schools, college dorms and some retail stores. It has a circulation of about 20,000.

## Contempora Magazine
**1818 Morena St. • (615) 321-3268**

This monthly, slick-stock magazine is tar-geted to the Mid-South's minority community, with an emphasis on the middle- and upper-income African-American community. Similar to *Ebony* in look and focus, *Contempora* highlights noteworthy individuals and achievements, covering topics, issues and news that often are overlooked by mainstream media. Nearly 100 percent of the magazine's circulation of 45,000 goes to subscribers in Nashville, Memphis, Chattanooga and Knoxville. A one-year subscription is $15. *Contempora* is published by Perry & Perry Publications, which also publishes the slick-stock, full-color *Contempora Brides* ($5 a copy) at the beginning of the year and the *Tennessee Tribune* newsweekly.

## Nashville Medical News
**4004 Hillsboro Pk., Suite 219**
**• (615) 385-4421**

*Nashville Medical News,* founded in 1989, is a monthly newspaper focusing on the healthcare industry. It is direct-mailed free to some 4,600 practicing physicians in Middle Tennessee; 3,500 top healthcare professionals, such as hospital administrators; and about 6,700 members of the Nashville Area Chamber of Commerce. There are also some subscribers, such as pharmaceutical reps and others who want to stay up to date on the local news. Averaging about 40 pages, the paper is published the first of each month. The company also publishes the *Dallas-Fort Worth Healthcare Journal, Houston Healthcare Journal* and the *Mississippi Medical News.*

## Nashville Parent Magazine
**2228 MetroCenter Blvd.**
**• (615) 256-2158**

A marvelous resource for parents, *Nashville Parent* is chock-full of information that every parent needs at some time or another. You'll find everything here from medical advice to kiddie video reviews. Founded in 1992, the free magazine has a circulation of more than 34,000; it's available free at various locations around town. *Nashville Parent* also pub-

---

**INSIDERS' TIP:**

Nashville's oldest and best-known radio talk show, Teddy Bart's *Round Table,* airs on WAMB-1160 AM.

lishes a private-school directory twice a year as well as a child-care and activity directory. It's invaluable for anyone with kids. This publisher also publishes *Murfreesboro Parent* and *Williamson County Parent.*

### Nashville Pride
**941 44th Ave. N. • (615) 292-9150**
This weekly newspaper is geared to the African-American community and has a circulation of 30,000. Published since 1987, *Nashville Pride* covers community news with a positive slant. You can pick up a newsstand copy for 50¢.

### Nfocus
**City Press Publishing Inc., 2120 Eighth Ave. S. • (615) 244-7989**
This free monthly publication covers the Nashville social scene. It is published by City Press Publishing Inc., publisher of the *Nashville Scene.* You can find it at 50 or so select retail stores and restaurants, including Kroger (Belle Meade, Bellevue, Brentwood and Green Hills), Davis-Kidd Booksellers, Bookstar, Illusions Salon, Jewish Community Center, McClure's and West Side Athletic Club.

### Query
**(615) 259-4135**
This free newsweekly covers gay and lesbian issues. It's published on Fridays and is available at bookstores and at some bars and restaurants. The mailing address is P.O. Box 2424, Nashville TN 37202.

### The Tennessee Conservationist
**401 Church St. • (615) 532-0060**
*The Tennessee Conservationist* is a glossy, full-color magazine published every other month by the Tennessee Department of Environment & Conservation. It features articles on history, parks, the environment and conservation. Readers skew toward middle- and upper-class 20- to 45-year-olds. The

magazine's circulation is about 15,000, and most of that is subscription. An annual subscription is $10.

### Tennessee Register
**2400 21st Ave. S. • (615) 383-6393**
Established in 1937, *Tennessee Register* is the official newspaper for the Catholic diocese of Nashville. This biweekly newspaper has 20 to 24 pages devoted to news of importance to Middle Tennessee's Catholic community. The publication has a circulation of 17,500. Subscriptions are $21 a year.

### Tennessee Tribune
**1818 Morena St. • (615) 321-3268**
Targeted to the African-American community, *Tennessee Tribune* is a weekly tabloid that focuses on consumer-oriented news and information geared to better living. It has been published since 1992 and has a circulation of 25,000. *Tennessee Tribune* is available free at school libraries and selected Kroger stores and retail outlets. A one-year subscription is $35.

### The Urban Journal
**3250 Dickerson Pk. • (615) 254-5176**
This free weekly newspaper has represented the African-American community in Nashville, and across the state, since 1980. It is distributed Wednesdays at libraries and other locations.

## Senior Citizens

### The Senior Sentinel
**1801 Broadway • (615) 327-4551**
This monthly tabloid newspaper is filled with articles on state and national issues that are of concern to seniors, such as health insurance and Social Security, as well as features on health, travel and politics. *The Senior Sentinel* is published by Senior Citizens Inc., a nonprofit organization that operates five se-

nior centers in the area. The paper carries the monthly schedule of activities for the senior centers. You can pick up a free copy at local Kroger stores, banks, senior centers, libraries, Shoney's and other locations.

# Music and Entertainment

## American Songwriter
**1009 17th Ave. S. • (615) 321-6096**

*American Songwriter* is a bimonthly magazine with 6,000 subscribers worldwide. Published since 1984, it focuses on topics of concern to songwriters. The magazine covers all genres of music, and most issues have a cover story about an individual songwriter. Past cover stories have featured artists ranging from Jimmy Buffett to Harlan Howard to Elton John. The magazine publishes several special editions annually, including a country music issue, a Christian music issue, an awards issue and the publishers special, which lists song publishers throughout the United States. Most of *American Songwriter's* readers are subscribers, but you can find copies at select newsstands around town, and in L.A. and New York. A single copy is $4, a one-year subscription is $22.

## Amusement Business
**49 Music Sq. W. • (615) 321-4290**

This entertainment-industry newsweekly covers all facets of live entertainment, from concert tours to theme parks to sports. The publication's weekly "Boxscore" lists grosses from concerts around the world. *Amusement Business* has an international circulation of approximately 14,000 and is read by booking agents, concert promoters, arena managers, fair managers, festival producers, sports management and others involved in the business of live entertainment. Today's *Billboard* (see next entry) evolved from this publication, which has been published continuously since 1894. Except for special editions, most single copies are $5; a yearly subscription is $129 to $149. *Amusement Business* and *Billboard* are published by New York-based BPI Communications, which also publishes the *Hollywood Reporter* and other well-known arts, media and entertainment magazines.

## Billboard
**49 Music Sq. W. • (615) 321-4290**

*Billboard's* country music bureau is based in Nashville. *Billboard*, based in New York, is the world's most recognized publication covering the music, video and home entertainment industries. The weekly publication dates back to 1894. A single copy is $5.95; a one-year subscription is $289.

## CCM Magazine
**107 Kenner Ave. • (615) 386-3011**

*CCM Magazine* is a favorite among fans of contemporary Christian music. Founded in 1978, *CCM* has a worldwide circulation of at least 85,000 and costs $3.50 a copy; a subscription is $21.95. The magazine's target audience is Christian music consumers in their 20s. The magazine is published by CCM Communications, which also publishes *Worship Leader*, read by about 50,000 church worship leaders; *CCM Update*, a weekly trade publication distributed to the Christian music industry; and *Youth Worker Journal*, a publication for church youth workers. The company also produces two weekly radio shows heard on stations around the country: *CCM Radio Magazine* and *CCM Countdown with Gary Chapman*.

## Country Airplay Monitor
**49 Music Sq. W. • (615) 321-4290**

*Country Airplay Monitor* is one of *Billboard's* four *Airplay Monitor* publications. The weekly magazine has editorial and charts geared to country radio and country record promotion. The annual subscription rate is $219. Or, you can pick up a single copy for $4.95 at one of the publisher's offices.

## Country Music
**7 Music Sq. W. • (615) 251-0106**

Published every other month, this fan magazine is chock full of artist interviews, features and news about country music stars. It has a circulation of 400,000. A one-year subscription is $15.98. A single copy is $2.99.

## Journal of Country Music
**4 Music Sq. E. • (615) 256-1639**

The *Journal of Country Music* usually is published three times a year by the Country Music Foundation. The magazine features interpretive articles on country music history plus articles on current artists and record and book reviews. It has a select readership of music industry people, collectors and others interested in country music history. A single copy is $5.95, and a one-year subscription is $18. You can find it at good newsstands and bookstores or order a subscription.

## Country Weekly
**118 16th Ave. S., Suite 230**
**• (615) 259-1111**

*Country Weekly* is based in Lantana, Florida, but the Nashville bureau can be found right on Music Row. This consumer publication has lots of features on country music artists. Its circulation is 400,000. A single copy is $1.99; a 20-issue subscription is $24.95.

## Gospel Today
**761 Old Hickory Blvd. • (615) 376-5656**

*Gospel Today* is a Christian lifestyle magazine geared mainly to the African American audience. Published since 1989, the magazine features articles on politics, gospel music and other subjects. The magazine is published eight times a year and has a circulation of 250,000. A single copy is $3.50; a one-year subscription is $20.

## Gospel Industry Today
**761 Old Hickory Blvd. • (615) 376-5656**

This publication is geared to gospel music performers and those who work in the business side of the gospel music industry. It is published 10 times per year and has a circulation of about 3,000. A single copy is $3; a one-year subscription is $36.

## The Gospel Voice
**812 Wren Rd., Goodlettsville**
**• (615) 851-1841**

*The Gospel Voice* is a monthly publication covering Southern gospel, traditional gospel

and other types of gospel music. Its readership is about 70,000. Published since 1987, *The Gospel Voice* presents its annual Diamond Awards to the best of the Southern gospel industry. A subscription is $20 a year; a single copy is $2.95.

## Music City News
**50 Music Sq. W., Ste. 601**
**• (615) 329-2200**

*Music City News* is a fan-oriented country music publication with a circulation of about 80,000. Published monthly, the magazine has two or three artist features in each issue as well as regular features such as the "StarGazing" personal news column and the "Ask MCN" Q&A column. *Music City News* teams up with TNN to present the TNN Music City News Awards. Fans vote for their favorites through TNN and the magazine, and TNN carries the awards show. A single copy of the magazine is $2.95; a one-year subscription $18.95.

## Music Row
**1231 17th Ave. S. • (615) 321-3617**

Published twice a month, *Music Row* features new-artist profiles, articles on finance, marketing and other topics of concern to artists, songwriters and other music-biz types, and regular features such as "Musical Chairs," which reports on the latest job changes, promotions and other business news. "Bobby Karl Works The Room" is a who-was-seen-at-what-party column written by longtime Nashville journalist Bob Oermann. And don't miss Oermann's always entertaining "Disclaimer" column, a series of brutally honest record reviews. Published since 1981, *Music Row* has a circulation of 4,000 and a readership of 16,000. A copy at the newsstand costs $4; a yearly subscription is $99. Music Row Publications also puts out several handy annual guides, including "In Charge," a comprehen-

---

**INSIDERS' TIP**

If you're a bluegrass fan, you'll want to tune into WRVU's (91.1 FM) popular bluegrass program, *George The Bluegrass Show*, from 2 to 4 PM Sundays and to WLPN's (90.3 FM) *Bluegrass Breakdown*, on Saturdays from 8 to 9 PM.

Photo: Cathy Summerlin

Pam Tillis performs at Fan Fair.

sive listing of the top people in the music business that comes out in April, and "Artist Roster," a list of artists, labels and producers that's published in September.

### Radio & Records
**1106 16th Ave. S. • (615) 244-8822**

*R&R*, as this trade weekly is known, tracks radio airplay. The Los Angeles-based magazine is published weekly and has a circulation of about 9,000. The country section of *R&R* is compiled at the Nashville office. *R&R* has been published since 1973. A one-year subscription is $299. *R&R's* daily and various weekly HotFaxes are available for an extra $100 to $190 a year.

### Session Guide
**(615) 321-4787**

*Session Guide* is an annual directory of session players, producers, engineers, recording studios, support services and other businesses related to the recording industry. In 1998, a separate *Session Guide* will be published for the Nashville, New York, Los Angeles and Canada markets. Guides for London, Australia, Northern Europe and Southern Europe are planned. The Nashville guide is pub-

lished in late summer. The book is available in some bookstores and by mail order for $25; write to P.O. Box 10589, Nashville TN 37216.

# Television

What's on TV? In Nashville, just about anything. We have all the major networks, local independent stations and a community access station. Cable and satellite viewers can choose from dozens more stations. There are a number of cable networks and cable programming providers in the area, such as CMT: Country Music Television, TNN (The Nashville Network) and Trinity Music City USA.

Here's the rundown on the TV scene.

## Major Local Stations

C.A.T. Channel 19 (Community Access
    Television)
WDCN Channel 8 (PBS)
WHTN Channel 39 (Independent)
WJXA Channels 12, 24 and 68
    (Independent)
WKRN Channel 2 (ABC)
WNAB Channel 58 (Warner Brothers)
WSMV Channel 4 (NBC)

WTVF Channel 5 (CBS)
WUXP Channel 30 (UPN)
WZTV Channel 17 (FOX)

# Cable Programming Providers

## CMT: Country Music Television
**2806 Opryland Dr. • (888) CMT-1997**

CMT: Country Music Television programs country music videos and original programming around the clock. Special video programs, such as *Top Twelve*, *Jammin' Country* and *The Delivery Room*, are scheduled in regular time slots. Among the network's original programs are the *All Access* live concert series; the weekly *CMT Showcase*, a 30-minute spotlight on a particular artist; and *CMT Hit Trip*, a weekly traveling show that features artist interviews. The CMT Request Line is a weekly series that features videos requested by fans as well as special dedications; for a cost of 99¢, you can make a video request by calling (900) 288-4CMT.

CMT is owned by CBS Cable. CMT International, owned by Gaylord Entertainment Co., is seen by nearly 6 million viewers in Latin America and the Pacific Rim.

## TNN
**2806 Opryland Dr. • (615) 889-6840,
(615) 883-7000 (information services)**

Though it's hard to imagine country music without TNN, the cable network has steadily been changing its lineup since Gaylord Entertainment sold it to CBS Cable in 1997. These changes, such as adding wrestling and roller derby programming, have primarily been targeted at young males. Still, since its 1983 premier, TNN has done much to promote country music and related lifestyle programming. It is seen in more than 74 million American homes.

TNN airs the annual *TNN Music City News*

*Country Awards Show*, the only fan-voted country awards program on TV, as well as special performance events.

One indication of TNN's shifting focus came in late summer 1999, when it was reported that the network planned to drop its flagship program, *Prime Time Country*, by year's end. That show, with host Gary Chapman, was an entertainment variety series. Also on the block are *Crook & Chase* and *This Week in Country Music*, reflecting a further move from TNN's country roots.

## Z Music Television
**One Gaylord Dr. • (615) 316-6170**

Z Music Television is a 24-hour "positive hit" music video network owned by Gaylord Entertainment. The network features contemporary Christian as well as urban, Southern and traditional gospel music. In addition to videos, Z Music has original programs such as concerts and artist profiles. Launched in 1993, the network reaches more than 7 million cable television homes.

## Community Access Television
**(615) 320-7800**

Nashville's Community Access Television, Channel 19 on Intermedia in Nashville, has been on the air for more than a decade. Most of the station's programming originates here and is locally produced. CATV/Nashville airs taped programs from about 8 AM to midnight daily.

Some of CATV's features are *Watch TV*, a 30-minute program of pastoral scenes in the area; *Old-Time Southern Cooking*; and various local music shows. One of the station's most popular shows is *The Bat Poet Show*, a bizarre, you-have-to-see-it-to-understand type of show that airs Friday and Saturday at 10 PM.

CATV membership is $25, $50 or $100 a year, and you must be a member to produce a program on the station. Members of the community who are interested in producing a show for CATV must submit a program proposal. If

**INSIDERS' TIP**

***Nashville Scene*** **has the most comprehensive listings of entertainment and arts schedules. The Thursday, Friday and Sunday editions of** ***The Tennessean*** **contain entertainment listings too.**

the proposal is approved, members must take the station's free training session in television production, after which they will be allowed to check out cameras and video equipment from the studio or produce their shows at the studio.

Longtime Nashville TV reporter Jim Gilchrist is the station's executive director. For more information on CATV, call the listed number, or write to P.O. Box 280718, Nashville TN 37228.

# Radio

Radio played the key role in Nashville's emergence as a country music capital. In the 1920s, as Americans became enamored with the new technology of radio, Nashville became an important broadcasting center. Local merchants and insurance com-

Friday and Saturday broadcasts of the *Grand Ole Opry* include appearances by *Opry* cast members like Dolly Parton.

panies established their own stations. Cain-Sloan's John E. Cain Jr., for example, founded WEBX in 1924, and in following years, stations were established by several other merchants.

National Life and Accident Insurance Company's WSM, which signed on the air in October 1925, and Life and Casualty's WLAC, which arrived on the dial a year later, were the city's major stations. Both are still on the air today, but it was WSM that put the spotlight on Nashville. WSM began broadcasting the *Grand Ole Opry*, originally known as the *WSM Barn Dance*, less than two months after it went on the air (see our History chapter for more details). The station took country music into homes and businesses around the country.

Today, WSM 650 AM continues to broadcast the *Grand Ole Opry* every Friday and Saturday night. WSM is one of the nation's few

clear-channel stations, meaning that no other station in a 750-mile radius has the same frequency for nighttime broadcasts. This and the station's 50,000-watt transmitter mean that the *Opry* can be heard across a large portion of the United States and parts of Canada.

In 1941 WSM launched WSM-FM, the nation's first commercially operated FM station. WSM-FM (95.5 on the dial) can be heard today in Middle Tennessee, southern Kentucky and northern Alabama. A WSM radio announcer is credited with giving Nashville the nickname Music City U.S.A. in 1950.

While WSM is Nashville's most famous station, for years the No. 1 rated station here has been WSIX-FM, which has been broadcasting since 1948. Gerry House is WSIX's most popular air personality and has been named the top medium-market local air personality at a country station in the nation.

Today, Nashville has plenty of country music stations, but, as you will hear with a touch of a button or a turn of the dial, most other forms of music are represented on Nashville and Nashville area radio. There are a lot of Christian and gospel stations, and we also have jazz, adult contemporary, urban, a wonderful public radio station and more. The large number of college radio stations in our market means that we hear a nice mix of everything from cutting-edge alternative rock to reggae to bluegrass.

In any market of this size, stations frequently change their formats, so what was a country station in the fall might be an adult contemporary or news/talk station in the spring. The following is a listing of most of the stations your radio will pick up in Nashville. Major stations are indicated in bold.

## Adult Contemporary
**WJXA 92.9 FM** (light rock)

## Christian and Gospel
**WAYM 97.7 FM** (contemporary Christian)
WBOZ 104.9 FM (gospel)
WENO 760 AM (Christian talk)
WNAH 1360 AM (gospel)
WNAZ 89.1 FM (adult contemporary Christian; will be changing to praise and worship)
WNQM 1300 AM (Christian talk)
WNSG 1240 AM (gospel)
WVOL 1470 AM (gospel)
WVRY 105.1 FM (gospel)
WYFN 980 AM (Christian)

## Classical
WPLN 90.3 FM (Nashville Public Radio; classical, news and information, talk)

## College Radio
WENO 760 AM (Trevecca Nazarene University; Christian talk)

WFSK 88.1 FM (Fisk University; jazz, gospel, urban, eclectic)
WNAZ 89.1 FM (Trevecca Nazarene University; adult contemporary Christian; will be changing to praise and worship)
WRVU 91.1 FM (Vanderbilt University; alternative rock, eclectic)
WVCP 88.5 FM (Volunteer State Community College; eclectic)
WMOT 89.5 FM (Middle Tennessee State University; jazz)

## Contemporary Hit Radio/Top-40
**WQZQ 102.5 FM**
**WRVW 107.5 FM**

## Country
WAKM 950 AM
WDBL 94.3
WENO 760 AM
WFGZ 94.5 FM
WHIN 1010 AM
**WKDF 103.3 FM**
WPFD 850 AM (classic country)
WSGI 1100 AM
**WSIX 97.9 FM**
**WSM 650 AM** (home of the *Grand Ole Opry*)
**WSM 95.5 FM**
WYXE 1130 AM (country and bluegrass)
**WYYB 93.7 FM**

## Jazz
WFSK 88.1 FM (Fisk University; eclectic)
**WJZC 101.1 FM**
WMOT 89.5 FM

## News/Talk
WCTZ 1550 AM
WGNS 1450 AM (news, talk, sports)
**WLAC 1510 AM** (news, talk, sports)
WPLN 90.3 FM (National Public Radio; classical, news and information)

## INSIDERS' TIP

**Have you been trying to catch your favorite performer's new country music video on CMT? If you're online, you can find out what time it will air next by checking out CMT's video schedule on country.com, a great country music website chock-full of interesting and fun information on country artists, CMT, TNN and more.**

WMAK 1430 AM (News Channel 5 Radio)
WNQM 1300 AM (Christian talk)
WWTN 99.7 FM

## Oldies

WAMB 1160 AM (adult standards, nostalgia, Big Band)

WAMB 98.7 FM (nostalgia, Big Band; nighttime only)

**WGFX 104.5 FM**

WMRO 1560 AM (rock oldies)

**WNPL 106.7 FM** (R&B oldies)

**WRMX 96.3 FM**

## Rock

WDBL 1590 AM (daytime simulcast of WRLG 93.7 FM; nighttime R&B)

**WNRQ 105.9 FM**

WRLG 94.1 FM simulcast of WRLT)

**WRLT 100.1 FM** (adult alternative)

**WZPC 102.9 FM** (modern rock)

WYYB 93.7 FM (new rock, alternative, Americana)

## Spanish

WHEW 1380 AM

## Sports

WNSR 560 AM

**WWTN 99.7 FM** (talk, sports, news)

## Urban

WDBL 1590 AM (daytime simulcast of WRLG; nighttime R&B)

WMDB 880 AM

**WQQK 92.1 FM**

A high quality of life
combined with a
relatively low cost of
living (and no income
tax) make Nashville an
especially desirable
place for retired people.

# Retirement

Lots of people apparently have chosen to live their "golden years" in the Nashville area. According to an estimate by the Nashville Area Chamber of Commerce, slightly more than 10 percent of the 1,134,744 residents in the eight-county metropolitan statistical area are 65 and older.

The same benefits that make Nashville such an attractive place for all ages — in a nutshell, a high quality of life combined with a relatively low cost of living (and no income tax) — make it an especially desirable place for retired people. Those who have left the rigors of the work world now have even more time to take advantage of Nashville's thousands upon thousands of acres of parks and waterways, its golf courses, swimming pools, country clubs, tennis courts, historical attractions, shopping opportunities, music and much more.

A number of retirement communities offer a range of living options, from independent to assisted living. A fine senior citizens center, with convenient branches throughout the area, provides activities for recreation, travel, relaxation and even volunteerism with friends old and new.

For many retired people, the issue of healthcare becomes increasingly important. With such well-respected institutions as Vanderbilt University Medical Center right in town, healthcare access is excellent in Nashville. The central location near major interstates, along with an international airport, makes getting in and out of town — whether you're going to see the grandkids or they're coming to see you — a snap. And plenty of public transportation is available as well.

Of course, being a senior means you get to enjoy many of the fine attractions detailed in this book at a reduced cost! So enjoy your stay and stick around for awhile. The Nashville area is a great place to grow old and stay young at the same time.

## Activities for Seniors

### 55 Plus
**Baptist Hospital, 2000 Church St.**
**• (615) 329-5500, (615) 284-5566**
**(recorded trip and seminar info)**

Baptist Hospital's 55 Plus program offers a variety of activities, trips and seminars for people 55 and older. Recent trips have been to Australia and New Zealand, the British Isles, Texas and Kentucky. Options also include group excursions to Titans football and Predators hockey games, "55 Alive" classes for older drivers, and a changing lineup of seminars on such topics as reducing heart attack risk, osteoporosis screening and managing stress. Membership is free, as are many of the seminars. Call Baptist at for a membership application.

### Senior Citizens Center Inc.
**1801 Broadway • (615) 327-4551**

Senior Citizens Center Inc. is a private, nonprofit organization for adults 55 years old or older. Under the leadership of Executive Director Janet Jernigan, the organization offers more than 60 classes, including computers, exercise classes, Spanish and French, social dancing, square dancing, quilting, art and woodcarving.

The group also has a winning swim team that competes in the national Senior Games, and a Senior Citizens Orchestra that performs Wednesday afternoons. Friday night dances with Big Bands draw visitors from throughout Middle Tennessee. (A writer acquaintance of ours used to drive down from Lebanon with a couple of his lady friends, who loved to dance as much as he did.)

Services offered include a nonprofit travel agency, Seniors Employment Services, (615) 321-3401, and case management for homebound seniors that coordinate meals on wheels, referrals to various agencies, volunteer assistance and respite care that helps them remain in their homes as long as possible.

Members also keep young through their eager participation in a number of volunteer programs. The Foster Grandparents program serves about 1,000 area children with special needs. More than 500 seniors take part in RSVP (Retired Senior Volunteer Program), serving more than 90 sites in Davidson and Williamson counties. FLIP (Friends Learning in Pairs) provides mentors/tutors for at-risk early elementary students in public school classrooms. Phone Friends offers an opportunity for homebound adults to become after-school friends with kids who are home alone after school. Respite Caregivers provide about four hours of relief care for a frail elderly loved one being cared for at home.

Seniors Citizens Center Inc. has five full-time centers. Suzanne Ezell runs the main Knowles Senior Activity Center, 1801 Broadway, (615) 327-4551. Other locations are: Donelson Station Center, 108 Donelson Pike, (615) 883-8375; Hadley Park Center, 1029 28th Avenue N., (615) 320-5833; College Grove Center, 8607 Horton Highway, College Grove, (615) 368-7093; and Madison Station Center, 301 Madison Street, (615) 860-7180. There are also five branches that are open for varying days and hours: Brentwood Branch, 1301 Franklin Road, Brentwood; Nolensville Branch, in Nolensville Recreation Center, 7248 Nolensville Road; Lucky 13 Branch, at St. Andrew United Methodist Church, 4590 Clarksville Highway; Center South Branch, at St. Matthias Episcopal Church, 5325 Nolensville Road; and Bellevue Branch, at Bellevue Presbyterian Church, 100 Cross Timbers Drive.

Membership is a $35 annual donation, and scholarships are available. All members receive the monthly newspaper *Senior Sentinel*

(see Media) in the mail; free copies are also available at public libraries, Kroger grocery stores and other locations around town.

# Senior Services

The following local and national organizations serve as vital resource outlets and information clearinghouses for seniors.

**Greater Nashville Regional Council Area Agency on Aging**
**501 Union St., 6th Floor • (615) 862-8828**

The Area Agency on Aging serves Davidson County as well as Cheatham, Dickson, Houston, Humphreys, Montgomery, Robertson, Rutherford, Stewart, Sumner, Trousdale, Wilson and Williamson counties. The agency plans for the provision of federal Older American Act services and state-funded services to persons 60 and older. It performs a wide range of activities related to advocacy, planning, coordination, inter-agency linkages, information sharing, brokering, monitoring, technical assistance, training and evaluation. The agency funds services related to such areas as health promotion and disease prevention, homemaking, information and assistance, legal assistance, nutrition services, ombudsmen, public guardianship, respite care, retired senior volunteers, senior centers and transportation.

# Metro Nashville/Davidson County Social Services

### Adult Day Care Program
**1010 Camilla Caldwell Ln.**
**• (615) 862-6450**

Services of the Adult Day Care Program include nutrition, transportation, homemaker

---

**INSIDERS' TIP**

Seniors play for reduced rates at many area golf courses, including all seven Metro Parks courses.

Nashville is a great place to spend the golden years.

services and adult day care assisted living. Cost is based on a sliding-fee scale.

## Homemaker Services for Adults/ Handicapped
### 25 Middleton Ave. • (615) 862-6480

This agency provides homemaker services involving light housekeeping to persons 60 and older and disabled people. Services are intended to help program participants remain in their homes, avoiding more costly nursing home placement. Homemaker Services also runs essential errands, such as grocery shopping and picking up medication, and performs laundry services. Eligibility requirements are based on financial need.

## Senior Renaissance Center
### 4805 Park Ave. • (615) 269-4565

For more than a decade, the Senior Renaissance Center has been providing seniors with a hot meal and activities five days a week. Under the stated goal of "life maintenance, life enrichment, life celebration and life construction," the center offers a wealth of opportunities including education, ceramics, flower arranging, quilt making, line dancing, health screening, exercise, tai chi, walking, billiards, drama, bowling, parties, shopping trips and various games. A live band plays country, Western, bluegrass and religious music once a week. Attendance generally ranges from about 40 to 85. "We recycle skills, discover talents and celebrate life," says director Mary Lou Green.

The Senior Renaissance Center, operated by Metro Social Services, is in Room 120 of the Cohn Adult Learning Center. It is open from 9 AM to 1 PM Monday through Friday. Charge for the daily meal is a donation for guests 60 and older, $4 for those younger than 60.

### Nutrition Program for the Elderly
**806 Fourth Ave. S. • (615) 880-2292**

Nutrition Program for the Elderly serves about 1,400 lunches daily Monday through Friday to Davidson County residents 60 and older. Meals are served at 18 managed sites, such as high-rise apartment buildings and community centers, throughout the county. In addition to each day's set menu of low-sodium food, the Nutrition Program provides activities such as arts and crafts, field trips, games and classes to keep seniors active and involved. A home-delivered meals program serving homebound residents also is available. The Nutrition Program is partly funded by the federal government under the Older American Act; while there is no charge, donations are encouraged and make up a necessary part of the funding.

### Senior Solutions
**501 Union Street • (615) 255-1010**

Senior Solutions, a sort of "one-stop shopping" for senior needs, is an information referral and assistance program for seniors and those who love and care for them. Using an extensive, nationally used software program, workers assess callers' needs and then connect them to community resources that can meet their needs. Sometimes the answer can be provided with one call; in other instances follow-up is necessary. Senior Solutions often does the legwork for social workers, calling multiple agencies to find who can provide the needed assistance. Help covers a wide range: anything from finances and healthcare to de-

pression, residential facilities and housecleaning.

# National Organizations

### American Association of Retired Persons
**601 E St. NW, Washington, D.C. 20049 • (800) 424-3410**

AARP is the nation's leading organization for people 50 and older. It serves their needs and interests through legislative advocacy, research, informative programs and community services provided by a network of local chapters and volunteers throughout the country. The organization also offers members a wide range of benefits, including *Modern Maturity* magazine and the monthly *Bulletin*.

### National Institute on Aging
**(800) 222-2225**

The National Institute on Aging is responsible for the "conduct and support of biomedical, social and behavioral research, training, health-information dissemination and other programs with respect to the aging process and the diseases and other special problems and needs of the aged." It offers a wide variety of publications, both general and specific, about such issues as incontinence, menopause, medications, arthritis, Alzheimer's disease, depression, forgetfulness, stroke, nutrition, hearing, sexuality, accident prevention and much more. Write NIA at P.O. Box 8057, Gaithersburg MD 20898.

# Retirement Communities

### Blakeford at Green Hills
**11 Burton Hills Blvd. • (615) 665-9505**

Blakeford, with a prime location in Green Hills, is an upscale not-for-profit senior-living community. It is a life-care community, which means it offers lifetime assisted living and unlimited nursing care for those who need it. The board of directors is composed of distinguished community leaders.

Residents pay a monthly fee and a "resident deposit." This one-time deposit, which varies according to the size and design of the apartment home you choose, starts at $119,000 for a one-bedroom, 604-square-foot model. Ninety percent of this fee is refundable should you leave the community. All units have private balconies or patios, fully equipped all-electric kitchens with microwaves, washer and dryer, sound-resistant construction and an emergency call system.

Blakeford at Green Hills occupies a 10-acre site, with 4 acres dedicated to green areas and walking paths adjoining Lake Burton. Inside the community buildings is a library, beauty salon/barber shop, exercise room and creative arts center. Guest accommodations are available for visitors, and a private dining room can accommodate private gatherings.

Included in the monthly fee, which ranges from $1,334 to $2,487, are a daily meal, weekly housekeeping and scheduled transportation. Restaurant-style dining is available for three meals daily in the main dining room; again, one meal a day is included in the plan, and additional meals may be purchased.

## McKendree Village
### 4343 Lebanon Rd., Hermitage
### • (615) 889-6990

McKendree Village, a nonprofit, continuing-care retirement community, has been serving the area for more than 35 years. Offerings range from total independent living in The Cottages and The Towers to varying levels of assisted living in The Manor and The Health Center.

Residents, who must be 55 or older, can choose from a variety of programs. The 42-acre complex includes an indoor swimming pool and whirlpool, exercise room, woodworking shop, activities/craft room and a chapel with a full-time chaplain and various Bible study classes throughout the week. McKendree Vil-

lage is affiliated with Vanderbilt University Medical Center and has a "covenant relationship" with the Tennessee Annual Conference of the United Methodist Church, which essentially means that the church provides money through offerings but is not involved in daily management or operations.

Monthly Manor leases range from $1,463 for a studio apartment to $2,808 for a deluxe one-bedroom unit. Rates include three meals daily and housekeeping weekly. The 40 cottages that make up The Cottages — priced from $80,000 — are individually owned and range from 1,100 to 3,000 square feet. The Towers apartments, which are for sale or lease, include home healthcare, a security system with emergency call and a resident dining room serving three meals daily. The Manor offers private apartment living that bridges the gap between total independent living and nursing care.

## Morningside of Belmont
### 1710 Magnolia Blvd. • (615) 383-2557

Morningside of Belmont, which has been in operation since 1980, offers a variety of floor plans for independent living in the Belmont/Hillsboro area. Services and amenities include housekeeping, laundry facilities, two or three meals a day, a library and beauty salon. Residents also may audit classes at Belmont University.

Apartments are furnished with residents' own furnishings. All have accessible bathrooms, kitchens and large picture windows overlooking Belmont or the city. Many also have balconies. No long-term leases, entrance fees or endowments are required.

An assisted-living program is available 24 hours a day, and a resident assistant can be reached by activating a call button in each apartment. Weekly shopping trips and a variety of social and community activities are available for residents who wish to participate.

Monthly rents for independent living, for instance, range from $1,040 for a one-bedroom unit to $1,865 for a two-bedroom unit.

## INSIDERS' TIP

**Senior citizens receive reduced admission to many Nashville-area attractions.**

Rates include three meals daily, complete dietary services and housekeeping.

## Park Manor
### 115 Woodmont Blvd. • (615) 383-7303

This nonprofit community in the prestigious Belle Meade area of west Nashville is owned and operated by the Presbyterian Church and governed by an independent board of directors. Park Manor, built in 1962, offers efficiencies and one- and two-bedroom apartments — all with fire- and sound-resistant construction, smoke detectors and 24-hour intercom systems — within a country-style environment on 7 acres.

The monthly fee — $1,083 for an efficiency to $1,930 for a two-bedroom — includes housekeeping services twice a month, all utilities except telephone and cable and a five-course lunch and dinner every day in an elegant dining room. Private dining rooms are available for entertaining family and friends. Organized activities and seminars are offered, and limousine transportation is also available.

The community has its own certified home health agency serving Park Manor exclusively. This allows you to remain in your apartment and receive skilled nursing care and speech, physical and occupational therapy. Park Manor requires no endowment or entry fees.

## Richland Place
### 500 Elmington Ave. • (615) 269-4200

Richland Place Inc. is a Tennessee not-for-profit corporation that consists of a 137-apartment continuing-care retirement community attached to a licensed, 131-bed long-term healthcare center. It is on the site of the former Richland Country Club near Interstate 440 at West End Avenue.

The community bills itself as "a distinctive luxury retirement community designed for successful, active seniors over the age of 55 desiring the peace-of-mind, convenience and comforts of a comprehensive residential package." Entry fees range from $135,000 to $500,000 depending upon the unit square footage; this fee is entirely refundable within the first four months and 90 percent refundable after 10 months.

Monthly service fees, which range from $1,200 to $4,000 according to unit size, include one chef-prepared meal a day, weekly housekeeping and flat linen service; apartment, building and grounds maintenance; scheduled transportation; apartment insurance; property taxes; all utilities except phone; additional storage space; and a medical-alert system.

The fees also cover such activities as fitness programs in the fitness center and long-term healthcare services, which are provided in a semiprivate accommodation in the project's healthcare center for up to 180 days a year with a lifetime maximum of 360 days at no additional charge. After the annual 180 days and the lifetime maximum, residents can have a semiprivate accommodation at the healthcare center for 85 percent of the prevailing rate in lieu of the monthly service fee.

Richland Place also has walking paths that meander through 7.5 acres, a stock room with real-time price quotations and computers for stock trading, an indoor swimming pool designed like a Roman spa with marble columns and floor, a restaurant, deli, soda fountain and sundries shop, on-site banking, pharmacy, laundry, dry-cleaning pickup, postal facilities and storage.

Apartments feature recessed fixtures, crown moldings, state-of-the-art appliances, carpeting throughout, decorator wallpaper, brass bathroom fixtures, dining room chandeliers and 9-foot ceilings. Entry gates are monitored by closed-circuit TV.

## St. Paul Senior Living Community
### 5031 Hillsboro Rd. • (615) 298-2400

St. Paul Senior Living Community is for residents 62 or older who are able to maintain an independent lifestyle. It features 130 suites in a prime Green Hills location, with "an atmosphere that will accentuate your favorite furnishings and family heirlooms."

The St. Paul has a community drawing room with fireplace, private dining rooms, beautifully landscaped grounds with a walking track, an exercise room, library, laundry facilities on each floor and maximum soundproof construction. The rent — $1,750 to $2,400 per month — includes all utilities except phone, one meal daily in the full-service dining room, biweekly housekeeping services, a medical-alert system, cable TV and chauffeured transportation.

## Sunpointe Senior Living
### 202 Walton Ferry Rd., Hendersonville
### • (615) 822-7520

Sunpointe, formerly Cumberland Green, is the only all-ground-floor retirement community in Nashville. It offers both independent and assisted living. The one- and two-bedroom apartments feature private patios and gardens and private outside entrances.

Residents pay a $500 non-refundable community service entrance fee. The monthly fee for independent living — $680 to $1,245 — includes weekly housekeeping, maintenance, 24-hour emergency response system and three meals daily in the community dining room. The complex contains a beauty/barber shop, free laundry facilities and activity room with exercise equipment, whirlpool, scheduled transportation and minimal supervision.

## Trevecca Towers
## Retirement Community
### 60 Lester Ave. • (615) 244-6911

More than 600 senior citizens live at Trevecca Towers: three 15-story buildings with apartments for retirees capable of independent apartment living "at prices senior citizens can afford to pay" — up to $410 per month.

On-site amenities include lounges and solariums, hobby and craft rooms, library, grocery store, beauty shop, heated indoor swimming pool, sauna and exercise equipment. No meals are included, but all maintenance is provided except housekeeping inside the apartments. The towers' location beside the 55-acre campus of Trevecca Nazarene University gives residents access to many university activities, and residents can audit courses free of charge. Organized programs, tours, shopping trips and activities are also available.

## Wellington Place
### Maryland Farms, 209 Ward Cir.,
### Brentwood • (615) 377-1221

Wellington Place offers respite care, or temporary assistance with bathing, dressing and other needs while residents are away from their own homes during recovery from illness or injury. In addition, short-term care is available for elderly parents while their care-giver children are on vacation. The new MaxLife program offers rehabilitation care. The cost of short-term–recovery assistance or respite care averages about $100 per day.

## Windlands South
### 3800 Sam Boney Dr. • (615) 834-1951

Windlands South, an 11-story high-rise situated on 10 acres, offers retirement living in one-, two-bedroom and two-bedroom deluxe apartments. Month-to-month rents — $1,350 to $1,995 — include three meals a day, all utilities except phone, weekly housekeeping and linen services, free laundry facilities, an emergency-call system, cable TV and local transportation in a van. Daily exercise programs and regular excursions to points of interest are available. No buy-in or lease is required. Facilities also include a craft room, meeting room, billiard and card room, TV room, library and beauty/barber shop.

Nashville is known as the buckle of the Bible Belt and even has been called the Protestant Vatican.

# Worship

Religion has always played an important role in the lives of Nashvillians. Since the first settlers walked across the frozen Cumberland River on a cold December day in 1779, bringing with them their Bibles, hymns, spirituals and religious traditions, religion has become an increasingly prominent fixture in Nashville. Today, with more than 800 houses of worship, numerous Bible schools, religious publishing houses and several denominational headquarters, Nashville continues to grow as a center of religious activity.

Nashville is known as the buckle of the Bible Belt and even has been called the Protestant Vatican. While the city is indeed dominated by Protestantism, particularly Southern Baptist and Church of Christ, Nashville embraces people of many faiths. More than 50 different faiths have houses of worship here, including African Methodist Episcopal, Buddhist, Hindu, Roman Catholic, Judaic (Orthodox, Conservative and Reform), Greek Orthodox and Islamic.

You've probably heard it said that Nashville has "a church on every street corner." Well, that's pretty close to the truth. In Bellevue, for example, at the corner of Colice Jeanne Road and U.S. Highway 70 S., you'll find Bellevue Baptist Church, Bellevue Church of Christ and Bellevue Presbyterian Church. In a short stretch along Hillsboro Road in Green Hills, you'll find Woodmont Baptist, Woodmont Christian, Calvary United Methodist and several others nearby.

A quick count of Protestant churches showed about 300 that are considered "Baptist," more than 110 Church of Christ locations, more than 85 Methodist churches and around 60 Presbyterian churches. It's not uncommon to find churches with memberships of 3,000 or more. Some congregations number more than 6,000.

In addition to the many places of worship, Nashville is home to religious publishers, denominational headquarters, various associations and service organizations, and it's the center of the Christian music business. The huge Southern Baptist Convention has offices in the tower downtown that features a huge cross on each of two sides.

Also here are LifeWay Christian Resources of the Southern Baptist Convention (formerly known as the Baptist Sunday School Board); The Gideons International (who make sure hotel and motel rooms have Bibles), Gospel Music Association (presenter of the annual Dove Awards), National Association of Free Will Baptists, National Baptist Convention USA, National Baptist Publishing Board, Thomas Nelson Publishers (the world's largest Bible publisher), United Methodist Publishing House and World Convention of Churches of Christ. And that's just for starters. The list of religious organizations in the Yellow Pages includes dozens of groups, from the African Christian Schools Foundation to the Disciples of Christ Historical Society, Kentucky-Tennessee Conference of Seventh Day Adventists, the Tennessee Baptist Convention and the Tennessee Baptist Missionary & Educational Convention.

Nashville is also known as a center of religious education. Some of the city's educational institutions are devoted to preparing clergy, while others offer religious study as part of a general curriculum. There are several institutions of higher learning tied to denominations: Belmont University and the Southern Baptist Convention, David Lipscomb University and Church of Christ, Trevecca Nazarene University and Church of the Nazarene. American Baptist College and Free Will Baptist Bible College are here too. Vanderbilt University was affiliated with Southern Methodists until 1914, when the denomination founded Southern Methodist University in Dallas and Emory University in Atlanta. Vanderbilt has been nonsectarian since, and today, the nationally prominent Vanderbilt Divinity School is part of a small league of nondenominational divinity schools that includes Harvard, Yale, Chicago and Union in New York.

In this chapter, we offer a brief look at some of the history of religion in Nashville. Unlike in most of our other chapters, we do not break out separate write-ups on individual locations here. There are far too many houses of worship to list them all, and in an effort to be fair, we will not attempt to do so. We do want to provide useful information, so we will give you a brief overview of some of the churches, temples and synagogues that are popular in Nashville as well as some of the locations, faiths and organizations that are not as widely known. You might use this information as a starting point in your search for a house of worship that suits you.

## Historical Highlights

Eugene Teselle, retired professor of church history and theology at Vanderbilt's Divinity School, says Methodists and Presbyterians were the first two religious groups to enter the Middle Tennessee area. Scots-Irish Presbyterians came to America from Britain in the 1700s to escape drought, religious persecution and British domination. They first settled in Pennsylvania and South Carolina, but eventually pushed westward.

According to *Faithful Volunteers: The History of Religion in Tennessee* by Stephen Mansfield and George Grant (Cumberland House, 1997), "Thomas Craighead (a graduate of Princeton) . . . mounted a stump on a Saturday afternoon in 1785 and preached the first Presbyterian sermon ever heard in Middle Tennessee." That same year, he established Davidson Academy, Nashville's first school, which later became the University of Nashville. "The Scots-Irish Presbyterians," according to *Faithful Volunteers*, "possessed a theology perfectly suited to their rugged character." Another early Middle Tennessee preacher prepared his sermons while doing manual la-

bor. As he ploughed, he would have a pen and paper on a stump at the end of the field so he could write down his thoughts.

By 1796, Presbyterians had established 27 congregations from East Tennessee to Nashville. While the Presbyterians were largely upper and middle class, Methodists were a bit more broad-based. Both groups were financially able to send traveling ministers into the area that became Middle Tennessee. One of the area's earliest Methodist leaders was a Revolutionary War veteran named Benjamin Ogden, who preached regularly in Nashville, Clarksville and Gallatin. Methodist societies eventually began springing up in the area, and Nashville followers built a stone meeting house in 1790.

According to the Metropolitan Nashville Historical Commission, Nashville's first church was a Methodist church built in 1796, 17 years after the first settlers arrived. The church was on the public square, near the courthouse, jail and stocks. In 1796, the year Tennessee became a state, Nashville's Methodist community numbered about 550 and included the city's founder, James Robertson. Traveling preachers pastored the Nashville group. One of Nashville's oldest churches, McKendree United Methodist Church — formerly known as Spring Street Church — at 523 Church Street, was organized in 1787.

The movement of Baptists into Tennessee was "quite different" from that of Presbyterians, who dominated both early religious life and education, says *Faithful Volunteers*. Baptists did not require an educated clergy and didn't follow strict hierarchies. Their style had great appeal to Middle Tennessee's early settlers, and their numbers quickly multiplied. According to *Faithful Volunteers*:

*The early Baptist congregations were communities in the truest sense, and a pastor was profitable only as a single constituent of that community — and even then if he had a clear "call" from God and if he refused to rise above his people in any way other than in character and godliness. These unique values caused the Baptists to grow far more rapidly than their*

*Presbyterian brethren, whose learned "divines"
and insistence on structure were rather difficult for the rough new breed of frontier settlers
flooding into the region to understand.*

Tennessee Baptists organized their first convention at the Mill Creek Church in Nashville in 1835. In 1842, the group changed to a general association, resulting in three organizations in each of the main divisions of the state. The present convention was formed at Murfreesboro in 1874, uniting the three groups.

## Continued Growth

In the 1800s, religious denominations underwent a period of tremendous growth in Tennessee, as revivals swept through the state, drawing hundreds of new converts into their folds. Denominations began forming state organizations, and numerous other denominations and churches were established. In 1820, Nashville's first Sunday School class was begun. Nashville's first public Mass was celebrated that year; the city's Catholics for a time shared a church with Protestants and were visited twice a year by priests. A decade later, a parish was formed, and in 1847, the state's first permanent Roman Catholic Church was completed.

The Greek Revival–style St. Mary's Catholic Church, at 330 Fifth Avenue N., is the oldest remaining church in downtown Nashville. It was built with the support of numerous denominations by mechanics who had come to Nashville to build a bridge over the Cumberland River. During the Civil War, the church was used as a military hospital. Masses are scheduled at 12:10 PM Monday, Tuesday, Thursday and Friday; 5 PM Saturday; and 9 AM Sunday.

Judaism arrived in Nashville as early as 1790. The census of 1840 counted 160 Jewish families in Davidson County. According to "Seven Early Churches of Nashville," a series of lectures presented at the Nashville public library, the first Jewish religious organization, a benevolent society that also met for religious services, dates to 1851. The first rabbi arrived in fall 1852. The state granted a charter for the Nashville congregation, known as Kahl Kodesh Mogen David, in March 1852. A Reform con-

gregation was established in 1864. Construction began on the Vine Street Temple, on the east side of Seventh Avenue, in 1874, and the building was dedicated in 1876. It moved to its present location at 5015 Harding Road in 1955 and today is known as The Temple.

Other Jewish congregations in Nashville today include the conservative West End Synagogue, at 3814 West End Avenue; the orthodox Sherith Israel Synagogue, 3600 West End Avenue; and the reform Congregation Micah, 2001 Old Hickory Boulevard. Congregation Yeshuat Yisrael is a Messianic congregation at 2100 Woodmont Boulevard. The Jewish Community Center, 801 Percy Warner Boulevard, (615) 356-7170, offers a variety of activities and special programs and has information for Jewish families new to the area.

The historic Downtown Presbyterian Church, at the corner of Fifth Avenue and Church Street, was completed in 1851. The Egyptian Revival–style building was designed by William Strickland, architect of the State Capitol. The church was originally organized in 1814 as First Presbyterian Church, but was later reorganized as the Downtown Presbyterian Church. The building served as a hospital during the Civil War. The 4,013-pound church bell was the gift of Adelicia Acklen (see the Belmont Mansion entry in the Attractions chapter). The church is a National Historic Landmark; call (615) 254-7584 to arrange a guided tour. Another historic church, Vine Street Christian Church, 104 Seventh Avenue N., was founded in 1890, but had beginnings in 1820.

As the number of houses of worship grew, and as religion became more organized, religious-based business, especially religious publishing, was beginning to take shape in Nashville. In 1854, the United Methodist Publishing House was established. Its publications include the *Upper Room*, which has a circulation in the millions. The *United Methodist Hymnal* has been the group's most successful publication; more than 4 million are distributed. UMPH produces more than 1,000 new products each year under the Abingdon Press, Cokesbury, Kingswood Books and Dimensions for Living imprints. Cokesbury Books, 301 Eighth Avenue S., (615) 749-6123 or (800) 672-1789, carries most of UMPH's publications. The 70-store Cokesbury chain is UMPH's retail arm and is also an official distributor for various other denominations.

LifeWay Christian Resources of the Southern Baptist Convention, today among the world's largest religious publishers, was established in 1891. Formerly known as The Baptist Sunday School Board, it employs some 1,200 people and produces 180 quarterly and monthly publications and 500 to 600 undated products annually. The board is self-supporting through the sale of church literature, books, music, films, recordings, videotapes, Bibles and church supplies. Any income above operating expenses is returned to the denominations to help fund missions. Baptist Bookstores and Lifeway Christian Stores handle more than 3 million transactions a year.

# The Civil War and Postwar Times

The issue of slavery had a great impact on Nashville churches in the 1800s. Rifts over abolition and related issues had occurred as early as the 1820s. Presbyterians and Baptists each split over the issues; eventually, so did Methodists, who early on had been firm in their opposition to slavery. Among Baptists, those in the North were against slavery, while Southern Baptists took a different view. There was a falling out over the national foreign missions board's refusal to appoint a slaveholder as a missionary, and Baptists from the South organized the Southern Baptist Convention in 1845, gathering in Augusta, Georgia. The convention met in Nashville in 1851.

During these times, blacks had considerable influence in religious matters. In Nashville, Rev. Nelson Merry, the city's first ordained black minister and pastor of the black First Baptist Church, was Tennessee's most prominent black minister before the Civil War. After the war, northern denominations assisted in the establishment of churches and schools for newly freed blacks.

In 1896, 31 years after the Civil War had ended, the Rev. Richard Henry Boyd, who had been born a slave in Mississippi, moved to Nashville and established a religious publishing house to publish materials for the African-American community. His business later became known as the National Baptist Publishing Board. He contracted with a white man to bid for printing presses, because the law prohibited blacks from taking part in such business activities. His business, originally at 523 Second Avenue N., quickly became one of the largest black-owned businesses in the United States. Now at 6717 Centennial Boulevard, the National Baptist Publishing Board is still operated by family members and today publishes more than 14 million books and periodicals annually. Boyd also co-founded the One-Cent Savings Bank, the first minority-owned bank in Tennessee, and established the Nashville *Globe*, a newspaper that served the local African-American community until 1960.

After the war, one of the important events in Nashville's religious history was the arrival of revivalist Sam Jones, who was invited by the city's clergy to preach here. One of his converts was Capt. Thomas Ryman, owner of 35 steamboats, "some of which were floating dens of iniquity" (*Faithful Volunteers*). Ryman built a venue that could accommodate the large crowds Jones drew. In 1892, the building, called the Union Gospel Tabernacle, was completed. It was eventually renamed the Ryman Auditorium and earned its place in history as "the mother church of country music," serving as home of the *Grand Ole Opry* for many years. (See our History and Music City chapters for more about that.)

In the early 1900s, religious diversity increased, as new opinions and movements, such as Unitarianism and transcendentalism, found followers. The Darwinian theory of the latter half of the 1800s spawned the evolution-creation debate, and Tennessee was right in the thick of it. In 1923, thousands of Nashvillians cheered as political leader Will-

## INSIDERS' TIP

**First Church Unity's Dial-A-Prayer offers uplifting daily messages of encouragement. The number is (615) 832-1885.**

iam Jennings Bryan bashed Darwin's theory of evolution in his speech "Is The Bible True?" Two years later Bryan was the prosecutor of Dayton, Tennessee, teacher John T. Scopes, who was under fire for talking about evolution in a classroom, an act that was prohibited by state law.

During the Great Depression of the 1930s, overall church membership throughout the state declined about 10 percent. Church of Christ declined 31 percent, while Baptists and Methodists declined by 16 percent each. The Presbyterian Church actually gained 11 percent during this period.

In 1960, the civil rights movement provided the backdrop for an interesting story in Nashville's religious history. During that year, a young black man named James Lawson was attending Vanderbilt Divinity School when sit-ins started taking place in protest to segregation. Before the sit-ins began, training sessions took place, and Lawson, who had studied principles of nonviolent demonstration with Mahatma Ghandi, was one of the trainers.

When Vanderbilt chancellor Harvie Branscomb learned of Lawson's involvement in the protests, Lawson was expelled. The Divinity School faculty then threatened to resign, and the Board of Trustees threatened to close the school. Professors from other schools at Vanderbilt also threatened to resign. Eventually, a compromise was reached, and the school stayed open. Lawson didn't graduate from Vandy, however. He was reinstated but took his degree from Boston University. Lawson, who had been one of the first blacks to come to Vanderbilt, became a nationally known pacifist and promoter of reconciliation.

Years later, the story took a triumphant twist: ironically, in October 1996, Lawson, then 68, met with the 101-year-old former chancellor Branscomb, the man who expelled him 36 years previously. The occasion? Lawson was presented Vanderbilt Divinity School's first Distinguished Alumnus Award — a dignified, if long overdue, happy ending to a chapter in the city's race relations.

# Well-established and Growing

Today, Nashville has numerous well-established churches with growing memberships. Among the largest are the nondenominational Christ Church, 15354 Old Hickory Boulevard, (615) 834-6171, which lists 6,800 members, and on an average Sunday welcomes 3,500 to 4,000 at its services, and Two Rivers Baptist, 2800 McGavock Pike, (615) 889-3950, which has a membership of 6,500. Christ Church, founded in 1949, is home to the nationally known Christ Church Choir. Two Rivers's pastor, Jerry Sutton, hosts a taped service that airs on Channel 4 (WSMV) at 10 AM each Sunday.

Woodmont Baptist, 2100 Woodmont Boulevard, (615) 297-5303, is the only church in Nashville to have a live TV broadcast. This church's service airs on Channel 2 (WKRN) at 10:30 AM each Sunday. Woodmont Baptist has about 1,350 members. A Korean church and Jewish fellowship meet at this site too.

First Baptist Church Downtown, Seventh and Broadway, (615) 664-6000, has 2,650 members. This church has been in Nashville for 180 years. There are also African American, Hispanic and Arabic Sunday services at the church.

West End United Methodist Church, 2200 West End Avenue, (615) 321-8500, was founded in 1869, when it began as a mission of McKendree Methodist Episcopal Church. Today, the church has about 1,200 members. Well-known nondenominational churches include Belmont Church, 68 Music Square E., (615) 256-2123, and Bethel World Outreach Center, 5670 Granny White Pike, (615) 371-1000. One of the fastest-growing nondenominational churches in Nashville is Bellevue Community Church, (615) 356-2500, which welcomes about 2,000 in five services each weekend. The church meets in Bellevue Middle School, but will move to its new facility off Highway 70 at the end of 1999.

# Diversity

Nashville has far too many houses of worship, service organizations and other groups to try to list them all here. Since it's easy to find a Baptist, Church of Christ, Methodist or Presbyterian church, we will provide you with a little information on some of the other faiths and houses of worship here that are especially popular or that may be a bit harder to track down. A few of these follow, listed in alphabetical order.

The **Baha'i Faith** holds an 11 AM Sunday discussion at 2026 Clifton Avenue, (615) 321-5926.

The **Celebrity Center Church of Scientology**, 1907 Old Murfreesboro Pike, (615) 399-2555, is open daily. It offers spiritual counseling and courses on such topics as improving relationships as well as services that aid artists in their careers.

The **Eckankar Tennessee Satsung Society** meets at 235 White Bridge Road, (615) 353-0623. Eckankar is a non-Christian religion whose teachings relate to two aspects of the Holy Spirit — light and sound — through spiritual exercises and daily contemplation. There are worldwide study groups, and this group of approximately 150 members has been in Nashville since 1973.

**First Church Unity**, 5125 Franklin Road, (615) 333-1323, has been present in Nashville for about 80 years. This Christian nondenominational church's services feature guest musicians in addition to the church choir. Sunday school is at 11 AM. The church's drama group presents two major productions (the sanctu-

ary is turned into a theater for plays with a spiritual theme). The church also has an interpretive dance group called Spirit in Motion that occasionally performs. The church holds a "Course in Miracles" and also makes available space for a variety of support groups to meet, including singles and parenting groups and groups not affiliated with the church, such as Zen and Sufi meditation.

The temple at 521 Old Hickory Boulevard in Bellevue is the **Hindu Cultural Center of Tennessee**, (615) 356-7207. The center is open daily, and a variety of classes are held here during the week. The Sunday congregation typically numbers about 100, but sometimes is as high as 500.

The **Islamic Center of Nashville**, 2515 12th Avenue S. at Sweetbriar, (615) 385-9379, has been in Nashville since 1994. Sunday noontime classes on Islamic religion draw around 20 participants.

**Nashville Cowboy Church**, 2416 Music Valley Drive, (615) 885-0028, is the kind of church that you won't find just anywhere. A country band, T-shirts for sale and a bit of an old-time revival-style atmosphere set this nondenominational church apart from the crowd. Founding pastor Dr. Harry Yates arrives clad in jeans, cowboy boots, hat and Western shirt. His wife, JoAnne Cash Yates, is Johnny Cash's sister. Sunday meetings take place at the Texas Troubador Theater near Opryland and are broadcast on the radio. This is a Christian church that goes by the book — the Good Book, that is — in its beliefs. The mixed congregation of regulars and tourists passes a Stetson hat for donations at the upbeat, joyous services.

The **Nashville Religious Society of Friends Meeting House**, 2804 Acklen Avenue, (615) 269-0225, holds unprogrammed Quaker meetings.

**Nashville Spiritual Community**, a small

---

**INSIDERS' TIP**

**The Nashville Area Chamber of Commerce publishes a "Church Resource Directory," a comprehensive guide to local congregations. The booklet lists addresses, phone numbers, names of clergy and some membership figures. It costs $20, or $10 for members of the chamber. For more information, call (615) 259-4710.**

group that meets at the Nashville Peace and Justice Center, 1016 18th Avenue S., (615) 321-9066, was organized in Nashville in the early 1990s. This group's members come from varied backgrounds and consider themselves spiritual rather than belonging to a particular religion. Services — really more of a discussion period — often consist of guest lecturers who may speak on Buddhism or meditation, or discuss a particular book.

One of Nashville's low-profile (but internationally known) religious attractions is the **Scarritt-Bennett Center**, 1008 19th Avenue S., (615) 340-7500, described in its literature as a "nonprofit conference, retreat and educational center committed to empowerment through cross-cultural understanding, education, creativity and spiritual formation." The center is owned by the United Methodist Church but is open to people of all denominations. Its 10-acre site includes meeting rooms, a library, gift shop, dining hall, the Hartzler-Towner Museum (see the Attractions chapter), a dormitory, organic garden and 350-seat Wightman Chapel. Among the goals of the Scarritt-Bennett Center are the eradication of racism and the empowerment of women. The center offers one-day to one-week programs on topics such as spiritual formation and worship. The staff and volunteers come from a variety of cultural, social and economic backgrounds.

# Index of Advertisers

# Index

# Going Somewhere?

Insiders' Publishing presents these current and upcoming titles to popular destinations all over the country — and we're planning on adding many more. To order a title, go to your local bookstore or call (800) 582-2665 and we'll direct you to one.